Cognitive-Behavioural Therapy for Insomnia (CBT-I) Across the Life Span

Cognitive-Behavioural Therapy For Insomnia (CBT-I) Across The Life Span

Guidelines and Clinical Protocols for Health Professionals

Edited by Chiara Baglioni, Colin A. Espie and Dieter Riemann

Endorsed by
European Sleep Research Society
European Insomnia Network
European Academy for Cognitive Behavioural Therapy for Insomnia

WILEY Blackwell

This edition first published 2022

Registered Office(s)
John Wiley & Sons, Inc., 111 River Street, Hoboken, NJ 07030, USA
John Wiley & Sons Ltd, The Atrium, Southern Gate, Chichester, West Sussex, PO19 8SQ, UK

Editorial Office
9600 Garsington Road, Oxford, OX4 2DQ, UK

For details of our global editorial offices, customer services, and more information about Wiley products visit us at www.wiley.com.

Wiley also publishes its books in a variety of electronic formats and by print-on-demand. Some content that appears in standard print versions of this book may not be available in other formats.

Library of Congress Cataloging-in-Publication Data applied for

Paperback: 9781119785132

Cover Design: Wiley
Cover Image: Cover Art by Susanne Eva Riemann, inspired by Hypnos, the Greek God of sleep

Set in 9.5/12.5pt STIXTwoText by Straive, Pondicherry, India
Printed and bound by CPI Group (UK) Ltd, Croydon, CR0 4YY

C115095_300622

Chiara Baglioni: "To my father, Maurizio, for all love, support and inspiration he gave me and still does."
Colin A. Espie: "To my children (Craig, Carolyn, and Robbie) and grandchildren (Mia, Ella, Callum, and Charlie). Thank you for all your love!"
Dieter Riemann: " To my daughters Constanze and Susanne and my wife Beatrice for always being there for me."

Contents

List of Contributors

Editors

Prof. Dr. Chiara Baglioni
Department of Human Sciences, University of Rome Guglielmo Marconi, Rome, Italy and Department of Psychiatry and Psychotherapy, Medical Center – University of Freiburg, Faculty of Medicine, University of Freiburg, Freiburg, Germany
chiara.baglioni@uniklinik-freiburg.de

Prof. Dr. Colin A. Espie
Sir Jules Thorn Sleep & Circadian Neuroscience Institute (SCNi), Nuffield Department of Clinical Neurosciences, University of Oxford, UK
colin.espie@ndcn.ox.ac.uk

Prof. Dr. Dieter Riemann
Department of Psychiatry and Psychotherapy, Medical Center – University of Freiburg, Faculty of Medicine, University of Freiburg, Freiburg, Germany
dieter.riemann@uniklinik-freiburg

Authors

Dr. Pamela Alfonso-Miller
Northumbria University, Faculty of Health and Life Sciences, Northumbria University, UK
pam.alfonso-miller@northumbria.ac.uk

Dr. Ellemarije Altena
INCIA – Neuroimaging and Human Cognition, University of Bordeaux, France
ellemarije.altena@u-bordeaux.fr

Dr. Valeria Bacaro
Department of Human Sciences, University of Rome Guglielmo Marconi, Rome, Italy
v.bacaro@unimarconi.it

Prof. Dr. Chiara Baglioni
Department of Human Sciences, University of Rome Guglielmo Marconi, Rome, Italy & Department of Psychiatry and Psychotherapy, Medical Center – University of Freiburg, Faculty of Medicine, University of Freiburg, Freiburg, Germany
chiara.baglioni@uniklinik-freiburg.de

Dr. Andrea Ballesio
Department of Psychology, Sapienza University of Rome, Italy
andrea.ballesio@uniroma1.it

Fee Benz, MSc
Department of Psychiatry and Psychotherapy, Medical Center – University of Freiburg, Faculty of Medicine, University of Freiburg, Freiburg, Germany
fee.benz@uniklinik-freiburg.de

Prof. Dr. Bjørn Bjorvatn
Department of Global Public Health and Primary Care, University of Bergen, Norway
bjorn.bjorvatn@uib.no

Prof. Dr. Kerstin Blom
Centre for Psychiatry Research, Karolinska Institute Stockholm, Haukeland University Hospital, Stockholm, Sweden
kerstin.blom@ki.se

Dr. Silvia Cerolini
Department of Psychology, Sapienza University of Rome, Italy
silvia.cerolini@uniroma1.it

Dr. Greg Elder
Northumbria University, Faculty of Health and Life Sciences, Northumbria University, UK
g.elder@northumbria.ac.uk

Prof. Dr. Jason G. Ellis
Director of the Northumbria Centre for Sleep Research, Northumbria University, UK
jason.ellis@northumbria.ac.uk

Prof. Dr. Colin A. Espie
Sir Jules Thorn Sleep & Circadian Neuroscience Institute (SCNi), Nuffield Department of Clinical Neurosciences, University of Oxford, UK
colin.espie@ndcn.ox.ac.uk

Dr. Lukas Frase
Department of Psychiatry and Psychotherapy, Medical Center – University of Freiburg, Faculty of Medicine, University of Freiburg, Freiburg, Germany
lukas.frase@uniklinik-freiburg.de

Prof. Dr. Daniel Freeman
Department of Psychiatry, University of Oxford, UK
daniel.freeman@psych.ox.ac.uk

Dr. Dimitri Gavriloff
Sir Jules Thorn Sleep and Circadian Neuroscience Institute (SCNi), Nuffield Department of Clinical Neurosciences, University of Oxford, UK
dimitri.gavriloff@ndcn.ox.ac.uk

Dr. Elisabeth Hertenstein
University Hospital of Psychiatry and Psychotherapy, University of Bern, Switzerland
Elisabeth.Hertenstein@upd.ch

Dr. Heli Järnefelt
Finnish Institute of Occupational Health, Finland
heli.jarnefelt@ttl.fi

Prof. Dr. Susanna Jernelöv
Division of Psychology & Centre for Psychiatry Research, Karolinska Institute, Stockholm, Sweden
susanna.jernelov@ki.se

Anna F. Johann, MSc
Department of Psychiatry and Psychotherapy/ Department of Medical Psychology & Medical Sociology, Medical Center – University of Freiburg, Faculty of Medicine, University of Freiburg, Freiburg, Germany
anna.johann@uniklinik-freiburg.de

Dr. Simon D. Kyle
Sir Jules Thorn Sleep & Circadian Neuroscience Institute (SCNi), Nuffield Department of Clinical Neurosciences, University of Oxford, UK
simon.kyle@ndcn.ox.ac.uk

Prof. Dr. Caterina Lombardo
Department of Psychology, Sapienza University of Rome, Italy
caterina.lombardo@uniroma1.it

Dr. Annemarie I. Luik
Dept of Epidemiology & Dept of Child and Adolescent Psychiatry/Psychology, Erasmus MC University Medical Center, Rotterdam, The Netherlands
a.luik@erasmusmc.nl

Dr. Leonie F. Maurer
Sleep & Circadian Neuroscience Institute, Nuffield Department of Clinical Neurosciences, University of Oxford, Oxford, UK
leonie.maurer@ndcn.ox.ac.uk

Prof. Dr. Christoph Nissen
University Hospital of Psychiatry and Psychotherapy, University of Bern, Switzerland
Christoph.Nissen@upd.ch

Dr. Laura Palagini
Psychiatric Unit Department of Neuroscience and Rehabilitation, University of Ferrara Italy Department of Clinical and Experimental Medicine, University of Pisa, School of Medicine, Pisa, Italy
lpalagini@tiscali.it

Prof. Dr. Dieter Riemann
Department of Psychiatry and Psychotherapy, Medical Center – University of Freiburg, Faculty of Medicine, University of Freiburg, Freiburg, Germany
dieter.riemann@uniklinik-freiburg.de

Dr. Nayantara Santhi
Northumbria University, Faculty of Health and Life Sciences, Northumbria University, UK
nayantara.santhi@northumbria.ac.uk

Prof. Dr. Angelika Schlarb
Department of Psychology, University of Bielefeld, Germany
angelika.schlarb@uni-bielefeld.de

Prof. Dr. Kai Spiegelhalder
Department of Psychiatry and Psychotherapy, Medical Center – University of Freiburg, Faculty of Medicine, University of Freiburg, Freiburg, Germany
kai.spiegelhalder@uniklinik-freiburg.de

Prof. Dr. Nicole K. Y. Tang
Department of Psychology, University of Warwick, UK
n.tang@warwick.ac.uk

Prof. Dr. Cristiano Violani
Department of Psychology, Sapienza University of Rome, Italy
cristiano.violani@uniroma1.it

Preface

This textbook on cognitive behavioural therapy for insomnia (CBT-I) would not have been possible without the support and endorsement of the European Sleep Research Society (ESRS). We have been closely involved in the work of the ESRS over several decades, and especially engaged in founding the European Insomnia Network and the European Academy for Cognitive Behavioural Therapy for Insomnia to promote sleep medicine and research related to insomnia in Europe.

Who would have guessed 20 years ago that Cognitive Behavioural Therapy for Insomnia (CBT-I) would be considered as the first-line treatment for the disorder? As of now, practically all published guidelines from the last six years support that point of view. Medication still plays a certain role in the treatment of insomnia, especially short-term, but CBT-I, as we teach and practice it, has attained the highest level of evidence, especially with respect to long-term sustainability. In order to support clinical guideline implementation in practice we decided two years ago to put together a state of the science textbook of CBT-I. With the invaluable help of more than 30 experienced colleagues, we have been able to compile this comprehensive textbook encompassing 24 chapters divided into six sections, which cover all important aspects of insomnia and its treatment with CBT. Each chapter aims at providing clinical recommendations based on the most updated research evidence on specific issues related to CBT-I. Our aim is to encourage a closer link between research and clinical practice with respect to the psychological treatment of the disorder of insomnia.

We sincerely hope that our work will help researchers and clinicians world-wide to understand that CBT-I is not just one homogenous treatment, but a family of evidence-based treatments. We also hope that our endeavour will help professionals involved in providing insomnia treatment to devise personalized solutions for each individual patient suffering from this widespread sleep disorder.

Chiara Baglioni (Rome)
Colin A. Espie (Oxford)
Dieter Riemann (Freiburg)

1

Introduction to Insomnia Disorder

Dieter Riemann, Kai Spiegelhalder, Colin A. Espie, Dimitri Gavriloff, Lukas Frase and Chiara Baglioni

Key points

- Insomnia, encompassing day- and night-time symptoms, is a frequent health complaint with manifold negative consequences for somatic and mental health and for quality of life.
- The evaluation of insomnia includes a clinical interview, a physical and psychiatric examination, sleep diaries and questionnaires. Technical procedures like actigraphy or polysomnography may be used in certain circumstances and differential-diagnosis needs to evaluate medical and psychiatric co-morbidities, as well as other sleep disorders.
- Etiological and pathophysiological insomnia concepts range from genetic and neurobiological to cognitive-behavioural models.
- Cognitive-behavioural therapy for insomnia (CBT-I) is presently considered world-wide as first line treatment.

Learning objectives

- To understand the importance of insomnia for somatic and mental health and quality of life.
- To be able to conduct an appropriate clinical evaluation including differential-diagnosis of patients with insomnia.
- To understand the present illness concepts of insomnia ranging from neurobiology to cognitive-behavioural concepts.
- To be familiar with the ingredients of CBT-I and to understand why CBT-I is presently the first line of treatment for insomnia.

Abstract

The clinical picture of insomnia encompasses day- and night-time symptoms. Typical night-time complaints are prolonged sleep latency, increased frequency of awakenings, difficulties getting back to sleep and early morning awakening. Day-time sequelae encompass fatigue, tiredness, reduced attention, impaired cognition, irritability, nervousness, anxiety and mood swings, including dysphoric or even depressed mood. DSM-5 (*Diagnostic and Statistical Manual of the American Psychiatric Association*, 5th edition), ICSD-3 (*International Classification of Sleep Disorders*, 3rd edition) and ICD-11 (*International Classification of Diseases*, 11th edition) summarise this condition as Insomnia Disorder (ID). Epidemiological studies demonstrated that ID is an important risk factor for somatic and mental health. The prevalence of ID is higher in women than in men and increases with age. Apart from a clinical interview, questionnaires should be used for the evaluation of insomnia. The core instrument is a standardised 7–14 day sleep diary that includes questions on sleep-related and daytime symptoms. Actigraphy and polysomnography can be considered for a subgroup of patients presenting with therapy-refractory insomnia or suspected occult sleep disorders. A thorough medical and psychiatric evaluation is advisable to evaluate clinically relevant comorbidities.

Cognitive-Behavioural Therapy for Insomnia (CBT-I) Across the Life Span: Guidelines and Clinical Protocols for Health Professionals,
First Edition. Edited by Chiara Baglioni, Colin A. Espie and Dieter Riemann.

Present illness concepts range from genetic and neurobiological to cognitive-behavioral models, forming the basis for Cognitive Behavioural Therapy for insomnia (CBT-I) encompassing sleep hygiene and education, relaxation methods, stimulus control, sleep restriction and cognitive techniques to reduce nocturnal ruminations. Recently published guidelines agree that CBT-I should be the first line treatment for insomnia.

Keywords *insomnia, night-time complaints, day-time symptoms, sleep diary, insomnia models, CBT-I, guidelines*

Introduction

This chapter serves as an introduction to the topic of insomnia and to prepare the ground for the reader to understand why Cognitive Behavioural Therapy for Insomnia (CBT-I) is presently considered to be the gold standard and first line treatment for this disorder. As the main focus of this book is on CBT-I, other aspects concerning insomnia, such as diagnosis and differential-diagnosis, epidemiology and costs/ risks of the disorder, as well as pathophysiological and aetiological concepts, are summarised here in order to provide a concise overview. Readers who want to broaden their horizon beyond this are referred to our previous work (Baglioni et al., 2020; Espie, 2002, 2007, 2009, 2022; Espie, Broomfield, MacMahon, Macphee & Taylor, 2006; Harris et al., 2015; MacMahon, Broomfield, & Espie, 2006; Morin et al., 2015; Perlis, Ellis, Spiegelhalder & Riemann, 2022; Riemann et al., 2010, 2011, 2015, 2017a, 2017b; Riemann, Krone, Wulff & Nissen, 2020;). These texts go into further detail concerning the above-mentioned aspects of insomnia (please note that there is some unavoidable overlap between these published works and the present book chapter).

Insomnia definition/diagnostic criteria

In the last five decades several diagnostic systems have been developed that include chapters on insomnia. Whereas the DSM (*Diagnostic and Statistical Manual of the American Psychiatric Association*) in its previous versions, DSM-III-R or DSM-IV, suggested a distinction between primary and secondary insomnias, DSM-5 (American Psychiatric Association, 2013) established a change of paradigm by introducing 'insomnia disorder' (ID) as an overarching diagnostic category, removing distinctions in primary/secondary forms of insomnia. ICSD (*International Classification of Sleep Disorders*) in its third version followed this approach; the diagnostic criteria for chronic insomnia disorder according to ICSD-3 (American Association of Sleep Medicine, 2014) are shown in Table 1.1.

ICD-10, in contrast, still distinguishes between organic and non-organic sleep disorders, but ICD-11 will follow the path taken by DSM-5 and ICSD-3. It is noteworthy, when considering the criteria for insomnia disorder (ID), that both night-time and day-time symptoms are listed. Furthermore, concerning night-time symptoms, non-restorative sleep has been dropped from the catalogue of criteria due to its lack of specificity for insomnia.

Giving up the distinction between primary and secondary insomnia was a tremendous step forward in acknowledging that insomnia in many cases is not just a symptom of any other somatic or mental disorder, but constitutes a distinct disease entity in its own right, deserving specific consideration in clinical practice. Formerly held widespread beliefs that treating the 'underlying' disorder would eliminate the insomnia 'symptoms' had turned out not to be valid and an increasing literature (see below) indicates that by detecting and properly treating insomnia disorder with CBT-I, a significant positive effect can be exerted on somatic/mental co-morbidities and quality of life with the additional benefit of having a preventive effect on future somatic/mental disorders as well.

Diagnostic and differential diagnostic procedure for insomnia

Clinical picture and complaints

Insomnia is seen primarily as a sleep disorder. Parameters of sleep continuity, such as sleep onset latency (SOL), wake-time after sleep onset (WASO), number of awakenings (NOA), early morning awakening (EMA), sleep efficiency (SE) and total sleep time (TST), are usually altered in insomnia and are used to describe the sleep of afflicted patients. Most insomnia patients will display both symptoms of difficulties initiating and maintaining sleep. However,

Table 1.1 Diagnostic criteria for chronic insomnia disorder according to ICSD-3 (AASM, 2014).

A) **The patient reports, or the patient's parent or caregiver observes, one or more of the following:**
  1) Difficulty initiating sleep.
  2) Difficulty maintaining sleep.
  3) Waking up earlier than desired.
  4) Resistance to going to bed on appropriate schedule.
  5) Difficulty sleeping without parent or caregiver intervention.

F) **The patient reports, or the patient's parent or caregiver observes, one or more of the following related to the night-time sleep difficulty:**
  1) Fatigue/malaise.
  2) Attention, concentration or memory impairment.
  3) Impaired social, family, occupational or academic performance.
  4) Mood disturbance/irritability.
  5) Day-time sleepiness.
  6) Behavioural problems (e.g., hyperactivity, impulsivity, aggression).
  7) Reduced motivation/energy/initiative.
  8) Proneness for errors/accidents.
  9) Concerns about or dissatisfaction with sleep.

J) **The reported sleep/wake complaints cannot be explained purely by inadequate opportunity (i.e., enough time is allotted for sleep) or inadequate circumstances (i.e., the environment is safe, dark, quiet, and comfortable) for sleep.**

K) **The sleep disturbance and associated day-time symptoms occur at least three times per week.**

L) **The sleep disturbance and associated day-time symptoms have been present for at least three months.**

M) **The sleep/wake difficulty is not better explained by another sleep disorder.**

subgroups of patients will be characterised by distinct complaints of only prolonged sleep latency or only trouble in maintaining sleep, which may inform the therapeutic process. Clinicians should probe differentially for information about sleep on weekends compared to weekdays and daytime sleep episodes (i.e., naps). Overall sleep quality may be altered and be described as poor. A general subjective judgement of sleep parameters during a clinical interview may yield rather inaccurate or distorted values. Thus, this information should be complemented by data from a sleep diary (see below), which is typically filled out over a period of 2 weeks on a day-to-day basis. Patients suffering from insomnia may complain of symptoms relating to a nocturnal hyperactivity of the autonomous nervous system, presenting as increased heart rate, palpitations, sweating or general restlessness, which have been interpreted as reflecting a chronic psychophysiological hyperarousal (Perlis, Giles, Mendelson, Bootzin & Wyatt, 1997; Riemann et al., 2010, 2015; Kyle & Espie, 2014; Morin et al., 2015). It is also important to ask about night-time behaviours when awake (clock watching, going to the toilet, etc.). Beyond, it is essential to evaluate cognitive-emotional aspects of insomnia; e.g., what thoughts, emotions, ruminations and worries are experienced when the patient is unable to sleep. These complaints are related to cognitive aspects (for cognitive models of insomnia see Harvey, 2002; Espie, 2002), including worries, ruminations or specific dysfunctional sleep-related thoughts. Many of these cognitions will be accompanied by unpleasant emotions like anxiety, anger, frustration or dysphoria. It is important to evaluate how intense these feelings are during the night, as insomnia is linked with emotion regulation (Baglioni, Spiegelhalder, Lombardo & Riemann, 2010) and constitutes an independent risk factor for depressive and anxiety disorders (see below). As it has been recognized that insomnia is associated with impaired cognitive functioning (Orff, Drummond, Nowakowski & Perlis, 2007; Shekleton, Rogers & Rajaratnam, 2010; Fortier-Brochu, Beaulieu-Bonneau, Ivers & Morin, 2012), any clinical interview should try to ascertain if and how insomnia impacts on day-time functioning. Typically, subjectively reported day-time symptoms and signs include tiredness or fatigue (although rarely sleepiness), decreased attention and concentration, impaired memory function, heightened irritability, decreased energy, anxiety or negative mood. Neuropsychological and psychometric tests and psychiatric assessment may be of help to evaluate the severity and/or origin of these symptoms.

Consistent with the diagnostic position that night-time symptoms of insomnia need to be associated with day-time complaints, people with insomnia typically report at least as much concern about the effects of insomnia on their quality of life (Kyle, Morgan & Espie, 2010).

Clinical evaluation including psychiatric assessment

Clinical evaluation starts with an open interview in which the clinician will leave room for the patient to describe his or her symptoms. Patients may state 'I have not slept a wink for years', 'I can't sleep at all' or 'I am afraid I will go crazy if this does not stop!' To get a more specific picture, it is necessary to turn to a more structured interview (see also Morin & Espie, 2003; Espie, 2022), including questions about sleep history (for an overview see Table 1.2).

The presence of periodic limb movement disorder, restless legs syndrome or sleep apnea should be probed actively. For this purpose, a structured interview such as the clinical interview for DSM-5 (*Diagnostic and Statistical Manual of the American Psychiatric Association*, 5th revision) sleep disorders (Taylor et al., 2018) can be used. Besides this sleep-related part, the clinical evaluation should include a medical and psychiatric assessment. A physical examination of the patient (including taking a medical history) should be performed and a blood sample (when clinically indicated) should be drawn to evaluate blood count as well as renal, hepatic and thyroid function. In some cases (if clinically indicated), the medical evaluation may include an ECG (Electrocardiogram), EEG (Electroencephalogram) or a radiological method (CT = Computer Tomography; MRI = Magnetic Resonance Imaging). During a first consultation many patients will be hesitant to talk about psychiatric symptoms; thus, a good rapport should be established between the patient and clinician beforehand. As most mental disorders are associated with sleep disturbance, the major psychiatric disorders should be routinely assessed for, including anxiety disorders, affective disorders, schizophrenia spectrum disorders, substance-related disorders and personality disorders.

The next part of the evaluation should include questions about precipitating factors for the insomnia (for example, psychosocial stressors) and general life circumstances (financial, work and familial situation). Beyond this, circadian factors, e.g., shift work and morningness/eveningness, should be evaluated.

Last but not least the clinical evaluation should focus on the prior or current intake of over the counter (OTC), prescribed and illegal/illicit medications or substances. Many prescribed medications have a negative effect on sleep (for an overview see Riemann and Nissen, 2012). Nicotine and/or caffeine not only immediately prior to bedtime will

Table 1.2 Questions about sleep history – overview.

How long have you suffered from insomnia?
Were there any specific predisposing/ triggering factors?
How did the insomnia develop over the years – constantly progressing or with periods of remission?
How have you responded to previous treatments?
When do you go to bed?
When do you get up?
What do you do when you go to bed?
Do you switch off the light immediately or do you read a book?
How long does it take you to fall asleep on average?
How frequently do you wake up on average?
How much time do you sleep on average?
How do you rate your sleep quality?
How do you feel during the day?
How do you feel in the morning?
How is your attention and concentration during the day?
Do you ever fall asleep during the day?
Are you tired/fatigued during the day?
What is the quality of the bedroom and of the bed?
Does the bedpartner snore?
How noisy is the environment?
Do you suffer from frequent dreams/nightmares?
Do you suffer from other sleep disorders?

disrupt sleep. Alcohol may help to initiate sleep but can have a detrimental effect on sleep maintenance. Knowledge of medication and substance/drug intake history is of the utmost importance for any clinician diagnosing and treating insomnia.

Questionnaires to assess insomnia and related complaints

Several questionnaires have been developed to assess day- and night-time complaints of patients with insomnia and to measure related symptoms like anxiety or depressed mood. Chapter 5 will describe these instruments in detail.

Actigraphy

Actigraphy is a technically sophisticated approach to collect information on patients' sleep–wake behaviour by measuring motor activity over long periods of time (up to four weeks or longer depending on the specific storage capacities of the device). The collected information typically shows alternating periods of high motor activity indicating wakefulness and periods of low motor activity mirroring rest/sleep. These data may reveal otherwise unnoticed episodes of day-time sleep (for example in front of the TV) or patterns of highly irregular bedtimes or weekend shifts of bedtimes. It is important to note that actigraphy cannot accurately measure sleep and gives only estimates of times of rest and activity, although many manufacturers of actigraphs provide software that claims to directly measure sleep onset latency or total sleep time. In clinical practice, actigraphs are used in combination with sleep diaries, as only the latter can provide valid information on the subjective experience of sleep.

Polysomnography

It is a controversial issue as to whether cardiorespiratory polysomnography (PSG) should be used to diagnose insomnia. There is no doubt concerning the use of polysomnography in case of a suspected occult pathology of sleep, for example when periodic limb movements during sleep or sleep apneas are suspected, as there might be co-morbidity with many other sleep disorders and insomnia. US guidelines veto the use of PSG as a diagnostic instrument for insomnia (Kushida et al., 2005). The insomnia guidelines of the German Sleep Society (Riemann et al., 2017a) and the European Sleep Research Society (Riemann et al., 2017b) have broadened this perspective by suggesting PSG for patients with therapy-refractory insomnia who have not responded to a previous adequate 'dose' of pharmaco- or psychotherapy. The discussion about the discrepancy between subjective (i.e., data from sleep diaries) and objective data (polysomnography) in insomnia still constitutes a major clinical and scientific challenge. In general, polysomnography in contrast to subjective data does not reveal as pronounced disturbances of sleep as indicated by subjective data (Feige et al., 2008). Newer data suggest that the long-term health consequences of insomnia may be related to the objectively documented impairment of sleep (Vgontzas, Fernandez-Mendoza, Liao & Bixler, 2013). This line of evidence shows an increased risk for obesity and cardiovascular disease in patients with insomnia and objective short sleep duration (≤ 6 hours). Furthermore, the hypothesis that polysomnographic data, i.e., the degree of objectively documented sleep disturbance, may be of relevance for differential therapy, i.e., pharmacotherapy versus psychotherapy (Vgontzas, Fernandez-Mendoza, Liao & Bixler, 2013), has yet to be resolved (see Riemann et al., 2011) and deserves further consideration. A meta-analysis of polysomnographic studies in insomnia (Baglioni et al., 2014a) demonstrated significant differences between primary insomnia patients and healthy good sleepers with respect to sleep latency, nocturnal wake times, total sleep time and sleep efficiency. Percentages of Rapid Eye Movement (REM) sleep and Slow Wave Sleep (SWS) were significantly reduced in insomnia patients. With respect to total sleep time a 30-minute reduction of polysomnographically recorded sleep was noted in insomnia patients compared to healthy good sleepers, whereas subjective data from sleep diaries revealed a 120-minute difference between the two groups. In clinical practice, polysomnography may be used when patients complain of extreme nocturnal disturbances, e.g., claiming not to sleep at all. In this example, it is likely that PSG will reveal more sleep than is subjectively experienced and the data can be used to inform the patient in an empathic way that the objective sleep problem is not as pronounced as expected, possibly reassuring the patient and having positive effects on sleep (Tang & Harvey, 2004). Spectral analysis of the sleep EEG has not yet become a routine analytical method in clinical practice. From a research perspective, several studies have shown that the spectral power in the beta band of NREM sleep was specifically increased in primary insomnia patients compared with good sleepers (e.g., Perlis, Smith, Andrews, Orff & Giles, 2001; Spiegelhalder et al., 2012), though not unequivocally (Bastien, Leblanc, Carrier & Morin, 2003). However, confirmatory evidence in this field is still too sparse to include this type of analysis in the routine clinical procedure for the assessment of insomnia (see Feige et al., 2013).

Nevertheless, the occurrence of increased fast EEG waves during nightly sleep has given rise to assumptions that these phenomena indeed reflect cognitive hyperarousal, i.e., increased information processing (thinking, worrying, ruminations) during objectively measured EEG sleep in patients suffering from insomnia.

Multiple Sleep Latency Test

An MSLT (Multiple Sleep Latency Test) should only be used in the assessment of an insomnia patient when the patient is complaining of clinically relevant sleepiness during the day (e.g., falling asleep at the wheel). The MSLT is routinely used to evaluate excessive daytime sleepiness in hypersomnia, e.g., patients with suspected sleep apnea syndrome or narcolepsy.

Interestingly, on average, the MSLT revealed prolonged sleep latencies in patients with insomnia, contrary to expectations derived from studies on the impact of sleep loss. Bonnet and Arand (e.g., see 2000) have thoroughly investigated this effect confirming increased sleep latencies during the day in chronic insomnia patients. These findings are in line with a 24-hour hyperarousal in insomnia (see below).

Other diagnostic tests in insomnia

Several diagnostic tests mentioned here may be used in specific subpopulations of insomnia patients or for atypical cases. When patients present with severe complaints about daytime fatigue/impairments of concentration, tests to evaluate attention/concentration can be used, like the PVT (psychomotor vigilance test). However, the PVT is more a research than a clinical tool and its usefulness on an individual basis may be challenged. It is suggested that for any relevant neuropsychological indication appropriately trained clinicians should apply standard test batteries (see, for example, Benton, 1995). For research purposes, several paradigms have been developed that tap into specific aspects of insomnia. One of these paradigms is the attentional bias paradigm (e.g., see Espie, Broomfield, MacMahon, Macphee & Taylor, 2006; MacMahon, Broomfield & Espie, 2006; Spiegelhalder, Espie, Nissen & Riemann, 2008; Spiegelhalder et al., 2010). It is based on the assumption that patients with chronic insomnia are biased with respect to their perception and processing of stimuli related to insomnia. The paradigm is not yet ready for standard clinical practice, but it is imaginable that it might be used in the future to measure responsiveness to CBT-I, specifically targeting this type of learned sleep-preventing associations.

It should be noted, however, that there are well-established self-report inventories that usefully measure cognitive sequelae (e.g., Everyday Cognitive Failures Questionnaire (Broadbent, Cooper, Fitzgerald & Parkes, 1982); British Columbia Cognitive Complaints Inventory (Iverson & Lam, 2013)) and these have recently been shown to respond to CBT for insomnia (Kyle et al., 2020). Likewise, the Flinders Fatigue Scale (Gradisar et al., 2007) has been specifically validated for use in insomnia populations.

Epidemiology and costs/risks of insomnia

Insomnia more frequently affects women than men (60 : 40%) and its prevalence increases with age (for overview, see Ohayon, 2002). The European Academy for CBT-I has summarized epidemiological data on the prevalence of insomnia disorder in European countries (Baglioni et al., 2020). The prevalence of insomnia disorder varies considerably from one European country to another. Data for Germany indicate a prevalence of 5.7 to 7.7%, whereas data from France indicate figures up to 20%. On average, approximately 10% of the adult European population seem to suffer from chronic insomnia. The heterogenous data clearly call for a prospective pan-European study to investigate the prevalence of insomnia, using agreed and standardised criteria, to fully grasp the present situation.

The costs of insomnia are high: it has been shown (mostly on a meta-analytic level) that insomnia conveys increased risks for cardiovascular diseases (Li, Zhang, Hou & Tang, 2014; Sofi et al., 2014; Spiegelhalder, Scholtes & Riemann, 2010), obesity and diabetes (*Anothaisintawee, Reitrakul, van Cauter & Thakkinstan, 2*016; Chan, Levsen & McCrae, 2018), depression (Baglioni et al., 2011; Hertenstein et al., 2019), anxiety (Hertenstein et al., 2019) and suicide (Pigeon, Pinkwart & Conner, 2012). Wickwire (2019) reported that untreated insomnia leads to increased all-cause health care utilization based on a randomly selected and nationally representative sample from the US. Data from Norway indicate that insomnia strongly predicts sick leave and disability pension (Øverland et al., 2008; Sivertsen, Krokstad, Øverland & Mykletun, 2009). Data for Germany have demonstrated that the direct or indirect costs for insomnia are around 40 to 50 billion euros annually (Thiart et al., 2016). Data for France indicated a sum of 2 billion USD in 1995 (Léger, Levy & Paillard, 1999). Data for the US indicate a sum of

150 billion US dollars for direct and indirect costs of insomnia (Reynolds and Ebben, 2017). A study from Canada (Daley, Morin, LeLanc, Gregoire & Savard, 2009) reported total annual costs for insomnia disorder alone to be around 6.5 billion Canadian dollars. Recent data indicate that treatment using digital CBT may be associated with reduced health care expenditure (Miller, Carl & Baker, 2020), and Markov health economic modelling indicates that digital CBT (dCBT) may be highly cost-effective when offered at scale (Darden et al., 2021). Further details of the costs and risks of insomnia are given in the European Academy for Cognitive Behavioral Therapy for Insomnia Report (Baglioni et al., 2020).

Aetiology and pathophysiology of insomnia

In the last five decades, several influential aetiological models for insomnia have been published. We have summarized the state of the art concerning aetiology and pathophysiology in previous publications. Figure 1.1 (taken from Riemann, Krone,

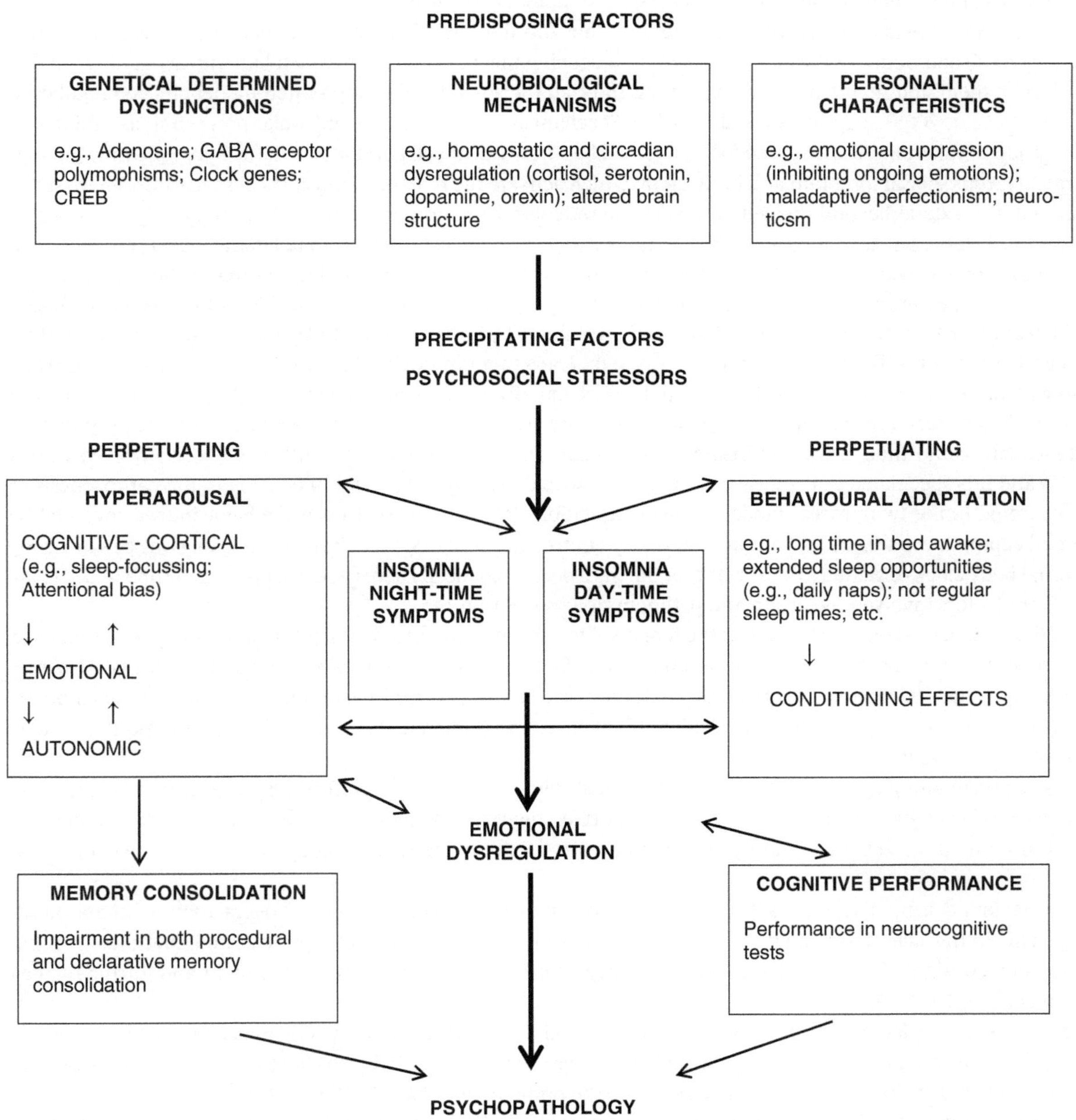

Figure 1.1 A comprehensive Insomnia Model (from Riemann, Krone, Wulff, and Nissen, 2020).

Wulff & Nissen, 2020) gives an overview and synthesis of current neurobiological and cognitive behavioural models for insomnia and for its relationship to psychopathology.

As can be seen from the figure, theoretical approaches range from purely behavioural models to neurobiological models and models taking both levels, i.e., cognitive-behavioural factors and neurobiology, into account.

This overview model integrates different strands of research from the fields of genetics, neurobiology, personality research, psychophysiology and cognitive behavioural research to develop a comprehensive understanding of the mechanisms involved in the aetiology and pathophysiology of insomnia.

The basic structure of this model is taken from the so-called 3P model of insomnia as suggested by Spielman, Saskind and Thorpy (1987). The three P's stand for: predisposing, precipitating and perpetuating factors. Predisposing factors can stem from the field of genetics, neurobiology and personality.

In brief, genetic and epigenetic factors have been shown to be involved in the aetiology of insomnia by family and twin studies (overview given in Palagini, Biber & Riemann, 2014). Genome-wide association studies point to an involvement of a large number of specific genes (e.g., Lane et al., 2019). This study also showed tentative evidence for a causal link between insomnia symptoms and cardiovascular diseases, depressive symptoms and well-being.

Neurobiological mechanisms, as described by the so-called flip-flop switch model of Saper and colleagues (Saper, Scammell & Lu, 2005) and homeostatic and biological time-keeping mechanisms have to be taken into account when discussing the development and maintenance of insomnia. In brief, the so-called flip-flop switch model of sleep regulation (Saper, Scammell & Lu, 2005) suggests a bistable switch mechanism between sleep and wake-promoting assemblies of neuronal cell groups. Wakefulness is assumed to be governed by a network of cell populations in the hypothalamus (including orexinergic neurons), basal forebrain and brain stem, which activate the thalamus and cortical structures. These structures include but also extend beyond the cell groups in the reticular formation of the brainstem (originally described as ARAS, or Ascending Reticular Activating System). The main sleep-inducing centres are located in the VLPO (ventrolateral-preoptic nucleus), which becomes active during sleep and inhibits all major wake-promoting centres in the hypothalamus and brain stem, using the neurotransmitters galanin and GABA (gamma-amino-butyric-acid). The VLPO receives afferent input from each of the major monoaminergic systems and is inhibited by noradrenaline and serotonin. A mutual inhibitory circuit between both systems, the wake and the sleep system, leads to a flip-flop switch with 'sharp' transitions between sleeping and waking. Thus, insomnia on this level can be conceptualized as imbalance between sleep inducing and wake (i.e., arousal) inducing mechanisms. Either a hyperactivity of the arousal system or a hypoactivity of the sleep system, or both simultaneously, could thus 'drive' the insomnia. Circadian and homeostatic mechanisms are also involved in this switch process and it is speculated that a dysfunctional "key switch" (see above) plays a major role in the pathogenesis of insomnia. According to the two-process model of sleep regulation (Borbely, 1982) sleep–wake behaviour is governed by circadian time-keeping mechanisms and a homeostatically controlled process S, i.e., Sleep Drive. Being out of synchrony with the internal body clock (e.g., due to shift work) or having a decreased Sleep Drive (due to a prolonged time in bed) may thus be important factors involved the origin and pathophysiology of insomnia.

For personality variables, sleep reactivity, i.e., the tendency to exhibit pronounced, albeit transient, sleep disturbance in response to stressful events, has been shown to be a major risk factor for insomnia (Drake, Pillai & Roth, 2014). Also, several personality traits have been linked to insomnia, including neuroticism, perfectionism, sensitivity to anxiety symptoms and the tendency to internalize problems (e.g., Dekker, Blanken, & Van Someren, 2017; van de Laar, Verbeek, Pevernagie, Aldenkamp & Overeem, 2010).

In many cases, precipitating factors can be readily identified. These are usually significant life events that facilitate the onset of acute episodes of insomnia. Most frequently, reported triggers of acute episodes of insomnia are stressful life events related to a threat of security to family, health and work–school living that are coupled with negative emotional valence.

Perpetuating factors can be discussed with respect to hyperarousal, an overexcitation or overactivity of the arousal-promoting systems to the sleep-inducing systems. Hyperarousal includes physiological, cognitive and emotional components and has been considered a stable characteristic of people with insomnia both during the night and during the day (e.g., Riemann et al., 2010, 2015).

Behavioural perpetuating factors include prolonged time in bed, irregular sleep–wake schedules, daytime napping and other maladaptive behaviours, such as using alcohol to combat insomnia. Usually these strategies are compensatory attempts to catch up on lost sleep, but in the end exacerbate the problem by decreasing Sleep Drive.

Cognitive perpetuating factors have been identified as a major factor driving insomnia (e.g., Harvey, 2002; Espie, 2002). Undoubtedly, focusing on the insomnia and its consequences is done by many, if not all, patients with insomnia. In recent years, the literature has emphasised the role of selective attention processes in people with insomnia. Specifically, it has been argued that the attentional system of patients with insomnia is abnormally sensitive to sleep-related information (Harris et al., 2015). This leads to increased rumination and direct efforts and intention towards sleeping (Harvey, 2002; Espie, Broomfield, MacMahon, Macphee & Taylor, 2006). Furthermore, sleep-related cognitions such as faulty beliefs, worry and attentional bias play an important role in perpetuating insomnia (Morin, Vallieres & Ivers, 2007). These cognitions include unrealistic beliefs about sleep requirements and excessive worry for not meeting these standards.

Emotional perpetuating factors have been less studied. Nevertheless, sleep is being conceptualized as a basic psychophysiological process that is fundamental for stress, behaviour and emotion regulation (Hagger, 2010; Palmer & Alfano, 2017). Consistently, most mental disorders are associated with sleep impairment (Baglioni et al., 2016) and insomnia-related problems in children have been linked with difficulties in socioemotional development (Sadeh, Tikotzky & Kahn, 2014). Furthermore, in adults, insomnia has been found to be a predictor of depression and anxiety disorders (Baglioni et al., 2011; Hertenstein et al., 2019). Experimental studies have found that patients with insomnia report more negative emotions than good sleepers (e.g., McCrae et al., 2008; Scott & Judge, 2006). Psychophysiological studies have also evidenced an emotional bias in people with insomnia to sleep-related stimuli with negative valence compared to good sleepers (e.g., Baglioni et al., 2010, 2014b).

Summarising, beyond the assumption that genetic factors and alterations of neurobiological mechanisms responsible for sleep–wake regulation are assumed to play a role in the aetiology and pathophysiology of insomnia, it is also clear that aspects of personality (i.e., perfectionism) are important to understand insomnia. Acute precipitating life events 'set the wheels in motion' – thus acute insomnia is triggered. The question of why most individuals who develop acute insomnia do not go on to develop the chronic condition has not yet been settled (see Ellis, Gehrman, Espie, Riemann & Perlis, 2012); maybe a genetic vulnerability, neurobiological dysfunction or personality traits might help to keep 'the train rolling'. Either cognitive–emotionalcortical (hyper-) arousal or maladaptive behaviours might keep the furnace burning. It is widely assumed that sleep preventing learned associations (conditioning effects) are strongly involved in this process as well, giving credit to Bootzin's assumption that in insomnia the original connection between the bed (stimulus) and the behaviour of sleep (response) has been lost or 'unlearned' (Bootzin, Epstein & Wood, 1991). This theory is deepened in Chapter 2.

CBT-I mainly targets the perpetuating factors, e.g., relaxation techniques and mindfulness aim to address psychophysiological hyperarousal, sleep hygiene, stimulus control and sleep restriction try to correct maladaptive behaviours and enhance sleep drive, whereas cognitive strategies aim to alter 'racing thoughts', dysfunctional beliefs and attitudes and to reduce nocturnal worrying and ruminations.

Introduction to CBT-I

Cognitive behavioural treatment for insomnia comprises a family of interventions and is not 'one' homogenous therapeutic strategy *per se* (see Table 1.3).

CBT-I ingredients range from sleep restriction, stimulus control, sleep hygiene education to relaxation methods, cognitive *reappraisal, cognitive control techniques and paradoxical intention therapy. A brief description of these techniques is given in the table. As CBT-I is the main focus of the rest of this book, no further details will be given here.*

Present treatment guidelines

In 2016, the American College of Physicians (ACP) published four guideline articles for chronic insomnia disorder relating to psychological (i.e., CBT-I) and pharmacological treatment, describing challenges to implementation and summarising the guidelines for patients (Quaseem, Kansagara, Forciea, Cooke & Denberg, 2016; Brasure et al., 2016; Wilt et al., 2016; Kathol & Arnedt, 2016). Following strict criteria for the formulation of clinical guidelines according to evidence-based principles, the authors concluded that 'ACP recommends that all adult patients receive cognitive behavioural therapy for insomnia (CBT-I) as the initial treatment for chronic insomnia disorder. (Grade: strong recommendation, moderate-quality evidence)'. A second recommendation was 'ACP recommends that clinicians use a shared decision-making approach, including a discussion of the benefits, harms, and costs of short-term use of medications, to decide whether to add pharmacological therapy in adults with chronic insomnia disorder in whom cognitive behavioural therapy for insomnia (CBT-I) alone was unsuccessful. (Grade: weak recommendation, low-quality evidence)'. Thus, a clear-cut statement was made that

Table 1.3 CBT-I ingredients (from Baglioni et al., 2020).

CBT-I strategy	Description
Sleep restriction	*Behavioural strategy*: A method which aims at strengthening homeostatic sleep pressure and stabilize circadian control of sleep and wakefulness, by decreasing the opportunity to sleep over successive nights. Patients are instructed to restrict their time in bed to match their average (self-report in sleep diaries) total sleep duration. The time in bed is then gradually increased until reaching patients' optimal sleep need. An alternative method, called *sleep compression*, consists in gradual constriction of time in bed until reaching the optimal sleep need.
Stimulus control	*Behavioural strategy*: Several instructions aiming at strengthening the bed as a cue for sleep, weakening it as a cue for activities that might interfere with sleep, and helping the insomniac acquire a consistent sleep rhythm, based on operant conditioning model: (1) lie down to go to sleep only when you are sleepy; (2) do not use your bed for anything except your sleep and sexual activity; (3) if you find yourself unable to fall asleep, get up and go to another room; stay up as long as you wish, and come back to bed when you feel sleepy; (4) if you still cannot fall asleep, repeat step 3 and do this as often as is necessary throughout the night; (5) set your alarm and get up at the same time every morning irrespective of how much sleep you got during the night; (6) no napping during daytime.
Sleep hygiene education	*Behavioural and educational strategy*: General health instructions about internal and external factors that might influence sleep (e.g., sport, light, temperature, etc.).
Relaxation	*Behavioural and cognitive strategy*: A set of methods aiming at reducing somatic or cognitive hyperarousal (e.g., progressive muscle relaxation, autogenic training imagery training, meditation).
Cognitive reappraisal	*Cognitive strategy*: Strategies directed to reduce dysfunctional beliefs, attitudes, concerns, and false beliefs about the cause of insomnia and about the inability to sleep.
Cognitive control/ Worry time	*Cognitive strategy*: The patient is instructed to sit comfortably in an armchair and write down a list of worries and list of what to do the next day. The rationale of this strategy is to prevent emotionally loaded intrusive thoughts during the sleep-onset period, as all worries have been "already" processed before going to bed.
Paradoxical intention	*Cognitive strategy*: Strategy aimed at reducing the anticipatory anxiety at the time of falling asleep. Patients are instructed to remain still in bed with the eyes closed and to try to keep awake as long as they can. This takes away the responsibility to try to fall asleep, which in turn often leads to falling asleep quicker.

CBT-I should be the first-line treatment. Furthermore, the authors of the guideline were aware of the fact that at present CBT-I is not available to the vast majority of patients around the world and they acknowledge this difficulty and make reference to web-based approaches as adjunct approaches to treatment dissemination. In addition, they stress that a stepped-care model will be of the utmost importance to establish CBT-I in different medical settings.

Sateia and colleagues from the American Academy of Sleep Medicine (Sateia, Buysse, Krystal, Neubauer & Head, 2017) summarised and evaluated the evidence concerning the pharmacological treatment of chronic insomnia in adults. They came to the conclusion that most of the published data relate to short-term treatment over a time span of 3 to 4 weeks. A main conclusion was that eszopiclone, ramelteon, temazepam, triazolam, zaleplon and zolpidem are recommended for treating sleep onset insomnia whereas doxepin, eszopiclone, temazepam, suvorexant and zolpidem are recommended for sleep maintenance insomnia. Not recommended were drugs like diphenhydramine, melatonin, tiagabine, trazodone, l-tryptophan and valerian. In a similar way, guidelines by the German Sleep Society (Riemann et al., 2017a) concluded that CBT-I should be the first-line treatment whereas benzodiazepine receptor agonists (BZRA) and SAD (sedating antidepressants) may be used for short-term pharmacological treatment.

The European guideline for the diagnosis and treatment of insomnia will be reviewed in more detail. Riemann and colleagues (2017b), as members of a task force of the European Sleep Research Society, aimed at providing clinical recommendations for the management of adult patients with chronic insomnia. The guideline was based on a systematic review of relevant meta-analyses concerning insomnia treatment published till June 2016. Recommendations concerning treatment are shown in Table 1.4.

The European guideline stresses that CBT-I should be the first-line treatment for insomnia, whereas pharmacological interventions can or should be offered if CBT-I is not sufficiently effective or not available. Pharmacological agents, specifically BZRA and SAD were recommended as main substances for insomnia treatment in the short term. None of these medications were recommended for long-term treatment. Antipsychotics, antihistaminics, melatonin, phytotherapy and

Table 1.4 Recommendations for insomnia treatment according to the European guideline for the diagnosis and treatment of insomnia (Modified from Riemann et al., 2017b).

In the presence of co-morbidities, clinical judgement should decide whether the insomnia or co-morbid condition is treated first, or whether both are treated at the same time.

Cognitive behavioural therapy for insomnia (CBT-I)

- CBT-I is recommended as first-line treatment for chronic insomnia in adults of any age (strong recommendation, high-quality evidence).

Pharmacological interventions

- A pharmacological intervention can be offered if CBT-I is not sufficiently effective or not available.

Benzodiazepine receptor agonists (BZRA)

- BZRA are effective in the short-term treatment of insomnia (≤ 4 weeks) (high-quality evidence)
- The newer BZRA (i.e., Z-substances are equally effective as the older ones (moderate-quality evidence).
- Long-term treatment of insomnia with BZRA is not generally recommended because of a lack of evidence and possible side effects/risks (strong recommendation, low-quality evidence).

Sedating antidepressants

- Sedating antidepressants are effective in the short-term treatment of insomnia; contraindications have to be carefully considered (moderate-quality evidence). Long-term treatment of insomnia with sedating antidepressants is not generally recommended because of a lack of evidence and possible side effects/risks (strong recommendation, low-quality evidence).

Antihistaminics

- Because of insufficient evidence, antihistaminics are not recommended for insomnia treatment (strong recommendation, low-quality evidence).

Antipsychotics

- Because of insufficient evidence and in light of their side effects, antipsychotics are not recommended for insomnia treatment (strong recommendation, very low-quality evidence). As an exception, low-potency antipsychotics may be considered in psychogeriatric patients with insomnia (weak recommendation, low-quality evidence).

Melatonin

- Melatonin is not generally recommended for the treatment of insomnia because of low efficacy (weak recommendation, low-quality evidence).

Phytotherapy

- Valerian and other phytotherapeutics are not recommended for the treatment of insomnia because of poor evidence (weak recommendation, very low-quality evidence).

Light therapy and exercise

- Light therapy and exercise regimes may be useful as adjunct regimes (weak recommendation, low-quality evidence).

Complementary and alternative medicine

- Aroma therapy, acupuncture, food reflexology, homeopathy, light therapy and music therapy are not recommended for the treatment of insomnia because of poor evidence (weak recommendation, very low-quality evidence).

complementary and alternative medicines were also not recommended for general insomnia treatment due to lack of evidence or possible adverse effects (e.g., antipsychotics).

Similarly, the British Association for Psychopharmcology consensus statement (Wilson et al., 2019) identifies CBT-I as the first-line treatment for insomnia disorder and does so at the statement's highest level of recommendation. It goes on to suggest that in cases of treatment failure, unavailability of CBT-I, or an inability to engage with CBT-I, evidence-based pharmacotherapy should be offered.

Accompanying the publications of the European guideline, Morin (2017) commented on critical issues and challenges in implementing the clinical practice guideline for the management of chronic insomnia. It is well acknowledged that though the evidence base for CBT-I is excellent, especially for the treatment of the chronic disorder, the availability of CBT-I trained clinicians may vary and is far from being sufficient world-wide. Several strategies are suggested by Morin (2017): the inclusion of web-based/eCBT-I in the standard treatment of insomnia, via, for example, prescription by a general practitioner. Stepped-care models for insomnia (Espie, 2009; Espie, Hames & McKinstry, 2013) have also been suggested, encompassing the levels of self-help (books, eCBT-I), nurses and other health professionals, general practitioners, specialists like neurologists, psychiatrists, psychologists, psychotherapists and sleep medicine specialists (see Chapter 24).

Most recently, the AASM (Edinger et al., 2021a, 2021b) reiterated its point of view concerning CBT-I: accordingly, CBT-I should be considered as the main strategy to treat insomnia.

References

American Academy of Sleep Medicine (2014). *International classification of sleep disorders* (3rd ed.). Rochester: AASM.

American Psychiatric Association (2013). *Diagnostic and statistical manual of mental disorders* (5th ed.: DSM-5). Washington, DC: APA.

Anothaisintawee, T., Reutrakul, S., Van Cauter, E., & Thakkinstian, A. (2016). Sleep disturbances compared to traditional risk factors for diabetes development: Systematic review and meta-analysis. *Sleep Medicine Reviews, 30*, 11–24. https://doi.org/10.1016/j.smrv.2015.10.002.

Baglioni, C., Spiegelhalder, K., Lombardo, C., & Riemann, D. (2010). Sleep and emotions: A focus on insomnia. *Sleep Medicine Reviews, 14*, 227–238.

Baglioni, C., Lombardo, C., Bux, E., Hansen, S., Salveta, C., Biello, S.,Violani, C., & Espie, C. A. (2010). Psychophysiological reactivity to sleep-related emotional stimuli in primary insomnia. *Behaviour Research and Therapy, 48*, 467–475. https://doi.org/10.1016/j.brat.2010.01.008.

Baglioni, C., Battagliese, G., Feige, B., Spiegelhalder, K., Nissen, C., Voderholzer, U., Lombardo, C., & Riemann, D. (2011). Insomnia as a predictor of depression: A meta-analytic evaluation of longitudinal epidemiological studies. *Journal of Affective Disorders, 135*, 10–19. https://doi.org/10.1016/j.jad.2011.01.011.

Baglioni, C., Regen, W., Teghen, A., Spiegelhalder, K., Feige, B., Nissen, C., & Riemann, D. (2014a). Sleep changes in the disorder of insomnia: A meta-analysis of polysomnographic studies. *Sleep Medicine Reviews, 18*, 195–213.

Baglioni, C., Spiegelhalder, K., Regen, W., Feige, B., Nissen, C., Lombardo, C., & Riemann, D. (2014b). Insomnia disorder is associated with increased amygdala reactivity to insomnia-related stimuli. *Sleep, 37*, 1907–1917. https://doi.org/10.5665/sleep.4240.

Baglioni, C., Nanovska, S., Regen, W., Spiegelhalder, K., Feige, B., Nissen, C., Reynolds, C. F., & Riemann D. (2016). Sleep and mental disorders: A meta-analysis of polysomnographic research. *Psychological Bulletin, 142* (9), 969–990.

Baglioni, C., Altena, E., Bjorvatn, B., Blom, K., Bothelius, K., Devoto, A., Espie, C. A., Frase, L., Gavriloff, D., Tuuliki, H, Hoflehner, A., Högl, B., Holzinger, B., Järnefelt, H., Jernelöv, S., Johann, A. F., Lombardo, C., Nissen, C., Palagini, L., Peeters, G., Perlis, M. L., Posner, D., Schlarb, A., Spiegelhalder, K., Wichniak. A., & Riemann, D. (2020). The European Academy for Cognitive Behavioural Therapy for Insomnia: An initiative of the European Insomnia Network to promote implementation and dissemination of treatment. *Journal of Sleep Research, 29*, 1–29. https://doi.org/10.1111/jsr.12967.

Bastien, C., LeBlanc, M., Carrier, J., & Morin, C. M. (2003). Sleep EEG power spectra, insomnia and chronic use of benzodiazepines. *Sleep*, 26, 313–317.

Benton, A. L. (1995). Neuropsychological assessment. *Annual Review of Psychology, 45*, 1–23.

Bonnet, M., & Arand, D. (2000). Activity, arousal and the MSLT in patients with insomnia. *Sleep*, 23, 1–8.

Bootzin, R. R., Epstein, D., & Wood, J. M. (1991). Stimulus control instructions. In P. Hauri (Ed.), *Case studies in insomnia* (pp. 19–28). New York and London: Plenum.

Borbely, A. A. (1982). A two-process model of sleep regulation. *Human Neurobiology*, 1, 195–204.

Brasure, M., Fuchs, E., MacDonald, R., Nelson, V. A., Koffel, E., Olson, C. M., Khawaja, I. S., Diem, S., Carlyle, M., Wilt, T. J., Ouellette, J., Butler, M., & Kane, R. L. (2016). Psychological and behavioral interventions for managing insomnia disorder: An evidence report for a clinical practice guideline by the American College of Physicians. *Annals of Internal Medicine, 165*, 113–124.

Broadbent, D. E., Cooper, P. F., FitzGerald, P., & Parkes, K. R. (1982). The cognitive failures questionnaire (CFQ) and its correlates. *British Journal of Clinical Psychology, 21*, 1–6.

Chan, W. S., Levsen, M. P., & McCrae, C. S. (2018). A meta-analysis of associations between obesity and insomnia diagnosis and symptoms. *Sleep Medicine Reviews, 40*, 170–182. https://doi.org/10.1016/j.smrv.2017.12.004.

Daley, M., Morin, C. M., LeBlanc, M., Grégoire, J. P., & Savard, J. (2009). The economic burden of insomnia: Direct and indirect costs for individuals with insomnia syndrome, insomnia symptoms, and good sleepers. *Sleep*, 32, 55–64.

Darden, M., Espie, C. A., Carl, J. R., Henry, A. L., Kanady, J. C., Krystal, A. D., & Miller, C. M. (2021). Cost-effectiveness of digital CBT (*Sleepio*) for insomnia: A Markov simulation model. *Sleep, Apr.,44* (4), zsaa223.

Dekker, K., Blanken, T. F., & Van Someren, E. J. (2017). Insomnia and personality – A network approach. *Brain Sciences, 7*, 28. doi: 10.3390/brainsci7030028. Drake, C. L., Pillai, V., & Roth, T. (2014). Stress and sleep reactivity: A prospective investigation of the stress-diathesis model of insomnia. *Sleep, 37*, 1295–1304.

Edinger, J. D., Arnedt, J. T., Bertisch, S., Carnesy, C. C., Harrington, J., Lichstein, K., Sateia, M. J., Troxel, W. M., Zhou, E. S., Kazmi, U., Heald, J. L., & Martin, J. (2021a). Behavioral and psychological treatments for chronic insomnia disorder in adults:

An American Academy of Sleep Medicine clinical practice guideline. *Journal of Clinical Sleep Medicine*, *17*, 255–262. doi: 10.5664/jcsm.8986.

Edinger, J. D., Arnedt, J., Bertisch, S., Carnesy, C. C., Harrington, J. J., Lichstein, K., Sateia, M. J., Troxel, W. M., Zhou, E. S., Kazmi, U., Heald, J. L, & Martin, J. (2021b). Behavioral and psychological treatments for chronic insomnia disorder in adults: An American Academy of Sleep Medicine systematic review, meta-analysis, and GRADE assessment. *Journal of Clinical Sleep Medicine*, *17*, 263–298. doi: 10.5664/jcsm.8988.

Ellis, J., Gehrman, P., Espie, C. A., Riemann, D., & Perlis, M. (2012). Acute insomnia: Current conceptualizations and future directions. *Sleep Medicine Reviews*, *16*, 5–14.

Espie, C. A. (2002). Insomnia: Conceptual issues in the development, persistence, and treatment of sleep disorder in adults. *Annual Review of Psychology*, *53*, 215–243. https://doi.org/10.1146/annurev.psych.53.100901.135243.

Espie, C. A. (2007). Understanding insomnia through cognitive modelling. *Sleep Medicine, Suppl.* 4, S3–S8.

Espie, C. A. (2009). Stepped care: A health technology solution for delivering cognitive behavioral therapy as a first line insomnia treatment. *Sleep*, *32*, 1549–1558.

Espie, C. A. (2022) *A Clinician's Guide to Cognitive and Behavioural Therapeutics (CBTx) for Insomnia*. Cambridge, UK: Cambridge University Press.

Espie, C. A., Broomfield, N. M., MacMahon, K. M., Macphee, L. M., & Taylor, L. M. (2006). The attention–intention–effort pathway in the development of psychophysiologic insomnia: A theoretical review. *Sleep Medicine Reviews*, *10*, 215–245.

Espie, C. A., Hames, P., & McKinstry, B. (2013). Use of the internet and mobile media for delivery of cognitive-behavioral insomnia therapy. *Sleep Medicine Clinics*, *8*, 407–419.

Feige, B., Al-Shajlawi, A., Nissen, C., Voderholzer, U., Hornyak, M, Spiegelhalder, K., Kloepfer, C., Perlis, M. L., & Riemann, D. (2008). Does REM sleep contribute to subjective wake time in primary insomnia? A comparison of polysomnographic and subjective sleep in 100 patients. *Journal of Sleep Research*, *17*, 180–190.

Feige, B., Baglioni, C., Spiegelhalder, K., Hirscher, V., Nissen, C., & Riemann, D. (2013). The microstructure of sleep in primary insomnia: A review and new data. *International Journal of Psychophysiology*, *89*, 171–180.

Fortier-Brochu, E., Beaulieu-Bonneau, S., Ivers, H., & Morin, C. M. (2012). Insomnia and daytime cognitive performance: A meta-analysis. *Sleep Medicine Reviews*, *16*, 83–94.

Gradisar, M., Lack, L. Richards, H., Harris, J., Gallasch, J., Boundy, M., & Johnston, A. (2007). The flinders fatigue scale: Preliminary psychometric properties and clinical sensitivity of a new scale for measuring daytime fatigue associated with insomnia. *Journal of Clinical Sleep Medicine*, *3*, 722–728.

Hagger, M. S. (2010). Sleep, self-regulation, self-control, and health. *Stress and Health*, 26 (3), 181–185. https://doi.org/10.1002/smi.1345.

Harris, K., Spiegelhalder, K., Espie, C. A., MacMahon, K. M., Woods, H. C., & Kyle, S. D. (2015). Sleep-related attentional bias in insomnia: A state-of-the-science review. *Clinical Psychology Review*, *42*, 16–27. https://doi.org/10.1016/j.cpr.2015.08.001.

Harvey, A. G. (2002). A cognitive model of insomnia. *Behaviour Research and Therapy*, *40*, 869–893.

Hertenstein, E., Feige, B., Gmeiner, T., Kienzler, C., Spiegelhalder, K., Johann, A., Jansson-Fröjmark, M., Palagini, L., Rücker, G., Riemann, D., & Baglioni, C. (2019). Insomnia as a predictor of mental disorders: A systematic review and meta-analysis. *Sleep Medicine Reviews*, *43*, 96–105. https://doi.org/10.1016/J.smrv.2018.10.006.

Iverson, G. L., & Lam, R. W. (2013). Rapid screening for perceived cognitive impairment in major depressive disorder. *Annuals of Clinical Psychology*, 25, 135–140.

Kathol, R. G., & Arnedt, J. T. (2016) Cognitive behavioral therapy for chronic insomnia: Confronting the challenges to implementation. *Annals of Internal Medicine*, *165*, 149–150.

Kushida, C. A., Littner, M., Morgenthaler, T., Alessi, C. A., Bailey, D., Coleman, J., Friedman, L., Hirshkowitz, M., Kapen, S., Kramer, M., Lee-Chiong, T., Loube, D. L., Owens, J., Pancer, J. P., & Wise, M. (2005). Practice parameters for the indications for polysomnography and related procedures: An update for 2005. *Sleep*, *28*, 499–521.

Kyle, S. D., & Espie, C. A. (2014). Insomnias: Classification, Evaluation and Pathophysiology. In S. Chokroverty and L. Ferini-Strambi (Eds.), *Oxford Textbook of Sleep Disorders*. Oxford, UK: Oxford University Press. eScholarID:227090.

Kyle, S. D., Morgan, K., & Espie, C. A. (2010). Insomnia and health-related quality of life. *Sleep Medicine Reviews*, *14*, 69–82.

Kyle, S. D., Hurry, M. E. D., Emsley, R., Marsden, A., Omlin, X., Juss, A., Spiegelhalder, K., Bisdounis, L., Luik, A. I., Espie, C. A., & Sexton, C. E. (2020). The effects of digital cognitive behavioural therapy for insomnia on cognitive function: A randomised, controlled trial. *Sleep, Sept.*, *43* (9), zsaa034. doi: 10.1093/sleep/zsaa034.

Lane, J. M., Jones, S., Dashti, H. S., Wood, A. R., Aragam, K., Van Hees, V., Strand, L. B., Winsvold, B. S., Wang, H., Bowden, J., Song, Y., Patel, K., Anderson, S. G., Beaumont, R. N., Bechtold, D. A, Cade, B. E., Haas, M., Kathiresan, S., Little, M. A., Luik,

A. I., Loudon, A. S., Purcell, S., Richmond, R. C., Scheer, F. A. J. L., Schormair, B., Tyrrell, J., Winkelman, J. W., Winkelmann, J., Hveem, K., Zhao, C., Nielsen, J. B., Willer, C. J., Redline, S., Spiegelhalder, K., Kyle, S. D., Ray, D. W., Zwart, J. A., Brumpton, B., Frayling, T. M., Lawlor, D. A., Rutter, M. K., Weedon, M. N., & Saxena, R. (2019). Biological and clinical insights from genetics of insomnia symptoms. *Nature Genetics*, *51*, 387–393.

Léger, D., Levy, E., & Paillard, M. (1999). The direct costs of insomnia in France. *Sleep*, *22*, S394–401.

Li, M., Zhang, X. W., Hou, W. S., & Tang, Z. Y. (2014). Insomnia and risk of cardiovascular disease: A meta-analysis of cohort studies. *International Journal of Cardiology*, *176*, 1044–1047.

MacMahon, K. M., Broomfield, N. M., & Espie, C. A. (2006). Attention bias for sleep-related stimuli in primary insomnia and delayed sleep phase syndrome using the dot-probe task. *Sleep*, *29*, 1420–1427.

McCrae, C., McNamara, J., Rowe, M., Dzierzewski, J., Dirk, J., Marsiske, M., & Craggs, J. (2008). Sleep and affect in older adults: Using multilevel modeling to examine daily associations. *Journal of Sleep Research*, *17*, 42–53.

Miller, C. M., Carl, J. R., Baker, L. (2020). A Health Economic Evaluation of Sleepio at a Fortune 500 Company. White paper published online by Big Health in collaboration with a Fortune 500 Company, IBM Watson Health, and Professor Laurence Baker, Stanford University, California.

Morin, C. M. (1993). *Insomnia: Psychological assessment and management*. New York and London: Guilford Press.

Morin, C. M. (2017) Issues and challenges in implementing clinical practice guideline for the management of chronic insomnia. *Journal of Sleep Research*, 26, 673–674.

Morin, C. M. & Espie, C. A. (2003). *Insomnia: A clinical guide to assessment and treatment*. New York: Kluwer Academic/ Plenum Publishers [ISBN 0-306-47750-5].

Morin, C. M., Vallières, A., & Ivers, H. (2007). Dysfunctional beliefs and attitudes about sleep (DBAS): Validation of a brief version (DBAS-16). *Sleep*, *30*, 1547–1554.

Morin, C., Drake, C., Harvey, A., Krystal, A. D., Manber, R., Riemann, D., & Spiegelhalder, K. (2015). Insomnia disorder. *Nature Reviews Disease Primers, Sept.*, *1*, 15026. doi: 1038/nrdp.2015.26.

Ohayon, M. M. (2002). Epidemiology of insomnia: What we know and what we still need to learn. *Sleep Medicine Reviews*, *6* (2), 97–111.

Orff, H. J., Drummond, S. P., Nowakowski, S., & Perlis, M. L. (2007). Discrepancy between subjective symptomatology and objective neuropsychological performance in insomnia. *Sleep*, *30*, 1205–1211.

Øverland, S., Glozier, N., Sivertsen, B., Stewart, R., Neckelmann, D., Krokstad, S., & Mykletun, A. (2008). A comparison of insomnia and depression as predictors of disability pension: The HUNT Study. *Sleep*, *31*, 875–880. https://doi.org/10.1093/ sleep/ 31.6.875.

Palagini, L., Biber, K., & Riemann, D. (2014). The genetics of insomnia – Evidence for epigenetic mechanisms. *Sleep Medicine Reviews*, *18*, 225–235.

Palmer, C. A., & Alfano, C. A. (2017). Sleep and emotion regulation: An organizing, integrative review. *Sleep Medicine Reviews*, *31*, 6–16. https://doi.org/10.1016/j.smrv.2015.12.006.

Perlis, M. L., Ellis, J., Spiegelhalder, K., & Riemann, D. (2022). Etiology and pathophysiology of insomnia. In M. Kryger, T. Roth and W. C. Dement (Eds.), *Principles and practice of sleep medicine* (7th ed.), pp. 835–849. Philadelphia, PA: Elsevier.

Perlis, M. L., Giles, D. E., Mendelson, W. B., Bootzin, R. R., & Wyatt, J. K. (1997). Psychophysiological insomnia: The behavioural model and a neurocognitive perspective. *Journal of Sleep Research*, *6*, 179–188.

Perlis, M. L., Smith, M. T., Andrews, P. J., Orff, H., & Giles, D. E. (2001). Beta/gamma EEG activity in patients with primary and secondary insomnia and good sleeper controls. *Sleep*, *24*, 110–117.

Pigeon, W. R., Pinquart, M., & Conner, K. (2012). Meta-analysis of sleep disturbance and suicidal thoughts and behaviors. *Journal of Clinical Psychiatry*, *73*, e1160–e1167. https://doi.org/10.4088/JCP.11r07586.

Qaseem, A., Kansagara, D., Forciea, M. A., Cooke, M., & Denberg, T. D. (2016). Management of chronic insomnia disorder in adults: A clinical practice guideline from the American College of Physicians. *Annals of Internal Medicine*, *165*, 125–133.

Reynolds, S. A., & Ebben, M. R. (2017). The cost of insomnia and the benefit of increased access to evidence-based treatment: Cognitive Behavioral Therapy for Insomnia. *Sleep Medicine Clinics*, *12*, 39–46. https://doi.org/10.1016/j.jsmc.2016.10.011.

Riemann, D., Krone, L.B., Wulff, K., & Nissen, C. (2020). Sleep, insomnia, and depression. *Neuropsychopharmacology*, *45*, 74–89.

Riemann, D., & Nissen, C. (2012). Sleep and psychotropic drugs In C. A. Espie and C. M. Morin (Eds.), *Oxford handbook of sleep and sleep disorders*, pp. 190–222. Oxford: Oxford Press.

Riemann, D., Spiegelhalder, K., Feige, B., Voderholzer, U., Berger, M., Perlis, M. L., & Nissen, C. (2010). The hyperarousal model of insomnia: A review of the concept and its evidence. *Sleep Medicine Reviews*, *14*, 19–31.

Riemann, D., Spiegelhalder, K., Espie, C., Pollmächer, T., Leger, D., Bassetti, C., & van Someren, E. (2011). Chronic insomnia: Clinical and research challenges – An agenda. *Pharmacopsychiatry*, *44*, 1–14.

Riemann, D., Nissen, C., Palagini, L., Otte, A., Perlis, M. L., & Spiegelhader, K. (2015). The neurobiology, investigation and treatment of chronic insomnia. *Lancet Neurology*, *14*, 547–558.

Riemann, D., Baum, E., Cohrs, S., Crönlein, T., Hajak, G., Hertenstein, E., Klose, P., Langhorst, J., Mayer, G., Nissen, C., Pollmächer, T., Rabstein, S., Schlarb, A., Sitter, H., Weeß, H.G., Wetter, T., & Spiegelhalder, K. (2017a). S-3 Leitlinie Nicht erholsamer Schlaf/ Schlafstörungen. Kapitel Insomnie bei Erwachsenen (AWMF Registriernummer 063-003), Update 2016. *Somnologie*, *20* (Suppl. s2), S97–S180.

Riemann, D., Baglioni, C., Bassetti, C., Bjorvatn, B., Dolenc Groselj, L., Ellis, J. G., Espie, C. A., Garcia-Borreguero, D., Gjerstad, M., Gonçalves, M., Hertenstein, E., Jansson-Fröjmark, M., Jennum, P. J., Leger, D., Nissen, C., Parrino, L., Paunio, T., Pevernagie, D., Verbraecken, J., Weeß, H. G., Wichniak, A., Zavalko, I., Arnardottir, E. S., Deleanu, O. C., Strazisar, B., Zoetmulder, M., & Spiegelhalder, K. (2017b). European guideline for the diagnosis and treatment of insomnia. *Journal of Sleep Research*, *26*, 675–700.

Sadeh, A., Tikotzky, L., & Kahn, M. (2014). Sleep in infancy and childhood: Implications for emotional and behavioral difficulties in adolescence and beyond. *Current Opinion in Psychiatry*, *27*, 453–459. doi: 10.1097/YCO.0000000000000109.

Saper, C. B., Scammell, T. E., & Lu, J. (2005). Hypothalamic regulation of sleep and circadian rhythms. *Nature*, 437, 1257–1263.

Sateia, M. J., Buysse, D. J., Krystal, A. D., Neubauer, D. N., & Head, J. L. (2017). Clinical practice guideline for the pharmacological treatment of chronic insomnia in adults: An American Academy of Sleep Medicine clinical practice guideline. *Journal of Clinical Sleep Medicine*, *2*, 307–349.

Scott, B. A., & Judge, T. A. (2006). Insomnia, emotions, and job satisfaction: A multilevel study. *Journal of Management*, *32* (5), 622–645. doi: 10.1177/0149206306289762.

Shekleton, J. A., Rogers, N. L., & Rajaratnam, S. M. (2010). Searching for the daytime impairments of primary insomnia. *Sleep Medicine Reviews*, *14*, 47–60.

Sivertsen, B., Krokstad, S., Øverland, S., & Mykletun, A. (2009). The epidemiology of insomnia: Associations with physical and mental health: The HUNT-2 study. *Journal of Psychosomatic Research*, *67*, 109–116.

Sofi, F., Cesari, F., Casini, A., Macchi, C., Abbate, R., & Gensini, G. F. (2014). Insomnia and risk of cardiovascular disease: A meta-analysis. *European Journal of Preventive Cardiology*, *21*, 57–64. https ://doi.org/10.1177/20474 87312 460020.

Spiegelhalder, K., Espie, C., Nissen, C., & Riemann, D. (2008). Sleep-related attentional bias in patients with primary insomnia compared with sleep experts and healthy controls. *Journal of Sleep Research*, *17*, 191–196.

Spiegelhalder, K., Scholtes, C., & Riemann, D. (2010). The association between insomnia and cardiovascular diseases. *Nature and Science of Sleep*, *2*, 71. https://doi.org/10.2147/NSS.S7471.

Spiegelhalder, K., Kyle, S. D., Feige, B., Prem, M., Nissen, C., Espie, C. A., & Riemann, D. (2010). The impact of sleep-related attentional bias on polyomnographically measured sleep in primary insomnia. *Sleep*, *33*, 107–112.

Spiegelhalder, K., Regen, W., Feige, B., Holz, J., Piosczyk, H., Baglioni, C., Riemann, D., & Nissen, C. (2012). Increased EEG sigma and beta power during NREM sleep in primary insomnia. *Biological Psychology*, *91*, 329–333.

Spielman, A. J., Saskin, P., & Thorpy, M. J. (1987). Treatment of chronic insomnia by restriction of time in bed. *Sleep*, *10* (1), 45–56.

Tang, N. K., & Harvey, A. G. (2004). Correcting distorted perception of sleep in insomnia: A novel behavioural experiment? *Behaviour Research and Therapy*, *42*, 27–39.

Taylor, D., Wilkerson, A. K., Pruiksma, K. E., Williams, J. M., Ruggero, C. J., Hale, W., Mintz, J., Organek, K. M., Nicholson, K. L., Litz, B. T., Young-McCaughan, S., Dondanville, K. A., Borah, E. V., Brundige, A., & Peterson, A. L. (2018) Reliability of the structured clinical interview for DSM-5 sleep disorders module. *Journal of Clinical Sleep Medicine*, *14*, 459–464.

Thiart, H., Ebert, D. D., Lehr, D., Nobis, S., Buntrock, C., Berking, M., & Riper, H. (2016). Internet-based cognitive behavioral therapy for insomnia: A health economic evaluation. *Sleep*, *39*, 1769–1778. https://doi.org/10.5665/sleep.6152.

van de Laar, M., Verbeek, I., Pevernagie, D., Aldenkamp, A., & Overeem, S. (2010). The role of personality traits in insomnia. *Sleep Medicine Reviews*, *14*, 61–68.

Vgontzas, A. N., Fernandez-Mendoza, J., Liao, D., & Bixler, E. O. (2013). Insomnia with objective short sleep duration: The most biologically severe phenotype of the disorder. *Sleep Medicine Reviews*, *17*, 241–254.

Wickwire, E. M. (2019). The value of digital insomnia therapeutics: What we know and what we need to know. *Journal of Clinical Sleep Medicine*, *15*, 11–13.

Wilson, S., Anderson, K., Baldwin, D., Dijk, D. J., Espie, A., Espie, C. A., Espie, C., Gringras, P., Krystal, A., Nutt, D., Selsick, H., & Sharpley, A. (2019). British association for psychopharmacology consensus statement on evidence-based treatment of insomnia, parasomnias and circadian rhythm disorders: An update. *Journal of Psychopharmacology*. doi: 10.1177/0269881119855343.

Wilt, T. J., MacDonald, R., Brasure, M., Olson, C. M., Carlyle, M., Fuchs, E., Khawaja, I. S, Diem, S., Koffel, E., Ouellette, J., Butler, M., & Kane, R. L. (2016). Pharmacological treatment of insomnia disorder: An evidence report for a clinical practice guideline by the American College of Physicians. *Annals of Internal Medicine*, *165*, 103–112.

Section I

Cognitive Behavioural Therapy for Insomnia (CBT-I). An Introduction for Health Professionals

Section Editor: Dieter Riemann

2

Standard CBT-I Protocol for the Treatment of Insomnia Disorder

Colin A. Espie

Key points

- CBT is not a treatment for insomnia, but a system of evidence-based therapeutics that may be combined to deliver clinically meaningful insomnia outcomes.
- CBT is typically delivered as a multicomponent treatment, but the form, content and sequencing of its elements may vary.
- The standard CBT protocol should include at least one behavioural therapeutic and one cognitive therapeutic. Relaxation methods, sleep education and sleep hygiene are less essential but may be useful therapy adjuncts.
- The standard CBT protocol is therapy, not a set of instructions, and for treatment to be effective consistent home implementation is essential. CBT therefore should be informed by clinical expertise and address individual needs.

Learning objectives

- To understand what comprises the standard ingredients of CBT for insomnia that need to be evidence-based and faithfully implemented if therapy is to be clinically effective.
- To understand the scientific and historical foundations of behavioural and cognitive therapeutics for insomnia.
- To understand how to use the standard protocol as a foundation for clinical work with insomnia patients.
- To understand how to present CBT therapeutics to patients, and to support them to implement them in real world situations.

Abstract

The purpose of this chapter is to provide an overview of what you might expect to find in a CBT program for insomnia. That is, what would comprise the *standard treatment protocol*. I have taken the perspective that the published literature provides us with the greatest confidence in knowing what is effective, and so have included, as standard, those elements of CBT that have the strongest evidence base. That said, a feature of the insomnia trials literature is that CBT has typically been evaluated as a *multicomponent* therapy, so discrete elements have not necessarily been investigated as fully as one might wish, and the contribution of those elements to the overall treatment effect remains largely unknown. Consequently, where a given intervention has been a common component in trials demonstrating the effectiveness of CBT, I have taken the view that there are good grounds for thinking of that intervention as part of the standard protocol. In other words, it is at the very core of CBT for insomnia. Inevitably, I have had to make some choices and some judgements in proposing this standard protocol, and I recognise that others may take a different view.

Cognitive-Behavioural Therapy for Insomnia (CBT-I) Across the Life Span: Guidelines and Clinical Protocols for Health Professionals,
First Edition. Edited by Chiara Baglioni, Colin A. Espie and Dieter Riemann.

My intention is that the chapter is practical, in keeping with the purpose of this book, rather than heavily referenced to source materials, so I have relied mainly on clinical guidelines, practice parameters and systematic reviews when citing evidence. It is important to note, however, that clinical trials, of which there are many, are readily accessible through these overviews and I would recommend that you look at some of those to see just how varied CBT for insomnia can be, in content, content ordering, in treatment duration and in format of delivery. There are situations, however, where I have felt it helpful, and interesting perhaps, to provide more referencing[1]; for example, to the scientific and historical roots of CBT. I often feel that these are overlooked. It is very important to appreciate the strength, depth and longevity of our field, even if the terminology we use (and sometimes re-brand) appears as if it is novel! Our confidence that CBT works is also based on this provenance, and the diligent work of countless clinicians and researchers over many decades.

Finally, this chapter is provided as a platform upon which other chapters may build. By presenting this standard protocol, focussed primarily in relation to adults with insomnia, applications of CBT to other populations, age groups and circumstances, protocol variations, and emerging approaches to therapeutics can compare, contrast and evolve through the course of the textbook. I have also tried to write as much as possible in plain language, and to share personal accounts of how I would deliver CBT, to make this chapter as clinically informative as possible. If you would like further insight into my approach to the actual delivery of CBT-I, I would refer you to two recent books, one for patients (Espie, 2021) and the other for clinicians (Espie, 2023).

Keywords *insomnia, CBT, therapeutic, protocol, component, implementation*

Minimal characteristics of a CBT protocol

I consider CBT to be a construct referring to a system of therapeutics, rather than a specific treatment (Espie, 2023). Accordingly, if you said that you 'gave your patient CBT', I would not know exactly what you did. Moreover, it might not be obvious to me what I did with one of my own 'CBT patients'! The treatment journey is often unique, and the course of treatment usually departs from what you at first expected or intended. Indeed, one of the great assets of CBT, as a system of therapeutics, is that it is well suited to this *formulation-driven* approach, where *case conceptualization* (Kuyken, Padesky & Dudley, 2011) leads to the personalised selection of CBT components and the ways in which they are introduced and delivered. You might be forgiven then for thinking that a standard protocol for CBT is a rather far-fetched idea!

In reviewing the literature on CBT for insomnia, the practice parameters task force of the American Academy of Sleep Medicine (AASM) recently grappled with the question of what were the *minimal characteristics* of effective CBT (Edinger et al., 2021). I think this is helpful, for us, as we try to discern what should be in a standard protocol. They were faced with the evidence, as we know, that multicomponent CBT has the strongest treatment claim, yet the large number of studies included in their review did not use a highly standardised approach to delivering and formatting multicomponent CBT. Importantly, however, the AASM task force found that an identical approach was not necessary to achieve clinically meaningful benefit to patients. Edinger et al. (2020) concluded that 'all studies included sleep restriction therapy, stimulus control and some form of cognitive therapy; however, the cognitive component varied widely. Whether or not relaxation strategies or sleep hygiene were included in the CBT-I regimen varied across studies as well. It was beyond the scope of this (group) to recommend a specific CBT protocol, and these variations did not appear to systematically impact the effectiveness of the treatment' (p. 261).

Consider carefully that last phrase '. . . these variations did not appear to systematically impact the effectiveness of the treatment'. Protocol variation is OK! Indeed, in my view, it is more than OK, it is a great thing, because it evidences the versatility and robustness of CBT. I disagree with the notion that everyone should use the same CBT content, and in the same order. We are not technicians at the mercy of a regimen. We are clinicians, and we should care about the best way of bringing clinically meaningful benefit to each patient, consistent with a personalised behavioural sleep medicine approach (Espie, Hames & McKinstry, 2013). The simple truth is that research studies require per protocol delivery of CBT in randomised controlled trials (RCTs) to ensure within trial treatment fidelity, but the different research labs who have been responsible for the RCTs have not used the same protocol as each other. In the hands of individual clinicians delivering CBT services for insomnia there is a very much wider bandwidth than this.

All these things taken into account, I am very confident that we can establish the minimal characteristics of multicomponent CBT, and that we can be confident that the CBT we are about to describe is the treatment of first choice for persistent insomnia (Qaseem, Kansagara, Forciea, Cooke & Denberg, 2016; Riemann et al., 2017; Wilson et al., 2019).

In Figure 2.1 I have summarized what I would be regarded as the core requirements of the standardised CBT protocol. Let me explain the overarching structure.

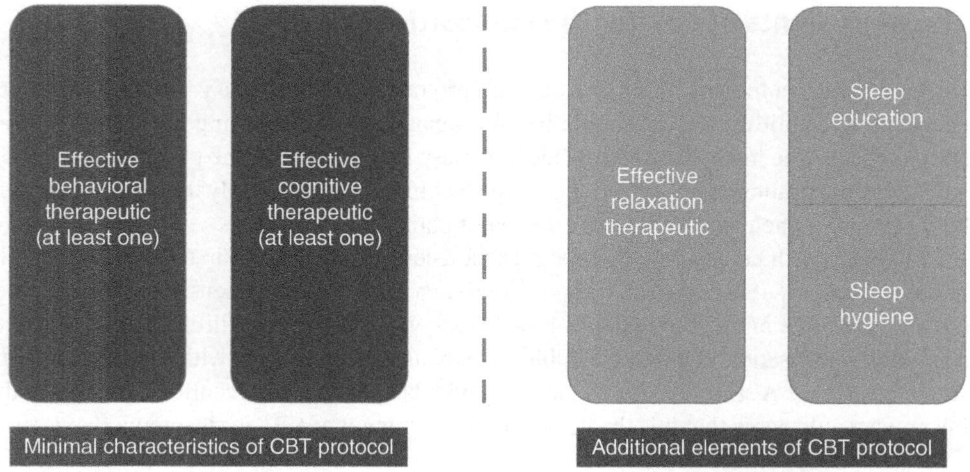

Figure 2.1 Minimal Characteristics of the Standard CBT Protocol for Effective Insomnia Treatment.

First, I would advise that the standard protocol has to comprise one or more effective *behavioural therapeutics*. The principal options here are *stimulus control therapy* and *sleep restriction therapy*. Although most protocols do include sleep restriction, some do not, and use stimulus control as the behavioural intervention. Stimulus control and sleep restriction may also be delivered sequentially or combined with one another. We often do the latter in our lab protocols, using the term 'sleep scheduling'. This is in part because these therapeutics can be combined quite readily and in part because stimulus control and sleep restriction are complex terms that many patients find hard to grasp. It should also be recognised that there are variants of, or alternatives to, these established behavioural therapies. *Sleep compression* is sometimes preferred to sleep restriction. Second, the standard protocol should include an effective *cognitive therapeutic*. There are relatively few trials of cognitive interventions as standalone treatment. However, as the name suggests, CBT always incorporates a 'C' in some way. Again, considerable variability is observed in the published literature. Cognitive elements range through adaptations of therapeutics that are widely adopted across mental disorders, such as *cognitive restructuring* and *imagery training*, to more specific techniques, such as *paradoxical intention* and *cognitive control*, sometimes known as worry control. These are the interventions that I will focus on in this chapter. However, there are others and some of these are featured elsewhere in the present textbook. For example, I consider (behavioural) *problem solving* to be a cognitive therapeutic option (Espie, 2023). Although clearly based on solution-focused planning principles it can also be interpreted as a reframing approach that drives self-control and self-efficacy. Likewise, and again in my personal view, the third wave, *mindfulness-based* interventions, are cognitive therapeutics. Finally, cognitive therapeutics may involve less well-known techniques, such as *articulatory suppression*, which has a more limited evidence base to date.

The first two columns in Figure 2.1 therefore represent the minimal ingredients for CBT. In addition to these, as represented in the third column, an effective *relaxation therapeutic* has often been part of CBT programs that have been tested in clinical trials. Whereas relaxation as a standalone therapeutic for insomnia has not been much evaluated for decades, it is often part of multicomponent CBT. That said, consistent with Edinger et al. (2021), I would not regard it as an essential part of the minimal protocol. The most commonly used relaxation approach by a long way has been *abbreviated progressive muscle relaxation*. However, elements of *cue-controlled relaxation*, exercises involving *diaphrammatic breathing* and *autogenic training* are often packaged into a combined form of relaxation therapy. Finally, there has been some resurgent interest in *biofeedback* as a method of self-regulation and relaxation because of sensors incorporated into wearable devices. However, the scientific literature on biofeedback is historical with few contemporary device developers testing products with any rigour.

In the final column of Figure 2.1, I have positioned sleep education and sleep hygiene as adjuncts to the standard protocol, but they are not part of the minimal requirements. This is because in the case of sleep hygiene there is limited evidence that sleep hygiene has clinical effects as a therapy in its own right (Chung et al., 2018), and indeed people with insomnia do not have particularly poor sleep hygiene in the first place. Nevertheless, sleep hygiene is typically included as an element in multicomponent CBT. Likewise, specific modules on sleep education would not be essential, in terms of sleep knowledge for the sake of knowing more about sleep, sleep processes and sleep disorders. Where sleep information and education are important is in relation to the active therapeutics themselves, for example, when explaining to your patient how and why sleep restriction might work for them. My assumption is that the rationale that you provide for a treatment should be an intrinsic component of collaboration around treatment formulation. Consequently, I would stress that knowledge and understanding are important, but just not as detached components.

The ingredients of CBT for the standard protocol

Having provided a framework for the standard protocol I will now take you through the CBT techniques in turn, using the behavioural, cognitive, and relaxation-based domains as the organising principle. I will also cover sleep education and sleep hygiene. The intention is to provide summary information on the provenance and content of each technique, along with some illustration of how you may use the technique in therapy. My descriptions are not detailed executional manuals but overviews to help you understand the major points.

I will begin with behavioural therapeutics for a couple of reasons. First, the origins of what we now know as CBT were in the application of behavioural interventions such as systematic desensitisation to phobic conditions. Cognitive adaptations of, and additions to, the evidence-based therapy tradition came a little later. Of course, from early days, relaxation was used in desensitisation to develop inhibitory responses incompatible with the feeling of anxiety, so my approach is not a strict chronology. A second reason for starting with behavioural intervention, however, is that most authorities on CBT for insomnia would agree that it is the behavioural component of CBT for insomnia that is the most effective.

Behavioural therapeutics

In this section I will focus on stimulus control therapy and sleep restriction, at least one of which should be included in effective multicomponent CBT.

Stimulus control

This well-established behavioural intervention focuses on strengthening the connection between bed and successful sleep. Stimulus control therapy is applicable both during the approach to sleep with a view to achieving rapid sleep-onset and during attempts to return to sleep during the night. Stimulus control also involves weakening maladaptive sleep associations that might arise when napping during the day or napping in non-sleep environments.

The scientific basis of stimulus control

The term *stimulus control* was first used in the mid-1800s during the early days of the *behavioural school* of thought. Pioneering psychologists such as Morgan, Thorndike, Pavlov and Guthrie conducted studies on animal behaviour from which theories of *associative learning* emerged. In *Classical Conditioning*, an animal learns to associate a stimulus (e.g., a bell) with the appearance of something important (e.g., food). The bell then becomes a conditioned stimulus (paired with the food) to the extent that ringing the bell signals, and so elicits, the conditioned response of salivation. In *Operant Conditioning*, these researchers found that an animal learns which of its own actions (e.g., pressing a lever) cause important things to happen. Those learned responses are then reinforced and so the animal acts *instrumentally* upon its environment via those conditioned/learned behaviours to obtain *reinforcement* (in this case food). In other words, within the operant framework, a behaviour is learnt through the consequences of that behaviour. The later work of Watson observing children under experimental conditions led to the conclusion that parents could 'shape' their child's behaviour by controlling such stimulus–response associations. Skinner in the 1950s extended the theoretical model of reinforcement and introduced the notion of there being different types of *reinforcement schedule*.

Stimulus control as a therapy for insomnia

By the mid-1960s stimulus control principles were being utilised in behaviour modification programmes for psychosis, such as the 'token economy'. Stimulus control also became adopted in the behaviour therapy literature of the early 1970s as a therapeutic component for a wide range of conditions including anxiety, depression, alcoholism and autistic disorder. However, the most successful translation of stimulus control to the clinical setting was achieved by Richard (Dick) Bootzin (1972).

Bootzin's stimulus control therapy for insomnia recognised that, for good sleepers, the bed and bedroom environment serve as strong discriminant stimuli for the operant reinforcer of sleepiness and sleep – something that he hypothesised to have become disrupted in people with insomnia (Bootzin, 1972; Bootzin, Epstein & Wood, 1991). Moreover, for these poor sleepers, the bed and bedroom may take on their own strong (and unhelpful) association with states of restlessness, wakefulness and of somatic and mental arousal, much as a conditioned stimulus triggers anxiety in an anxiety disorder. There may also be present in the bedroom other discriminative stimuli for activity that interferes with sleep (e.g., computer for work, television).

The principal purpose of stimulus control for insomnia is to re-establish the bed and bedroom as strong discriminant stimuli for rapid sleep initiation upon retiring to bed, or re-initiation following an awakening, and to remove other stimuli that may serve to promote wakefulness or disrupt sleep-onset and maintenance. Stimulus control instructions to remain out of bed until sleepy, to rise from bed if wakeful, and to use the bed only for sleep strengthen that bed–sleep connection. In addition, stimulus control treatment encourages the patient not to nap. This is because napping may lead to sleep being associated with day-time hours and waking environments, as well as interfering with the homeostatic drive for sleep at night (Bootzin, Epstein & Wood, 1991).

By virtue of the fact that sleep is a natural *intrinsic reinforcer*, I believe that the stimulus control approach is particularly well suited to insomnia, where this desired outcome of falling asleep is inherent to the principal (instrumental) intention underlying bedtime behaviour, i.e., I go to bed in order to obtain sleep, I close my eyes to get (to) sleep. Moreover, I suggest that *Premack's principle* may help to understand how stimulus control works as a therapy. This is a principle of reinforcement (from 1959), which stated that an opportunity to engage in a *high probability behaviour* (or activity) will reinforce or increase the likelihood of a *low probability behaviour* (or activity) occurring. For example, you can go out to play (more probable) *if* you finish your homework assignment (less probable). So, we can increase the probability and predictability of sleep by establishing behavioural contingencies such as: (a) you can go to bed *if* you are sleepy at night-time and (b) you can stay in bed *if* you fall asleep or fall back to sleep (within a quarter of an hour).

So, bringing these two factors together, that is the intrinsic reinforcement of sleep and the manipulation of probability contingencies, we can establish a situation where going to bed and being in bed reliably delivers the reward of successful sleep. Favourable conditions for success are also met by another stimulus control instruction to maintain a regular daily wake time, which reduces night to night variability in sleep timings and helps to entrain the circadian rhythm.

Stimulus control treatment instructions

Stimulus control therapy centres on five principal instructions (see Table 2.1) that are introduced and explored therapeutically with the patient. This is a more nuanced therapeutic approach than it might initially appear and is a far cry from simple administration of a set of arbitrary 'rules' that the patient is asked to follow. Walking the patient through the rationale for each instruction and in-depth planning of how they will be implemented are crucial steps to optimal delivery of stimulus control. The behavioural thinking underlying stimulus control assumes that the bedtime routine of the person with insomnia no longer acts as an *automated setting condition for successful sleep* in the way that it does for the good sleeper (Espie, 2002, p. 227). Even if what the person with insomnia is doing is unremarkable, and is not substantially different from a person who sleeps well, the problem is that it is not working as an automatic behavioural pathway to sleep. Moreover, it has become habitual and self-perpetuating. This needs to be explained and understood.

Only go to bed when sleepy In order to re-establish a good sleep pattern, the best place to start is with the most reliable predictor of sleep, and that is feeling sleepy. This is where you can discuss what sleepiness entails, and how it differs from tiredness or fatigue. Going to bed contingent upon feeling sleepy requires an understanding of what it is like to experience the symptoms and to exhibit the signs of a struggle to remain awake (e.g., yawning, rubbing eyes, losing consciousness, 'nodding off'). Many people with insomnia may have lost their familiarity with their body's own endogenous cues for sleep and instead have got into the habit of retiring to bed at a time that maximises their opportunity to achieve perceived adequate nightly sleep. Indeed, preliminary work shows that patients with insomnia have a shorter phase angle compared to normal sleepers. That is, they tend to attempt sleep closer to – or indeed before – their dim-light melatonin onset (DLMO) time (Flynn-Evans et al., 2017) and therefore at an inappropriate circadian phase. Undoubtedly some of this is driven by anxiety.

Table 2.1 Treatment instructions for stimulus control therapy.

1) Only go to bed when you feel sleepy.
2) Your bed should only be used for sleep. Other than sexual activity, all other activities (e.g., TV, work, eating) should take place elsewhere.
3) If you don't manage to fall asleep within approximately a 'quarter of an hour', get out of bed and find somewhere quiet and dimly lit in which you can do a relaxing activity (e.g., read a book).
4) When you feel sleepy again, head back to bed.
5) Repeat steps 3 and 4 as often as necessary, including if you wake up during the night and don't manage to get back to sleep.
6) Maintain a fixed rise time each morning.
7) Refrain from day-time naps.

Helping to ensure that your patient only goes to bed when sleepy not only helps to reinforce the association between being sleepy whilst in bed, but also serves to help re-acquaint the individual with their body's own cues for sleep. Of course, this takes time and perhaps many *reconditioning trials*. It is useful to encourage your patient to see that an old habit needs to be broken and a new one to be established. Consider with your patient how they are going to spend their time before going to bed, or until they feel sleepy. Walking through behavioural adjustments helps make the plan feel real and helps patients make the necessary preparations at home.

Use the bed only for sleep Many patients will ask what they are meant to do if activities apart from sexual activity are to be avoided in bed. They may feel anxious about this, and it may be difficult for them to abandon their *safety behaviours* (Harvey, 2002), such as having a book to read to keep their mind occupied. They may also comment that plenty of people look at their devices in bed and sleep normally. Again, it is important to explain conditioning history differences. That their reaction to bed is arousal not de-arousal and that the goal is to change that. It is important also to explain that the intention in stimulus control is always to achieve rapid sleep or return to sleep; hence going to bed only when sleepy and spending no longer than a quarter of an hour at any one time, awake in bed.

The hope is that across repeated nights the patient will go to bed sleepy and will learn that they can fall asleep naturally, because they are sleepy. As I would explain it, this is the bed–sleep connection, rather than the bed–read or the bed–work connection. An exclusion is made for sexual activity.

Follow the quarter of an hour rule Although most people are likely to be amenable to limiting use of the bed to just sleep, for many patients, the idea of leaving the bed during the night is anathema! It may even come across to them as the very antithesis of an effective sleep treatment. A thorough explanation and exploration of the theory behind the *quarter of an hour rule*, as I call it, is therefore key to maximising engagement. Central to that is the fact that good sleepers generally fall asleep within this time period, so it is long enough as a goal to work towards. I never say 15 minutes to patients because that seems much more like you are suggesting they time themselves and they may end up literally clock-watching. Rather I direct them to evidence that estimating a quarter of an hour (give or take) is relatively easy to do (Harrow & Espie, 2010).

I strongly recommend collaborative generation of a clear step-by-step plan for what the patient will do when they leave the bed at night, because this greatly increases the likelihood of implementation of this challenging rule. This might include planning details such as what they will wear to keep warm, where in the house they are going to sit, placing an interesting book on a comfortable chair, etc. Helping the patient to visualise and prepare for what to do helps them move from the contemplative frame of mind, when they may intend to follow the plan, to the action stage of actually doing it.

Rise at the same time each morning This element of stimulus control requires less elaboration. You should explain that you understand the importance of the flexibility, and indeed the pleasure, of having a longer 'lie-in' or a 'catch-up' sleep, for example on the weekend, and that you understand that good sleepers are not entirely rigid in their sleep habits and rising time. However, once again this instruction is about creating a consistent sleep habit of getting out of bed when you awaken in the morning and trying to do this at the same time. It is what needs to be done for now to resolve the insomnia problem and not necessarily for the long-term future.

Do not nap during the day Within the stimulus control model, having sleeps, even short ones, in other environments may weaken the bed–sleep and the sleep–bedtime connections, as well as reducing the sleepiness drive that we need to use as the precondition for going to bed at night. Naps should therefore be avoided if possible and mitigated, for example by using *behavioural activation* strategies that help alertness and engagement in alternative behaviours. In many cases this will be more about helping your patient to respond to low energy levels or fatigue. However, a tendency to nap or to have a behavioural tendency towards falling asleep without wanting to also needs to be assessed in case there is risk of accident or injury, or in differential diagnosis the possibility of another type of sleep disorder. You should also bear in mind that napping is common as a social norm in some cultures and in older adults. You need to make a judgement about whether or not napping is indicative of an unhelpful conditioned behaviour that is interfering with sleep stimulus control, before simply advising patients not to nap. If your patient needs to nap I would advise them that 10 minutes constitutes 'taking a nap' and that anything longer constitutes 'having a sleep'.

Sleep restriction

Sleep restriction is also firmly established as a behavioural therapeutic for insomnia, and is incorporated in the majority of CBT protocols. It is regarded amongst behavioural sleep medicine specialists as the most powerful intervention in the CBT toolbox, but it is also the most challenging for patients to put into practice.

The scientific basis for sleep restriction

Consolidated periods of sleep and wakefulness rely on synchrony between the homeostatic drive for sleep and the underlying endogenous circadian rhythm. This *two-process model* (Borbély, 1982; Borbély, Daan, Wirz-Justice & Deboer, 2016) posits that the homeostatic drive for sleep (Process S) interacts with a process controlled by the circadian pacemaker (Process C), with time-courses derived from both physiological and behavioural variables. These variables are particularly important for CBT of course. During the night the homeostat discharges us into sleep, during the day the circadian pacemaker renders us awake and alert, and when the biological night comes round again, this timing system releases us into sleep once more to repay the accumulated sleep debt. Sleep–wake regulation is also dependent upon and responsive to behavioural inputs. It is possible, for example, to reduce the homeostatic drive for sleep at night by choosing to sleep during the day and to 'delay the clock' by working late. The two processes also feedback reciprocally on one another in response to behavioural changes, so that influencing the homeostat affects the clock and vice versa. It should also be noted that the homeostatic drive is evident, not just in relation to total sleep, but also at the level of sleep stages, particularly REM sleep and NREM stage 3 sleep (N3, or SWS) (Dijk & Czeisler, 1995).

Recognising that behaviour may have a direct effect on the expression of our sleep, Arthur (Art) Spielman postulated that, in response to acute sleep disruption, people who go on to develop chronic insomnia may have implemented behaviours that dysregulate their sleep, for example, spending excessive amounts of time in bed, napping during the day and keeping an irregular sleep–wake schedules biology (Spielman, Saskin & Thorpy, 1983, 1987). Although there may be limited evidence that people with insomnia actively extend time in bed during acute stress (relative to their own preinsomnia baseline), it is clear that a mismatch exists between night-time sleep opportunity and sleep ability. This mismatch, coupled with increased frequency of day-time napping, increases the likelihood of experiencing fragmented and inefficient sleep and contributes to frustration and arousal in bed, which, over time, may become associated with the bedroom environment, further potentiating wake-promoting arousal. Moreover, one of the most reliable ways to strengthen the homeostatic sleep drive and thereby increase the propensity for sleep during upcoming nights is to limit the amount of sleep currently being accumulated (Webb & Agnew, 1965, 1974; Spielman, Yang & Glovinsky, 2010). Restricting time in bed over a number of nights is a simple way to limit sleep accumulation and therefore opens a door to the treatment of insomnia.

Sleep restriction as a therapy for insomnia

Sleep restriction therapy is a treatment founded upon the inevitability of sleep. However, the mere notion of restricting sleep will immediately seem counter-intuitive to your patient. It is therefore important to help your patient to understand how it works.

As clinicians we may know that by increasing homeostatic sleep pressure, overriding cognitive and physiological arousal, and strengthening circadian control of sleep, there is a strong possibility that sleep will ensue, but how can we convey that to the average person? Some clinics use a graphic of the two-process model to demonstrate the science. However, I have seldom had success with that. In my experience it is not a 'patient-friendly' illustration. I find that the most accessible approach is to explain the concept of *sleep efficiency* and to illustrate that from their own data – they may typically be in bed for 8 hours but sleep only a total of 6 hours made up of broken pieces, i.e., 75% sleep efficiency. It is then possible to explain the value of consolidating sleep and of squeezing out wakefulness to move towards sleeping 90% or more of your time in bed. People can understand the notion of a homeostat as a pressure/squeezing system and of the body clock as a sleep timer.

The idea of a treatment that restricts your sleep is challenging. Perhaps it could be more appropriately referred to as 'time in bed restriction therapy' because it aims to: (a) restrict the time in bed in order to increase sleep efficiency; (b) regularize the timing of sleep and wake, standardizing exposure to zeitgebers to help improve sleep predictability, and (c) recondition the bed–sleep association through suppression of wake time in bed (Maurer, Espie & Kyle, 2018). We should bear in mind, however, that the data do in fact show that sleep restriction therapy is associated with a short-term reduction in total sleep time, likely because this is part of sleep restriction's mechanism of effect (Kyle et al., 2014). The tailored recommendation of bed time and rise time over several weeks leads to improved sleep consolidation and quality, and patients often respond well to this prescription-like model, as well as to the relatively rapid successes they experience when they implement therapy. Being able to increase the sleep window with improvement in sleep efficiency is also a reinforcer to progress, to self-empowerment and having a sense of control, as well as to continuing with the programme.

Sleep restriction treatment instructions

I have summarised sleep restriction in Table 2.2. As I mentioned earlier, I often use the term *sleep scheduling* and refer to getting your sleep back into 'good shape', or a 'healthy pattern'. However you present it, the first step in sleep restriction is calculation of the patient's *average nightly sleep duration*, usually taken from at least 1, but preferably 2, weeks of sleep diary data. If diary data are not available you may wish to estimate average sleep from discussion during the clinical consultation. In cases where their average sleep is less than 5 hours, make 5 hours the sleep window, to protect the patient from sleep deprivation. If there are health concerns I would make the minimum window 6 hours.

Following this, you should ask your patient to select a *rise time* that you can use to anchor their *sleep window*. You should explain that the idea behind the rise time is for it to become one edge of the window, and you can use this window metaphor to explain that you are trying to find the right size space for sleep so you can begin the treatment journey.

The third step is to introduce the idea of what I call the *threshold time*. This is the time after which they can cross the threshold into the bedroom environment. Explain that you are not wanting them to pick a bed time, but a time at which they are permitted to get into bed at the beginning of the sleep period. This is the other end of the sleep window. Threshold time is arrived at by subtracting the nightly average sleep duration from the agreed habitual rise time.

By the fourth step when you are putting this all together, your patient may be getting anxious, as they realise that they are not to get into bed until after the threshold time has been reached and not to leave bed any later than the agreed rise time, *7 days a week*. This is challenging, and they will probably say that they cannot afford to get even less sleep than they are at present. They will be feeling that they can barely cope with the present situation. I encourage them to see this as an experiment to see what happens. Discuss the fact that they have a chronic problem that has been difficult so far to solve, and that sleep restriction is very effective, even though it is tough.

Once the programme is under way, step 5 is very important. Do advise your patient that sleep restriction will make them sleepy. Although they will find this reassuring and it will help them consolidate their sleep, they must also take care. Sleepiness is sometimes a necessary *side effect* of the treatment. More accurately, perhaps, it is part of the *mechanism* of treatment; but patients need to stay safe and take responsibility for any sleepiness they experience during the day. In particular, with shorter sleep windows, of less than 6 hours, you should consider advising your patient not to drive because they may be sleepy.

Table 2.2 Treatment instructions for sleep restriction therapy.

1) Get your patient to record sleep diary data for at least a week to establish baseline values for average nightly sleep duration. Use this nightly sleep duration (i.e., total time in bed spent asleep across one night) as your patient's initial 'sleep window'. Round average time down to the nearest 15 minutes to simplify titration (e.g., 5 hours, 45 minutes).
2) Agree with your patient a habitual rise time, after which the patient should be awake and out of bed (e.g., 6:00 a.m.). It is preferable to keep the rising time the same throughout treatment.
3) Using the baseline average nightly sleep duration (e.g., 5 hours, 45 minutes), work backwards to agree on a threshold time, after which your patient is permitted to get into bed (e.g., 12.15 a.m.). This is done by subtracting average nightly sleep duration from the agreed rise time (e.g., 6:00 a.m. - 5 hours, 45 minutes = 12.15 a.m.).
4) Advise your patient not to enter bed before the specified threshold time and to leave bed no later than their applied rise time, even on weekends and holidays.
5) Advise your patient that acute increases in daytime sleepiness can result from sleep restriction. Remind them to avoid driving, operating heavy machinery or activities that include significant risk of injury or death if they experience any daytime sleepiness.
6) Titrate the sleep window with your patient on a weekly basis, based on sleep efficiency calculations from the past week (total time asleep/total time in bed × 100). Suggested titration criteria for changes to the sleep window are as follows:
   - If sleep efficiency is > 85%, sleep window is increased by 15 minutes.
   - If sleep efficiency is between 80 and 85%, sleep window remains unchanged.
   - If sleep efficiency is < 80%, sleep window is reduced by 15 minutes.

Finally, step 6 may involve several iterations of adjustment depending on sleep efficiency data. Acute restriction of the sleep window results in a reduced opportunity for sleep and so sleep efficiency is likely to increase. The sleep window can then be *titrated* over the course of subsequent weeks in line with changes to the patient's sleep efficiency. There is no evidence-based consensus on titration guidelines for sleep efficiency; however, most protocols remain broadly in line with the original formulation (Kyle et al., 2015). At the weekly review of sleep efficiency, time in bed should be gradually increased – contingent on achieving the sleep efficiency values in Table 2.2. Over the course of several weeks it then becomes possible to arrive at the patient's approximate natural sleep requirement.

Cognitive therapeutics

We have known for some time that people with insomnia stress mental events as the determinant of their trouble sleeping (Lichstein & Rosenthal, 1980). Consequently, in this section we will focus on four cognitive therapeutics that are commonly included in CBT protocols. We will start with cognitive control, because this is an approach that helps with mental preparation for bed, before moving on to imagery training, a technique that can be learnt and applied in bed to help with the racing mind. We will then cover paradoxical intention, an approach designed to prevent your patient's efforts to sleep, and we will conclude with cognitive restructuring, which helps patients to de-catastrophise their insomnia fears and experiences.

Cognitive control

Cognitive control is also known as worry control or in lay terms I prefer *putting the day to rest*. It is commonly incorporated in CBT as a way to eliminate over-thinking in bed. It can be readily incorporated into a prebedtime wind-down routine.

The scientific basis for cognitive control

Just as the psychodynamic tradition was challenged by the emergence of the more scientific, evidence-based psychological approach known as behaviour therapy, so the behavioural tradition was challenged in the 1970s by emergent cognitive theories and associated therapeutics. Of course, cognitive influences had been there for some time. As far back as the 1930s, for example, Edward Tolman had demonstrated that animals could 'anticipate' the consequences of their actions and develop 'cognitive maps' of their environment. Over time it was natural therefore that psychologists became interested in the application of stimulus control principles to mental events.

Tom Borkovec, for example, recognised that anxious cognitive events can occur under a wide variety of environmental conditions, and so discriminative control may be suboptimal for a patient to manage them well (Borkovec, Wilkinson, Folensbee & Lerman, 1983). He experimented with a novel stimulus control treatment of worry whereby subject-initiated restriction of the temporal and environmental cues for the occurrence of worried thinking could reduce worry frequency. *Scheduled worry time* is now a standard component of CBT for anxiety disorders (e.g., Shafran, Brosan & Cooper, 2013).

Cognitive control as a therapy for insomnia

The application of stimulus control principles to mental events is important for insomnia because the dominant complaint in the great majority of insomnia relates to having an *overactive or racing mind*. Based on some early work on insomnia by Mitchell and White (1977) and on our own clinical work on *worry control for insomnia* (Espie & Lindsay, 1987), we have incorporated this approach in our manualised treatment (e.g., Espie, Inglis, Tessier & Harvey, 2001), as have others, for example Carney and Walters (2006) who called the approach *constructive worry*.

In our work we have consistently preferred the term *cognitive control* in order to be agnostic as to the thought content that interferes with sleep. In our experience the applicability of cognitive control is particularly to thoughts that are not necessarily intrusive nor worrying (cf. Espie, 1991). Indeed, these thoughts often simply relate to reflecting on the past day and planning ahead for the next day. They may be quite normal to think about and are not necessarily worries, so we frame cognitive control as *putting the day to rest* in the evening as a 'pre-emptive strike' to deal with thought content that might otherwise bubble up into thinking while awake in bed.

Cognitive control treatment instructions

Although this is a cognitive strategy, cognitive control is very much a behavioural prescription to be followed every evening. In our lab protocol we explain that it is important to get into the habit of making good preparations for bed and that this begins with signing off on the day past and by getting things in good order for the next day. We explain to patients that by having this *mental window* in which to *put the day to rest*, they create a natural break from the activity of the day. By *closing the book on the day* they signal their commitment to become more relaxed in the latter part of the evening before they go to bed. I have provided the detailed instructions in Table 2.3, which are quite self-explanatory.

Paradoxical intention

Paradoxical intention therapy is less well known and less widely practised than many other elements of multicomponent CBT, yet it has been part of the insomnia evidence base for more than 40 years. The concept of paradox is also central to the majority of empirically supported therapies, although the term itself may not be used.

The scientific basis for paradoxical intention

Therapists were using paradoxical techniques long before Viktor Frankl coined the term *paradoxical* intention (Frankl, 1955, 1960). In reviewing historical applications of paradox, Seltzer (1986), for example, refers to Dubois and Adler in the early part of the twentieth century encouraging their psychotherapy patients to approach their symptoms with a sense of humour, and Stekel treated impotence by the simultaneous prescription of intimate physical contact and the prohibition of sexual intercourse. The latter became the central instruction in Masters and Johnson's research programme on *sensate focus* therapy. Indeed, many elements of behavioural therapeutics could reasonably be regarded as paradoxical. Examples include using negative practice to break undesirable habits (Dunlap), tensing muscles as a precursor to relaxation (Jacobsen), and exposure therapy to reduce fear responses (Cover-Jones), all of which originate from the 1920s to the 1930s. Wolpe (1958) regarded Cover-Jones, for example, as the 'mother of behaviour therapy', and Bernstein and Borkovec (1973) created a manual for progressive relaxation training that adapted and abbreviated Jacobsen's approach. Moreover, paradox is by no means confined to behavioural methods. Motivational interviewing (Miller & Rollnick, 1991) can be intrinsically paradoxical, as is asking a patient 'what is the worst that could happen' during rational emotive behaviour therapy or cognitive restructuring (Ellis & Harper, 1961; Beck, 1979), and embracing symptoms and feelings in acceptance and commitment therapy (Hayes, Strosahl & Wilson, 1999) goes beyond exposure and response prevention to, in my view, developing a more paradoxical mindset.

It is, however, to Frankl (1955, 1960) that we owe the explicit use of paradoxical intention or *prescribing the symptom* as a therapeutic in its own right. He recognised that encouraging the patient to do the things he or she fears, and even wishing

Table 2.3 Treatment instructions for cognitive control (putting the day to rest).

1) Set aside 20 min in the early evening, the same time every night if possible (e.g., 19:00 hours).
2) Sit down somewhere you are not going to be disturbed.
3) All you need is a notebook, your diary and a pen.
4) Think of what has happened during the day, how events have gone and how you feel about the kind of day it has been.
5) Write down some of the main points, put them to rest by committing them to paper. Write down what you feel good about and also what has troubled you.
6) Write down anything you feel you need to do on a 'to do' list, with steps that you can take to tie up any loose ends of unfinished business.
7) Now think about tomorrow and what is coming up. Consider things that you are looking forward to as well as things that may cause you worry.
8) Write down your schedule in your diary or check it if it is already there.
9) Write down anything you are unsure about and make a note in your diary of a time in the morning when you are going to find out about that.
10) Try to use your 20 min to leave you feeling more in control. 'Close the book on the day.'
11) When it comes to bedtime, remind yourself that you have already dealt with all these things if they come into your mind.
12) If new thoughts come up in bed, note them down on a piece of paper at your bedside to be dealt with the following morning.

for them to happen, is an optimal way to counteract stubbornly maladaptive problems that we spend too much time fretting about and trying to prevent.

Paradoxical intention as a therapy for insomnia

Sleep is a perfect example of a need that does not respond well to a power struggle. A famous quote by Frankl, that he attributes to the French psychiatrist Dubois, illustrates this point. 'Sleep is like a dove which has landed near one's hand and stays there as long as one does not pay any attention to it; but if one attempts to grab it, it quickly flies away' (Frankl, 1955, p. 253). I often use this quote with patients to illustrate the natural and spontaneous presence of sleep, but also to show just how easily sleep can flee when we focus our attention and behaviour upon it. Essentially, we scare it off, because sleep is not there because we choose it to be. We do not know how to sleep and we cannot turn sleep on. On the other hand, we are very capable of maintaining or heightening our waking arousal levels and of turning sleep off.

Michael Ascher was largely responsible for adapting paradoxical intention therapy to address insomnia (Ascher & Turner, 1979; Turner & Ascher, 1979). In the paradoxical framework, sleep initiation is seen as an involuntary physiological process, and so attempts to actively control it serve to inhibit sleep's natural progression. I call this the 'attention–intention–effort' pathway (Espie, Broomfield, MacMahon, Macphee & Taylor, 2006), and often discuss comparable involuntary behaviours that are either interrupted by focusing on trying to perform them (e.g., breathing, sexual responses) or made worse when you try to stop them (e.g., blushing, stammering). Analogies can help the person with insomnia stand back from their sleep problem to see how they are making things worse. It can also help if you ask them to consider the case of the good sleeper. How do they do it? What techniques or skills do they use? Good sleepers are good sleepers because they do not do anything special and it never crosses their minds to try to control their sleep. Or to put it simply, good sleepers are not good at sleeping. Patients should be helped to appreciate the *automaticity* of sleep and how sleep is a process over which control and anxious effort are, perhaps counterintuitively, antithetical to their goal (Espie, 2002). Indeed, you may be more likely to sleep when you are trying to remain awake than when you are trying to sleep.

Paradoxical intention treatment instructions

There are two methods for administering paradoxical intention therapy. I will briefly outline each of these, but for more detailed information I would refer you elsewhere (Espie, 2023).

The first is more directly *prescribing the symptom*, and this is the *try to stay awake* method (see Table 2.4: left panel). As you can see, the patient is encouraged to resist closing their eyes and to resist any urges to fall asleep or to try to fall asleep, and to do this repeatedly, even in the face of symptoms and signs of sleepiness (like involuntary eye closure, yawning). An analogy might be that holding your breath is likely to restore normal breathing when you are hyperventilating and worried that you cannot breathe. In the alternative *give up trying* method (Table 2.4: right panel), there is less specific instruction to attempt to remain awake. Rather the focus is on reducing *performance anxiety* and allowing sleep to come naturally. An analogy might be a golfer trying too hard to hit the ball straight down the middle with the result that they hit a wayward shot.

Table 2.4 Treatment instructions for paradoxical intention therapy.

Method 1	Method 2
Lie comfortably in your bed with the lights off, but keep your eyes open.	Lie comfortably in your bed with the lights off. You can close your eyes or keep them open as you prefer.
When your eyelids feel like they want to close, resist that gently. Keep them open.	That's all you need to do. Your goal is to allow sleep to come naturally.
Say to yourself 'just stay awake for another couple of minutes. I'll fall asleep naturally when I'm ready.'	Give up any effort to fall asleep. Don't try to sleep. Don't try at all.
Don't purposefully make yourself stay awake. Just focus, eyes open, perhaps on a spot on the ceiling.	Give up any concern about being awake. Sleep is not something you can switch on.
Keep this approach going for as long as you can.	Keep this approach going for as long as you can.

For many patients you can combine these methods into a single set of instructions. As you can see, the central idea is that sleepiness will overtake or capture the patient and that they will fall asleep involuntarily. In the context of it being bed time, and the patient being sleepy, paradoxical intention therapy allows the patient to discover that trying to control the sleep process does not work, but that conversely sleep is powerful and inevitable and will overcome them. Essentially, paradoxical intention helps the patient re-learn how to *abandon wakefulness*.

It is important to say that paradoxical instructions are readily misunderstood by patients, so it is important to take time to explain the rationale for therapy and, as with all therapeutics, to establish a collaborative working relationship. Your patient needs to recognise that this is a treatment for insomnia, and the goal is to help them overcome their insomnia, rather than just to stay awake all night because you think that does not matter! Encourage your patient therefore not to take the instructions too literally. You do not want them finding ways to stimulate themselves with exercise, caffeine or anxious thoughts so they can remain awake. Rather they should adopt a more passive attitude towards trying to remain awake or to giving up trying to sleep. Remind them that good sleepers are not walking a tightrope. As may have become clear, the use of humour can be very helpful with paradoxical intention!

Imagery training

Imagery training is often reported as a relaxation technique, and indeed offers a natural therapeutic segue from a focus on muscle tension release and diaphrammatic breathing. It is also a component in mindfulness. However, imagery is also a cognitive technique for managing negative or intrusive thoughts and images.

The scientific basis for imagery training

Visualisation has a long history in psychotherapy research. In Wolpe's (1958) *systematic desensitisation*, the anxious patient, while relaxed, is invited to imagine a series of progressively more fear-provoking situations. Here relaxation is intended to dissipate (reciprocally inhibit) the fear that is engendered using imagery. Likewise, Cautela's (1966) *covert sensitisation* asks patients to pair an image of a maladaptive behaviour with an aversive image, with the intention of reducing the maladaptive behaviour. Although these approaches purported to demonstrate conditioning paradigms, more explicitly cognitive hypotheses were recognised early on as equally plausible. Meichenbaum (1977), for example, introduced the use of *coping imagery* in his *cognitive-behaviour modification* programs whereby patients visualise themselves using, for example, deep breaths to reduce their anxiety level. So, we can see that the active use of visualisation and imagery as part of the therapeutic process has a long tradition. Indeed, *guided imagery* has been shown to result in reduced symptoms across a wide range of mental health and medical conditions. Besides, for decades there has been an established practice of using imagery successfully to enhance children's learning, memory and problem solving, as well as self-control skills and in the sports domain to enhance learning and elite performance. The neural foundations of the imagination are indeed fascinating (e.g., Kosslyn, Ganis and Thompson, 2001).

Imagery training as a therapy for insomnia

Intrusive and preoccupying thoughts are typically accompanied by unwelcome mental images. Indeed, it is hard for a person with insomnia to harbour a sleep-related thought without an associated negative image (Harvey, 2000, 2002; Harvey & Payne, 2002). This has also been found in PTSD, social anxiety and depression, where negative rather than pleasant or affirming images also dominate. Patients seem to know that this is self-defeating. They try instead to think about good times, and they try to picture pleasant scenes, but it seems that the negative stream of thoughts and images wins the battle. For this reason, when you suggest imagery as a treatment approach, they are often very sceptical. They may also say that they do not have much imagination. Certainly, imagery techniques are useful for some but not all patients, partly because there are individual differences in the ability to visualize (Cocude & Demis, 1988). However, it is possible to increase the prospect of success, because some imagery methods are more effective than others.

Active imagery is the evidence-based option. This is where mental images are rehearsed and replayed from memory (Kosslyn, Thompson & Ganis, 2006). Images that re-create previous, real sensory experiences, do so, not just visually, but also by way of sounds, tastes, smells, movements, and representations of touch, such as texture, temperature and pressure. Importantly, they relate to the re-telling of an engaging story. By contrast, it is very difficult to sustain attention on spontaneously generated, involuntary images. This is what patients with insomnia often try to do when they cannot get to sleep or cannot get back to sleep. They say they try to generate a pleasant scene to focus on, rather than having one to hand.

It has been known for some time that visual imagery is effective in insomnia (Woolfolk & McNulty, 1983) and my own long-standing view is that imagery training is particularly useful for agitated, unfocused and fleeting thoughts that flit from topic to topic, rather than for thoughts that 'need' consideration, processing or resolution (Espie, 1991, pp.154–155).

Imagery training treatment instructions

The first point to make is that imagery is firstly a training, before it is a treatment. Therefore, your patient will need to be helped to construct the exercise itself. What you should be aiming for is a set of imagery sequences, the content of which is based upon a place or places that the patient knows and likes. Typically, the patient will suggest a scene from a park, a forest or a beach. It is your role to engage in dialogue and content creation around which particular park, forest, or beach the patient is referring to. This is not an abstract exercise. Ask your patient to call to mind the actual scene that they have chosen. Then ask them to gradually embellish the image with ever increasing layers of detail, helping to make it more realistic and tangible. You can do this by means of prompts to connect the patient with experiences of their five senses within the scene (e.g., 'experience the feeling of the sunlight on your face or the gentle breeze in your hair. What can you smell?'). Explain to your patient that their actual memory of a place and their experiences are crucial from the outset because this will be more readily retained in memory. Help them to understand that you are not asking them to make things up but to think and recall in detail. However, you can also explain that over time they might be able to extend the imagery experience using more creative thought.

I have summarised my approach to imagery training in Table 2.5. As you will see, I use the analogy of the patient becoming the director of a movie. Taking the lead from the introduction that you have given, the patient is to develop the scenes, the settings, the participants, the sights and sounds and smells, and tell the story through the screenplay. The goal is to create a mental film lasting about 10 minutes. Importantly, because the patient is the creator of it, and because they are going to 'shoot' and 're-shoot' the movie, they will get plenty of practice. They will need that practice. Patients should be encouraged to find a dedicated time, and a quiet and comfortable place in which to lie down, practice and learn their imagery exercise. After a period of training, they will know it well, will have learnt it, and so can easily 'run the reel' at night when they go to bed or when they wake up at night. The creative piece is largely done so encourage them to settle down to enjoy and become absorbed in being on that beach, in that forest or walking in those hills.

Cognitive restructuring

This is a term that describes therapeutic techniques that aim to identify and target unhelpful beliefs and thinking errors that serve to induce or maintain a patient's mental health problem or impaired emotional adjustment. It's 'parent' intervention, cognitive therapy, has been less successfully applied to insomnia than cognitive restructuring by itself, which is often incorporated into multicomponent CBT.

The scientific basis for cognitive restructuring

When one thinks of cognitive therapeutics it is more likely that cognitive restructuring would come to mind than the interventions (cognitive control, paradoxical intention and imagery training) I have so far described. So let us turn finally to this important approach.

The pioneers of the more explicit cognitive therapy approaches are several. Ellis and Beck both have claims to an overarching theory that the way we think determines how we function, and that rational thinking can correct conceptual distortions and improve mental health (Ellis and Harper, 1961; Beck, 1979). As early as 1966, Cautela taught clients to say to themselves 'I am

Table 2.5 Treatment instructions for imagery training.

Be prepared. Don't just wait until the time comes and try to think something up. Develop a screenplay! You are the director, so shoot the scenes and edit them until you have got what you want. Your imagery sequence should take about 10 minutes to go through in your mind's eye.
Practice regularly. You are also a participant! You must learn the scenes and the sequences so that they flow as the movie rolls! You need to set time aside to learn the 'script' and you should practice in the evening or during the day too.
Get good quality images and scenes. Vivid and clear in your mind's eye is what you want. Notice the colours, the smells, the sounds, the sensations that you make part of your imagery routine.
Relax and enjoy! Who wants to watch a movie that is uninteresting? This is something that you should look forward to. But at the same time remember you want to develop an imagery story that is calming, soothing and not evocative of strong emotions!

calm and relaxed' in stressful situations and observed that 'in a while, the mere words calmed them down' and Meichenbaum (1977) incorporated such self-instructional training into cognitive behavioural modification, a narrative approach to therapy that encouraged the patient to develop a different, more positive story. This is not dissimilar to Ellis's and Beck's theories that people's emotions and behaviours are influenced primarily by their perceptions and interpretation of events, and the later development of *cognitive restructuring* as therapy. Somewhat in parallel, Lazarus and Folkman (1984) stressed the importance of appraising an event, thus developing their long-held thesis about the connection between emotion and cognition (Lazarus, 1966). All these approaches recognise the role of self-talk, inner speech or *internal dialogue*, a term first adopted from philosophy into therapy by Meichenbaum and later also adopted by Beck.

Cognitive restructuring (after Ellis) or *cognitive reframing* includes practical techniques such as using a *thought record* to capture *negative automatic thoughts*, the veracity of which are then systematically reappraised by the patient and therapist. Learning to challenge these thoughts begins by having the patient simply acknowledge their manifestation in the mind and the effect that they have on physiological arousal, emotion and behaviour. The next step typically involves the generation of evidence for and against the thought, helping the patient to then make a more nuanced appraisal of the original thought and notice the effect of this on their subsequent state of arousal.

Cognitive restructuring is a collaborative process used in therapy with all manner of mental health conditions, and typically involves the use of *Socratic questioning*. Beck advised the Socratic method rather than disputation or indoctrination in his original book on cognitive therapy for depression (Beck, Rush, Shaw & Emery, 1979). Examples include: 'Are my thoughts on the event accurate?', 'What objective facts are there to support my view?' and 'What alternative views are there of the event?' The commonly cited 'What is the worst that can happen (if my view of the event is correct)?' was also a cornerstone of Ellis's REBT. Cognitive restructuring is then followed up by *behavioural experiments*, particularly where salient links between unhelpful cognitions and maladaptive safety behaviours have been identified. Behavioural experiments are used to test negative automatic thoughts and to re-evaluate underlying beliefs and assumptions, and so reduce future vulnerability (Bennet-Levy et al., 2004).

Cognitive restructuring as a therapy for insomnia

Many CBT protocols include sessions dedicated to cognitive restructuring and tackling unhelpful beliefs and attitudes about sleep. Patients with insomnia have been shown to experience higher levels of dysfunctional beliefs about sleep than people without insomnia (Morin, 1993; Morin, Vallières & Ivers, 2007), in a manner parallel to those with other mental health concerns. These negative sleep-related cognitions occur not only at night but also through the day, as events are interpreted through attentional and attributional biases to sleep. Most established models of insomnia recognise the role of these cognitions and underlying beliefs, in driving behaviours that perpetuate the insomnia problem (e.g., Espie, 1991, 2002; Morin, 1993; Perlis, Giles, Mendelson, Bootzin & Wyatt, 1997; Harvey, 2002).

A commonly occurring unhelpful belief is the idea that everyone requires 8 hours of sleep to be able to function (see Morin et al., 2007). This may result in increased preoccupation about sleep when sleep is perceived to be in deficit, and results in sleep-disruptive 'safety' behaviours such as spending excessive time in bed, which is more likely to fragment sleep and maintain the problem (Harvey, 2002). Another example would be believing that you will be unable to cope the next day if you sleep poorly. This belief may cause anxiety and worry, even before going to bed, an attentional and effortful focus on sleep itself, and considerable preoccupation about the potential consequences of insomnia when (perhaps inevitably) lying awake. Likewise, during the day the patient with this dysfunctional belief may be subject to further *thinking errors*, *misattributions* and *overgeneralisations*, that the reason for any observed problem is because they did not sleep well and that their insomnia is causing them harm and that their sleep is out of control.

Once these patient-specific beliefs have been identified, often using thought records, the therapist and patient can collaboratively work to explore and test their validity in a systematic fashion using reappraisal, restructuring and behavioural experiments to test alternate hypotheses.

Cognitive restructuring treatment instructions

An example of the thought record that I use in cognitive restructuring therapy is presented in Table 2.6. As you can see, it is good practice to ask patients to write their thoughts down in their own words, exactly as they think them, so that they can recognise and respond to their own internal dialogue. I do not always use the terms cognitive restructuring or reframing, because for some people these can be unhelpful jargon, but I do explain to them about the importance of thinking

Table 2.6 Cognitive restructuring for insomnia – some examples.

My thoughts about sleep and sleepiness	How this makes me feel	A more accurate version of my thoughts would be	How this version makes me feel
'It seems as if I am awake half the night and everyone else is sleeping.'	Anxious, Annoyed, lonely, jealous	*'I probably sleep around 6 hours and have 2 hours awake in bed; that's 75% (three-quarters) not 50%. Also, if there are 1 million people living in this city and half of them are adults, maybe 50,000 are having serious problems. Everyone else is not sleeping!'*	Reassured, more optimistic, less angry
'I'm never going to get to sleep tonight.'	Demoralized, out of control	*'Almost certainly I will fall asleep. I always get some sleep. The average in my Diary was 6 hours and I never got less than 3–4 hours.'*	More accepting, relieved, more relaxed
'I'm so tired I just can't concentrate. It's because I slept so badly last night.'	Hopeless, pre-occupied with sleep, irritable	*'My concentration is not just down to my sleep. I've slept worse than I did last night and felt better during the day. Maybe I'm bored, or doing too much at once, or. . . . .'*	More in control, able to focus

through their thoughts and concerns about sleep and sleeplessness clearly, honestly and accurately. I encourage them to see that they can evaluate their thinking, and to decide whether or not their thought and their initial reaction to it is fair and reasonable. I explain to them in plain language about common thinking errors like overgeneralizing and catastrophizing and once they start recording their thoughts and feelings, they usually begin to see just how emotional and upsetting their automatic thoughts can make them feel.

Cognitive restructuring helps patients take the fight to their insomnia by not letting it get the better of them, and often you see how empowering it is to patients when they realise that they can change the way they think. As you can see in Table 2.6, the process is for the patient: (1) to record the thought as carefully as they can; (2) to consider how thinking this thought makes them feel, and to write that down; (3) to reconsider the thought critically – that is, to evaluate it and to write down a new and more accurate version of the thought; and (4) to reconsider how thinking this new way makes them feel. After keeping thought diaries for a week or two, it is likely that no new thoughts will come up, or those that do will be versions of previous thoughts. Your patient should also get better at 'spotting them' as live cognitions, and so, given time and practice, cognitive restructuring becomes a more fluid process that people are able to use more naturally, as they go along, to disarm intrusive negative thinking related to poor sleep. Sometimes I explain that they are learning to cool down their *hot cognitions* (Safran & Goldberg, 1982) or hot thoughts, the ones that were so full of catastrophe, emotion and stress, and learning to manage them more normally just like other people do.

Relaxation therapeutics

In this section we will briefly cover the evening wind-down routine before consideration of relaxation as a form of therapy. Some aspect of relaxation is often included in multicomponent CBT, even if relaxation therapy is not the most potent treatment for chronic insomnia.

Evening wind-down routine

Whether or not you plan to include formal relaxation training in a patient's CBT program, you may wish to consider giving some general advice about winding down in the pre-bedtime period. Insomnia has for long been considered a disorder of excess arousal or of difficulty in down-regulating arousal (de la Pena, 1978; Riemann et al, 2010), so how readily your patient relaxes in the evening may be important. I often ask my patients to consider how 'sleep-friendly' their wind-down to bed time is, and work with them to optimise preparation for bed. This also serves as a good general introduction to relaxation therapy itself if you do decide to make it part of their CBT.

Often people hope that they will just fall into bed and fall asleep because it is 'bed time'. This may be more possible for the good sleeper of course, but for people with insomnia it is rather unlikely. This is why I suggest that a *wind-down* routine should start at least 60–90 minutes before bed so that the patient can start relaxing and preparing for sleep. Their evening routine should include things like slowing down their work/activity and then stopping it. A relaxed hour or more to wind down, before getting into the immediate pre-bed activities of locking up, changing for bed and so on, can be helpful. The wind-down routine should be, on the one hand, carefully planned, but, on the other hand, should not be rigid or inflexible, and I encourage patients to plan it out, write it down and follow the plan until it becomes a habit each night. If people are using the cognitive control procedure for putting the day to rest this can be incorporated at the start of the wind-down period.

It is a good idea to have an actual deadline to mark the transition from busy-ness to relaxation, but what people choose to do in this new-found time can be quite varied. Some people get over-concerned about exactly what they should or should not do. Do reassure them that it is not about getting a perfect routine and observe with them that to over-think it would not be a relaxed approach! You may also find that some patients want to keep busy rather than relax, perhaps so they do not have to start acknowledging and worrying about whether or not they will sleep. You might consider this a type of safety behaviour (Harvey, 2002).

Relaxation therapy

The scientific basis for relaxation therapy

The origins of relaxation therapeutics go back to the pioneering work of Edmund Jacobsen and his classic book on *progressive relaxation* published in 1929. Jacobsen's approach comprised an extensive set of exercises for tensing and relaxing muscle groups progressively around the body. His work became particularly influential with the emergence of behaviour therapy when relaxation was adopted to support the counter-conditioning of fear and as a means to inhibit anxiety responses (e.g., Wolpe, 1958). Relaxation exercises were later condensed into the more usable format of *abbreviated progressive muscle relaxation* by Bernstein and Borkovec (1973). Somewhat in parallel, Schultz and Luthe (1959) published their more passive approach to relaxation. *Autogenic training* trains people to adopt simple standard phrases, referring, for example, to experiences of warmth and heaviness in the extremities (such as 'my right arm is feeling warm and heavy'), to instruct the body to a state of low arousal and to attend to associated pleasant sensations. In practice, and as I will demonstrate below, abbreviated progressive muscle relaxation and autogenic elements are often integrated. Another early pioneer of relaxation methods was Yates, in the 1940s. His *association set technique* involved helping the client to relax by thinking of a soothing word, such as 'calm', an approach that was a forbearer of *cue-controlled relaxation* that became widely used in early behaviour therapy.

Relaxation became a mainstay of clinical behaviour therapy from the 1970s onwards and was reinforced in the 1970s and 1980s by the emergent field of biofeedback and self-regulation where protocols using alpha EEG, EMG and GSR feedback were used to help patients manage anxiety and cognitive/emotional threat across a range of medical and psychiatric conditions. Huge interest emerged also in 'deconstruction' studies in an effort to establish which relaxation approaches and components were the most effective (King, 1980, provided a review). As it transpires, there is little evidence that relaxation therapeutics are differentially effective from one another. Variants of relaxation – in terms of activity, visualisation, focus, attentional process, imagery, meditative content and even philosophical stance – can be traced throughout the history of psychotherapy to the present day with the (re-)emergence of mindfulness, and all seem to offer a relatively similar benefit.

Relaxation as a therapy for insomnia

From the outset relaxation therapy was a natural fit for treating insomnia. The notion of tension and relaxation being mutually incompatible was proving valuable in the anxiety disorders, and seemed equally applicable to insomnia. Relaxation appeared to address both the somatic and cognitive determinants of emotional states, and insomnia, which could be readily understood as a disorder of hyperarousal, had both mental and physiological components. Importantly, relaxation exercises were also attractive from both a procedural and a learning perspective. Here was a practical treatment that was readily translatable to insomnia. Over a productive 15–20 year period there was much theorizing and a great deal of research on relaxation, meditation and biofeedback (reviewed in Espie, 1991). As with the wider literature, no particular relaxation approach emerged as superior, and even with the recent re-emergence of biofeedback it remains unclear whether or not biofeedback per se is crucial to therapeutic response over and above the generic relaxation process (Schabus et al., 2017).

A common thread in relaxation therapeutics is the importance of practice. Relaxation is seen as a skill to be learned or even a way of life to be adopted. Understandably, patients wish to have relaxation techniques available to deploy at night and during periods of high psychophysiological arousal. However, this is the least optimal time at which to develop familiarity with relaxation practices and is likely to result in suboptimal engagement with relaxation techniques. Consequently, patients are first encouraged to practise relaxation during the day and during periods of low stress. The evidence is that once the techniques are adequately internalised, they can then be implemented at night or during periods of high arousal with a much greater chance of success. With this in mind, I always emphasise to patients the value of scheduling daytime and evening practice, recognising that dedicated sessions can so easily get lost in the multiple demands of busy lives. I also always provide them with an audio-recording where I guide them through a practice session. The goal of relaxation is of course to be able to relax, to 'let go', not to fall asleep. Becoming skilled in relaxation therefore is a useful pathway to sleep, not a hypnotic procedure.

Relaxation therapy instructions

The technique I use is based upon abbreviated progressive muscle relaxation but incorporates elements of autogenic training of breathing control and imagery of relaxation responses. The script Provided in Box 2.1 generally takes about 12 minutes to deliver. Hopefully it is self-explanatory.

Box 2.1 Relaxation

Relaxation instructions

These exercises are designed to help you relax. Relaxation is a skill that you can learn. It is just like any other skill, so don't be surprised if you find it takes practice, because that is how we learn skills. So do practice. Practice a couple of times a day, especially as you start to learn.

It is best to practice at a time when you know you won't be disturbed. The exercises will last around 12 minutes, so you will need to set aside at least 15 minutes for each session. You will get the sense of how to pace them, and make sure you go slow, if anything, rather than rushing. When you do your relaxation exercises in your bed you will also be able to listen to the recording there. But after a while you will have learned what to do and you will be able to follow the exercises in your own mind. Let's get started.

Settle yourself down. Lie down with your hands and arms by your sides; have your eyes closed. That's good.

We will start by just thinking about your breathing. Your breathing can help you relax; the more deep and relaxed it is, the better you will feel and the more in control you will feel. So begin by taking some slow regular breaths. Do that now. Breathe in fully and fill up your lungs fully; breathe in, hold your breath for a few seconds now, and let go, breathe out . . .. Do that again, another deep breath, filling your lungs fully when you breathe in, hold it . . . and relax, breathe out. Continue in your own time, noticing that each time you breathe in the muscles in your chest tighten up, and as you breathe out there is a sense of letting go. You can think the word 'relax" each time you breathe out. This will remind you that breathing out helps you relax. It will also help you use this word to tell yourself to relax whenever you need to. You will find that your body will begin to respond. Breathing slowly, comfortably, regularly, and deeply; thinking the word "relax" every time you breathe out; enjoying just lying still and having these moments to relax, concentrating on the exercises.

Now I'd like you to turn your attention to your arms and hands. I'd like you to create some tension in your hands and arms by pressing your fingers into the palms of your hands and making fists. Do that with both hands now. Feel the tension in your hands, feel the tension in your fingers and your wrists, feel the tension in your forearms. Notice what it is like. Keep it going . . . and now relax. Let those hands flop. Let them do whatever they want to do; just let them relax. Notice the difference that's taken place between tension and relaxation. Breathing slowly and deeply, you will find that your fingers will just straighten out and flop, and your hands and arms will feel more relaxed. Allow them to sink into the couch or into the bed; just allow your arms to be heavy. Breathing slowly and deeply, thinking the word 'relax' each time you breathe out, and finding that your hands and arms just relax more and more and more. Your arms and your hands are so heavy and rested. It's almost as if you couldn't be bothered moving them. Just because you have let go of the energy and tension that was in the muscles there. Breathing slowly and deeply, both your hands, both your arms, heavy and rested. Let go of the energy and tension that was in the muscles there, breathing slowly and deeply. Both your hands, both your arms, heavy and rested and relaxed.

I'd like you to turn your attention now to your neck and shoulders. Again, we're going to get your neck and shoulders into a state of relaxation following some tension we're going to introduce. I'd like you to do that by pulling your shoulders up towards your ears. Now, do that; pull your shoulders up towards your ears. Feel the tension across the back of your neck,

(Continued)

Box 2.1 (Continued)

across the top of your back and in your shoulders. Feel the tension, keep it going not so much that it's sore, but keep it constant. Feel it, and now let go . . . relax; go back to breathing slowly and deeply. Let that tension drain away, let it go. Breathe deeply and, as you do so, notice that the tension, almost like a stream, drains away from your neck, across your shoulders, down the upper part of your arms, down the lower part of your arms and out through your fingertips. Draining out and leaving a sense of warmth and relaxation deep in your muscles. Breathing slowly and deeply and allowing that to take place. Just let the tension go. If it doesn't seem to go, don't force it, it will go by itself. Be confident about that. Just breathe slowly and deeply and allow yourself to be relaxed, remembering to think the word 'relax' each time you breathe out. Using that word 'relax' to focus on the sense of relaxation that you get, using the word 'relax' to remind you of the success you are having in relaxing your body.

I'd like you to concentrate now on your face, and on your jaw, and on your forehead. I'd like you to create some tension in these parts of your body by doing two things together at the same time. These things are to screw up your eyes really tightly and bite your teeth together. Do these things together now. Bite your teeth together; feel the tension in your jaw. Screw up your eyes; feel the tension all around your eyes, in your forehead, in your cheeks, throughout your face, wherever there is tension. Now keep it going . . . and relax; breathing in through your nose and out through your mouth, slowly and deeply. Notice how your forehead smoothes out and then your eyelids and your cheeks. Allow your jaw to hang slightly open. Allow your whole head to feel heavy and to sink into the pillow; breathing slowly and deeply. Allow there to be a spread of relaxation across the surface of your face and into all those muscles in your face. Allow your eyelids to feel heavy and comfortable, your jaw and your whole head; breathing slowly and deeply, enjoying the relaxation which you feel in your body. Relax each time you breathe out. Relax just that little bit more each time you breathe out.

Concentrating now on your legs and feet, I want you to create some tension here by doing two things at the same time; these things are to press the backs of your legs downwards and to pull your toes back towards your head. Do these things together now. Create the tension in your legs, press the backs of your legs downwards and pull your toes back towards your head. Feel the tension in your feet, in your toes, in your ankles, in the muscles in your legs. Feel what it is like. Don't overdo it; just notice what it is like . . . hold it . . . and now relax. Breathing slowly and deeply once more; just allow your feet to flop any old way. Thinking the word 'relax' each time you breathe out. Allow the muscles to give up their energy, give up their tension. Let it go, breathing slowly and deeply. Notice how your feet just want to flop to the side. Notice how your legs feel heavy as if you couldn't be bothered moving them. Heavy and comfortable and rested and relaxed. Just that little bit more relaxed each time you breathe out.

Be thinking about your whole body now; supported by the bed or couch, sinking into it, but supported by it. You've let go the tension throughout your body. Your body feels rested, comfortable. Enjoy each deep breath you take. Just use these few moments now to think about any part of your body that doesn't feel quite so rested and allow the tension to go. It will go. Breathe slowly and deeply; thinking the word 'relax' each time you breathe out. Just let any remaining tension drain away; from your hands, your arms, your neck and your back. Heavy and rested, comfortable and relaxed. From your face and your eyes, from your forehead; letting the muscles give up their energy. Like a stream of relaxation flowing over your whole body. Let your legs and feet feel relaxed; sinking into the bed. Breathing slowly and deeply.

In a few moments, the exercises will be finished; but you can continue to relax. You may wish to repeat some of the exercises yourself and that is fine. You may wish to enjoy just continuing as you are. It's up to you . . . but continue to relax.

Sleep education and sleep hygiene

Although sleep education and sleep hygiene are not active treatment components of CBT-I, they nonetheless represent an important foundation upon which the wider treatment approach is built. Many protocols incorporate aspects of sleep education and sleep hygiene, either within a dedicated therapy session or more commonly integrated alongside the more active therapeutics.

Sleep education

Providing a patient with better knowledge of their condition does not in itself constitute a sufficient treatment, but there can be little doubt that it is of therapeutic value to patients to have a better understanding of their health needs. Most people prefer to have accurate information and they are likely to have questions that require answering. Not least, patients are interested in what is wrong with them (diagnostics) and whether it will get better and how quickly (prognostics). They will also want to know what treatments are available and if they are effective. All this is the case for any disorder and it is certainly true for insomnia. In Table 2.7 I have summarised some of the most common questions that are on patients' minds and provided, in broad terms, the sleep education content that I think is most appropriate.

It is important, however, to recognise that sleep education is integral to the practice of CBT as a therapy, rather than an activity in its own right. I suggest that you regard it as the process of guided discovery, through exploring myths and misunderstandings, addressing misattributions and other cognitive challenges, and through the conduct of behavioural experiments, rather than through didactic learning. Individual patient needs for information and explanation varies, and the level of detail required also varies. Some people will want to understand sleep architecture or the molecular clock, while others will be more focused on pragmatic factors. Sleep education is therefore something that often needs to be tailored to the individual. It should, however, always be delivered in an accessible way. You will also see from Table 2.7 that the content of the educational process has much to do with addressing the patient's motivational state (cf. Prochaska & DiClemente, 1983). CBT is a collaborative therapy, but you should bear in mind that it is demanding of patients.

Table 2.7 Sleep education as part of the CBT program.

Common sleep questions	Sleep education content
1. What is sleep?	Sleep is not a unitary state but an orderly set of phases and stages. Each element is important. Sleep and circadian factors interact to deliver sleep and wakefulness at the right times.
2. Why does sleep matter?	Sleep serves important physiological, emotional and cognitive functions throughout our lives. The role of sleep in learning, memory and regulation of our mood is crucial.
3. What are the consequences of poor sleep?	Having insufficient sleep at night causes unwanted symptoms the next day. In the long-term chronic sleep problems can be associated with the development of physical and mental disorders.
4. How much sleep do I need?	There are recommended amounts of sleep depending on your age and stage in life. These are not exact figures because everyone is different. It is important to get the amount of sleep you require every night.
5. What is insomnia?	Difficulty getting to sleep, getting back to sleep or waking too early, 3 or more nights per week for 3 months or longer. Insomnia is associated with daytime symptoms attributable to poor sleep. Insomnia is very common.
6. What treatments work for insomnia?	CBT is the treatment recommended in clinical guidelines. There is a lot of strong evidence for CBT. Medication can be used but is recommended as the second rather than the first choice of treatment. Sleep hygiene alone is not CBT.
7. Why does CBT work?	CBT addresses the behavioural aspects of insomnia by getting sleep back into a consistent and well-timed pattern, and the cognitive aspects by addressing the racing mind and excess arousal that keep us awake.
8. What does CBT involve?	CBT involves working through a program, usually in step-by-step sessions over several weeks supported by a therapist. You then put agreed therapy actions into practice at home. You review your progress with your therapist.
9. Is there not an easier solution?	CBT can be quite demanding, but it is very effective. CBT will help your sleep drive and your pattern become stronger, and it will help you to worry less and to focus less on sleep so that you fall asleep more naturally. CBT is worth the effort.
10. Will CBT work for me?	CBT helps 3 out of 4 people even when they have severe and long-term insomnia. Much depends on putting CBT into effect each night at home. Your therapist will help you discover the parts of CBT that you most need.
11. How long will this take?	Most people begin to improve with CBT within a week or two, and a full course of CBT is often 5–8 weeks long. You should observe improvements not just in sleep but also in how you feel during the day (e.g., energy, mood, concentration).
12. Will treatment effects last?	CBT has lasting effects because CBT addresses the behavioural and mental factors that otherwise would keep insomnia going. You also learn skills that will help you manage any future episodes of poor sleep.

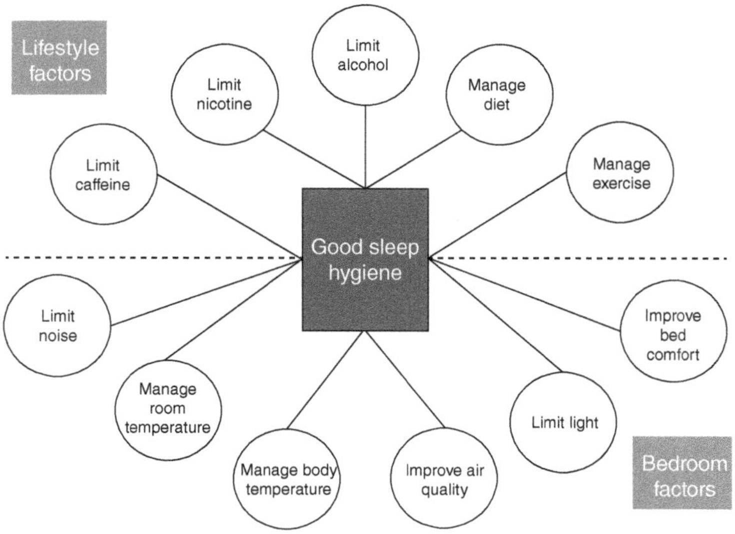

Figure 2.2 Sleep Hygiene Factors to Consider.

Sleep hygiene

Although the term 'sleep hygiene' was first coined by Kleitman in 1939, it was not systematically delineated until Hauri's work, much more recently (1977, 1991). Sleep can be affected by a range of factors that include diet, environment and lifestyle, and the aim of sleep hygiene is to provide patients with information on how such factors affect sleep with a view to developing healthy sleep habits. Typically, sleep hygiene is split into lifestyle habits (e.g., diet, exercise and use of substances) and bedroom environmental factors (e.g., temperature, light, noise and bedding). Figure 2.2 provides an illustration of the main elements of sleep hygiene that you could use with patients as a visual checklist. This provides the opportunity to consider whether or not there is any 'low hanging fruit', as it were, that might assist your patient. For example, you could suggest reducing or eliminating caffeine and alcohol in the evening because both can have adverse effects upon normal sleep, or keeping the bedroom cool and well aired can facilitate sleep. Some patients with insomnia do not observe good sleep hygiene, and so some corrective action may be advised. On the other hand, many patients will have sleep hygiene that is well within the range of what good sleepers normally do.

When talking about bedroom and lifestyle behaviours you should bear in mind that exposure to a sleep hygiene leaflet may well have been your patient's first experience of a non-drug sleep treatment. They may have been given a handout by a family physician or gleaned information on sleep hygiene from searches on the internet. Thus, the advice may already be familiar to them and they may feel that you are going over old ground that they already know about. Most importantly perhaps, they may mistake sleep hygiene for CBT. Patients will often say that they have 'tried everything' and may think of CBT as just another set of 'sleep tips'. This is where it is essential to explain what CBT is, and how it works, and to differentiate CBT as an evidence-based treatment for insomnia rather than a well-being program or a list of 'do's and don'ts'.

Conclusions

In this chapter I have sought to provide an overview of what we have termed the standard CBT treatment protocol for insomnia, as well as offering some clinical insights into the 'how' of CBT. We are fortunate to have such a well-established and robust evidence base to support so many effective components of CBT, and in this regard would do well to remember that CBT is indeed more of a system of therapeutics than a unidimensional treatment. CBT is often constructed into a multicomponent package, where behavioural and cognitive therapeutics (the two domains that form the core) may be supported by relaxation methods and sleep hygiene. It is perhaps the very reliability of CBT as an effective treatment for insomnia that permits the flexibility and tailoring of treatment to different populations and settings. We know that the selection of components, their sequencing, the frequency and timing of sessions, the format of therapy (be it individual, group, telehealth or digital), and the skills and attributes of the therapist may vary, yet CBT is likely to yield clinically meaningful outcomes to our patients. Other chapters in this book illustrate this strength and diversity by showing how the standard protocol can be adapted to meet the needs of our many patients who do not sleep well.

Note

1 In this chapter I have mainly referred to historical milestones, rather than specifically referencing them. For detailed citation of the historical origins, see Espie (2001).

References

Ascher, L.M., & Turner, R. (1979). Paradoxical intention and insomnia: An experimental investigation. *Behaviour Research and Therapy*, *17* (4), 408–411.

Beck, A. T. (1979). *Cognitive therapy and the emotional disorders*. New York: Penguin Books.

Beck, A. T., Rush, J. T., Shaw, B. F., & Emery, G. (1979). *Cognitive therapy of depression* (11th ed.). New York: The Guilford Press.

Bennett-Levy, J., Butler, G., Fennell, M., Hackman, A., Mueller, M., & Westbrook, D. (Eds.). (2004). *Cognitive behaviour therapy: Science and practice series. Oxford guide to behavioural experiments in cognitive therapy*. Oxford, UK: Oxford University Press.

Bernstein, D. A., & Borkovec, T. D. (1973). *Progressive relaxation training: A manual for the helping professions*. Champaign, IL: Research Press.

Bootzin, R. (1972). A stimulus control treatment for insomnia. *Proceedings of the American Psychological Association*, *7*, 395–396.

Bootzin, R. R., Epstein, D., & Wood, J. M. (1991). Stimulus control instructions. In P. J. Hauri (Ed.), *Case studies in insomnia. Critical issues in psychiatry (an educational series for residents and clinicians)*. Boston, MA: Springer.

Borbély, A. A. (1982). A two-process model of sleep regulation. *Human Neurobiology*, *1* (3), 195–204. PMID: 7185792.

Borbély, A. A., Daan, S., Wirz-Justice, A., & Deboer, T. (2016, April). The two-process model of sleep regulation: A reappraisal. *Journal of Sleep Research*, *25* (2), 131–143. doi: 10.1111/jsr.12371. Epub 2016 Jan. 14. PMID: 26762182.

Borkovec, T. D., Wilkinson, l., Folensbee, R., & Lerman, C. (1983). Stimulus control applications to the treatment of worry. *Behaviour Research and Therapy*, *21*, 247–251.

Carney, C. E., & Waters, W. F. (2006). Effects of a structured problem-solving procedure on pre-sleep cognitive arousal in college students with insomnia. *Behaviour and Sleep Medicine*, *4* (1), 13–28.

Cautela, J. R. (1966). Treatment of compulsive behavior by covert sensitization. *The Psychological Record*, *16* (1), 33–41.

Chung, K.-F., Lee, C.-T., Yeung, W.-F., Chan, M.S., Chung, E. W.-Y., & Lin, W.-L. (2018). Sleep hygiene education as a treatment of insomnia: A systematic review and meta-analysis. *Family Practice*, *35* (4), 365–375.

Cocude, M., & Denis, M. (1988). Measuring the temporal characteristics of visual images. *Journal of Mental Imagery*, *12* (1), 89–101.

de la Pena, A. (1978). Toward a psychophysiologic conceptualization of insomnia. In R. L. Williams and I. Karacan (Eds.), *Sleep disorders: Diagnosis and treatment* (pp. 101–143). New York: Wiley.

Dijk, D.J., & Czeisler, C.A. (1995, May). Contribution of the circadian pacemaker and the sleep homeostat to sleep propensity, sleep structure, electroencephalographic slow waves, and sleep spindle activity in humans. *Journal of Neuroscience*, *15* (5, Pt 1), 3526–3538.

Edinger, J. D., Arnedt, J. T., Bertisch, S. M., Carney, C. E., Harrington, J. J., Lichstein, K. L., Sateia, M. J., Troxel, W. M., Zhou, E. S., Kazmi, U., Heald, J. L., & Martin, J. L. (2021). Behavioral and psychological treatments for chronic insomnia disorder in adults: An American Academy of Sleep Medicine clinical practice guideline. *Journal of Clinical Sleep Medicine (JCSM): Official publication of the American Academy of Sleep Medicine*, *17* (2), 255–262. htpps://doi.org/10.5664/jcsm.8986.

llis, A., & Harper, R. A. (1961). *A guide to rational living*. Englewood Cliffs, NJ: Prentice-Hall.

Espie, C. A. (1991). *The psychological treatment of insomnia*. Chichester, UK: Wiley.

Espie, C. A. (2002) Insomnia: Conceptual issues in the development, persistence, and treatment of sleep disorder in adults. *Annual Review of Psychology*, *53*, 215–243.

Espie, C. A. (2021). *Overcoming insomnia and sleep problems: A self-help guide using cognitive behavioral techniques* (2nd ed.). London: Little, Brown Book Group.

Espie, C. A. (2023). *A clinician's guide to cognitive and behavioural therapeutics (CBTx) for Insomnia*. Cambridge, UK: Cambridge University Press.

Espie, C. A., Broomfield, N. M., MacMahon, K. M. A., Macphee, L. M., & Taylor, L. M. (2006). The attention–intention–effort pathway in the development of psychophysiologic insomnia: A theoretical review. *Sleep Medicine Reviews*, *10*, 215–245. https://doi.org/10.1016/j.smrv.2006.03.002.

Espie, C. A., Hames P., & McKinstry, B. (2013). Use of the internet and mobile media for delivery of cognitive-behavioral insomnia therapy. *Sleep Medicine Clinics*, *8*, 407–419.

Espie C. A., Inglis, S.J., Tessier, S., and Harvey, L. (2001). The clinical effectiveness of cognitive behaviour therapy for chronic insomnia: Implementation and evaluation of a sleep clinic in general medical practice. *Behaviour and Research Therapy, Jan.*, *39* (1), 45–60.

Espie, C. A., & Lindsay, W. R. (1987). Cognitive strategies for the management of severe sleep-maintenance insomnia: A preliminary investigation. *Behavioural Psychotherapy*, *15* (4), 388–395.

Flynn-Evans, E. E., Shekleton, J. A., Miller, B., Epstein, L. J., Kirsch, D., Brogna, L. A., Burke, L. M., Bremer, E., Murray, J. M., Gehrman, P., Rajaratnam, S., & Lockley, S. W. (2017). Circadian phase and phase angle disorders in primary insomnia. *Sleep*, *40* (12), 10. https://doi.org/10.1093/sleep/zsx163.

Frankl, V. E. (1955). *The doctor and the soul: From psychotherapy to logotherapy*. New York: Knopf.

Frankl, V. E. (1960). Paradoxical intention. A logotherapeutic technique. *American Journal of Psychotherapy*, *14*, 520–535.

Harrow, L., & Espie, C. A. (2010). Applying the Quarter Hour Rule: Can people with insomnia accurately estimate 15 minute periods during the sleep onset phase? *Journal of Sleep Research*, *19*, 19–26.

Harvey, A. G. (2000). Pre-sleep cognitive activity: A comparison of sleep-onset insomniacs and good sleepers. *British Journal of Clinical Psychology*, *39*, 275–286.

Harvey, A. G. (2002). A cognitive model of insomnia. *Behaviour Research and Therapy*, *40*, 869–893.

Harvey, A. G., & Payne, S. (2002). The management of unwanted pre-sleep thoughts in insomnia: distraction with imagery versus general distraction. *Behaviour Research and Therapy*, *40* (3), 267–277.

Hauri, P. J. (1977). *Current concepts: The sleep disorders*. Kalamazoo, MI: Upjohn.

Hauri, P. J. (1991). Sleep hygiene, relaxation therapy, and cognitive interventions. In P. J. Hauri (Ed.), *Case studies in insomnia*. Boston, MA: Springer.

Hayes, S. C., Strosahl, K. D., & Wilson, K. G. (1999). *Acceptance and commitment therapy: An experiential approach to behavior change*. Guilford, UK: Guilford Press.

Jacobsen, E. (1929). *Progressive relaxation*. Chicago, IL: University of Chicago Press.

Kleitman, N. (1939). *Sleep and wakefulness*. Chicago, IL: University of Chicago Press.

Kosslyn, S. M., Ganis, G., & Thompson, W. L. (2001). Neural foundations of imagery. *Nature Reviews Neuroscience*, *2* (9), 635–642.

Kosslyn, S. M., Thompson, W. L., & Ganis, G. (2006). *The case for mental imagery*. New York: Oxford University Press, Inc.

Kuyken, W., Padesky, C. A., & Dudley, R. (2011). *Collaborative case conceptualization: Working effectively with clients in cognitive-behavioral therapy*. New York: Guilford Press.

Kyle, S. D., Miller, C. B., Rogers, Z., Siriwardena, A. N., Macmahon, K. M, Espie, C. A. (2014). Sleep restriction therapy for insomnia is associated with reduced objective total sleep time, increased daytime somnolence, and objectively impaired vigilance: implications for the clinical management of insomnia disorder. *Sleep*, Feb., *37* (2), 229–237.

Kyle, S. D., Aquino, M. R., Miller, C. B., Henry, A. L., Crawford, M. R., Espie, C. A., & Spielman, A. J. (2015). Towards standardisation and improved understanding of sleep restriction therapy for insomnia disorder: A systematic examination of CBT-I trial content. *Sleep Medicine Reviews*, *23*, 83–88.

Lazarus, R. S. (1966). *Psychological stress and the coping process*. New York: McGraw-Hill.

Lazarus, R. S., & Folkman, S. (1984). *Stress, appraisal, and coping*. New York: Springer Publishing Company.

Lichstein, K. L., & Rosenthal, T. L. (1980). Insomniacs' perceptions of cognitive versus somatic determinants of sleep disturbance. *Journal of Abnormal Psychology*, *89* (1), 105–107.

Maurer, L. F., Espie, C. A., & Kyle, S. D. (2018). How does sleep restriction therapy for insomnia work? A systematic review of mechanistic evidence and the introduction of the Triple-R model. *Sleep Medicine Reviews*, *42*, 127–138.

Meichenbaum, D. (1977). *Cognitive-behavior modification: An integrative approach*. New York: Plenum.

Miller, W. R., & Rollnick, S. (1991). *Motivational interviewing: Preparing people to change addictive behavior*. New York: Guilford Press.

Mitchell, K. R., & White, R. G. (1977). Self-management of severe predormital insomnia. *Journal of Behavior Therapy and Experimental Psychiatry*, *8*, 57–63.

Morin, C. M. (1993). *Insomnia: Psychological assessment and management*. New York: Guilford Press.

Morin, C.M., Vallières, A., & Ivers H. (2007). Dysfunctional beliefs and attitudes about sleep (DBAS): Validation of a brief version (DBAS-16). *Sleep*, Nov., *30* (11), 1547–1554.

Perlis, M. L., Giles, D. E., Mendelson, W. B., Bootzin, R. R., & Wyatt, J. K. (1997). Psychophysiological insomnia: The behavioural model and a neurocognitive perspective. *Journal of Sleep Research*, Sept., *6* (3), 179–188.

Prochaska, J.O., & DiClemente, C.C. (1983). Stages and processes of self-change in smoking: Toward an integrative model of change. *Journal of Consulting and Clinical Psychology*, *5*, 390–395.

Qaseem, A., Kansagara, D., Forciea, M. A., Cooke, M., & Denberg, T.D. (2016). Clinical Guidelines Committee of the American College of Physicians. Management of chronic insomnia disorder in adults: A clinical practice guideline from the American College of Physicians. *Annals of Internal Medicine*, *165* (2), 125–133.

Riemann, D., Spiegelhalder, K., Feige, B., Voderholzer, U., Berger. M., Perlis, M., & Nissen, C. (2010). The hyperarousal model of insomnia: A review of the concept and its evidence. *Sleep Medicine Reviews, Feb.*, *14* (1), 19–31.

Riemann, D., Baglioni, C., Bassetti, C., Bjorvatn, B., Dolenc Groselj, L., Ellis, J. G., Espie, C. A., Garcia-Borreguero, D., Gjerstad, M., Gonçalves, M., Hertenstein, E., Jansson-Fröjmark, M., Jennum, P. J., Leger, D., Nissen, C., Parrino, L., Paunio, T., Pevernagie, D., Verbraecken, J., Weeß, H. G., & Spiegelhalder, K. (2017). European guidelines for the diagnosis and treatment of insomnia. *Journal of Sleep Research*, *26* (6), 675–700. https://doi.org/10.1111/jsr.12594.

Safran, J., & Greenberg, L. (1982). Eliciting 'hot cognitions' in cognitive behaviour therapy: Rationale and procedural guidelines. *Canadian Psychology*, *23*, 83–87.

Schabus, M., Griessenberger, H., Gnjezda, M. T., Heib, D. P. J., Wislowska, M., & Hoedlmoser, K. (2017). Better than sham? A double-blind placebo-controlled neurofeedback study in primary insomnia. *Brain, Apr.*, *140* (4), 1041–1052.

Schultz, J. H., & Luthe, W. (1959). *Autogenic training: A psychophysiologic approach to psychotherapy*. New York: Grune & Stratton.

Seltzer, L. F. (1986). *Paradoxical strategies in psychotherapy: A comprehensive overview and guidebook*. Wiley series on personality processes. New York: John Wiley & Sons.

Shafran, R., Brosan, L., & Cooper P. (2013). *The complete CBT guide for anxiety: A self-help guide for anxiety, panic, social anxiety, phobias, health anxiety and obsessive compulsive disorder*. London, UK: Constable & Robinson.

Spielman, A. J., Saskin, P., & Thorpy, M. J. (1983). Sleep restriction: A new treatment of insomnia. *Sleep Research*, *12*, 286.

Spielman, A. J., Saskin, P., & Thorpy, M. J. (1987). Treatment of chronic insomnia by restriction of time in bed. *Sleep*, *10* (1), 45–56.

Spielman, A. J., Yang, C. M., & Glovinsky, P. B. (2010). Sleep restriction therapy. In M. Perlis, M. Aloia, & B. Kuhn (Eds.), *Behavioral treatments for sleep disorders* (pp. 9–19). New York: Elsevier Inc.

Turner, R. M., & Ascher, L. M. (1979). Controlled comparison of progressive relaxation, stimulus control, and paradoxical intention therapies for insomnia. *Journal of Consulting and Clinical Psychology*, *47* (3), 500–508.

Webb, W. B., and Agnew, H. (1965). Sleep: Effects of a restricted regime. *Science*, *150*, 1745–1747.

Webb, W. B., & Agnew, H. (1974). The effects of a chronic limitation of sleep length. *Psychophysiology*, *11*, 265–274.

Wilson, S., Anderson, K., Baldwin, D., Dijk, D. J., Espie, A., Espie, C., Gringras, P., Krystal, A., Nutt, D., Selsick, H., & Sharpley, A. (2019). British Association for Psychopharmacology consensus statement on evidence-based treatment of insomnia, parasomnias and circadian rhythm disorders: An update. *Journal of Psychopharmacology, Aug.*, *33* (8), 923–947.

Wolpe, J. (1958). *Psychotherapy by reciprocal inhibition* (pp. 53–62). Stanford, CA: Stanford University Press.

Woolfolk, R. L., & McNulty, T. F. (1983). Relaxation treatment for insomnia: A component analysis. *Journal of Consulting & Clinical Psychology, Aug.*, *51* (4), 495–503.

3

Efficacy of Multicomponent CBT-I and Its Single Components

Leonie F. Maurer and Simon D. Kyle

Key points

- Compared to control groups, CBT-I is an effective treatment for insomnia, producing medium-to-large effect sizes across self-reported global insomnia and sleep measures, and small-to-medium effects on daytime functioning.
- Treatment effects are reliably observed for up to 12 months postrandomisation although the magnitude appears to decline over time.
- Current evidence for brief behavioural interventions and standalone sleep restriction therapy suggest that treatment effects could be similar in magnitude to full CBT-I.
- Relaxation therapy and stimulus control have yielded promising results, but more research is needed.
- Evidence for cognitive components and sleep hygiene is insufficient at present.
- Similar to other psychological treatments in other conditions, non-specific treatment factors may play a role in the treatment of insomnia.

Learning objectives

- To become familiar with the current evidence for the efficacy of CBT-I and its components.
- To gain knowledge about research areas and outcomes that are still lacking evidence.
- To understand the need to conduct meta-analyses and systematic reviews.

Abstract

This chapter provides an overview of contemporary evidence (as of 2021) for the efficacy of CBT-I and its components. The scientific support for the clinical use of CBT-I has emerged over the last 40 years and now comprises over 100 randomised controlled trials (RCTs). These trials have informed numerous meta-analyses that have, as a consequence, shaped the treatment guidelines we use today. The evidence considered in this chapter focuses on the most recent meta-analyses that report on the effects of CBT-I and its components on insomnia symptoms and measures of sleep continuity. The overarching conclusion from meta-analyses is that CBT-I is effective in improving night-time insomnia symptoms in both the short term and the long term. In addition, CBT-I improves daytime functioning and its efficacy seems to be independent of co-morbid conditions, age and use of medication. The efficacy of CBT-I components as standalone therapies has been examined to a lesser extent but shows promising results, especially for behavioural components.

Keywords *insomnia, CBT-I, evidence, meta-analysis, systematic review, single component therapy*

Cognitive-Behavioural Therapy for Insomnia (CBT-I) Across the Life Span: Guidelines and Clinical Protocols for Health Professionals, First Edition. Edited by Chiara Baglioni, Colin A. Espie and Dieter Riemann.

Evidence for the efficacy of CBT-I

The aim of this chapter is to provide a comprehensive overview of up-to-date evidence for the efficacy of CBT-I. We will accomplish this goal by focusing on systematic reviews and meta-analyses on full CBT-I and its constituent components. Primary target areas of insomnia treatment comprise the night- and day-time symptoms experienced by patients. In order to determine whether CBT-I is an effective treatment, research therefore needs to show that it consistently performs better than control conditions on these key areas, with systematic reviews and meta-analyses being placed at the top of the hierarchical pyramid of evidence (Murad, Asi, Alsawas & Alahdab, 2016). The outcomes of interest are changes in self-reported global insomnia measures (e.g., the insomnia severity index (ISI); see Chapter 5) and sleep parameters derived from sleep diaries such as sleep onset latency (SOL), sleep efficiency (SE), wake after sleep onset (WASO) and sleep quality (SQ). Although total sleep time (TST) is also commonly reported, we specifically focus on sleep continuity variables, since these are considered chief outcomes of CBT-I. To aid interpretation and comparability, mean differences between groups are typically converted to effect sizes (Cohen's D or Hedges' g) and averaged across studies, and the levels 0.2, 0.5 and 0.8 are interpreted as small, medium and large respectively (Cohen, 1977; Hedges, 1981). An overview of standardised effect sizes for global insomnia symptoms and sleep continuity measures is provided in Figure 3.1.

Sleep outcomes

To date, the most comprehensive meta-analyses on the efficacy of CBT-I at post-treatment (immediately after treatment) were conducted by Van Straten and colleagues in 2018 (Van Straten et al., 2018) and by the American Academy of Sleep Medicine (AASM) task force in 2020 (Edinger et al., 2021b). Van Straten and colleagues identified 87 randomised-controlled trials (RCT) that compared at least one CBT-I component to a non-active control group (e.g., waiting list or no treatment) in the adult insomnia population. Out of the 87 trials, 51 met criteria for full CBT-I (educational + cognitive + behavioural component). The largest effect sizes were observed for the ISI ($g = 0.82$). Effect sizes for SOL ($g = 0.47$) and SE ($g = 0.63$) were smaller, but also in favour of CBT-I (see Figure 3.1). Furthermore, treatment effects were not modified by the presence of co-morbid conditions, sleep medication or age. However, face-to-face treatments and treatments with four or more sessions

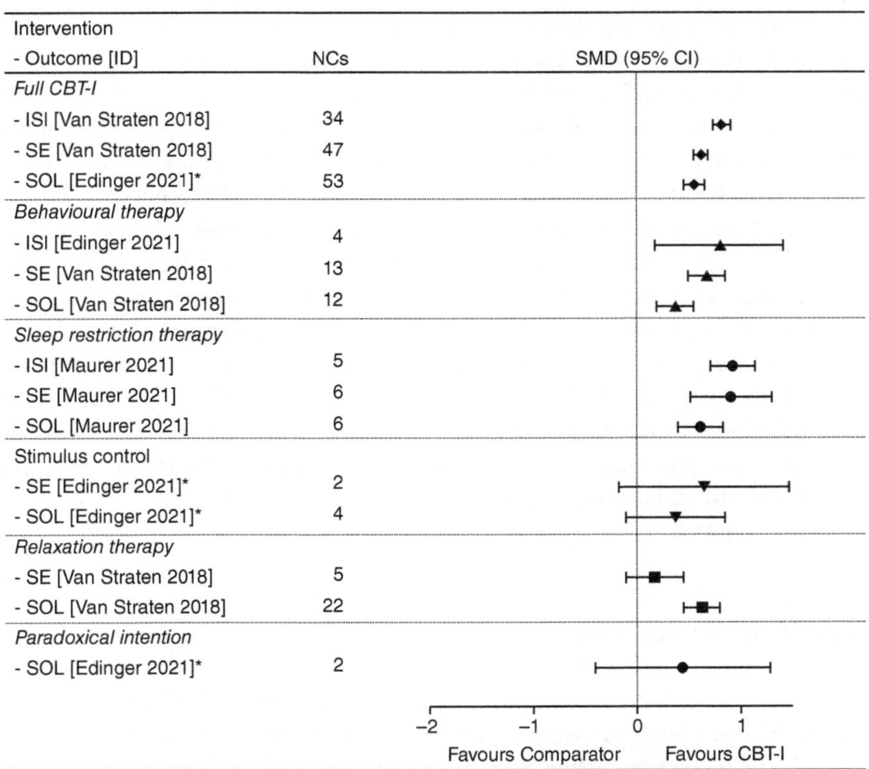

Figure 3.1 Overview of standardised mean differences for insomnia severity (ISI) and sleep diary derived sleep efficiency (SE), and sleep onset latency (SOL) across CBT-I and its components. Standardised mean differences (SMD) and 95% confidence intervals (95% CI) are derived from meta-analyses (ID presented in form of the first author and the year of publication) or were manually calculated with data provided by the meta-analysis (marked with an asterisk). Whenever more than one meta-analysis provided relevant outcome data, we included the meta-analysis that was based on a higher number of comparisons (NCs), or provided outcome data in SMD format.

were found to be more effective than self-help interventions or treatments with fewer sessions. Meta-analyses of CBT-I trials in patients with medical and/or psychiatric co-morbidities similarly show medium-to-large treatment effects (Geiger-Brown et al., 2015; Wu, Appleman, Salazar & Ong, 2015). Effects for online or digital CBT-I are generally found to be comparable to face-to face interventions (Soh, Ho, Ho & Tam, 2020), with large effect sizes on the ISI ($g = 1.09$) and medium effect sizes for SQ, SOL, WASO and SE ($g = 0.41$–0.58), whereby longer treatment duration and more involvement of personal support appears to be related to larger effect sizes (Zachariae, Lyby, Ritterband & O'Toole, 2016).

A follow-up meta-analysis by van der Zweerde, Bisdounis, Kyle, Lancee and van Straten (2019) showed that CBT-I sleep improvements are also maintained over time. Results from 30 RCTs providing data at 3, 6 or 12 months indicate that effects decline over time but remain significant 12 months after treatment (e.g., ISI at 12 months, $g = 0.25$). These results are also supported by RCTs comparing CBT-I to pharmacological treatments; findings from a meta-analysis in 2012 showed that long-term studies consistently favour CBT-I across sleep outcomes when compared to benzodiazepines and non-benzodiazepines (Mitchell, Gehrman, Perlis & Umscheid, 2012).

The aim of the recent AASM task force review was to inform and update AASM treatment guidelines (Edinger et al., 2021a). As a consequence, outcomes of interest were mostly reported in the form of mean differences and in comparison to previously specified thresholds for critical outcomes. The thresholds were set to a between-group standard mean difference (SMD) of 0.5 for sleep quality, a between-group difference of 20 minute for SOL and WASO, and a 10% group difference in remission and responder rates. Remission and responder rates were based on the ISI, sleep diary, or PSQI (Pittsburgh sleep quality index) (see Edinger et al., 2021b, for details). The authors identified 49 CBT-I trials providing at least one critical outcome. The mean differences from which outcomes were derived included RCTs and indicated a significant clinical benefit for CBT-I on SQ (derived from the PSQI; see Chapter 5), remission rate (the percentage of patients achieving remission was 33% higher than control) and responder rate (the percentage of patients achieving responder status was 45% higher than control). Criteria were not met for SOL (−12.68 min), WASO (−18.96 min) and diary defined SQ (SMD = 0.44) when all evidence was considered, but were met for the subgroups 'insomnia with no co-morbidities' (SQ (2 RCTs) and WASO (9 RCTs) only) and 'insomnia with psychiatric comorbidities' (SQ (1 RCT) and SOL/WASO (8 RCTs)). Comparable to the results from Van Straten et al. (2018), large between-group effects were found for global insomnia measures (e.g., ISI, $g = 0.95$). In line with previous findings, effects for participants with medical or psychiatric co-morbidities were of comparable magnitude for most outcomes. Indeed, a recently published chart review of a clinical sample of 'real world' patients ($n = 455$) also found that pretreatment symptoms of depression, anxiety and stress did not alter the effectiveness of CBT-I (Sweetman et al., 2020).

In addition to self-reported outcomes, actigraphy and polysomnography (PSG) can be used to track sleep improvements objectively. In contrast to self-reported sleep outcomes, a recent meta-analysis of 15 RCTs (five provided data for PSG outcomes) failed to find reliable changes in favour of CBT-I across PSG-defined sleep parameters, indicating a discrepancy between subjective and objective sleep measures. In comparison, results from actigraphy indicated small reductions for SOL and, intriguingly, moderate reductions for TST (Mitchell, Bisdounis, Ballesio, Omlin & Kyle, 2019). Reductions in actigraphy-defined TST were also reported by the AASM task force (Edinger et al., 2021a). The loss of sleep time is typically expected during the implementation of CBT-I and has been linked to the SRT component (Kyle et al., 2014; Maurer et al., 2020) as well as stimulus control. These reductions are assumed to be transient and, unlike improvements in SOL and WASO, increases in self-reported TST are not typically (or are only marginally) observed as a result of CBT-I (Van Straten et al., 2018). Overall, the absence of marked effects of CBT-I on objective sleep continuity measures is preliminary, but surprising. Indeed, they are in contrast to findings from pharmacological trials (Rösner, Englbrecht, Wehrle, Hajak & Soyka, 2018) and question the sleep improvement processes underlying CBT-I. Changes in subjective but not objective markers could be indicative of a potential correction of sleep perception, whereby sleep parameters are estimated more accurately following CBT-I (Lund, Rybarczyk, Perrin, Leszczyszyn & Stepansky, 2013). However, more studies are needed to test this hypothesis – and to further investigate the role of objective markers in the treatment of insomnia.

Day-time functioning

Day-time dysfunction is a common complaint of insomnia patients and the driving motivation in seeking treatment (Kyle, Espie & Morgan, 2010; Buysse et al., 2007; Morin, LeBlanc, Daley, Gregoire & Mérette, 2006). Consequently, its consideration is of central importance when examining treatment efficacy (Kyle et al., 2013; Kyle, Morgan & Espie 2010). Compared to sleep outcomes, day-time symptoms are less commonly studied, but a few recent meta-analyses have been performed. Benz and colleagues (2020) reported on a comprehensive network meta-analysis (see Chaimani, Caldwell, Li, Higgins & Salanti, 2021) for various day-time symptoms, including depressive symptoms, anxiety and worry, daytime sleepiness, fatigue, quality of life, day-time and social functioning, physical functioning, mental state and stress. In comparison to control conditions, results revealed predominantly small-to-medium effects (except for physical functioning and stress). These results are also supported by the AASM task force, who reported a medium effect size for day-time fatigue ($g = 0.56$). While promising, researchers suggest that day-time symptoms could further improve if they were directly targeted by intervention (Benz et al., 2020; Harvey, Sharpley, Ree, Stinson & Clark, 2007).

Evidence for the efficacy of CBT-I components

Brief behavioural therapy

Brief behavioural therapies (BBTs) may offer a cost-effective solution to treat insomnia, whereby an abbreviated version of CBT-I, with only 1–4 sessions focused on behavioural components, is typically implemented over a short time frame (Troxel, Germain, and Buysse, 2012). The meta-analyses by Van Straten and colleagues (2018) and the AASM task force (2020) both address the question of whether behavioural therapy is an effective treatment for insomnia. Van Straten et al. identified 13 RCTs that tested behavioural therapy (stimulus control + sleep restriction therapy) and showed small-to-medium effects for SOL ($g = 0.38$), medium-to-large effects for SE ($g = 0.68$) and large effects on the ISI ($g = 0.90$). However, results for the ISI were only based on two RCTs. The AASM task force identified nine RCTs investigating brief therapies, revealing large effect sizes for sleep quality ($g = 1.73$) and insomnia severity (ISI, $g = 0.81$; see Figure 3.1). Between-group comparisons for SOL and WASO showed a mean difference of –10.54 min and –16.16 min respectively, favouring brief therapy. The remission rate was 34% higher compared to the control. Similarly, data from two RCTs showed a responder rate that was 26% higher than control.

Sleep restriction therapy

Sleep restriction therapy (SRT) is claimed to be the most effective component of CBT-I and has gained more attention in the trial literature than most of its counterparts. Similar to BBT, SRT may provide a cost-effective solution to treat insomnia. The AASM task force also appraised results from SRT trials against their pre-set clinical significance thresholds (Edinger et al., 2021b). Four RCTs were identified and results showed a medium effect size for sleep quality ($g = 0.49$) and small reductions for SOL and WASO (6.4–11.7 min), favouring SRT. The remission rate was estimated to be between 13 and 24% (two RCTs only). Our team recently performed a dedicated meta-analysis on SRT trials, finding eight RCTs for quantitative appraisal (Maurer, Schneider, Miller, Espie & Kyle, 2021). In favour of SRT, results revealed medium-to-large effects on the ISI ($g = 0.93$), for SE ($g = 0.93$), SOL ($g = 0.62$; see Figure 3.1) and WASO ($g = 0.83$). Preliminary results from three RCTs also suggest that effects on the ISI ($g = 0.83$) and for WASO ($g = 0.31$) may decline over time (the follow-up period ranged from 3 to 6 months).

Stimulus control

Meta-analytical evidence for stimulus control is limited to the report by the AASM task force (Edinger et al., 2021b). The authors identified four RCTs that reported on relevant outcomes. At post-treatment, between-group comparisons revealed a mean difference of ~19 min for WASO and ~10 min for SOL, favouring stimulus control. Sleep efficiency was 13% higher when compared to control. The small number of RCTs highlights the limitations of the current evidence and demands for more effectiveness trials on standalone stimulus control therapy.

Relaxation therapy

As regards relaxation therapy, eight RCTs were regarded as suitable for meta-analysis by the AASM task force (2021). In favour of relaxation therapy, results showed a medium effect size for SQ ($g = 0.52$) and small reductions for SOL and WASO (7–16 min). The responder rate was 16% higher and SE was 4.5% higher when compared to control groups. Results were also supported by the meta-analysis from Van Straten and colleagues (2018), who reported a medium-to-large effect size for SOL ($g = 0.63$), favouring relaxation therapy. No significant effect was found for SE ($g = 0.18$; see Figure 3.1).

Cognitive therapies

Compared to the behavioural components of CBT-I, cognitive therapy for insomnia is less protocolised and standardised (see Chapter 1). In 2018, Jansson-Fröjmark and Norell-Clarke published a comprehensive systematic review on cognitive treatment components in which they identified 32 RCTs and 16 different cognitive components for insomnia. Results from this review suggest that paradoxical intention and cognitive therapy (the latter as formulated by Allison G. Harvey in 2007) may be efficacious in their own right (Jansson-Frojmark and Norell-Clarke, 2018). These components have also been investigated by the AASM task force for quantitative appraisal, but no suitable studies were identified for cognitive therapy as a standalone therapy (Edinger et al., 2021b) and only 2 RCTs were found for paradoxical intention, revealing a mean reduction of ~18 min for SOL (Edinger et al., 2021b). One head-to-head comparison between cognitive therapy and full CBT-I showed that the proportion of treatment responders was lower at post-treatment (42.4% vs 67.3%) but comparable at 6-month follow-up (62.3% vs 67.3%), suggesting that cognitive therapy may take longer to achieve therapeutic potency (Harvey et al., 2014). These results were also confirmed by Sunnhed and colleagues, who reported comparable treatment effects for most outcomes when comparing internet-delivered cognitive and behavioural therapy (Sunnhed et al., 2020). Evidently, more studies are needed to determine the efficacy of cognitive therapies. An overview of the evidence base for CBT-I and its components is presented in Figure 3.1.

Sleep hygiene

Sleep hygiene advice (also known as psychoeducation) is typically delivered as part of usual care for insomnia (Everitt et al., 2014), but at the same time often serves as a control group in CBT-I trials (Van Straten et al., 2018). Since it is used as a control group, comparisons between sleep hygiene and other control groups are rare (e.g., Edinger, Wohlgemuth, Krystal & Rice, 2005) and thus available evidence focuses on within-group changes or comparisons between sleep hygiene and full CBT-I (Chung et al., 2018). Results from 15 RCTs showed small to medium effect sizes for within-group changes on sleep and insomnia outcomes (e.g., SOL, $g = 0.23$; ISI, $g = 0.68$), thereby suggesting that sleep hygiene may be effective. However, when compared to full CBT-I, sleep hygiene was inferior across all self-reported sleep continuity and insomnia measures (Chung et al., 2018).

Considerations and future directions

Addressing risk of bias

At the beginning of this chapter we highlighted the importance of meta-analyses in determining the efficacy of an intervention. While meta-analysis combines evidence from a broad literature and helps to estimate the true level of a treatment effect, results are nevertheless influenced by the quality of included studies and (usually) are restricted to published studies. The quality of a study is typically evaluated with a risk of bias assessment that takes into account the methodological rigour of each study (Higgins et al., 2019). Across all meta-analyses included in this overview, the relatively high risk of bias was of general concern and highlighted by the various authors, potentially overestimating the true effectiveness (e.g., Van Straten et al., 2018). One reason for a high risk of bias seems to be a combination of the nature of cognitive-behavioural interventions (i.e., participants are aware that they are receiving a treatment), the choice of outcome measure (typically self-reported) and the lack of well-designed control groups (e.g., awareness of being assigned to the control group increasing the risk for bias; Gold et al., 2017). For example, Van Straten and colleagues (2018) reported that (1) the choice of control group was associated with treatment effects, whereby larger effect sizes favouring CBT-I were reported when the control condition was a waitlist control, and (2) studies that did not report concealment of treatment allocation indicated larger treatment effects. Another important consideration is the number of comparisons (number of studies providing relevant outcomes), which was typically low for meta-analyses of single-component interventions. It is questionable whether meta-analyses with less than five studies can exceed the power of an individual study, especially when heterogeneity between studies is high (Jackson and Turner, 2017). As a consequence, results from single-component meta-analyses should be interpreted with caution and demand for more well-designed RCTs.

Risk-benefit analysis

We also want to stress that the benefit of CBT-I and its components should not solely be determined by effect sizes on treatment outcomes. Indeed, a relevant consideration may be to ask whether the benefits outweigh the risks of the intervention. This aspect is typically neglected in psychotherapy research and CBT-I is no exception (Condon, Maurer, and Kyle, 2021). Side-effects of full CBT-I have previously been reported (e.g., Espie et al., 2019), especially in relation to the behavioural components (Sunnhed et al., 2020) and SRT in particular (Kyle, Morgan, Spiegelhalder & Espie, 2011; Kyle et al. 2014; Maurer et al., 2020; Maurer, Ftouni, Espie, Bisdounis & Kyle, 2020). Although it is generally assumed that the benefits of CBT-I strongly outweigh these potential risks (Edinger et al., 2021b), particularly relative to pharmacotherapies, better assessment is needed to make formal conclusions (Condon, Maurer, and Kyle, 2021).

Variability in treatment response

Another important consideration is individual variability in treatment response. We have reported above that treatment effects were neither related to the presence of a co-morbid condition, nor to medication or age. Yet, remission and responder rates indicate that not everyone benefits from CBT-I. One of the underlying assumptions of psychotherapy is that an intervention can only be as good as its implementation. Consequently, adherence and engagement with CBT-I have been hypothesised as predictors of treatment outcomes (Matthews, Arnedt, McCarthy, Cuddihy & Aloia, 2013). However, lack of consistent adherence measures and reporting have hitherto hindered the assessment of such a relationship, with mixed findings demanding more research (Agnew et al., 2021). Besides the lack of an established association between treatment adherence and treatment outcomes, barriers to treatment engagement have been identified and should be considered. For behavioural therapy, Vincent, Lewychy and Finnegan (2008) have reported the perception of barriers and the experience of sleepiness before the beginning of the treatment as indicators for lower treatment adherence, while for full CBT-I, Cui and Fiske (2020) have shown younger age, variability in bed and rise times, and co-occurring depression and anxiety symptomatology as indicators for lower adherence. Additionally, the recent proposal of multiple insomnia subtypes may pave the way for targeted therapeutic approaches based on phenotypic features (Blanken et al., 2019).

Co-morbid populations

Finally, we want to comment on other health areas in which insomnia has a key role, and consequently, in which CBT-I has the potential to reduce the symptoms and the burden of the co-morbid disorder. For example, preliminary evidence from CBT-I trials in patients with insomnia and co-morbid depression identified CBT-I as a potentially promising intervention for unipolar depression with effect sizes comparable in magnitude to antidepressant medication (Cunningham and Shapiro, 2018). Furthermore, a recent meta-analysis by Selvanathan and colleagues (2021) investigated the efficacy of CBT-I in the treatment of co-morbid insomnia and chronic pain. Besides showing robust effects on sleep outcomes, the authors reported that the probability of experiencing less pain after CBT-I treatment was 57–58% at post treatment and follow-up. The first evidence from RCTs also shows that CBT-I may yield beneficial effects on cognitive functioning in those with insomnia and mild cognitive impairment (Cassidy-Eagle, Siebern, Unti, Glassman & O'Hara, 2018), but more studies are needed (Blackman et al., 2020). Since sleep plays a central role in brain functioning, CBT-I has also been identified as a potential treatment to improve symptoms and recovery after traumatic brain injury and the first large RCT is currently ongoing (Dietch and Furst, 2020). Additionally, the improvement of sleep may also be an important target in those with sleep disturbances and abnormal glucose metabolism (Kothari, Cardona, Chirakalwasan, Anothaisintawee & Reutrakul, 2021). With more studies in various study populations under way, we believe the future will tell whether the treatment effects of CBT-I can reach beyond the improvement of sleep and day-time functioning.

Research agenda

In order to improve our understanding of CBT-I efficacy, future studies should aim to:

- Carefully design RCTs to mitigate the risk of bias (e.g., verification through objective markers, comparing against active control groups).
- Systematically assess the risk–benefit ratio of CBT-I (e.g., including side effect measures).

- Identify predictors of non-responders (e.g., baseline characteristics, treatment barriers, treatment trajectories, adherence measures).
- Investigate CBT-I benefits beyond sleep (e.g., mood, pain, metabolism, cognitive functioning) and beyond insomnia (e.g., depression, anxiety, chronic fatigue).

References

Agnew, S., Vallières, A., Hamilton, A., McCrory, S., Nikolic, M., Kyle, S. D., Fleming, L., & Crawford, M. R. (2021). Adherence to cognitive behavior therapy for insomnia: An updated systematic review. *Sleep Medicine Clinics*, *16*, 155–202. https://doi.org/10.1016/j.jsmc.2020.11.002.

Benz, F., Knoop, T., Ballesio, A., Bacaro, V., Johann, A. F., Rücker, G., Feige, B., Riemann, D., & Baglioni, C. (2020). The efficacy of cognitive and behavior therapies for insomnia on daytime symptoms: A systematic review and network meta-analysis. *Clinical Psychology Review*, 101873. https://doi.org/10.1016/j.cpr.2020.101873.

Blackman, J., Swirski, M., Clynes, J., Harding, S., Leng, Y., & Coulthard, E. (2020). Pharmacological and non-pharmacological interventions to enhance sleep in mild cognitive impairment and mild Alzheimer's disease: A systematic review. *Journal of Sleep Research*, e13229. https://doi.org/10.1111/jsr.13229.

Blanken, T. F., Benjamins, J. S., Borsboom, D., Vermunt, J. K., Paquola, C., Ramautar, J., Dekker, K., Stoffers, D., Wassing, R., Wei, Y., & Van Someren, E. J. W. (2019). Insomnia disorder subtypes derived from life history and traits of affect and personality. *The Lancet Psychiatry*, *6*, 151–163. https://doi.org/10.1016/S2215-0366(18)30464-4.

Buysse, D. J., Thompson, W., Scott, J., Franzen, P. L., Germain, A., Hall, M., Moul, D. E., Nofzinger, E. A., & Kupfer, D. J. (2007). Daytime symptoms in primary insomnia: A prospective analysis using ecological momentary assessment. *Sleep Medicine*, *8*, 198–208. https://doi.org/10.1016/j.sleep.2006.10.006.

Cassidy-Eagle, E., Siebern, A., Unti, L., Glassman, J., & O'Hara, R. (2018). Neuropsychological functioning in older adults with mild cognitive impairment and insomnia randomized to CBT-I or control group. *Clinical Gerontologist*, *41*, 136–144. https://doi.org/10.1080/07317115.2017.1384777.

Chaimani, A., Caldwell, D. M., Li, T., Higgins, J. P., & Salanti, G. (2021). Chapter 11: Undertaking network meta-analyses. Available from: www.training.cochrane.org/handbook.

Chung, K.-F., Lee, C.-T., Yeung, W.-F., Chan, M.-S., Chung, E. W.-Y., & Lin, W.-L. (2018). Sleep hygiene education as a treatment of insomnia: A systematic review and meta-analysis. *Family Practice*, *35*, 365–375. https://doi.org/10.1093/fampra/cmx122.

Cohen, J. (1977). *Statistical power analysis for the behavioral sciences*. New York: Academic Press.

Condon, H., Maurer, L., & Kyle, S. (2021). Reporting of adverse events in cognitive behavioural therapy for insomnia: A systematic examination of randomised controlled trials. *Sleep Medicine Reviews*, *56*. https://doi.org/10.1016/j.smrv.2020.101412.

Cui, R., & Fiske, A. (2020). Predictors of treatment attendance and adherence to treatment recommendations among individuals receiving Cognitive Behavioral Therapy for Insomnia. *Cognitive Behaviour Therapy*, *49*, 113–119. https://doi.org/10.1080/16506073.2019.1586992.

Cunningham, J. E. A., & Shapiro, C. M. (2018). Cognitive Behavioural Therapy for Insomnia (CBT-I) to treat depression: A systematic review. *Journal of Psychosomatic Research*, *106*, 1–12. https://doi.org/10.1016/j.jpsychores.2017.12.012.

Dietch, J. R., & Furst, A. J. (2020). Perspective: Cognitive Behavioral Therapy for Insomnia is a promising intervention for mild traumatic brain injury. *Frontiers in Neurology*, *11*. https://doi.org/10.3389/fneur.2020.530273.

Edinger, J. D., Wohlgemuth, W. K., Krystal, A. D., & Rice, J. R. (2005). Behavioral insomnia therapy for fibromyalgia patients: a randomized clinical trial. *Archives of Internal Medicine*, *165*, 2527–2535. https://doi.org/10.1001/archinte.165.21.2527.

Edinger, J. D., Arnedt, J. T., Bertisch, S. M., Carney, C. E., Harrington, J. J., Lichstein, K. L., Sateia, M. J., Troxel, W. M., Zhou, E. S., Kazmi, U., Heald, J. L., & Martin, J. L. (2021a). Behavioral and psychological treatments for chronic insomnia disorder in adults: An American Academy of Sleep Medicine clinical practice guideline. *Journal of Clinical Sleep Medicine*, *17*, 255–262. https://doi.org/10.5664/jcsm.8986.

Edinger, J. D., Arnedt, J. T., Bertisch, S. M., Carney, C. E., Harrington, J. J., Lichstein, K. L., Sateia, M. J., Troxel, W. M., Zhou, E. S., Kazmi, U., Heald, J. L., & Martin, J. L. (2021b). Behavioral and psychological treatments for chronic insomnia disorder in adults: An American Academy of Sleep Medicine systematic review, meta-analysis and GRADE assessment. *Journal of Clinical Sleep Medicine*, *17*, 263–298. https://doi.org/10.5664/jcsm.8988.

Espie, C. A., Emsley, R., Kyle, S. D., Gordon, C., Drake, C. L., Siriwardena, A. N., Cape, J., Ong, J. C., Sheaves, B., Foster, R., Freeman, D., Costa-Font, J., Marsden, A., & Luik, A. I. (2019). Effect of digital cognitive behavioral therapy for insomnia on health, psychological well-being, and sleep-related quality of life: A randomized clinical trial. *JAMA Psychiatry*, *76* (1). https://doi.org/10.1001/jamapsychiatry.2018.2745.

Everitt, H., McDermott, L., Leydon, G., Yules, H., Baldwin, D., & Little, P. (2014). GPs' management strategies for patients with insomnia: A survey and qualitative interview study. *British Journal of General Practice*, 64, e112–e19. https://doi.org/10.1016/j.smrv.2018.09.004.

Geiger-Brown, J. M., Rogers, V. E., Liu, W., Ludeman, E. M., Downton, K. D., & Diaz-Abad, M. (2015). Cognitive behavioral therapy in persons with comorbid insomnia: A meta-analysis. *Sleep Medicine Reviews*, *23*, 54–67. https://doi.org/10.1016/j.smrv.2014.11.007.

Gold, S. M., Enck, P., Hasselmann, H., Friede, T., Hegerl, U., Mohr, D. C., & Otte, C. (2017). Control conditions for randomised trials of behavioural interventions in psychiatry: A decision framework. *The Lancet Psychiatry*, *4*, 725–732. https://doi.org/10.1016/S2215-0366(17)30153-0.

Harvey, A. G., Sharpley, A. L., Ree, M. J., Stinson, K., & Clark, D. M. (2007). An open trial of cognitive therapy for chronic insomnia. *Behavioural Research Therapy*, *45*, 2491–501. https://doi.org/10.1016/j.brat.2007.04.007.

Harvey, A. G., Bélanger, L., Talbot, L., Eidelman, P., Beaulieu-Bonneau, S., Fortier-Brochu, É., Ivers, H., Lamy, M., Hein, K., Soehner, A. M., Mérette, C., & Morin, C. M. (2014). Comparative efficacy of behavior therapy, cognitive therapy, and cognitive behavior therapy for chronic insomnia: a randomized controlled trial. *Journal of Consulting and Clinical Psychology*, *82*, 670–683. https://doi.org/10.1037/a0036606.

Hedges, L. V. (1981). Distribution theory for Glass's estimator of effect size and related estimators. *Journal of Educational Statistics*, *6* (2), 107–128.

Higgins, J. P., Thomas, J., Chandler, J., Cumpston, M., Li, T., Page, M. J., & Welch, V. A. (2019). *Cochrane handbook for systematic reviews of interventions*. John Wiley & Sons.

Jackson, D., & Turner, R. (2017). Power analysis for random-effects meta-analysis. *Research Synthesis Methods*, *8*, 290–302. https://doi.org/10.1002/jrsm.1240.

Jansson-Frojmark, M., & Norell-Clarke, A. (2018). The cognitive treatment components and therapies of cognitive behavioral therapy for insomnia: A systematic review. *Sleep Medicine Reviews*, *42*, 19–36. https://doi.org/10.1016/j.smrv.2018.05.001.

Kothari, V., Cardona, Z., Chirakalwasan, N., Anothaisintawee, T., & Reutrakul, S. (2021). Sleep interventions and glucose metabolism: Systematic review and meta-analysis. *Sleep Medicine*, *78*, 24–35. https://doi.org/10.1016/j.sleep.2020.11.035.

Kyle, S. D., Espie, C. A., & Morgan, K. (2010). '. . . Not just a minor thing, it is something major, which stops you from functioning daily': Quality of life and daytime functioning in insomnia. *Behavioural Sleep Medicine*, *8*, 123–140. https://doi.org/10.1080/15402002.2010.487450.

Kyle, S. D., Morgan, K., & Espie, C. A. (2010). Insomnia and health-related quality of life. *Sleep Medicine Reviews*, *14*, 69–82. https://doi.org/10.1016/j.smrv.2009.07.004.

Kyle, S. D., Morgan, K., Spiegelhalder, K., & Espie, C. A. (2011). No pain, no gain: An exploratory within-subjects mixed-methods evaluation of the patient experience of sleep restriction therapy (SRT) for insomnia. *Sleep Medicine*, *12*, 735–747. https://doi.org/10.1016/j.sleep.2011.03.016.

Kyle, S. D., Crawford, M. R., Morgan, K., Spiegelhalder, K., Clark, A. A., & Espie, C. A. (2013). The Glasgow Sleep Impact Index (GSII): A novel patient-centred measure for assessing sleep-related quality of life impairment in insomnia disorder. *Sleep Medicine*, *14*, 493–501. https://doi.org/10.1016/j.sleep.2012.10.023.

Kyle, S. D., Miller, C. B., Rogers, Z., Siriwardena, A. N., MacMahon, K. M., & Espie, C. A. (2014). Sleep restriction therapy for insomnia is associated with reduced objective total sleep time, increased daytime somnolence, and objectively impaired vigilance: Implications for the clinical management of insomnia disorder. *Sleep*, *37*, 229–237. https://doi.org/10.5665/sleep.3386.

Lund, H. G., Rybarczyk, B. D., Perrin, P. B., Leszczyszyn, D., & Stepanski, E. (2013). The discrepancy between subjective and objective measures of sleep in older adults receiving CBT for comorbid insomnia. *Journal of Clinical Psychology*, *69*, 1108–1120. https://doi.org/10.1002/jclp.21938.

Matthews, E. E., Arnedt, J. T., McCarthy, M. S., Cuddihy, L. J., & Aloia, M. S. (2013). Adherence to cognitive behavioral therapy for insomnia: A systematic review. *Sleep Medicine Reviews*, *17*, 453–464. https://doi.org/10.1016/j.smrv.2013.01.001.

Maurer, L. F., Ftouni, S., Espie, C. A., Bisdounis, L., and Kyle, S. D. (2020). The acute effects of sleep restriction therapy for insomnia on circadian timing and vigilance. *Journal of Sleep Research*, *30* (4), e13260. https://doi.org/10.1111/jsr.13260.

Maurer, L. F., Schneider, J., Miller, C. B., Espie, C. A., & Kyle, S. D. (2021). The clinical effects of sleep restriction therapy for insomnia: A meta-analysis of randomised controlled trials. *Sleep Medicine Reviews, 58*. https://doi.org/10.1016/j.smrv.2021.101493.

Maurer, L. F., Espie, C. A., Omlin, X., Reid, M. J., Sharman, R., Gavriloff, D., Emsley, R., & Kyle, S. D. (2020). Isolating the role of time in bed restriction in the treatment of insomnia: A randomized, controlled, dismantling trial comparing sleep restriction therapy with time in bed regularization. *Sleep, 43*. https://doi.org/10.1093/sleep/zsaa096.

Mitchell, L. J., Bisdounis, L., Ballesio, A., Omlin, X., & Kyle, S. D. (2019). The impact of cognitive behavioural therapy for insomnia on objective sleep parameters: A meta-analysis and systematic review. *Sleep Medicine Reviews, 47*, 90–102. https://doi.org/10.1016/j.smrv.2019.06.002.

Mitchell, M. D., Gehrman, P., Perlis, M., & Umscheid, C. A. (2012). Comparative effectiveness of cognitive behavioral therapy for insomnia: A systematic review. *BMC Family Practitioner, 13*, 40. https://doi.org/10.1186/1471-2296-13-40.

Morin, C. M., LeBlanc, M., Daley, M., Gregoire, J. P., & Mérette, C. (2006). Epidemiology of insomnia: Prevalence, self-help treatments, consultations, and determinants of help-seeking behaviors. *Sleep Medicine, 7*, 123–130. https://doi.org/10.1016/j.sleep.2005.08.008.

Murad, M. H., Asi, N., Alsawas, M., & Alahdab, F. (2016). *New evidence pyramid. Evidence Based Medicine, 21*, 125. https://doi.org/10.1136/ebmed-2016-110401.

Rösner, S., Englbrecht, C., Wehrle, R., Hajak, G., & Soyka, M. (2018). Eszopiclone for insomnia. *Cochrane Database of Systematic Reviews.* https://doi.org/10.1002/14651858.CD010703.pub2.

Selvanathan, J., Pham, C., Nagappa, M., Peng, P. W. H., Englesakis, M., Espie, C. A., Morin, C. M., & Chung, F. (2021). Cognitive behavioral therapy for insomnia in patients with chronic pain – A systematic review and meta-analysis of randomized controlled trials. *Sleep Medicine Reviews, 60*, 101460. https://doi.org/10.1016/j.smrv.2021.101460.

Soh, H. L., Ho, R. C., Ho, C. S., & Tam, W. W. (2020). Efficacy of digital cognitive behavioural therapy for insomnia: A meta-analysis of randomised controlled trials. *Sleep Medicine, 75*, 315–325. https://doi.org/10.1016/j.sleep.2020.08.020.

Sunnhed, R., Hesser, H., Andersson, G., Carlbring, P., Morin, C. M., Harvey, A. G., & Jansson-Fröjmark, M. (2020). Comparing internet-delivered cognitive therapy and behavior therapy with telephone support for insomnia disorder: A randomized controlled trial. *Sleep, 43*. https://doi.org/10.1093/sleep/zsz245.

Sweetman, A., Lovato, N., Micic, G., Scott, H., Bickley, K., Haycock, J., Harris, J., Gradisar, M., & Lack, L. (2020). Do symptoms of depression, anxiety or stress impair the effectiveness of cognitive behavioural therapy for insomnia? A chart-review of 455 patients with chronic insomnia. *Sleep Medicine, 75*, 401–410. https://doi.org/10.1016/j.sleep.2020.08.023.

Troxel, W. M., Germain, A., & Buysse, D. J. (2012). Clinical management of insomnia with brief behavioral treatment (BBTI). *Behavioral Sleep Medicine, 10*, 266–279. https://doi.org/10.1080/15402002.2011.607200.

van der Zweerde, T., Bisdounis, L., Kyle, S. D., Lancee, J., & van Straten, A. (2019). Cognitive behavioral therapy for insomnia: A meta-analysis of long-term effects in controlled studies. *Sleep Medicine Reviews, 48*, 101208. https://doi.org/10.1016/j.smrv.2019.08.002.

Van Straten, A., van der Zweerde, T., Kleiboer, A., Cuijpers, P., Morin, C. M., & Lancee, J. (2018). Cognitive and behavioral therapies in the treatment of insomnia: A meta-analysis. *Sleep Medicine Reviews, 38*, 3–16. https://doi.org/10.1016/j.smrv.2017.02.001.

Vincent, N., Lewycky, S., and Finnegan, H. (2008). Barriers to engagement in sleep restriction and stimulus control in chronic insomnia. *Journal of Consulting and Clinical Psychology, 76*, 820. https://doi.org/10.1037/0022-006X.76.5.820.

Wu, J. Q., Appleman, E. R., Salazar, R. D., & Ong, J. C. (2015). Cognitive behavioral therapy for insomnia comorbid with psychiatric and medical conditions: A meta-analysis. *JAMA Internal Medicine, 175*, 1461–1472. https://doi.org/10.1001/jamainternmed.2015.3006.

Zachariae, R., Lyby, M. S., Ritterband, L. M., and O'Toole, M. S. (2016). Efficacy of internet-delivered cognitive-behavioral therapy for insomnia – A systematic review and meta-analysis of randomized controlled trials. *Sleep Medicine Reviews, 30*, 1–10. https://doi.org/10.1016/j.smrv.2015.10.004.

4

Psychophysiological Mechanisms of CBT-I

Ellemarije Altena

Key points

- Effectiveness of CBT-I depends on different factors with aspects of behaviour, cognition and hyperarousal each playing a role.
- Differential contribution of these factors to the effectiveness of CBT-I provides an insight into the psychophysiological mechanisms of CBT-I.
- Behavioural and cognitive factors in particular contribute to CBT-I effectiveness, while hyperarousal effects do not change consistently with CBT-I.
- Neuroimaging data possibly support reductions in selective attention for sleep-related stimuli and normalization of neural representations of cognitive functions and hyperarousal, though data are sparse.
- Replication by well-designed behavioural and physiological research studies and meta-analyses are awaited to draw conclusions on psychophysiological mechanisms of CBT-I, particularly concerning debated mechanisms of hyperarousal.

Learning objectives

- To understand the underlying psychophysiological mechanisms of CBT-I.
- To understand which factors contribute more to CBT-I effectiveness and which less.
- To understand how research on mediators of CBT-I effectiveness is designed.
- To understand the gap in research investigating underlying psychophysiological mechanisms of CBT-I, in particular concerning physiological mediators.

Abstract

Models describing insomnia symptoms have focused on behaviour (time in bed, bedroom activities), cognition (worry, rumination, dysfunctional beliefs) and hyperarousal (elevated cortisol, heartrate, EEG frequency). When investigating those psychophysiological mechanisms explaining effectiveness of CBT-I through mediator research, behavioural and cognitive factors emerge as stronger predictors of CBT-I effectiveness than hyperarousal factors. In particular, sleep restriction and stabilizing bedtimes have been found to contribute to CBT-I effectiveness on a behavioural level, while on a cognitive level, reductions in dysfunctional beliefs, worrying and selective attention to sleep-related stimuli contribute to CBT-I effectiveness. Neuroimaging results confirm some of those findings in terms of corresponding brain activity of cognitive and behavioural factors. Well-designed replicated studies with larger sample sizes are needed to verify these very limited findings on psychophysiological mechanisms of CBT-I.

Keywords *psychophysiological mechanisms, CBT-I, mediators, insomnia, behaviour, cognition, hyperarousal*

Cognitive-Behavioural Therapy for Insomnia (CBT-I) Across the Life Span: Guidelines and Clinical Protocols for Health Professionals,
First Edition. Edited by Chiara Baglioni, Colin A. Espie and Dieter Riemann.

Introduction

Models to describe, categorise and explain insomnia symptoms, their underlying psychophysiological mechanisms and effects of cognitive-behavioural therapy can be categorised into behavioural, cognitive and hyperarousal models (Schwartz & Carney, 2012). This division will be respected below when addressing both insomnia models and effects of cognitive-behavioural therapy. Of note, insights on these categorisations are constantly changing and debated as many more scientific findings emerge (Bastien, St-Jean, Morin, Turcotte & Carrier, 2008; Bastien, 2020; Vargas et al., 2020), with findings from behavioural (clinical interviews, questionnaires) as well as physiological measures (muscle tone, heartrate, EEG, structural MRI and functional MRI) contributing to these changing insights.

Investigating effectiveness of CBT-I and its underlying mechanisms is often undertaken by studying mediators of CBT-I. A mediator is a factor that can statistically explain the relationship between a dependent and independent variable (Kraemer, Wilson, Fairburn & Agras, 2002; Nock, 2007) and has been helpful to explain treatment effects in many conditions including insomnia (Schwartz & Carney, 2012; Sunnhed & Jansson-Fröjmark, 2015). More research into these mediators, which has been limited thus far, may improve treatment adherence rates, which are estimated at approximately 60% for in-person CBT-I (Morin, 2006) and 50% for digital CBT-I (Horsch, Lancee, Beun, Neerincx & Brinkman, 2015).

Neuroimaging studies have been performed to investigate underlying physiological models of insomnia, though those investigating effects of CBT-I are sparse. Results of brain activity differences and changes can be measured during task presentation, in the absence of task presentation (resting state) or when asleep. Several reviews have attempted to arrive on common ground based upon results from functional and structural neuroimaging studies in insomnia. However, these reviews concluded that variability in diagnosis criteria of insomnia as well as differences in MRI and task setups, types of analyses and statistical thresholds applied, as well as the limited sample size of most studies, have hampered conclusions on the pathophysiological brain mechanisms of insomnia (Spiegelhalder, Regen, Baglioni, Riemann & Winkelmann, 2013; O'Byrne, Berman Rosa, Gouin & Dang-Vu, 2014; Spiegelhalder et al., 2015; Tahmasian, 2018). It is therefore important to pursue high quality imaging studies so meta-analyses can be performed on more studies, such as has been done in other psychiatric conditions (Goodkind et al., 2015).

Furthermore, to arrive at conclusions about intervention effects, a well-defined control group or control condition is a major requirement in any study, but this is particularly the case in physiological studies. Without adequate control, any changes, for instance in brain activity, could be due to a placebo effect, a habituation effect to undergoing fMRI, etc. Combining imaging data from large freely accessible databases for future analyses, such as is done in other psychiatric conditions (Kempton et al., 2011; Nichols et al., 2017), could help to clarify the psychophysiological mechanism(s) that underly insomnia and its treatment effects.

Behavioural models of insomnia

Insomnia can be regarded as an imbalance between sleep-inducing and wake-inducing mechanisms (Saper, Scammell & Lu, 2005), which can be further enhanced by dysfunctional behaviour (see Chapter 1). Prolonged wakefulness naturally leads to a build-up of the sleep drive, which when released at the opening of the circadian gate, determines night-time sleep quantity and quality through increased sleep pressure (Borbély, 1982). Behavioural patterns such as day-time napping and spending excessive time in bed can serve as perpetuating factors of insomnia, disrupting homeostatic regulation and maintaining sleep difficulties (Schwartz et al., 2012). Going to bed and getting up at variable times, having naps throughout the day, disrupting natural sleep onset triggers by being exposed to bright light, consuming heavy meals, alcohol, drugs or sleep disruptive medication in the evening are examples of sleep disrupting behaviour typical of insomnia (Harvey, Dong, Bélanger & Morris, 2017).

Cognitive models of insomnia

Cognitive aspects of insomnia include increased worry and rumination about both sleep-related and non-sleep-related issues, according to the 'cognitive model of insomnia' of Harvey (2002). This also includes overattributing the consequences of insomnia, such as the impact of sleep disturbance on day-time functioning. Further, selective attention to sleep-related information is found to be increased in insomnia (Morin, Blais & Savard, 2002; Woods, Marchetti,

Biello & Espie, 2009; Spiegelhalder, Espie, Nissen & Riemann, 2008) although this might depend on the type of stimulus presented (e.g., pictures instead of words; Spiegelhalder et al., 2018).

A dysfunctional tendency to consciously address a natural process such as the wake-to-sleep transition, by increasing attention and intention to sleep, is represented in the 'attention–intention–effort model' (A-I-E) of Espie, Broomfield, MacMahon, Macphee & Taylor (2006), a component of Espie's (2002) broader psychobiological inhibition framework. This A-I-E model states that when individuals selectively attend to sleep, explicitly intend to sleep and engage in efforts to produce sleep, the natural and automatic sleep process is disrupted (Espie et al., 2006; Schwartz et al., 2012).

Support for these cognitive models can be found in a limited number of behavioural and neuroimaging studies. When presented with sleep-related emotional stimuli, insomnia patients show attentional bias (MacMahon, Broomfield & Espie, 2006; Lundh, Froding, Gyllenhammar, Broman & Hetta, 1997; see Harris et al., 2015, for a review) and increased activity in brain regions typically active in those tasks, such as the amygdala (Baglioni et al., 2014), as well as increased connectivity patterns in the brain reward network (Sanz-Arigita et al., 2021). When performing a cognitive task in fMRI or fNIRS, however, insomnia patients show hypoactivity in those regions usually implicated in the task, whether it be tasks of cognitive flexibility, planning or working memory (Altena et al., 2008; Drummond et al., 2013; Stoffers et al., 2014; Sun et al., 2017). Moreover, increased functional connectivity in a hippocampal–prefrontal network typically active during rumination, but silent during sleep, has been found to be related to insomnia severity (Leerssen et al., 2019). These findings may, though based on few studies, thus offer neural support for selective attention of sleep-related information and excessive rumination, while increased brain activity is not observed during other cognitive tasks.

Hyperarousal models of insomnia

Hyperarousal refers to a constantly present increased level of arousal in insomnia, independent of task or stressor presentation (Bonnet & Arand 1995, 1998; Perlis, Giles, Mendelson, Bootzin & Wyatt, 1997; Riemann et al., 2010) with a typical distinction made between somatic hyperarousal and cortical hyperarousal (Perlis, Merica, Smith & Giles, 2001; Pigeon & Perlis, 2006; Cortoos, Verstraeten & Cluydts, 2006). Somatic hyperarousal refers to findings of increased heart rate, altered galvanic skin response and heart rate variability in insomnia patients (Riemann et al., 2002; Lushington, Dawson & Lack, 2000; Monroe, 1967; Borbély, 1982; Vgontzas et al., 1998; Perlis, Smith & Pigeon, 2005; Bonnet & Arand, 2010). Cortical arousal refers to findings showing increased evoked response potentials (ERPs) in the evening and morning in insomnia (Bastien et al., 2008), as well as high frequency EEG activity at or around sleep onset (Bastien, Turcotte, St-Jean, Morin & Carrier, 2013; Fernandez-Mendoza et al., 2016), increased EEG power during REM sleep (alpha, sigma) and NREM sleep (theta, alpha, sigma) and during wakefulness (theta, gamma: Zhao et al., 2021). Through cortical hyperarousal, it is hypothesised, sensory and information processing as well as long-term memory formation continues, whilst these processes should be diminished to facilitate the sleep process. Both somatic and cognitive hyperarousal can prevent the transition from wake to sleep (Bonnet & Arand, 2010) and are directly linked to sleep continuity disturbance (Perlis, Ellis, Kloss & Riemann, 2017).

These models are supported by several physiological findings. Next to enhanced states of arousal and vigilance observable in day-time wake EEG (Oh, Park & Choi, 2020; Losert et al., 2020), a typical pattern of hyperarousal and increased vigilance is also observed in fMRI, through increased brain activity in the insula network (Chen, Chang, Glover & Gotlib, 2014; for an overview see also Kay & Buysse, 2017). Somatic hyperarousal is also represented in elevated levels of the stress hormone cortisol in insomnia (Vargas et al., 2018), while levels of the inhibitory neurotransmitter GABA, typically high during sleep, tend to be lower in insomnia patients as compared to controls (Winkelman et al., 2008; Morgan et al., 2012). Sleep is particularly fragmented during REM sleep in insomnia (Riemann et al., 2012), and when woken from REM sleep, insomnia patients report having been awake more often than controls, suggestive of elevated levels of consciousness during REM sleep and of hyperarousal (Feige et al., 2018). Neuroimaging findings show that metabolism in several cortical regions is also higher during sleep in insomnia patients than controls, while prefrontal metabolism is in fact lower during wake, suggestive of an imbalance of brain activity during both sleep and wake in insomnia (Nofzinger et al., 2004; Van Someren, 2021). Altered thalamic connectivity in insomnia during both wake and NREM sleep further supports physiological hyperarousal models of insomnia, given the role of the thalamus in sleep–wake regulation (Zou et al., 2021. The concept of hyperarousal in insomnia has been the fruit of discussions in recent debates, however, in particular its occurrence in the absence of stress-provoking stimuli and its specificity for insomnia alone and not co-morbid disorders (Kalmbach et al., 2018; Bastien, 2020; Vargas et al., 2020).

Effects of CBT-I on behavioural, cognitive and hyperarousal aspects of insomnia

Those effects of insomnia observable from group comparisons with healthy controls, such as hyperarousal before sleep and during sleep onset, local brain hypoactivity when performing cognitive tasks or local brain hyperactivity when presented with emotional stimuli, could be expected to (partially) normalise after successful insomnia treatment through cognitive behavioural therapy. Although studies investigating CBT-I effects using neuroimaging methods have often lacked a proper control group, some of the published findings, if replicated, may give insight into psychophysiological mechanisms underlying CBT-I.

Behavioural effects of CBT-I

Through sleep restriction, as part of CBT-I, sleep pressure is increased, which further increases the homeostatic sleep drive (Borbely, 1982). Effects of sleep restriction as part of CBT-I are noticeable in a more rapid decline in EEG delta power over the night, which is related to the therapeutic effect of CBT and to an increase in the homeostatic sleep drive (Krystal & Edinger, 2010). Sleep restriction not only ensures that time in bed is spent asleep, but also reverses the typical negative association of the bed with not-sleeping. Research by Maurer et al. shows that sleep restriction improves sleep continuity, reduces insomnia severity (Maurer, Ftouni, Espie, Bisdounis & Kylie, 2020a) and is superior to time in bed regularization in improving objective and self-reported sleep variables and sleep-related quality of life (Maurer et al., 2020b). Other studies did find that stabilizing bedtimes, and its resulting reduction of bedtime variability, was a mediator for reductions in insomnia severity (Sunnhed & Jansson-Fröjmark, 2015). Maurer, Espie & Kylie (2018) propose the 3-R model, in which restricting sleep leads to recondition on the cognitive-behavioural level, such as a more positive bed–sleep association, and to regularization on the physiological level, such as improving the circadian sleep–wake cycle (Maurer, Espie & Kylie, 2018) (see Table 4.1).

Cognitive effects of CBT-I

On cognitive aspects, changes in beliefs and attitudes about sleep as well as locus of control has been shown to be associated with diminished insomnia complaints as well as improvements in objective sleep through CBT-I (Edinger, Wohlgemuth, Radtke, Marsh & Quillian, 2001; Chow et al.,2018; Thakral, Von Korff, McCurry, Morin & Vitiello, 2020). Introducing a rumination moment during the day, which is part of CBT-I interventions (see Chapter 2), prevents night-time rumination, at moments when emotion regulatory functions are not optimal, such as during REM sleep (Tempesta, Socci, De Gennaro & Ferrara, 2018). Decreased rumination has been found to be a mediator in the beneficial effects of CBT-I on both insomnia and depression symptoms (Cheng, Kalmbach, Castelan, Murugan & Drake, 2020). The more patients achieve to reduce worrying, rumination and unhelpful beliefs about sleep, the more effective CBT is, reflected in reduced insomnia severity and improved day-time functioning (Sunnhed & Jansson-Fröjmark, 2015). For improved sleep efficiency, particularly sleep-related worry and rumination were found to be mediators, but not dysfunctional beliefs (Lancee et al., 2019).

Hypoactivity in prefrontal regions that are typically implicated in a task for cognitive flexibility partially normalised after effective cognitive behavioural therapy as compared to a waitlist control group (Altena et al., 2008). The same research group found that hypoactivity in task-related brain regions on a planning and working memory task, however, did not change after effective CBT-I (Stoffers et al., 2014).

Changes in brain structure after CBT-I, as measured through increases in cortical thickness, have been related to decreased wake after sleep onset (WASO) in co-morbid insomnia and fibromyalgia (McCrae et al., 2018). These findings, which included a control group, could be in line with findings of baseline reduction of grey matter volume in insomnia patients compared to controls (Altena, Vrenken, Van der Werf, van den Heuvel & Van Someren, 2010; Stoffers et al., 2012; Yu et al., 2018). In these studies, particularly the orbitofrontal cortex is affected, a brain region particularly important for emotional decision making and impulse regulation (Rudebeck & Rich, 2018).

In an fMRI study by Kim et al. (2019), cortical hyperactivity in response to sleep-related sounds, indicative of selective attention to sleep-related stimuli, decreased after CBT-I in 14 insomnia patients, but a control group and condition was lacking in this study. Hyper-reactivity to other sleep-related stimuli decreased after CBT-I, which was related to less wake after sleep onset (WASO) (Kim et al., 2017), but again no control group comparisons after CBT-I were included. The same researchers showed that in the absence of performance or brain activity changes after CBT-I, ISI improvement was related to activity changes in the supramarginal gyrus, normally involved in performance of the cognitive task described by

Table 4.1 Overview: Psychophysiological mechanisms of CBT-I.

CBT effect type	CBT elements	Effect	References
Behavioural effects	Sleep restriction	Increased sleep pressure, reduced negative association of bed with not sleeping, improved sleep continuity, improves sleep-related quality of life	Borbély et al., 1982 Krystal et al., 2010 Maurer et al., 2020a Maurer et al., 2020b Maurer et al., 2018
	Stabilizing bedtime variability	Reduced insomnia severity	Sunnhed et al., 2015
Cognitive effects	Changes in beliefs and attitudes about sleep	Reduced insomnia severity, better objective sleep, better daytime functioning	Edinger et al., 2001 Chow et al., 2018 Thakral et al., 2020 Sunnhed et al., 2015
	Change in locus of control	Reduced insomnia severity, better objective sleep	Edinger et al., 2001 Chow et al., 2018 Thakral et al., 2020
	Reducing night-time rumination	Reduced insomnia severity, improved daytime functioning, improved sleep efficiency	Tempesta et al., 2018 Sunnhed et al., 2015 Lancee et al., 2019
Hyperarousal effects	Computerized CBT-I	Reduced pre-sleep cognitive arousal	Vincent et al., 2009
	Sleep restriction	Decreased body temperature	Miller et al., 2015
	Multicomponent CBT-I	Increased cerebral blood flow basal ganglia	Smith et al., 2004
	Multicomponent CBT-I	Functional connectivity changes basal ganglia, amygdala, OFC	Lee et al., 2017
	Multicomponent CBT-I vs sleep restriction	Reduced pre-sleep somatic hyperarousal, more for CBT than for SR	Kalmbach et al., 2019

Hwang et al. (2019), but again without control group comparisons. These results thus might indicate that increased selective attention for sleep-related stimuli decreases after CBT-I and that brain activity related to cognitive tasks possibly normalises after CBT-I, but the results await replication and comparison with a control group (see Table 4.1).

Hyperarousal effects of CBT-I

Often, treatment components of CBT-I are proposed to reduce hyperarousal by enhancing parasympathetic activation (e.g., relaxation), limiting bed-related activities to sleep and sex only (stimulus control) and by enhancing the sleep drive (e.g., sleep restriction). However, evidence of reduced hyperarousal as a CBT-I mechanism is limited. As measured by the Presleep State Arousal Scale, reductions in hyperarousal have been found as a result of effective CBT-I (Rosen, Lewin, Goldberg & Woolfolk, 2000; Vincent & Lewycky, 2009; Wu, Bao, Zhang, Deng & Long, 2006). In particular, Vincent and Lewycky (2009) found that reduced pre-sleep cognitive hyperarousal mediated the effect of computerised CBT on sleep, while an improved sleep schedule consistency did not. Kalmbach et al. (2019) found that somatic hyperarousal was reduced after sleep restriction, but more strongly so after cognitive behavioural therapy. Body temperature decreases following CBT-I have also been found (Miller et al., 2015), but changes in heart rate variability (Jarrin et al., 2016) and cortisol (Miller et al., 2015) were in a contrary direction to those expected for reduced hyperarousal.

Smith, Perlis, Chengazi, Soeffing and McCann (2004) showed increased regional cerebral blood flow in the basal ganglia during sleep after CBT-I, as measured by SPECT in an exploratory study of four insomnia patients without a control group. Lee et al. (2017) showed functional connectivity changes after CBT-I within 14 insomnia patients, including in the thalamus, amygdala, caudate nucleus and orbitofrontal cortex, but again no control group was included, and changes did not correspond to those showing differences from controls on the baseline. Park et al. (2020) found, in 35 dialysis patients with insomnia, that improvement of sleep after CBT-I was correlated with increased connectivity between the default-mode network and the premotor/dorsolateral prefrontal cortex, but this study also lacked a control group. Taken together, neuroimaging findings during day- and night-time resting state and task presentation that show changes with cognitive behavioural therapy point more at partial restoration of the disbalance in wake and sleep psychophysiological processes than at hyperarousal reductions per se (Kay & Buysse, 2017) (see Table 4.1).

Conclusion

The limited literature on psychophysiological mechanisms of cognitive behavioural therapy for insomnia and mediator effects indicates that changes in behavioural and cognitive factors, such as changing dysfunctional beliefs and attitudes about sleep, are stronger predictors of CBT-I effectiveness than other factors such as hyperarousal. Future studies should focus on increasing the limited knowledge about physiological mechanisms underlying CBT-I effects. In particular, well-controlled studies focusing on changes after CBT in those physiological features typical of insomnia, such as differences in heart rates, cortisol levels and brain activity, would be of interest.

References

Altena, E., Van Der Werf, Y. D., Sanz-Arigita, E. J., Voorn, T. A., Rombouts, S. A. R. B., Kuijer, J. P. A., & Van Someren, E. J. W. (2008). Prefrontal hypoactivation and recovery in insomnia. *Sleep*, *31* (9), 1271–1276.

Altena, E., Vrenken, H., Van Der Werf, Y. D., van den Heuvel, O. A., & Van Someren, E. J. W. (2010). Reduced orbitofrontal and parietal gray matter in chronic insomnia: A voxel-based morphometric study. *Biological Psychiatry*, *67* (2), 182–185. https://doi.org/10.1016/j.biopsych.2009.08.003.

Baglioni, C., Spiegelhalder, K., Regen, W., Feige, B., Nissen, C., Lombardo, C., Violani, C., Hennig, J., & Riemann, D. (2014). Insomnia disorder is associated with increased amygdala reactivity to insomnia-related stimuli. *Sleep*, *37* (12), 1907–1917. https://doi.org/10.5665/sleep.4240.

Bastien, C. (2020). Does insomnia exist without hyperarousal? What else can there be? *Brain Sciences*, *10* (4), 225. https://doi.org/10.3390/brainsci10040225.

Bastien, C. H., St-Jean, G., Morin, C. M., Turcotte, I., & Carrier, J. (2008). Chronic psychophysiological insomnia: Hyperarousal and/or inhibition deficits? *An ERPs investigation. Sleep*, *31* (6), 887–898. https://doi.org/10.1093/sleep/31.6.887.

Bastien, C. H., Turcotte, I., St-Jean, G., Morin, C. M., & Carrier, J. (2013). Information processing varies between insomnia types: Measures of N1 and P2 during the night. *Behavioral Sleep Medicine*, *11* (1), 56–72. https://doi.org/10.1080/15402002.2012.660896.

Bonnet, M. H., & Arand, D. L. (1995). 24-Hour metabolic rate in insomniacs and matched normal sleepers. *Sleep*, *18* (7), 581–588. https://doi.org/10.1093/sleep/18.7.581.

Bonnet, M. H., & Arand, D. L. (1998). Heart rate variability in insomniacs and matched normal sleepers. *Psychosomatic Medicine*, *60* (5), 610–615. https://doi.org/10.1097/00006842-199809000-00017.

Bonnet, M. H., & Arand, D. L. (2010). Hyperarousal and insomnia: State of the science. *Sleep Medicine Reviews*, *14* (1), 9–15. https://doi.org/10.1016/j.smrv.2009.05.002.

Borbély, A. A. (1982). A two process model of sleep regulation. *Human Neurobiology*, *1* (3), 195–204.

Chen, M. C., Chang, C., Glover, G. H., & Gotlib, I. H. (2014). Increased insula coactivation with salience networks in insomnia. *Biological Psychology*, *97*, 1–8. https://doi.org/10.1016/j.biopsycho.2013.12.016.

Cheng, P., Kalmbach, D. A., Castelan, A. C., Murugan, N., & Drake, C. L. (2020). Depression prevention in digital cognitive behavioral therapy for insomnia: Is rumination a mediator? *Journal of Affective Disorders*, *273*, 434–441. https://doi.org/10.1016/j.jad.2020.03.184.

Chow, P. I., Ingersoll, K. S., Thorndike, F. P., Lord, H. R., Gonder-Frederick, L., Morin, C. M., & Ritterband, L. M. (2018). Cognitive mechanisms of sleep outcomes in a randomized clinical trial of internet-based cognitive behavioral therapy for insomnia. *Sleep Medicine*, *47*, 77–85. https://doi.org/10.1016/j.sleep.2017.11.1140.

Cortoos, A., Verstraeten, E., & Cluydts, R. (2006). Neurophysiological aspects of primary insomnia: Implications for its treatment. *Sleep Medicine Reviews*, *10* (4), 255–266. https://doi.org/10.1016/j.smrv.2006.01.002.

Drummond, S. P. A., Walker, M., Almklov, E., Campos, M., Anderson, D. E., & Straus, L. D. (2013). Neural correlates of working memory performance in primary insomnia. *Sleep*, *36* (9), 1307–1316. https://doi.org/10.5665/sleep.2952.

Edinger, J. D., Wohlgemuth, W. K., Radtke, R. A., Marsh, G. R., & Quillian, R. E. (2001). Does cognitive-behavioral insomnia therapy alter dysfunctional beliefs about sleep? *Sleep*, *24* (5), 591–599. https://doi.org/10.1093/sleep/24.5.591.

Espie, C.A. (2002). Insomnia: Conceptual issues in the development, persistence and treatment of sleep disorder in adults. *Annual Review of Psychology*, *53*, 215–243.

Espie, C. A., Broomfield, N. M., MacMahon, K. M. A., Macphee, L. M., & Taylor, L. M. (2006). The attention–intention–effort pathway in the development of psychophysiologic insomnia: A theoretical review. *Sleep Medicine Reviews*, *10* (4), 215–245. https://doi.org/10.1016/j.smrv.2006.03.002.

Feige, B., Nanovska, S., Baglioni, C., Bier, B., Cabrera, L., Diemers, S., Quellmalz, M., Siegel, M., Xeni, I., Szentkiralyi, A., Doerr, J-P., & Riemann, D. (2018). Insomnia – perchance a dream? Results from a NREM/REM sleep awakening study in good sleepers and patients with insomnia. *Sleep*, *41* (5), zsy032. https://doi.org/10.1093/sleep/zsy032.

Fernandez-Mendoza, J., Li, Y., Vgontzas, A. N., Fang, J., Gaines, J., Calhoun, S. L., Liao, D., & Bixler, E. O. (2016). Insomnia is associated with cortical hyperarousal as early as adolescence. *Sleep*, *39* (5), 1029–1036. https://doi.org/10.5665/sleep.5746.

Goodkind, M., Eickhoff, S. B., Oathes, D. J., Jiang, Y., Chang, A., Jones-Hagata, L. B., Ortega, B. N., Zaiko, Y. V., Roach, E. L., Korgaonkar, M. S., Grieve, S. M., Galatzer-Levy, I., Fox, P. T., & Etkin, A. (2015). Identification of a common neurobiological substrate for mental illness. *JAMA Psychiatry*, *72* (4), 305–315. https://doi.org/10.1001/jamapsychiatry.2014.2206.

Harris, K., Spiegelhalder, K., Espie, C. A., MacMahon, K. M., Woods, H. C., & Kyle, S. D. (2015). Sleep-related attentional bias in insomnia: A state-of-the-science review. *Clinical Psychology Review*, *42*, 16–27.

Harvey, A. G. (2002). A cognitive model of insomnia. *Behaviour Research and Therapy*, *40* (8), 869–893. https://doi.org/10.1016/s0005-7967(01)00061-4.

Harvey, A. G., Dong, L., Bélanger, L., & Morin, C. M. (2017). Mediators and treatment matching in behavior therapy, cognitive therapy and cognitive behavior therapy for chronic insomnia. *Journal of Consulting and Clinical Psychology*, *85* (10), 975–987. https://doi.org/10.1037/ccp0000244.

Horsch, C., Lancee, J., Beun, R. J., Neerincx, M. A., & Brinkman, W.-P. (2015). Adherence to technology-mediated insomnia treatment: A meta-analysis, interviews, and focus groups. *Journal of Medical Internet Research*, *17* (9), e214. https://doi.org/10.2196/jmir.4115.

Hwang, J. Y., Kim, N., Kim, S., Park, J., Choi, J.-W., Kim, S. J., Kang, C.-K., & Lee, Y. J. (2019). Stroop task-related brain activity in patients with insomnia: Changes after cognitive-behavioral therapy for insomnia. *Behavioral Sleep Medicine*, *17* (5), 621–633. https://doi.org/10.1080/15402002.2018.1435546.

Jarrin, D. C., Chen, I. Y., Ivers, H., Lamy, M., Vallières, A., & Morin, C. M. (2016). Nocturnal heart rate variability in patients treated with cognitive-behavioral therapy for insomnia. *Health Psychology: Official Journal of the Division of Health Psychology, American Psychological Association*, *35* (6), 638–641. https://doi.org/10.1037/hea0000347.

Kalmbach, D. A., Cuamatzi-Castelan, A. S., Tonnu, C. V., Tran, K. M., Anderson, J. R., Roth, T., & Drake, C. L. (2018). Hyperarousal and sleep reactivity in insomnia: Current insights. *Nature and Science of Sleep*, *10*, 193–201. https://doi.org/10.2147/NSS.S138823.

Kalmbach, D. A., Cheng, P., Arnedt, J. T., Anderson, J. R., Roth, T., Fellman-Coutre, C., Williams, R. A., Drake, C. L (2019). Treating insomnia improves depression, maladaptive thinking, and hyperarousal in postmenopausal women: Comparing cognitive-behavioral therapy for insomnia (CBTI), sleep restriction therapy, and sleep hygiene education. *Sleep Medicine*, *55*, 124–134. doi: 10.1016/j.sleep.2018.11.019.

Kay, D. B., & Buysse, D. J. (2017). Hyperarousal and beyond: New insights to the pathophysiology of insomnia disorder through functional neuroimaging studies. *Brain Sciences*, *7* (3). https://doi.org/10.3390/brainsci7030023.

Kempton, M. J., Salvador, Z., Munafò, M. R., Geddes, J. R., Simmons, A., Frangou, S., & Williams, S. C. R. (2011). Structural neuroimaging studies in major depressive disorder. Meta-analysis and comparison with bipolar disorder. *Archives of General Psychiatry*, *68* (7), 675–690. https://doi.org/10.1001/archgenpsychiatry.2011.60.

Kim, S. J., Lee, Y. J., Kim, N., Kim, S., Choi, J.-W., Park, J., Gwak, A. R., Kang, C.-K., Kang, S.-G., & Jeong, D.-U. (2017). Exploration of changes in the brain response to sleep-related pictures after cognitive-behavioral therapy for psychophysiological insomnia. *Scientific Reports*, *7* (1), 12528. https://doi.org/10.1038/s41598-017-13065-0.

Kim, N., Kang, S.-G., Lee, Y. J., Kim, S. J., Kim, S., Choi, J.-W., Oh, S. M., Park, J., Gwak, A. R., Kim, H.-K., & Jeong, D.-U. (2019). Decreased regional brain activity in response to sleep-related sounds after cognitive behavioral therapy for psychophysiological insomnia. *Psychiatry and Clinical Neurosciences*, *73* (5), 254–261. https://doi.org/10.1111/pcn.12822.

Kraemer, H. C., Wilson, G. T., Fairburn, C. G., & Agras, W. S. (2002). Mediators and moderators of treatment effects in randomized clinical trials. *Archives of General Psychiatry*, *59* (10), 877–883. https://doi.org/10.1001/archpsyc.59.10.877.

Krystal, A. D., & Edinger, J. D. (2010). Sleep EEG predictors and correlates of the response to cognitive behavioral therapy for insomnia. *Sleep*, *33* (5), 669–677. https://doi.org/10.1093/sleep/33.5.669.

Lancee, J., Effting, M., van der Zweerde, T., van Daal, L., van Straten, A., & Kamphuis, J. H. (2019). Cognitive processes mediate the effects of insomnia treatment: Evidence from a randomized wait-list controlled trial. *Sleep Medicine*, *54*, 86–93. https://doi.org/10.1016/j.sleep.2018.09.029.

Lee, Y.-J. G., Kim, S., Kim, N., Choi, J.-W., Park, J., Kim, S. J., Gwak, A. R., & Lee, Y. J. (2017). Changes in subcortical resting-state functional connectivity in patients with psychophysiological insomnia after cognitive-behavioral therapy: Changes in resting state FC after CBT for insomnia. *Neuroimage: Clinical* 12, 115–123. doi: 10.1016/j.nicl.2017.10.013.

Leerssen, J., Wassing, R., Ramautar, J., Stoffers, D., Lakbila-Kamal, O., Perrier, J. Bruijel, J., Foster-Dingley, J. C., Aghajani, M., & Van Someren, E. J. W. (2019). Increased hippocampal–prefrontal functional connectivity in insomnia. *Neurobiology of Learning and Memory*, *160*, 144–150). doi: 10.1016/j.nlm.2018.02.006.

Losert, A., Sander, C., Schredl, M., Heilmann-Etzbach, I., Deuschle, M., Hegerl, U., & Schilling, C. (2020). Enhanced vigilance stability during daytime in insomnia disorder. *Brain Sciences*, *10* (11), 830. https://doi.org/10.3390/brainsci10110830.

Lundh, L. G., Froding, A., Gyllenhammar, L., Broman, J. E., & Hetta, J. (1997). Cognitive bias and memory performance in patients with persistent insomnia. *Scandinavian Journal of Behaviour Therapy*; *26*, 27–35.

Lushington, K., Dawson, D., & Lack, L. (2000). Core body temperature is elevated during constant wakefulness in elderly poor sleepers. *Sleep*, *23* (4), 504–510.

MacMahon, K. M. A., Broomfield, N. M., & Espie, C. A. (2006). Attention bias for sleep-related stimuli in primary insomnia and delayed sleep phase syndrome using the dot-probe task. *Sleep*, *29*,1420–1427. doi: 10.1093/sleep/29.11.1420.

McCrae, C. S., Mundt, J. M., Curtis, A. F., Craggs, J. G., O'Shea, A. M., Staud, R., Berry, R. B., Perlstein, W. M., & Robinson, M. E. (2018). Gray matter changes following cognitive behavioral therapy for patients with comorbid fibromyalgia and insomnia: A pilot study. *Journal of Clinical Sleep Medicine: JCSM: Official Publication of the American Academy of Sleep Medicine*, *14* (9), 1595–1603. https://doi.org/10.5664/jcsm.7344.

Maurer, L. F., Espie, C. A., & Kyle, S. D. (2018). How does sleep restriction therapy for insomnia work? A systematic review of mechanistic evidence and the introduction of the Triple-R model. *Sleep Medicine Reviews*, *42*, 127–138. doi: 10.1016/j.smrv.2018.07.005.

Maurer, L. F., Ftouni, S., Espie C. A., Bisdounis, L., & Kyle, S. D. (2020a). The acute effects of sleep restriction therapy for insomnia on circadian timing and vigilance. *Journal of Sleep Research*, 13, e13260. doi: 10.1111/jsr.13260.

Maurer, L. F., Espie, C. A., Omlin, X., Reid, J. M., Sharman, R., Gavriloff, D., Emsley, R., & Kyle, S. D. (2020b). Isolating the role of time in bed restriction in the treatment of insomnia: A randomized, controlled, dismantling trial comparing sleep restriction therapy with time in bed regularization. *Sleep*, *43* (11), zsaa096. doi: 10.1093/sleep/zsaa096.

Miller, C. B., Kyle, S. D., Gordon, C. J., Espie, C. A., Grunstein, R. R., Mullins, A. E., Postnova, S., & Bartlett, D. J. (2015). Physiological markers of arousal change with psychological treatment for insomnia: A preliminary investigation. *PloS One*, *10* (12), e0145317. https://doi.org/10.1371/journal.pone.0145317.

Monroe, L. J. (1967). Psychological and physiological differences between good and poor sleepers. *Journal of Abnormal Psychology*, *72* (3), 255–264. https://doi.org/10.1037/h0024563.

Morgan, P. T., Pace-Schott, E. F., Mason, G. F., Forselius, E., Fasula, M., Valentine, G. W., & Sanacora, G. (2012). Cortical GABA levels in primary insomnia. *Sleep*, *35* (6), 807–814. https://doi.org/10.5665/sleep.1880.

Morin, C. M. (2006). Cognitive–behavioral therapy of insomnia. *Sleep Medicine Clinics*, *1* (3), 375–386. https://doi.org/10.1016/j.jsmc.2006.06.008.

Morin, C. M., Blais, F., & Savard, J. (2002). Are changes in beliefs and attitudes about sleep related to sleep improvements in the treatment of insomnia? *Behaviour Research and Therapy*, *40* (7), 741–752. https://doi.org/10.1016/s0005-7967(01)00055-9.

Nichols, T. E., Das, S., Eickhoff, S. B., Evans, A. C., Glatard, T., Hanke, M., Kriegeskorte, N., Milham, M. P., Poldrack, R. A., Poline, J.-B., Proal, E., Thirion, B., Van Essen, D. C., White, T., & Yeo, B. T. T. (2017). Best practices in data analysis and sharing in neuroimaging using MRI. *Nature Neuroscience*, *20* (3), 299–303. https://doi.org/10.1038/nn.4500.

Nock, M. K. (2007). Conceptual and design essentials for evaluating mechanisms of change. *Alcoholism, Clinical and Experimental Research*, *31* (10 Suppl.), 4s–12s. https://doi.org/10.1111/j.1530-0277.2007.00488.x.

Nofzinger, E. A., Buysse, D. J., Germain, A., Price, J. C., Miewald, J. M., & Kupfer, D. J. (2004). Functional neuroimaging evidence for hyperarousal in insomnia. *The American Journal of Psychiatry*, *161* (11), 2126–2128. https://doi.org/10.1176/appi.ajp.161.11.2126.

O'Byrne, J. N, Berman Rosa, M., Gouin, J.-P., & Dang-Vu, T. T. (2014). Neuroimaging findings in primary insomnia. *Pathology and Biology (Paris)*, *62* (5), 262–269. doi: 10.1016/j.patbio.2014.05.013.

Oh, D. Y., Park, S. M., & Choi, S. W. (2020). Daytime neurophysiological hyperarousal in chronic insomnia: A study of qEEG. *Journal of Clinical Medicine*, *9* (11). https://doi.org/10.3390/jcm9113425.

Park, H. Y., Lee, H., Jhee, J. H., Park, K. M., Choi, E. C., An, S. K., Namkoong, K., Lee, E., & Park, J. T. (2020). Changes in resting-state brain connectivity following computerized cognitive behavioral therapy for insomnia in dialysis patients: A pilot study. *General Hospital Psychiatry*, *66*, 24–29. https://doi.org/10.1016/j.genhosppsych.2020.05.013.

Perlis, M. L. (2001). Response to 'Do increases in beta EEG activity uniquely reflect insomnia?' (C. H. Bastien and M. H. Bonnet). *Sleep Medicine Reviews*, *5* (5), 379–383. https://doi.org/10.1053/smrv.2001.0171.

Perlis, M. L., Ellis, J. G., Kloss, J. D., & Riemann, D. W. (2017). Chapter 82: Etiology and pathophysiology of insomnia. In M. Kryger, T. Roth, & W. C. Dement (Eds.), *Principles and practice of sleep medicine* (6th ed.), pp. 769–784.e4. Amsterdam, The Netherlands: Elsevier. https://doi.org/10.1016/b978-0-323-24288-2.00082-9.

Perlis, M. L., Giles, D. E., Mendelson, W. B., Bootzin, R. R., & Wyatt, J. K. (1997). Psychophysiological insomnia: The behavioural model and a neurocognitive perspective. *Journal of Sleep Research*, *6* (3), 179–188. https://doi.org/10.1046/j.1365-2869.1997.00045.x.

Perlis, M. L., Merica, H., Smith, M. T., & Giles, D. E. (2001). Beta EEG activity and insomnia. *Sleep Medicine Reviews*, *5* (5), 363--374. https://doi.org/10.1053/smrv.2001.0151.

Perlis, M. L., Smith, M. T., & Pigeon, W. R. (2005). Chapter 60: Etiology and pathophysiology of insomnia. In M. Kryger, T. Roth, & W. C. Dement (Eds.), *Principles and practice of sleep medicine* (4th ed.), pp. 714–725. Amsterdam, The Netherlands, Elsevier. https://doi.org/10.1016/B0-72-160797-7/50067-7.

Pigeon, W. R., & Perlis, M. L. (2006). Sleep homeostasis in primary insomnia. *Sleep Medicine Reviews*, *10* (4), 247–254. https://doi.org/10.1016/j.smrv.2005.09.002.

Riemann, D., Klein, T., Rodenbeck, A., Feige, B., Horny, A., Hummel, R., Weske, G., Al-Shajlawi, A., & Voderholzer, U. (2002). Nocturnal cortisol and melatonin secretion in primary insomnia. *Psychiatry Research*, *113* (1–2), 17–27. https://doi.org/10.1016/s0165-1781(02)00249-4.

Riemann, D., Spiegelhalder, K., Feige, B., Voderholzer, U., Berger, M., Perlis, M., & Nissen, C. (2010). The hyperarousal model of insomnia: A review of the concept and its evidence. *Sleep Medicine Reviews*, *14* (1), 19–31. https://doi.org/10.1016/j.smrv.2009.04.002.

Riemann, D., Spiegelhalder, K., Nissen, C., Hirscher, V., Baglioni, C., & Feige, B. (2012). REM sleep instability – A new pathway for insomnia? *Pharmacopsychiatry*, *45* (5),167–176. doi: 10.1055/s-0031-1299721.

Rosen, R. C., Lewin, D. S., Goldberg, L., & Woolfolk, R. L. (2000). Psychophysiological insomnia: Combined effects of pharmacotherapy and relaxation-based treatments. *Sleep Medicine*, *1*, 279–288.

Rudebeck, P. H., & Rich, E. L. (2018). *Orbitofrontal cortex. Current Biology: CB*, *28* (18), R1083–R1088. https://doi.org/10.1016/j.cub.2018.07.018.

Sanz-Arigita, E. J., Daviaux, Y., Joliot, M., Dilharreguy, B., Micoulaud-Franchi, J. A., Bioulac, S., Taillard, J., Philip, P., & Altena, E. (2021). Brain reactivity to humorous films is affected by insomnia. *Sleep*. https:/doi.org/10.1093/slleep/zsab081.

Saper, C. B., Scammell, T. E., & Lu, J. (2005). Hypothalamic regulation of sleep and circadian rhythms. *Nature*, *437*, 1257–1263.

Schwartz, D. R., & Carney, C. E. (2012). Mediators of cognitive–behavioral therapy for insomnia: A review of randomized controlled trials and secondary analysis studies. *Clinical Psychology Review*, *32* (7), 664–675. https://doi.org/10.1016/j.cpr.2012.06.006.

Smith, M. T., Perlis, M. L., Chengazi, V. U., Soeffing, J., & McCann, U. (2004). NREM sleep cerebral blood flow before and after behavior therapy for chronic primary insomnia: Preliminary single photon emission computed tomography (SPECT) data. *Sleep Medicine*, *6* (1), 93–94. doi: 10.1016/j.sleep.2004.10.003.

Spiegelhalder, K., Espie, C., Nissen, C., & Riemann, D. (2008). Sleep-related attentional bias in patients with primary insomnia compared with sleep experts and healthy controls. *Journal of Sleep Research*, *17* (2), 191–196. https://doi.org/10.1111/j.1365-2869.2008.00641.x.

Spiegelhalder, K., Regen, W., Baglioni, C., Riemann, D., & Winkelman, J. W. (2013). Neuroimaging studies in insomnia. *Current Psychiatry Reports*, *15* (11), 405. doi: 10.1007/s11920-013-0405-0.

Spiegelhalder, K., Regen, W., Baglioni, C., Nissen, C., Riemann, D., & Kyle, S.D. (2015). Neuroimaging insights into insomnia. *Current Neurology and Neuroscience Reports*,*15* (3), 9. doi: 10.1007/s11910-015-0527-3.

Spiegelhalder, K., Baglioni, C., Regen, W., Kyle, S. D., Nissen, C., Hennig, J., Doerr, J.-P., Feige, B., & Riemann, D. (2018). Brain reactivity and selective attention to sleep-related words in patients with chronic insomnia. *Behavioral Sleep Medicine*, *16* (6), 587–600. https://doi.org/10.1080/15402002.2016.1253014.

Stoffers, D., Moens, S., Benjamins, J., van Tol, M.-J., Penninx, B. W. J. H., Veltman, D. J., Van der Wee, N. J. A., & Van Someren, E. J. W. (2012). Orbitofrontal gray matter relates to early morning awakening: A neural correlate of insomnia complaints? *Frontiers in Neurology*, *3*, 105. https://doi.org/10.3389/fneur.2012.00105.

Stoffers, D., Altena, E., van der Werf, Y. D., Sanz-Arigita, E. J., Voorn, T. A., Astill, R. G., Strijers, R. L. M., Waterman, D., & Van Someren, E. J. W. (2014). The caudate: A key node in the neuronal network imbalance of insomnia? *Brain: A Journal of Neurology*, *137* (Pt 2), 610–620. https://doi.org/10.1093/brain/awt329.

Sun, J.-J., Liu, X.-M., Shen, C.-Y., Zhang, X.-Q., Sun, G.-X., Feng, K., Xu, B., Ren, X.-J., Ma, X.-Y., & Liu, P.-Z. (2017). Reduced prefrontal activation during verbal fluency task in chronic insomnia disorder: A multichannel near-infrared spectroscopy study. *Neuropsychiatric Disease and Treatment*, *13*, 1723–1731. https://doi.org/10.2147/NDT.S136774.

Sunnhed, R., & Jansson-Fröjmark, M. (2015). Cognitive arousal, unhelpful beliefs and maladaptive sleep behaviors as mediators in cognitive behavior therapy for insomnia: A quasi-experimental study. *Cognitive Therapy and Research*, *39* (6), 841–852. https://doi.org/10.1007/s10608-015-9698-0.

Tahmasian, M., Noori, K., Samea, F., Zarei, M., Spiegelhalder, K., Eickhoff, S. B., Van Someren, E., Khazaie, H., & Eickhoff, C. R. (2018). A lack of consistent brain alterations in insomnia disorder: An activation likelihood estimation meta-analysis. *Sleep Medicine Reviews*, *42*, 111–118. https://doi.org/10.1016/j.smrv.2018.07.004.

Tempesta, D., Socci, V., De Gennaro, L., & Ferrara, M. (2018). Sleep and emotional processing. *Sleep Medicine Reviews*, *40*, 183–195. https://doi.org/10.1016/j.smrv.2017.12.005.

Thakral, M., Von Korff, M., McCurry, S. M., Morin, C. M., & Vitiello, M. V. (2020). Changes in dysfunctional beliefs about sleep after cognitive behavioral therapy for insomnia: A systematic literature review and meta-analysis. *Sleep Medicine Reviews*, *49*, 101230. https://doi.org/10.1016/j.smrv.2019.101230.

Van Someren, E. J. W. (2021). Brain mechanisms of insomnia: New perspectives on causes and consequences. *Physiological Reviews*, *101*, 995–1046. https://doi.org/10.1152/physrev.00046.2019.

Vargas, I., Vgontzas, A. N., Abelson, J. L., Faghih, R. T., Morales, K. H., & Perlis, M. L. (2018). Altered ultradian cortisol rhythmicity as a potential neurobiologic substrate for chronic insomnia. *Sleep Medicine Reviews*, *41*, 234–243. https://doi.org/10.1016/j.smrv.2018.03.003.

Vargas, I., Nguyen, A. M., Muench, A., Bastien, C. H., Ellis, J. G., & Perlis, M. L. (2020). Acute and chronic insomnia: What has time and/or hyperarousal got to do with It? *Brain Sciences*, *10* (2). https://doi.org/10.3390/brainsci10020071.

Vgontzas, A. N., Tsigos, C., Bixler, E. O., Stratakis, C. A., Zachman, K., Kales, A., Vela-Bueno, A., & Chrousos, G. P. (1998). Chronic insomnia and activity of the stress system: A preliminary study. *Journal of Psychosomatic Research*, *45* (1), 21–31. https://doi.org/10.1016/s0022-3999(97)00302-4.

Vincent, N., & Lewycky, S. (2009). Logging on for better sleep: RCT of the effectiveness of online treatment for insomnia. *Sleep*, *32*, 807–815.

Vincent, N., & Walsh, K. (2013). Hyperarousal, sleep scheduling, and time awake in bed as mediators of outcome in computerized cognitive-behavioral therapy (cCBT) for insomnia. *Behaviour Research and Therapy*, *51* (3), 161–166. https://doi.org/10.1016/j.brat.2012.12.003.

Wassing, R., Schalkwijk, F., Lakbila-Kamal, O., Ramautar, J. R., Stoffers, D., Mutsaerts, H. J. M. M., Talamini, L. M., & Van Someren, E. J. W. (2019). Haunted by the past: Old emotions remain salient in insomnia disorder. *Brain: A Journal of Neurology*, *142* (6), 1783–1796. https://doi.org/10.1093/brain/awz089.

Winkelman, J. W., Buxton, O. M., Jensen, J. E., Benson, K. L., O'Connor, S. P., Wang, W., & Renshaw, P. F. (2008). Reduced brain GABA in primary insomnia: Preliminary data from 4T proton magnetic resonance spectroscopy (1H-MRS). *Sleep*, *31* (11), 1499–1506. https://doi.org/10.1093/sleep/31.11.1499.

Woods, H., Marchetti, L. M., Biello, S. M., & Espie, C. A. (2009). The clock as a focus of selective attention in those with primary insomnia: An experimental study using a modified Posner paradigm. *Behaviour Research and Therapy*, *47* (3), 231–236. https://doi.org/10.1016/j.brat.2008.12.009.

Wu, R., Bao, J., Zhang, C., Deng, J., & Long, C. (2006). Comparison of sleep condition and sleep-related psychological activity after cognitive-behavior and pharmacological therapy for chronic insomnia. *Psychotherapy and Psychosomatics*, *75*, 220–228.

Yu, S., Shen, Z., Lai, R., Feng, F., Guo, B., Wang, Z., Yang, J., Hu, Y., & Liang Gong, L. (2018). The orbitofrontal cortex gray matter is associated with the interaction between insomnia and depression. *Front Psychiatry*, *9*, 651. doi: 10.3389/fpsyt.2018.00651.

Zhao, W., Van Someren, E. J. W., Li, C., Chen, X., Gui, W., Tian, Y., Liu, Y., & Lei, X. (2021). EEG spectral analysis in insomnia disorder: A systematic review and meta-analysis. *Sleep Medicine Reviews*, *59*, 101457. https://doi.org/10.1016/j.smrv.2021.101457.

Zou, G., Li, Y., Liu, J., Zhou, S., Xu, J., Qin, L., Shao, Y., Yao, P., Sun, H., Zou, Q., & Gao, J.-H. (2021). Altered thalamic connectivity in insomnia disorder during wakefulness and sleep. *Human Brain Mapping*, *42* (1), 259–270. https://doi.org/10.1002/hbm.25221.

5

CBT-I Assessment Instruments

Jason G Ellis, Pamela Alfonso-Miller and Nayantara Santhi

Key points
• Whilst there are many scales for measuring sleep, a measure that is specific to insomnia is required in the context of CBT-I. • Sleep diaries are integral to CBT-I and should be obtained for at least one week prior to the commencement of CBT-I (in particular the behavioural components), completed over successive days and continued over the entire course of CBT-I. • A measurement of day-time sleepiness is core in the context of CBT-I. • Supplementary measures can and should be included but these should be tailored to the populations and contexts that you are working with.

Learning objectives
• To be able to determine which measurement strategies are core and which are supplementary. • To discuss the relative value of subjective and objective measures over the course of CBT-I. • To understand why a measure of sleepiness is important during CBT-I. • To be able to employ a sleep diary in the context of CBT-I.

Abstract

The aim of this chapter is to provide an overview of the different measures and instruments used within the context of CBT-I, from initial intake to outcome and follow-up. Throughout the chapter, there are some measures and instruments that are considered as core and others as recommended. The rationale for this is finding a balance between comprehensive assessment and patient burden. As you will note, a great deal of attention is paid to the sleep diary – arguably the most important instrument used within the context of delivering CBT-I. Finally, we discuss additional measures and instruments that may be helpful when applying CBT-I in complex cases and situations, such as a co-morbid illness.

Keywords *measures, sleep diary, scales, sleepiness, insomnia*

Introduction

This chapter starts with the premise that a clinical interview, or something similar, will have been conducted prior to commencing CBT-I, taking into account known physical and psychological co-morbidities (including medication use), occupational and lifestyle factors (including substance use) and the differential diagnosis of Insomnia Disorder according

Cognitive-Behavioural Therapy for Insomnia (CBT-I) Across the Life Span: Guidelines and Clinical Protocols for Health Professionals,
First Edition. Edited by Chiara Baglioni, Colin A. Espie and Dieter Riemann.

to the ICSD-3, DSM-5 or ICD-11 (*American Academy of Sleep Medicine*, 2014; American Psychiatric Association, 2013; World Health Organisation, 2018). This is invaluable for determining suitability for CBT-I (e.g., identifying a contraindicated co-morbidity) and/or where additional gatekeeping/planning may be needed (e.g., an occupation that involves driving long distances) prior to the initiation of treatment.

Identifying 'other' sleep disorders

In addition to collecting information on co-morbidities, medication and substance use and lifestyle factors, it is important to identify whether any other sleep disorders are present. This not only provides information that may be relevant to the diagnosis of Insomnia Disorder itself (i.e., does the other sleep disorder 'adequately' or 'better' explain the insomnia) but can also inform whether CBT-I is contraindicated until the other sleep disorder is managed. For example, there is considerable overlap between insomnia and obstructive sleep apnoea (OSA), with 39–58% of those with a diagnosis of OSA reporting insomnia symptoms and between 29 and 67% of individuals with insomnia meeting criteria for OSA (i.e., an Apnoea Hypopnea Index of five or more; Luyster, Buysse & Strollo, 2010). As such, a sleep disorder screener is recommended in order to 'flag' other potential sleep disorders for additional assessment or referral.

The Sleep Disorders Checklist-25 (SDSCL-25) (Klingman, Jungqvist & Perlis, 2017) is a comprehensive tool that assesses the presence of 13 potential sleep disorders by the number of times a symptom is experienced within a given week, over the previous three months. Its main advantage is that it is easy to administer and score (a positive response to three or more times a week) suggests the potential for that specific sleep disorder category (see Figures 5.1 and 5.2). It can also be used to examine the severity of each of the potential sleep disorders by summing the scores in each category. It should be noted, however, that the SDS-CL-25 can only be used to identify potential sleep disorders as the algorithm has yet to be validated against diagnosed sleep disorders. It should also be noted that the possible presence of another sleep disorder does not preclude the treatment of insomnia as a co-morbid sleep problem.

Core instruments

Assessing Insomnia Symptoms

Whilst a myriad of scales exist that have great sensitivity in detecting insomnia, such as the Pittsburgh Sleep Quality Index (PSQI) (Buysse, Reynolds, Monk, Berman & Kupfer, 1989), the Jenkins Sleep Questionnaire (Jenkins et al., 1988), and the two sleep-specific Patient Reported Outcomes Information System measures (Buysse et al., 2010) – Sleep Disturbance (PROMIS-SD) and Sleep-Related Impairments (PROMIS-SRI) – they lack the specificity to differentiate insomnia from other sleep disturbances and disorders and are not preferred in the context of CBT-I. As such, we recommend using one of the two most popular insomnia-specific measures for use at intake, outcome and at any follow-up. Both scales that we recommend have been used within a variety of contexts (e.g., clinics, primary care, research) and populations (e.g., cancer patients, depressed patients) and have been translated into numerous languages – further making them the scales of choice at present.

The Sleep Condition Indicator (SCI) (Espie et al, 2014) is an eight-item scale that asks individuals to report their daytime and night-time symptoms over the previous month (Figure 5.3). It also includes questions about the frequency and duration of these symptoms. Items are summed to give a range between 0 and 32, with higher scores indicating less insomnia symptomology and ≤ 16 being the cut-off for Insomnia Disorder. In a study examining the psychometric properties of the SCI, age and sex appropriate norms were provided and it was reported that an increase of seven points, or more (if using the whole scale), demonstrates a 'reliable improvement' in symptoms, which can be applied in the context of understanding treatment effectiveness (Espie et al., 2018). Its main advantage is that of all the scales for assessing insomnia it is the only one that has been developed since the new diagnostic criteria for Insomnia Disorder, according to the DSM-5 and ICSD-3, were introduced. More recently, a brief two-item version of the SCI was introduced to aid identification of insomnia in busy practices, such as in primary care. This brief measure has been validated in 200,000 adults who had completed it online and a score of ≤ 2 suggests probable insomnia (Luik, Machado, Siriwardena & Espie, 2019).

SDS-CL-25

Date:__/__/__ID/Initials____Age:____Sex:_ Height_____Weight_____ H1: Work Shift: n/a First (9–5 pm) Second (4–12 am) Third (12 to 8 am) H2: Work Hours: __0 __10–19 __20–40 __ > 40 Hours per week H3: Do you regularly have a bed partner? (3 or more days/week)(Yes/No) H4: How much sleep do you typically get per night?____hours (e.g., 8.5 hrs.) H5: How much time do your typically spend in bed per night?__hours (e.g., 9.0 hrs.) **Answer all questions for what has been typical for you for the last 3 months**	NEVER 0	ONCE A MONTH 1	1–2 TIMES WEEK 2	3–5 TIMES WEEK 3	>5 TIMES WEEK 4
1. My work or other activities prevent me from getting at least 6 hours of sleep					
2. My bedtime or waketime varies by more than 3 hours					
3. It takes me 30 minutes or more to fall asleep					
4. I am awake for 30 minutes or more during the night					
5. I wake up 30 or more minuts before I have to and can't fall bak asleep					
6. I am tired, fatigued, or sleepy during the day					
7. I sleep better if I go to bed before 9pm and wake up before 4:30 am					
8. I sleep better if I go to bed late (after 1 am) and wake up late (after 9 am)					
9. I am prone to fall asleep at inappropriate times or places					
10. I snore					
11. I wake up with a dry mouth in the morning (cotton mouth)					
12. My snoring is so loud, that my bed partner complains					
13. I have to been told that I stop breathing in my sleep					
14. I wake up choking or gasping for air					
15. I feel uncomfortable sensations in my legs, especially when sitting or lying down, that are relieved by moving them					
16. I have an urge to move my legs that is worse in the evenings and nights					
17. I wake up frequently during the night for no reason					
18. When angered, humored, frightened, I experiences sudden muscle weakness					
19. When falling asleep or waking up, I experience scary dream like images					
20. When I am first awakening, I feel like I can't move					
21. I have nighmares					
22. For no reason, I awaken suddenly, feeling startled and afraid					
23. I have been told that I walk, talk, eat, act strangely or violently when asleep					
24. I grind my teeth or clench my jaw while I sleep					
25. My sleep difficulties interfere with my daily activities					

Figure 5.1 The Sleep Disorders Symptom Checklist-25.

The Insomnia Severity Index (ISI) (Morin, 1993; Bastien, Vallières and Morin, 2001) is a seven-item scale that is intended to screen for the presence of insomnia symptoms over the previous month. Items are summed to give a range between 0 and28, with higher scores indicating more severe insomnia symptomology (Figure 5.4). The original scale identified a series of cut-off scores (i.e., 0–7 = no clinically significant insomnia, 8–14 = subthreshold insomnia, 15–21 = moderate severity clinical insomnia and 22–28 = severe clinical insomnia). Specific values on the ISI, which

Figure 5.2 Scoring Criteria for the SDS-CL-25.

Item	Content
Header	Age, sex, height, weight H1: work shift H2: hours worked per week H3: presence or bed partner H4: amount of sleep each night H5: amount of time in bed each night
Q1	Work/activity interferes w/sufficient sleep
Q2	Bed or wake time variability
Q3	Time to fall asleep
Q4	Time awake during sleep period
Q5	Early awakening
Q6	Daytime sleepiness or fatigue
Q7	Prefers early bed & wake times
Q8	Prefers late bed & wake times
Q9	Inappropriately falling asleep
Q10	Snores
Q11	Morning dry mouth
Q12	Snoring interferes w/others' sleep
Q13	Stops breathing while asleep
Q14	Gasps while asleep
Q15	Leg sensations
Q16	Urge to move legs at night
Q17	Frequent nighttime awakenings for unknown reason
Q18	Muscle weakness w/strong emotions
Q19	Frightening images as awakens
Q20	Can't move as awakens
Q21	Nightmares
Q22	Wake up afraid for no reason
Q23	Strange behaviors while sleeping
Q24	Grind teeth while sleep
Q25	Sleep problems interfere with daytime function

SDS-CL-25: Sleep Disorders Symptom Checklist-25.

Item	Score 4	3	2	1	0
Thinking about a typical night in the last month ...					
1. ... how long does it take you to fall asleep?	0–15 min	16–30 min	31–45 min	46–60 min	≥61 min
2. ... if you then wake up during the night ... how long are you awake for in total? (add all the wakenings up)	0–15 min	16–30 min	31–45 min	46–60 min	≥61 min
3. ... how many nights a week do you have a problem with your sleep?	0–1	2	3	4	5–7
4. ... how would you rate your sleep quality?	Very good	Good	Average	Poor	Very poor
Thinking about the past month, to what extent has poor sleep...					
5. ... affected your mood, energy, or relationships?	Not at all	A little	Somewhat	Much	Very much
6. ... affected your concentration, productivity, or ability to stay awake	Not at all	A little	Somewhat	Much	Very much
7. ... troubled you in general	Not at all	A little	Somewhat	Much	Very much
Finally ...					
8. ... how long have you had a problem with your sleep?	I don't have a problem/<1 mo	1–2 mo	3–6 mo	7–12 mo	>1 yr

Scoring instructions:
Add the item scores to obtain the SCI total (minimum 0, maximum 32).
A higher score means better sleep.
Scores can be converted to 0–10 format (minimum 0, maximum 10) by dividing total by 3.2.
Item scores in grey area represent threshold criteria for Insomnia Disorder.

Figure 5.3 The Sleep Condition Indicator.

Insomnia Severity Index

The Insomnia Severity Index has seven questions. The seven answers are added up to get a total score. When you have your total score, look at the 'Guidelines for Scoring/Interpretation' below to see where your sleep difficulty fits.

For each question, please CIRCLE the number that best describes your answer.

Please rate the CURRENT (i.e. LAST 2 WEEKS) SEVERITY of your insomnia problem(s).

Insomnia Problem	None	Mild	Moderate	Severe	Very Severe
1. Difficulty falling asleep	0	1	2	3	4
2. Difficulty staying asleep	0	1	2	3	4
3. Problems waking up too early	0	1	2	3	4

4. How SATISFIED/DISSATISFIED are you with your CURRENT sleep pattern?

Very Satisfied	Satisfied	Moderately Satisfied	Dissatisfied	Very Dissatisfied
0	1	2	3	4

5. How NOTICEABLE to others do you think your sleep problem is in terms of impairing the quality of your life?

Not at all Noticeable	A Little	Somewhat	Much	Very Much Noticeable
0	1	2	3	4

6. How WORRIED/DISTRESSED are you about your current sleep problem?

Not at all Worried	A Little	Somewhat	Much	Very Much Worried
0	1	2	3	4

7. To what extent do you consider your sleep problem to INTERFERE with your daily functioning (e.g. daytime fatigue, mood, ability to function at work/daily chores, concentration, memory, mood, etc.) CURRENTLY?

Not at all Interfering	A Little	Somewhat	Much	Very Much Interfering
0	1	2	3	4

Guidelines for Scoring/Interpretation:

Add the scores for all seven items (questions 1 + 2 + 3 + 4 + 5 + 6 + 7) = _______ your total score

Figure 5.4 The Insomnia Severity Index.

are indicative of the threshold of insomnia, in both community (≤ 10) and clinical (≤ 11) populations, have also been provided (Morin, Belleville, Bélanger & Ivers, 2011). Its main advantage is that it has been used extensively within the context of CBT-I, providing a great deal of comparative data, and is the only scale, at present, that provides a variety of treatment efficacy benchmarks (i.e., reductions of 4.7 points relates to a slight improvement treatment response, 8.4 points to a moderate treatment response and 9.9 to a marked improvement treatment response). Further, a score of < 8 following treatment can be used as an index of recovery in the short term and remission in the longer term. This can be helpful, not only at the individual patient level but also for auditing purposes.

An alternative measure of insomnia, albeit less well reported in the context of CBT-I, is the Athens Insomnia Scale (AIS) (Soldatos, Dikeos & Paparrigopoulos, 2000). As with the SCI and ISI, it asks individuals to self-report problems with sleep over the previous month. It contains eight items, which are scored between 0 and 3 (scale ranges between 0 and 24). The AIS has the advantage that the instructions ask the individual to only respond to sleep difficulties experienced at least three times per week, aligning it with the DSM-5 and ICSD-3. Additionally, unlike the SCI and ISI, the AIS has one item specifically asking about early morning awakenings (if that is of particular interest). In one study a score of six correctly identified 90% of patients with insomnia (Soldatos, Dimitris & Paparrigopoulos, 2003).

The Sleep Diary

Although sleep diaries come in many different forms, essentially, they all rely on the patient self-reporting information about their previous night's sleep. In its simplest form, the sleep diary asks the patient: (i) what time they got into bed with the intention of sleeping, (ii) how long it took them to get off to sleep – after intending to sleep, (iii) how many times they woke up in the night and (iv) for how long they were awake in the night, (v) what time they woke up in the morning and (vi) what time they got out of bed (see Figures 5.5 and 5.6 for examples). Together, this information provides a basic understanding of how well, or poorly, the individual reports they are sleeping and in the case of someone with insomnia, it provides an indication of where the problem(s) appear to lie. Most sleep diaries also ask the patient to record how well they felt they slept the previous night and how refreshed and alert they feel that morning. These last two questions are general indicators of overall sleep quality. If you are working with a specific population you may want to include other pertinent behaviours (e.g., the timing and frequency of food or liquid intake, exercise, caffeine consumption, medication use). That said, it is important not to overwhelm the patient with too many questions in the diary as that may result in non-completion. A very useful guide of what to include when working with different populations comes from Carney et al. (2012) who introduced the Consensus Sleep Diary with the aim of creating a set of minimum measurement standards for sleep diaries, with additional items based upon the population being worked with.

Sleep diaries can be delivered through a multitude of media (e.g., hand-written, app-delivered, completed online) and the choice of which media should be made largely depending upon the needs and circumstances surrounding treatment (e.g., remote therapy). That said, we should be mindful that if an automated diary only generates averaged data or if the patient is not signposted to look at individual nights, the richness of these data can be lost, preventing the patient, or indeed therapist, from seeing patterns in behaviour that may impact on sleep and recovery (e.g., I did x on Tuesday and that night I slept horribly and yet I did not do it on Wednesday and I slept well that night – Figure 5.6).

How many nights of information are enough?

As we know that even normal sleepers have the occasional poor night of sleep, the question we have to ask ourselves is: how many nights of diary data are needed to provide meaningful information? Most clinicians and researchers agree that seven nights is the minimum number needed to identify meaningful patterns and highlight any issues.

MEASURING THE PATTERN OF YOUR SLEEP	Day 1	Day 2	Day 3	Day 4	Day 5	Day 6	Day 7
1. What time did you wake this morning?							
2. At what time did you get out of bed?							
3. At what time did you go to bed last night?							
4. Lights Out: At what time did you put the lights out to go to sleep?							
5. How long did it take you to fall asleep (minutes)? (After Lights Out)							
6. How many times did you wake up during the night?							
7. How long were you awake during the night (in total)?							
8. About how long did you sleep altogether (hours/mins)?							
9. Did you use anything to help you sleep (medication, herbal, alcohol)? (Y/N)							

MEASURING OTHER ACTIVITIES

1. How was the quality of your sleep last night? 0 1 2 3 4 very poor moderately ok very good							
2. How physically tense were you last night at bedtime? 0 1 2 3 4 not at all moderately very good							
3. How mentally alert were you last night at bedtime? 0 1 2 3 4 not at all moderately very good							
4. Did you nap in the daytime and for how long? (time and duration)							

Figure 5.5 An example of a Sleep Diary.

MEASURING THE PATTERN OF YOUR SLEEP	Mon 14/06/21	Tues 15/06/21	Wed 16/06/21	Thur 17/06/21	Fri 18/06/21	Sat 19/06/21	Sun 20/06/21
1. What time did you wake this morning?	07.30	07.30	07.30	07.30	07.30	09.45	08.30
2. At what time did you get out of bed?	07.40	07.30	07.30	0730	07.30	10.15	09.15
3. At what time did you go to bed last night?	00.30	23.15	23.00	22.30	22.00	01.00	01.30
4. Lights Out: At what time did you put the lights out to go to sleep?	00.30	23.30	23.00	22.30	23.30	01.15	01.30
5. How long did it take you to fall asleep (minutes)? (After Lights Out)	30	0	5	40	60	5	40
6. How many times did you wake up during the night?	2	3	1	2	2	1	2
7. How long were you awake during the night (in total)?	120	120	5	90	40	100	110
8. About how long did you sleep altogether (hours/mins)?	340	360	500	410	380	435	270
9. Did you use anything to help you sleep (medication, herbal, alcohol)? (Y/N)	Y	Y	N	N	N	N	N
MEASURING OTHER ACTIVITIES							
1. How was the quality of your sleep last night? 0 1 2 3 4 (very poor; moderately ok; very good)	3	2	4	2	2	3	1
2. How physically tense were you last night at bedtime? 0 1 2 3 4 (not at all; moderately; very good)	3	0	0	3	3	1	3
3. How mentally alert were you last night at bedtime? 0 1 2 3 4 (not at all; moderately; very good)	3	0	0	3	3	1	3
4. Did you nap in the daytime and for how long? (time and duration)	N	N	N	N	N	Y 90 minutes @ 2 p.m.	N

Figure 5.6 An example of a Completed Sleep Diary.

Ideally there should be two weeks of sleep diary information at intake, but this can be difficult to get in practice. Not only is a one-week minimum good for identifying patterns, but also it is important to have information about sleep on work days and non-work days (if applicable), as in some cases sleep patterns may differ substantially between days when the patient has morning commitments and days they do not. The final point is the diary should be completed over consecutive days.

Using sleep diaries for outcome data

As sleep diaries are completed throughout therapy, they can be an excellent reference point for assessing changes in the main symptoms (i.e., getting off to sleep, number of awakenings, time awake during the night). In many instances these data can be graphed and shared with the patient to demonstrate changes in symptoms (Figure 5.7). The question remains as to what are considered clinically relevant changes in sleep diary data. One method may be to use the quantitative criteria for insomnia, as outlined by Lichstein and colleagues (2003). In this respect, if the patient reports achieving an endpoint of <= 31 minutes sleep latency and/or wake after sleep onset, then this could be considered a proxy for recovery/remission. In terms of magnitude of change, a 50% reduction, from intake, on sleep onset latency and/or wake after sleep onset (in this instance WASO incorporates Early Morning Awakenings) has been proposed as clinically meaningful in a series of meta-analyses (Morin, Cubert & Schwartz, 1994; van Straten et al., 2018). For example, one meta-analysis demonstrated a mean pre–post treatment reduction of 51.66% in sleep latency and 53.37% in wake after sleep onset (Koffel, Koffel & Gehrmon, 2015).

Sleepiness

Another core measure that should be collected prior to initiating CBT-I, and perhaps on a regular basis during therapy where a behavioural intervention is applied, is day-time sleepiness. Although not a measure with high specificity for insomnia per se, it is sensitive and specific to sleepiness and any changes in this dimension. At intake, this may provide an additional indication of an occult sleep disorder, which may be masking as insomnia, an occult co-morbidity or another factor that could impact on an individual's suitability/timing for CBT-I. The main rationale for a measure of day-time sleepiness being incorporated throughout therapy is to identify if, and the extent to which, the sleep restriction or stimulus

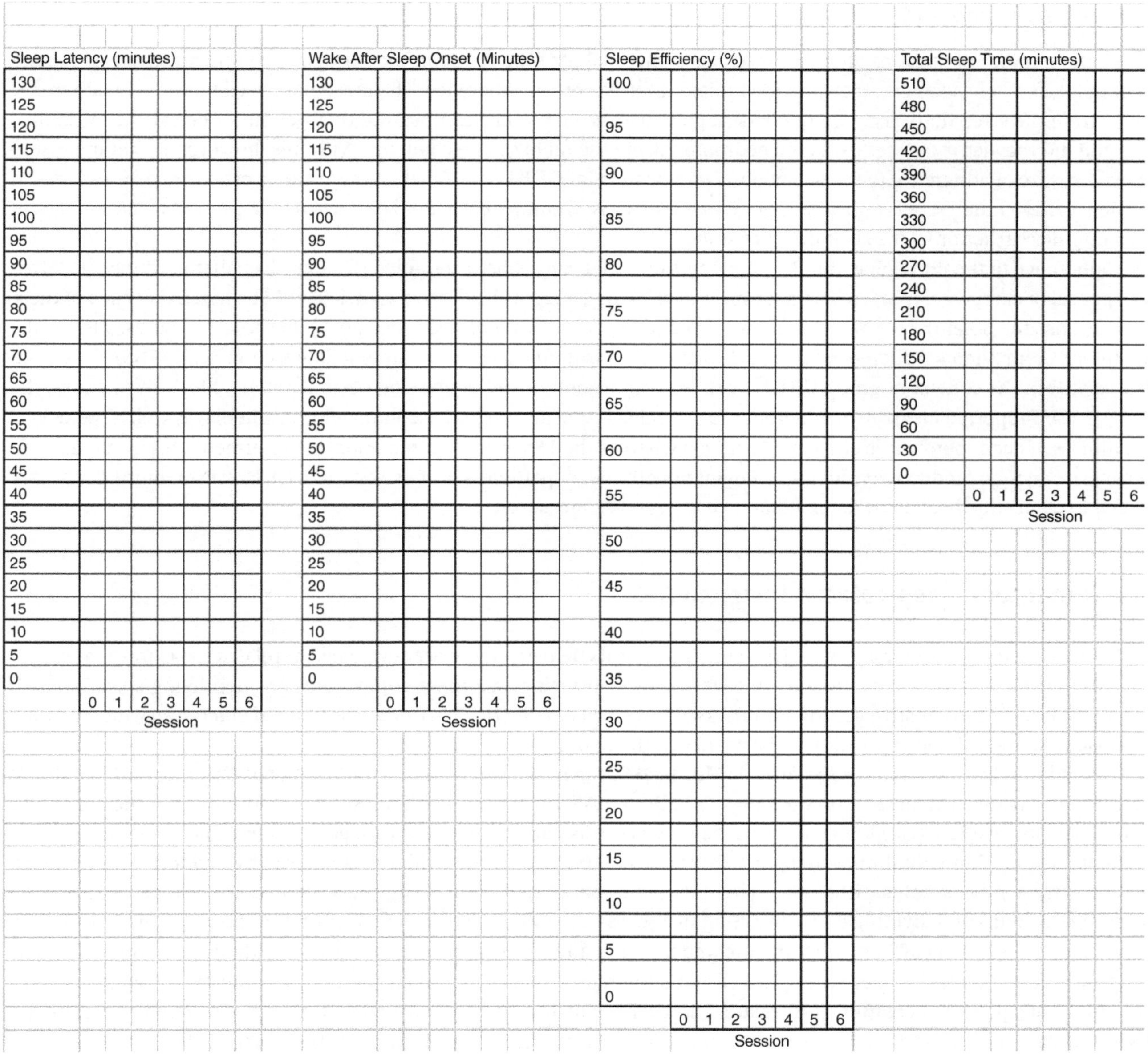

Figure 5.7 Examples for graphing changes during CBT-I.

control components of CBT-I may be impacting, albeit briefly, on day-time performance and safety during the delivery of CBT-I. In essence, whilst not necessarily a barrier to CBT-I, any condition that is characterised by excessive day-time sleepiness needs to be tracked throughout treatment to determine the impact of therapy on this other condition. If there is significant excessive day-time sleepiness or an unexpected change in sleepiness then it is good to pause CBT-I whilst an investigation of the source of the excessive day-time sleepiness occurs.

Apart from enquiring about day-time sleepiness as part of the clinical review process, the most well-established sleepiness scale is the Epworth Sleepiness Scale (ESS) (Johns, 1991), which is a brief scale that asks the individual to report the chances of dozing in eight different situations (0–3). Scores are summed, providing a range between 0 and 24, and a score of ≤11 is indicative of excessive day-time sleepiness. Although the ESS is copyrighted, it can be used, without charge, under some conditions (see: https://eprovide.mapi-trust.org/instruments/epworth-sleepiness-scale#contact_and_conditions_of_use). Alternative measures of sleepiness include the Karolinska Sleepiness Scale (Akerstedt & Gillberg, 1990) and the Stanford Sleepiness Scale (Hoddes, Dement & Zarcone, 1972), although they are time-specific (how are you feeling right now) and have not been used regularly in the context of CBT-I.

Measuring Adherence to CBT-I

Whilst the number of sessions attended/modules completed (or time spent on modules) can be direct measures of treatment uptake and engagement, they provide limited information on adherence. The most often used measure of adherence comes from the sleep diary (i.e., did the patient go to bed at the prescribed time, did they get out of bed at the prescribed time and did they leave and return to the bedroom during the night?). The challenge with this, however, is that it is a self-report measure of adherence to the behavioural components of CBT-I only. Further, there are no established boundaries as to when an individual is, or is not, adherent in this context (is 5 minutes earlier or later to bed than prescribed non-adherent vs 15 minutes earlier or later to bed than prescribed?).

As adherence to the non-behavioural components of CBT-I cannot be ascertained through sleep diaries, direct questioning, spousal or caregiver report (where appropriate) or therapist report have been used, it should be noted that each of these strategies has the potential for bias (Matthews, Arnedt, McCarthy, Cuddihy & Aloia, 2013). Bespoke measures, such as the Treatment Components Adherence Scale (TCAS) and the insomnia-specific Treatment Satisfaction Scale (TSS), have been created within the context of group CBT-I for those with insomnia and depression (Manber et al., 2011). In this case, the TCAS is a self-reported measure of adherence to the behavioural and cognitive components (six items) as well as perceived helpfulness of each therapeutic element (17 items) whereas the TSS examined the impact of treatment on seven main outcomes (i.e., energy, productivity, coping, enjoyment with life, hopefulness, self-esteem, mood). However, more studies are needed to determine benchmarks for adherence using these measures.

Supplementary sleep-related instruments

Whilst not core to the assessment for CBT-I suitability, or its delivery, there are several sleep-related measures that can be used, in practice, to guide the therapist in tailoring or prioritising treatment components by identifying specific target areas. This is not an exhaustive list and for further scales, the book *STOP, THAT and one hundred other sleep scales* (Shahid, Wilkinson, Marcu & Shapiro, 2012) may be a good starting point.

Dysfunctional Beliefs about Sleep (DBAS) (Morin, 1993) measure sleep-related dysfunctional attitudes and beliefs. Of the various versions available, it is common to see the DBAS-16 (Morin, Vallières & Ivers, 2007) used in the context of CBT-I, as it has excellent psychometric properties and is not as burdensome as the longer versions. The DBAS-16 contains 16 statements the individual rates along a 100-mm visual analogue scale, which is anchored by endorsement (strongly agree vs strongly disagree) at either end. The individual marks each item along the scale and an average is derived by summing the items and dividing by 16, resulting in a score of 0–100 (note that there is no cut-off score for the DBAS). The DBAS can be helpful in CBT-I as both an outcome measure and as a way to help identify individuals' catastrophic beliefs about the consequences of poor sleep. Two recent systematic reviews identified the DBAS as the most frequently used measure of sleep-related cognitions in relation to CBT-I. Further, they found that DBAS scores respond to treatment, observing moderate to large effect sizes (Thakral, Von Korff, McCurry, Morin & Vitiello, 2020; Parsons, Zachariae, Landberger & Young, 2021).

The Pre-Sleep Arousal Scale (PSAS) (Nicassio, Mendlowitz, Fussell & Petras, 1985) is a 16-item scale that asks about experiences when attempting to initiate sleep. Each item is scored (1–5) and then two composite scores are derived, one for somatic arousal (eight items: range 8–40) and one for cognitive arousal (eight items: range 8–40) by summing the individual items. Cut-off scores of ≤14 for somatic arousal and ≤20 for cognitive arousal have been recently suggested (Puzino, Amatrudo, Sullivan, Vgontzas & Fernandez-Mendoza, 2020). Within the context of CBT-I the PSAS may provide an indication of which aspect(s) of arousal (somatic or cognitive) to address as a priority through relaxation/cognitive strategies.

The Glasgow Sleep Effort Scale (GSES) (Broomfield and Espie, 2005) is a seven-item scale that examines levels of sleep effort over the previous week. Each item is scored 0–3 and summed with a score of ≤3 showing good discriminatory value. It is independent of general anxiety levels, making it a specific target area of focus and can be helpful when explaining, and implementing, paradoxical intention.

The Flinders Fatigue Scale (FFS) (Gradisar et al., 2007) is a seven-item scale that examines the frequency and severity of fatigue symptoms over the previous two weeks. The first six items are scored 0–4 and the final item is scored on a range between 0 and 7. Scores from each item are summed, providing a range between 0 and31, with higher levels indicating greater fatigue. An advantage of the FFS is that it is independent of sleepiness, as measured by the ESS, and has been shown to respond in line with treatment gains following CBT-I – i.e., a mean reduction of 5.29 points pre- to post-CBT-I and a mean reduction of 8.53 points pre-treatment to two months post-treatment (Gradisar et al., 2007).

The Sleep Preoccupation Scale (SPS) (Ellis, Mitchell & Hogh, 2007) is a 22-item scale that measures the frequency of: (i) day-time thoughts and behaviours and (ii) affective responses to a typical night of poor sleep over the previous month. The SPS is scored on a scale of 0–6 (range of scores 0–132). Although the SPS has not been examined within the context of CBT-I, to date, its potential importance was recently highlighted in the context of acute insomnia, whereby the affective dimension of the SPS was a significant predictor of the transition from acute to chronic insomnia (Ellis et al., 2021), making it a target for relapse prevention within the context of CBT-I.

The role of objective measures in CBT-I (polysomnography and actigraphy)

Considering that objective sleep measures are not indicated in the diagnosis of Insomnia Disorder, it might stand to reason that these techniques are not required in the treatment. That said, objective measures can, and often do, have a place in the context of CBT-I. For example, if there is a suspected co-morbid sleep disorder, such as OSA or Restless Legs Syndrome, then PSG may be indicated; or if it is believed that this may be a case of 'masked' insomnia where symptoms appear to match insomnia but there is a likelihood of Circadian Rhythm Sleep Wake Disorder, then actigraphy may be warranted. Moreover, if there is a suspected case of paradoxical insomnia, that is when there is a significant mismatch between self-reported insomnia symptoms – including day-time dysfunction – and objective measures of the complaint, then PSG or actigraphy is useful to identify the scale of mismatch before commencement of CBT-I. During treatment there may also be occasion to use actigraphy, which generally occurs when the patient reports following the treatment protocol but treatment gains are lower than what would be expected. Whilst this can happen naturally (not everyone benefits from CBT-I), actigraphy can be used in this context to determine whether this is actually the case or whether the patient is being non-adherent to the behavioural components of CBT-I (i.e., getting into and out of bed at the prescribed times, following stimulus control instructions).

Non-sleep-related associated measures

Whilst this is subject to the specific contexts and populations the therapist is working with (e.g., in a pain clinic a measure of pain tolerance could be introduced), due to the intimate relationship between sleep and mood and the established impact of CBT-I on mood outcomes (Cunningham & Shapiro, 2018), it may be helpful to include measures of anxiety, depression and/or health-related quality of life (HRQoL). One thing to be mindful of is that some scales measuring depression may include items relating to sleep disturbance (e.g., the Patient Health Questionnaire (PHQ-9): Kroenke, Spitzer & Williams, 2001). As such, it may be helpful to incorporate a scale that does not rely on somatic symptoms if you wish to examine the impact of CBT-I on mood, independently of sleep. Here, the Hospital Anxiety and Depression Scale (HADS: Zigmund & Snaith, 1983), the State and Trait Anxiety Inventory (STAI: Spielberger, Gorsuch, Lushene & Jacobs, 1983) or the Depression Anxiety Stress Scales (DASS: Lovibond & Lovibond, 1995) may be good alternatives. With regard to HRQoL, the Medical Outcomes Study, a short-form health survey – 36 (SF-36: Ware, Brook & Williams, 1980), has been the most often reported in the insomnia literature and in relation to CBT-I (e.g., Léger et al., 2012; Dixon, Morgan, Mathers, Thompson & Tomeny, 2006; Wickwire, Shaya & Scharf, 2016). There is one insomnia-specific measure of HRQoL, the 16-item Hotel Dieu (HD-16; Léger et al., 2005), although pre-post data, following CBT-I, is rare, precluding comparisons.

Conclusion

The aim of this chapter was to provide an overview of the core, sleep-specific and non-sleep-specific associated instruments and measures suitable for use within the context of CBT-I (see Table 5.1). This was by no means an exhaustive list but, rather, provided a set of tools from which you can then tailor additions depending upon your practice, expertise and the specific populations you work with.

Table 5.1 Overview of instruments for CBT-I.

Measure type	Suggested measure	When to administer				
Core		I	E	P	F	A
Other sleep disorders	SCS-CL-25	x				
Insomnia symptoms	SCI or ISI	x		x	x	
Sleep diary	Sleep diary	x	x	x	x	
Sleepiness	ESS	x	x	x	x	
Adherence	Bespoke Sleep diary/Actigraphy	x	x			x
Sleep-related associated		I	E	P	F	A
Dysfunctional beliefs	DBAS -16	x		x	x	
Pre-sleep arousal	PSAS	x		x	x	
Sleep effort	GSCS	x		x	x	
Fatigue	FFS	x		x	x	
Sleep preoccupation	SPS	x		x	x	
Non-sleep associated		I	E	P	F	A
Depression	PHQ-9; HADS; DASS	x		x	x	
Anxiety	GAD-7; HADS; STAI; DASS	x		x	x	
Quality of life	SF-36; HD-16	x		x	x	
Objective measures		I	E	P	F	A
Polysomnography		x*				
Actigraphy		x*				

I = Intake; E = Every session; P = Post-treatment; F = Follow up; A = If adherence issues suspected
SDS-CL-25 = Steep Disorders Symptom Checklist; SCI = Steep Condition Indicator; ISI = Insomnia Severity Index
ESS = Epworth Sleepiness Scale; DBAS-16 = Dysfunctional Attitudes and Beliefs about Sleep – 16 item version
PSAS = Pre-Sleep Arousal Scale; GSES = Glasgow Sleep Effort Scale; FFS = Flinders Fatigue Scale
SPS = Sleep Preoccupation Scale; PHQ-9 = Patient Health Questionnaire; HADS = Hospital Anxiety and Depression Scale
DASS = Depression, Anxiety and Stress Scale; GAD-7 = Generalized Anxiety Disorder
STAI = State and Trait Anxiety Inventory; SF-36 = Short Form Health Survey; HD-16 = Hotel Dieu
* If another sleep disorder is suspected

References

Akerstedt, T., & Gillberg, M. (1990). Subjective and objective sleepiness in the active individual. *International Journal of Neuroscience*, *52*, 29–37.

American Academy of Sleep Medicine (2014). *International classification of sleep disorders* (3rd ed.) *(ICSD-3)*. Darien, IL: American Academy of Sleep Medicine.

American Psychiatric Association (2013). *Diagnostic and statistical manual of mental disorders (DSM-5®)*. Washington, DC: American Psychiatric Publishers.

Bastien, C. H., Vallières, A., & Morin, C. M. (2001). Validation of the Insomnia Severity Index as an outcome measure for insomnia research. *Sleep Medicine*, 2 (4), 297–307.

Broomfield, N. M., & Espie, C. A. (2005). Towards a valid, reliable measure of sleep effort. *Journal of Sleep Research*, *14* (4), 401–407.

Buysse, D. J., Reynolds III, C. F., Monk, T. H., Berman, S. R., & Kupfer, D. J. (1989). The Pittsburgh Sleep Quality Index: A new instrument for psychiatric practice and research. *Psychiatry Research*, *28* (2), 193–213.

Buysse, D. J., Yu, L., Moul, D. E., Germain, A., Stover, A., Dodds, N. E., Johnston, K. L., Shablesky-Cade, M. A., & Pilkonis, P. A. (2010). Development and validation of patient-reported outcome measures for sleep disturbance and sleep-related impairments. *Sleep*, *33* (6), 781–792.

Carney, C. E., Buysse, D. J., Ancoli-Israel, S., Edinger, J. D., Krystal, A. D., Lichstein, K. L., & Morin, C. M. (2012). The consensus sleep diary: Standardizing prospective sleep self-monitoring. *Sleep*, *35* (2), 287–302.

Cunningham, J. E., & Shapiro, C. M. (2018). Cognitive Behavioural Therapy for Insomnia (CBT-I) to treat depression: A systematic review. *Journal of Psychosomatic Research*, *106*, 1–12.

Dixon, S., Morgan, K., Mathers, N., Thompson, J., & Tomeny, M. (2006). Impact of cognitive behavior therapy on health-related quality of life among adult hypnotic users with chronic insomnia. *Behavioral Sleep Medicine*, *4* (2), 71–84.

Ellis, J., Mitchell, K., & Hogh, H. (2007). Sleep preoccupation in poor sleepers: Psychometric properties of the Sleep Preoccupation Scale. *Journal of Psychosomatic Research*, *63* (6), 579–585.

Ellis, J. G., Perlis, M. L., Espie, C. A., Grandner, M. A., Bastien, C. H., Barclay, N. L., Altena, E., & Gardani, M. (2021). The natural history of insomnia: Predisposing, precipitating, coping, and perpetuating factors over the early developmental course of insomnia. *Sleep*, *44* (9), zsab095.

Espie, C. A., Kyle, S. D., Hames, P., Gardani, M., Fleming, L., & Cape, J. (2014). The Sleep Condition Indicator: A clinical screening tool to evaluate insomnia disorder. *BMJ Open*, *4* (3), e004183.

Espie, C. A., Farias Machado, P., Carl, J. R., Kyle, S. D., Cape, J., Siriwardena, A. N., & Luik, A. I. (2018). The Sleep Condition Indicator: Reference values derived from a sample of 200 000 adults. *Journal of Sleep Research*, *27* (3), e12643.

Gradisar, M., Lack, L., Richards, H., Harris, J., Gallasch, J., Boundy, M., & Johnston, A. (2007). The Flinders Fatigue Scale: Preliminary psychometric properties and clinical sensitivity of a new scale for measuring daytime fatigue associated with insomnia. *Journal of Clinical Sleep Medicine*, *3* (7), 722–728.

Hoddes, E., Dement, W., & Zarcone, V. (1972). The development and use of the Stanford Sleepiness Scale (SSS). *Psychophysiology*, *9*, 150.

Jenkins, C. D., Stanton, B. A., Niemcryk, S. J., & Rose, R. M. (1988). A scale for the estimation of sleep problems in clinical research. *Journal of Clinical Epidemiology*, *41* (4), 313–321.

Johns, M. W. (1991). A new method for measuring daytime sleepiness: The Epworth Sleepiness Scale. *Sleep*, *14* (6), 540–545.

Klingman, K. J., Jungquist, C. R., & Perlis, M. L. (2017). Introducing the sleep disorders symptom checklist-25: A primary care friendly and comprehensive screener for sleep disorders. *Sleep Medicine Research*, *8* (1), 17–25.

Koffel, E. A., Koffel, J. B., & Gehrman, P. R. (2015). A meta-analysis of group cognitive behavioral therapy for insomnia. *Sleep Medicine Reviews*, *19*, 6–16.

Kroenke, K., Spitzer, R. L., & Williams, J. B. (2001). The PHQ-9: Validity of a brief depression severity measure. *Journal of General Internal Medicine*, *16* (9), 606–613.

Léger, D., Scheuermaier, K., Raffray, T., Metlaine, A., Choudat, D., & Guilleminault, C. (2005). HD-16: A new quality of life instrument specifically designed for insomnia. *Sleep Medicine*, *6* (3), 191–198.

Léger, D., Morin, C. M., Uchiyama, M., Hakimi, Z., Cure, S., & Walsh, J. K. (2012). Chronic insomnia, quality-of-life, and utility scores: Comparison with good sleepers in a cross-sectional international survey. *Sleep Medicine*, *13* (1), 43–51.

Lichstein, K. L., Durrence, H. H., Taylor, D. J., Bush, A. J., & Riedel, B. W. (2003). Quantitative criteria for insomnia. *Behaviour Research and Therapy*, *41* (4), 427–445.

Lovibond, P. F., & Lovibond, S. H. (1995). The structure of negative emotional states: Comparison of the Depression Anxiety Stress Scales (DASS) with the Beck Depression and Anxiety Inventories. *Behaviour Research and Therapy*, *33*, 335–343.

Luik, A. I., Machado, P. F., Siriwardena, N., & Espie, C. A. (2019). Screening for insomnia in primary care: Using a two-item version of the Sleep Condition Indicator. *British Journal of General Practice*, *69* (679), 79–80.

Luyster, F. S., Buysse, D. J., & Strollo Jr, P. J. (2010). Comorbid insomnia and obstructive sleep apnea: Challenges for clinical practice and research. *Journal of Clinical Sleep Medicine*, *6* (2), 196–204.

Manber, R., Bernert, R. A., Suh, S., Nowakowski, S., Siebern, A. T., & Ong, J. C. (2011). CBT for insomnia in patients with high and low depressive symptom severity: Adherence and clinical outcomes. *Journal of Clinical Sleep Medicine*, *7* (6), 645–652.

Matthews, E. E., Arnedt, J. T., McCarthy, M. S., Cuddihy, L. J., & Aloia, M. S. (2013). Adherence to cognitive behavioral therapy for insomnia: A systematic review. *Sleep Medicine Reviews*, *17* (6), 453–464.

Morin, C. M. (1993). *Insomnia: Psychological assessment and management*. New York: Guilford Press.

Morin, C. M., Belleville, G., Bélanger, L., & Ivers, H. (2011). The Insomnia Severity Index: Psychometric indicators to detect insomnia cases and evaluate treatment response. *Sleep*, *34* (5), 601–608.

Morin, C. M., Culbert, J. P., & Schwartz, S. M. (1994). Nonpharmacological interventions for insomnia: A meta-analysis of treatment efficacy. *American Journal of Psychiatry*, *151* (8), 1172–1180.

Morin, C. M., Vallières, A., & Ivers, H. (2007). Dysfunctional beliefs and attitudes about sleep (DBAS): Validation of a brief version (DBAS-16). *Sleep, 30* (11), 1547–1554.

Nicassio, P. M., Mendlowitz, D. R., Fussell, J. J., & Petras, L. (1985). The phenomenology of the pre-sleep state: The development of the pre-sleep arousal scale. *Behaviour Research and Therapy*, 23 (3), 263–271.

Parsons, C. E., Zachariae, R., Landberger, C., & Young, K. S. (2021). How does cognitive behavioural therapy for insomnia work? A systematic review and meta-analysis of mediators of change. *Clinical Psychology Review, 86* (102027), 1–14.

Puzino, K., Amatrudo, G., Sullivan, A., Vgontzas, A. N., & Fernandez-Mendoza, J. (2020). Clinical significance and cut-off scores for the Pre-Sleep Arousal Scale in chronic insomnia disorder: A replication in a clinical sample. *Behavioral Sleep Medicine*, 18 (6), 705–718.

Shahid, A., Wilkinson, K., Marcu, S., & Shapiro, C. M. (Eds.) (2012). *STOP, THAT and one hundred other sleep scales*. New York: Springer Science & Business Media.

Soldatos, C. R., Dikeos, D.G., & Paparrigopoulos, T.J. (2000). Athens insomnia scale: Validation of an instrument based on ICD-10 criteria. *Journal of Psychosomatic Research, 48* (6), 555–560.

Soldatos, C. R., Dimitris, G. D., & Paparrigopoulos, T.J. (2003). The diagnostic validity of the Athens insomnia scale. *Journal of Psychosomatic Research, 55*, 263–267.

Spielberger, C. D., Gorsuch, R. L., Lushene, R., Vagg, P. R., & Jacobs, G. A. (1983). *Manual for the State-Trait Anxiety Inventory*. Palo Alto, CA: Consulting Psychologists Press.

Thakral, M., Von Korff, M., McCurry, S. M., Morin, C. M., & Vitiello, M. V. (2020). Changes in dysfunctional beliefs about sleep after cognitive behavioral therapy for insomnia: A systematic literature review and meta-analysis. *Sleep Medicine Reviews, 49* (101230), 1–9.

van Straten, A., van der Zweerde, T., Kleiboer, A., Cuijpers, P., Morin, C. M., & Lancee,J. (2018). Cognitive and behavioral therapies in the treatment of insomnia: A meta-analysis. *Sleep Medicine Reviews, 38*, 3–16.

Ware, J. E., Brook, R. H., & Williams, K. N. (1980). *Conceptualisation and measurement of health care in adults in the health insurance study*, Vol. 1, *Model of health and methodology*. Santa Monica, CA: Rand Corp.

Wickwire, E. M., Shaya, F. T., & Scharf, S. M. (2016). Health economics of insomnia treatments: The return on investment for a good night's sleep. *Sleep Medicine Reviews, 30*, 72–82.

World Health Organization (2018). *International classification of diseases for mortality and morbidity statistics* (11th Revision). Retrieved from: https://icd.who.int/browse11/l-m/en.

Zigmond, A. S., & Snaith, R. P. (1983). The hospital anxiety and depression scale. *Acta Psychiatrica Scandinavica, 67* (6), 361–370.

6

CBT-I and Pharmacological Treatment

Lukas Frase

Key points
• Pharmacotherapy for insomnia disorder (ID) should be considered, if CBT-I is not effective or not available. • Following evidence-based treatment guidelines, the therapist should either select the benzodiazepine (BZ) triazolam (0.25 mg daily dose, DD) or temazepam (15 mg DD), or the benzodiazepine receptor agonist (BZRA) zolpidem (10 mg DD) or (es-) zopiclone (2–3 mg DD). Nevertheless, guidelines should be considered in each country context, as not all medicines are available everywhere. • If BZ and BZRA need to be avoided, for example due to age, past substance dependence or other contraindications, low-dose doxepine (3–6 mg DD) appears to be the most favourable alternative. • In case of medication, treatment needs to be carefully and regularly administered by professional care providers and limited to short-term treatment of <4 weeks. • Pharmacotherapy can and should be combined with CBT-I. • Benzodiazepines should be avoided in patients older than 64. • If hypnotics need to be deprescribed, a gradual dose reduction of 12.5 to 25% every two weeks accompanied by frequent clinical monitoring and behavioural changes/CBT-I should be chosen.

Learning objectives
• To understand underlying physiological concepts of sedating agents used to improve sleep. • To know in which scenarios pharmacotherapy for insomnia is recommended and effective. • To be able to choose the correct medication for the individual patient. • To be familiar with recommendations regarding deprescribing of hypnotics.

Abstract

Pharmacotherapy for insomnia disorder (ID) should be considered if CBT-I is not effective or not available. A combination of pharmacotherapy with CBT-I is feasible and effective and can be considered if CBT-I alone does not lead to remission. Following evidence-based treatment guidelines, the therapist should either select the benzodiazepines (BZ) triazolam (0.25 mg daily dose, DD) or temazepam (15 mg DD), or the benzodiazepine receptor agonists (BZRA) zolpidem (10 mg DD) or (es)zopiclone (2–3 mg DD). Guidelines should be considered in each country context, as not all medicines are available everywhere. As an example, triazolam is not available in the UK. If BZ and BZRA need to be avoided, for example due to age, past substance dependence or other contraindications, low-dose doxepine (3–6 mg DD) appears to be the most favourable alternative. In case of medication, treatment

Cognitive-Behavioural Therapy for Insomnia (CBT-I) Across the Life Span: Guidelines and Clinical Protocols for Health Professionals,
First Edition. Edited by Chiara Baglioni, Colin A. Espie and Dieter Riemann.

needs to be carefully and regularly administered by professional care providers and limited to short-term treatment of <4 weeks. BZ and BZRA should be deprescribed in all ID patients older than 64 years regardless of treatment duration and in all younger patients after 4 weeks of treatment. Deprescribing should follow published clinical recommendations and include frequent clinical monitoring and initiation of behavioural changes/CBT-I. Tapering should be gradual, with only 12.5–25% dose reduction every two weeks. Sedating antidepressants are considered effective in the short-term treatment of insomnia, but contraindications have to be carefully considered. Melatonin appears to only show effectiveness in ID treatment in the elderly and usage should therefore be limited to this population.

Keywords *pharmacotherapy, hypnotics, benzodiazepines, deprescribing, reduction, withdrawal*

Pharmacotherapy for insomnia – theoretical background and general recommendations

Pharmacological interventions to improve sleep quality and/or quantity remain in high demand. Despite rising evidence for the superiority of CBT-I, in practice it is often not available at the scale required to meet clinical guidelines. Targeting the natural brain pathways regulating arousal and brain state represents the common mechanisms of all medications used with varying effectiveness in treating sleep disturbances including insomnia disorder (ID) (Frase, Nissen, Riemann, & Spiegelhalder, 2018). In general, medication either increases sleep drive and relaxation by increasing GABAergic transmission (e.g., benzodiazepines) or decreases vigilance and arousal by inhibiting monoaminergic transmission in the ascending reticular activating system (ARAS; e.g., sedating antidepressants) (Frase et al., 2018). In addition, the melatonin and orexin pathways represent two additional potential targets for pharmacological intervention.

Historically, increasing or modulating GABAergic transmission represents the most common approach. To date, several benzodiazepines (BZ), mainly flunitrazepam, flurazepam, lormetazepam, nitrazepam, temazepam and triazolam, and hypnotic benzodiazepine receptor agonists (BZRA; zaleplon, zolpidem and [es-]zopiclone) are approved for the short-term treatment of insomnia but some of these may not be available in certain countries. Several meta-analyses have concluded as small to medium, but with robust positive effects on objective and subjective sleep parameters for both BZ and BZRA hypnotics (e.g., Winkler, Auer, Doering, & Rief, 2014).

Several medications have demonstrated inhibiting characteristics on monoaminergic transmission in the ARAS. This effect can either limit therapeutic effectiveness by diminishing vigilance and quality of life in patients or can be sought out deliberately to improve sleep. The strongest sedation can be expected from substances with antihistaminergic properties as exhibited by traditional antihistamines (such as diphenhydramine, doxylamine or hydroxyzine), sedating antidepressants (such as doxepine, mirtazapine or trimipramine) or sedating antipsychotics (such as quetiapine, prothipendyl, chlorprothixene or levomepromazin). The second transmitter system with strong sedating effects can be identified as anticholinergic effects, as mainly expected under treatment with doxepine, trimipramine, amitriptyline, chlorprothixene or levomepromazin. Additional sedating effects possibly include antiserotonergic (trazodone) or adrenolytic influences (doxepine, melperone).

As described, potential agents for inhibiting monoaminergic transmission in the ARAS are abundantly available and regularly used. However, scientific evidence for their use in ID is mostly lacking. In a recent Cochrane Database Review, the authors corroborate these limitations by only stating limited evidence in favour of the short-term use of low-dose doxepin or trazodone while highlighting the lacking justification for other substances including amitriptyline and for long-term antidepressant treatment of ID (Everitt et al., 2018).

Melatonin as well as the newly developed melatonin receptor agonists (MRA), ramelteon and tasimelteon, and the structurally similar antidepressant agomelatine have been promoted as a more 'natural' way of improving sleep by increasing the physiological melatonin signal at the beginning of the night. While melatonin and MRAs appear to be effective in circadian rhythm sleep–wake disorders such as jet lag, evidence on effectiveness in ID has been mixed (Frase et al., 2018). While melatonin itself does not induce sedating effects and shows no effectiveness in ID, the MRA ramelteon significantly reduced sleep onset latency without effecting sleep maintenance, leading to its FDA approval in ID (Sateia, Buysse, Krystal, Neubauer, & Heald, 2017). It is noteworthy, however, that the European Agency for the Evaluation of Medicinal Products differed in its evaluation of ramelteon's effectiveness and did not approve its therapeutic use in ID patients (European Medicines Agency, 2008).

Since its identification as the main neurotransmitter involved in narcolepsy, a very severe hypersomnia in which sleep maintenance as well as vigilance sustainability are highly disturbed, orexin (synonym: hypocretin) has been a promising target for the development of new hypnotics. The first FDA approved selective, dual orexin receptor antagonist suvorexant, has demonstrated a slight improvement in total sleep time in clinical trials (Sateia et al., 2017). Several similar substances are under investigation, including almorexant, daridorexant and seltorexant. So far, no orexin receptor antagonists are approved for ID treatment in the European Union.

In keeping with the stated evidence, the European guideline for the diagnosis and treatment of insomnia recommends BZ or BZRA for the short-term treatment of insomnia if CBT-I is not effective or not available (Riemann et al., 2017). Sedating antidepressants are considered effective only in the short-term treatment of insomnia, but contraindications have to be carefully considered (Riemann et al., 2017). No pharmacological treatment options are recommended for long-term treatment >4 weeks. Other substance groups, e.g., antihistamines, antipsychotics and phytotherapy (herbal therapy) are not recommended, either due to lack of evidence for their effectiveness and/or unfavourable adverse effect rates. The AASM guideline slightly differs from these recommendations by differentiating between sleep-onset and sleep maintenance insomnia (Sateia et al., 2017). For the improvement of sleep latency, the melatonin receptor agonist ramelteon is recommended next to BZ (triazolam, temazepam) and the BZRAs.

For sleep maintenance, doxepine and the orexin receptor antagonist suvorexant are recommended in addition to BZ (temazepam) and BZRA (zolpidem and [es]zopiclone) drugs. This guideline explicitly advises against the use of antihistamines, melatonin, the anticonvulsant tiagabine, trazodone, L-tryptophan and valerian (Sateia et al., 2017).

In summary, pharmacotherapy for ID treatment should be considered if CBT-I is not effective or not available. Following evidence-based treatment guidelines, clinicians should either select the BZ triazolam (0.25 mg daily dose, DD) or temazepam (15 mg DD), or the BZRA zolpidem (10 mg DD) or (es-)zopiclone (2–3 mg DD), with a slight preference for BZRA due to the optimised pharmacokinetics. If BZ and BZRA need to be avoided, for example due to age, past substance dependence or other contraindications, low-dose doxepine (3–6 mg DD) appears to be the most favourable alternative. In all uses of medication, treatment needs to be carefully and regularly administered by professional care providers and limited to short-term treatment of <4 weeks.

Pharmacotherapy for insomnia – Special populations

Several clinical populations experience a higher prevalence rate of ID while on the other hand exhibit a reduced tolerability regarding adverse effects of potential medical interventions; e.g., very young (<18 years) or elderly patients (>64 years), or ID occurring during pregnancy (Frase et al., 2018). The resulting clinical challenge is noticeable in the absence of specifications concerning these subgroups in all the published guidelines (Riemann et al., 2017; Sateia et al., 2017). However, several consensus papers try to complement the existing guidelines (e.g., Bruni et al., 2015). For children and adolescents, BZ, BZRA and antihistamines should be avoided, while the use of antidepressants and antipsychotics should be limited to severe cases with co-morbid mental disorders (Frase et al., 2018). Of note, melatonin appears to be more effective in ID treatment in children and adolescents, especially in cases with co-morbid ADHD, autism or other developmental disorders (Bruni et al., 2015). In the elderly, BZ and BZRA are now considered inappropriate (American Geriatrics Society, 2015), as well as antihistamines. Antidepressants and antipsychotics should be closely monitored, mainly due to more severe anticholinergic adverse effects, and limited to severe cases, potentially with co-morbid mental disorders (Frase et al., 2018). Of note, prolonged-release melatonin (circadin) appears to show slightly more effectiveness in ID treatment in the elderly, leading to its approval for patients older than 55 years in the European Union. During pregnancy, ID prevalence reaches as high as 80%, but a completely safe pharmacological treatment option is lacking (Frase et al., 2018). Treatment decisions should therefore always carefully consider the potential risk for mother and child due to the medication in contrast to the risk and burden of untreated insomnia (Chaudhry & Susser, 2018).

Combining pharmacotherapy and CBT-I

As stated earlier, treatment guidelines prominently highlight the importance of CBT-I as the first-line treatment of ID, with pharmacotherapy only being recommended if CBT-I is not effective or not available. However, the question of combining pharmacotherapy and CBT-I regularly arises, as patients either might need additional treatment while waiting for an eligible CBT-I therapist, respond only partially while receiving CBT-I or already are receiving long-term hypnotic pharmacotherapy when beginning CBT-I. In theory, sedating substances such as BZ and BZRA might interfere with concurrent CBT-I by hindering neural plasticity and thereby interfering with learning new cognitive concepts or behaviours. On the other hand, short-term sleep benefits induced by medication might increase the patient's ability to engage in psychotherapy and apply behavioural changes.

Empirical evidence supporting the combination of pharmacotherapy with CBT-I

A recent network meta-analysis included 28 randomized controlled trials on ID treatment for elderly patients using PSQI scores as the main outcome criteria (Kwon et al., 2020). The authors reported acupuncture, benzodiazepines and CBT-I as more effective than a wait-list. Interestingly, combined protocols, e.g., benzodiazepines combined with CBT-I, appeared superior to either intervention alone (Kwon et al., 2020). Another review compared several commonly used interventions for insomnia regarding effectiveness and safety and concluded that short-term application of melatonin, zolpidem, suvorexant or doxepin can be added to non-pharmacological therapy (Rios et al., 2019). Although only preliminary data have been published so far, a novel trial on remote CBT-I enhanced by ACT (acceptance commitment therapy) elements specifically targeted patients with ID and co-morbid hypnotic dependence, and reported significant improvements in insomnia symptoms, a reduction in hypnotic use and a general quality of life increase compared to a waiting-list condition (Chapoutot et al., 2021).

It can be summarised that a combination of pharmacotherapy with CBT-I is feasible and effective according to the literature and can be considered if CBT-I alone does not lead to remission.

Deprescribing of hypnotic medications

As stated earlier, the use of BZ or BZRA in insomnia should be limited to <4 weeks due to lack of effectiveness and highly relevant adverse effects, including dependence during long term treatment. However, many patients experience difficulties in reducing use, which leads to a high prevalence of up to 70% chronic users (Neutel, 2005). While many guidelines recommend limited BZ/BZRA use (Riemann et al., 2017; Sateia et al., 2017), only limited evidence on optimal deprescribing strategies exists (Lee, Farrell & Holbrook, 2019). Difficulties include motivational aspects, providing effective treatment alternatives for the sleep disturbances and precise tapering protocols (Lee et al., 2019). In their deprescribing algorithm published in 2018, an expert group of Canadian physicians and pharmacists recommended BZ and BZRA deprescribing for all ID patients older than 64 years regardless of treatment duration and for all younger patients after 4 weeks of treatment (Pottie et al., 2018).

Clinical tapering protocol

The BZ and BZRA Deprescribing Algorithm (Pottie et al., 2018) recommends the following steps:

- Detailed patient information regarding benefits of deprescribing, symptoms of withdrawal and tapering, as well as all planned steps during tapering.
- Gradual dose reduction of ~25% every two weeks, with dose reduction of ~12.5% near the end.
- Inclusion of planned intermittent drug-free days during tapering.
- Concomitant behavioural sleep advice or CBT-I if available.
- Monitoring by a qualified therapist every 1–2 weeks for expected benefits and/or withdrawal symptoms.
- In case of an ID symptom relapse, maintaining of the current dose for 1–2 weeks and then continuing of tapering at a reduced rate.

Conclusion

Pharmacotherapy for ID should be considered as a second line treatment if CBT-I is not effective or not available. A combination of pharmacotherapy with CBT-I is feasible and effective, and can be considered if CBT-I alone does not lead to remission. Pharmacological treatment options should be limited to short-term treatment because of a lack of evidence supporting long-term treatment. Therefore, therapeutic challenges in treating chronic insomnia arise frequently and include deprescribing difficulties.

References

American Geriatrics Society (2015). Updated beers criteria for potentially inappropriate medication use in older adults. *Journal of the American Geriatrics Society*, *63* (11), 2227–2246. https://doi.org/10.1111/jgs.13702.

Bruni, O., Alonso-Alconada, D., Besag, F., Biran, V., Braam, W., Cortese, S., Moavero, R., Parisi, P., Smits, M., Van der Heijden, K., & Curatolo, P. (2015). Current role of melatonin in pediatric neurology: Clinical recommendations. *European Journal of Paediatric Neurology (EJPN): Official Journal of the European Paediatric Neurology Society*, *19* (2), 122–133. https://doi.org/10.1016/j.ejpn.2014.12.007.

Chapoutot, M., Peter-Derex, L., Schoendorff, B., Faivre, T., Bastuji, H., & Putois, B. (2021). Telehealth-delivered CBT-I programme enhanced by acceptance and commitment therapy for insomnia and hypnotic dependence: A pilot randomized controlled trial. *Journal of Sleep Research*, *30* (1), e13199. https://doi.org/10.1111/jsr.13199.

Chaudhry, S. K., & Susser, L. C. (2018). Considerations in treating insomnia during pregnancy: A literature review. *Psychosomatics*. Advance online publication. https://doi.org/10.1016/j.psym.2018.03.009.

European Medicines Agency (2008). Questions and answers on recommendation for the refusal of the marketing authorization for ramelteon. Document Reference EMEA/CHMP/268216/2008. Retrieved from: www.emea.europa.eu/pdfs/human/opinion/Ramelteon_26821608en.pdf.

Everitt, H., Baldwin, D. S., Stuart, B., Lipinska, G., Mayers, A., Malizia, A. L., Manson, C. C., & Wilson, S. (2018). Antidepressants for insomnia in adults. *The Cochrane Database of Systematic Reviews*, *5*, CD010753. https://doi.org/10.1002/14651858.CD010753.pub2.

Frase, L., Nissen, C., Riemann, D., & Spiegelhalder, K. (2018). Making sleep easier: Pharmacological interventions for insomnia. *Expert Opinion on Pharmacotherapy*, *19* (13), 1465–1473. https://doi.org/10.1080/14656566.2018.1511705.

Kwon, C.-Y., Lee, B., Cheong, M. J., Kim, T.-H., Jang, B.-H., Chung, S. Y., & Kim, J. W. (2020). Non-pharmacological treatment for elderly individuals with insomnia: A systematic review and network meta-analysis. *Frontiers in Psychiatry*, *11*, 608896. https://doi.org/10.3389/fpsyt.2020.608896.

Lee, J. Y., Farrell, B., & Holbrook, A. M. (2019). Deprescribing benzodiazepine receptor agonists taken for insomnia: A review and key messages from practice guidelines. *Polish Archives of Internal Medicine*, *129* (1), 43–49. https://doi.org/10.20452/pamw.4391.

Neutel, C. I. (2005). The epidemiology of long-term benzodiazepine use. *International Review of Psychiatry (Abingdon, England)*, *17* (3), 189–197. https://doi.org/10.1080/09540260500071863.

Pottie, K., Thompson, W., Davies, S., Grenier, J., Sadowski, C. A., Welch, V., Holbrook, A., Boyd, C., Swenson, R., Ma, A., & Farrell, B. (2018). Deprescribing benzodiazepine receptor agonists: Evidence-based clinical practice guideline. *Canadian Family Physician Medecin De Famille Canadien*, 64(5), 339–351.

Riemann, D., Baglioni, C., Bassetti, C., Bjorvatn, B., Dolenc Groselj, L., Ellis, J. G., Espie, C. A., Garcia-Borreguero, D., Gjerstad, M., Gonçalves, M., Hertenstein, E., Jansson-Fröjmark, M., Jennum, P. J., Leger, D., Nissen, C., Parrino, L., Paunio, T., Pevernagie, D., Verbraecken, J., Weeß, H. G., Wichniak, A., Zavalko, I., Arnardottir, E. S., Deleanu, O. C., Strazisar, B., Zoetmulder, M., & Spiegelhalder, K. (2017). European guideline for the diagnosis and treatment of insomnia. *Journal of Sleep Research*, *26* (6), 675–700. https://doi.org/10.1111/jsr.12594.

Rios, P., Cardoso, R., Morra, D., Nincic, V., Goodarzi, Z., Farah, B., Harricharan, S., Morin, C. M., Leech, J., Straus, S. E., & Tricco, A. C. (2019). Comparative effectiveness and safety of pharmacological and non-pharmacological interventions for insomnia: An overview of reviews. *Systematic Reviews*, *8* (1), 281. https://doi.org/10.1186/s13643-019-1163-9.

Sateia, M. J., Buysse, D. J., Krystal, A. D., Neubauer, D. N., & Heald, J. L. (2017). Clinical Practice Guideline for the Pharmacologic Treatment of Chronic Insomnia in Adults: An American Academy of Sleep Medicine Clinical Practice Guideline. *Journal of Clinical Sleep Medicine (JCSM): Official Publication of the American Academy of Sleep Medicine*, *13* (2), 307–349. https://doi.org/10.5664/jcsm.6470.

Winkler, A., Auer, C., Doering, B. K., & Rief, W. (2014). Drug treatment of primary insomnia: A meta-analysis of polysomnographic randomized controlled trials. *CNS Drugs*, 28 (9), 799–816. https://doi.org/10.1007/s40263-014-0198-7.

Section II

A Focus on Lifespan and Professional Factors

Section Editor: Colin A. Espie

7

Protocols for Sleep Initiation and Maintenance Problems in Paediatric Populations

Dimitri Gavriloff, Valeria Bacaro, Angelika Schlarb and Chiara Baglioni

Key points

- Sleep problems are common in children and young people and often result in a range of functional impairments across cognitive, emotional, behavioural and academic domains.
- Sleep plays a crucial role in healthy human development but data from many countries indicates that significant proportions of children and adolescents do not regularly achieve the recommended sleep durations outlined in clinical guidance.
- There is a robust evidence base for the cognitive-behavioural treatment of sleep problems in children and young people.

Learning objectives

- To understand how sleep changes across childhood and adolescence.
- To be able to recommend healthy sleep habits for children and young people and explain their theoretical rationale.
- To be able to implement evidence-based cognitive-behavioural interventions for child and adolescent sleep problems.

Abstract

Sleep plays a crucial role in healthy human development. Nevertheless, burgeoning societal data from many countries indicates that significant proportions of children and adolescents do not regularly achieve the recommended sleep duration outlined in clinical guidance. Furthermore, there is a high prevalence of sleep initiation and maintenance disorders in paediatric populations. These disorders are strongly associated with behavioural and emotional problems, which in turn impact educational progress and social development. Despite their widespread prevalence and the deleterious impact they have on the health and quality of life of both children and their families, paediatric sleep disorders are generally poorly understood and remain undertreated in many clinical settings. Improving clinical education on the cognitive-behavioural management of paediatric insomnia for clinicians at all levels of paediatric care is, therefore, of great importance. This chapter is intended to be used as a primer for clinicians undertaking the assessment and cognitive-behavioural treatment of sleep problems in paediatric patients in the childhood and adolescent years. It will focus on presenting cognitive-behavioural protocols for problems initiating and/or maintaining sleep, as well as discussion of issues surrounding assessment and diagnosis.

Keywords *CBT-I, sleep initiation, sleep maintenance, insomnia, children, adolescents, paediatric*

Cognitive-Behavioural Therapy for Insomnia (CBT-I) Across the Life Span: Guidelines and Clinical Protocols for Health Professionals, First Edition. Edited by Chiara Baglioni, Colin A. Espie and Dieter Riemann.

Introduction

Sleep plays a crucial role in healthy human development (e.g., Dahl, 1996; Mindell, Leichman, DuMond & Sadeh, 2017; Williamson, Mindell, Hiscock & Quach, 2020). During infancy and toddlerhood, children spend more time asleep than they spend awake and continue to require higher than adult sleep durations until the end of adolescence (Mindell & Owens, 2015). Nevertheless, burgeoning societal data from many countries indicates that significant proportions of children and adolescents do not achieve the recommended sleep durations outlined in clinical guidance (summarised in Table 7.1; Matricciani, Olds & Petkov, 2012).

The prevalence of sleep disorders in paediatric populations is generally high. Furthermore, these disorders are strongly associated with behavioural and emotional problems, which in turn impact educational progress and social development (e.g., Mindell et al., 2017; Hysing, Harvey, Linton, Askeland & Sivertsen, 2016). Prevalence rates for specific paediatric sleep disorders range from 1 to 3% for obstructive sleep apnoea to as high as 20–30% for insomnia disorder (Owens, 2008). Insomnia, in particular, is often underdiagnosed and poorly managed in paediatric clinical practice (Meltzer, Johnson, Crosette, Ramos & Mindell, 2010). This is underpinned by insufficient training of paediatric clinicians in the appropriate assessment and treatment of behavioural sleep problems, something reported by both parents of patients and by the clinicians themselves (Bruni et al., 2004).

Comprehensive assessment and formulation of paediatric sleep disorders should have as its basis a foundational understanding of the characteristics of normative sleep across the developmental trajectory. Additionally, it should ideally follow a biopsychosocial approach where contextual, parental, familial, societal and environmental influences are given due consideration. This is particularly the case where there is a strong family dynamic that has a bearing upon the sleep problem, such as with cases of poor parental understanding of sleep–wake regulation or normative circadian developmental change, or lack of appropriate limit setting and routines. These interactions are represented graphically in Figure 7.1.

Table 7.1 Recommended sleep duration during development.

	Newborns	Infants	Toddlers	Preschoolers	School-aged children	Adolescents
May be appropriate	11–19 hours	10–18 hours	9–16 hours	8–14 hours	7–12 hours	7–11 hours
Recommended	14–17 hours	12–15 hours	11–14 hours	10–13 hours	9–11 hours	8–10 hours

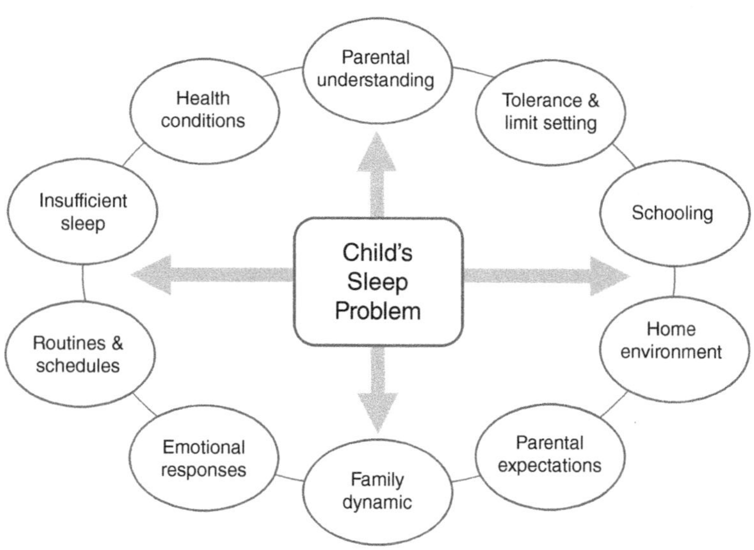

Figure 7.1 Dynamic family interactions with regard to sleep behaviours.

Despite their widespread prevalence and the deleterious impact that they have on the lives of both children and their families, paediatric sleep disorders are generally poorly understood and undertreated in many clinical settings (Meltzer, Plaufcan, Thomas & Mindell, 2010; 2014; Honaker & Meltzer, 2016). Improving clinical education on behavioural management of paediatric insomnia for clinicians at all levels of paediatric care is, therefore, a vital means of improving access to such interventions. However, it is also important to consider cultural, familial and parental attitudes to the child's sleep problem and to allow a choice of approach that aligns with the patient's, or their parents', preference.

This chapter is intended to be a primer for clinicians undertaking the assessment and cognitive-behavioural treatment of sleep problems in paediatric patients of all ages. It will focus on presenting cognitive-behavioural protocols for problems initiating and/or maintaining sleep, as well as a discussion of issues surrounding assessment and diagnosis. Clinical protocols will be presented for three aggregated developmental stages: infancy and toddlerhood, preschool and school-aged children and adolescents.

Diagnosis of insomnia

A diagnosis of chronic insomnia disorder is given where there is a regular (≥ 3 nights per week) and persistent (> 3 months) difficulty initiating or maintaining sleep that is associated with day-time functional impairment (e.g., mood, concentration, fatigue). In the two most widely used diagnostic schedules, the *Diagnostic and Statistical Manual of Mental Disorders*, 5th edition (DSM-5; American Psychiatric Association (APA), 2013) and the *International Classification of Sleep Disorders*, 3rd edition (ICSD-3; American Academy of Sleep Medicine (AASM), 2014), there is no longer a diagnostic distinction made between insomnia experienced by paediatric and adult patients. However, it is worth noting that clinical presentations of insomnia are markedly different in children and adults. Additionally, particularly for younger children, complaints are generally reported by parents as opposed to the patient themselves, and difficulties may be exacerbated by child–parent dynamics. Aetiologically speaking, there are several underlying issues that commonly result in a child's difficulty initiating and maintaining sleep. Often these include the development of unhelpful sleep onset associations (Owens, 2008), typically requiring parental involvement in the facilitation of sleep onset (e.g., presence, rocking, patting). This is often then required to facilitate sleep re-initiation when the child experiences normative nocturnal arousals following the natural ultradian rhythm of sleep cycles. Other common reasons why children may present with bed-time resistance and prolonged sleep onset latency include being put to bed at a time that is incompatible with their own endogenous circadian timings (LeBourgeois, Gomez, Pinto & Mérian, 2013), problems with parental limit setting (Owens, 2008) and absence of consistent bed-time routines (Mindell & Owens, 2015; Mindell & Williamson, 2018). Symptoms of insomnia may also be associated with poor sleep hygiene, such as the child's use of caffeinated beverages, inappropriate sleep schedules (e.g., staying up or sleeping in late) or inappropriately timed use of technology (e.g., TV, smartphone, video games). Finally, the household and bedroom environment also have an effect on a child's sleep. Environmental light, noise, family dynamics and temperature of the room can all influence sleep onset and continuity.

Epidemiology

Behavioural sleep problems in paediatric populations are extremely common. Epidemiological data suggests that approximately 20 to 30% of infants, toddlers and preschool age children regularly experience problems with sleep initiation and maintenance (Lozoff, Wolf & Davis, 1985; Mindell, Kuhn, Lewin, Meltzer & Sadeh, 2006; Sadeh, Mindell, Luedtke & Wiegand, 2009). Although the trajectories of specific sleep problems vary across childhood, these problems often become chronic, with early problems predictive of later difficulties (Stein, Mendelsohn, Obermeyer, Amromin, & Benca, 2001; Mindell et al., 2006; Williamson, Mindell, Hiscock & Quach, 2020).

The development and persistence of sleep problems throughout childhood is associated with several risk factors, including lower socioeconomic status, and maternal and paternal family risks (Williamson et al., 2020). Symptoms of insomnia are also frequently reported during adolescence and are often associated with fatigue and daytime sleepiness (de Zambotti, Goldstone, Colrain & Baker, 2018). Epidemiological estimates suggest that approximately 4–10% of adolescents exhibit symptoms of insomnia (Gau & Soong, 2003; Ohayon, Roberts, Zully, Smirne & Priest, 2000; Johnson, Roth, Schultz & Breslau, 2006).

Differential diagnosis

Given the prevalence of paediatric insomnia in childhood and the overlap in symptomatology between several aetiologically distinct sleep disorders, a crucial aspect in the clinical evaluation of paediatric insomnia is differential diagnosis. Comprehensive and considered assessment of all potential factors that may be contributing to the sleep disturbance is essential in ensuring optimally tailored interventions and treatment success. For example, a child with a later chronotype may have difficulties falling asleep at an earlier bed-time, despite its general appropriateness for the age group, but may easily fall asleep later. As long as this does not impede the child achieving their required nightly sleep need this can be considered non-problematic. However, if the child is unable to achieve adequate sleep at this later bed-time, consideration of a diagnosis and treatment for delayed sleep–wake phase disorder may be appropriate (Auger et al., 2015). Similarly, motor restlessness in a child before bed may be an indication of restless legs syndrome, the symptoms of which younger children may not be able to verbalise or describe. Other sleep disorders, such as periodic limb movement disorder (PLMD), or sleep-related breathing disorders (e.g., obstructive sleep apnoea (OSA)) are also associated with night wakings, difficulties maintaining sleep and both day-time sleepiness and behavioural problems. Careful screening for associated symptoms and signs (e.g., motor restlessness, snoring, observed respiratory pauses) is crucial in confirming a diagnosis of insomnia. Comprehensive assessment is often easier to perform using parental questionnaires completed in advance of the clinical consultation (e.g., Owens, Spirito & McGuinn, 2000). Where another sleep disorder is suspected, appropriate clinical investigations and/or further assessment by a sleep medicine specialist is indicated.

Importantly, individual differences in sleep duration should also be taken into consideration. Although recommended sleep durations for age groups are reported in normative ranges (Hirshkowitz et al., 2015; see Table 7.1), some children may need less time asleep than their peers, and some may need more. Unlike those with insomnia, these children may not complain of day-time insomnia symptoms and, despite a relatively short sleep duration, should not be given a diagnosis of insomnia.

Co-morbidity

Insomnia is often co-morbid with depression and anxiety (Calhoun, Fernandez-Mendoza, Vgontzas, Liao & Bixler, 2014), as well as with medical disorders (Roth et al., 2006), and until relatively recently was regularly considered symptomatic of other underlying conditions. Where it presented alongside another disorder, it was generally towards the comorbid condition that clinical intervention was focused. However, current clinical understanding and guidance suggests that insomnia should be treated wherever it presents, either comorbid with another disorder or in isolation (APA, 2013; AASM, 2014). Nevertheless, adequate assessment of co-morbid conditions is strongly recommended, as it may be necessary for parallel treatment to be initiated.

Infancy and toddlerhood (0–3 years)

Definition of the population in terms of sleep characteristics

The first three years of life constitute a period of rapid and dynamic developmental change, including changes to both sleep architecture and sleep-related behaviours (Coons & Guilleminault, 1984; Acebo et al., 2005; Henderson, France & Blampied, 2011). These continue to evolve throughout childhood along with a tendency to spend progressively less time asleep and more time awake throughout the 24-hour period. In healthy babies born at term, it is possible to discern the two distinct sleep states of 'active' and 'quiet' sleep, corresponding to REM and NREM sleep states respectively. A newborn's total sleep is approximately equally distributed across both active and quiet sleep states with total sleep times typically around 16 to 17 hours across the 24-hour period, irregularly punctuated by feeding (Sheldon, Ferber, Kryger & Gozal, 2014). Although the development of circadian rhythms begins in utero, photic entrainment of circadian rhythmicity and establishment of circadian patterns of core body temperature have been shown to take place by approximately three months (Rivkees, 2003; Lodemore, Petersen & Wailoo, 1991). Average total sleep times across the 24-hour period between birth and three months range between 14 and 17 hours (Hirshkowitz et al., 2015). Over the child's first year ever more consolidated sleep takes place at night, supplemented by day-time naps (Henderson, France, Owens & Blampied, 2010; Henderson, France & Blampied, 2011). Between 4 and 12 months, total sleep needs decrease to a range of between 12 and 15 hours

(Hirshkowitz et al., 2015), including day-time naps of on average totalling three to four hours. Napping may take place as several brief naps, or fewer longer periods of day-time sleep. There is a trend towards a decrease in the number of naps to one by approximately 18 months (Galland, Taylor, Elder & Herbison, 2012). At this age, a sleep onset latency of up to 30 minutes and up to one period of wake after sleep onset of over five minutes is considered appropriate (Ohayon et al., 2017). Between the ages of one and three years old, total sleep times drop to 11 to 14 hours, with approximately two to three hours of day-time napping, generally discontinuing after the age of three (Jenni & Carskadon, 2000). Similarly, a sleep onset latency of up to 30 minutes and up to one night-time awakening of more than five minutes may be considered appropriate at this age (Ohayon et al., 2017).

Definition of common developmental issues with respect to sleep

The centrality of healthy sleep to optimal human development is now well established with robust evidence demonstrating that insufficient sleep in young children is associated with functional and developmental deficits across a range of domains (Sadeh, Gruber & Raviv, 2002; Beebe, 2011; Sadeh, Tikotzky & Kahn, 2014; Owens & Adolescent Sleep Walking Group, 2014; Miller, Lumeng & LeBourgeois, 2015; Williamson et al., 2020). When defining behavioural sleep problems in very young children, a comprehensive understanding of what constitutes normative sleep at this age is crucial. This may, for example, include an appreciation of the irregular sleep-wake patterns of newborns and infants, as well as the disturbances to sleep in infants and toddlers that may result from approaching and achieving developmental milestones, phenomena that may not align with parental expectations. The establishment of photic entrained circadian rhythmicity by approximately three months (Rivkees, 2003) means that infants of this age are physiologically capable of sleeping for consolidated periods at night, however, sleep periods are still punctuated by the drive to feed. In typically developing children, night feeding can often be discontinued by the parents at around six months given daytime nutritional intake is often sufficient to maintain healthy development (Mindell & Owens, 2015).

The most prevalent behavioural sleep problems experienced by families of infants and toddlers are those involving excessive sleep onset latencies, difficulties with independent child sleep initiation and frequent night wakings that necessitate parental involvement in resettling the child (Anders, Halpern & Hua, 1992; Burnham, Goodlin-Jones, Gaylor & Anders, 2002; Bayer, Hiscock, Hampton & Wake, 2007; Mindell et al., 2006; Wake et al., 2006; Sadeh et al., 2009; Touchette et al., 2005). In fact, epidemiological estimates suggest that as many as 30% of young children may experience these problems on a regular basis (Lozoff, Wolf & Davis, 1985; Mindell et al., 2006; Sadeh et al., 2009). Where diagnostic criteria are met, these problems are now classified as insomnia disorder (see introduction) and evidence-based intervention is indicated (Mindell & Owens, 2015). This is not least because these are often persistent sleep problems that, in addition to being associated with poorer child outcomes, convey increased risks to parental mental health and family stress (Hiscock & Wake, 2002; Lam, Hiscock & Wake, 2003; Sadeh, Tikotzky & Scher, 2010; Byars, Yolton, Rausch, Lanphear & Beebe, 2012; Meltzer, Plaufcan, Thomas & Mindell, 2014).

The formulation of these problems is complex and necessitates consideration of the bidirectional relationships between parental (e.g., cognitive, emotional) factors and child sleep (see Sadeh, Tikotsky & Scher, 2010). However, a central perpetuating behavioural factor often seen in infant and toddler sleep problems is the development of maladaptive sleep onset associations (Burnham et al., 2002; Sadeh et al., 2009; Sadeh et al., 2010; Touchette et al., 2005). These associations typically involve excessive parental involvement in the facilitation of sleep onset, such as by rocking, patting or feeding to sleep, but can also develop around passive parental presence during sleep initiation. These associations are then again required following the child's normative nocturnal arousals that happen as part of the ultradian rhythm of sleep cycles (Honaker & Metzler, 2016). The development of the ability of the child to 'self-soothe' and therefore reinitiate sleep independently has long been highlighted as a crucial factor in improving these behaviourally underpinned sleep problems (Keener, Zeanah & Anders, 1988; Burnham et al., 2002; Goodlin-Jones, Burnham, Gaylor & Anders, 2001; Mindell et al., 2006).

Several other important factors should be given adequate consideration in the understanding of difficulties initiating sleep and frequent night wakings in young children. First, ensuring consistency and appropriateness of bed-time or 'wind down' routines prior to sleep initiation has been shown to be associated with better sleep in younger children (Mindell & Owens, 2015; Mindell & Williamson, 2018). Consistency of approach is important to convey to parents, not least because night to night variability in behaviours is often seen routinely in young children. Additionally, abrupt and transient change in both day-time and sleep-related behaviour is often associated with the approach to or achievement of developmental milestones or, indeed, periods of illness (Mindell et al., 2006). Although the sleep problems experienced during these periods are temporary, where parents begin to engage in behaviours that reinforce difficulties with sleep onset or night waking, they may persist. The inappropriateness of a child's bed-time relative to their chronotype has also been highlighted as a potential perpetuating factor in the emergence of difficulties initiating sleep, or 'bed-time resistance' as it is also known (LeBourgeois et al., 2013). Specifically, LeBourgeois and colleagues (2013) found that children put to bed with narrower phase angles (i.e., a time that was closer to their natural dim light melatonin onset (DLMO)) and those with naturally later DLMO experienced on average longer sleep onset latencies and more bed-time resistance. Another central factor that may mediate excessive parental involvement in children's sleep onset is the degree of a parents' tolerance for their child crying (Sadeh et al., 2016; Kahn et al., 2020). Lower parental cry tolerance in parents of children with sleep problems is associated with higher attribution of child distress and shorter delays in intervening, suggesting an innate susceptibility for these parents to need to intervene more readily and soothe their children to sleep (Sadeh et al., 2016). Comprehensive appreciation of such parental factors, including their informed choice of intervention, is crucial in ensuring optimal behavioural treatment outcomes for both children and their parents. Co-sleeping, defined as room-sharing and bed-sharing typically with siblings or adult caregivers, is also often a source of problems with independent sleep initiation and maintenance. Co-sleeping is a contentious area because it is variously associated with both positive and negative health-related outcomes (Mindell & Owens, 2015; Keller & Goldberg, 2004). Additionally, it is often associated with cultural attitudes and lifestyle factors (Okami, Weisner & Olmstead, 2002) that may not be pertinent to all families (Sadeh et al., 2010). Appreciation of these factors is important in the assessment of the impact of co-sleeping, and whether or not the co-sleeping has been implemented in response to a child's sleep difficulties. Additionally, appropriate assessment of risk to the safety of infants who co-sleep is important, as is provision of advice to parents around how to do so safely (e.g., American Academy of Pediatrics, 2005) should they choose to do so.

Preschool and school years

Definition of the population in terms of sleep characteristics

Recommended total sleep times vary greatly across the preschool and school years, with preschoolers (3–5 years) recommended between 10 and 13 hours and school-aged children (6–12 years) recommended to have between 9 and 11 hours. Importantly, during the preschool years, most children will also discontinue their day-time naps (Jenni & Carskadon, 2000). Similar to younger aged children, being able to fall asleep independent of parental presence and without excessive parental involvement continues to be important at these ages. Recommendations from the National Sleep Foundation (Ohayon et al., 2017; Hirshkowitz et al., 2015) suggest that an appropriate sleep onset latency would be less than 30 minutes and wake after sleep onset should not be longer than 20 minutes. Although individual differences in circadian preference should be considered, later bedtimes (i.e., those that result in insufficient opportunity for sleep) are associated with reduced total sleep time and increased wake after sleep onset in children of all ages (Mindell, Meltzer, Carskadon & Chervin, 2009).

Definition of common developmental issues with respect to sleep

The preschool years are associated with large-scale psychosocial and developmental changes that include nursery and school attendance. During this period, the development of language, cognition and social skills continue apace and there are opportunities for these to impact sleep and sleep-related behaviour. Examples of these may include greater independence in the bed-time routine (e.g., reading before bed) and progressively later bed-times, but may also include the development of night-time fears and nightmares in relation to fantasy–reality differentiation (Zisenwine, Kaplan, Kushnir & Sadeh, 2013). In addition to this, and in association with age-appropriate development of more independent thinking and behaviours, bed-time resistance may become more explicit. As children mature and become more independent, many maladaptive sleep behaviours may see signs of improvement (Williamson, Mindell, Hiscock & Quach, 2020). However, this change is often slow, and reinforcement and modelling of healthy sleep behaviours during this period continues to be very important for promoting good sleep in both children and their families (Allen, Howlett, Coulombe & Corkum, 2016). Sleep problems which impact other members of the family (e.g., co-sleeping, requiring parental presence at bedtime) continue to be relatively common and are likely to persist with sustained behavioural reinforcement by parents and caregivers (Williamson et al., 2020). Despite this, the behavioural treatment of sleep problems in children of this age is effective using a range of evidence-based approaches (Mindell et al., 2006). These may even be relatively low intensity interventions, such as simply ensuring consistency of bed-time routine, which has been shown to be associated with improved sleep in preschool children (Mindell, Li, Sadeh, Kwon, & Goh, 2015).

In school-age children, participation in extra-curricular activities and duties may be associated with relatively delayed bed-times (Zhang, Li, Fok & Wing, 2010). Furthermore, the increased importance of and nuance surrounding peer relationships and academic homework may increase anxiety, which may in turn affect sleep (Rubin, Coplan & Bowker, 2009). In recent years, overuse of electronic devices at this age has garnered much attention in the media, and their use, especially at bed-time, has been associated with poor sleep in preschool and school-aged children (Cain & Gradisar, 2010). As children reach older childhood and adolescence, there is a natural delay in circadian sleep–wake timings that may lead to an inability to achieve sufficient nightly sleep. During this period, difficulties with sleep onset that may be biologically driven may be exacerbated by worries and frustrations associated with the sleep problem (Saxvig, Pallesen, Wilhelmsen-Langeland, Molde & Bjorvatn, 2012). Additionally, school-aged children may display high variability in sleep–wake patterns between weekdays and weekends, which may be associated with sleep problems (Mishra, Pandey, Minz & Arora, 2017).

Adolescence

Definition of the population in terms of sleep characteristics

Recommendations from the National Sleep Foundation suggest that adolescents should get between 8 and10 hours of nocturnal sleep (Hirschkowitz et al., 2015). Prolonged sleep onset latency is defined by the *Diagnostic and Statistical Manual of Mental Disorders* (5th edition (DSM-5); American Psychiatric Association (APA), 2013) as taking more than 30 minutes to fall asleep, with problematic nocturnal awakenings defined in similar terms. However, natural changes in circadian rhythms during adolescence, including evening melatonin secretion and sleep–wake timings, often result in difficulties with initiating sleep sufficiently early to allow an adequate opportunity for nightly sleep needs to be met on school days. The often ensuing significant sleep deficits in this age group also then impact day-time function (Saxvig et al., 2012). Many adolescents may also manage this with afternoon naps that further impact later bed-times (Malone et al., 2016).

Definition of common developmental issues with respect to sleep

Adolescence is a period of dynamic developmental change along biological, psychological and social lines. Besides the many physiological changes that take place during puberty, adolescence is also a time for important lifestyle, psychosocial and behavioural changes (e.g., peer-group social activities, part-time jobs, increased media usage) that are also likely to influence sleep. Despite the increasing independence of the young person and parents playing less of a role in terms of sleep management at this developmental stage, parental limit-setting – especially rules concerning bed-times and evening screen-use – seem to be important factors that influence sleep quality and duration.

Smartphone usage in adolescents is associated with later bed-times, shorter sleep duration, longer sleep onset latency, insomnia or sleep difficulties, worse sleep quality and sleep efficiency, impaired day-time function, and day-time sleepiness (Thomée, Härenstam & Hagberg, 2011). It is, however, important to consider young people's motivation for their smartphone use, as these may be used in bed to avoid worries and rumination by offering distraction (Kater & Schlarb, 2020). Also characteristic of the sleep patterns associated with this age group are day-time functional impairments seen alongside truncated weekday sleep, relative to the improved function and longer sleep durations seen on weekends. Understandably, many adolescents will regularly sleep in much later on weekends as a means of managing the sleep deficits accrued during the week. An unintended consequence of this approach is, however, subsequent difficulty falling asleep on Sunday evenings, resulting in particular difficulties with day-time sleepiness on Monday mornings for up to 70% of adolescents (Taylor, Wright & Lack, 2008).

Clinical assessment of behavioural sleep problems in paediatric populations

Assessment of sleep problems in young children (infants, toddlers and preschoolers, 0–5 years) is generally based solely on parental report and must take into account parental perception of the sleep problem and expectations regarding normal sleep. For school-aged children (6–12 years), assessment of the sleep problem is still principally directed at parents but may also involve the child themselves. Finally, assessment of sleep problems in adolescents will be principally directed by the self-report of the young person themselves but may still include information from parents. Assessment of the latter must also take into account the young person's own perception of their sleep problem and their motivation for change.

Comprehensive assessment may include:

- Sleep history for both parents and for the child, including the presence of any family history of sleep disorders and onset of a current problem.
- Information on the child's sleep, including:
  - Presence of a set bed-time and its appropriateness
  - Degree of parental involvement at bed-time
  - Bed-time routines: presence, content, timings and duration
  - Use of electronic devices (particularly in the two hours prior to bed-time)
  - Any sleep onset associations (e.g., nursing, rocking)
  - Any examples of bed-time resistance (e.g., calling out, tantrums)
  - Whether the child can fall asleep independently
  - Levels of day-time sleepiness and difficulties waking independently
  - Information on the child's bedroom (e.g., whether they have their own room, whether it is shared, whether they fall asleep elsewhere and are transferred to bed, etc.)
  - Duration and timing of any day-time naps
  - Presence and description of any night-time behaviours
  - Reports of any day-time behaviours that are suspected to be associated with the sleep disturbance (e.g., difficulties maintaining wakefulness, challenging behaviour, mood impairment)
  - Use of any prescription or non-prescription sleep aids (e.g., melatonin, OTC products)
- Any relevant family medical and psychosocial history
- Assessment of school functioning and related impairments (e.g., impaired concentration)
- A full psychological and medical history (including use of psychometric questionnaires and/or semi-structured diagnostic interviews where appropriate).
- Behavioural assessment of the sleep problem
- Presence of any symptoms of other sleep disorders (e.g., loud snoring, sleepwalking)

Several standardised questionnaires for assessing childhood sleep problems exist and can be used alongside the above (e.g., Children's Sleep Habits Questionnaire (CSHQ); Owens, Spirito, & McGuinn, 2000).

Considerations for parental assessment

Before initiating treatment for suspected behavioural sleep problems, appropriate and comprehensive assessment of the presenting problems should be made. Whilst assessment should include a full clinical and developmental history, it is also important to collect information on several other factors that may impact treatment.

These factors might include cultural attitudes towards certain sleep practices (e.g., co-sleeping), parental attitudes towards particular behavioural approaches (e.g., extinction-based approaches), parental expectations, any previous treatment and, of course, a comprehensive overview of the sleep patterns and sleep-related behaviours of the child. The latter may be elicited effectively by asking parents to relate a typical example of a 24-hour period, in which both day (e.g., timing of meals, activity and day-time naps) and night-time contextual factors can be elicited, including any differences in consistency between weekday and weekends. In addition to excluding the presence of other sleep disorders with different aetiological foundations and clinical indications, this ensures an optimal 'fit' of treatment approach that aligns with parental expectations and may enhance treatment adherence and outcomes. For example, parents with lower cry tolerance and higher distress attribution may well find certain behavioural interventions more challenging and may either require amended treatment approaches or more support in adhering to treatment (Etherton, Blunden & Hauck, 2016; Kahn et al., 2020).

Considerations for assessment with school-aged children

For school-aged children, more information can be collected both by talking to the child about his/her own perception of the problem and by using questionnaires designed for this age group. An innovative and useful psychometric tool that can be used here is the Children's Sleep Comic (CSC) (Schwerdtle, Kanis, Kubler & Schlarb, 2016). The CSC is a tool for self-reporting and assessing sleeping habits and sleep problems in children 5 to 11 years old and was validated based on other tools like the CSHQ (Owens et al., 2000) and a diagnostic interview of paediatric sleep disorders.

Considerations for assessment with adolescents

Although adolescent assessment is principally based on the young person's self-report, it is still important to consider the wider impact of the family dynamic relative to this. Thus, it may be useful to include questionnaires for parents and single sessions dedicated to all family members together.

Instruments: Sleep diaries and ancillary assessment tools

Sleep diaries

It is recommended that use of a standardised sleep diary (e.g., Consensus Sleep Diary; Carney et al., 2012) is routinely included in the comprehensive assessment of insomnia in both adults and children (American Academy of Sleep Medicine (AASM), 2014). Diaries are typically kept for a period of two weeks prior to an assessment consultation, to provide the clinician with an overview of current sleep–wake patterns and sleep parameters. If the sleep–wake pattern is considered representative of current sleep, one week of sleep diary may be sufficient to inform diagnosis. Sleep parameters that are calculated from sleep diaries include mean sleep onset latency (SOL), mean time spent awake during the night (i.e., wake after sleep onset (WASO)), sleep efficiency (i.e., total sleep time/total time in bed × 100), number of night awakenings, ratings of sleep quality, etc. (see Chapter 7.4). Parental perceptions and observations can also be noted, which provide yet more data to inform treatment. These observations may include information on the child or young person's emotional state, their activity during the day, any particular stressors and any sleep-related behaviours. School-aged children can also be included in the process of recording a sleep diary. In Appendix I a standard paediatric sleep diary is illustrated.

As sleep diaries provide a window into any differences in sleep patterns for weekdays relative to weekends, their data can be crucial in determining whether a young person's sleep patterns may be the result of a circadian rhythm sleep–wake disorder, such as delayed sleep–wake phase disorder (DSWPD). Differential diagnosis of disorders such as DSWPD from insomnia is important in ensuring that the young person receives an appropriate treatment approach. Although sleep diaries are important for informing diagnosis, their use is encouraged throughout the active treatment and follow-up phases so that appraisal of a change in sleep can be monitored by both the clinician and patient.

Questionnaires

Several validated and standardised sleep-specific questionnaires and psychometrics can be used by the assessing clinician to inform their formulation. For infants and toddlers, there is the Brief Infant Sleep Questionnaire (BISQ) (Sadeh, 2004), which is available to parents in two formats (11-item and 33-item versions) and designed for use with children from birth to 29 months. Another widely used questionnaire for younger children is the Children's Sleep Habits Questionnaire (CSHQ) (Owens, 2000), a 35-item questionnaire for use with children from 4 to 10 years old. The Sleep Self Report (Owens et al., 2000) is an 18-item self-report measure that corresponds to the CSHQ and can be used from ages 7 to 12 to elicit the perspectives of the child or young person themselves. Additionally, there is the Sleep Disturbance Scale for Children (SDSC) (Bruni et al., 1996), which is a 26-item measure that assesses a range of sleep-related problems and behaviours in children from 6 to 15 years old.

Although not routinely used in the assessment of behavioural sleep problems in children, the Epworth Sleepiness Scale for Children (Melendres, Lutz, Rubin, & Marcus, 2004) may be helpful where there is significant day-time somnolence. This seven-item measure has been designed for children and adolescents from 6 to 19 years old.

Protocols for the behavioural treatment of paediatric sleep problems in infants and toddlers

Sleep education and healthy sleep practices

A common starting point for intervention in children's sleep problems is to discuss the characteristics of normative sleep in children, including recommended total sleep durations, day-time napping and timing, and effects of developmental changes on sleep and sleep-related circadian processes. Additionally, this typically includes an in-depth discussion of healthy sleep practices, often termed *sleep hygiene*, relating to both behavioural and environmental factors that impact sleep (see Mindell & Owens, 2015, pp. 59–67). Typical sleep hygiene recommendations include information on the importance of:

- Consistency of sleep–wake timings (including napping), as well as activity and meal timings: recommendations on regular bed-times (regular sleep schedules with consistent nap-times, bed-times and wake-times).
- Napping schedules (i.e., ensuring optimal periods of wake in between napping, avoiding excessive delays to napping and ensuring napping does not take place too close to bed-time).
- Ensuring a consistent and conducive sleep environment (e.g., dark, cool, quiet room).
- Sleep-related safety information (e.g., particularly relating to the reduction of Sudden Infant Death Syndrome (SIDS) risk).
- Consistency of positive sleep onset associations and routines (e.g., regular and appropriate bed-time routine): consider what activities to include in bed-time routines, and keeping activities in bed-time routines consistent. Routines that are generally associated with positive sleep outcomes are quiet calming activities (e.g., bath time, saying goodnight, giving a kiss/hug, softly singing, reading a book).
- Reduction of potential negative sleep onset associations (e.g., putting child down to sleep *drowsy but awake*).
- Avoidance of sleep-disrupting technology use close to bed or nap times: electronic devices should be kept out of children's bedrooms to limit access to electronics during and after bed-time, and to prevent children engaging with electronic devices (e.g., smartphones, televisions, iPods, computers, etc.) too close to bed-time (i.e., within approximately one hour of bed-time).
- Discussion of co-sleeping and its relative merits and disadvantages, in relation to parents personal or cultural beliefs.
- Consistency of day-time routines: ensuring that scheduled day-time activities are not competing with or interfering with sleep time; recommendation to limit or totally eliminate caffeine consumption and to have a healthy balanced diet. Children should be engaged in physical activity on a daily basis, but not too close to bed-time.

Rather than being provided as a list of practices to which parents should adhere, provision of sleep hygiene information is an opportunity for the clinician to work collaboratively with the family to help develop knowledge and confidence in their agency relating to the child's sleep problem. Furthermore, these practices provide a solid and consistent foundation upon which to begin an intervention, increasing the likelihood of successful treatment.

Evidence-based behavioural interventions for infants and toddlers

Behavioural treatments for infant and toddler sleep problems have been extensively reviewed (Mindell et al., 2006; Morgenthaler et al., 2006; Meltzer & Mindell, 2014; Allen, Howlett, Coulombe & Corkum, 2016) with evidence suggesting widespread efficacy. Meta-analytic data suggest that these interventions produce significant effects on sleep-onset latency, number of night wakings, duration of night wakings, and sleep efficiency (Metzler & Mindell, 2014). Many have also been shown to be rapidly effective even when instituted as a relatively low-intensity intervention (Mindell et al., 2017).

Extinction

The behavioural term *extinction* refers to the discontinuation of reinforcement for a given behaviour (in this case an undesirable behaviour, such as a child's insistence on parental presence at bed-time) resulting in the termination of the behaviour. Broadly speaking, this approach is separated into both *unmodified* extinction and *modified* extinction approaches, the latter being a group of approaches known generally as graduated extinction.

Typically, unmodified extinction involves the parent or caregiver ignoring any undesired behaviours (e.g., calling out, crying) from the point of putting the child to bed until a designated time the following morning. The exceptions are in situations where there is concern about the child coming to harm or when the child is unwell. For this reason, this technique is referred to colloquially as the 'cry it out' method. Although unmodified extinction has been shown to be highly effective at improving sleep problems in both younger and older children (Mindell et al., 2006), it is an approach that many parents find particularly stressful and to which many struggle to adhere (Etherton et al., 2016). The unfortunate consequences of this are that when parents find themselves unable to tolerate the sounds of their child crying and intervene, a strong reinforcement of the undesired behaviour takes place, via an intermittent behavioural reinforcement schedule. This risk is often compounded by the experience of an 'extinction burst', a brief increase in the undesired behaviours at the start of the treatment (Owens, France & Wiggs, 1999). Furthermore, if presented as the sole option, 'failure' with unmodified extinction may demotivate parents to try behavioural approaches to managing the sleep problem.

Extinction with parental presence

A minor modification to the standard extinction approach is for parents to be present in the room until the child falls asleep, whilst ignoring any undesirable behaviour such as tantrums or crying. This modification is informally known as 'camping out' and may be a preferable alternative to unmodified extinction for some parents (Mindell et al., 2006). Over successive days parents can gradually increase the distance from where they sit and their child at bed-time, moving closer towards the door and eventually outside it.

Graduated extinction

Although graduated extinction also focuses on discontinuation of reinforcers for an undesired behaviour, it does so in a gradual rather than an abrupt manner. These approaches typically involve parents checking on the child after a given period of time and briefly (generally less than one minute) comforting them before leaving the room again. The intervals can either be kept static (e.g., every 5 minutes), ad hoc (e.g., whenever the parent feels the need to check) or they can increase in duration following successive checks (e.g., 5, 10, 15 minutes). The key factor in this process is that the child learns to fall asleep without parental presence, and hence why parents are entreated to make only brief visits and not to pick up the child to comfort them. Understandably, this is often better tolerated by parents and therefore an approach with which adherence may be optimised by taking into account parental preference (Etherton et al., 2016). Graduated extinction protocols have been found to be similarly highly effective at improving sleep problems in both younger and older children (Mindell et al., 2006).

Faded bed-time with response cost

Another approach to managing the typically lengthy sleep onset latencies, with which many children with sleep problems present, is the faded bed-time with a response cost approach. This method involves using baseline data to determine a time at which sleep onset latency is likely to be 15 minutes or less and pairing this later bed-time with positive sleep associations (e.g., use of transitional objects, child falling asleep without parental presence). The response cost element entails removing the child from bed for a specified period of time if sleep onset has not taken place within 15 minutes. Additionally, a fixed rise time must be kept. This approach and its variants have similarly been found to be effective at reducing sleep onset latency and improving sleep problems in children, although has been most extensively studied in populations of children with developmental disorders (Mindell et al., 2006).

Bed-time passes

Bed-time passes are an extinction-based intervention aimed at providing an alternative to unmodified extinction (Friman et al., 1999). In this approach, children are given a card (a 'Bedtime Pass'), which they are able to trade in with their parents for sanctioned parental attention (e.g., a hug) and other specific behaviours (e.g., leaving the room to get a drink). Parents are instructed that other sleep-disruptive behaviours are to be ignored throughout the rest of the night. The card is then returned to the child the next night and the procedure begins anew. Although not yet extensively studied, it has been shown to produce significant improvements in the reduction of disruptive bed-time behaviours without the extinction burst often seen when using unmodified extinction (Moore, Meltzer & Mindell, 2007). Additionally, it may be augmented by adding an element of positive behavioural reinforcement, whereby when the child retains any passes throughout the night, they receive a pre-specified reward (e.g., a sticker on a reward chart) the following morning (see positive reinforcement strategies below).

Excuse me technique

The 'Excuse Me' approach (EMA) (Kuhn, 2011) was also developed as an alternative to unmodified extinction and utilises both an extinction component (i.e., ignoring sleep-disruptive behaviours) and differential reinforcement of an alternative behaviour (DRA) (see Kuhn, 2011; Kuhn, LaBrot, Ford & Roane, 2020). Parents are instructed to begin with implementing a positive bed-time routine and on putting the child to bed then excuse themselves briefly from the room. Leaving the room is initially done very briefly and the child is then given positive reinforcement (e.g., hugs, praise) for any positive sleep behaviours (e.g., staying in bed). Over subsequent nights the parents can take longer outside the room such that the child gets used to longer periods of being alone and is secure in their expectation of the parent returning. If the child exhibits any sleep incompatible behaviours (e.g., crying), the parents are instructed to ignore these until there is a pause in the behaviour, upon which they can re-enter the room and reinforce any positive sleep-related behaviours (e.g., being in bed). Although not yet extensively studied, EMA has been shown to not only reduce disruptive bed-time behaviours and increase independent sleep onset, but to provide an acceptable alternative to parents who may struggle to implement unmodified extinction (Kuhn et al., 2020).

Evidence-based behavioural interventions for preschool and school children

The cognitive-behavioural treatment of paediatric insomnia in preschoolers is principally a parental therapy, whereas for those at school age inclusion of the child in some parts of the treatment may be recommended. Protocols should be seen as guidelines for treatment and should be modified and adapted according to the specifics of the sleep problem, the motivation and availability of parents, and the needs and capacity of the child (e.g., include sessions together with the child; plan home visits). For this reason, here we consider six fundamental treatment components that should be considered and adapted accordingly. First, components will be described in line with a 'parent only' approach to treatment for both preschool and school-age children. Following this, active involvement of school-age children in the therapeutical process will be described.

Psychoeducation and recommendations for healthy sleep practices or 'Sleep Hygiene'

Table 7.2 displays core topics typically included in the psychoeducation component of a cognitive-behavioural intervention for sleep problems. Psychoeducation principally focuses on providing parents with important information about optimising positive sleep-related behaviours and creating an optimal and conducive sleep-friendly environment. For instance, it is

Table 7.2 Psychoeducation component in CBT-I for preschool and school-aged children.

Core topics	Points of importance
Sleep changes in the specific age groups	• Sleep onset latency < 30 minutes • Nocturnal awakenings < 20 minutes Total sleep time: 10–13 hours for pre-schoolers 9–11 hours for school-aged children • Age-related changes in pre-sleep behaviour (e.g., pre-bed routines) • Gradual delaying of bed-time and reduction in co-sleeping
Negative consequences associated with poor sleep	• Cognitive impairment • Academic difficulties • Impairments to social function • Fatigue • Development of Psychopathology • Deterioration in daytime behaviour • Increased risk of obesity
Psychoeducation principles	• Basics of sleep-wake regulation • Age appropriate sleep needs • Appropriate bed-time routine (reading or being read to, singing lullabies, listening to soft music, putting on pajamas, brushing teeth) • Not using bed for punishment (e.g., time out) • Discontinuing stimulating play at least an hour before bed-time • Reducing cognitive and emotional stimulation before bed-time • Including activities in the bed-time routine that are relaxing and calming, such as reading • Maintaining a safe and comfortable sleeping environment

here that the clinician might explain that the bedroom should not be used as a place of punishment, as this will set up an unhelpful paired association for the young person. Instead, the bedroom should be associated with sleep, safety and calming activities that promote sleep.

Healthy sleep practices are especially important to establish during childhood, particularly as unhelpful behaviours will become more difficult to change the longer they have been present. Guidance on healthy sleep practices should include:

1) Keeping regular sleep timings (e.g., going to bed and getting up at roughly the same time each day).
2) Maintaining a regular and consistent bed-time routine.
3) Minimising variation in sleep patterns on weekdays and weekends.
4) Maintaining regular meal times and advocating dynamic activity in the morning and early afternoon.
5) Avoiding bright light exposure in the evening, particularly within an hour of bed-time.
6) Avoiding the use of televisions, smartphones, tablets and electronic devices when in bed and in the bedroom.
7) Avoiding stimulants that may interfere with sleep (e.g., caffeine from soft drinks).
8) Encouraging exposure to natural bright light in the morning after waking (e.g., sitting near a window whilst eating breakfast).
9) Avoiding spending time in bed when not sleeping.

Sleep hygiene practices could also be explained to school-aged children with the use of pictures and cartoons (e.g., illustrated posters with pictures of routine pre-bed activities). An example is given in Figure 7.2.

Bed-time routine

Establishment of a consistent and age-appropriate bed-time routine is an important first-line intervention for childhood sleep problems and has been demonstrated to be associated with better sleep outcomes in children. Based on conditioning theories (see Chapter 1), bed-time routines provide important behavioural stimuli that prime children for sleep and positively reinforce sleep promoting processes. Moreover, bed-time or 'wind-down' routines provide time and space for the effective transition from alertness to drowsiness in a consistent and predictable manner. Bed-time should be able to be a pleasant time of day for both the child and their caregivers.

Keeping the bedtime routine consistent entails maintaining a predictable running order for both parent and child and events should be increasingly relaxing in nature as bed-time approaches. A general structure might be along the following lines:

1) Brushing teeth
2) Getting dressed into pyjamas
3) Reading a story together
4) Goodnight hugs and kisses
5) Lights out

Parents should be advised that the bed-time routine should last no longer than approximately an hour.

Additionally, parents might consider:

1) Letting the child model sleep promoting behaviour by putting a favourite toy to sleep.
2) Helping the child to imagine a calming story: parents and child can think of a story that the child might tell himself/herself when alone in bed before falling asleep.
3) Use of a night light for children who are averse to sleeping in total darkness.
4) Doing relaxation exercises together before bed, such as mindfulness practices, diaphragmatic breathing or progressive muscle relaxation.

Figure 7.2 Example progression of the bedtime routine.

Behavioural interventions

Behavioural sleep interventions used in adult insomnia practice are also indicated to improve sleep in preschool and school-age children. Nevertheless, as there is a scarcity of empirical evidence, these strategies should be prescribed with caution (Meltzer & Mindell, 2014; Åslund, Arnberg, Kanstrup & Lekander, 2018). This may especially be true for prescription of sleep restriction, which may induce sleep deprivation in young children and adolescents; thus, diurnal side effects should be carefully monitored and appropriately supported.

Stimulus control

This approach centres on fostering a strong bed–sleep association, such that the bed and bedroom act as strong discriminant stimuli for sleep. Parents are asked to ensure that the bed is used solely for sleep and that any sleep incompatible behaviours (e.g., watching television, worrying, lying in bed awake) are done elsewhere. Not only do these activities degrade the bed–sleep association, but they often serve as cues for wakefulness rather than sleepiness. Periods of wakefulness at night are encouraged to be spent somewhere comfortable in the bedroom (e.g., a beanbag), rather than in bed. Ensuring that the child is comfortable with and aware of the approach and its rationale in advance is key in optimising treatment outcomes.

Sleep restriction

This approach involves restricting the time spent in bed to the child's average total sleep time across a baseline assessment period. This is never less than six hours in children and adolescents. The aim with this approach is to increase sleep efficiency by consolidating sleep. In line with stimulus control, above, it may also have the effect of disrupting learned associations between being awake and in bed, rather than asleep when in bed. Consistent and accurate recording of sleep patterns using a sleep diary is essential to allow weekly titration of the sleep window in line with changes to sleep efficiency.

Cognitive interventions

Cognitive exercises to address children's dysfunctional thoughts about sleep can be implemented during therapy. For example, therapeutic bed-time stories, adapted to the level of the child, might help to change sleep disturbing cognitions in children (Schlarb & Brandhorst, 2012). Moreover, guided visual imagery and exploring alternative ways to respond to the fears could help the child to manage sleep-related anxiety symptoms (e.g., imagining a beach or another favourite scene or memory) and to fall asleep more easily (Mindell & Owens, 2015). The use of relaxation training, guided imagery and positive self-statements, has been found to be helpful for children with sleep problems (Owens et al., 1999). Mindfulness-based approaches may also be implemented at bed-time: for example, encouraging the child to put their hands on their belly and carefully pay attention to the movements of their abdomen as they breathe calmly (Snel, Kabat-Zinn & Kabat-Zinn, 2014). This may offer a useful means of distraction from unhelpful pre-sleep mentation and help to reduce physiological arousal.

Positive reinforcement strategies

Sticker charts and other reward systems are an effective means of reinforcing desirable behaviours using a positive behavioural reinforcement paradigm (Luersen et al., 2012). These systems are best utilised where rewards are given using a variable or intermittent schedule, rather than a fixed ratio schedule. Ensuring that there is 'buy-in' from the child is an important means of enhancing adherence and optimising motivation. This often entails having the child choose their own rewards and co-designing the system (e.g., helping to draw up the reward chart). Positive behavioural reinforcement can also be used alongside behavioural strategies such as 'bed-time passes' (see above). Visual displays of rewards (e.g., sticker charts, jars of pieces of pasta/beans) are often helpful for both children and parents and serve as an additional reinforcing stimulus by giving an indication of progress. Small rewards can also be given interspersed with larger rewards for having reached waypoints on the chart (e.g., three consecutive nights of going to bed without protest; one week of complete pre-bed routine, etc.).

Relapse prevention

Each intervention should include an extensive discussion and summary of the strategies learned and progress made. Furthermore, helping parents identify their own strengths and weaknesses and walking through imagined scenarios of how poor sleep might again show up in the future and what can be done are important means of reducing risk of relapse. Creating a 'blueprint' for treatment during a final consultation with parents is a practical way to consolidate learning and to summarise strategies with which they will now be intimately familiar, but which may become less well remembered at a future date. It is often helpful to ask the parent to imagine if things deteriorated once again, what their future self would need to know in order to get things back on track (e.g., by writing a letter to their future self). This, of course, should include any bespoke amendments to particular treatment approaches and any reflections on their own child and situation.

Issues to consider for including school-aged children in therapy

Adaptation of these techniques for children of different ages and presenting them in age-appropriate language is important in encouraging motivation and treatment engagement by the child themselves. An example of this has been proposed in a manual in the German language developed by Schlarb and colleagues (2018), called the KiSS (**Ki**ds **S**leep **S**essions) programme. This CBT-I programme targets children from five to 10 years old suffering from insomnia and/or nightmares. KiSS entails six sessions (three for children and three for parents) based on the above-mentioned techniques. The CBT techniques are introduced with the help of a soft toy called Kalimba, a stuffed leopard. Kalimba walks the children through the various elements of the programme and fulfils several functions. First, Kalimba models strength, courage, speed and fearlessness; second, Kalimba encourages a sense of security by protecting the children so that they feel less lonely and more supported at bed-time and during the night; and third it serves as a memory aid for the KiSS strategies so that the children, who have often not yet learned to read or write, may easily recall the techniques.

Evidence-based behavioural interventions for adolescents

Unlike approaches for younger patients, CBT-I treatment for adolescents should be directed primarily at the patient, rather than conveyed via a parent. However, including parents at appointments or offering additional sessions to parents may still be helpful in facilitating parental support of the young person in their treatment. This may be the case particularly for those teenagers who struggle with mood problems, low motivation or for those who find adherence to protocols too challenging to do independently. Depending on the needs of the individual, it may also be helpful to include teachers in the development of a plan, such that support for the young person can be comprehensive and the potential for treatment success optimised.

The presentation of insomnia in adolescents will often more closely resemble that of adults than that of younger children, necessitating an approach that caters to these differences. For instance, it is likely that teenagers will experience more negatively toned sleep-related cognitions than younger children and so cognitive therapeutics will play a more substantial role in treatment at this age. Although CBT-I protocols with older adolescents may more closely resemble those designed for adults, the clinician should be conscious of the need to modify their language and delivery of the content such that age-appropriateness is ensured. Additionally, it is important for the clinician to have a comprehensive appreciation of the developmental changes to sleep that take place during adolescence, and how these changes may affect the presentation of their sleep problem. For most adolescents this includes a significant delay to their sleep–wake timings relative to both their timings as younger children and to the societally determined schedules to which they must adhere (e.g., school start times).

As with both younger children and adults, cognitive-behavioural treatment of adolescent sleep problems typically begins with a foundational psychoeducation component that covers basic sleep science and information on healthy sleep practices. Behavioural treatments can include stimulus control instructions and sleep restriction therapy, although the latter should be used with caution where teenagers present with symptoms of a significantly delayed sleep–wake phase (see Delayed Sleep-Wake Phase Disorder below). Additionally, general practice is to not restrict the sleep window to below six hours in adolescents. Cognitive therapeutics, including imagery techniques and cognitive restructuring, as well as relaxation therapeutics (e.g., progressive muscle relaxation), can also form central components to the treatment approach.

Considering Delayed Sleep–Wake Phase Disorder (DSWPD) in adolescence

During adolescence there is a developmentally normal tendency towards a delay in the timing of the circadian rhythm that often results in later sleep–wake timings. For many young people, this natural delay to the timing of sleep onset often results in insufficient opportunity for adequate sleep to take place before being required to wake in time for school the following day. Successive nights of insufficient sleep often result in day-time impairments to domains such as mood, cognitive function and increased day-time fatigue or sleepiness. Many young people will find this increased sleep onset latency triggers pre-sleep cognitive arousal and may resort to the use of electronics (e.g., smartphones) to pass the time before sleep takes place, something that may well have a secondary effect on sleep onset latency. Ensuring that both the parents and the young person themselves understand that consistent difficulties with late sleep onset are the result of developmentally driven circadian changes may help in reducing interpersonal tension in the home dynamic. Additionally, it is important to link these explanations to those of stimulus control (see Lack and Wright, 2007) and convey to both the young person and their parents that trying for sleep before the young person is sleepy-tired will likely result in difficulties with sleep onset. It may also be appropriate to discuss the use of alerting stimuli (e.g., video games, smartphones) that may further impact the ability of the young person to relax and fall asleep. In general, mild delays can be managed by maximising sleep opportunity at night, such as by preparing for the next day in advance and allowing the young person to sleep in later in the morning and by encouraging exposure to morning sunlight soon after waking. Where more significant delays present, this may require the attention of a sleep medicine specialist who can prescribe a phase advancement treatment using either sleep scheduling (chronotherapy), exposure to light (phototherapy) at the appropriate time and/or oral melatonin taken to affect phase advancement.

Psychoeducation

As with children of all ages, age-appropriate information and psychoeducation should be provided to both parents and the patient themselves. In adolescence this would include providing information on recommended age-appropriate ranges for sleep durations, explanations of sleep–wake regulation, and discussions around optimising opportunity for sleep by removing sleep disturbing stimuli (e.g., smartphone use). It is also of the utmost importance to explain the nature of circadian changes that tend to manifest during adolescence (e.g., normalisation of the tendency towards eveningness, which may affect as much as 40% of adolescents; Gradisar, Gardner & Dohnt, 2011). This may also include an explanation of why many adolescents may struggle with early morning academic work and why sport and exercise performance may improve in the afternoon (e.g., Gau et al., 2007; Short, Gradisar, Lack, Wright & Dohnt, 2013; Adan, Natali, Caci & Prat, 2010; Negriff, Dorn, Pabst & Susman, 2011; Susman et al., 2007). Another important recommendation is that adolescents do their best to maintain schedules that fluctuate as little as is possible between weekdays and weekends. Sleeping in too long on the weekends can result in an eastward-direction 'jet lag-like' situation by the end of the weekend, which may negatively impact sleep onset.

Sleep hygiene recommendations

In addition to the aforementioned sleep hygiene advice for children above (consistent sleep habits, age-appropriate wind-down practice, day-time activities, etc.), sleep hygiene recommendations for adolescents may include:

- Maximising exposure to sunlight in the morning. Not only does this help with alertness, but the circadian phase advancing properties of morning exposure to bright light may help to maintain earlier bed-times. Similarly, evening and night-time light exposure should be minimised.
- Avoiding use of a clock on the bedside table may be useful in reducing anxiety associated with clock-watching when unable to sleep.
- Careful use of smartphones and electronic devices is important. Whilst so-called 'electronics curfews' may be implemented in many households, these may set up unhelpful and antagonistic parent–child dynamics. Education on the effects of smartphone use (e.g., on how they stimulate both body and mind at a time when sleep requires us to be relaxed) is crucial in helping a young person take control of their own sleep problem.
- Avoiding use of stimulants where there is a sleep problem (e.g., Coke, caffeine, energy drinks) and any use of alcohol in the evening and pre-sleep period.

Wind-down routines

Just as with children of other ages, appropriate wind-down routines are important for adolescents. Using the hour or so before bed to pursue calming activities that are associated with relaxation and getting ready for bed not only help by directly reducing arousal but also act as useful behavioural cues for sleep. For teens who spend evenings on video games or chatting to friends online, helping them set clear boundaries will be important in ensuring that these activities do not negatively impact sleep onset. This may also mean making time for these activities at other points in the day, rather than removing them from the teenager's schedule completely. As children mature, they may also become more receptive to approaches such as mindfulness, where pre-sleep meditation or relaxation techniques could be a useful means of reducing arousal.

Behavioural intervention

Stimulus control therapy.

A thorough explanation of stimulus control and its underlying rationale should be a hallmark of this treatment approach for adolescents. Use of metaphor to explain the conditioning of behavioural associations and how spending excessive time in bed not sleeping, or being frustrated at not being able to sleep, can lead to deconditioning of the bed–sleep association is often a helpful means of elucidating the rationale for treatment. This is especially important given the way in which many adolescents may use their bed and their room as their primary 'personal space' within the house, and as a space into which they can escape from the rest of the world during the day. As with adults, this approach should not become overly prescriptive but should encourage the young person to utilise their engagement with the strategies as a means of developing confidence in their ability to improve their sleep. A full list of stimulus control instructions is provided in Chapter 2.

Sleep restriction therapy

Just as with adults, sleep restriction therapy has been shown to be an effective treatment for insomnia in adolescents. An important consideration for young people undergoing this treatment component is that the minimum sleep window is typically taken no lower than six hours. This is to allow for the greater sleep need that young people of this age require compared to adults. Circadian factors are particularly important to take into consideration when choosing a sleep window with adolescent patients, as many will have significantly delayed sleep–wake phases, which may preclude earlier sleep onset. A full protocol for sleep restriction therapy is provided in Chapter 2.

Cognitive intervention

Relative to younger children, more adult-oriented cognitive interventions are also likely to be helpful for adolescent patients, particularly those with a significant anxiety-based component to their presentation. Here, cognitive challenging, worry time and even behavioural experiments can be useful elements to broadening the treatment approach and addressing unhelpful day-time cognitive-behavioural patterns. As with other elements of the cognitive-behavioural therapeutic approach, tailoring language and tone with adolescents to maximise engagement is important.

Relaxation techniques

Relaxation techniques used in the treatment of insomnia in children and adults more generally are also appropriate for use with adolescents. The relaxation therapeutics used in a cognitive-behavioural treatment approach to insomnia typically involve techniques such as progressive muscle relaxation, which should be encouraged to be practised during the day as well as at night when the individual has trouble sleeping. Imagery-based relaxation exercises can also be helpful and should be tailored to the preferences of the young person themselves (Schlarb, Liddle & Hautzinger, 2010). Incorporating the use of apps that offer guided relaxation exercises can also be a useful way of encouraging more regular practice of these techniques. However, it should be emphasised that avoidance of phone use at night is optimal.

Positive reinforcement strategies

As with younger children, adolescents may still benefit from the use of positive behavioural reinforcement paradigms (Roeser, Schwerdtle, Kübler & Schlarb, 2016). This may be particularly helpful for those younger adolescents with sleep problems or those with less inclination to adhere to clinical advice.

Issues to consider for therapy with adolescents

Several manualised protocols have been developed for adolescents with sleep problems, including one in German called the JuSt programme (adolescent sleep training). In this particular approach, sleep–wake rhythm problems and development-related chronotype changes are considered. This CBT-I training for adolescents encompasses six sessions with five sessions for the adolescents and one for their parents. Although therapy for adolescents is generally directed solely at the young person, inclusion of a parent session is deemed important because parents are often not familiar with information such as developmental sleep-related changes and recommended sleep durations. The structure of the training was based on an interactive game-type format to encourage therapeutic engagement. The JuSt programme has been shown to display good acceptability to adolescent patients and their parents and participants showed significant improvements after the training (Schlarb et al., 2010), an effect that persisted to 12 months post-treatment (Roeser et al., 2016).

Although the adolescent CBT-I literature is less extensive than that of adults and older adults, this treatment approach has been shown to be acceptable to and effective for this age group, albeit with minor modifications (e.g., de Bruin, Oort, Bögels & Meijer, 2014; Schlarb et al., 2018; Blake, Sheeber, Youssef, Raniti & Allen, 2017; Åslund et al., 2018). There is also a suggestion that internet-based therapy may be well suited to adolescents, particularly for those who may be reluctant to seek psychological help. Furthermore, therapy may need to focus on motivational issues that support the independence of the adolescent in their behaviour change and wider life goals.

Children with disabilities or somatic/mental disorders

Children with neurodevelopmental disabilities, such as autism spectrum disorder (ASD), have a much higher likelihood of experiencing sleep problems than typically developing children. Additionally, the sleep problems are often more severe, chronic and treatment-resistant (Mindell & Owens, 2015). Epidemiological estimates suggest it is likely that about 50–80% of children with ASD experience insomnia (Couturier et al., 2005; Krakowiak, Goodlin-Jones, Hertz-Picciotto, Croen & Hansen, 2008; Richdale & Schreck, 2009; Souders et al., 2009). As well as experiencing greater severity of insomnia symptoms themselves, it is also clear that these problems have a significant impact on parental sleep (Goldman et al., 2011; Malow et al., 2006; Schreck, Mulik & Smith, 2004). Since the aetiology of insomnia in children with ASD is multifactorial, insomnia treatment should take a broad-spectrum approach. The Autism Treatment Network recommend behavioural sleep intervention as the first-line treatment (Malow et al., 2012). More recently, McCrae and colleagues (2020) suggested the use and the efficacy of Cognitive Behavioural Treatment for Childhood Insomnia (CBT-CI) in order to manage crucial factors that could interfere with sleep at school age (e.g., anxiety, bullying, academic and social demands). The application of cognitive techniques and the involvement of both child and parent as agents of change are important factors in CBT-CI that could ameliorate the development of self-management and self-initiation of sleep strategies and potentially maximizing long-term effects of the treatment (McCrae et al., 2020). Important factors to consider for treatment of insomnia of children with ASD include:

- Use of Visual support
- Repetition and practice of strategies
- An awareness of Sensory integration issues (e.g., weighted vests and blankets for children with tactile sensory issues, 'white noise' generators that produce a mixture of all frequencies and can mask environmental sounds, body pillows)
- Incorporation of special interests
- Adaptation of cognitive strategies (cartoons to illustrate cognitive concepts, concrete language and metaphors)
- Adaptation of relaxation strategies
- Consideration of the sleep Environment (e.g., temperature, noise level, ambient light)
- Monitoring Scheduling (e.g., regular sleep–wake patterns)
- Alarm systems that alert caregivers when a child has left the bedroom may be necessary, as some children may wander around the house during the night.
- Bedroom lighting may need to be adapted; although a dark sleeping environment is preferable, some anxious children might benefit from a dim night-light, or lights adapted to sensory needs.

Conclusion

Poor sleep and insomnia are common across the developmental age range and are associated with negative consequences for health, daytime function and quality of life. In spite of this, these problems are often underdiagnosed and undertreated in clinical practice. This chapter aims to provide clinical guidelines for the health professionals for early recognition of insomnia and its appropriate treatment. It covers three age ranges: infancy and toddlerhood; preschool and school age; adolescence. General issues and clinical aspects associated with assessment and treatment are discussed for each age range. Finally, a section for children with specific disorders is considered. Treating insomnia in the early stages of life may be associated with important short-term positive sequelae but are also likely to have protective value for adult mental and physical health.

References

Acebo, C., Sadeh, A., Seifer, R., Tzischinsky, O., Hafer, A., & Carskadon, M. A. (2005). Sleep/wake patterns derived from activity monitoring and maternal report for healthy 1- to 5-year-old children. *Sleep*, *28* (12), 1568–1577.

Adan, A., Natale, V., Caci, H., & Prat, G. (2010). Relationship between circadian typology and functional and dysfunctional impulsivity. *Chronobiology International*, *27* (3), 606–619.

Allen, S. L., Howlett, M. D., Coulombe, J. A., & Corkum, P. V. (2016). ABCs of SLEEPING: A review of the evidence behind pediatric sleep practice recommendations. *Sleep Medicine Reviews*, *29*, 1–14.

American Academy of Sleep Medicine (2014). *International classification of sleep disorders* (3rd ed.). Darien, IL: American Academy of Sleep Medicine.

American Academy of Pediatrics Task Force on Sudden Infant Death Syndrome (2005). The changing concept of sudden infant death syndrome: Diagnostic coding shifts, controversies regarding the sleeping environment, and new variables to consider in reducing risk. *Pediatrics*, *116* (5), 1245–1255. https://doi.org/10.1542/peds.2005-1499.

American Psychiatric Association (2013). *Diagnostic and statistical manual of mental isorders* (5th ed.): *DSM-5*. Washington, DC: American Psychiatric Publishers.

Anders, T. F., Halpern, L. F., & Hua, J. (1992). Sleeping through the night: A developmental perspective. *Pediatrics*, *90* (4), 554–560.

Åslund, L., Arnberg, F., Kanstrup, M., & Lekander, M. (2018). Cognitive and behavioral interventions to improve sleep in school-age children and adolescents: A systematic review and meta-analysis. *Journal of Clinical Sleep Medicine*, *14* (11), 1937–1947.

Auger, R. R., Burgess, H. J., Emens, J. S., Deriy, L. V., Thomas, S. M., & Sharkey, K. M. (2015). Clinical practice guideline for the treatment of intrinsic circadian rhythm sleep–wake disorders: Advanced sleep–wake phase disorder (ASWPD), delayed sleep–wake phase disorder (DSWPD), non-24-hour sleep-wake rhythm disorder (N24SWD), and irregular sleep-wake rhythm disorder (ISWRD). An update for 2015: An American Academy of Sleep Medicine Clinical Practice Guideline. *Journal of Clinical Sleep Medicine: JCSM*, *11* (10), 1199–1236. https://doi.org/10.5664/jcsm.5100.

Bayer, J. K., Hiscock, H., Hampton, A., & Wake, M. (2007). Sleep problems in young infants and maternal mental and physical health. *Journal of Paediatrics and Child Health*, *43* (1–2), 66–73.

Beebe, D. W. (2011). Cognitive, behavioral, and functional consequences of inadequate sleep in children and adolescents. *Pediatric Clinics*, *58* (3), 649–665.

Blake, M. J., Sheeber, L. B., Youssef, G. J., Raniti, M. B., & Allen, N. B. (2017). Systematic review and meta-analysis of adolescent cognitive-behavioral sleep interventions. *Clinical Child and Family Psychology Review*, *20* (3), 227–249.

Bruni, O., Ottaviano, S., Guidetti, V., Romoli, M., Innocenzi, M., Cortesi, F., & Giannotti, F. (1996). The Sleep Disturbance Scale for Children (SDSC) construct on and validation of an instrument to evaluate sleep disturbances in childhood and adolescence. *Journal of Sleep Research*, *5* (4), 251–261.

Bruni, O., Violani, C., Luchetti, A., Miano, S., Verrillo, E., Di Brina, C., & Valente, D. (2004). The sleep knowledge of pediatricians and child neuropsychiatrists. *Sleep and Hypnosis*, *6*, 130–138.

Burnham, M. M., Goodlin-Jones, B. L., Gaylor, E. E., & Anders, T. F. (2002). Nighttime sleep-wake patterns and self-soothing from birth to one year of age: A longitudinal intervention study. *Journal of Child Psychology and Psychiatry*, *43* (6), 713–725.

Byars, K. C., Yolton, K., Rausch, J., Lanphear, B., & Beebe, D. W. (2012). Prevalence, patterns, and persistence of sleep problems in the first 3 years of life. *Pediatrics*, *129* (2), e276–e284.

Cain, N., & Gradisar, M. (2010). Electronic media use and sleep in school-aged children and adolescents: A review. *Sleep Medicine*, *11* (8), 735–742.

Calhoun, S. L., Fernandez-Mendoza, J., Vgontzas, A. N., Liao, D., & Bixler, E. O. (2014). Prevalence of insomnia symptoms in a general population sample of young children and preadolescents: Gender effects. *Sleep Medicine*, *15* (1), 91–95.

Carney, C. E., Buysse, D. J., Ancoli-Israel, S., Edinger, J. D., Krystal, A. D., Lichstein, K. L., & Morin, C. M. (2012). The consensus sleep diary: Standardizing prospective sleep self-monitoring. *Sleep*, *35* (2), 287–302.

Coons, S., & Guilleminault, C. (1984). Development of consolidated sleep and wakeful periods in relation to the dav/night cycle in infancy. *Developmental Medicine & Child Neurology*, *26* (2), 169–176.

Couturier, J. L., Speechley, K. N., Steele, M., Norman, R., Stringer, B., & Nicolson, R. (2005). Parental perception of sleep problems in children of normal intelligence with pervasive developmental disorders: Prevalence, severity, and pattern. *Journal of the American Academy of Child & Adolescent Psychiatry*, *44* (8), 815–822.

Dahl, R. E. (1996). The regulation of sleep and arousal: Development and psychopathology. *Development and Psychopathology*, *8* (1), 3–27.

de Bruin, E. J., Oort, F. J., Bögels, S. M., & Meijer, A. M. (2014). Efficacy of internet and group-administered cognitive behavioral therapy for insomnia in adolescents: A pilot study. *Behavioral Sleep Medicine*, *12* (3), 235–254.

de Zambotti, M., Goldstone, A., Colrain, I. M., & Baker, F. C. (2018). Insomnia disorder in adolescence: Diagnosis, impact, and treatment. *Sleep Medicine Reviews*, *39*, 12–24.

Etherton, H., Blunden, S., & Hauck, Y. (2016). Discussion of extinction-based behavioral sleep interventions for young children and reasons why parents may find them difficult. *Journal of Clinical Sleep Medicine*, *12* (11), 1535–1543.

Friman, P. C., Hoff, K. E., Schnoes, C., Freeman, K. A., Woods, D. W., & Blum, N. (1999). The bedtime pass: An approach to bedtime crying and leaving the room. *Archives of Pediatrics & Adolescent Medicine*, *153* (10), 1027–1029.

Galland, B. C., Taylor, B. J., Elder, D. E., & Herbison, P. (2012). Normal sleep patterns in infants and children: A systematic review of observational studies. *Sleep Medicine Reviews*, *16* (3), 213–222.

Gau, S. F., & Soong, W. T. (2003). The transition of sleep–wake patterns in early adolescence. *Sleep*, *26* (4), 449–454.

Gau, S.-F., Shang, C.-Y., Merikangas, K. R., Chiu, Y.-N., Soong, W.-T., & Cheng, A.T.-A. (2007). Association between morningness–eveningness and behavioral/emotional problems among adolescents. *Journal of Biological Rhythms*, *22* (3), 268–274.

Goldman, S. E., McGrew, S., Johnson, K. P., Richdale, A. L., Clemons, T., & Malow, B. A. (2011). Sleep is associated with problem behaviors in children and adolescents with autism spectrum disorders. *Research in Autism Spectrum Disorders*, *5* (3), 1223–1229.

Goodlin-Jones, B. L., Burnham, M. M., Gaylor, E. E., & Anders, T. F. (2001). Night waking, sleep-wake organization, and self-soothing in the first year of life. *Journal of Developmental and Behavioral Pediatrics: JDBP*, *22* (4), 226.

Gradisar, M., Gardner, G., & Dohnt, H. (2011). Recent worldwide sleep patterns and problems during adolescence: A review and meta-analysis of age, region, and sleep. *Sleep Medicine*, *12* (2), 110– 118.

Henderson, J. M., France, K. G., & Blampied, N. M. (2011). The consolidation of infants' nocturnal sleep across the first year of life. *Sleep Medicine Reviews*, *15* (4), 211–220.

Henderson, J. M., France, K. G., Owens, J. L., & Blampied, N. M. (2010). Sleeping through the night: The consolidation of self-regulated sleep across the first year of life. *Pediatrics*, *126* (5), e1081–e1087.

Hirshkowitz, M., Whiton, K., Albert, S. M., Alessi, C., Bruni, O., DonCarlos, L., Hazen, N., Herman, J., Katz, E. S., Kheirandish-Gozal, L., Neubauer, D. N., O'Donnell, A. E., Ohayon, M., Peever, J., Rawding, R., Sachdeva, R. C., Setters, B., Vitiello, M. V., Ware, J. C., & Adams Hillard, P. J. (2015). National Sleep Foundation's sleep time duration recommendations: Methodology and results summary. *Sleep Health*, *1* (1), 40–43. https://doi.org/10.1016/j.sleh.2014.12.010.

Hiscock, H., & Wake, M. (2002). Randomised controlled trial of behavioural infant sleep intervention to improve infant sleep and maternal mood. *British Medical Journal*, *324* (7345), 1062.

Honaker, S. M., & Meltzer, L. J. (2016). Sleep in pediatric primary care: A review of the literature. *Sleep Medicine Reviews*, *25*, 31–39. https://doi.org/10.1016/j.smrv.2015.01.004.

Hysing, M., Harvey, A. G., Linton, S. J., Askeland, K. G., & Sivertsen, B. (2016). Sleep and academic performance in later adolescence: Results from a large population-based study. *Journal of Sleep Research*, *25* (3), 318–324.

Jenni, O. G., & Carskadon, M. A. (2000). Sleep Research Society. *SRS Basics of Sleep Guide* (pp. 11–19). Westchester, IL: Sleep Research Society.

Johnson, E. O., Roth, T., Schultz, L., & Breslau, N. (2006). Epidemiology of DSM-IV insomnia in adolescence: Lifetime prevalence, chronicity, and an emergent gender difference. *Pediatrics*, *117* (2), e247–e256.

Kahn, M., Livne-Karp, E., Juda-Hanael, M., Omer, H., Tikotzky, L., Anders, T. F., & Sadeh, A. (2020). Behavioral interventions for infant sleep problems: The role of parental cry tolerance and sleep-related cognitions. *Journal of Clinical Sleep Medicine*, *16* (8), 1275–1283.

Kater, M.-J., & Schlarb, A. A. (2020). Smartphone usage in adolescents – Motives and link to sleep disturbances, stress and sleep reactivity. *Somnologie*, *24*, 1–8. 10.1007/s11818-020-00272-7.

Keener, M. A., Zeanah, C. H., & Anders, T. F. (1988). Infant temperament, sleep organization, and nighttime parental interventions. *Pediatrics*, *81* (6), 762–771.

Keller, M. A., & Goldberg, W. A. (2004). Co-sleeping: Help or hindrance for young children's independence? *Infant and Child Development: An International Journal of Research and Practice*, *13* (5), 369–388.

Krakowiak, P., Goodlin-Jones, B. E. T. H., Hertz-Picciotto, I. R. V. A., Croen, L. A., & Hansen, R. L. (2008). Sleep problems in children with autism spectrum disorders, developmental delays, and typical development: A population-based study. *Journal of Sleep Research*, *17* (2), 197–206.

Kuhn, B. (2011). The excuse-me drill: A behavioral protocol to promote independent sleep initiation skills and reduce bedtime problems in young children. In M. Perlis, M. Aloia, & B. Kuhn (Eds.), *Behavioral treatments for sleep disorders: A comprehensive primer of behavioural sleep medicine interventions* (pp. 299–309). London: Academic Press.

Kuhn, B. R., LaBrot, Z. C., Ford, R., & Roane, B. M. (2020). Promoting independent sleep onset in young children: Examination of the excuse me drill. *Behavioral Sleep Medicine, 18* (6), 730–745.

Lack, L. C., & Wright, H. R. (2007). Clinical management of delayed sleep phase disorder. *Behavioral Sleep Medicine, 5* (1), 57–76.

Lam, P., Hiscock, H., & Wake, M. (2003). Outcomes of infant sleep problems: A longitudinal study of sleep, behavior, and maternal well-being. *Pediatrics, 111* (3), e203–e207.

LeBourgeois, F., Gomez, N., Pinto, P., & Mérian, P. (2013). Mixed stands reduce Abies alba tree-ring sensitivity to summer drought in the Vosges Mountains, western Europe. *Forest Ecology and Management, 303*, 61–71.

Lodemore, M., Petersen, S. A., & Wailoo, M. P. (1991). Development of night time temperature rhythms over the first six months of life. *Archives of Disease in Childhood, 66* (4), 521–524.

Lozoff, B., Wolf, A. W., & Davis, N. S. (1985). Sleep problems seen in pediatric practice. *Pediatrics, 75* (3), 477–483.

Luersen, K., Davis, S. A., Kaplan, S. G., Abel, T. D., Winchester, W. W., & Feldman, S. R. (2012). Sticker charts: A method for improving adherence to treatment of chronic diseases in children. *Pediatric Dermatology, 29* (4), 403–408.

Malone, S. K. (2011). Early to bed, early to rise? An exploration of adolescent sleep hygiene practices. *The Journal of School Nursing, 27* (5), 348–354.

Malone, S. K., Zemel, B., Compher, C., Souders, M., Chittams, J., Thompson, A. L., & Lipman, T. H. (2016). Characteristics associated with sleep duration, chronotype, and social jet lag in adolescents. *The Journal of School Nursing: The Official Publication of the National Association of School Nurses, 32* (2), 120–131. https://doi.org/10.1177/1059840515603454.

Malow, B. A., Marzec, M. L., McGrew, S. G., Wang, L., Henderson, L. M., & Stone, W. L. (2006). Characterizing sleep in children with autism spectrum disorders: A multidimensional approach. *Sleep, 29* (12), 1563–1571.

Malow, B. A., Byars, K., Johnson, K., Weiss, S., Bernal, P., Goldman, S. E., Panzer, R., Coury, D. L., & Glaze, D. G. (2012). A practice pathway for the identification, evaluation, and management of insomnia in children and adolescents with autism spectrum disorders. *Pediatrics, 130* (Suppl. 2), S106–S124. https://doi.org/10.1542/peds.2012-0900I

Matricciani, L., Olds, T., & Petkov, J. (2012). In search of lost sleep: Secular trends in the sleep time of school-aged children and adolescents. *Sleep Medicine Reviews, 16* (3), 203–211.

McCrae, C. S., Chan, W. S., Curtis, A. F., Nair, N., Deroche, C. B., Munoz, M., Takamatsu, S., McLean, D., Davenport, M., Muckerman, J. E., Takahashi, N., McCann, D., McGovney, K., Sahota, P., & Mazurek, M. O. (2020). Telehealth cognitive behavioral therapy for insomnia in children with autism spectrum disorder: A pilot examining feasibility, satisfaction, and preliminary findings. *Autism, The International Journal of Research and Practice, 25* (3) 667–680. https://doi.org/10.1177/1362361320949078.

Melendres, C. S., Lutz, J. M., Rubin, E. D., & Marcus, C. L. (2004). Daytime sleepiness and hyperactivity in children with suspected sleep-disordered breathing. *Pediatrics, 114*, 768–775.

Meltzer, L. J., Johnson, C., Crosette, J., Ramos, M., & Mindell, J. A. (2010). Prevalence of diagnosed sleep disorders in pediatric primary care practices. *Pediatrics, 125* (6), e1410–e1418.

Meltzer, L. J., & Mindell, J. A. (2014). Systematic review and meta-analysis of behavioral interventions for pediatric insomnia. *Journal of Pediatric Psychology, 39* (8), 932–948.

Meltzer, L. J., Plaufcan, M. R., Thomas, J. H., & Mindell, J. A. (2014). Sleep problems and sleep disorders in pediatric primary care: Treatment recommendations, persistence, and health care utilization. *Journal of Clinical Sleep Medicine, 10* (4), 421–426.

Miller, A. L., Lumeng, J. C., & LeBourgeois, M. K. (2015). Sleep patterns and obesity in childhood. *Current Opinion in Endocrinology, Diabetes, and Obesity, 22* (1), 41.

Mindell, J. A., Kuhn, B., Lewin, D. S., Meltzer, L. J., & Sadeh, A., & American Academy of Sleep Medicine (2006). Behavioral treatment of bedtime problems and night wakings in infants and young children. *Sleep, 29* (10), 1263–1276.

Mindell, J. A., Li, A. M., Sadeh, A., Kwon, R., & Goh, D. Y. (2015). Bedtime routines for young children: A dose-dependent association with sleep outcomes. *Sleep, 38* (5), 717–722.

Mindell, J. A., Leichman, E. S., DuMond, C., & Sadeh, A. (2017). Sleep and social-emotional development in infants and toddlers. *Journal of Clinical Child & Adolescent Psychology, 46* (2), 236–246.

Mindell, J. A., Meltzer, L. J., Carskadon, M. A., & Chervin, R. D. (2009). Developmental aspects of sleep hygiene: Findings from the 2004 National Sleep Foundation Sleep in America Poll. *Sleep Medicine, 10* (7), 771–779.

Mindell, J. A., & Owens, J. A. (2015). *A clinical guide to pediatric sleep: Diagnosis and management of sleep problems.* Philadelphia, PA: Lippincott Williams & Wilkins.

Mindell, J. A., & Williamson, A. A. (2018). Benefits of a bedtime routine in young children: Sleep, development, and beyond. *Sleep Medicine Reviews*, *40*, 93–108.

Mindell, J. A., Owens, J., Alves, R., Bruni, O., Goh, D. Y., Hiscock, H., Kohyama, J., & Sadeh, A. (2011). Give children and adolescents the gift of a good night's sleep: A call to action. *Sleep Medicine*, *12* (3), 203–204. https://doi.org/10.1016/j.sleep.2011.01.003.

Mishra, A., Pandey, R. K., Minz, A., & Arora, V. (2017). Sleeping habits among school children and their effects on sleep pattern. *Journal of Caring Sciences*, *6* (4), 315.

Moore, M., Meltzer, L. J., & Mindell, J. A. (2007). Bedtime problems and night wakings in children. *Sleep Medicine Clinics*, *2* (3), 377–385.

Morgenthaler, T., Kramer, M., Alessi, C., Friedman, L., Boehlecke, B., Brown, T., Coleman, J., Kapur, V., Lee-Chiong, T., Owens, J., Pancer, J., Swick, T., & American Academy of Sleep Medicine (2006). Practice parameters for the psychological and behavioral treatment of insomnia: An update. An American Academy of Sleep Medicine Report. *Sleep*, *29* (11), 1415–1419.

Negriff, S. Dorn, L. D., Pabst, S. R., & Susman, E. J. (2011). Morningness/eveningness, pubertal timing, and substance use in adolescent girls. *Psychiatry Research*, *185* (3), 408–413.

Ohayon, M. M., Roberts, R. E., Zulley, J., Smirne, S., & Priest, R. G. (2000). Prevalence and patterns of problematic sleep among older adolescents. *Journal of the American Academy of Child & Adolescent Psychiatry*, *39* (12), 1549–1556.

Ohayon, M., Wickwire, E. M., Hirshkowitz, M., Albert, S. M., Avidan, A., Daly, F. J., Dauvilliers, Y., Ferri, R., Fung, C., Gozal, D., Hazen, N., Krystal, A., Lichstein, K., Mallampalli, M., Plazzi, G., Rawding, R., Scheer, F. A., Somers, V., & Vitiello, M. V. (2017). National Sleep Foundation's sleep quality recommendations: First report. *Sleep Health*, *3* (1), 6–19. https://doi.org/10.1016/j.sleh.2016.11.006.

Okami, P., Weisner, T., & Olmstead, R. (2002). Outcome correlates of parent–child bedsharing: An eighteen-year longitudinal study. *Journal of Developmental & Behavioral Pediatrics*, *23* (4), 244–253.

Owens, J. (2008). Classification and epidemiology of childhood sleep disorders. *Primary care: clinics in office practice*, *35*(3), 533–546.

Owens, J., & Adolescent Sleep Working Group (2014). Insufficient sleep in adolescents and young adults: An update on causes and consequences. *Pediatrics*, *134* (3), e921–e932.

Owens, J. A., France, K. G., & Wiggs, L. (1999). Behavioural and cognitive-behavioural interventions for sleep disorders in infants and children: A review. *Sleep Medicine Reviews*, *3* (4), 281–302.

Owens, J. A., Spirito, A., & McGuinn, M. (2000). The Children's Sleep Habits Questionnaire (CSHQ): Psychometric properties of a survey instrument for school-aged children. *Sleep*, *23* (8), 1043–1051.

Owens, J. A., Spirito, A., McGuinn, M., & Nobile, C. (2000). Sleep habits and sleep disturbance in elementary school-aged children. *Journal of Developmental and Behavioral Pediatrics*, *21* (1), 27–36.

Richdale, A. L., & Schreck, K. A. (2009). Sleep problems in autism spectrum disorders: Prevalence, nature, & possible biopsychosocial aetiologies. *Sleep Medicine Reviews*, *13* (6), 403–411.

Rivkees, S. A. (2003). Time to wake-up to the individual variation in sleep needs. *The Journal of Clinical Endocrinology & Metabolism*, *88* (1), 24–25.

Roeser, K., Schwerdtle, B., Kübler, A., & Schlarb, A. A. (2016). Further evidence for the JuSt program as treatment for insomnia in adolescents: Results from a 1-year follow-up study. *Journal of Clinical Sleep Medicine*, *12* (2), 257–262.

Roth, T., Jaeger, S., Jin, R., Kalsekar, A., Stang, P. E., & Kessler, R. C. (2006). Sleep problems, comorbid mental disorders, and role functioning in the national comorbidity survey replication. *Biological Psychiatry*, *60* (12), 1364–1371.

Rubin, K. H., Coplan, R. J., & Bowker, J. C. (2009). Social withdrawal in childhood. *Annual Review of Psychology*, *60*, 141–171.

Sadeh, A. (2004). A brief screening questionnaire for infant sleep problems: Validation and findings for an internet sample. *Pediatrics*, *113* (6), e570–e577.

Sadeh, A., Gruber, R., & Raviv, A. (2002). Sleep, neurobehavioral functioning, and behavior problems in school-age children. *Child Development*, *73* (2), 405–417.

Sadeh, A. V. I., Mindell, J. A., Luedtke, K., & Wiegand, B. (2009). Sleep and sleep ecology in the first 3 years: A web-based study. *Journal of Sleep Research*, *18* (1), 60–73.

Sadeh, A., Tikotzky, L., & Kahn, M. (2014). Sleep in infancy and childhood: Implications for emotional and behavioral difficulties in adolescence and beyond. *Current Opinion in Psychiatry*, *27* (6), 453–459.

Sadeh, A., Tikotzky, L., & Scher, A. (2010). Parenting and infant sleep. *Sleep Medicine Reviews*, *14* (2), 89–96.

Sadeh, A., Juda-Hanael, M., Livne-Karp, E., Kahn, M., Tikotzky, L., Anders, T. F., Calkins, S., & Sivan, Y. (2016). Low parental tolerance for infant crying: An underlying factor in infant sleep problems. *Journal of Sleep Research*, *25* (5), 501–507. https://doi.org/10.1111/jsr.12401.

Saxvig, I. W., Pallesen, S., Wilhelmsen-Langeland, A., Molde, H., & Bjorvatn, B. (2012). Prevalence and correlates of delayed sleep phase in high school students. *Sleep Medicine*, *13* (2), 193–199.

Schlarb, A. A., Bihlmaier, I., Velten-Schurian, K., Poets, C. F., & Hautzinger, M. (2018). Short-and long-term effects of CBT-I in groups for school-age children suffering from chronic insomnia: The KiSS-program. *Behavioral Sleep Medicine*, *16* (4), 380–397.

Schlarb, A. A., & Brandhorst, I. (2012). Mini-KiSS online: An internet-based intervention program for parents of young children with sleep problems – Influence on parental behavior and children's sleep. *Nature and Science of Sleep*, *4*, 41.

Schlarb, A. A., Liddle, C. C., & Hautzinger, M. (2010). JuSt – a multimodal program for treatment of insomnia in adolescents: A pilot study. *Nature and Science of Sleep*, *3*, 13.

Schreck, K. A., Mulick, J. A., & Smith, A. F. (2004). Sleep problems as possible predictors of intensified symptoms of autism. *Research in Developmental Disabilities*, *25* (1), 57–66.

Schwerdtle, B., Kanis, J., Kübler, A., & Schlarb, A. A. (2016). The children's sleep comic: Psychometrics of a self-rating instrument for childhood insomnia. *Child Psychiatry & Human Development*, *47* (1), 53–63.

Sheldon, S. H., Ferber, R., Kryger, M. H., & Gozal, D. (Eds.) (2014). *Principles and practice of pediatric sleep medicine e-book.* Elsevier Health Sciences.

Short, M. A., Gradisar, M., Lack, L. C., Wright, H. R., & Dohnt, H. (2013). The sleep patterns and well-being of Australian adolescents. *Journal of Adolescence*, *36* (1), 103–110.

Snel, E. (2014). *Mindfulness matters: Mindfulness for children, ages: 5–8* (Vol. 1). Amsterdam, The Netherlands: Trainer's Handbook.

Snel, E., Kabat-Zinn, M., & Kabat-Zinn, J. (2014). *Sitting still like a frog: Mindfulness exercises for kids (and their parents).* Shambhala Publications.

Souders, M. C., Mason, T. B., Valladares, O., Bucan, M., Levy, S. E., Mandell, D. S., & Pinto-Martin, J. (2009). Sleep behaviors and sleep quality in children with autism spectrum disorders. *Sleep*, *32* (12), 1566–1578.

Stein, M. A., Mendelsohn, J., Obermeyer, W. H., Amromin, J., & Benca, R. (2001). Sleep and behavior problems in school-aged children. *Pediatrics*, *107* (4), e60.

Susman, E. J., Dockray, S., Schiefelbein, V. L., Herwehe, S., Heaton, J. A., & Dorn, L. D. (2007). Morningness/eveningness, morning-to-afternoon cortisol ratio, and antisocial behavior problems during puberty. *Developmental Psychology*, *43* (4), 811–822.

Taylor, A., Wright, H. R., & Lack, L. C. (2008). Sleeping-in on the weekend delays circadian phase and increases sleepiness the following week. *Sleep and Biological Rhythms*, *6* (3), 172–179.

Thomée, S., Härenstam, A., & Hagberg, M. (2011). Mobile phone use and stress, sleep disturbances, and symptoms of depression among young adults – A prospective cohort study. *BMC Public Health*, *11* (1), 1–11.

Touchette, É., Petit, D., Paquet, J., Boivin, M., Japel, C., Tremblay, R. E., & Montplaisir, J. Y. (2005). Factors associated with fragmented sleep at night across early childhood. *Archives of Pediatrics & Adolescent Medicine*, *159* (3), 242–249.

Wake, M., Morton-Allen, E., Poulakis, Z., Hiscock, H., Gallagher, S., & Oberklaid, F. (2006). Prevalence, stability, and outcomes of cry-fuss and sleep problems in the first 2 years of life: Prospective community-based study. *Pediatrics*, *117* (3), 836–842.

Williamson, A. A., Mindell, J. A., Hiscock, H., & Quach, J. (2020). Longitudinal sleep problem trajectories are associated with multiple impairments in child well-being. *Journal of Child Psychology and Psychiatry*, *61* (10), 1092–1103. https://doi.org/10.1111/jcpp.13303.

Zhang, J., Li, A. M., Fok, T. F., & Wing, Y. K. (2010). Roles of parental sleep/wake patterns, socioeconomic status, and daytime activities in the sleep/wake patterns of children. *The Journal of Pediatrics*, *156* (4), 606–612.

Zisenwine, T., Kaplan, M., Kushnir, J., & Sadeh, A. (2013). Nighttime fears and fantasy –Reality differentiation in preschool children. *Child Psychiatry & Human Development*, *44* (1), 186–199.

Appendix: Children's Sleep Diary (Parent Version)

(Please Complete Daily) Parent's name: ____________________ Child's name: ____________________

Today's Date	5/10/2021							
1. Has your child had any naps today? If so, at what time and for how long?	1 nap at 1 p.m. for 1 hour and 30 min							
2. What time did your child go to bed?	7:30 p.m.							
3. What time did they fall asleep?	7:45 p.m.							
4. How long did it take them to fall asleep?	15 min							
5. Did they wake during the night? If so: - what time did they wake? - what did they do?- how did you/partner respond? - how long did it take child to resettle?	Yes9 p.m.: cried loudly for 5 min and then resettled herself 11 p.m.: as above 1 a.m.: crying – gave a bottle (30 min to resettle)							
6. What time did they wake for the day? What woke them? What did they do?	5 a.m.: woke spontaneously Came into bed with us, went back to sleep							
7. What time did they get out of bed to start the day?	7.15 a.m.							
8. How would you rate the quality of their sleep?	☐ Very poor ☐ Poor ☐ Fair ☐ Good ☐ Very good	☐ Very poor ☐ Poor ☐ Fair ☐ Good ☐ Very good	☐ Very poor ☐ Poor ☐ Fair ☐ Good ☐ Very good	☐ Very poor ☐ Poor ☐ Fair ☐ Good ☐ Very good	☐ Very poor ☐ Poor ☐ Fair ☐ Good ☐ Very good	☐ Very poor ☐ Poor ☐ Fair ☐ Good ☐ Very good	☐ Very poor ☐ Poor ☐ Fair ☐ Good ☐ Very good	☐ Very poor ☐ Poor ☐ Fair ☐ Good ☐ Very good
10. Comments/Notes (if applicable)	Very hot in her room due to weather							

Sleep diary instructions

In order to understand your child's sleep better and assist us in any diagnosis and treatment, we need to collect some important information. Please follow the instructions below and keep the sleep diary (overleaf):

for a period of at least **two weeks** prior to your assessment appointment

or

as directed by your clinician for post-assessment recording

What is a sleep diary?

A sleep diary is the most commonly used way to track someone's sleep over a period of time. In younger children or those who might find it difficult to record this information themselves, we ask that a parent or guardian who is with the child overnight complete the diary.

How should I fill in the sleep diary?

We ask that you please complete the sleep diary **every day**. If possible, please try to complete the bed-time questions in the evening and the night-time/morning questions within one hour of getting up. This is to ensure greater accuracy.

Guide for individual questions

1) Record the time and duration of your child's day-time naps (this includes both **planned/regular** naps and **unplanned/irregular** naps, e.g., falling asleep in the car).
2) Record the time that your child got into bed at bed-time.
3) Record the time that your child fell asleep (please give as accurate an estimate as possible without disturbing your child to check that they are asleep).
4) Record the length of time between the child getting into bed to go to sleep and them actually falling asleep.
5) Record whether or not your child woke during the night after having fallen asleep. If they did wake during the night, record what they did (i.e., how you knew they were awake), what you or your partner (if applicable) did to respond (e.g., waited for 5 minutes, went in and gave them a cuddle, sat on their bed), and how long it took the child to resettle back to sleep.
6) Record the time that your child woke up for the day. What woke them (e.g., did they wake spontaneously by themselves or did they have to be woken up by an alarm or by you)? What did they do next (e.g., came into your room and got into bed with you, fell back to sleep)?
7) Record the time that your child got up to start their day.
8) How well do you think that your child slept during the night?
9) Any further comments or important information. This space is for you to record anything about the **day** or **night** that you feel might have affected your child's sleep (e.g., illness, parent coming home late, special occasion, busy day of activity, weather, noise, etc.).

8

CBT-I Protocols for Older Adults

Fee Benz and Anna F. Johann

Key points
• Insomnia prevalence is higher in the elderly population, probably due to an increase in co-morbid disorders and multiple medication use, in addition to natural aging. • Insomnia in older adults is associated with a number of negative consequences. • While international guidelines recommend CBT-I for late-life insomnia, hypnotics are often prescribed that are associated with serious risks and side effects. • The group of older adults suffering from insomnia is very heterogeneous and, thus, there is not just one single specific CBT-I treatment protocol.

Learning objectives
• To understand normal age-related changes in sleep patterns and specific problems related to the elderly. • To understand that clinical insomnia is not an inevitable consequence of aging. • To gain practical understanding of how CBT-I can be adapted in older adults.

Abstract

Insomnia prevalence is higher in older adults and is associated with a wide range of negative consequences. Besides normal age-related changes, further factors such as co-morbid conditions, multiple medication intake and different life circumstances increase the risk for developing insomnia in older age. While CBT-I has proven to be effective also in late-life insomnia and is recommended as the first-line treatment, in general practice, hypnotics are often prescribed. However, these are associated with severe risks and side effects. In this chapter, it will be outlined how CBT-I can be modified to meet the challenges linked to older age.

Keywords *late-life insomnia, CBT-I, elderly, older adults*

Introduction

About half of older adults suffer from difficulties in initiating and maintaining sleep (Crowley, 2011). Insomnia disorder prevalence is even higher in the elderly than in the younger population, which might be a consequence of the physical and mental health co-morbidities of aging as well as multiple medication use and not aging itself (Hemmeter, Thum & Krieg, 2007; Rodriguez, Dzierzewski & Alessi, 2015; Vitiello, Moe & Prinz, 2002).

Cognitive-Behavioural Therapy for Insomnia (CBT-I) Across the Life Span: Guidelines and Clinical Protocols for Health Professionals,
First Edition. Edited by Chiara Baglioni, Colin A. Espie and Dieter Riemann.

In fact, sleep architecture changes are part of the normal aging process (Gulia & Kumar, 2018). The sleep of older adults is characterized by a decrease in slow wave sleep (stage N3) and REM sleep, accompanied by an increase in lighter non-REM sleep (stage N1). Furthermore, sleep in the elderly tends to be more fragmented than in younger adults. While total sleep time may only slightly decline, many older adults spend more time in bed, resulting in decreased sleep efficiency (Ohayon, Carskadon, Guilleminault & Vitiello, 2004). Additionally, they often show an advanced circadian tendency, i.e., they go to bed earlier and have an associated earlier wake time in the morning (Dzierzewski, O'Brien, Kay & McCrae, 2010).

Besides normative changes in sleep, further age-related factors increase the risk of sleep disturbance in later life. These include an increased incidence of health problems and increased use of multiple medications. Additionally, transition to retirement is often life-changing and may lead to less structured daily routine, less social activity, reduced light exposure, decreased exercise and increased day-time napping (Dzierzewski et al., 2010).

Insomnia in elderly people is associated with a number of negative consequences such as decreased quality of life (Schubert et al., 2002), increased risk of falls (Stone, Ensrud & Ancoli-Israel, 2008), development of cognitive impairment (Yaffe, Falvey & Hoang, 2014) and difficulty with concentration and memory (Cricco, Simonsick & Foley, 2001). Further research suggests that insomnia may be involved in the development of neurodegenerative disease, especially dementia (Osorio et al., 2011). Due to increased life expectancy, the percentage of the elderly population is growing rapidly (https://www.un.org/en/sections/issues-depth/ageing/). Thus, adequate treatment of insomnia is very important. Unfortunately, insomnia in older adults often remains unrecognized and untreated, probably because of the common belief that insomnia is an inevitable consequence of aging (Bélanger, LeBlanc & Morin, 2012). Nevertheless, not all age-related changes are pathological and most of them are not associated with complaints of poor sleep and daytime impairments (Bélanger et al., 2012). CBT-I, the first-line treatment for insomnia (Riemann et al., 2017), has proven to be effective also in later life (McCurry, Logsdon, Teri & Vitiello, 2007; Irwin, Cole & Nicassio, 2006) and in patients who suffer from other medical and psychological conditions (Smith, Huang & Manber, 2005). Although guidelines recommend CBT-I as the first-line treatment, many older people receive hypnotics (Abad & Guilleminault, 2018). However, these drugs are contraindicated and should be avoided in older individuals because of associated risks and side effects, such as rebound insomnia, tolerance, dependency, hangover, nocturnal confusion, motor incoordination, cognitive impairment and increased risk of falls (see Chapter 6). Polypharmacy can aggravate these side effects, especially in older adults (Riemann et al., 2017). In the following, possible adaptations in the assessment of insomnia and of CBT-I will be presented.

Assessment

Initially and before starting CBT-I, a comprehensive assessment of sleep complaints (see also Chapter 5) is strongly recommended. Due to the increased prevalence of co-morbid health conditions (e.g., chronic pain, health conditions, cognitive decline), polypharmacy and psychosocial changes (e.g., social isolation, less daily routine), it is very important to carefully evaluate patients' medical and psychiatric history as well as lifestyle and environmental factors (Roepke & Ancoli-Israel, 2010). Medication use should be reviewed since many substances can interfere with sleep (Patel, Steinberg & Patel, 2018). In older adults the prevalence of sleep-disordered breathing, periodic limb movements in sleep and restless legs syndrome (Roepke & Ancoli-Israel, 2010) are increased, highlighting the importance of identifying intrinsic sleep disorders that cannot be treated effectively with CBT-I alone. Assessment includes the use of sleep diaries, sleep questionnaires, objective measurements (if required) and a comprehensive clinical interview. Due to multimorbidity, close cooperation with the patient's primary care physician is even more important in elderly people.

Suggestions for CBT-I adaptations

In the literature, late-life insomnia is commonly defined as insomnia occurring at the age of 60 and above (McCurry, Gibbons, Logsdon, Vitiello & Teri, 2005). Hence, older adults suffering from insomnia comprise a very heterogeneous group, because patients' conditions (co-morbid somatic or psychiatric illness, medication intake) as well as life circumstances (e.g., retirement, decreased mobility, loneliness, etc.) vary widely in people > 60 years. Therefore, there is not one specific modification for elderly people suffering from insomnia and the following ideas for adaptations do not apply to all older adults. In the literature, there have not been major fundamental modifications of CBT-I in elderly people (Lichstein & Morin, 2000). Nevertheless, we present several suggested adaptations of CBT-I that older adults may benefit from. For older adults with co-morbid conditions, please also see the corresponding chapters in Section III.

Therapy setting

Before introducing adaptations of different CBT-I components, general aspects of the treatment setting should be considered. For example, therapy materials might be reduced in complexity and adapted in type size. Older adults with cognitive impairment might benefit from shorter therapy sessions and memory notes. Further, written reminders placed in strategic places at home could help with treatment adherence in these patients (Bélanger et al., 2012). Since older adults may suffer from loneliness, they might benefit from a group therapy setting as it provides the opportunity for social interactions with persons experiencing similar problems (Bélanger et al., 2012).

Psychoeducation

Psychoeducation should include information about age-related sleep changes in order to help patients to differentiate between normative and pathophysiological changes in sleep patterns. Psychoeducation should also include information on how to stay active during the day, which can help to resist sleepiness and boredom (Bélanger et al., 2012).

Relaxation

Older adults more often experience physical discomfort or suffer from pain that may make progressive muscle relaxation (PMR) ineffective or very unpleasant since tensing and relaxing muscles may exacerbate the pain (Dzierzewski et al., 2010). Thus, other relaxation techniques, such as relaxation through autogenic training, self-hypnosis or guided imagery may be more suitable for these patients.

Sleep restriction/stimulus control

Sleep restriction and stimulus control should be conducted with greater flexibility depending on the patient's condition. For example, some older adults might be satisfied with a sleep efficiency of 80%, making it unnecessary to further reduce bed-time. Moreover, there are a number of specific age-related risks for this particular group of patients. Since sleep restriction therapy may lead to transient increases in somnolence and objectively impaired vigilance (Kyle et al., 2014), it can only be recommended without restrictions if there are no safety concerns (Riemann et al., 2017). If patients are taking hypnotics, which may lead to the side-effects described above, it should be carefully considered whether a less strict sleep restriction regime can be applied or whether hypnotics should be tapered first.

Stimulus control therapy should be adapted in patients taking hypnotic medication because leaving the bed when feeling awake can lead to falls. Also, for older adults with restricted mobility or ambulatory difficulties, getting out of bed during long awakenings can be challenging and thus should be avoided or modified (Bélanger et al., 2012). One possibility could be to sit up in a chair placed next to the bed or even to just sit up in bed. Then, the patient could follow a quiet and relaxing activity (e.g., crossword puzzles, listening to quiet music, reading) until he or she feels sleepy again (Bootzin & Epstein, 2000).

For some individuals, it might be beneficial to permit a brief scheduled day-time nap. This can increase alertness and reduce day-time sleepiness as well as postpone bed-time in the evening. Nevertheless, it should be time-limited (10–15 minutes) and taken regularly in the early afternoon (Bélanger et al., 2012; Joshi, 2008; Rybarczyk, Lund, Garroway & Mack, 2013). Together with the patient, it should be evaluated whether napping is beneficial. Is napping important for the individual or is it sufficient to relax? Is napping necessary because of a medical condition or just used to kill time?

In fact, sleep restriction and stimulus control usually result in more time awake prior to and after the sleep period. This might be a problem, especially for older adults who suffer from loneliness, and may result in less adherence. Further, some elderly people lack daily routines as a consequence of retirement. Therefore, patients and therapists should particularly focus on possible activities to fill the time and to counteract day-time sleepiness (see the following list). Activities should be chosen with regard to a patient's condition.

Ideas for possible activities:

- Going for a walk (to increase light exposure)
- Walk the dog
- Knitting
- Cooking
- Playing jigsaw puzzles
- Playing cards/boardgames
- Listening to music
- Playing an instrument
- Writing letters/emails
- Painting
- Doing handicraft
- Yoga/meditation
- Reading
- Singing in a choir
- Voluntary work
- Dancing
- Learning a new language
- Socializing/meeting friends

Cognitive strategies

Cognitive therapy in older adults should especially focus on age-related changes in sleep patterns and individual differences in sleep needs (Bélanger et al., 2012). Some elderly people may struggle because they think they should be able to sleep like they did when they were young (Bélanger et al., 2012; Rybarczyk et al., 2013). Distinguishing normal age-related changes in sleep from clinical insomnia might be helpful to change unrealistic expectations. Some patients believe that insomnia is an inevitable consequence of aging. In this case, it should be emphasised that a number of factors are involved in the regulation of sleep and that people do have an influence on their sleep. Further common false beliefs among older adults refer to the time they spend in bed, i.e., some older adults believe that napping during the day or longer bed-times are good ways to cope with poor sleep (Rybarczyk et al., 2013). Hence, patients should be advised about the fact that these intuitive but maladaptive coping strategies may play a decisive role in the maintenance of insomnia. Since cognitive impairment can be an issue in elderly people, quantity and complexity of cognitive strategies should be adapted towards the individual needs of patients (Bélanger et al., 2012). Being explicit and providing practical examples might help these patients (Bélanger et al., 2012).

CBT-I in long-term care settings

CBT-I for patients in long-term care settings requires several adaptations. In care homes, for example, elderly people often have to go to bed very early and may, thus, suffer from sleep problems during the night. Other factors associated with the setting may exacerbate sleep problems, such as a disruptive night-time environment/routine care, noise, lighting, etc. (Schnelle et al., 1998). In addition, the cooperation of the caregiver/nursing staff is of the utmost importance. Management of insomnia in these patients is beyond the scope of this chapter. For further information on this topic the reader is referred elsewhere (e.g., Bliwise, Breus, Lichtstein & Morin, 2000; McCurry et al., 2005; Schnelle et al., 1998). In general, regular schedules (meals, etc.), sufficient light exposure, regular social interactions and adequate physical activity should be integrated in the institutional care of the handicapped elderly, either by motivating and/or directly assisting the patients.

References

Abad, V. C., & Guilleminault, C. (2018). Insomnia in elderly patients: Recommendations for pharmacological management. *Drugs & Aging, 35* (9), 791–817.

Bélanger, L., LeBlanc, M., & Morin, C. M. (2012). Cognitive behavioral therapy for insomnia in older adults. *Cognitive and Behavioral Practice, 19* (1), 101–115.

Bliwise, D. L., Breus, M. J., Lichtstein, K. L., & Morin, C. M. (2000). Insomnia in dementia and in residential care. *Treatment of Late-Life Insomnia*, 321–344.

Bootzin, R. R., & Epstein, D. R. (2000). Stimulus control. In K. L. Lichstein & C. M. Morin (Eds.), *Treatment of late-life insomnia* (pp. 167–184). Thousand Oaks, CA: Sage Publications.

Cricco, M., Simonsick, E. M., & Foley, D. J. (2001). The impact of insomnia on cognitive functioning in older adults. *Journal of the American Geriatrics Society, 49* (9), 1185–1189.

Crowley, K. (2011). Sleep and sleep disorders in older adults. *Neuropsychology Review, 21* (1), 41–53.

Dzierzewski, J. M., O'Brien, E. M., Kay, D., & McCrae, C. S. (2010). Tackling sleeplessness: Psychological treatment options for insomnia in older adults. *Nature and Science of Sleep, 2*, 47.

Gulia, K. K., & Kumar, V. M. (2018). Sleep disorders in the elderly: A growing challenge. *Psychogeriatrics, 18* (3), 155–165.

Hemmeter, U. M., Thum, A., & Krieg, J. C. (2007). *Altersinsomnie. Somnologie-Schlafforschung und Schlafmedizin, 11* (2), 84–98.

Irwin, M. R., Cole, J. C., & Nicassio, P. M. (2006). Comparative meta-analysis of behavioral interventions for insomnia and their efficacy in middle-aged adults and in older adults 55+ years of age. *Health Psychology, 25* (1), 3.

Joshi, S. (2008). Nonpharmacologic therapy for insomnia in the elderly. *Clinics in Geriatric Medicine, 24* (1), 107–119.

Kyle, S. D., Miller, C. B., Rogers, Z., Siriwardena, A. N., MacMahon, K. M., & Espie, C. A. (2014). Sleep restriction therapy for insomnia is associated with reduced objective total sleep time, increased daytime somnolence, and objectively impaired vigilance: Implications for the clinical management of insomnia disorder. *Sleep, 37* (2), 229–237.

Lichstein, K. L., & Morin, C. M. (Eds.). (2000). *Treatment of late-life insomnia*. Thousand Oaks, CA: Sage.

McCurry, S. M., Gibbons, L. E., Logsdon, R. G., Vitiello, M. V., & Teri, L. (2005). Nighttime insomnia treatment and education for Alzheimer's disease: A randomized, controlled trial. *Journal of the American Geriatrics Society, 53* (5), 793–802.

McCurry, S. M., Logsdon, R. G., Teri, L., & Vitiello, M. V. (2007). Evidence-based psychological treatments for insomnia in older adults. *Psychology and Aging, 22* (1), 18.

Ohayon, M. M., Carskadon, M. A., Guilleminault, C., & Vitiello, M. V. (2004). Meta-analysis of quantitative sleep parameters from childhood to old age in healthy individuals: Developing normative sleep values across the human lifespan. *Sleep, 27* (7), 1255–1273.

Osorio, R. S., Pirraglia, E., Agüera-Ortiz, L. F., During, E. H., Sacks, H., Ayappa, I., Walsleben, J., Mooney, A., Hussain, A., Glodzik, L., Frangione, B., Martinez-Martin, P., & de Leon, M. J. (2011). Greater risk of Alzheimer's disease in older adults with insomnia. *Journal of the American Geriatrics Society, 59* (3), 559.

Patel, D., Steinberg, J., & Patel, P. (2018). Insomnia in the elderly: A review. *Journal of Clinical Sleep Medicine, 14* (6), 1017–1024.

Riemann, D., Baglioni, C., Bassetti, C., Bjorvatn, B., Dolenc Groselj, L., Ellis, J. G., Ellis, J. G., Espie, C. A., Garcia-Borreguero, D., Gjerstad, M., Goncalves, M., Hertenstein, E., Jansson-Fröjmark, M., Jennum, P. J., Leger, D., Nissen, C., Parrino, L., Paunio, T., Pevernagie, D., Verbraecken, J., Weeß, H.-G., Wichniak, A., Zavalko, I., Arnardottir, E. S., Deleanu, O.-C., Strazisar, B., Zoetmulder, M., & Spiegelhalder, K. (2017). European guideline for the diagnosis and treatment of insomnia. *Journal of Sleep Research, 26* (6), 675–700.

Rodriguez, J. C., Dzierzewski, J. M., & Alessi, C. A. (2015). Sleep problems in the elderly. *Medical Clinics, 99* (2), 431–439.

Roepke, S. K., & Ancoli-Israel, S. (2010). Sleep disorders in the elderly. *Indian Journal of Medical Research, 131* (2), 302.

Rybarczyk, B., Lund, H. G., Garroway, A. M., & Mack, L. (2013). Cognitive behavioral therapy for insomnia in older adults: Background, evidence, and overview of treatment protocol. *Clinical Gerontologist, 36* (1), 70–93.

Schnelle, J. F., Cruise, P. A., Alessi, C. A., Ludlow, K., Al-Samarrai, N. R., & Ouslander, J. G. (1998). Sleep hygiene in physically dependent nursing home residents: Behavioral and environmental intervention implications. *Sleep, 21* (5), 515–523.

Schubert, C. R., Cruickshanks, K. J., Dalton, D. S., Klein, B. E., Klein, R., & Nondahl, D. M. (2002). Prevalence of sleep problems and quality of life in an older population. *Sleep, 25* (8), 48–52.

Smith, M. T., Huang, M. I., & Manber, R. (2005). Cognitive behavior therapy for chronic insomnia occurring within the context of medical and psychiatric disorders. *Clinical Psychology Review*, *25* (5), 559–592.

Stone, K. L., Ensrud, K. E., & Ancoli-Israel, S. (2008). Sleep, insomnia and falls in elderly patients. *Sleep Medicine*, *9*, S18–S22.

Vitiello, M. V., Moe, K. E., & Prinz, P. N. (2002). Sleep complaints cosegregate with illness in older adults: Clinical research informed by and informing epidemiological studies of sleep. *Journal of Psychosomatic Research*, *53* (1), 555–559.

Yaffe, K., Falvey, C. M., & Hoang, T. (2014). Connections between sleep and cognition in older adults. *The Lancet Neurology*, *13* (10), 1017–1028.

9

CBT-I Protocols Across the Female Lifespan

Chiara Baglioni and Laura Palagini

Key points

- Prevalence of insomnia is higher in women compared to men, particularly considering the phases of puberty, pregnancy and menopause.
- Data indicate that insomnia is underdiagnosed and undertreated in women health care.
- Emergent empirical evidence supports the use of CBT for insomnia disorder during adolescence and for women during pregnancy and menopause.
- Specific clinical protocols for puberty, pregnancy and menopause are provided.

Learning objectives

- To understand clinical aspects of insomnia considering gender differences.
- To understand the scientific and clinical importance of offering treatment for insomnia for women across the lifespan.
- To learn CBT-I protocols adaptations for specific stages of a woman's lifespan.

Abstract

The prevalence of insomnia is higher in women than in men. Menarche, pregnancy and menopause are specific periods of women`s lifespan and are associated with marked gender differences in the prevalence of insomnia. Complex interactions between hormonal, psychological, societal and environment factors are associated with peaks of insomnia prevalence during these times of life. Despite this knowledge, not much is done to combat these difficulties from a clinical perspective and, so far, women's sleep has not received sufficient attention from health professionals, either in the research or the clinical context. The result is that insomnia in women during these three important and sensitive life stages is underdiagnosed and undertreated. This chapter aims at providing clinical guidelines for professionals for offering high quality CBT for insomnia to women.

Keywords *CBT-I, insomnia, women, puberty, adolescence, pregnancy, menopause*

Cognitive-Behavioural Therapy for Insomnia (CBT-I) Across the Life Span: Guidelines and Clinical Protocols for Health Professionals,
First Edition. Edited by Chiara Baglioni, Colin A. Espie and Dieter Riemann.

Insomnia during puberty

Puberty respresents an important phase for gender differences in insomnia prevalence. Female adolescents present insomnia symptomatology more frequently compared to male adolescents (Suh, Cho & Zang, 2018; Pengo, Won & Bourjeily, 2018). Menarche is associated with the first evidence of gender differences with respect to risk for mood disturbances and insomnia in female adolescents and also seems to be associated with personality aspects, such as self-oriented critical perfectionism (Richardson & Gradisar, 2020) and emotional and relationship problems (Chang, Chen, Hayter & Lin, 2009). Psychological, societal, environmental factors and stereotypes associated with educational issues may play a key role in explaining gender differences at puberty.

Evidence for CBT-I targeting the transition to puberty

To our knowledge, no specific clinical study has been conducted to evaluate the efficacy of CBT-I in reducing insomnia symptomatology in the transition to puberty in female preadolescents and adolescents.

CBT-I for female preadolescents and adolescents

While scarce evidence is available as background for targeting sleep difficulties during preadolescence to minimize the impact of puberty and menarche on sleep, we do know that CBT-I has positive beneficial effects in children and adolescents (see Chapter 7). Targeting insomnia at an early age may be important for reducing the cascade of psychobiological events that contribute to sleep gender differences. Insomnia being an important psychophysiological process for psychopathology, early treatment of insomnia could impact and reduce risk for mental disorders in women, thus promoting gender equality in development and early adulthood.

It may be important to prepare parents and paediatricians for the fact that changes in sleep patterns, which may be triggered by biological changes, may be stabilized by social contexts. Thus, early interventions could prevent a cascade of negative events that has been associated with gender gaps.

Insomnia during peripartum

Peripartum is a life period that is associated with many life changes for women and their families. Empirical data show that during pregnancy and postpartum, mental health is challenged by hormonal, physiological, relational, emotional and environmental factors (Yanıkkerem, Altıparmak & Karadeniz, 2006; Workman, Bartha & Galea, 2012). The prevalence of maternal psychopathology during peripartum, including depression and anxiety, is high (Gavin et al., 2005; Goodman, Watson & Stubbs, 2016) and is associated with alarming direct and indirect societal costs (Bauer, Knapp & Parsonage, 2016). Insomnia seems to be associated with negative gestational and birth outcomes, as for example premature birth, emergency caesarean section and gestational diabetes (Okun, Schetter & Glynn, 2011; August et al., 2013; Naghi, Keypour, Ahari, Tayalai & Khak, 2011). Insomnia is furthermore a key risk factor for mental disorders in general (Baglioni et al., 2011; Hertenstein et al., 2019) and during peripartum (Emamian, Khazaie, Okun, Tahmasian & Sepehry, 2019). Symptoms of insomnia are common during pregnancy in women, and in all family members (Baglioni et al., 2020). We propose here that a standard assessment of insomnia during pregnancy may be easily implemented and extremely useful to help women sleep better, as well as for early detection of cases of vulnerabilities for mental health problems.

Up to 78% of women complain about disturbed sleep during the third trimester of pregnancy (Baker, Wolfson & Lee, 2009). However, pregnant women experience alterations in sleep duration, quality and pattern across all gestational weeks, and not only during late pregnancy (Mindell, Cook & Nikoloyski, 2015). Sleep problems during pregnancy may be explained by several reasons, including hormonal, societal, environmental, emotional and physical changes (Palagini et al., 2014). Common problems during all three trimesters include short sleep duration, poor sleep quality and insomnia, which persists and worsens during postpartum. Sleep problems are likely both an outcome and a predictor of increased levels of stress during pregnancy, which may be linked to a cascade of negative consequences for the birth, the mother and the child (Palagini et al., 2014). Currently, assessment of sleep and insomnia is not included in standard pregnancy care in most countries. As a consequence, insomnia during pregnancy is underdiagnosed and undertreated (e.g., Bacaro et al., 2020).

Assessment

Assessment of insomnia during pregnancy is not significantly different to the standard protocol (see Chapters 2 and 5). Nevertheless, some specific issues related to pregnancy-related factors and to family members dynamic interactions may be important to be considered in the evaluation phase. These issues are listed in Table 9.1.

Insomnia may trigger and may be triggered by co-morbidity with other mental disorders. Early assessment of mental health problems is crucial for prevention and good clinical practice for taking care of postpartum quality of the life of the mother and the child. Structured clinical interviews to assess psychopathology should be used. Similarly, appropriate questionnaires for mental disorder symptoms should be included in the assessment procedure. A widely used questionnaire during peripartum is the Edinburgh Perinatal Depression Scale (Cox, Chapman, Murray & Jones, 1996). This is a short and easy to administer scale that gives information on depressive symptoms during peripartum.

Sleep disorders are prevalent during pregnancy (see Table 9.2). It is important to carefully assess symptoms and to provide differential diagnosis, in order to evaluate whether multidisciplinary treatment is needed. Restless Leg Syndrome (RLS) is characterized by an uncomfortable feeling of the legs, generally under the knee, which often occurs when lying in bed before falling asleep. The uncomfortable feeling is often relieved by standing up and moving, which affects easiness of falling asleep and impairs sleep quality. Similar to RLS, another sleep problem may be Periodic Limb Movement Disorder (PLMD), in which a person repetitively jerks or kicks during sleep. As these problems often are associated with lack of iron, a condition often present during pregnancy, it is not surprising that their prevalence is enhanced in pregnant women compared to the general population. Snoring is also very prevalent during pregnancy for several physiological reasons related to gestational course and may interfere with good quality sleep and family relationships (e.g., co- sleeping with the partner may be disturbed). Sleep apnoea, a breathing disorder in which a person has repetitive episodes of upper airway obstruction during sleep, is frequent during pregnancy and should get clinical attention. It is beyond the purposes of this book to describe treatment options for sleep disorders co-morbid with insomnia. Nevertheless, accurate diagnosis is particularly important during pregnancy and should lead to therapeutical decisions (e.g., a multidisciplinary team approach vs exclusive psychological intervention).

Table 9.1 Specific pregnancy-related issues to be considered during assessment.

Specific issues	Possible useful instruments
How sleep is perceived as changed during pregnancy compared to before	Subjective retrospective report in clinical interview
How sleep changes during pregnancy	If you have the possibility to follow your patient through pregnancy it is adequate to assess insomnia through the ISI (see Chapter 5) in every trimester.
Specific health issues related to pregnancy and past pregnancies	Clinical interview
Day-time sleepiness	Specific questionnaires (see Chapter 5)
Fatigue	Specific questionnaires (see Chapter 5)
Attachment	Specific questionnaires or interviews (e.g., Adult Attachment Interview; George, Kaplan & Main, 1996)
Work–family balance	Clinical interview
Sleep quality of other family members (partner, children, other family members)	Clinical interview, specific questionnaires for other family members (to be filled in by the father or by the mother for other children)
Sleep habits (e.g., co-sleeping with partner, children; preferred bed-time for all family members, etc.)	Clinical interview
Health issues (mental and physical health) of other family members	Clinical interview, specific questionnaires for other family members (to be filled in by the father or by the mother for other children)

Table 9.2 Sleep psychoeducation for pregnancy-related issues.

How sleep changes during pregnancy	**1st trimester**: day-time sleepiness increases; night awakenings may increase. Stress, nausea and emotional overload may be associated with sleep initiating problems. Behaviours to compensate sleepiness and fatigue during the day, as naps, may impact on nocturnal sleep quality. **2nd trimester**: day-time sleepiness and fatigue gets better; nocturnal awakenings may persist due to need to urinate and discomfort with sleep position. **3rd trimester**: late pregnancy is associated with shorter sleep duration, increased number of night awakenings; prolonged sleep onset latency. All these changes are caused both by pregnancy course and by social, environmental, emotional and behavioural changes. Sleep duration may even be increased during the first two trimesters, but it may be a result of increased sleep interruptions. As insomnia is a problem of sleep continuity, and not much of sleep duration, interrupted sleep may affect health more than shortened sleep duration.
Sleep disorders prevalence during pregnancy	**Insomnia**: up to 78% (National Sleep Foundation, 2007). **RLS**: 12–27% (Manconi et al., 2004) **Snoring**: 14–45% (Silvestri et al., 2019) **Sleep Apnoea**: 4–9% (Silvestri et al., 2019)
Consequences of poor sleep	Being resistant to sleep loss could be associated with positive feelings of resilience and good parenting. Nevertheless, ***good balance between resistance and dedicating good time to sleep should be found***. Negative consequences of poor sleep for birth, maternal and child's health should be discussed during clinical sessions.
Number of pregnancies	Sleep problems seem to be more severe during the first pregnancy (Mindell et al., 2015). Experienced mothers may have learned that prioritizing sleep is key for good functioning during the day, including maternal emotional availability and sensitivity.
Age and career	Pregnant women over 35 years are more likely to have a career, spend less time in bed and report the shortest sleep duration compared to pregnant women with less than 35 years (Mindell, 2007). Nevertheless, sleep duration is not that much associated with insomnia, as sleep continuity, so more clinical attention should be dedicated to reach continuous sleep.
Sleep hygiene	Obviously, smoking, alcohol, caffeine are even more important to be considered in psychological programs for healthy pregnancy compared to the general population. Similar attention to healthy eating, regular and well-balanced physical activity, and healthy sleep are dynamically interrelated.
Comfort when sleeping	Some attention should be dedicated to a comfortable sleep environment, including to choose the right pyjamas (some women prefer to sleep with a bra when pregnant), a good pillow (specific pregnancy pillows are available) and to make your bedroom comfortable.
Co-sleeping with partner/husband	Sleep during pregnancy may be challenging (increase of snoring, moving to find the right position, night awakenings). There is no good or bad solution, but at best each couple should negotiate the solution that best suits them. Some couples prefer to sleep separately for a while. Instead, others may prefer to sleep together but use specific pregnancy pillows to improve sleep comfort.
Napping	Pregnant women may be often tempted to sleep during the day. This may however be risky, as day-time sleep may interfere with adequate sleep pressure at times to go to bed in the evening. Short naps (around 15–30 minutes) at early afternoon may be adequate.
Liquids	Drinking a lot during the day should be reinforced. Nevertheless, women should be alerted to avoid drinking too much in the evening.
Nausea	During early pregnancy, sleep onset may be disturbed by nausea. A light snack before going to bed could help in reducing nausea and facilitate sleep initiation.
Bed time	Women may feel sleepy in the evening. They should be encouraged to go to bed earlier than usual and avoid falling asleep on the couch.
Presence of other children	If other children with sleep problems are present, mothers should be guided to solve these problems before the new baby arrives. In general, some rest during the day should be planned to not exceed personal resources. A nap for younger children may be essential. Otherwise, a plan of quiet activities after lunch should be encouraged in which expecting mothers may have some time to relax.

Evidence for CBT-I applied during pregnancy

Four randomized controlled studies have evaluated the efficacy of psychological interventions for sleep difficulties during pregnancy. Tested experimental interventions consisted of four sessions of therapy including Sleep Hygiene Education (SHE) and instructions for stimulus control (Rezaei, Moghadam, Nejat & Dehghannaveri, 2014); five sessions of CBT-I including SHE, stimulus control, strategies for reducing cognitive and somatic arousal, and modified sleep restriction therapy (SRT) (Manber et al., 2019), and six sessions of digital CBT-I (using Sleepio, see Chapter 23) including the standard protocol with adapted SRT (Felder, Epel, Neuhaus, Krystal & Prather, 2020; Kalmbach et al., 2019). In total, 278 expectant mothers received experimental interventions compared to 267 pregnant women receiving control interventions. Altogether, these studies suggest that CBT-I improves maternal sleep and related mood symptoms; SRT should be adapted to minimize related stress and fatigue and in some cases it may not be indicated during pregnancy.

CBT-I adaptation for expectant mothers

Insomnia during pregnancy can be treated using the standard protocol (Chapter 2) and following general principles of the stepped care model (Section V, Chapter 23, Figure 23.1). Nevertheless, the treatment protocol may benefit from some pregnancy-related adaptions. These may be summarized as follows:

1) Sleep psychoeducation should be adapted to pregnancy-related issues.
2) SRT should be modified to reduce excessive related increase of fatigue and stress.
3) Strategies targeting emotional aspects may be emphasised and deserve a more central role than in the standard CBT-I protocol.
4) Family issues should be taken into consideration.
5) Balance between working and family lives may be important to target.
6) Sleep psychoeducation for postpartum should be included.

1. Sleep psychoeducation for pregnancy-related issues

Sleep psychoeducation should focus on specific aspects of pregnancy and post-partum. Furthermore, patients should be advised that while insomnia during pregnancy is very common, it is not inevitable. Instead, insomnia during pregnancy has been associated with several negative outcomes for the mother and the child (e.g., Palagini et al., 2014). Data on risks of insomnia and efficacy of CBT-I should be shared with the patient during the psychoeducation session. These are described in Table 9.2.

2. Adaptation of SRT

SRT is highly effective for insomnia, even when administered alone (see Chapter 2). Nevertheless, this strategy may be associated with increased fatigue, stress and tiredness, which if excessive may be not helpful during pregnancy. For this reason, several adaptations of this strategy have been proposed to minimize its potential adverse effects. All approaches aim at restricting the time spent in bed to the actual time spent asleep in order to reach optimal sleep efficiency. Proposed modifications of SRT are:

a) **Sleep compression.** Whereas SRT abruptly curtails time in bed to a minimal quantity and afterwards gradually expands bed-time duration to optimal sleep efficiency, sleep compression interventions comprise the gradual constriction of time in bed to optimal duration.
b) **Addition of 30 minutes.** Calculation of an SRT window + 30 minutes has proved to be efficacious in a randomized controlled trial (Manber et al., 2019).
c) **Six hours at least.** Some authors suggest using SRT with the minimal time in bed ≥ 6 hours (Kalmbach et al., 2019).

3. Strategies targeting emotional processes

Sleep quality during peripartum may be triggered by several emotional factors, which may interact with sleep processes. Dedicating a specific module to clinical strategies directed to emotional processes may be associated with important benefits. See Chapters 17, 18 and 19 for clinical protocols based on strategies targeting emotional processes applied to patients with insomnia disorder.

4. Family issues should be taken into consideration

Maternal insomnia during pregnancy may be triggered by the sleep difficulties of other family members. If other children complain of sleep difficulties, parents should be guided to solve these problems before the new baby arrives. This is important to avoid situations in which sleep problems of older children, combined with sleep characteristics of new babies, may cause extremely poor nights for both parents, and especially mothers (see Chapter 7 for interventions for insomnia in children). Fathers' sleep issues may also interfere with mothers' sleep quality. Accurate assessment is needed and treatment for the father may need to be suggested. CBT-I for fathers should follow standard protocols (Chapter 2). Nevertheless, as for mothers, peripartum issues and family dynamics should be considered.

5. Balance between working and family life

Many expectant mothers may experience stress in balancing working and family life. This stress may trigger insomnia problems. Dedicating a therapy session to this life theme may be important. This session should be focused upon helping women in prioritizing, planning and organizing their time in order to reach their aims. Assertiveness training may also be useful for pregnant women in understanding and recognizing their feelings, improving communication, improving their abilities to manage job satisfaction and their new role as mothers.

6. Psychoeducation for sleep at postpartum

CBT-I during pregnancy may benefit for inclusion of a session module that comprehensively prepares expectant mothers for postpartum sleep issues. Refer to Chapter 7 for clinical protocols for sleep training for babies' and infants' sleep.

Conclusions

Several practical aspects should be targeted when offering CBT-I to pregnant women. CBT-I during pregnancy may offer important benefits towards a healthy course of pregnancy, birth and during the postpartum period. The literature suggests that CBT-I is well accepted by women, particularly those who may be resistant to medication during such a sensitive time (Sedov, Goodman & Tomfohr-Madsen, 2017). In Table 9.3 a possible seven sessions of CBT-I intervention for pregnant women are proposed.

Insomnia during menopause

The menopausal transition is associated with fluctuating hormone levels and the emergence of physiological and psychological symptoms, including hot flashes, sleep disturbances and mood changes, which may vary among women in terms of frequency, severity and duration (for an overview see Caruso, Masci, Cipollone & Palagini, 2019; Silvestri et al., 2019). Midlife women transitioning through menopause are more likely than women in other stages of their lives

Table 9.3 Suggestion of seven weeks of CBT-I during pregnancy.

First session	Psychoeducation adapted to pregnancy-related issues
Second session	Stimulus control and adapted SRT
Third session	Cognitive therapy
Fourth session	Strategies directed to emotional processes
Fifth session	Family dynamics and work–life balance
Sixth session	Psychoeducation for post-partum
Seventh session	Conclusion and prevention of relapses

to report sleep difficulties. The prevalence of symptoms of insomnia may range from 39 to 60%, with 26% of perimenopausal women experiencing a chronic form of insomnia with a negative impact on day-time functioning, quality of life and overall health (for an overview see Caruso et al., 2019; Silvestri et al., 2019; Proserpio et al., 2020). It has been shown that amongst other factors, insomnia and disturbed sleep may contribute to depressive disorders during the menopausal transition (Caruso et al., 2019; Silvestri et al., 2019). Development of insomnia at this time can be considered as multifactorial (Caruso et al., 2019; Proserpio et al., 2020). Among the psychological/psychopathological factors, personality traits, such as obsessive–compulsive traits and neuroticism, may predispose to the development of insomnia. In addition, a history of severe premenstrual symptoms may increase a woman's vulnerability to insomnia during the menopausal transition, as may a history of depression or previous episodes of insomnia. Endocrine and hormonal changes are also predisposing factors for insomnia during the perimenopause; for instance, the decrease in estradiol hormone medication levels is associated with a worse sleep quality (Caruso et al., 2019; Silvestri et al., 2019; Proserpio et al., 2020). In addition, since estrogen and progesterone regulate and stabilize the circadian system, a decreased sensitivity to estrogens in the hypothalamus during menopause has been related to circadian rhythm disturbances. These circadian rhythm alterations, together with age-related sleep changes, may contribute to the development of sleep difficulties during the perimenopause (Caruso et al., 2019; Silvestri et al., 2019; Proserpio et al., 2020). All these factors may interact with precipitating factors, providing a complex basis for the development of insomnia in midlife women. Among the factors precipitating insomnia, age-related stress, poor health, sleep-related breathing and movement disorders and chronic pain may play a role during the menopause (Silvestri et al., 2019; Proserpio et al., 2020). In addition, as estrogen levels decline, vasomotor symptoms, which are a hallmark of the menopausal transition, tend to emerge, and the presence of hot flashes is consistently associated with insomnia and may contribute to its precipitation (Silvestri et al., 2019; Proserpio et al., 2020). Factors perpetuating insomnia include the persistence of hot flashes, which, during the perimenopause, tend to occur in the early hours of the night and, by interrupting sleep, perpetuate insomnia with a self-reinforcing feedback loop. In particular, a 'domino effect' has been postulated with hot flashes, insomnia and depressive symptoms all contributing to the perpetuation of both insomnia and depressive symptoms (Baker, Lampio, Saaesranta & Polo-Kantola, 2018; Caruso et al., 2019; Silvestri et al., 2019, Proserpio et al., 2020). In addition, physiological hyperarousal has been described in the peri-menopause and may contribute to the maintenance of insomnia through associations with dysfunctional cognitions such as worry and rumination about sleep and misattribution of the cause of sleep problems. It may also trigger maladaptive sleep habits (an excessive time in bed, an irregular sleep schedule), and alterations in mood and quality of life. Therefore, the physiological hyperarousal seen in the perimenopause may contribute to the vicious cycle of insomnia during this period of a woman's life (Baker et al., 2018; Caruso et al., 2019; Silvestri et al., 2019; Proserpio et al., 2020).

Assessment

An assessment of insomnia (see Chapters 2 and 5) during menopause is not substantially different to standard protocols. Nevertheless, some specific issues related to menopausal factors may be important to be considered in the evaluation phase. As for pregnancy, patients should be advised that, although sleep changes are triggered by biological processes, their maintenance is often dependent on several psychosocial factors, which may be effectively contrasted with appropriate treatment. These issues are listed in Table 9.4.

As mentioned before, a 'domino effect' has been postulated and may contribute to the perpetuation of both insomnia and depressive symptoms and an early assessment of vasomotor and depressive symptoms is of key importance. Appropriate questionnaires for hot flashes (HF) and night sweating (NS) and for depressive symptoms should be included in the assessment procedure.

Other sleep disorders are prevalent during menopause. It is important to carefully assess symptoms and to provide differential diagnosis, in order to evaluate carefully whether multidisciplinary treatment is needed. RLS occurs about twice as often in women as in men and symptom severity increases after menopause.

Snoring is also another factor that is very prevalent during menopause. It is beyond the scope of this book to describe treatment options for sleep disorders co-morbid with insomnia. Nevertheless, accurate diagnosis is particularly important during menopause and should lead to appropriate clinical decision-making (i.e., the multidisciplinary team approach vs exclusive psychological intervention).

Table 9.4 Specific menopause-related issues to be considered during assessment.

Specific issues	Possible useful instruments
How sleep is perceived as changed during menopause compared to before	Subjective retrospective report in a clinical interview
How sleep changes during menopause	If you have the possibility to follow your patient through menopause it is adequate to assess insomnia through the ISI (see Chapter 3 of Section I)
Daytime sleepiness, fatigue	Specific questionnaires (see Chapter 3 of Section I)
Hot flushes, night sweating	Specific questionnaires (Hot Flush Rating Scale: frequency of HF/NS experienced in the previous week and/or twenty-four-hour hot-flush diary for monitoring their HF/NS prospectively for 24 h)
Depressive symptoms	Specific questionnaires or interviews (see Chapter 5 of Section I)
Sleep habits and other sleep disorders	Clinical interview
Health issues: mental and physical health	Clinical interview

Evidence for CBT-I during menopause

Five clinical studies on CBT-I have been undertaken and are described below. Two studies come from the Menopause Strategies Finding Lasting Answers for Symptoms and Health research network (MsFLASH). The trial conducted by McCurry et al. (2016) was a single-site, randomized controlled trial of a telephone CBT-I intervention versus telephone-delivered menopause education over 8 weeks in 104 perimenopausal women with insomnia symptoms assessed with the Insomnia Severity Index scale (ISI) and sleep diaries (see Chapter 5). The CBT-I and menopause education interventions both consisted of six 20–30-minute telephone sessions over eight weeks. The CBT-I protocol provided information about age/menopause-related sleep changes and the rationale for a behavioural approach, implemented by re-scheduling sleep using sleep restriction and stimulus control instructions, changing beliefs/attitudes about sleep and applying sleep hygiene recommendations. The menopausal education protocol included educational content and texts relevant to women's health and quality of life. Sessions were designed to reduce uncertainty about changes occurring during menopause and to help women identify symptom self-management strategies with no practice or instruction in CBT-I principles. This first randomized controlled trial showed that brief, telephone-delivered CBT-I resulted in significant 8- and 24-week improvements in self-reported insomnia symptoms, overall sleep quality, sleep latency, wake-time after sleep onset, and sleep efficiency compared with the menopausal educational protocol. In addition, CBT-I was able to reduce self-reported Hot Flashes interference with sleep at 8 and 24 weeks compared with the menopausal educational protocol. The authors hypothesised that the cognitive strategies taught during CBT-I may reduce day-time dysfunction associated with sleep loss dependent on the vasomotor symptoms response. A second paper from MsFLASH (Guthrie et al., 2018) compared the results of several randomized control trials studying the effects of different interventions on insomnia and vasomotor symptoms. As previously seen, findings from these pooled analyses suggested that telephone-delivered CBT-I was more effective for reducing moderate to severe symptoms of insomnia in menopausal women with hot flashes than other commonly used pharmacological or lifestyle modification options considered. A controlled trial by Drake et al. (2019) evaluated 150 postmenopausal women with chronic insomnia according to DSM-5 criteria and assessed them with the ISI and sleep diaries. Interventions were: sleep hygiene education, versus sleep restriction therapy, versus face-to-face CBT-I. Blinded assessments were performed at baseline, post-treatment, and 6 months after treatment. CBT-I and sleep restriction were more effective in the treatment of insomnia than sleep hygiene education. Although the responses to CBT-I and sleep restriction were similar, CBT-I treatment out-performed sleep restriction alone in improving sleep maintenance, a common problem following the menopausal transition.

Importantly CBT-I delivered via face-to-face or telemedicine boasts much larger reductions in menopause-related insomnia symptoms than hormone replacement therapy, antidepressant medication, yoga and exercise (Guthrie et al., 2018). These data support CBT-I and SRT as first-line treatments for menopausal insomnia. Taken together, all three studies demonstrate the efficacy of CBT-I in the treatment of menopausal insomnia, confirming it as an effective intervention for these symptoms.

Interestingly, Kalmbach et al. (2019) tested whether CBT-I improves depressive symptoms, maladaptive thinking and somatic hyperarousal in postmenopausal women with insomnia and whether sleep restriction therapy (SRT) is equally efficacious. Also,117 postmenopausal women with peri- or postmenopausal onset of chronic insomnia were randomized to three treatment conditions: sleep hygiene education control (SHE), SRT and multicomponent CBT-I. Multicomponent CBT-I patients received six weekly sessions, which covered behavioural (sleep restriction and stimulus control) and cognitive (e.g., cognitive restructuring) components, as well as relaxation strategies (e.g., progressive muscle relaxation and autogenic training) and sleep hygiene education. Blinded assessments were performed at baseline, post-treatment and 6-month follow-up. The authors concluded that CBT-I produced the larger reductions in depressive symptoms, whereas SRT produced moderate reductions but not until 6 months post-treatment. CBT-I and SRT both produced large improvements in dysfunctional beliefs about sleep, but weaker influences on presleep cognitive arousal, rumination and worry. CBT-I produced the largest and most durable improvements in presleep somatic hyperarousal. Although CBT-I and SRT both produced improvements in these areas, CBT-I was the superior treatment option based on more immediate, durable and larger reductions in depression, dysfunctional beliefs about sleep and presleep somatic hyperarousal. Even so, treatment effects on overall cognitive arousal, including worry, rumination and presleep perseverative cognitions, were less robust. This suggests that postmenopausal women with insomnia would be likely to benefit from ensuring that CBT-I and SRT sufficiently target cognitive arousal and stress dysregulation, which may improve treatment effects for both insomnia and depression, as well as reduce the risk for future relapse of these disorders.

These results are consistent with prior findings showing that CBT-I improves symptoms of insomnia and depression in patients with both disorders. Further, research data suggest that postmenopausal women with insomnia disorder and co-morbid major depression may experience reductions in both sleep and mood symptoms via cognitive-behavioural insomnia interventions. A more recent study from the MsFLASH network (Diem et al., 2020) tested six interventions treating vasomotor symptoms and menopause-related quality of life. Interventions included escitalopram of 10–20 mg/day, yoga/aerobic exercise, 1.8 g/day of omega-3-fatty acids, oral 17-beta-estradiol of 0.5 mg/day, venlafaxine XR of 75 mg/day and cognitive-behavioural therapy for insomnia (CBT-I). Significant improvements in total menopause-specific Quality of Life and psychosocial, physical and sexual factors were observed with CBT-I indicating that it may improve quality of life and all the physical and mental factors associated with menopause.

Adaptation of CBT- I in menopause

No specific CBT-I adaptations have been proposed for treating insomnia during menopause. Insomnia during menopause can be treated using the standard protocol (Chapter 2) and following the general principles of the stepped care model (see Section V, Chapter 23, Figure 23.1). CBT-I delivered face-to-face or via telephone have both been reported as effective during the menopause. Nevertheless, treatment protocols may benefit from some menopause-related adaptation. These may be summarized as follows:

1) Sleep psychoeducation should be adapted to age-related sleep modification and menopause-related sleep issues (Table 9.5).
2) SRT has emerged as a key component of the CBT-I protocol in menopause and should be applied as part of CBT-I in treating insomnia in menopausal women.
3) Progressive muscle relaxation and autogenic training might decrease sympathetic tone, contributing to a reduction in vasomotor symptoms, and so also merits inclusion in the CBT-I protocol during the menopause.
4) Strategies targeting cognitive arousal including worry, rumination, presleep perseverative cognitions and stress dysregulation should be part of the CBT-I menopause protocol as they are likely to improve treatment effects for both insomnia and depression.

Conclusions

Several aspects should be targeted when offering CBT-I to menopausal women. CBT-I during menopause may have important benefits for menopausal women. Significant improvements in total menopause-specific quality of life, psychosocial, physical and sexual factors and in depressive symptoms have been observed, indicating that CBT-I may be a key intervention during menopause. In Table 9.6 a possible six sessions of CBT-I intervention for menopausal women is proposed.

Table 9.5 Sleep psychoeducation for menopause-related issues.

How sleep changes during menopause	Endocrine and hormonal changes are predisposing factors for insomnia and circadian sleep dysregulation during peri-menopause. These circadian rhythm alterations, together with age-related sleep changes, may predispose to insomnia in perimenopause. All these factors may interact with precipitating factors during menopause, such as age-related stress, poor health, other sleep disturbances and chronic pain. In addition, as estrogen levels decline, vasomotor symptoms with hot flushes are consistently associated with insomnia. Factors perpetuating insomnia include the persistence of hot flushes, which, during the perimenopause, tend to occur in the early hours of the night and, by interrupting sleep, perpetuate insomnia with a self-reinforcing feedback loop.
Other sleep disorders during menopause	Snoring and rest leg syndrome are frequent during menopause and may contribute to precipitate insomnia.
Consequences of poor sleep	A 'domino effect' has been postulated among hot flashes, insomnia and depressive symptoms and may contribute to the perpetuation of both insomnia and depressive symptoms.
Sleep hygiene	Healthy eating, regular and well-balanced physical activity, and healthy sleep are dynamically interrelated.

Table 9.6 Suggestion of six weeks of CBT-I during menopause.

First session	Psychoeducation adapted to sleep-related changes and menopause-related issues
Second session	SRT and SC
Third session	Strategies directed to cognitive arousal and stress dysregulation
Fourth session	Progressive muscle relaxation and autogenic training
Fifth session	Sleep hygiene education and sleep disturbances in CBT-I adaptation
Sixth session	Conclusion and prevention of relapses

References

August, E. M., Salihu, H. M., Biroscak, B. J., Rahman, S., Bruder, K., & Whiteman, V. E. (2013). Systematic review on sleep disorders and obstetric outcomes: Scope of current knowledge. *American Journal of Perinatology*, *30* (04), 323–334. https://doi.org/10.1055/s-0032-1324703.

Bacaro, V., Benz, F., Pappaccogli, A., De Bartolo, P., Johann, A. F., Palagini, L., Lombardo, C., Feige, B., Riemann, D., & Baglioni, C. (2020). Interventions for sleep problems during pregnancy: A systematic review. *Sleep Medicine Reviews*, *50*, 101234. https://doi.org/10.1016/j.smrv.2019.101234.

Baglioni, C., Battagliese, G., Feige, B., Spiegelhalder, K., Nissen, C., Voderholzer, U., Lombardo, C., & Riemann, D. (2011). Insomnia as a predictor of depression: A meta-analytic evaluation of longitudinal epidemiological studies. *Journal of Affective Disorders*, *135* (1–3), 10–19. https://doi.org/10.1016/j.jad.2011.01.011.

Baglioni, C., Tang, N.K.Y., Johann, A.F., Altena, E., Bramante, A., Riemann, D., Palagini, L. (2020). Insomnia and poor sleep quality during peripartum: A family issue with potential long term consequences on mental health. *Journal of Maternal-Fetal and Neonatal Medicine*, 1–9. https://doi.org/10.1080/14767058.2020.1854718.

Baker, F. C., Lampio, L., Saaresranta, T., & Polo-Kantola, P. (2018). Sleep and sleep disorders in the menopausal transition. *Sleep Medicine Clinics*, *13* (3), 443–456. https://doi.org/10.1016/j.jsmc.2018.04.011.

Baker, F. C., Wolfson, A. R., & Lee, K. A. (2009). Association of sociodemographic, lifestyle, and health factors with sleep quality and daytime sleepiness in women: Findings from the 2007 National Sleep Foundation 'Sleep in America Poll'. *Journal of Women's Health*, *18* (6), 841–849. https://doi.org/10.1089/jwh.2008.0986.

Bauer, A., Knapp, M., & Parsonage, M. (2016). Lifetime costs of perinatal anxiety and depression. *Journal of Affective Disorders*, *192*, 83–90. https://doi.org/10.1016/j.jad.2015.12.005.

Caruso, D., Masci, I., Cipollone, G., & Palagini, L. (2019). Insomnia and depressive symptoms during the menopausal transition: Theoretical and therapeutic implications of a self-reinforcing feedback loop. *Maturitas*, *123*, 78–81. https://doi.org/10.1016/j.maturitas.2019.02.007.

Chang, Y. T., Chen, Y. C., Hayter, M., & Lin, M. L. (2009). Menstrual and menarche experience among pubescent female students in Taiwan: Implications for health education and promotion practice. *Journal of Clinical Nursing, 18* (14), 2040–2048. https://doi.org/10.1111/j.1365-2702.2008.02545.x.

Cox, J. L., Chapman, G., Murray, D., & Jones, P. (1996). Validation of the Edinburgh Postnatal Depression Scale (EPDS) in non-postnatal women. *Journal of Affective Disorders, 39* (3), 185–189.

Diem, S. J., LaCroix, A. Z., Reed, S. D., Larson, J. C., Newton, K. M., Ensrud, K. E., Woods, N. F., & Guthrie, K. A. (2020). Effects of pharmacologic and nonpharmacologic interventions on menopause-related quality of life: A pooled analysis of individual participant data from four MsFLASH trials. *Menopause, 27* (10), 1126–1136. https://doi.org/10.1097/gme.0000000000001597.

Drake, C. L., Kalmbach, D. A., Arnedt, J. T., Cheng, P., Tonnu, C. V., Cuamatzi-Castelan, A., & Fellman-Couture, C. (2019). Treating chronic insomnia in postmenopausal women: A randomized clinical trial comparing cognitive-behavioral therapy for insomnia, sleep restriction therapy, and sleep hygiene education. *Sleep, 42* (2), zsy217. https://doi.org/10.1093/sleep/zsy217.

Emamian, F., Khazaie, H., Okun, M. L., Tahmasian, M., & Sepehry, A. A. (2019). Link between insomnia and perinatal depressive symptoms: A meta-analysis. *Journal of Sleep Research, 28* (6), e12858. https://doi.org/10.1111/jsr.12858.

Felder, J. N., Epel, E. S., Neuhaus, J., Krystal, A. D., & Prather, A. A. (2020). Efficacy of digital cognitive behavioral therapy for the treatment of insomnia symptoms among pregnant women: A randomized clinical trial. *JAMA Psychiatry, 77* (5), 484–492. https://doi.org/10.1001/jamapsychiatry.2019.4491.

Gavin, N. I., Gaynes, B. N., Lohr, K. N., Meltzer-Brody, S., Gartlehner, G., & Swinson, T. (2005). Perinatal depression: A systematic review of prevalence and incidence. *Obstetrics & Gynecology, 106* (5), 1071–1083. https://doi.org/10.1097/01.AOG.0000183597.31630.db.

George, C., Kaplan, N., & Main, M. (1996). Adult attachment interview. Unpublished manuscript, Department of Psychology, University of California at Berkeley, Berkeley, CA.

Goodman, J. H., Watson, G. R., & Stubbs, B. (2016). Anxiety disorders in postpartum women: A systematic review and meta-analysis. *Journal of Affective Disorders, 203*, 292–331. https://doi.org/10.1016/j.jad.2016.05.033.

Guthrie, K. A., Larson, J. C., Ensrud, K. E., Anderson, G. L., Carpenter, J. S., Freeman, E. W., Joffe, H., LaCroix, A. Z., Manson, J. A. E., Morin, C. M., Newton, K. M., Otte, J., Reed, S. D., McCurry, S. M., (2018). Effects of pharmacologic and nonpharmacologic interventions on insomnia symptoms and self-reported sleep quality in women with hot flashes: A pooled analysis of individual participant data from four MsFLASH trials, *Sleep, 41* (1), Zsx190. https://doi.org/10.1093/sleep/zsx190ù.

Hertenstein, E., Feige, B., Gmeiner, T., Kienzler, C., Spiegelhalder, K., Johann, A., Jansson-Fröjmark, M., Palagini, L., Rücker, G., Riemann, D., & Baglioni, C. (2019). Insomnia as a predictor of mental disorders: A systematic review and meta-analysis. *Sleep Medicine Reviews*, 43, 96–105. https://doi.org/10.1016/j.smrv.2018.10.006.

Kalmbach, D. A., Cheng, P., Arnedt, J. T., Anderson, J. R., Roth, T., Fellman-Couture, C., Williams, R. A., & Drake, C. L. (2019). Treating insomnia improves depression, maladaptive thinking, and hyperarousal in postmenopausal women: Comparing cognitive-behavioral therapy for insomnia (CBTI), sleep restriction therapy, and sleep hygiene education. *Sleep Medicine*, 55, 124–134. https://doi.org/10.1016/j.sleep.2018.11.019.

Manber, R., Bei, B., Simpson, N., Asarnow, L., Rangel, E., Sit, A., & Lyell, D. (2019). Cognitive behavioral therapy for prenatal insomnia: A randomized controlled trial. *Obstetrics and Gynaecology, 133* (5), 911. https://doi.org/10.1097/AOG.0000000000003216.

Manconi, M., Govoni, V., De Vito, A., Economou, N. T., Cesnik, E., Mollica, G., & Granieri, E. (2004). Pregnancy as a risk factor for restless legs syndrome. *Sleep Medicine, 5* (3): 305–308. https://doi.org/10.1016/j.sleep.2004.01.013.

McCurry, S. M., Guthrie, K. A., Morin, C. M., Woods, N. F., Landis, C. A., Ensrud, K. E., Larson, J. C., Joffe, H., Cohen, L. S., Hunt, J. R., Newton, K. M., Otte, J. L., Reed, S. D., Sternfeld, B., Tinker, L. F., & LaCroix, A. Z. (2016). Telephone-based cognitive behavioral therapy for insomnia in perimenopausal and postmenopausal women with vasomotor symptoms. *JAMA Internal Medicine, 176* (7), 913. https://doi.org/10.1001/jamainternmed.2016.1795.

Mindell, J. A., Cook, R. A., & Nikolovski, J. (2015). Sleep patterns and sleep disturbances across pregnancy. *Sleep Medicine, 16* (4), 483–488. https://doi.org/10.1016/j.sleep.2014.12.006.

Naghi, I., Keypour, F., Ahari, S. B., Tavalai, S. A., & Khak, M. (2011). Sleep disturbance in late pregnancy and type and duration of labour. *Journal of Obstetrics and Gynaecology, 31* (6), 489–491. https://doi.org/10.3109/01443615.2011.579196.

Okun, M. L., Schetter, C. D., & Glynn, L. M. (2011). Poor sleep quality is associated with preterm birth. *Sleep, 34* (11), 1493–1498. https://doi.org/10.5665/sleep.1384.

Palagini, L., Gemignani, A., Banti, S., Manconi, M., Mauri, M., & Riemann, D. (2014). Chronic sleep loss during pregnancy as a determinant of stress: Impact on pregnancy outcome. *Sleep Medicine, 15* (8), 853–859. https://doi.org/10.1016/j.sleep.2014.02.013.

Pengo, M. F., Won, C. H., & Bourjeily, G. (2018). Sleep in women across the life span. *Chest*, *154* (1), 196–206. https://doi.org/10.1016/j.chest.2018.04.005.

Proserpio, P., Marra, S., Campana, C., Agostoni, E. C., Palagini, L., Nobili, L., & Nappi, R. E. (2020). Insomnia and menopause: A narrative review on mechanisms and treatments. *Climacteric*, *23* (6), 539–549. https://doi.org/10.1080/13697137.2020.1799973.

Rezaei, E., Moghadam, Z. B., Nejat, S., & Dehghannayeri, N. (2014). The impact of sleep healthy behavior education on the quality of life in the pregnant women with sleep disorder: A randomized control trial in the year 2012. *Iranian Journal of Nursing and Midwifery Research*, *19* (5), 508.

Richardson, C., & Gradisar, M. (2020). Perfectionism and insomnia in adolescents: The role of vulnerability to stress and gender. *Journal of Adolescence*, *85*, 70–79. https://doi.org/10.1016/j.adolescence.2020.10.003.

Sedov, I. D., Goodman, S. H., & Tomfohr-Madsen, L. M. (2017). Insomnia treatment preferences during pregnancy. *Journal of Obstetric, Gynecologic & Neonatal Nursing*, *46* (3), e95–e104. https://doi.org/10.1016/j.jogn.2017.01.005.

Silvestri, R., Aricò, I., Bonanni, E., Bonsignore, M., Caretto, M., Caruso, D., Di Perri, M. C., Galletta, S., Lecca, R. M., Lombardi, C., Maestri, M., Miccoli, M., Palagini, L., Provini, F., Puligheddu, M., Savarese, M., Spaggiari, M. C., & Simoncini, T. (2019). Italian Association of Sleep Medicine (Associazione Italiana Medicina del Sonno: AIMS) position statement and guideline on the treatment of menopausal sleep disorders. *Maturitas*, *129*, 30–39. https://doi.org/10.1016/j.maturitas.2019.08.006.

Suh, S., Cho, N., & Zhang, J. (2018). Sex differences in insomnia: From epidemiology and etiology to intervention. *Current Psychiatry Reports*, *20*, 1–12. https://doi.org/10.1007/s11920-018-0940-9.

Workman, J. L., Barha, C. K., & Galea, L. A. (2012). Endocrine substrates of cognitive and affective changes during pregnancy and postpartum. *Behavioral Neuroscience*, *126* (1), 54. https://doi.org/10.14288/1.0369059.

Yanıkkerem, E., Altıparmak, S., & Karadeniz, G. (2006). Review of the physical health problems experienced in pregnancy. Family and Community Education. *Culture and Research Journal*, *3*, 35–42.

10

CBT-I Protocols for Shift Workers and Health Operators

Heli Järnefelt and Kai Spiegelhalder

Key points

- High prevalence rates of sleep disorders and symptoms among shift workers probably reflect the temporal misalignment of the homeostatic and circadian processes of sleep in this group of people.
- Screening of insomnia among shift workers requires distinction between shift work disorder and insomnia disorder.
- Few CBT-I studies have been conducted on shift workers and the results of these studies vary.
- The standard CBT-I components can be used among shift workers in an unmodified manner except for sleep restriction therapy and stimulus control therapy because these are based on recommending fixed rise-times.

Learning objectives

- To be familiar with and understand the consequences of shift work on sleep.
- To be able to distinguish between insomnia disorder and shift work disorder.
- To be familiar with CBT-I studies on shift workers.
- To be familiar with and to be able to use modifications of sleep restriction therapy and stimulus control therapy for shift workers.

Abstract

High prevalence rates of sleep disorders and related symptoms among shift workers probably reflect the temporal misalignment of the homeostatic and circadian processes of sleep in this group of people. The health and safety consequences of shift work and insufficient sleep are very similar, suggesting that they share common mechanisms. In the screening of insomnia among shift workers it can be difficult to distinguish between shift work disorder and insomnia disorder. Both disorders can also coexist, which complicates screening and treatment planning. Sleep diaries or actigraphy are recommended to use as screening tools for shift work disorder. A questionnaire with shift-specific questions on insomnia and sleepiness can be used in the screening as well. Few CBT-I studies have been conducted among shift workers. A couple of non-randomised studies have shown that CBT-I may be as effective among shift workers as it is for day workers. However, one RCT among both day and shift workers found that CBT-I was effective only when shift workers were not included in the analyses and another RCT showed similar sleep improvements both after CBT-I and a brief sleep hygiene control intervention among shift workers. The standard CBT-I components (Chapter 2) can be used for shift workers in an unmodified manner except for sleep restriction therapy and stimulus control therapy because these two components are based on the recommendation of fixed rise-times. There is only preliminary scientific evidence for sleep restriction and stimulus control therapy modifications in those who have irregular sleeping hours. One option is to apply the sleep restriction therapy step by step: first only to night sleep, then to day sleep and lastly to naps.

Cognitive-Behavioural Therapy for Insomnia (CBT-I) Across the Life Span: Guidelines and Clinical Protocols for Health Professionals,
First Edition. Edited by Chiara Baglioni, Colin A. Espie and Dieter Riemann.

An option to handle shift work-related sleep debt is to allow one extra hour of bed-time during sleep restriction therapy in one to three sleep periods after having a shift with a brief time for sleeping. An option for enhancing solidity and regularity of sleep is to give education on how to schedule sleep and how to time light exposure while working in shifts. In addition to common information regarding sleep hygiene, additional recommendations including instructions for work alertness management can be used. It is also important to notice that sleep–wake disturbances connected to shift work can be prevented and decreased through ergonomic shift scheduling.

Keywords *CBT-I among shift workers, shift work disorder, modifications of behavioural strategies, alertness management*

Introduction

Nowadays one-fifth of European Union (EU) employees work shifts (Eurofound, 2017), making shift workers a significant group of people whose potential insomnia should be managed using effective interventions. Higher prevalence rates of sleep disorders and symptoms among shift workers compared to day workers probably reflect the temporal misalignment of the homeostatic and circadian processes of sleep associated with shifts (West & Bechtold, 2015). Sleep difficulties are associated especially with night and early morning shifts (Sallinen & Kecklund, 2010) and short rest periods between shifts (Karhula et al., 2013; Vedaa et al., 2016). In a study by Kerkhof (2018), the prevalence of symptoms of sleep disorders was 39.0% for shift workers and 24.6% for day workers, and more than one sleep disorder was present in twice as many shift workers (18.8%) than day workers (8.1%). On the other hand, in a follow-up study of hospital employees night shifts were associated with longer sleep, probably reflecting a higher need for recovery (Härmä et al., 2019).

Definition of most common sleep problems among shift workers

Shift work disorder (SWD) is a circadian rhythm sleep–wake disorder defined as insomnia and/or excessive sleepiness that lasts at least three months, and is associated with a shift work schedule that overlaps with the habitual sleeping time (American Academy of Sleep Medicine, 2014). In other words, insomnia symptoms and impairments of day-time functioning may coexist or occur alone in SWD. Its etiology is primarily attributed to circadian disruption and misalignment due to shift work (Wright, Boban, & Wyatt, 2013). Diverse diagnostic criteria and instruments have resulted in different prevalence rates of SWD between studies on shift work populations (Järnefelt, Vanttola, Waage & Bjorvatn, 2020). For example, using the criteria of the International Classification of Sleep Disorders (ICSD-3) (American Academy of Sleep Medicine, 2014), which includes a reduction of total sleep time due to the work schedule and a symptom duration of 3 months, and, in addition, using ≥ 3 days with SWD symptoms a month as a frequency cut-off, provided lower estimates for SWD prevalence (3–6%) among Finnish hospital employees than the earlier ISCD-2 criteria (9–18%) (Vanttola, Puttonen, Karhula, Oksanen & Härmä, 2019).

In a field study of Finnish airport ground staff members SWD was related to disturbed sleep and alertness in association with both morning and night shifts, and also to less compensatory sleep on days off (Vanttola, et al., 2020). In addition, SWD was associated with poorer sleep quality and feeling less relaxed at bedtime. Among Finnish hospital workers those with SWD may need a longer time to overcome excessive sleepiness than allowed by their roster (Vanttola, Puttonen, Karhula, Oksanen & Härmä, 2020). Thus, these studies show that SWD-related sleeping problems may disrupt sleep also on days off.

In the screening of insomnia among shift workers it can be difficult to distinguish between insomnia symptoms in the context of SWD and insomnia disorder. Both disorders can also coexist, which complicates screening and treatment planning (Drake, Roehrs, Richardson, Walsh & Roth, 2004). In this case, insomnia may initially be associated with the shift work schedule but may progress into chronic insomnia disorder with symptoms even on days off (Wright et al., 2013). Sleep diaries or actigraphy are recommended to use as screening tools for SWD (American Academy of Sleep Disorders, 2014). A questionnaire with shift-specific questions on insomnia and sleepiness (Shift-Specific Questionnaire (SS-Q); see Table 10.1) can be used in the screening as well (Vanttola et al., 2019). Based on the SS-Q, patients are categorized as having

Table 10.1 Shift-specific questions on insomnia and sleepiness (SS-Q) for screening shift work disorder (Based on Vanttola et al., 2019).

	Never	Rarely	Sometimes	Often	Always	Not applicable
1. How often during the last three months have you experienced insomnia? By insomnia we mean difficulties in initiating sleep, recurrent awakenings during sleep period, or difficulties in staying asleep.						
In connection to morning shifts	( )	( )	( )	( )	( )	( )
In connection to evening shifts	( )	( )	( )	( )	( )	( )
In connection to night shifts	( )	( )	( )	( )	( )	( )
While on holiday over two weeks	( )	( )	( )	( )	( )	-
2. How often during the last three months have you experienced excessive sleepiness?						
During morning shifts	( )	( )	( )	( )	( )	( )
During evening shifts	( )	( )	( )	( )	( )	( )
During night shifts	( )	( )	( )	( )	( )	( )
While on holiday over two weeks	( )	( )	( )	( )	( )	-

Criteria for ICSD-2-based SWD based on the survey: SWD cases had to report at least the other primary SWD symptom (insomnia and/or excessive sleepiness) 'never' or 'rarely' after over two weeks on holiday and the never or rarely occurring symptom 'often' or 'always' in connection to some shift type/types (morning, evening and/or night).

SWD features if they have 'always' or 'often' suffered from insomnia symptoms and/or sleepiness on working days during the last three months, and 'never' or 'rarely' on holidays. Vanttola et al. (2019) also suggest that a clinically plausible cut-off for days with SWD symptoms is three per month.

Consequences of poor sleep and insomnia among shift workers

Insufficient and disturbed sleep may be a central causal pathway for the adverse health effects associated with shift work (Kecklund & Axelsson, 2016). The health and safety consequences of shift work and insufficient sleep are very similar, suggesting that they share common mechanisms. There are associations between shift/night work and occupational accidents and injuries, obesity, type 2 diabetes, coronary heart disease, stroke, and cancer of the breast, prostate and colorectum. Fatigue and insomnia related to shift work can also lead to reduced work performance, processing errors, accidents at work, absenteeism, reduced quality of life and symptoms of depression (Richter, Acker, Adam & Niklewski, 2016).

The evidence base for treating insomnia among shift workers

Few CBT-I studies have been conducted among shift workers. A couple of non-randomised studies have shown that CBT-I may be as effective among shift workers as it is in day workers (Järnefelt et al., 2012; Peter, Reindl, Zauter, Hillemacher & Richter, 2019). However, one RCT among both day and shift workers found that CBT-I was effective only when shift workers were not included in the analyses (Schiller, Soderstom, Lekander, Rjaleid & Kecklund, 2018) and another RCT showed similar sleep improvements both after CBT-I and a brief sleep hygiene control intervention among shift workers with insomnia disorder (Järnefelt et al., 2020). In the latter study, an alleviation of mood symptoms seemed to be the added value of the CBT-I intervention compared to the control intervention. In this study, half of the shift workers with insomnia had features of SWD. Compared to insomnia patients with SWD features, the clinical condition of those without SWD (i.e., having insomnia, also during days off) was more severe, as demonstrated by more prevalent co-morbid diseases, more sleep-promoting medications, more severe insomnia symptoms, more sleep-related dysfunctional beliefs and more severe depression symptoms. However, the insomnia patients without SWD features benefitted more from the interventions than those with SWD features. Based on this study, Järnefelt et al. (2020) recommended that sleep hygiene combined with ergonomic shift scheduling and circadian adaptation tools should be used as treatment options in SWD. However, if a shift worker has insomnia independent of the work schedule, standard treatment guidelines of chronic insomnia are recommended to be followed.

Clinical protocol for treating insomnia among shift workers

The standard CBT-I components can be used among shift workers in an unmodified manner except for sleep restriction therapy and stimulus control therapy because these two components are based on the recommendation of fixed rise-times. Thus, sleep restriction therapy and/or stimulus control therapy need to be modified in those who have irregular sleeping hours. However, there is only preliminary scientific evidence for modifications to these behavioural strategies.

In a study of Vallières, Roy, Bastille-Denis, Claveau & Simon (2015), sleep restriction therapy was applied step by step: first only to night sleep, then to day sleep and lastly to naps. A certain sleep efficiency level had to be reached at each step before going to the next step. In the studies of Järnefelt et al. (2012, 2020), one extra bed-time hour was allowed during sleep restriction therapy in one to three sleep periods after having a shift that permitted a relatively brief opportunity for sleeping (e.g., having only a short rest period between shifts). In addition, participants received information on how to schedule sleep (main sleep periods and naps) and how to time light exposure while working shifts (based, for example, on Akerstedt, 1998; Wickwire, Geiger-Brown, Scharf & Drake, 2017; see Table 10.2). The so-called 'anchor sleep' suggested by

Table 10.2 Instructions on how to schedule sleep and how to time light exposure on the basis of circadian principles while working in differently timed and distributed shifts (Järnefelt et al., 2012, 2020, based on shift work related studies and recommendations). Instructions support a return to a regular sleep–wake pattern if the rotation speed is fast and on a contrary adaptation to a shift-based sleep–wake pattern if the rotation speed is slow.

	Early morning shift	Evening shift	Night shift
Regardless of shift rotation speed	- Set your alarm clock a little earlier than normal on the pre-shift morning - Start settling down and go to bed a little earlier than normal before the shift	- Start settling down and go to bed a little later than normal on the pre-shift evening - Sleep a little later than normal on the pre-shift morning	- Go to bed later than normal on the pre-shift evening and set your alarm clock later on the pre-shift morning - Nap near the beginning of the shift - Discuss opportunities to take naps during the shift with the employer
Fast rotation speed (1–3 similarly timed shifts)	- Nap shortly soon after the morning shift if needed	- Set your alarm clock at the regular time after the evening shift	- Sleep soon after the night shift - Do not nap if you have only one night shift in a row - If you have two or three night shifts in a row, try to sleep in two main sleep periods, one soon after the shift and the other one before the next shift
Slow rotation speed (≥ 4 similarly timed shifts)	- Do not nap after the morning shift - Expose yourself to bright light early in the morning - Avoid bright light in the evening	- If needed, nap in the early afternoon before the evening shift	- Try to sleep in two main sleep periods, one soon after the shift and the other one before the next shift - Try to position your main sleep period just before the night shift - Expose yourself to bright light from 23:00 to 05:00 - Avoid bright light from 05:00 to 11:00 and use sunglasses while being outside (e.g., when commuting from the night shift) - Expose yourself to bright morning light after the last night shift - Sleep only couple of hours right after the last shift and do not take any more naps

Table 10.3 Instructions for work alertness management of shift workers (Järnefelt et al., 2012, 2020, based on shift work related studies and recommendations).

- Allocate enough time for sleeping before the shift.
- Do not drink alcohol in the evening before the shift and avoid physically demanding sports just before the shift.
- Make sure you take breaks for recovery during the shift.
- If possible, vary your tasks and avoid monotonous tasks when you are tired.
- Eat light, small meals that are high in fibre and low in carbs. Favour cold drinks.
- Although coffee or other caffeinated beverages generally increase alertness, drink coffee moderately, and mainly at the beginning of the shift.
- If possible and needed, nap for 10–20 minutes during the night shift. A nap is even more effective if you consume caffeine just before it.
- Good lightning helps maintain alertness. However, take your sleeping times into account, because strong lightning just before a sleep period can delay sleep onset.
- If you have to work or drive a car (e.g., commuting home) at night (01:00–06:00), you should closely monitor the variations in your alertness and have more breaks if possible.
- It is recommended that you stop working after a maximum of 16 continuous awake hours.

Glovinsky and Spielman (2006) was also introduced to make the sleep rhythm as regular as possible, whenever possible. Anchor sleep means that in a 24-hour period at least four hours of sleep are taken at a regular time of day, even though other sleeping hours are taken irregularly because of shift work.

One thing to consider is that sleep restriction therapy may temporarily increase day-time sleepiness and decrease objective performance (Kyle et al., 2014). Because of that, patients that suffer from day-time sleepiness before treatment should be assigned to a more liberal sleep window when using sleep restriction therapy. This may often be the case with shift workers. Increasing sleepiness may also be particularly problematic for some shift workers like professional drivers or nurses in intensive care. However, if sleep restriction is mild (the total sleep time does not decrease more than 30 minutes), this does not appear to place insomnia patients at risk of significant impairments in sleepiness and reaction times (Whittall, Pillion & Gradisar, 2018).

In addition to general information regarding sleep hygiene, additional recommendations can be used (Richter et al., 2016; Wickwire et al., 2017). These include instructions on how to support good sleep by, for example, using eye covers and earplugs, and gaining social support from the family to enable good sleeping conditions in the required time. It also includes recommendations for work alertness management (see Table 10.3) and sleep education regarding temporal misalignment of the homeostatic and circadian processes of sleep when working in different shifts, which helps to understand the vulnerability of shift workers to sleeping problems and sleepiness.

From an organisational perspective, sleep and alertness problems related to shift work must be handled within the broader context of fatigue risk management and prevention (Wickwire et al., 2017). Sleep–wake disturbances connected to shift work can be decreased through ergonomic shift scheduling by, for example, minimising the proportion of night shifts and avoiding shift combinations with short rest periods between shifts, like, for example, between evening and early morning shifts (Harma et al., 2006, 2018; Neil-Sztramko, Pahwa, Demers & Gotay, 2014; Vedaa et al., 2017).

References

Akerstedt, T. (1998). Is there an optimal sleep–wake pattern in shift work? *Scandinavian Journal of Work, Environment & Health, 24*, 18–27.

American Academy of Sleep Medicine (2014). *International classification of sleep disorders; Diagnostic and coding manual* (3rd ed.). Darien, IL: American Academy of Sleep Medicine.

Drake, C. L., Roehrs, T., Richardson, G., Walsh, J. K., & Roth, T. (2004). Shift work sleep disorder: Prevalence and consequences beyond that of symptomatic day workers. *Sleep, 27* (8), 1453–1462.

Eurofound (2017). *Sixth European Working Conditions Survey – Overview report*. Luxembourg: Publications Office of the European Union.

Glovinsky, P., & Spielman, A. (2006). Answer for broken or irregular sleep. *The insomnia answer* (pp. 187–211). New York: Penguin Group.

Härmä, M., Hakola, T., Kandolin, I., Sallinen, M., Virkkala, J., Bonnefond, A., & Mutanen, P. (2006). A controlled study on the effects of a very rapidly forward rotating shift system on sleep–wakefulness and well-being among young and elderly shift workers. *International Journal of Psychobiology*, *59* (1), 70–79.

Härmä, M., Karhula, K., Ropponen, A., Puttonen, S., Koskinen, A., Ojajärvi, A., Hakola, T., Pentti, J., Oksanen, T., Vahtera, J., & Kivimäki, M. (2018). Association of changes in work shifts and shift intensity with change in fatigue and disturbed sleep: a within-subject study. *Scandinavian Journal of Work, Environment & Health, 44* (4), 394-402.

Härmä, M., Karhula, K., Puttonen, S., Ropponen, A., Koskinen, A., Ojajärvi, A., & Kivimäki, M. (2019). Shift work with and without night work as a risk factor for fatigue and changes in sleep length: A cohort study with linkage to records on daily working hours. *Journal of Sleep Research, 28* (3), e12658.

Järnefelt, H., Vanttola, P, Waage, S., & Bjorvatn, B. (2020). Assessment and treatment of shift work disorder. In M. Härmä & K. Karhula (Eds), *Working hour, health, well-being and participation in working life. Current knowledge and recommendations for health and safety* (pp. 65–67). Helsinki: Finnish Institute of Occupational Health.

Järnefelt, H., Lagerstedt, R., Kajaste, S., Sallinen, M., Savolainen, A., & Hublin, C. (2012). Cognitive behavioral therapy for shift workers with chronic insomnia. *Sleep Medicine*, *13* (10), 1238–1246.

Järnefelt, H., Härmä, M., Sallinen, M., Virkkala, J., Paajanen, T., Martimo, K.-P., & Hublin, C. (2020). Cognitive behavioural therapy interventions for insomnia among shift workers: RCT in an occupational health setting. *International Archives of Occupational and Environmental Health*, *93*, 535–550.

Karhula, K., Härmä, M., Sallinen, M., Hublin, C., Virkkala, J., Kivimäki, M., Vahtera, J., & Puttonen, S. (2013). Association of job strain with working hours, shift-dependent perceived workload, sleepiness and recovery. *Ergonomics*, *56* (11), 1640–1651.

Kecklund, G., & Axelsson, J. (2016). Health consequences of shift work and insufficient sleep. *British Medical Journal*, *355*, i5210.

Kerkhof, G. A. (2018). Shift work and sleep disorder comorbidity tend to go hand in hand. *Chronobiology International*, *35* (2), 219–228.

Kyle, S. D., Miller, C. B., Rogers, Z., Siriwardena, A. N., MacMahon, K. M., & Espie C. A. (2014). Sleep restriction therapy for insomnia is associated with reduced objective total sleep time, increased daytime somnolence, and objectively impaired vigilance: Implications for the clinical management of insomnia disorder. *Sleep*, *37* (2), 229–237.

Neil-Sztramko, S. E., Pahwa, M., Demers, P. A., & Gotay, C. C. (2014). Health-related interventions among night shift workers: a critical review of the literature. *Scandinavian Journal of Work Environment and Health*, *40* (6), 543–556.

Peter, L., Reindl, R., Zauter, S., Hillemacher, T., & Richter, K. (2019). Effectiveness of an online CBT-I intervention and a face-to-face treatment for shift work sleep disorder: A comparison of sleep diary data. *International Journal of Environmental Research and Public Health*, *16* (17), 3081.

Richter, K., Acker, J., Adam, S., & Niklewski G (2016). Prevention of fatigue and insomnia in shift workers – A review of non-pharmacological measures. *The EPMA Journal*, *7* (1), 16.

Sallinen, M., & Kecklund, G. (2010). Shift work, sleep, and sleepiness - differences between shift schedules and systems. *Scandinavian Journal of Work, Environment & Health, 36*, 121–133.

Schiller, H., Soderstrom, M., Lekander, M., Rajaleid, K., & Kecklund, G. (2018). A randomized controlled intervention of workplace-based group cognitive behavioral therapy for insomnia. *International Archives of Occupational and Environmental Health, 91* (4), 413–424.

Vallières, A., Roy, M., Bastille-Denis, E., Claveau, S., & Simon, T. (2015). Exploring a behavioural therapy for insomnia in shift workers. *Journal of Sleep Disorders & Therapy*, *4* (3), 1–13.

Vanttola, P., Puttonen, S., Karhula, K., Oksanen, T., & Härmä, M. (2019). Prevalence of shift work disorder among hospital personnel: A cross-sectional study using objective working hour data. *Journal of Sleep Research*, *29* (3), e12906.

Vanttola, P., Puttonen, S., Karhula, K., Oksanen, T., & Härmä, M. (2020). Employees with shift work disorder experience excessive sleepiness also on non-work days: A cross-sectional survey linked to working hours register in Finnish hospitals. *Industrial Health*, *58* (4), 366–374.

Vanttola, P., Härmä, M., Viitasalo, K., Hublin, C., Virkkala, J., Sallinen, M., Karhula, K., & Puttonen, S. (2020). Sleep and alertness in shift work disorder: Findings of a field study. *International Archives of Occupational and Environmental Health*, *92* (4), 523–533.

Vedaa, Ø., Pallesen, S., Waage, S., Bjorvatn, B., Sivertsen, B., Erevik, E., Svensen, E., & Harris, A. (2017). Short rest between shift intervals increases the risk of sick leave: A prospective registry study. *Occupational and Environmental Medicine*, *74* (7), 496–501.

West, A. C., & Bechtold, D. A. (2015). The cost of circadian desynchrony: Evidence, insights and open questions. *Bioessays*, *37* (7), 777–788.

Whittall, H., Pillion, M., & Gradisar M. (2018). Daytime sleepiness, driving performance, reaction time and inhibitory control during sleep restriction therapy for Chronic Insomnia Disorder. *Sleep Medicine*, *45*, 44–48.

Wickwire, E. M., Geiger-Brown, J., Scharf, S. M., & Drake, C. L. (2017). Shift work and shift work sleep disorder: Clinical and organizational perspectives. *Chest*, *151* (5), 1156–1172.

Wright, K. P. Jr., Bogan, R. K., & Wyatt, J. K. (2013). Shift work and the assessment and management of shift work disorder (SWD). *Sleep Medicine Reviews, 17* (1), 41–54.

11

CBT-I Adaptation for Health Professionals under Stress Conditions

Andrea Ballesio, Caterina Lombardo and Cristiano Violani

Key points

- Health workers are a population at risk of sleep disturbances, especially when working under intense stress conditions (e.g., war scenarios, natural disasters, and pandemics).
- Sleep problems in this population are associated with individual consequences, including higher risk of mental and somatic disorders, altered immune responses, accidents, as well as potential medical errors and organizational and public health hazards.
- Evidence on the implementation of 'standard' CBT-I protocols is not available for this population, yet psychoeducational interventions and single CBT-I components could be effectively adapted to this target population, both in normal work circumstances and under intense work-related stress conditions.

Learning objectives

- To be able to identify common sleep problems experienced by health workers under stressful conditions.
- To be aware of the consequences of poor sleep and insomnia in this population.
- To be familiar with specific CBT-I components that can be adapted to interventions in this population.

Abstract

Health workers are a population at risk of sleep disturbances such as circadian rhythm disorders and insomnia. This risk is even greater when they are exposed to intense stress conditions such as public health emergencies. Sleep problems in this population have been associated with individual consequences, including burnout, depression and anxiety, altered immune responses, altered metabolism, cardiovascular diseases, accidents at work and while driving, career changes, as well as medical errors and organizational problems and public health hazards. The aim of the chapter is to propose specific adaptations of CBT-I for health professionals, both in normal work circumstances and under intense stress conditions.

Keywords *insomnia, Public Health, stress exposure, pandemic, emergency*

Introduction: Sleep problems in health professionals working under stress conditions

This chapter includes considerations of insomnia, the most frequently experienced sleep problems among health professionals, especially when working under intense stress conditions, and their consequences, as well as a discussion of CBT-I-derived strategies to deal with insomnia problems in this population. By 'stress conditions' we refer to a variety of

Cognitive-Behavioural Therapy for Insomnia (CBT-I) Across the Life Span: Guidelines and Clinical Protocols for Health Professionals,
First Edition. Edited by Chiara Baglioni, Colin A. Espie and Dieter Riemann.

scenarios, which go from prolonged working shifts in non-emergency situations to public health emergencies such as war scenarios, natural disasters, and global pandemics. By health professionals, we include not only physicians and nurses, but also a broader number of frontline professionals such as paramedics, medical interns, nursing assistants, ambulance drivers, rescuers and all staff contributing to emergency services and crisis management.

Under normal conditions, health professionals already often face a variety of stressors that include long working hours, psychological distress, burnout, stigma and pathogen exposure (World Health Organization, 2020) that may have detrimental effects on their health, including sleep disturbances. Several psychobiological factors involved in sleep regulation may trigger and perpetuate insomnia in health professionals even when they are not working under exceptional stress conditions. For example, irregular and prolonged work shifts are known to impact both homeostatic and circadian processes, leading to insufficient or inadequate sleep (Kancherla et al., 2020a, 2020b). Moreover, health professionals working in emergency departments and on life-threatening conditions are likely to experience a variety of negative emotions, such as anxiety concerning uncertain outcomes, feelings of guilt, and perceptions of impotence and loneliness, which may activate cognitive processes including repetitive health worries, ruminations and catastrophic thinking (e.g., Vandevala et al., 2017) that are deleterious for the quantity and quality of sleep (Ballesio, Ghezzi, Vacca, Ottaviani & Lombardo, 2019). Finally, there is evidence that emotion regulation may also play a role. For instance, health professionals are generally reported to suppress, rather than express, their emotional experience, especially when interacting with patients (Kafetsios, Anagnostopoulos, Lempesis & Valindra, 2014). However, emotional suppression is known to increase physiological arousal and disrupt sleep (Palmer & Alfano, 2017).

In addition to what might be regarded as 'normal' work circumstances, psychological distress and disrupted sleep are frequently reported in the aftermath of any disaster or life-threatening emergency. According to a recent report, up to 75% of individuals exposed to a disaster report emotional distress, while up to 20% experience mild to moderate anxiety and persistent insomnia (Cream, 2021). In a longitudinal study conducted among the 2011 East Japan earthquake and tsunami survivors, Li et al. (2018), showed that the inability to receive appropriate medical care and facilities predicted subjective poor sleep. Similarly, among the nuclear plant workers involved in the Fukushima nuclear disaster, many of those exposed to life-threatening danger and social stigma reported subsequent insomnia (Ikeda, Charvat, Shigemura, Kales & Tanigawa, 2019). Veterans exposed to war scenarios have a higher risk of developing sleep disorders including insomnia compared to non-exposed veterans (Chao, Abadjion, Esparza & Reeb, 2016).

In relation to the recent Covid-19 pandemic, it has been observed that 34% of physicians and nurses in Wuhan city reported insomnia (Lai et al., 2020). However, a recent meta-analysis showed that in China the pooled prevalence of sleep disturbances among health professionals was even higher, at 40%, even before the Covid-19 emergency (Qiu, Yu, Li, Li & Xiao, 2020).

Consequences of poor sleep and insomnia for health professionals under stress conditions

There is a substantial body of evidence on the high prevalence of stress and poor sleep and insomnia in health professionals while their consequences under intense stress conditions have been reported in a more fragmentary manner. A recent study with professional nurses confirmed that poor sleep satisfaction, efficiency and duration are associated with self-reported mood problems (Furihata et al., 2020a). Also, a biological investigation from the same group showed that nurses with insomnia and concomitant short sleep duration (<6 hours) compared to their healthy colleagues have a reduced level of serum brain-derived neurotrophic factor (BDNF) (Furihata et al., 2020b), a protein considered to be a biomarker for cognitive impairments and depression (Rahmani, Rahmani, & Rezaei, 2019). Short sleep duration in nurses was also associated with lower ratings of quality of care and patient safety (Witkoski Stimpfe, Fatehi & Kovner, 2020). In medical interns, sleep loss has been associated with lower quality of life (Belayachi et al., 2013), fatigue, lack of concentration, and objective cognitive impairments (Maltese et al., 2016; St Hilaire et al., 2019), whilst insomnia has been found to be predictive of anxiety (Kalmbach et al., 2019) and depression (Tafoya et al., 2019). In paramedics, poor subjective sleep quality has been associated with lower emotional empathy (Guadagniet, Cook, Hart, Burles & Iaria, 2018), higher depression and anxiety symptoms (Khan, Conduit, Kennedy & Jackson, 2020), acute and chronic stress symptoms, obesity and cardiovascular diseases (Hegg-Deloye et al., 2014).

Furthermore, it is well known from theoretical and experimental studies that adequate sleep in the aftermath of traumatic experiences may protect individuals from the development of intrusive memories, likely by improving memory consolidation and integration of traumatic memories into long-term memory (Kleim, Wysokowsky, Schmid, Seifritz & Rasch, 2016). Emerging empirical evidence in healthy sleepers suggests that sleep, especially REM sleep, consolidates fear memory in the human amygdala (e.g., Menz et al., 2013). Thus, REM sleep deprivation may play a key role in fear learning mechanisms after exposure to distressing events in anxiety and post-traumatic stress disorders. To the best of our knowledge, research on the role of sleep in the onset of traumatic memories in health professionals is lacking. However, there is evidence that health professionals with poor sleep tend to have less positive and more negative memories than healthy sleeper colleagues (e.g., Khormizi, Ali Salehinejad, Nitsche, & Nejati, 2019). Thus, it is plausible to hypothesise that disturbed sleep in health professionals in the aftermath of public emergencies and disasters may dampen sleep-related memory consolidation.

Strategies

To the best of our knowledge, evidence of the implementation of 'standard' CBT-I protocols in this population is not available yet. Rather, the use of single CBT-I components has been proposed to deal with the specific sleep problems of health professionals working under intense stress (Ballesio, Lombardo, Lucidi & Violani, 2020). Organising the provision of CBT-I for this population can be particularly difficult. Face-to-face individual counselling or therapy as well as group interventions may not be feasible in natural disasters due to logistic reasons and to time constraints; furthermore, during epidemics/pandemics they should be avoided in order to reduce social contact. Self-help therapy with remote (internet, telephone) professional support may instead be more accessible and preferable (Ballesio et al., 2020). Below, we discuss the adaptation of the main CBT-I techniques that can be included in psychoeducational and counselling interventions to treat the problems in initiating and maintaining sleep of health professionals working under intense stress. However, given the potential limitations of providing adequate therapy in emergency scenarios, it should be noted that sleep problems should be routinely addressed for health professionals as part of occupational health initiatives, even before the occurrence of intense stressful events, using low intensity psychoeducation interventions (Carter, Kathleen, & Mikan, 2013).

Sleep hygiene education

Poor sleep hygiene is a multifaceted set of habitual behaviours that are frequently involved in precipitating and perpetuating sleep disruption (Abe et al., 2011), which can be accentuated under stress and also once the stress condition has ended. Poor sleep hygiene behaviours include: irregular sleep schedules and excessive day-time napping; sleeping in uncomfortable and inappropriate environments; use of substances (e.g., alcohol, nicotine, caffeine) with negative effects on sleep; and poor lifestyle (e.g., sedentary life, excessive food intake before sleep). Napping is a common habit implemented to buffer the effects of health professionals' sleep deprivation after shifts, although it may contribute to difficulties in initiating and in maintaining the ensuing nocturnal sleep because it reduces homeostatic pressure for sleep. In order to prevent this undesired effect and to reduce sleep inertia upon awakening, a nap should last no longer than 20–30 minutes. In this way the sleep deprived professional will obtain a smaller reduction of homeostatic pressure and of somnolence, which is necessary for adequate cognitive and psychomotor functioning, but will avoid arriving at the moment of initiating the nocturnal sleep period with a sleep pressure reduced to the point that it will cause difficulties in initiating sleep and trigger worries and the insomnia cognitive vicious cycle.

After a nap, wrists, hands and face soaking with cold water may reduce sleep inertia (Hayashi, Masuda, & Hori, 2003). Moreover, when sleeping or napping at work, the sleep environment should be made as adequate as possible and exposure to light and noise reduced using earplugs and eye masks. The effects on the sleep and circadian cycle of exposure to bright and blue should be considered. These and other indications and information on the relationship between sleep and stress should be included in psychoeducational interventions routinely offered to health professionals.

Stimulus control

There are no substantial contraindications to the use of standard pre-bed routines and the *quarter of an hour rule* during 'days off', even under stress conditions. Indeed, a wind down routine can be helpful in decreasing the psychophysiological arousal induced by stress exposure and therefore improve sleep. Health professionals should avoid work activities in the two hours before going to bed and avoid arousing activities such as checking emergency-related news. Moreover, as individuals cannot force themselves to sleep even if they have a short time available to sleep due to work schedule, the rule of going to sleep when feeling sleepy is also applicable to day-off, even under stress conditions.

Sleep restriction/compression

Health professionals working under stress conditions rarely spend lengthy periods of time in bed continuously, due to a prolonged work schedule. However, special attention should be given to days off, when health professionals could be tempted to compensate the lack of sleep experienced on work days by having long naps or oversleeping. While general advice to this population would be to set a regular time to wake up, sleep restriction/sleep compression could be suggested in those individuals who spend more time in bed both for sleeping and for relaxing. Prior to the proposal of the technique, the rationale for the intervention (i.e., knowledge on homeostatic sleep pressure) should be explained. It is important that the professional understands that while it is a normal desire to 'regain' the sleep lost in the previous nights, it is essential to maintain a robust homeostatic sleep drive in order not to impact sleep adversely in the medium–long term.

Cognitive therapy

There are no substantial contraindications to the use of cognitive control in health professionals working under stress conditions. Daily writing on emergency-related topics could help stop intrusive and repetitive thinking on health emergencies (e.g., in the case of a pandemic or natural disaster) (Ballesio et al., 2021). Paradoxically, though, cognitive control may foster further worry and rumination over the event by overfocusing attention on worrisome topics; thus it should not be implemented too close to bed-time. There are also no substantial contraindications to the use of cognitive restructuring and de-catastrophising strategies. However, therapists should be aware that in acute stress conditions directly focusing on traumatic content could paradoxically increase intrusive thoughts, worry and rumination, especially in individuals with high arousability. Psychoeducation on sleep, arousal and emotion may be helpful in such conditions. Creating a 'safe mental island' may also be a useful imagery technique during stressful events (Ballesio et al., 2020), particularly when the worry chair (cognitive control, see Chapter 2) strategy is not helpful. Creating a personal safe mental island comprising relaxing memories, fantasies and dreams may reduce pre-sleep worries and rumination and facilitate falling asleep.

Relaxation

Relaxation techniques aiming at decreasing autonomic arousal are highly recommended in this population due to their effects on stress-related activation. These techniques may include diaphragmatic breathing at the resonance frequency, progressive muscle relation and mindfulness. The implementation of these as functional pre-bed routines may be particularly useful.

Conclusion

Health professionals working under stress may experience poor sleep and insomnia with deleterious effects on individual, organisational and public health. Although 'standard' CBT-I protocols have not been specifically tested for their efficacy in this population using clinical or randomised controlled trials, several individual CBT-I-derived techniques can be effectively adapted as a first aid to deal with sleep problems in this population.

References

Abe, Y., Mishima, K., Kaneita, Y., Li, L., Ohida, T., Nishikawa, T., & Uchiyama, M. (2011). Stress coping behaviors and sleep hygiene practices in a sample of Japanese adults with insomnia. *Sleep and Biological Rhythms*, *9*, 35–45. https://doi.org/10.1111/j.1479-8425.2010.00483.x.

Ballesio, A., Ghezzi, V., Vacca, M., Ottaviani, C., & Lombardo, C. (2019). Effects of presleep cognitive intrusions on subjective sleep and next-day cognitive performance in insomnia. *Behavior Therapy*, *51* (5), 688–699. https://doi.org/10.1016/j.beth.2019.09.003.

Ballesio, A., Lombardo, L., Lucidi, F., & Violani, C. (2020). Caring for the carers: Advice for dealing with sleep problems of hospital staff during the COVID-19 outbreak. *Journal of Sleep Research, 30* (1), e13096. https://doi.org/10.1111/jsr.13096.

Ballesio, A., Bacaro, V., Vacca, M., Chirico, A., Lucidi, F., Riemann, D., Baglioni, C., & Lombardo, C. (2021). Does cognitive behaviour therapy for insomnia reduce repetitive negative thinking and sleep-related worry beliefs? A systematic review and meta-analysis. *Sleep Medicine Reviews, 55*, 101378. https://doi.org/10.1016/j.smrv.2020.101378.

Belayachi, J., Benjelloun, O., Madani, N., Abidi, K., Dendane, T., Zeggwagh, A. A., & Abouwal, R. (2013). Self-perceived sleepiness in emergency training physicians: Prevalence and relationship with quality of life. *Journal of Occupational Medicine and Toxicology, 8*, 24. https://doi.org/10.1186/1745-6673-8-24.

Carter, P. A., Kathleen, A. D., & Mikan, S. Q. (2013). Sleep disturbance, chronic stress, and depression in hospice nurses: testing the feasibility of an intervention. *Oncology Nursing Forum*, 40 (5), 368–373. https://doi.org/10.1188/13.ONF.E368-E373.

Chao, L. L., Abadjian, L. R., Esparza, I. L., & Reeb, R. (2016). Insomnia severity, subjective sleep quality, and risk for obstructive sleep apnea in veterans with Gulf War illness. *Military Medicine, 181*, 1127–1134. https://doi.org/10.7205/MILMED-D-15-00474.

Cream, J. (2021). Covid-19 recovery and resilience: What can health and care learn from other disasters? The King's Fund. https://www.kingsfund.org.uk/publications/covid-19-recovery-resilience-health-and-care#comments-top.

Furihata, R., Saitoh, K., Otsuki, R., Murata, S., Suzuki, M., Jike, M., Kaneita, Y., Ohida, T., & Uchiyama, M. (2020a). Association between reduced serum BDNF levels and insomnia with short sleep duration among female hospital nurses. *Sleep Medicine, 68*, 167–172. https://doi.org/10.1016/j.sleep.2019.12.011.

Furihata, R., Saitoh, K., Suzuki, M., Jike, M., Kaneita, Y., Ohida, T., Buysse, D. J., & Uchiyama, M. (2020b). A composite measure of sleep health is associated with symptoms of depression among Japanese female hospital nurses. *Comprehensive Psychiatry, 97*, 152151. https://doi.org/10.1016/j.comppsych.2019.152151.

Guadagni, V., Cook, E., Hart, C., Burles, F., & Iaria, G. (2018). Poor sleep quality affects empathic responses in experienced paramedics. *Sleep and Biological Rhythms, 16*, 365–368. https://doi.org/10.1007/s41105-018-0156-8.

Hayashi, M., Masuda, A., & Hori, T. (2003). The alerting effects of caffeine, bright light and face washing after a short daytime nap. *Clinical Neurophysiology, 114*, 2268–2278. https://doi.org/10.1016/S1388-2457(03)00255-4.

Hegg-Deloye, S., Brassard, P., Jauvin, N., Prairie, J., Larouche, D., Poirier, P., Tremblay, A., Corbeil, P. (2014). Current state of knowledge of post-traumatic stress, sleeping problems, obesity and cardiovascular disease in paramedics. *Emergency Medical Journal, 31*, 242–247. https://doi.org/10.1136/emermed-2012-201672.

Ikeda, A., Charvat, H., Shigemura, J., Kales, S. N., & Tanigawa, T. (2019). Longitudinal trends in disaster-related insomnia among Fukushima nuclear plant workers: The Fukushima Nuclear Energy Workers' Support Project study. *Sleep, 42*, 1–8. https://doi.org/10.1093/sleep/zsz043.

Kafetsios, K., Anagnostopoulos, F., Lempesis, E., & Valindra, A. (2014). Doctors' emotion regulation and patient satisfaction: A social–functional perspective. *Health Communication, 29* (2), 205–214. https://doi.org/10.1080/10410236.2012.738150.

Kalmbach, D. A., Abelson, J. L., Arnedt, J. T., Zhao, Z., Schubert, J. R., & Sen, S. (2019). Insomnia symptoms and short sleep predict anxiety and worry in response to stress exposure: A prospective cohort study of medical interns. *Sleep Medicine, 55*, 40–47. https://doi.org/10.1016/j.sleep.2018.12.001.

Kancherla, B. S., Upender, R., Collem, J. F., Rishi, M. A., Sullivan, S. S., Ahmed, O., Bernekinf, M., Flynn-Evans, E. E., Peters, B. R., Abassi-Feinberg, F., Aurora, N., Carden, K. A., Kirsch, D. B., Kristo, D. A., Malhotra, R. K., Martin, J. L., Olson, E. J., Ramar, K., Rosen, C. L., Rowley, J. A., Shelgikar, A. V., & Gurubhagavatula, I. (2020a). Sleep, fatigue and burnout among physicians: An American Academy of Sleep Medicine position statement. *Journal of Clinical Sleep Medicine, 16* (5), 803–805. https://doi.org/10.5664/jcsm.8408.

Kancherla, B. S., Upender, R., Collen, J. F., Rishi, M. A., Sullivan, S. S., Ahmed, O., Berneking, M., Flynn-Evans, E. E., Peters, B. R., & Gurubhagavatula, I. (2020b). What is the role of sleep in physician burnout? *Journal of Clinical Sleep Medicine, 16* (5), 807–810. https://doi.org/10.5664/jcsm.8412.

Khan, W. A. A., Conduit, R., Kennedy, G. A., & Jackson, M. L. (2020). The relationship between shift-work, sleep, and mental health among paramedics in Australia. *Sleep Health, 19*, 30264–30265. https://doi.org/10.1016/j.sleh.2019.12.002.

Khormizi, H.Z., Ali Salehinejad, M., Nitsche, M.A., & Nejati, V. (2019). Sleep-deprivation and autobiographical memory: Evidence from sleep-deprived nurses. *Journal of Sleep Research, 28* (1), e12683. https://doi.org/10.1111/jsr.12683.

Kleim, B., Wysokowsky, J., Schmid, N., Seifritz, E., & Rasch, B. (2016). Effects of sleep after experimental trauma on intrusive emotional memories. *Sleep, 39* (12), 2125–2132. https://doi.org/10.5665/sleep.6310.

Lai, J., Ma, S., Wang, Y., Cai, X., Hu, J., Wei, N., Wu, J., Du, H., Chen, T., Li, R., Tan, H., Kang, L., Yao, L., Huang, M., Wang, H., Wang, G., Liu, Z., & Hu, S. (2020). Factors associated with mental health outcomes among health care workers exposed to coronavirus disease 2019. *JAMA Network Open*, *3* (3), e203976. https://doi:10.1001/jamanetworkopen.2020.3976.

Li, X., Buxton, O. M., Hikichi, H., Haneuse, S., Aida, J., Kondo, K., & Kawachi, I. (2018). Predictors of persistent sleep problems among older disaster survivors: A natural experiment from the 2011 Great East Japan earthquake and tsunami. *Sleep*, *41*, 1–11. https://doi.org/10.1093/sleep/zsy084.

Maltese, F., Adda, M., Bablon, A., Hraeich, S., Guervilly, C., Lehingue, S., Wiramus, S., Leone, M., Martin, C., Vialet, R., Thirion, X., Roch, A., Forel, J. M., & Papazian, L. (2016). Night shift decreases cognitive performance of ICU physicians. *Intensive Care Medicine*, *42*, 393–400. https://doi.org/10.1007/s00134-015-4115-4.

Menz, M. M., Rihm, J. S., Salari, N., Born, J., Kalisch, R., Pape, H. C., Marshall, L., & Büchel, C. (2013). The role of sleep and sleep deprivation in consolidating fear memories. *Neuroimage*, *75*, 87–96. https://doi.org/10.1016/j.neuroimage.2013.03.001.

Palmer, C. A., & Alfano, C. A. (2017). Sleep and emotion regulation: An organizing, integrative review. *Sleep Medicine Reviews*, *31*, 6–16. http://dx.doi.org/10.1016/j.smrv.2015.12.006.

Qiu, D., Yu, Y., Li, R., Li, Y., & Xiao, S. (2020). Prevalence of sleep disturbances in Chinese healthcare professionals: A systematic review and meta-analysis. *Sleep Medicine*, *67*, 258–266. https://doi.org/10.1016/j.sleep.2019.01.047.

Rahmani, M., Rahmani, F., & Rezaei, N. (2019). The brain-derived neurotrophic factor: Missing link between sleep deprivation, insomnia, and depression. *Neurochemical Research*, *5*(2), 221–231. https://doi.org/10.1007/s11064-019-02914-1.

St Hilaire, M. A., Anderson, C., Anwar, J. Sullivan, J. P., Cade, B. E., Flynn-Evans, E. E., Czeisler, C. A., Lockley, S. W., & Harvard Work Hours Health and Safety Group (2019). Brief (<4 hr) sleep episodes are insufficient for restoring performance in first-year resident physicians working overnight extended-duration work shifts. *Sleep*, *42*, 1–6. https://doi.org/10.1093/sleep/zsz041.

Tafoya, S. A., Aldrete–Cortez, V., Ortiz, S., Fouilloux, C., Felipe, F., & Monterrosas, A. M. (2019). Resilience, sleep quality and morningness as mediators of vulnerability to depression in medical students with sleep pattern alterations. *Chronobiology International*, *36* (3), 381–391. https://doi.org/10.1080/07420528.2018.1552290.

Vandevala, T., Pavey, L., Chelidoni, O., Chang, N.F., Creagh-Brown, B., & Cox, A. (2017). Psychological rumination and recovery from work in intensive care professionals: Associations with stress, burnout, depression and health. *Journal of Intensive Care*, *5*, 16. https://doi.org/10.1186/s40560-017-0209-0.

Witkoski Stimpfe, A., Fatehi, F., & Kovner, C. (2020). Nurses' sleep, work hours, and patient care quality, and safety. *Sleep Health*, *6* (3), 314–320. https://doi.org/10.1016/j.sleh.2019.11.001.

World Health Organization (2020). Coronavirus disease (COVID-19) outbreak: Rights, roles and responsibilities of health workers, including key considerations for occupational safety and health. Zurich: World Health Organization.

Section III

A Focus on Co-Morbidities

Section Editor: Chiara Baglioni and Laura Palagini

12

CBT-I Protocol for Insomnia Co-morbid with Affective Disorders

Kerstin Blom and Susanna Jernelöv

Key points

- CBT-I is delivered in fundamentally the same way for patients with affective disorders as for those without. Thus similar rationales and therapeutic approaches are used.
- Patient motivation for treatment may be low in patients during a depressive episode. Therefore shaping procedures and a system for positive reinforcement are particularly useful in these patients.
- Cognitive functioning is often impaired and adaptations to facilitate treatment uptake are recommended.
- To minimize the risk of sleep deprivation, we encourage initial use of bed-time consistency with subsequent sleep compression rather than sleep restriction, for patients with type 1 bipolar disorder.
- As many patients with affective disorders have circadian rhythm disturbances, we also encourage adding behavioral components to address these, e.g., stable rise-times and systematic light/dark exposure.
- Another important specific element is the monitoring of affective symptom changes, most notably increases in manic symptoms, during treatment, and the adjustment of treatment if significant changes occur.

Learning objectives

- To understand how sleep is affected in affective disorders.
- To understand the specific difficulties for insomnia patients with co-morbid affective disorders.
- To understand how the standard protocol can be adjusted for work with insomnia patients with co-morbid affective disorder.

Abstract

The purpose of this chapter is to provide an overview of sleep problems in affective disorders, important aspects of CBT-I and adjustments to regular CBT-I for patients with affective disorders. The treatment is essentially the same for patients with affective disorders as for those without, with similar rationales and therapeutic approaches. However, due to the high occurrence of impaired cognitive functioning, lowered motivation and circadian rhythm disturbances, adaptions to treatment delivery are recommended, and to minimize the risk of sleep deprivation in bipolar type 1 patients, the use of sleep compression rather than sleep restriction is recommended.

Keywords *insomnia, CBT, affective disorders, bipolar disorder, depression*

Cognitive-Behavioural Therapy for Insomnia (CBT-I) Across the Life Span: Guidelines and Clinical Protocols for Health Professionals, First Edition. Edited by Chiara Baglioni, Colin A. Espie and Dieter Riemann.

Introduction to affective disorders and co-morbid insomnia

Affective disorders are common, with a lifetime prevalence of between 10 and 21% (Kessler et al., 2009) and a 12-month prevalence of around 9.1% for all affective disorders, including 8.3% for major depressive disorder and 0.8% for bipolar disorder (Wittchen & Jacobi, 2005).

Sleep in depression

Sleep problems are highly prevalent in patients with affective disorders. Co-morbidity of insomnia and depression is very common, with around two-thirds of patients with major depression also having insomnia disorder (Geoffroy et al., 2018). Hypersomnia is less common than insomnia (17–50 %; Geoffroy et al., 2018; Murru et al., 2019), but some patients present with both insomnia and hypersomnia. In terms of EEG, patients with depression have presented with alterations in both slow-wave sleep and REM sleep (Pillai, Kalmbach & Ciesla, 2011). Interestingly, patients with depression only, and patients with co-morbid insomnia and depression, have shown different EEG characteristics (Hein, Lanquart, Loas, Hubain & Linkowski, 2017).

Sleep in bipolar disorder

Studies have generally found that the vast majority of bipolar patients have sleep problems when in an illness episode, with both insomnia and hypersomnia being very prevalent (23–100 % depending on the study) and sometimes co-occurring (Harvey, Talbot & Gershon, 2009; Kaplan & Harvey, 2009). Sleep problems also tend to persist in the euthymic phase (Harvey, Schmidt, Scarna, Semler & Goodwin, 2005). Both longer sleep-onset latency and longer sleep duration, shifts in circadian rhythm and delayed sleep phase have been demonstrated (Jones, Hare & Evershed, 2005; Ritter et al., 2012), and circadian dysfunction has been suggested as an underlying cause of bipolar disorder (Murray & Harvey, 2010). In terms of EEG, increased sleep onset latency and alterations in REM sleep have been identified across all stages of bipolar disorder (Zangani et al., 2020).

Sleep disturbance impact and treatments

It has been suggested that sleep disturbance may directly contribute to mood disorders because it is a risk factor for episodes, can contribute to relapse, hinders recovery from depression, has an adverse impact on mood regulation, impairs cognitive functioning, compromises health and may contribute to substance use co-morbidity and suicidality (Baglioni et al., 2011; Harvey, 2011; Perlis, Giles, Buysse, Tu & Kupfer, 1997; Pigeon et al., 2008).

Depression

Traditionally, insomnia has been seen as a consequence or symptom of depression, expected to subside when the depression is successfully treated. However, depression treatments are often not adequate to improve co-morbid insomnia (Carney, Segal, Edinger & Krystal, 2007; Yon et al., 2014). By contrast, studies have shown that CBT-I is effective in alleviating insomnia in patients with co-morbid depression (Wu, Appleman, Salazar & Ong, 2015) and that CBT-I may alleviate depressive symptoms as effectively as CBT for depression (Blom et al., 2015). Indeed, reducing insomnia may play a causal role in addressing mental health symptoms (Scott, Webb, Martyn-St James, Rowse & Weich, 2021: Henry et al., 2021).

Bipolar disorder

In bipolar disorder, disturbed sleep is the most common prodromal symptom in mania and one of the most common in depression (Jackson, Cavanagh & Scott, 2003), and disordered sleep is included in the diagnostic criteria for both mania/hypomania and depression. Sleep deprivation correlates with day-time manic symptoms and sleep deprivation has been suggested to trigger manic episodes (Barbini, Bertelli, Colombo & Smeraldi, 1996). Accordingly, short total sleep time has been associated with increased mania severity, greater sleep variability with increases in both mania and depression severity (Gruber et al., 2011), and both short and long sleep duration with impaired functioning and quality of life (Gruber et al., 2009).

To date, few studies have examined the use of CBT-I exclusively in bipolar patients, but those that are available show promising results, suggesting improved sleep and even decreased risk for future mood episodes (Jernelöv et al., 2022; Harvey et al., 2015; Kaplan & Harvey, 2013). A recent review summarises the evidence on behavioural and circadian interventions in bipolar disorders (Bisdounis et al., 2022), and several studies on this patient group are ongoing as this chapter is written.

Theories of mechanisms of change

The underlying mechanisms of change that enable CBT-I to be effective in improving mood are not fully known. Several lines of reasoning have been put forward; for instance, most treatments that are delivered in a structured and qualitative manner will have a positive impact on depression (Barth et al., 2016; Cuijpers, Andersson, Donker & van Straten, 2011). At the same time, studies report that changes in insomnia or insomnia-related variables mediate improvements in depression (Manber et al., 2016; Norell-Clarke, Tilfors, Jansson-Fröjmark, Holländare & Engström, 2017), which indicates that there could be a specific sleep-related mechanism of change in the treatment of depression with CBT-I. Recently, a model was suggested where sleep is seen as the main regulator of several systems and processes whose dysregulation is involved in the pathogenesis of mood disorders (Palagini, Bastien, Marazziti, Ellis & Riemann, 2019). Very briefly, the model posits that sleep disruption acts as a neurobiological stressor, and that it may impair circadian rhythmicity and disturb emotion regulation. This could help to explain why disturbed sleep is so strongly linked to mood disorders and why treating sleep disturbances may alleviate affective episodes. Chapter 13 will provide an overview of CBT-I studies looking at all mental co-morbidities, including depression and bipolar disorder.

CBT-I for patients with co-morbid affective disorders

Suggestions for both depression and bipolar disorder

CBT-I components used for treating insomnia co-morbid with affective disorder reflect all the traditional components (see Chapter 2). The core standard protocol comprises a behavioural component and a cognitive component, and adaptations are described below. Patients with co-morbid affective disorders and insomnia tend to be heavily burdened and face varying challenges due to the heterogenous characteristics of affective disorders. Therapists therefore need to be skilled in therapeutic approaches, such as shaping procedures and establishing a system for positive reinforcement, in understanding psychiatric co-morbidities and in handling individual patients' challenges.

Patients with co-morbid insomnia and affective disorders, especially in depressive or manic episodes, may also have impaired cognitive functioning. This can manifest as difficulties understanding and remembering methods, and difficulties in executive functioning, such as getting started. In addition, increased fatigue may make it more difficult for patients with affective disorders to accept and stick with demanding strategies such as sleep restriction. Although longer treatment time is generally not associated with better outcomes in CBT (Cuijpers, Huibers, Ebert, Koole & Andersson, 2013), these patient groups may benefit from a slightly longer treatment time than a standard CBT-I, due to the patients' high level of insomnia and affective disorder symptoms.

Making sure patients understand, accept and remember methods and instructions

Table 12.1 includes a list of suggestions that have been collected from studies by Blom et al. (2016); Sadler, McLaren, Klein & Jenkins, (2020); Forsell et al. (2019) to increase patients' understanding, acceptance and compliance.

Adaptations of sleep restriction therapy

The standard protocol for sleep restriction therapy is described in Chapter 2 and, as discussed there, we tend to combine stimulus control and sleep restriction into 'sleep scheduling' also for patients with affective disorders.

Patients with affective disorders often have executive difficulties, low mood and low motivation. This makes it more challenging to fill out a sleep diary and to follow sleep restriction involving substantial shortening of time in bed. Therefore,

Table 12.1 Suggestions for increasing patients' attention, acceptance and compliance.

- Increase the frequency of contact, e.g., through therapeutic telephone calls in between sessions or by having several sessions per week.
- Make instructions and materials easy to understand and learn, and to help with memory difficulties, e.g., by providing pedagogically structured materials intended for repetition.
- A structured interview a few weeks into treatment, specifically targeting treatment progress and difficulties, is helpful for individualising treatment to suit the patient's specific needs, especially if treatment is given in groups or over the internet.
- Patients have suggested the use of multimodal learning methods, video or audio clips, and internet-based, group or individual treatment.
- Schedule brief sessions so patients can concentrate during the whole session.
- Take brief breaks during sessions to manage fatigue.
- Use telephone reminders in between sessions to help patients focus on the treatment and assignments.
- Send encouraging messages and session-related information after missed sessions.
- Engage support persons at home.

we often adapt sleep scheduling, for instance by not using a sleep diary. For patients with depression and no substantial executive difficulties, regular sleep restriction procedures are recommended as this has the strongest evidence.

A specific difficulty for patients with low mood is to actually get out of bed at the prescribed time, as motivation to get up and start the day may be virtually non-existent. Being observant that the patient is on board with the rationale for the strategy, discussing with the patient how they can make it work in their life, adding rewards for doing what needs be done and using an open and positive inquiring approach when evaluating the strategy after a week or so, is most helpful. For instance, for getting up in the morning, suggestions for making it work in the patient's life could be to set several alarms, and to ask for help from family or friends, and a reward could be meeting friends at a café or preparing a special breakfast at home.

Another difficulty that needs to be addressed is the additional time the patient has on their hands when using sleep restriction, as patients with an already low mood may feel overwhelmed when there is even more time to 'kill'. The therapist needs to validate this and help the patient reframe the situation; time can be better spent than 'killed'. Exploring the patient's wishes and gently guiding them to use the time to do something they have always wanted to (or used to want to do) is ideal, but also just taking an evening walk or folding clean laundry that usually stays unfolded for long times is a good first step which also serves the function of behavioural activation.

Napping

Napping is discussed in the context of the two-factor model (see also Chapter 2). If the patient is in a depressive or euthymic phase, the choice is preferably to skip napping, thus increasing sleep pressure in the evening.

However, as napping is an efficient way to decrease arousal during the day, patients with increased manic symptoms can benefit substantially from lying down in a dark room for about 30 minutes a couple of times during the day; a relaxation exercise can also be useful. Some patients will fall asleep during this period, in which case an option is to incorporate napping into their sleep schedule. If napping is included, it is important to discuss shortening the time in bed during the night and to phase out napping following improvements in manic symptoms.

Sleep medication use

The use of hypnotics may have its place, for instance in acute phases of affective disorders. However, we always encourage short-term use of hypnotics, as there is a problem when they are prescribed during an acute phase and then never discontinued. Patients who use hypnotics when starting CBT-I are encouraged, under medical guidance, to stabilize them in the early phase of treatment. We then offer a tapering and discontinuation schedule to be implemented when they experience sleep improvements from the cognitive and behavioural strategies.

Case example (Insomnia co-morbid with major depression)

Ms G, aged 64, struggled with insomnia since her menopause about 10 years previously. She intermittently used sleep medication, but had stopped several times due to side-effects and poor treatment effects after the first few weeks.

Her husband of 32 years died suddenly five years ago, and two years ago, about a year after her retirement from work, she became more and more depressed and decided to seek help. She had rather regular habits and went to bed early (around 9.30 p.m.) in order to get as much sleep as possible. She had difficulties falling asleep and woke up early in the morning, unable to go back to sleep. Her social life was limited due to fatigue and lack of initiative, and she often took naps or laid down to rest during the day. Ms G was reluctant to start doing sleep restriction since it seemed impossible to stay awake late and not nap. Instead, she started a regularised sleep schedule aiming at 8 hours of sleep – going to bed at 10.30 p.m. and getting up at 6.30 a.m. After three weeks with little or no improvement in her sleep, she was ready to try sleep restriction for a few weeks as an experiment. She then went to bed at midnight and was up at 6 a.m. for one week, with no napping scheduled. The strict schedule was combined with brief morning walks every day – just 10 minutes to get some sunlight. If the weather was nice she often extended the walk. Her therapist asked her to report back every morning using a text message, briefly describing her sleep times and the walk. The therapist sent back a very short message encouraging her to keep working with the method. In addition, they met weekly to set new bed times, and to problem solve and figure out ways to cope with the treatment and daily life. Ms G gradually increased her daily activity level both with physical exercise (mostly short walks) and social interaction. After two weeks with sleep restriction she noticed improvements in her sleep continuity, day-time functioning and mood, and decided to stick with the sleep restriction program in spite of the hard work it entailed. After another two weeks she started tapering her sleep medications slowly as per a schedule devised together with her therapist, while continuing to increase her bed-time weekly until her sleep was satisfactory. At this time her mood was also considerably improved and she was no longer clinically depressed.

Specific adaptations for patients with co-morbid bipolar disorder

The adaptations of CBT-I described above are applicable also in co-morbid bipolar disorder. In addition, components of chronotherapy (Wirz-Justice et al., 2005) tend to be useful in this patient group, and special attention to worry about sleep loss leading to manic episodes, and adaptations of sleep restriction and stimulus control procedures are also described below.

Handle worry about poor sleep leading to manic episode

It is well recognized that sleep is very important for patients with bipolar disorder. Indeed, most patients receive pharmacological treatment targeting insomnia and initial psychoeducation for bipolar patients commonly includes information about monitoring sleep pattern and sleep time. This is an important first step and helps both clinicians and patients to be appreciative of bipolar patients' sleep. However, for patients with chronic insomnia the worry of short sleep may be one of the most important barriers to sleeping well and may also be a barrier to engaging in CBT-I.

For patients with bipolar disorder, some practices of the mental health care staff they encounter may add to the worry; e.g., a strong focus on getting a specific number of hours of sleep including counter-productive advice to stay in bed in the morning to catch up on their sleep (also while the patient is in CBT-I) and emphasis on long-term intermittent use of hypnotics.

Educating the staff on sleep and CBT-I is therefore often needed and an important part of psychoeducation for both staff and patients is to address the difference between a few nights of poor sleep and a manic episode. Day-time fatigue is an important differentiator and a rule of thumb is that poor sleep accompanied by day-time fatigue is usually not a sign of a manic episode, whereas unusually short sleeps for several nights without day-time fatigue often accompany other manic symptoms, like elated mood.

Adaptations of sleep restriction therapy

Sleep restriction is at the very core of CBT-I, but sleep restriction may cause mild sleep deprivation and there has been concern that sleep deprivation could induce mania (Barbini et al., 1996; Colombo, Benedetti, Barbini, Campon & Smeraldi, 1999). Although the use of sleep restriction therapy in bipolar patients does not seem to increase the risk of manic episodes (Kaplan & Harvey, 2013), we recommend using consistent bed-times since this is often sufficient to resolve wakefulness in the night with bipolar patients (Jernelöv et al., 2022; Kaplan & Harvey, 2013). Thus, with bipolar patients, bed-time consistency is advised as the first step, with sleep compression as a second step if needed.

Bed-time consistency, i.e., keeping very regular sleeping hours, is thus the first step. Rise-time should ideally be kept constant throughout the treatment period, so it is important to discuss with the patient to find one that will work both during the week and during the week-end for some time.

Once rise-time has been decided, count backwards the number of hours **the patient wishes to sleep**, or believes that they **usually sleep**. Note that the length of the sleep window therefore is often set based on the patient's global estimation of how much sleep they need, not on data from a sleep diary. For many patients with affective disorders, establishing consistency in bed-times will improve their sleep substantially.

If bed-time consistency is not sufficient to improve sleep – e.g., if the patient still takes a long time to fall asleep or wakes up a lot during the night – and regular sleep restriction is not chosen, **sleep compression** is subsequently applied. In contrast to sleep restriction, where the sleep window is immediately set to correspond to average total sleep time as registered in the sleep diary, sleep compression encompasses a gradual shortening of the sleep window to approach the patients' sleep need. Thus, there may be less risk of sleep deprivation. Reductions stop when sleep (or sleep efficiency for patients using a sleep diary) is satisfactory. The size of the reductions can be negotiated, but unless the patient has extremely long wake-times, about 15 minutes weekly is often sufficient and practical.

Adaptations of stimulus control instructions

Interestingly, reduced sleep in mania may not be due to a reduced *need* for sleep, but rather due to a reduced *opportunity* for sleep (Harvey, 2011; Van Sweden, 1986), as patients during manic episodes tend to not lie down to sleep. Therefore, patients with bipolar disorder should be instructed to go to bed at the prescribed time even if they do not feel particularly sleepy, as 'feeling sleepy' may not happen. However, as per the regular stimulus control instructions, if the patient does not fall asleep within a reasonable time (about 15 minutes), they should get out of bed and engage in low arousing activities such as listening to calm music or doing a relaxation exercise. It is also important that the patient does not stay out of bed longer than necessary. Rather than staying out of bed 'until sleepy', about 15 minutes out of bed is usually sufficient. This rule of thumb is also used for patients with unipolar depression, as they too may have difficulties discerning sleepiness from other experiences. As discussed above, periodic darkness and relaxation exercises may be encouraged during the day if the patient displays increased manic symptoms, and a nap can be temporarily included in the patient's sleep schedule.

Chronotherapeutic components

With circadian dysregulation affecting both sleep and the bipolar disorder, the application of chronotherapeutic components (Wirz-Justice et al., 2005) may help improve sleep. Specifically, we apply systematic use of light and darkness to stabilize circadian rhythm, but also include other *zeitgebers*, such as meals, physical activity and social interaction (Frank et al., 2005; Frank, Swartz & Kupfer, 2000). Together with the patient, we discuss circadian rhythms and map their circadian preference, and jointly come up with a zeitgeber schedule to stabilize and improve their circadian rhythm that fits the patient's situation.

Scheduled rise-times alone have been shown to improve circadian rhythm in delayed sleep phase (Danielsson, Jansson-Frojmark, Broman & Markstrom, 2018; Saxvig et al., 2014). Scheduled rise-times are a part of sleep restriction therapy, but this component is especially important in bipolar disorder and may be used without restricting the time in bed, as described above.

Case example (insomnia co-morbid with bipolar disorder – late circadian phase)

Mr S, 35, was in a euthymic phase, had had insomnia 'as long as I can remember', with difficulties falling asleep in the evening. He lived on his own and was unemployed. At the beginning of treatment, he described that he was unable to wake up on his own until 11 in the morning or even later, and he usually did not leave bed for another few hours. He did not eat until later as he was too tired and not at all hungry during the day, and having breakfast made him feel nauseated. After having had something to eat towards the late afternoon he would most often finally feel a bit more energized and would want to start projects, meet up with friends or go to the (night-open) gym. His behaviours thus perpetuated his innate late circadian tendency. During treatment, Mr S and the therapist mapped his circadian rhythm behaviourally, by investigating his preferred rise-time and bed-time and mapping how energized he felt during different parts of the day. They then discussed how Mr S could use different zeitgebers to help align his circadian rhythm and jointly developed a zeitgeber schedule, which was evaluated weekly. The initial zeitgeber schedule included a stable wake-time at 9:30 a.m., getting daylight directly when he woke up, and having a very light breakfast (coffee and a biscuit) within 30 minutes of waking up. He then scheduled other activities to have regular meals, such as meeting up with friends for lunch, and being physically active during the day. From about seven o'clock in the evening, he was to use only low lights, and from about an hour and a half before going to bed he adopted a wind-down schedule including gradually less-arousing activities. He went to bed at half past midnight. These were enormous changes in Mr S's life, and they initially required a great deal of work, including asking friends for help and setting alarms not only for waking up but also to remember turning the lights down low in the evening. After the first week, a wake-up routine (Kaplan, Talavera & Harvey, 2018) was added as he had great difficulties getting out of bed, and he also added a reward (a massage) after having got out of bed in time for four days. Within a few weeks, he experienced improvements as getting out of bed was not such a struggle any more. After about a month, the schedule was adjusted somewhat, for instance he decided to set an earlier wake-time as he realized getting up earlier in the morning would be needed if he were to get a job, and so the bed-time was also set earlier. He also added a fruit to his breakfast as he felt he could eat a little more without feeling nauseous. After about two months he realized he did not have to think about the schedule so much, as most parts had turned into new habits, for instance getting out of the house in the morning and going to the gym during the day instead of the evening. However, he still did not feel sleepy in the evening and had to watch out for the tendency to start projects in the evening, since starting projects late would make him stay up very late during the night, and he had realized that very short nights of sleep tended to make him more aroused the next day.

Useful questionnaires

Co-morbid depression

There are a number of scales for continuously measuring depression severity that are well spread, tested, psychometrically sound and suited for self-rating: The Patient Health Questionnaire, PHQ-9 (Kroenke, Spitzer & Williams, 2001), the Beck Depression Inventory, BDI-II (Beck, Steer & Garbin, 1988) and the Montgomery Åsberg Depression Rating Scale, Self-rated, MADRS-S (Svanborg & Asberg, 1994) are some examples. They all include an item asking about suicidal ideation, which is important to follow-up on during treatment, since poor sleep is a predictor of increased suicide risk.

Co-morbid bipolar disorder

A sleep diary with columns for day-time symptoms of mania and depression is useful to follow day-to-day variations in mood. The Affective Self-Rating Scale (AS-18) (Adler, Liberg, Andersson, Isacsson & Hetta, 2008) is an 18-item self-rating scale with adequate psychometric properties assessing depressive, manic/hypomanic and mixed affective states, and includes an item on suicidal ideation. The five-item version of the Altman self-rated mania scale (ASRM-5) can also be used to monitor for manic symptoms (Meyer et al., 2020).

Conclusion

Insomnia disorder is often co-morbid with other conditions, especially affective disorders, including major depression and bipolar disorders. While treatment of co-morbid insomnia does not refer to different strategies or interventions for improving sleep, many aspects should be considered. Expert clinicians with good knowledge and practice of mental disorders should handle interventions. The key point is that insomnia treatment should be integrated into the general treatment plan. Motivational, emotional and circadian aspects have a relevant role in treatment of insomnia co-morbid with affective disorder. Sleep restriction should be prescribed carefully in patients with bipolar disorder, to avoid the provocation of hypomanic/maniac mood swings.

References

Adler, M., Liberg, B., Andersson, S., Isacsson, G., & Hetta, J. (2008). Development and validation of the Affective Self Rating Scale for manic, depressive, and mixed affective states. *Nordic Journal of Psychiatry*, *62* (2), 130–135. https://doi.org/10.1080/08039480801960354.

Baglioni, C., Battagliese, G., Feige, B., Spiegelhalder, K., Nissen, C., Voderholzer, U., Lombardo, C., & Riemann, D. (2011). Insomnia as a predictor of depression: A meta-analytic evaluation of longitudinal epidemiological studies. *Journal of Affective Disorders*, *135* (1–3), 10–19. https://doi.org/10.1016/j.jad.2011.01.011.

Barbini, B., Bertelli, S., Colombo, C., & Smeraldi, E. (1996). Sleep loss, a possible factor in augmenting manic episode. *Psychiatry Research*, *65* (2), 121–125. https://doi.org/10.1016/s0165-1781(96)02909-5.

Barth, J., Munder, T., Gerger, H., Nuesch, E., Trelle, S., Znoj, H., Juni, P., & Cuijpers, P. (2016). Comparative efficacy of seven psychotherapeutic interventions for patients with depression: A network meta-analysis. *Focus*, *14* (2), 229–243. https://doi.org/10.1176/appi.focus.140201.

Beck, A. T., Steer, R. A., & Garbin, M. G. (1988). Psychometric properties of the Beck Depression Inventory: Twenty five years of evaluation. *Clinical Psychology Review*, *8*, 77–100.

Bisdounis, L., Saunders, K. E. A., Farley, H. J., Lee, C. K., McGowan, N. M., Espie, C. A., & Kyle, S. D. (2022). Psychological and behavioural interventions in bipolar disorder that target sleep and circadian rhythms: A systematic review of randomised controlled trials. *Neuroscience & Biobehavioral Reviews*, *132*, 378–390. https://doi.org/https://doi.org/10.1016/j.neubiorev.2021.12.002.

Blom, K., Jernelov, S., Lindefors, N., & Kaldo, V. (2016). Facilitating and hindering factors in Internet-delivered treatment for insomnia and depression. *Internet Interventions*, *4*, 51–60. https://doi.org/10.1016/j.invent.2016.03.004.

Blom, K., Jernelov, S., Kraepelien, M., Bergdahl, M. O., Jungmarker, K., Ankartjarn, L., Lindefors, N., & Kaldo, V. (2015). Internet treatment addressing either insomnia or depression, for patients with both diagnoses: A randomized trial. *Sleep*, *38* (2), 267–277. https://doi.org/10.5665/sleep.4412.

Carney, C. E., Segal, Z. V., Edinger, J. D., & Krystal, A. D. (2007). A comparison of rates of residual insomnia symptoms following pharmacotherapy or cognitive-behavioral therapy for major depressive disorder. *Journal of Clinical Psychiatry*, *68* (2), 254–260. https://doi.org/10.4088/jcp.v68n0211.

Colombo, C., Benedetti, F., Barbini, B., Campori, E., & Smeraldi, E. (1999). Rate of switch from depression into mania after therapeutic sleep deprivation in bipolar depression. *Psychiatry Research*, *86* (3), 267–270.

Cuijpers, P., Andersson, G., Donker, T., & van Straten, A. (2011). Psychological treatment of depression: Results of a series of meta-analyses [Meta-Analysis]. *Nord Journal of Psychiatry*, *65* (6), 354–364. https://doi.org/10.3109/08039488.2011.596570.

Cuijpers, P., Huibers, M., Ebert, D. D., Koole, S. L., & Andersson, G. (2013). How much psychotherapy is needed to treat depression? A metaregression analysis. *Journal of Affective Disorders*, *149* (1–3), 1–13. https://doi.org/10.1016/j.jad.2013.02.030.

Danielsson, K., Jansson-Frojmark, M., Broman, J. E., & Markstrom, A. (2018). Light therapy with scheduled rise times in young adults with delayed sleep phase disorder: Therapeutic outcomes and possible predictors. *Behavioural Sleep Medicine*, *16* (4), 325–336. https://doi.org/10.1080/15402002.2016.1210150.

Forsell, E., Jernelov, S., Blom, K., Kraepelien, M., Svanborg, C., Andersson, G., Lindefors, N., & Kaldo, V. (2019). Proof of concept for an adaptive treatment strategy to prevent failures in internet-delivered CBT: A single-blind randomized clinical trial with insomnia patients. *American Journal of Psychiatry*, *176* (4), 315–323. https://doi.org/10.1176/appi.ajp.2018.18060699.

Frank, E., Swartz, H. A., & Kupfer, D. J. (2000). Interpersonal and social rhythm therapy: Managing the chaos of bipolar disorder. *Biological Psychiatry*, *48* (6), 593–604. https://doi.org/10.1016/s0006-3223(00)00969-0.

Frank, E., Kupfer, D. J., Thase, M. E., Mallinger, A. G., Swartz, H. A., Fagiolini, A. M., Grochocinski, V., Houck, P., Scott, J., Thompson, W., & Monk, T. (2005). Two-year outcomes for interpersonal and social rhythm therapy in individuals with bipolar I disorder. *Archives of General Psychiatry*, *62* (9), 996–1004. https://doi.org/10.1001/archpsyc.62.9.996.

Geoffroy, P. A., Hoertel, N., Etain, B., Bellivier, F., Delorme, R., Limosin, F., & Peyre, H. (2018). Insomnia and hypersomnia in major depressive episode: Prevalence, sociodemographic characteristics and psychiatric comorbidity in a population-based study. *Journal of Affective Disorders*, *226*, 132–141. https://doi.org/10.1016/j.jad.2017.09.032.

Gruber, J., Harvey, A. G., Wang, P. W., Brooks III, J. O., Thase, M. E., Sachs, G. S., & Ketter, T. A. (2009). Sleep functioning in relation to mood, function, and quality of life at entry to the Systematic Treatment Enhancement Program for Bipolar Disorder (STEP-BD). *Journal of Affective Disorders*, *114* (1–3), 41–49. https://doi.org/10.1016/j.jad.2008.06.028.

Gruber, J., Miklowitz, D. J., Harvey, A. G., Frank, E., Kupfer, D., Thase, M. E., Sachs, G. S., & Ketter, T. A. (2011). Sleep matters: Sleep functioning and course of illness in bipolar disorder. *Journal of Affective Disorders*, *134* (1–3), 416–420. https://doi.org/10.1016/j.jad.2011.05.016.

Harvey, A. G. (2011). Sleep and circadian functioning: Critical mechanisms in the mood disorders? *Annual Review of Clinical Psychology*, *7* (1), 297–319. https://doi.org/10.1146/annurev-clinpsy-032210-104550.

Harvey, A. G., Schmidt, D., Scarna, A., Semler, C. N., & Goodwin, G. M. (2005). Sleep-related functioning in euthymic patients with bipolar disorder, patients with insomnia, and subjects without sleep problems. *American Journal of Psychiatry*, *162* (1), 50–59. https://doi.org/10.1176/appi.ajp.162.1.50.

Harvey, A. G., Talbot, L. S., & Gershon, A. (2009). Sleep disturbance in bipolar disorder across the lifespan. *Clinical Psychology (New York), 16* (2), 256–277. https://doi.org/10.1111/j.1468-2850.2009.01164.x.

Harvey, A. G., Soehner, A. M., Kaplan, K. A., Hein, K., Lee, J., Kanady, J., Li, *D.*, Rabe-Hesketh, S., Ketter, T. A., Neylan, T. C. & Buysse, D. J. (2015). Treating insomnia improves mood state, sleep, and functioning in bipolar disorder: A pilot randomized controlled trial. *Journal of Consulting and Clinical Psychology, 83* (3), 564–577. https://doi.org/10.1037/a0038655.

Hein, M., Lanquart, J. P., Loas, G., Hubain, P., & Linkowski, P. (2017). Similar polysomnographic pattern in primary insomnia and major depression with objective insomnia: A sign of common pathophysiology? *BMC Psychiatry, 17* (1), 273. https://doi.org/10.1186/s12888-017-1438-4.

Henry, A. L., Miller, C. B., Emsley, R., Sheaves, B., Freeman, D., Luik, A. I., Littlewood, D. L., Saunders, K., Kanady, J. C., Carl, J. R., Davis, M. L., Kyle, S. D., & Espie, C. A. (2021). Insomnia as a mediating therapeutic target for depressive symptoms: A sub-analysis of participant data from two large randomized controlled trials of a digital sleep intervention. *Journal of Sleep Research, 30* (1), e13140. https://doi.org/10.1111/jsr.13140.

Jackson, A., Cavanagh, J., & Scott, J. (2003). A systematic review of manic and depressive prodromes. *Journal of Affective Disorders, 74* (3), 209–217. https://doi.org/10.1016/s0165-0327(02)00266-5.

Jernelöv, S., Killgren, J., Ledin, L., & Kaldo, V. (2022). Treatment feasibility and preliminary evaluation of group-delivered cognitive behavioral therapy for insomnia adapted for patients with bipolar and related disorders: A pragmatic within-group study. *Journal of Affective Disorders Reports, 7*, 100293. https://doi.org/10.1016/j.jadr.2021.100293.

Jones, S. H., Hare, D. J., & Evershed, K. (2005). Actigraphic assessment of circadian activity and sleep patterns in bipolar disorder. *Bipolar Disorders, 7* (2), 176–186. https://doi.org/10.1111/j.1399-5618.2005.00187.x.

Kaplan, K. A., & Harvey, A. G. (2009). Hypersomnia across mood disorders: A review and synthesis. *Sleep Medicine Reviews, 13* (4), 275–285. https://doi.org/10.1016/j.smrv.2008.09.001.

Kaplan, K. A., & Harvey, A. G. (2013). Behavioral treatment of insomnia in bipolar disorder. *American Journal of Psychiatry, 170* (7), 716–720. https://doi.org/10.1176/appi.ajp.2013.12050708.

Kaplan, K. A., Talavera, D. C., & Harvey, A. G. (2018). Rise and shine: A treatment experiment testing a morning routine to decrease subjective sleep inertia in insomnia and bipolar disorder. *Behaviour Research and Therapy, 111*, 106–112. https://doi.org/10.1016/j.brat.2018.10.009.

Kessler, R. C., Aguilar-Gaxiola, S., Alonso, J., Chatterji, S., Lee, S., Ormel, J., Ustun, T. B., & Wang, P. S. (2009). The global burden of mental disorders: An update from the WHO World Mental Health (WMH) surveys. *Epidemiologia e Psichiatria Sociale, 18* (1), 23–33. https://doi.org/10.1017/s1121189x00001421.

Kroenke, K., Spitzer, R. L., & Williams, J. B. (2001). The PHQ-9: Validity of a brief depression severity measure. *Journal of General Internal Medicine, 16* (9), 606–613. https://doi.org/10.1046/j.1525-1497.2001.016009606.x.

Manber, R., Buysse, D. J., Edinger, J., Krystal, A., Luther, J. F., Wisniewski, S. R., Trockel, M., Kraemer, H. C., & Thase, M. E. (2016). Efficacy of cognitive-behavioral therapy for insomnia combined with antidepressant pharmacotherapy in patients with comorbid depression and insomnia: A randomized controlled trial. *Journal of Clinical Psychiatry, 77* (10), e1316–e1323. https://doi.org/10.4088/JCP.15m10244.

Meyer, T. D., Crist, N., La Rosa, N., Ye, B., Soares, J. C., & Bauer, I. E. (2020). Are existing self-ratings of acute manic symptoms in adults reliable and valid? *A systematic review. Bipolar Disorders, 22* (6), 558–568. https://doi.org/10.1111/bdi.12906.

Murray, G., & Harvey, A. (2010). Circadian rhythms and sleep in bipolar disorder. *Bipolar Disorders, 12* (5), 459–472. https://doi.org/10.1111/j.1399-5618.2010.00843.x.

Murru, A., Guiso, G., Barbuti, M., Anmella, G., Verdolini, N., Samalin, L., Azorin, J. M., Angst, J. J., Bowden, C. L., Mosolov, S., Young, A. H., Popovic, D., Valdes, *M.*, Perugi, G., Vieta, E., Pacchiarotti, I., & For the BRIDGE-II-Mix Study Group, B.R.I.M.S. (2019). The implications of hypersomnia in the context of major depression: Results from a large, international, observational study. *European Neuropsychopharmacology, 29* (4), 471–481. https://doi.org/10.1016/j.euroneuro.2019.02.011.

Norell-Clarke, A., Tillfors, M., Jansson-Fröjmark, M., Holländare, F., & Engström, I. (2017). How does cognitive behavioral therapy for insomnia work? An investigation of cognitive processes and time in bed as outcomes and mediators in a sample with insomnia and depressive symptomatology. *International Journal of Cognitive Therapy, 10* (4), 304–329. https://doi.org/10.1521/ijct.2017.10.4.304.

Palagini, L., Bastien, C. H., Marazziti, D., Ellis, J. G., & Riemann, D. (2019). The key role of insomnia and sleep loss in the dysregulation of multiple systems involved in mood disorders: A proposed model. *Journal of Sleep Research, 28* (6), e12841. https://doi.org/10.1111/jsr.12841.

Perlis, M. L., Giles, D. E., Buysse, D. J., Tu, X., & Kupfer, D. J. (1997). Self-reported sleep disturbance as a prodromal symptom in recurrent depression. *Journal of Affective Disorders*, *42* (2–3), 209–212. https://doi.org/10.1016/s0165-0327(96)01411-5.

Pigeon, W. R., Hegel, M., Unutzer, J., Fan, M. Y., Sateia, M. J., Lyness, J. M., Phillips, C., & Perlis, M. L. (2008). Is insomnia a perpetuating factor for late-life depression in the IMPACT cohort? *Sleep*, *31* (4), 481–488. https://doi.org/10.1093/sleep/31.4.481.

Pillai, V., Kalmbach, D. A., & Ciesla, J. A. (2011). A meta-analysis of electroencephalographic sleep in depression: Evidence for genetic biomarkers. *Biological Psychiatry*, *70* (10), 912–919. https://doi.org/10.1016/j.biopsych.2011.07.016.

Ritter, P. S., Marx, C., Lewtschenko, N., Pfeiffer, S., Leopold, K., Bauer, M., & Pfennig, A. (2012). The characteristics of sleep in patients with manifest bipolar disorder, subjects at high risk of developing the disease and healthy controls. *Journal of Neural Transmission*, *119* (10), 1173–1184. https://doi.org/10.1007/s00702-012-0883-y.

Sadler, P., McLaren, S., Klein, B., & Jenkins, M. (2020). Cognitive behaviour therapy for insomnia and depression: Qualitative reflections from older adults who participated in a randomised controlled trial. *Aging Mental Health*, *24* (6), 932–938. https://doi.org/10.1080/13607863.2019.1571013.

Saxvig, I. W., Wilhelmsen-Langeland, A., Pallesen, S., Vedaa, O., Nordhus, I. H., & Bjorvatn, B. (2014). A randomized controlled trial with bright light and melatonin for delayed sleep phase disorder: Effects on subjective and objective sleep. *Chronobiology International*, *31* (1), 72–86. https://doi.org/10.3109/07420528.2013.823200.

Scott, A. J., Webb, T. L., Martyn-St James, M., Rowse, G., & Weich, S. (2021). Improving sleep quality leads to better mental health: A meta-analysis of randomised controlled trials. *Sleep Medicine Reviews*, *60*, 101556. https://doi.org/https://doi.org/10.1016/j.smrv.2021.101556.

Svanborg, P., & Asberg, M. (1994). A new self-rating scale for depression and anxiety states based on the Comprehensive Psychopathological Rating Scale. *Acta Psychiatrica Scandinavica*, *89* (1), 21–28. https://doi.org/10.1111/j.1600-0447.1994.tb01480.x.

Van Sweden, B. (1986). Disturbed vigilance in mania. *Biological Psychiatry*, *21* (3), 311–313. https://doi.org/10.1016/0006-3223(86)90052-1.

Wirz-Justice, A., Benedetti, F., Berger, M., Lam, R. W., Martiny, K., Terman, M., & Wu, J. C. (2005). Chronotherapeutics (light and wake therapy) in affective disorders. *Psychological Medicine*, *35* (7), 939–944. https://doi.org/10.1017/s003329170500437x.

Wittchen, H. U., & Jacobi, F. (2005). Size and burden of mental disorders in Europe – A critical review and appraisal of 27 studies. *European Neuropsychopharmacology*, *15* (4), 357–376. https://doi.org/10.1016/j.euroneuro.2005.04.012.

Wu, J. Q., Appleman, E. R., Salazar, R. D., & Ong, J. C. (2015). Cognitive behavioral therapy for insomnia comorbid with psychiatric and medical conditions: A meta-analysis. *JAMA Internal Medicine*, *175* (9), 1461–1472. https://doi.org/10.1001/jamainternmed.2015.3006.

Yon, A., Scogin, F., DiNapoli, E. A., McPherron, J., Arean, P. A., Bowman, D., Jamison, C. S., Karpe, J. A., Latour, D., Reynolds, C. F., 3rd, Rohen, N., Pardini, J. E., & Thompson, L. W. (2014). Do manualized treatments for depression reduce insomnia symptoms? *Journal of Clinical Psychology*, *70* (7), 616–630. https://doi.org/10.1002/jclp.22062.

Zangani, C., Casetta, C., Saunders, A. S., Donati, F., Maggioni, E., & D'Agostino, A. (2020). Sleep abnormalities across different clinical stages of bipolar disorder: A review of EEG studies. *Neuroscience and Biobehavioral Reviews*, *118*, 247–257. https://doi.org/10.1016/j.neubiorev.2020.07.031.

13

CBT-I Protocols for Insomnia Co-morbid with Other Mental Disorders

Elisabeth Hertenstein, Christoph Nissen and Daniel Freeman

Key points

- Almost 70% of patients with mental disorders report symptoms of insomnia. Insomnia in patients with mental disorders is associated with a more severe course of the mental disorder and reduced treatment efficacy.
- Cognitive Behavioral Therapy for Insomnia (CBT-I) is effective for the treatment of insomnia in patients with mood disorders, anxiety disorders, post-traumatic stress disorder and schizophrenia. In some patient groups, CBT-I can also have positive effects on the severity of the co-morbid disorder.
- Clinical adaptations of the CBT-I protocol have been described for several disorders.

Learning objectives

- To know the prevalence of insomnia in patients with mental disorders.
- To know about the impact of insomnia on the course of illness and treatment success in patients with insomnia and co-morbid mental disorders
- To know how insomnia can be treated in patients with mental disorders.

Abstract

Insomnia is a frequent co-morbidity of many mental disorders: Almost 70% of patients with mental disorders find it difficult to fall asleep or maintain sleep. Insomnia increases the risk of a negative course of the mental disorder and of poorer treatment efficacy. Cognitive behavioural therapy for insomnia (CBT-I) is effective for the reduction of insomnia in this patient group and has been recommended as a first-line treatment in European and American treatment guidelines. Among different mental disorders, depression is the best investigated co-morbidity (see Chapter 12). A wide range of studies demonstrates the efficacy of CBT-I for the reduction of insomnia. Whereas some studies found a positive effect of CBT-I also on depressive symptoms, other studies could not replicate these effects. Treatment efficacy of CBT-I has also been demonstrated for patients with post-traumatic stress disorder, bipolar disorder and schizophrenia. For depression, bipolar disorder and schizophrenia, research suggests that CBT-I may contribute to the prevention of further episodes of the disease. More research is needed to evaluate the efficacy of CBT-I for patients with yet under-investigated co-morbidities such as ADHD.

Keywords *Insomnia, depression, bipolar disorder, post-traumatic stress disorder, anxiety disorders, schizophrenia, cognitive behavioural therapy for insomnia, co-morbid insomnia*

Cognitive-Behavioural Therapy for Insomnia (CBT-I) Across the Life Span: Guidelines and Clinical Protocols for Health Professionals, First Edition. Edited by Chiara Baglioni, Colin A. Espie and Dieter Riemann.

Introduction

Insomnia is frequently co-morbid with mental disorders. Almost 70% of patients with mental disorders report difficulties falling asleep or sleep maintenance problems (Seow et al., 2018). One third of these patients fulfill the criteria for insomnia disorder (Seow et al., 2018). Insomnia has a negative impact on the course of the mental disorder and on treatment efficacy (Seow et al., 2018). CBT-I has been scientifically evaluated for patients with co-morbid insomnia and different mental disorders, mainly depression, but also bipolar disorder, anxiety disorders and psychosis. For some groups of patients, CBT-I protocols have been adapted to address specific symptoms of the co-morbid mental disorder; for example, nightmares in patients with post-traumatic stress disorder (PTSD) or sleep inertia in patients with bipolar disorder (Kaplan, Talavera & Harvey, 2018). The evidence clearly shows that CBT-I is also effective in patients with mental co-morbidity. According to current guidelines, CBT-I is the first-line treatment also in co-morbid insomnia (Riemann et al., 2017).

Most studies have been conducted in outpatients with comparatively mild mental disorders. CBT-I protocols for patients with severe neuropsychiatric disorders requiring inpatient treatment, however, are scarce. Traditionally, CBT-I protocols are adapted for patients with a specific mental disorder such as depression (see Chapter 12) or PTSD. Especially for patients with severe mental disorders, this approach has shifted towards a transdiagnostic adaptation (Schneider et al., 2020; Sheaves et al., 2018b). Patients in an acute psychiatric crisis often suffer from cognitive difficulties such as reduced concentration and memory, as well as problems with motivation and psychomotor drive. For this patient group, it is especially important to adapt CBT-I to make it easier to understand and apply and to offer support during the daily implementation of the therapeutic techniques. An additional adaption for specific disorders, on the other hand, would be difficult to implement on psychiatric wards and may be dispensable for this patient group.

Major depression

Among those with co-morbid insomnia and a mental disorder, depression is the best-investigated co-morbidity. A wide range of studies demonstrates the efficacy of CBT-I on the reduction of insomnia. Whereas some trials found that CBT-I also improves depression severity independent of specific antidepressant treatment, other studies did not replicate this effect. It needs to be kept in mind that there is an overlap in the day-time symptoms of insomnia and symptoms of mild depression: fatigue, reduced motivation and energy, reduced concentration and increased rumination can occur in both disorders. A newer approach is to treat insomnia with CBT-I with the aim of preventing the de novo onset of depression or further episodes in patients with known recurrent major depression.

Hsu et al. (2015) and Ashworth et al. (2015) have demonstrated in randomized-controlled trials that CBT-I is more effective than written sleep-related education for patients with insomnia and depression. CBT-I was delivered in four individual sessions in the Ashworth trial and in six group sessions in the Hsu trial. While Hsu et al. (2015) did not investigate the effect of CBT-I on depression, Ashworth et al. (2015) found a greater reduction in depression severity in the CBT-I group compared to the control group. In this study, all participants had been on antidepressant medication for at least six weeks prior to the study screening visit. From this study, it can be concluded that CBT-I may be an effective additional treatment.

Another randomized controlled trial by Norell-Clarke, Tillfors, Kansson-Fröjmark, Holländare and Engström (2017) compared group CBT-I to an active control condition, namely relaxation training. The participants received four two-hour bi-weekly sessions of group treatment. The results showed a significant reduction of insomnia severity in the CBT-I group, but the conditions were equally effective in reducing depressive symptomatology with a tendency towards better reduction in the CBT-I condition (Norell-Clarke et al., 2017).

Group CBT-I not only seems to work in a middle-aged population, but also showed therapeutic effects in older adults with insomnia and depression. Sadler, McLaren, Klein, Harvey & Jenkins (2018) compared three conditions in a randomized controlled trial in 72 elderly (mean age 75 $\pm$ 7 years; 56% females) using a small group format: standard CBT-I, an adapted protocol of CBT-I including additional strategies for mood regulation and a psychoeducation control group. Both CBT-I formats were delivered in eight weekly group-based sessions. The study demonstrated the superiority of the two CBT-I conditions over the control condition in improving insomnia and depression severity. The adapted protocol, however, was not significantly more effective than standard CBT-I (Sadler et al., 2018).

Glozier et al. (2019) investigated CBT-I in an online format. They compared online CBT-I to online sleep psychoeducation as an adjunct to pharmacological depression treatment according to guidelines (Glozier et al., 2019). The online CBT-I programme consisted of six 30–40 minute modules, which were completed weekly and successively. There was a significant group effect favouring CBT-I regarding insomnia but not depression directly after the intervention. No significant group difference was found six months later (Glozier et al., 2019). A meta-analysis, however, found that online CBT-I can be comparably effective as face-to-face treatment in patients with insomnia without co-morbidity (Zachariae et al., 2018). This discrepancy may point to the fact that patients with depression have more difficulties with online treatment since this is likely to be more demanding regarding self-organization and motivation compared to face-to-face treatment.

Since brief therapies are crucial in primary care settings, a brief version of CBT-I has been tested in a randomized controlled pilot trial by Pigeon, Funderburk, Bishop and Crean (2017). Twenty-seven participants were assigned to brief CBT-I, which consisted of two in-person sessions and two telephone sessions or two brief sessions of sleep hygiene (one in person and one via the telephone). The CBT-I sample improved significantly more than the control group across all sleep parameters. There was no significant group by time interaction for depression severity, which may be due to the study being underpowered (Pigeon et al., 2017).

Two further studies systematically compared antidepressant treatment alone with antidepressant treatment plus CBT-I. Manber et al. (2008) conducted a randomized pilot study in 30 co-morbid patients (mean age 35 ± 18 years, 61% females). The participants were randomized to either antidepressant treatment with escitalopram plus CBT-I or antidepressant treatment with escitalopram plus a quasi-desensitization placebo. The frequency of the treatments were 12 weeks of escitalopram and concomitantly seven individual sessions of CBT-I or control therapy. The results showed that the augmentation of antidepressant treatment with a brief CBT-I improved depression and insomnia symptoms (Manber et al., 2008). A subsequent randomized controlled trial by Manber et al. (2016) replicated the results described in the earlier study. In the later trial, the study sample consisted of 150 participants who were randomized to either CBT-I plus antidepressant treatment with escitalopram, sertraline and desvenlafaxine in a predefined sequence or a credible control therapy for insomnia plus the same antidepressant treatment. The treatments were delivered over a period of 16 weeks with medication management every 2 weeks and seven individual 45-minute sessions. The frequency and duration were the same for both conditions. CBT-I was more effective in reducing insomnia severity than the control condition. Depression remission as an outcome was not significantly different between groups. However, mediation analyses showed that insomnia remission improved depression remission (Manber et al., 2016). Carney et al. (2017) conducted a similar study by comparing three conditions in a randomized split-plot experimental study. The three conditions, antidepressant plus CBT-I, CBT-I plus placebo pill and antidepressant plus sleep hygiene, were compared in a sample of 107 participants (mean age 42 ± 11 years; 68% females). All groups received eight weeks of active individual treatment delivered in four bi-weekly sessions. All groups showed improvements in subjective sleep quality, but only the CBT-I group improved in sleep measured with polysomnography. Interestingly, all groups had a reduction in depression severity, even the CBT-I plus placebo group, which had no component consisting of depression treatment (Carney et al., 2017).

Since it has recently been demonstrated that insomnia increases the risk of *de novo* onset of depression (Baglioni et al., 2011; Hertenstein et al., 2019), research has been conducted with the aim of preventing depression with the help of CBT-I (e.g., Cheng et al., 2019). Patients with insomnia were randomized to digital CBT-I or an attentional control. The sample consisted of 658 patients at the follow-up time-point. The number of study participants who did not report depression at 1-year follow-up was 51% higher in the CBT-I group. The incidence rate of moderate and severe depression was 18.8% in the control group and 9.6% in the CBT-I group. Patients with chronic depression already at baseline were excluded from this trial.

Bipolar disorder

Whereas insomnia is by far the most frequent sleep complaint in patients with depression, patients with bipolar disorder may suffer not only from insomnia but also day-time sleepiness, sleep inertia and chronobiological sleep disorders, such as delayed sleep phase syndrome (Laskemoen et al., 2019).

Interpersonal and social rhythm therapy (ISRT) is a treatment developed for patients with bipolar disorder and sleep problems. The intervention focuses on the development and maintenance of stable daily routines including regular light exposure, meal times and social contacts (Frank, Swartz & Boland, 2007). In a randomized controlled trial, this treatment was compared to intensive clinical management, a psychoeducational and supportive approach, in patients with bipolar I disorder (175 in the initial phase and 125 in the maintenance phase). They were randomized to one of four groups: acute and maintenance ISRT, acute and maintenance intensive clinical management, acute ISRT and maintenance intensive clinical management or acute intensive clinical management and maintenance ISRT, all with appropriate pharmacotherapy.

There was a significant time by initial treatment interaction, such that those who received ISRT in the initial phase showed more rapid improvement of functioning. After the 2-year follow-up period, however, there was no difference between the groups.

Harvey at al. (2015) conducted a randomized controlled trial comparing a bipolar-disorder-specific modification of CBT-I (CBT-I BP) to psychoeducation in a sample of 58 patients with bipolar disorder and insomnia. The modified CBT-I programme was designed to target the unique features of sleep-in bipolar disorder. Elements of chronotherapy, ISRT and motivational interviewing were integrated in this intervention (Harvey et al., 2015). Both groups received eight sessions of 50–60 minutes in duration. The results showed a significant reduction of the likelihood of a relapse into either depression or mania and greater improvements in sleep in the CBT-I BP condition (Harvey et al., 2015). These results are highly promising, but have not been replicated so far.

Another randomized controlled trial targeted sleep inertia in patients with co-morbid bipolar disorder and insomnia (Kaplan et al., 2018). The CBT-I protocol was supplemented by an additional component called the 'RISE UP routine', including instructions to refrain from snoozing, increased activity for the first hour after getting up, shower or wash the face with cold water after getting up and an increased exposure to sunlight in the morning. The 40 study participants were randomized to CBT-I plus RISE UP or psychoeducation, whereby CBT-I plus RISE UP was significantly more effective in reducing sleep inertia and day-time sleepiness. Due to the design of the study, however, it remains unclear whether the adaptation of the protocol was necessary to achieve this effect.

Anxiety disorder

Anxiety disorders are frequently co-morbid with sleep difficulties. High levels of worry and arousal, often associated with anxiety disorders, can disturb sleep. The other way around, poor sleep may impair emotion regulation and make individuals more vulnerable to anxiety.

The effect of CBT-I on anxiety is moderate (effect size 0.4) according to a meta-analysis (Belleville, Cousineau, Levrier & St-Pierre-Delorme, 2011). A co-morbid anxiety disorder was not a mandatory inclusion criterion for this meta-analysis. Insomnia itself is associated with symptoms of anxiety, such as worries about the effects of poor sleep on day-time performance and health. Thus, it remains unclear whether CBT-I may have an effect on co-morbid anxiety, or whether it primarily reduces anxiety related to insomnia itself.

Studies investigating the efficacy of CBT-I in patients with anxiety disorders did not implement disorder-specific alterations to the CBT-I protocol. The authors of a randomized controlled trial found that a co-morbid anxiety diagnosis did not have an impact on the efficacy of CBT-I, compared to a subgroup with primary insomnia (Bélanger et al., 2016). However, if cognitive therapy or behavioral therapy were administered as a standalone treatment, this was less effective in patients with co-morbid anxiety. Patients with co-morbidity may thus be less likely to benefit from a minimal, shortened intervention protocol.

Taylor, Rybarczyk, Nay and Leszczyszyn (2015) conducted a study in which participants were randomized to either CBT-I or treatment as usual. The CBT-I intervention comprised five treatment sessions (three face-to-face sessions and two telephone sessions). The patients were 23 hypnotic-dependent psychiatry outpatients with different disorders, including anxiety disorders. The CBT-I condition improved sleep but not the secondary outcomes, including anxiety. The authors argued that despite improving sleep quality, CBT-I may not be helpful to improve mental health parameters (Taylor et al., 2015). Anxiety disorders require specialized treatment such as exposure with response prevention, but are unlikely to remit with psychotherapy that does not directly target the anxiety.

Post-traumatic stress disorder

'Persistent symptoms of increased psychological sensitivity and arousal' is one of the diagnostic criteria for post-traumatic stress disorder (PTSD). Up to 90% of patients with PTSD report difficulties falling or staying asleep (Maher et al., 2006). In addition, nightmares, often with re-experiencing aspects of the trauma, are highly prevalent in PTSD. In two studies, classical CBT-I protocols as an add-on to disorder-specific treatment of PTSD were investigated.

Talbot et al. (2014) conducted a two-arm randomized controlled trial in patients with PTSD to test whether a CBT-I improved sleep, nightmares, PTSD symptoms, depression symptoms and psychosocial functioning. In this study, CBT-I was not specifically adapted for PTSD. The sample comprised 45 adults (22–59 years; 37 females) with chronic PTSD who were in treatment for PTSD for at least 3 months. The participants were assigned to eight weekly individual CBT-I sessions delivered by a therapist, or a wait-list control group, whilst their PTSD treatment as usual was continued throughout the study. The results showed significant long-term improvements in sleep and psychosocial functioning in the CBT-I condition. The effects on nightmares and other PTSD symptoms were not significantly different between the CBT-I groups and the wait list arm.

In a trial by Pigeon, Funderburk, Cross, Bishop and Crean (2019), brief CBT-I plus disorder-specific treatment as usual was compared to treatment as usual alone. The participants who suffered from either depression or PTSD received four individual CBT-I sessions in six weeks. The results showed a large decrease of insomnia severity and depression severity in the CBT-I condition but no effect on PTSD.

The results of both the Talbot et al. and Pigeon et al. trials suggest that CBT-I is effective as an add-on to disorder-specific treatment of PTSD, but not as a standalone treatment.

Another approach is to integrate PTSD-specific adaptations into the CBT-I protocol, for example by using imagery rehearsal therapy (IRT) as an add-on to CBT-I. In IRT, patients keep a dream diary where they describe their nightmares every morning. Together with their therapist, they develop less distressing modified versions of their nightmares. For example, a patient who frequently dreams of being prosecuted could imagine growing wings and escaping his prosecutors. Patients imagine the modified version of their dream every evening before going to bed. This treatment is effective to reduce distress associated with nightmares and nightmare frequency (Yücel, van Emmerik, Souama & Lancee, 2019).

Margolies, Rybarczyk, Vrana, Leszczyszyn and Lynch (2013) investigated the effect of combined CBT-I and IRT. The sample comprised 40 combat veterans (mean age 37.7 years; 90% male) who were randomized to four sessions of CBT-I plus IRT or to a wait-list control condition. The combined intervention was successful for both sleep quality and PTSD-related night-time symptoms, but only half of the sample fully implemented the protocol (Margolies et al., 2013). The combined treatment package requiring considerable self-organization may be difficult to realize in outpatients with severe PTSD.

In a similar trial, 22 veterans meeting insomnia and PTSD criteria were randomized to a waitlist control condition or six bi-weekly 1-hour individual sessions of CBT-I and IRT. The authors reported large intervention effects on insomnia severity and PTSD symptoms (Ulmer, Edinger & Calhoun, 2011). These effects, however, were not replicated in a recent larger trial with 108 veterans with PTSD. Here, CBT-I plus IRT was not superior to CBT-I alone for the reduction of nightmare frequency and nightmare distress (Harb et al., 2019). In a similar vein, Belleville et al. did not find that the combination treatment was clearly superior to CBT-I alone (Belleville, Dubé-Frenette, Rousseau & Dubé-Frenette, 2018). Further research is needed to analyze whether this combined intervention may be suitable only for a specific subgroup of patients. Notably, sleep-focused psychotherapy is certainly not an alternative to a disorder-specific psychotherapy and pharmacotherapy, but an effective add-on targeting the sleep-related symptoms of PTSD.

Schizophrenia

Historically, sleep difficulties have been overlooked in the understanding and treatment of schizophrenia. This is starting to change. It is increasingly recognized that sleep disorders are very common in patients diagnosed with schizophrenia, that there is aetiological overlap between sleep disruption and psychotic experiences and that the sleep difficulties are a contributory causal factor in the occurrence of psychotic experiences such as paranoia and hallucinations (Freeman, Sheaves, Waite, Harvey & Harrison, 2020; Reeve, Sheaves & Freeman, 2015). Insomnia was found to be present in half of a cohort of 1800 patients with non-affective psychosis in contact with clinical services, with higher levels of insomnia associated with the presence of paranoia and hallucinations (Freeman, Taylor, Molodynski & Waite, 2019). In a study with over six hundred patients with schizophrenia and related disorders, clinician-rated sleep disturbance was found in three-quarters of patients (Laskemoen et al., 2019). In a diagnostic interview study with 60 patients with first episode psychosis, 80% of patients reported at least one sleep disorder, typically insomnia and nightmares, and patients had on average three sleep disorders (Reeve, Sheaves & Freeman, 2019). Circadian rhythm disruption is also common (Wulff, Dijk, Middleton, Foster & Joyce, 2012). Surveys of clinicians indicate that the potential importance of sleep disturbance in schizophrenia is recognized but that the use of formal assessments or recommended treatment is uncommon (Barrett et al., 2020).

Cognitive-behavioural treatments for insomnia are popular with patients diagnosed with schizophrenia (Waite et al., 2016a). The detailed adaptation of CBT-I for patients with schizophrenia (Waite et al., 2016b), including for in-patient settings (Sheaves et al., 2018b), have been described. These protocols include the need to address issues such as that a proportion of patients have very poor sleep environments, that activity levels throughout the day are often very limited and that sleep during the day may sometimes be used as a method to cope with psychotic experiences. There may also be a bidirectional relationship between sleep disturbance and psychotic experiences. The available evidence indicates that CBT for insomnia – setting appropriate sleep windows, learning to associate bed with sleep, and improving daytime activity levels – is very successful in reducing sleep problems in patients with schizophrenia. A pilot randomized controlled trial (BEtter Sleep Trial; BEST) with 50 patients experiencing persistent delusions and/or hallucinations showed that CBT-I delivered individually over eight sessions produced large effect size improvements in insomnia ($d = 1.9$) (Freeman et al., 2015). Large clinical effects persisted at a six-month follow-up. It is also potentially cost-effective (Tsiachristas, Waite, Freeman & Luengo-Fernandez, 2018). The BEST trial was underpowered to determine the effect of CBT-I on psychotic experiences, but the OASIS trial, which was designed to answer this question and suitably powered, clearly demonstrated that treating insomnia successfully using digital CBT-I ($d = 1.1$) leads to reductions in (non-clinical) paranoia and hallucinations, though of small effect size ($d = 0.2$) (Freeman et al., 2017). Group delivered CB-I for patients with schizophrenia may also be effective (Hwang, Nam & Lee, 2019), though it is likely with a lower effect size benefit for insomnia ($d = 0.5$) compared to individual treatment.

There are also other very interesting ways that sleep treatment is being evaluated for patients with schizophrenia. A pilot randomized controlled trial with 40 patients, including those with a diagnosis of schizophrenia, indicates that even at the stage of admission to psychiatric hospital, individual CBT-I can substantially improve sleep ($d = 0.9$) and that it may even lessen time hospitalized (Sheaves et al., 2018a). A case series indicates that CBT-I is likely to improve insomnia for patients at ultra-high risk of developing psychosis (Bradley et al., 2018), with the potential to prevent transition to psychosis, which is now starting to be evaluated in a pilot randomized controlled trial (Waite et al., 2020). Insomnia has been the typical target in clinical trials, but a pilot randomised controlled trial with 24 patients with persecutory delusions and nightmares provides evidence that nightmares can be successfully treated using imagery rehearsal therapy (IRT) (effect size = 1.1) (Sheaves et al., 2019). The use of IRT was also associated with reductions in insomnia ($d = 1.4$) and there were indications of reductions in paranoia ($d = 0.6$). Overall, established sleep interventions, suitably modified, look to be very efficacious for patients with schizophrenia and related diagnoses, and that successful treatment of sleep difficulties lessens psychotic experiences and brings other qualities of life benefits.

Attention Deficit Hyperactivity Disorder

Attention deficit hyperactivity disorder, especially hyperactivity, is associated with several sleep disorders such as insomnia, delayed sleep phase syndrome, restless legs syndrome and obstructive sleep apnea (Vogel et al., 2017). Evidence regarding the efficacy of CBT-I in adults with ADHD is scarce. In an uncontrolled within-group pilot study of 19 adults with ADHD and insomnia, CBT-I delivered in a group format successfully reduced insomnia severity (Jernelöv, Larsson, Llenas, Nasri & Kaldo, 2019). In this study, several adjustments to the standard CBT-I protocol were made to meet the needs of ADHD patients. CBT-I was delivered in weekly sessions over the course of 10 weeks. To address circadian rhythm related sleep problems, the circadian nadir of each patient was estimated and used to make recommendations for optimal meal times, activity times and times for light exposure. Alarms and calendar entries were used to deal with organizational problems common in this patient group. The format was adjusted to cope with short attention spans, i.e., by shortening sessions, lengthening the total treatment period and scheduling regular phone calls.

Protocol adaptations

Compelling evidence suggests that CBT-I in its standard format or modified versions is effective for the treatment of insomnia in patients with depression, schizophrenia, bipolar disorder, anxiety disorders and PTSD. CBT-I is clearly effective as an add-on to disorder-specific pharmarcological and psychotherapeutic treatment. In some patient groups, CBT-I also has a positive impact on the mental disorder, i.e., for the prevention of depressive episodes. Adaptations of the CBT-I protocol have been described for several disorders. A summary of these adaptations can be found in Table 13.1.

More research into adapted CBT-I protocols is needed to clarify which adaptations are needed for which disorder to address specific needs and problems of each patient. Another approach is a transdiagnostic adaptation of CBT-I for patients with severe mental illness, e.g., those treated as inpatients in acute psychiatric hospitals (Schneider et al., 2020; Sheaves et al., 2018b), including patients with psychosis, bipolar disorder, substance abuse, personality disorders and others. Here, adaptations focus on a simplification of CBT-I to allow feasibility in patients with different acute severe mental disorders.

Table 13.1 Adaptations of the CBT-I protocol for patients with different co-morbid mental disorders.

Depression
Sadler, McLaren, Klein, Harvey & Jenkins (2018) investigated an adapted protocol of CBT-I including additional strategies for mood regulation, and compared it to a psychoeducation control group. The adapted protocol, however, was not significantly more effective than standard CBT-I. Most authors investigating CBT-I for patients with depression did not adapt the protocol. For further information please refer to Chapter 12.
Bipolar Disorder
Harvey et al. (2015): CBT-I + chronotherapy, interpersonal and social rhythm therapy (ISRT), and motivational interviewing. ISRT focuses on the development and maintenance of stable daily routines including regular light exposure, meal times and social contacts. The results showed a significant reduction of the likelihood of a relapse into either depression or mania and greater improvements in sleep in the modified CBT-I condition. These results are highly promising, but have not been replicated so far. Kaplan et al. (2018): 'RISE UP routine' to target sleep inertia. The routine includes instructions to refrain from snoozing, increase activity for the first hour after getting up, shower or wash the face with cold water after getting up, an increase exposure to sunlight in the morning. CBT-I plus RISE UP was significantly more effective in reducing sleep inertia and day-time sleepiness than psychoeducation. Due to the design of the study, however, it remains unclear whether the adaptation of the protocol was necessary to achieve this effect. For further information please refer to Chapter 12.
Post-traumatic Stress Disorder
Margolies, Rybarczyk, Vrana, Leszczyszyn & Lynch (2013), Ulmer, Edinger & Calhoun (2011) and Harb et al. (2019) combined CBT-I and imagery rehearsal therapy (IRT) for nightmares. There is no clear evidence that CBT-I combined with IRT is more effective than CBT-I alone.
Schizophrenia
Waite et al. (2016b) describe different ways of adapting CBT-I for insomnia: planning activities in the evening to overcome phase advance, adapting the stimulus control to reset circadian rhythms using routines for morning (RISE UP) and evening (WIND DOWN), increasing the ability to cope with distressing voices, adding elements of CBT for psychosis, which lessen psychotic experiences. Freeman et al. (2015) found that standard care plus CBT-I adapted for patients with schizophrenia was more effective than standard care alone. Adaptations included, among others, a simplification of the protocol, the establishment of appropriate day-time activity and circadian rhythms, and adaptations needed for the particular problems of delusions and hallucinations interfering with sleep.
Attention Deficit Hyperactivity Disorder
Jernelöv, Larsson, Llenas, Nasri & Kaldo (2019): CBT-I adjusted for patients with ADHD, including shortening sessions, lengthening the total treatment period and scheduling regular phone calls. This was effective in an uncontrolled study but has not been compared to standard CBT-I yet.
Transdiagnostic Approach
Sheaves et al. (2018b) describe an adapted CBT-I protocol for patients with mixed diagnoses on psychiatric wards. Adaptations included sleep monitoring watches to engage patients in treatment, stabilizing circadian rhythms, reducing the impact of night-time observations and managing discharge as a sleep challenge. This adapted protocol was more effective than standard care on psychiatric wards. Schneider et al. (2020) followed a similar approach, adapting CBT-I for acute inpatients with mixed diagnoses on psychiatric wards. Adaptations included a shortening of the protocol, a focus on sleep restriction and circadian stabilization as main interventions and the use of simple metaphors. The protocol was effective in a small uncontrolled pilot study.

Conclusion

In summary, CBT-I is recommended as a first-line treatment for insomnia and also in patients with co-morbid mental disorders. Future research is needed to (i) test the efficacy of CBT-I in previously underinvestigated disorders such as ADHD or eating disorders, (ii) clarify which disorder-specific adaptations increase the efficacy of CBT-I compared to a standard protocol and (iii) compare efficacy of disorder-specific adaptations vs transdiagnostic approaches.

References

Ashworth, D. K., Sletten, T. L., Junge, M., Simpson, K., Clarke, D., Cunnington, D., & Rajaratnam, S. M. W. (2015). A randomized controlled trial of cognitive behavioral therapy for insomnia: An effective treatment for comorbid insomnia and depression. *Journal of Counseling Psychology*, *62* (2), 115–123. https://doi.org/10.1037/cou0000059.

Baglioni, C., Battagliese, G., Feige, B., Spiegelhalder, K., Nissen, C., Voderholzer, U., Lombardo, C., Riemann, D. (2011). Insomnia as a predictor of depression: A meta-analytic evaluation of longitudinal epidemiological studies. *Journal of Affective Disorders*, *135* (1–3), 10–19. https://doi.org/10.1016/j.jad.2011.01.011.

Barrett, E. A., Aminoff, S. R., Simonsen, C., & Romm, K. L. (2020). Opening the curtains for better sleep in psychotic disorders – Considerations for improving sleep treatment. *Comprehensive Psychiatry*, *103*, 152207. https://doi.org/10.1016/j.comppsych.2020.152207.

Bélanger, L., Harvey, A. G., Fortier-Brochu, É., Beaulieu-Bonneau, S., Eidelman, P., Talbot, L., Ivers, H., Hein, K., Lamy, M., Soehner, A., Mérette, C., & Morin, C. M. (2016). Impact of comorbid anxiety and depressive disorders on treatment response to cognitive behavior therapy for insomnia. *Journal of Consulting and Clinical Psychology*, *84* (8), 659–667. https://doi.org/10.1037/ccp0000084.

Belleville, G., Cousineau, H., Levrier, K., & St-Pierre-Delorme, M.-È. (2011). Meta-analytic review of the impact of cognitive-behavior therapy for insomnia on concomitant anxiety. *Clinical Psychology Review*, *31* (4), 638–652. https://doi.org/10.1016/j.cpr.2011.02.004.

Belleville, G., Dubé-Frenette, M., Rousseau, A., & Dubé-Frenette, M. (2018). Efficacy of imagery rehearsal therapy and cognitive behavioral therapy in sexual assault victims with posttraumatic stress disorder: A randomized controlled trial. *Journal of Traumatic Stress*, *31* (4), 591–601. https://doi.org/10.1002/jts.22306.

Bradley, J., Freeman, D., Chadwick, E., Harvey, A. G., Mullins, B., Johns, L., Sheaves, B., Lennox, B., Broome, M., & Waite, F. (2018). Treating sleep problems in young people at ultra-high risk of psychosis: A feasibility case series. *Behavioural and Cognitive Psychotherapy*, *46* (3), 276–291. https://doi.org/10.1017/s1352465817000601.

Carney, C.E., Edinger, J.D., Kuchibhatla, M., Lachowski, A.M., Bogouslavsky, O., Krystal, A.D., & Shapiro, C.M. (2017). Cognitive behavioral insomnia therapy for those with insomnia and depression: A randomized controlled clinical trial. *Sleep*, *40*, zsx019. https://doi.org/10.1093/sleep/zsx019.

Cheng, P., Kalmbach, D. A., Tallent, G., Joseph, C. L., Espie, C. A., & Drake, C. L. (2019). Depression prevention via digital cognitive behavioral therapy for insomnia: A randomized controlled trial. *Sleep*, *42* (10), zsz150. https://doi:10.1093/sleep/zsz150.

Frank, E., Swartz, H. A., & Boland, E. (2007). Interpersonal and social rhythm therapy: An intervention addressing rhythm dysregulation in bipolar disorder. *Dialogues in Clinical Neuroscience*, *9* (3), 325–332.

Freeman, D., Sheaves, B., Waite, F., Harvey, A. G., & Harrison, P. J. (2020). Sleep disturbance and psychiatric disorders. *The Lancet. Psychiatry*, *7* (7), 628–637. https://doi.org/10.1016/S2215-0366(20)30136-X.

Freeman, D., Taylor, K. M., Molodynski, A., & Waite, F. (2019). Treatable clinical intervention targets for patients with schizophrenia. *Schizophrenia Research*, *211*, 44–50. https://doi.org/10.1016/j.schres.2019.07.016.

Freeman, D., Sheaves, B., Goodwin, G. M., Yu, L.-M., Harrison, P. J., Emsley, R., Bostock, S., Foster, R. G., Wadekar, V., Hinds, C., & Espie, C. A. (2015a). Effects of cognitive behavioural therapy for insomnia on the mental health of university students: Study protocol for a randomized controlled trial. *Trials*, *16* (1), 236–236. https://doi.org/10.1186/s13063-015-0756-4.

Freeman, D., Waite, F., Startup, H., Myers, E., Lister, R., McInerney, J., Harvey, A. G., Geddes, J., Zaiwalla, Z., Luengo-Fernandes, R., Foster, R., Clifton, L., & Yu, L.-M. (2015b). Efficacy of cognitive behavioural therapy for sleep improvement in patients with persistent delusions and hallucinations (BEST): A prospective, assessor-blind, randomised controlled pilot trial. *The Lancet Psychiatry*, *2* (11), 975–983.

Freeman, D., Sheaves, B., Goodwin, G. M., Yu, L. M., Nickless, A., Harrison, P. J., Emsley, R., Luik, A., Foster, R. G., Wadekar. V, Hin, C., Gumley, A., Jones, R., Lightman, S., Jones, S., Bentall, R., Kinderman, P., Rowse, G., Brugha, T., Blagrove, M., Gregory, A. M., Fleming, L., Walklet, E., Glazebrook, C., Bethan Davies, E., Hollis, C., Haddock, G., John, B., Coulson, M., Fowler, D., Pugh, K., Cape, J., Moseley, P., Brown, G., Hughes, C., Obonsawin, M., Coker, S., Watkins, E., Schwannauer, M., MacMahon, K., Siriwardena, A. N., & Espie, C. A. (2017). The effects of improving sleep on mental health (OASIS): A randomised controlled trial with mediation analysis. *Lancet Psychiatry*, *4* (10), 749–758. https://doi.org/10.1016/s2215-0366(17)30328-0.

Glozier, N., Christensen, H., Griffiths, K. M., Hickie, I. B., Naismith, S. L., Biddle, D., Overland, S., Thorndike, F., & Ritterband, L. (2019). Adjunctive internet-delivered cognitive behavioural therapy for insomnia in men with depression: A randomised controlled trial. *The Australian and New Zealand Journal of Psychiatry*, *53* (4), 350–360.

Harb, G. C., Cook, J. M., Phelps, A. J., Gehrman, P. R., Forbes, D., Localio, R., Harpaz-Rotem, I., Gur, R. C., & Ross, R. J. (2019). Randomized controlled trial of imagery rehearsal for posttraumatic nightmares in combat veterans. *Journal of Clinical Sleep Medicine*, *15* (5), 757–767. https://doi.org/10.5664/jcsm.7770.

Harvey, A. G., Soehner, A. M., Kaplan, K. A., Hein, K., Lee, J., Kanady, J., Li, D., Rabe-Hesketh, S., Ketter, T. A., Neylan, T. C., & Buysse, D. J. (2015). Treating insomnia improves mood state, sleep, and functioning in bipolar disorder: A pilot randomized controlled trial. *Journal of Consulting and Clinical Psychology*, *83* (3), 564–577. https://doi.org/10.1037/a0038655.

Hertenstein, E., Feige, B., Gmeiner, T., Kienzler, C., Spiegelhalder, K., Johann, A., Jansson-Fröjmark, M., Palagini, L., Rücker, G., Riemann, D., & Baglioni, C. (2019). Insomnia as a predictor of mental disorders: A systematic review and meta-analysis. *Sleep Medicine Reviews*, *43*, 96–105. https://doi.org/10.1016/j.smrv.2018.10.006.

Hsu, H. M., Chou, K. R., Lin, K. C., Chen, K. Y., Su, S. F., & Chung, M. H. (2015). Effects of cognitive behavioral therapy in patients with depressive disorder and comorbid insomnia: A propensity score-matched outcome study. *Behavioural Research Therapy*, *73*, 143–150. https://doi.org/10.1016/j.brat.2015.07.016.

Hwang, D. K., Nam, M., & Lee, Y. G. (2019). The effect of cognitive behavioral therapy for insomnia in schizophrenia patients with sleep disturbance: A non-randomized, assessor-blind trial. *Psychiatry Research*, *274*, 182–188. https://doi.org/10.1016/j.psychres.2019.02.002.

Jernelöv, S., Larsson, Y., Llenas, M., Nasri, B., & Kaldo, V. (2019). Effects and clinical feasibility of a behavioural treatment for sleep problems in adult attention deficit hyperactivity disorder (ADHD): A pragmatic within-group pilot evaluation. *BMC Psychiatry*, *19* (1), 226. https://doi.org/10.1186/s12888-019-2216-2.

Kaplan, K. A., Talavera, D. C., & Harvey, A. G. (2018). Rise and shine: A treatment experiment testing a morning routine to decrease subjective sleep inertia in insomnia and bipolar disorder. *Behavioural Research Therapy*, *111*, 106–112. https://doi.org/10.1016/j.brat.2018.10.009.

Laskemoen, J. F., Simonsen, C., Büchmann, C., Barrett, E. A., Bjella, T., Lagerberg, T. V., Vedal, T. J., Andreassen, O. A., Melle, I., & Aas, M. (2019). Sleep disturbances in schizophrenia spectrum and bipolar disorders – A transdiagnostic perspective. *Comprehensive Psychiatry*, *91*, 6–12. https://doi.org/10.1016/j.comppsych.2019.02.006.

Maher, M. J., Rego, S. A., Asnis, G. M., Maher, M. J., Rego, S. A., & Asnis, G. M. (2006). Sleep disturbances in patients with post-traumatic stress disorder: Epidemiology, impact and approaches to management. *CNS Drugs*, *20* (7), 567–590. https://doi.org/10.2165/00023210-200620070-00003.

Manber, R., Edinger, J. D., Gress, J. L., San Pedro-Salcedo, M. G., Kuo, T. F., & Kalista, T. (2008). Cognitive behavioral therapy for insomnia enhances depression outcome in patients with comorbid major depressive disorder and insomnia. *Sleep*, (31), 489–495.

Manber, R., Buysse, D. J., Edinger, J., Krystal, A., Luther, J. F., Wisniewski, S. R., Trockel, M., Kraemer, H. C., & Thase, M. E. (2016). Efficacy of cognitive-behavioral therapy for insomnia combined with antidepressant pharmacotherapy in patients with comorbid depression and insomnia: A randomized controlled trial. *Journal of Clinical Psychiatry*, *77*, e1316–1323.

Margolies, S. O., Rybarczyk, B., Vrana, S. R., Leszczyszyn, D. J., & Lynch, J. (2013). Efficacy of a cognitive-behavioral treatment for insomnia and nightmares in Afghanistan and Iraq veterans with PTSD. *Journal of Clinical Psychology*, *69* (10), 1026–1042. https://doi.org/10.1002/jclp.21970.

Norell-Clarke, A., Tillfors, M., Jansson-Fröjmark, M., Holländare, F., & Engström, I. (2017). How does cognitive behavioral therapy for insomnia work? An Investigation of cognitive processes and time in bed as outcomes and mediators in a sample with insomnia and depressive symptomatology. *International Journal of Cognitive Therapy*, *10* (4), 304–329. https://doi.org/10.1521/ijct.2017.10.4.304.

Pigeon, W. R., Funderburk, J., Bishop, T. M., & Crean, H. F. (2017) Brief cognitive behavioral therapy for insomnia delivered to depressed veterans receiving primary care services: A pilot study. *Journal of Affective Disorders*, *217*, 105–111.

Reeve, S., Sheaves, B., & Freeman, D. (2015). The role of sleep dysfunction in the occurrence of delusions and hallucinations: A systematic review. *Clinical Psychology Review*, *42*, 96–115. https://doi.org/10.1016/j.cpr.2015.09.001.

Reeve, S., Sheaves, B., & Freeman, D. (2019). Sleep disorders in early psychosis: Incidence, severity, and association with clinical symptoms. *Schizophrenia Bulletin*, *45* (2), 287–295. https://doi.org/10.1093/schbul/sby129.

Riemann, D., Baglioni, C., Bassetti, C., Bjorvatn, B., Dolenc Groselj, L., Ellis, J. G., Espie, C. A., Garcia-Borreguero, D., Gjerstad, M., Goncalves, M., Hertenstein, E., Jansson-Fröjmark, M., Jennum, P. J., Leger, D., Nissen, C., Parrino, L., Paunio, T., Pevernagie, D., Verbraecken, J., Weess, H. G., Wichniak, A., Zavalko, I., Arnardottir, E. S., Deleanu, O. C., Strazisar, B., Zoetmulder, M., & Spiegelhalder, K. (2017). European guideline for the diagnosis and treatment of insomnia. *Journal of Sleep Research*, *26* (6), 675–700. https://doi.org/10.1111/jsr.12594.

Sadler, P., McLaren, S., Klein, B., Harvey, J., & Jenkins, M. (2018). Cognitive behavior therapy for older adults with insomnia and depression: A randomized controlled trial in community mental health services. *Sleep*, *41* (8), zsy104. https://doi.org/10.1093/sleep/zsy104.

Schneider, C. L., Hertenstein, E., Fehér, K., Maier, J. G., Cantisani, A., Moggi, F., Berger, T., & Nissen, C. (2020). Become your own SLEEPexpert: Design, implementation, and preliminary evaluation of a pragmatic behavioral treatment program for insomnia in inpatient psychiatric care. *SLEEP Advances*, *1*, zpaa005. https://doi.org/10.1093/sleepadvances/zpaa005.

Seow, L. S. E., Verma, S. K., Mok, Y. M., Kumar, S., Chang, S., Satghare, P., Hombali, A., Vaingankar, J., Chong, S. A., & Subramaniam, M. (2018). Evaluating DSM-5 insomnia disorder and the treatment of sleep problems in a psychiatric population. *Journal of Clinical Sleep Medicine: JCSM: Official Publication of the American Academy of Sleep Medicine*, *14* (2), 237–244. https://doi.org/10.5664/jcsm.6942.

Sheaves, B., Freeman, D., Isham, L., McInerney, J., Nickless, A., Yu, L.-M., Rek, S., Bradley, J., Reeve, S., Attard, C., Espie, C. A., Foster, R., Wirz-Justice, A., Chadwick, E., & Barrera, A. (2018a). Stabilising sleep for patients admitted at acute crisis to a psychiatric hospital (OWLS): An assessor-blind pilot randomised controlled trial. *Psychological Medicine*, *48* (10), 1694–1704. https://doi.org/10.1017/S0033291717003191.

Sheaves, B., Isham, L., Bradley, J., Espie, C., Barrera, A., Waite, F., Harvey, A.G., Attard, C., & Freeman, D. (2018b). Adapted CBT to stabilize sleep on psychiatric wards: A transdiagnostic treatment approach. *Behavioural Cognition Psychotherapy*, *46* (6), 661–675. https://doi.org/10.1017/s1352465817000789.

Sheaves, B., Holmes, E. A., Rek, S., Taylor, K. M., Nickless, A., Waite, F., Germain, A., Espie, C. A., Harrison, P. J., Foster, R., & Freeman, D. (2019). Cognitive behavioural therapy for nightmares for patients with persecutory delusions (Nites): An assessor-blind, pilot randomized controlled trial. *The Canadian Journal of Psychiatry*, *64* (10), 686–696. https://doi.org/10.1177/0706743719847422.

Talbot, L. S., Maguen, S., Metzler, T. J., Schmitz, M., McCaslin, S. E., Richards, A., Perlis, M. L., Posner, D. A., Weiss, B., Ruoff, L., Varbel, J., & Neylan, T. C. (2014). Cognitive behavioral therapy for insomnia in posttraumatic stress disorder: A randomized controlled trial. *Sleep*, 37, 327–341. https://doi.org/10.5665/sleep.3408.

Taylor, H. L., Rybarczyk, B. D., Nay, W., & Leszczyszyn, D. (2015). Effectiveness of a CBT intervention for persistent insomnia and hypnotic dependency in an outpatient Psychiatry Clinic. *Journal of Clinical Psychology*, *71*, 666–683. https://doi.org/10.1002/jclp.22186.

Tsiachristas, A., Waite, F., Freeman, D., & Luengo-Fernandez, R. (2018). Cost-effectiveness of cognitive-behavioural therapy for sleep disorder added to usual care in patients with schizophrenia: The BEST study. *British Journal of Psychology Open*, *4* (3), 126–135. https://doi.org/10.1192/bjo.2018.2.

Ulmer, C. S., Edinger, J. D., & Calhoun, P. S. (2011). A multi-component cognitive-behavioral intervention for sleep disturbance in veterans with PTSD: A pilot study. *Journal of Clinical Sleep Medicine*, *7* (1), 57–68.

Vogel, S. W. N., Bijlenga, D., Benjamins, J. S., Beekman, A. T. F., Kooij, J. J. S., & Van Someren, E. J. W. (2017). Attention deficit hyperactivity disorder symptom severity and sleep problems in adult participants of the Netherlands sleep registry. *Sleep Medicine*, *40*, 94–102. https://doi.org/10.1016/j.sleep.2017.09.027.

Waite, F., Evans, N., Myers, E., Startup, H., Lister, R., Harvey, A. G., & Freeman, D. (2016a). The patient experience of sleep problems and their treatment in the context of current delusions and hallucinations. *Psychology and Psychotherapy*, *89* (2), 181–193. https://doi.org/10.1111/papt.12073.

Waite, F., Myers, E., Harvey, A. G., Espie, C. A., Startup, H., Sheaves, B., & Freeman, D. (2016b). Treating sleep problems in patients with schizophrenia. *Behavioural and Cognitive Psychotherapy*, *44* (3), 273–287. https://doi.org/10.1017/S1352465815000430.

Waite, F., Kabir, T., Johns, L., Mollison, J., Tsiachristas, A., Petit, A., & Freeman, D. (2020). Treating sleep problems in young people at ultra-high-risk of psychosis: Study protocol for a single-blind parallel group randomised controlled feasibility trial (SleepWell). *British Medical Journal Open*, *10* (11), e045235. https://doi.org/10.1136/bmjopen-2020-045235.

Wulff, K., Dijk, D.-J., Middleton, B., Foster, R. G., & Joyce, E. M. (2012). Sleep and circadian rhythm disruption in schizophrenia. *The British Journal of Psychiatry: The Journal of Mental Science*, *200* (4), 308–316. https://doi.org/10.1192/bjp.bp.111.096321.

Yücel, D. E., van Emmerik, A. A. P., Souama, C., & Lancee, J. (2019). Comparative efficacy of imagery rehearsal therapy and prazosin in the treatment of trauma-related nightmares in adults: A meta-analysis of randomized controlled trials. *Sleep Medicine Reviews*, *50*, 101248. https://doi.org/10.1016/j.smrv.2019.101248.

Zachariae, R., Amidi, A., Damholdt, M. F., Clausen, C. D. R., Dahlgaard, J., Lord, H., Thorndike, F. P., & Ritterband, L. M. (2018). Internet-delivered cognitive-behavioral therapy for insomnia in breast cancer survivors: A randomized controlled trial. *Journal of the National Cancer Institute*, *110* (8), 880–887. https://doi.org/10.1093/jnci/djx293.

14

CBT-I Protocols for Insomnia Co-morbid with Somatic Disorders

Bjørn Bjorvatn

Key points

- Insomnia is often co-morbid with somatic conditions.
- Low-grade inflammation may play a role in the pathophysiological mechanism underlying the association between sleep and health.
- CBT-I is effective also among patients with insomnia co-morbid with somatic conditions.

Learning objectives

- To understand the strong association between insomnia and somatic health.
- To learn that CBT-I is recommended and effective in insomnia co-morbid with somatic conditions.
- To understand that CBT-I may need to be modified in patients with certain severe somatic diseases.

Abstract

This chapter focuses on the strong association between insomnia and somatic disorders and diseases. The pathophysiological mechanisms behind this association are unclear, but low-grade inflammation may play a role. Insomnia seems to be a risk factor for many somatic conditions and poor sleep may also impact the severity and outcome of somatic conditions. Insomnia is no longer considered only as a symptom or consequence of the somatic condition, but as a disorder in itself. CBT-I is recommended, also when insomnia is co-morbid with somatic conditions. Studies show that CBT-I improves sleep in such co-morbid cases and may furthermore positively impact the somatic condition. However, treatment modifications may be necessary in certain cases, such as when patients are bedridden or have severe illnesses.

Keywords *Insomnia, somatic health, somatic diseases, cancer, cardiovascular diseases, immune system, inflammation*

Sleep and health

Sleep is vital for cognitive, emotional and somatic functioning. Without proper sleep, the body and mind do not function well. Unfortunately, many people suffer from sleep problems. Poor sleep is a growing public health concern, with significant consequences both at an individual and socioeconomic level. Short sleep duration and insomnia are associated with a multitude of health problems, not only mental health issues such as anxiety, depression and dementia, but also somatic illnesses such as obesity, diabetes, cardiovascular diseases and cancer (Anothaisintawee, Reutrakul, Van Cauter & Thakkinstian, 2016; Conley

Cognitive-Behavioural Therapy for Insomnia (CBT-I) Across the Life Span: Guidelines and Clinical Protocols for Health Professionals, First Edition. Edited by Chiara Baglioni, Colin A. Espie and Dieter Riemann.

& Redeker, 2015; Kecklund & Axelsson, 2016; Morin et al., 2020; Riemann et al., 2017; Spiegelhalder, Scholtes & Riemann, 2010). Furthermore, insomnia is prospectively associated with sick leave and work disability (Sivertsen, Overland, Bjorvatn, Mæland & Mykletun, 2009).

Possible pathophysiological mechanisms

The underlying pathophysiological mechanisms behind the association between sleep and health are unclear. However, low-grade inflammation may play a role. This notion is supported by findings that prolonged sleep deficiency (e.g., chronic short sleep duration and sleep disturbances) can lead to chronic, systemic, low-grade inflammation and is associated with diseases that have an inflammatory component, such as diabetes, atherosclerosis and neurodegeneration (e.g., dementia) (Besedovsky, Lange & Haack, 2019; Irwin, Olmstead & Carroll, 2016). Short sleep duration, sleep disturbances and circadian misalignment have all been reported to be associated with increased levels of pro-inflammatory biomarkers such as interleukin-1 (IL-1), interleukin-6 (IL-6) and tumour necrosis factor (TNF) (Besedovsky et al., 2019; Irwin et al., 2016). In a systematic review and meta-analysis on the link between sleep disturbance, sleep duration and inflammation, Irwin et al. (2016) found 72 studies assessing IL-6, TNF-alpha and C-reactive protein (CRP). It was reported that sleep disturbance and short sleep duration were associated with higher levels of CRP, but not with levels of TNF-alpha. IL-6 was associated with sleep disturbance (higher values) but not short sleep duration. Furthermore, neither experimental sleep deprivation nor sleep restriction have been found to be associated with IL-6, TNF-alpha or CRP (Irwin et al., 2016). The authors concluded that sleep disturbance, but not short sleep duration, was associated with higher levels of markers of systemic inflammation (Irwin et al., 2016). In a recent study from my research group, short sleep duration (<6 hours) was associated with lower IL-1beta levels and higher TNF-alpha levels, whereas long sleep duration (8+ hours) was associated with higher IL-13 levels. However, we found no association between self-reported sleep quality and immunological biomarkers (Bjorvatn et al., 2020). Even though research shows an association between sleep and the immune system, more studies are clearly needed to elucidate the mechanisms involved.

Sleep and infection

The association between sleep and infectious diseases is not fully understood, but of special interest nowadays with the Covid-19 pandemic. Will insomnia, short sleep duration and/or circadian misalignment (i.e., due to shift work) increase the risk of becoming infected by the corona virus? And what about other types of infections? Will insomnia, short sleep duration and/or circadian misalignment have an impact on the severity of different types of infections, and how will sleep and insomnia symptoms impact on the effect of vaccination against viruses such as corona and influenza, and also other infectious diseases? An extensive review on the sleep-immune crosstalk in health and disease focuses on how sleep and the immune system interact and points to the need for more research (Besedovsky et al., 2019). Still, enhanced sleep during an infection is assumed to feed back to the immune system to promote host defence. Furthermore, sleep of sufficient duration and quality is assumed to reduce the risk of becoming infected and to improve infection outcome and vaccination responses (Besedovsky et al., 2019). This implies that patients with insomnia disorder may be at increased risk of infections and possibly have poorer vaccination responses. Interestingly, an influenza vaccination study compared habitual sleep with restricted sleep (the time in bed was restricted to 4 hours per night for 4 days before and 2 days after the vaccination) and found that influenza-virus-specific antibody titres after vaccination were doubled in participants with normal sleep compared to restricted sleep (Spiegel, Sheridan & Van Cauter, 2002). Furthermore, research shows that a single night without sleep following vaccination against hepatitis A, hepatitis B, and H1N1 (swine flu) reduced the antigen-specific antibody response (Besedovsky et al., 2019). These studies suggest that severe limitation of sleep impacts the effects of vaccination, but whether more modest sleep deprivation and/or insomnia affect the immune system and vaccination are more uncertain. Of great importance in this respect, a few studies suggest that improved sleep, for instance through treatment of insomnia by cognitive behavioural therapy (CBT-I), may counteract the sleep deficiency-induced changes in immune function (Besedovsky et al., 2019). For instance, in a study among patients with insomnia disorder, CBT-I resulted in lower levels of CRP in a 16-month follow-up period (Irwin et al., 2014). This highlights the importance of implementing CBT-I in the treatment of patients with chronic insomnia disorder.

Insomnia – diagnostic considerations

For a detailed description of the standard diagnostic and differential diagnostic procedures as well as useful diagnostic tools go back to Chapters 1 and 5.

It is now recognized that sleep disorders, including insomnia, can no longer be considered only as symptoms, but also as major causative factors of a wide array of problems. In keeping with this point of view, pain has been regarded as a sleep disturbing factor, but evidence also suggests that poor sleep and insomnia exacerbate pain (Finan, Goodin & Smith, 2013; see also Chapter 15). Sleep disturbance is further recognized as a strong feature of psychopathology as it has been associated with a wide array of psychiatric disorders, such as depression, bipolar disorder, psychotic disorders, anxiety disorders, ADHD and eating disorders (Sateia, 2009; see Chapters 12 and 13).

It is well known that several somatic illnesses, such as obesity, metabolic syndrome, diabetes, allergic conditions, asthma, chronic pain conditions, cardiovascular diseases, cancer, epilepsy, and rheumatic disorders (Anothaisintawee et al., 2016; Conley & Redeker, 2015; Lazaratou, Soldatou & Dikeos, 2012; Ma et al., 2021; Spiegelhalder et al., 2010), are associated with insomnia. Insomnia may be a result of the discomfort caused by the somatic condition or insomnia may be caused by the same pathophysiological mechanisms involved in insomnia disorder per se. Furthermore, but very importantly, insomnia may aggravate somatic illnesses, and vicious cycles in which sleep problems and somatic illnesses exacerbate each other reciprocally have been described (Conley & Redeker, 2015; Lazaratou et al., 2012; Ma et al., 2021). Sleep can also be impaired because of treatment regimens related to the comorbid condition. For instance, several types of medications may disturb sleep, such as medications for thyroid disease, hypertension, and depression (Hauser, Urrutia, Tort, Uceyler & Walitt, 2013; Ma et al., 2021; van der Wardt, Logan, Conrog, Harwood & Gladman, 2014). For many disorders and diseases where comorbidity with insomnia is present, CBT-I has been shown to improve sleep, and sometimes also to improve the symptoms of the comorbid condition (Belleville, Cousineau, Levrier & St-Pierre-Delorme, 2011; Blom et al., 2015; Ma et al., 2021; Wu, Appleman, Salazar & Ong, 2015). A meta-analysis of 23 randomized controlled trials using CBT-I among patients with insomnia co-morbid with medical or psychiatric conditions showed that CBT-I improved subjective sleep quality, with large treatment effects for the Insomnia Severity Index (ISI) and Pittsburgh Sleep Quality Index (PSQI) (Geiger-Brown et al., 2015). Furthermore, treatment effects were durable up to 18 months post-treatment (Geiger-Brown et al., 2015).

An overview of assessment and treatment guidelines for insomnia co-morbid with somatic disorders is given in Table 14.1.

Table 14.1 Assessment and treatment guidelines for insomnia co-morbid with somatic disorders.

1) Does the patient fulfill the criteria for chronic insomnia disorder?
   a) Problems sleeping at night with day-time consequences at least three days per week for a duration of at least three months.
   b) The insomnia symptoms are not better explained by another sleep disorder.
      i) Consider obstructive sleep apnea.
      ii) Consider circadian rhythm sleep–wake disorders.
      iii) Consider restless legs syndrome.
2) Consider whether the co-morbid condition(s) may be a contraindication for CBT-I.
   a) Unstable cardiovascular disease?
   b) Short life expectancy (cancer with metastasis)?
3) Use a sleep diary for 1–2 weeks to assess the insomnia symptoms.
4) Start treatment with CBT-I and follow how the insomnia and somatic condition(s) progress.
5) Follow up at 1–2 week intervals with the focus on both insomnia and the co-morbid condition.
6) If there is no improvement within a few weeks, consider referral to self-help therapies or secondary care specialists.
7) If the patient is taking hypnotics, I recommend to start with CBT-I without changing the dose. When the patient's sleep improves, the hypnotic may be gradually tapered off over several weeks.

Cognitive behavioural therapy for insomnia

The treatment-of-choice for chronic insomnia disorder is CBT-I, in which the behavioural treatment components *sleep restriction* and *stimulus control* are shown to be the most effective components (Brasure et al., 2016; Morin, Culbert & Schwartz, 1994; Riemann et al., 2017). The standard CBT-I protocol including stimulus control and sleep restriction has been described in detail in Chapter 2. Unfortunately, CBT-I is often not available for patients with chronic insomnia and most patients still receive insomnia treatment in terms of medications and/or general sleep hygiene advice (Cheung, Jarrin, Ballot, Bharwani & Morin, 2019; Everitt et al., 2014). This is certainly true also for patients with co-morbid somatic conditions. However, even though hypnotics may be effective in the short term, there is a lack of evidence for their effectiveness and safety beyond a few weeks of use (Rios et al., 2019). Moreover, hypnotics are known to be associated with unwanted effects like sedation, falls, accidents, amnesia, tolerance, dependence and abuse, and research also shows that such use may increase infection rates and mortality (Kripke, 2000; Parsaik et al., 2016). Of great interest, when asking patients who use hypnotics what they would prefer, 80% say they prefer non-pharmacological therapy compared with medications (Omvik et al., 2010). However, less than 10% of this group of hypnotic users had ever been offered anything other than pharmacological treatment (Omvik et al., 2010). Thus, easily implementable therapies are clearly needed, also in clinics focusing on somatic conditions. Several randomized controlled trials among patients with insomnia show that CBT-I delivered through the internet (Espie et al., 2012; Ritterband et al., 2009) or through self-help books (Bjorvatn, Fiske & Pallesen, 2011; Jernelov et al., 2012) are effective (for more details see Chapter 23).

CBT-I in insomnia co-morbid with somatic conditions

CBT-I, or components of CBT-I, are effective when given to patients with comorbid somatic conditions. In fact, among patients with cancer, studies show that CBT-I leads to improvement in insomnia severity, mood, cancer-related fatigue and overall quality of life (Espie et al., 2008; Garland et al., 2014; Jung, Yu & Kim, 2020; Savard, Ivers, Morin & Lacroix, 2021). A recent meta-analysis of the efficacy of CBT-I among patients with breast cancer found 14 randomized controlled trials, and, overall, CBT-I produced long-term reductions in insomnia symptoms and improvement in sleep quality with medium-to-large effect sizes (Ma et al., 2021). There are fewer studies on CBT-I among patients with co-morbid insomnia and cardiovascular diseases, but results are promising (Conley & Redeker, 2015). Although relatively few patients were included, studies show that CBT-I improves sleep among patients with heart diseases such as coronary heart disease and stable heart failure (Heenan, Pipe, Lemay, Davidson & Tulloch, 2020; Javaheri, Reid, Drerup, Mehra & Redline, 2020; Redeker et al., 2015; Rybarczyk, Macks, Harris & Stepanski, 2011).

Treatment considerations in co-morbid conditions

I recommend CBT-I whenever a patient has chronic insomnia disorder, regardless of co-morbid somatic conditions. CBT-I, or at least components of CBT-I, are likely to improve sleep in all somatic conditions in which insomnia symptoms occur. However, when treating patients with co-morbid insomnia and somatic conditions, some considerations are appropriate. For instance, sometimes the somatic condition may render the patient bedridden. In such cases, the stimulus control instruction to get out of bed when not sleeping is difficult to follow. Also sleep restriction is difficult in cases where the patient needs to stay in bed due to the somatic condition. In such cases it is still advisable to try to keep the bed and bedroom used at night separate from the bed and room the patient uses the rest of the day – if possible. If the somatic condition is associated with a lot of pain, pain treatment is recommended, preferably in combination with CBT-I. To rely solely on CBT-I in patients with high levels of pain is likely to be unsuccessful (see Chapter 15).

Another issue to consider is how severe the somatic condition is. If the patient suffers from intractable or terminal disease, for instance cancer with metastasis and poor prognosis, to recommend CBT-I may not be advisable. CBT-I is demanding and the patient needs to be motivated for such treatment. In cases where life expectancy is short, I do not think CBT-I is advisable, and the patient may be better off with hypnotics. In cases with a terminal disease, we do not need to worry about drug abuse or dependence. In my view CBT-I is therefore more appropriate among cancer patients with a good prognosis.

In certain cardiovascular diseases, it may be important to avoid stressful events. For instance, in patients with unstable angina pectoris or a high risk of cardiac arrythmias, the behavioural components of CBT-I may be too stressful to introduce. In such cases, a focus on cognitive strategies to reduce insomnia may be recommended.

Some patients with co-morbid somatic conditions may attribute the insomnia symptoms to the unresolved health problem or the medication regime. This may make these patients less motivated for CBT-I. In such cases, I believe we need to offer the rationale and explanations of the interplay between insomnia and somatic health, and how CBT-I may not only reduce the insomnia symptoms but also reduce the burden of the co-morbid somatic condition.

Who should provide CBT-I in insomnia co-morbid with somatic conditions?

For most somatic conditions, I do not see any problem with calling for implementing CBT-I in the treatment of the co-morbid insomnia disorder. One may discuss who should provide such treatment to patients with co-morbidity. Physicians treating somatic conditions co-morbid with insomnia may provide CBT-I as they already have these patients in their care. However, many of these physicians will need to be trained in CBT-I. I believe that physicians will implement CBT-I among their patients with insomnia disorder when given the rationale and explanations for why such treatment is preferable. However, obviously, doctors need to get formal training in CBT-I (Baglioni et al., 2020). If treatment by a physician is unsuccessful, the doctor may refer the patient to self-help therapies such as digital CBT-I or self-help books or consider referring to secondary care specialists - consistent with the suggested stepped care model (Baglioni et al., 2020; Espie, 2009; see Chapter 23, Figure 23.1).

CBT-I may not be indicated in patients where the insomnia symptoms clearly seem to be secondary to the somatic condition. In such cases, initial focus on the somatic condition is recommended. However, physicians need to be aware that insomnia symptoms may prevail (e.g., due to irrational compensatory behaviour and negative conditioning) after successful treatment of the main disorder/disease. If this is the case, the physician should consider shifting the focus to the insomnia symptoms and start treatment with CBT-I.

Conclusion

Many somatic disorders and diseases are associated with insomnia symptoms. Insomnia will obviously add to the disease burden and may also worsen the prognosis of the somatic condition. I would therefore call for implementing CBT-I in the treatment of chronic insomnia disorder in these patients with co-morbid illnesses.

References

Anothaisintawee, T., Reutrakul, S., Van Cauter, E., & Thakkinstian, A. (2016). Sleep disturbances compared to traditional risk factors for diabetes development: Systematic review and meta-analysis. *Sleep Medicine Reviews, 30*, 11–24. https://doi.org/10.1016/j.smrv.2015.10.002.

Baglioni, C., Altena, E., Bjorvatn, B., Blom, K., Bothelius, K., Devoto, A., Espie, C. A., Frase, L., Gavriloff, D., Tuuliki, H., Hoflehner, A., Hogl, B., Holzinger, B., Jarnefelt, H., Jernelov, S., Johann, A. F., Lombardo, C., Nissen, C., Palagini, L., Peeters, G., Perlis, M. L., Posner, D., Schlarb, A., Spiegelhalder, K., Wichniak, A., & Riemann, D. (2020). The European Academy for Cognitive Behavioural Therapy for Insomnia: An initiative of the European Insomnia Network to promote implementation and dissemination of treatment. *Journal of Sleep Research, 29* (2), e12967. https://doi.org/10.1111/jsr.12967.

Belleville, G., Cousineau, H., Levrier, K., & St-Pierre-Delorme, M. E. (2011). Meta-analytic review of the impact of cognitive-behavior therapy for insomnia on concomitant anxiety. *Clinical Psychology Review, 31* (4), 638–652. https://doi.org/10.1016/j.cpr.2011.02.004.

Besedovsky, L., Lange, T., & Haack, M. (2019). The sleep-immune crosstalk in health and disease. *Physiological Reviews, 99* (3), 1325–1380. https://doi.org/10.1152/physrev.00010.2018.

Bjorvatn, B., Fiske, E., & Pallesen, S. (2011). A self-help book is better than sleep hygiene advice for insomnia: A randomized controlled comparative study. *Scandinavian Journal of Psychology*, *52* (6), 580–585. https://doi.org/10.1111/j.1467-9450.2011.00902.x.

Bjorvatn, B., Axelsson, J., Pallesen, S., Waage, S., Vedaa, O., Blytt, K. M., Buchvold, H. V., Moen, B. E., & Thun, E. (2020). The association between shift work and immunological biomarkers in nurses. *Frontiers in Public Health*, *8*, 415. https://doi.org/10.3389/fpubh.2020.00415.

Blom, K., Jernelov, S., Kraepelien, M., Bergdahl, M. O., Jungmarker, K., Ankartjarn, L., Lindefors, N., & Kaldo, V. (2015). Internet treatment addressing either insomnia or depression, for patients with both diagnoses: a randomized trial. *Sleep*, *38* (2), 267–277. https://doi.org/10.5665/sleep.4412.

Brasure, M., Fuchs, E., MacDonald, R., Nelson, V. A., Koffel, E., Olson, C. M., Khawaja, I. S., Diem, S., Carlyle, M., Wilt, T. J., Ouellette, J., Butler, M., & Kane, R. L. (2016). Psychological and behavioral interventions for managing insomnia disorder: An evidence report for a clinical practice guideline by the American College of Physicians. *Annals of Internal Medicine*, *165* (2), 113–124. https://doi.org/10.7326/M15-1782.

Cheung, J. M. Y., Jarrin, D. C., Ballot, O., Bharwani, A. A., & Morin, C. M. (2019). A systematic review of cognitive behavioral therapy for insomnia implemented in primary care and community settings. *Sleep Medicine Reviews*, *44*, 23–36. https://doi.org/10.1016/j.smrv.2018.11.001.

Conley, S., & Redeker, N. S. (2015). Cognitive behavioral therapy for insomnia in the context of cardiovascular conditions. *Current Sleep Medicine Reports*, *1* (3), 157–165. https://doi.org/10.1007/s40675-015-0019-7.

Espie, C. A. (2009). 'Stepped care': A health technology solution for delivering cognitive behavioral therapy as a first line insomnia treatment. *Sleep*, *32* (12), 1549–1558. http://www.ncbi.nlm.nih.gov/entrez/query.fcgi?cmd=Retrieve&db=PubMed&dopt=Citation&list_uids=20041590.

Espie, C. A., Fleming, L., Cassidy, J., Samuel, L., Taylor, L. M., White, C. A., Douglas, N. J., Engleman, H. M., Kelly, H. L., & Paul, J. (2008). Randomized controlled clinical effectiveness trial of cognitive behavior therapy compared with treatment as usual for persistent insomnia in patients with cancer. *Journal of Clinical Oncology*, *26* (28), 4651–4658. https://doi.org/10.1200/JCO.2007.13.9006.

Espie, C. A., Kyle, S. D., Williams, C., Ong, J. C., Douglas, N. J., Hames, P., & Brown, J. S. (2012). A randomized, placebo-controlled trial of online cognitive behavioral therapy for chronic insomnia disorder delivered via an automated media-rich web application. *Sleep*, *35* (6), 769–781. https://doi.org/10.5665/sleep.1872.

Everitt, H., McDermott, L., Leydon, G., Yules, H., Baldwin, D., & Little, P. (2014). GPs' management strategies for patients with insomnia: A survey and qualitative interview study. *British Journal of General Practice*, *64* (619), e112–119. https://doi.org/10.3399/bjgp14X677176.

Finan, P. H., Goodin, B. R., & Smith, M. T. (2013). The association of sleep and pain: An update and a path forward. *The Journal of Pain*, *14* (12), 1539–1552. https://doi.org/10.1016/j.jpain.2013.08.007.

Garland, S. N., Johnson, J. A., Savard, J., Gehrman, P., Perlis, M., Carlson, L., & Campbell, T. (2014). Sleeping well with cancer: A systematic review of cognitive behavioral therapy for insomnia in cancer patients. *Neuropsychiatric Disease Treatment*, *10*, 1113–1124. https://doi.org/10.2147/NDT.S47790.

Geiger-Brown, J. M., Rogers, V. E., Liu, W., Ludeman, E. M., Downton, K. D., & Diaz-Abad, M. (2015). Cognitive behavioral therapy in persons with comorbid insomnia: A meta-analysis. *Sleep Medicine Reviews*, *23*, 54–67. https://doi.org/10.1016/j.smrv.2014.11.007.

Hauser, W., Urrutia, G., Tort, S., Uceyler, N., & Walitt, B. (2013). Serotonin and noradrenaline reuptake inhibitors (SNRIs) for fibromyalgia syndrome. *Cochrane Database of Systematic Reviews* (1), CD010292. https://doi.org/10.1002/14651858.CD010292.

Heenan, A., Pipe, A., Lemay, K., Davidson, J. R., & Tulloch, H. (2020). Cognitive-behavioral therapy for insomnia tailored to patients with cardiovascular disease: A Pre-Post Study. *Behavioral Sleep Medicine*, *18* (3), 372–385. https://doi.org/10.1080/15402002.2019.1594815.

Irwin, M. R., Olmstead, R., & Carroll, J. E. (2016). Sleep disturbance, sleep duration, and inflammation: A systematic review and meta-analysis of cohort studies and experimental sleep deprivation. *Biological Psychiatry*, *80* (1), 40–52. https://doi.org/10.1016/j.biopsych.2015.05.014.

Irwin, M. R., Olmstead, R., Carrillo, C., Sadeghi, N., Breen, E. C., Witarama, T., Yokomizo, M., Lavretsky, H., Carroll, J. E., Motivala, S. J., Bootzin, R., & Nicassio, P. (2014). Cognitive behavioral therapy vs. Tai Chi for late life insomnia and inflammatory risk: A randomized controlled comparative efficacy trial. *Sleep*, *37* (9), 1543–1552. https://doi.org/10.5665/sleep.4008.

Javaheri, S., Reid, M., Drerup, M., Mehra, R., & Redline, S. (2020). Reducing coronary heart disease risk through treatment of insomnia using web-based cognitive behavioral therapy for insomnia: A methodological approach. *Behavioral Sleep Medicine, 18* (3), 334–344. https://doi.org/10.1080/15402002.2019.1584896.

Jernelov, S., Lekander, M., Blom, K., Rydh, S., Ljotsson, B., Axelsson, J., & Kaldo, V. (2012). Efficacy of a behavioral self-help treatment with or without therapist guidance for co-morbid and primary insomnia -- a randomized controlled trial. *BMC Psychiatry, 12*, 5. https://doi.org/10.1186/1471-244X-12-5.

Jung, H. J., Yu, E. S., & Kim, J. H. (2020). Combined program of cognitive-behavioral therapy for insomnia and medication tapering in cancer patients: A clinic-based pilot study. *Behavioral Sleep Medicine, 18* (3), 386–395. https://doi.org/10.1080/15402002.2019.1597718.

Kecklund, G., & Axelsson, J. (2016). Health consequences of shift work and insufficient sleep. *British Medical Journal, 355*, i5210. https://doi.org/10.1136/bmj.i5210.

Kripke, D. F. (2000). Chronic hypnotic use: Deadly risks, doubtful benefit. *Sleep Medicine Reviews, 4* (1), 5–20. https://doi.org/10.1053/smrv.1999.0076.

Lazaratou, H., Soldatou, A., & Dikeos, D. (2012). Medical comorbidity of sleep disorders in children and adolescents. *Current Opinion in Psychiatry, 25* (5), 391–397. https://doi.org/10.1097/YCO.0b013e3283556c7a.

Ma, Y., Hall, D. L., Ngo, L. H., Liu, Q., Bain, P. A., & Yeh, G. Y. (2021). Efficacy of cognitive behavioral therapy for insomnia in breast cancer: A meta-analysis. *Sleep Medicine Reviews, 55*, 101376. https://doi.org/10.1016/j.smrv.2020.101376.

Morin, C. M., Culbert, J. P., & Schwartz, S. M. (1994). Nonpharmacological interventions for insomnia: A meta-analysis of treatment efficacy. *American Journal of Psychiatry, 151* (8), 1172–1180. http://www.ncbi.nlm.nih.gov/entrez/query.fcgi?cmd=Retrieve&db=PubMed&dopt=Citation&list_uids=8037252.

Morin, C. M., Jarrin, D. C., Ivers, H., Merette, C., LeBlanc, M., & Savard, J. (2020). Incidence, persistence, and remission rates of insomnia over 5 years. *JAMA Network Open, 3* (11), e2018782. https://doi.org/10.1001/jamanetworkopen.2020.18782.

Omvik, S., Pallesen, S., Bjorvatn, B., Sivertsen, B., Havik, O. E., & Nordhus, I. H. (2010). Patient characteristics and predictors of sleep medication use. *International Clinical Psychopharmacology, 25* (2), 91–100. https://doi.org/10.1097/YIC.0b013e328334e5e6.

Parsaik, A. K., Mascarenhas, S. S., Khosh-Chashm, D., Hashmi, A., John, V., Okusaga, O., & Singh, B. (2016). Mortality associated with anxiolytic and hypnotic drugs – A systematic review and meta-analysis. *The Australian and New Zealand Journal of Psychiatry*, 50(6), 520–533. https://doi.org/10.1177/0004867415616695.

Redeker, N. S., Jeon, S., Andrews, L., Cline, J., Jacoby, D., & Mohsenin, V. (2015). Feasibility and efficacy of a self-management intervention for insomnia in stable heart failure. *Journal of Clinical Sleep Medicine, 11* (10), 1109–1119. https://doi.org/10.5664/jcsm.5082.

Riemann, D., Baglioni, C., Bassetti, C., Bjorvatn, B., Dolenc Groselj, L., Ellis, J. G., Espie, C. A., Garcia-Borreguero, D., Gjerstad, M., Goncalves, M., Hertenstein, E., Jansson-Frojmark, M., Jennum, P. J., Leger, D., Nissen, C., Parrino, L., Paunio, T., Pevernagie, D., Verbraecken, J., Weess, H. G., Wichniak, A., Zavalko, I., Arnardottir, E. S., Deleanu, O. C., Strazisar, B., Zoetmulder, M., & Spiegelhalder, K. (2017). European guideline for the diagnosis and treatment of insomnia. *Journal of Sleep Research, 26* (6), 675–700. https://doi.org/10.1111/jsr.12594.

Rios, P., Cardoso, R., Morra, D., Nincic, V., Goodarzi, Z., Farah, B., Harricharan, S., Morin, C. M., Leech, J., Straus, S. E., & Tricco, A. C. (2019). Comparative effectiveness and safety of pharmacological and non-pharmacological interventions for insomnia: An overview of reviews. *Systematic Reviews, 8* (1), 281. https://doi.org/10.1186/s13643-019-1163-9.

Ritterband, L. M., Thorndike, F. P., Gonder-Frederick, L. A., Magee, J. C., Bailey, E. T., Saylor, D. K., & Morin, C. M. (2009). Efficacy of an internet-based behavioral intervention for adults with insomnia. *Archives of General Psychiatry, 66* (7), 692–698. https://doi.org/66/7/692[pii]10.1001/archgenpsychiatry.2009.66.

Rybarczyk, B., Mack, L., Harris, J. H., & Stepanski, E. (2011). Testing two types of self-help CBT-I for insomnia in older adults with arthritis or coronary artery disease. *Rehabilitation Psychology, 56* (4), 257–266. https://doi.org/10.1037/a0025577.

Sateia, M. J. (2009). Update on sleep and psychiatric disorders. *Chest, 135* (5), 1370–1379. https://doi.org/10.1378/chest.08-1834.

Savard, J., Ivers, H., Morin, C. M., & Lacroix, G. (2021). Video cognitive-behavioral therapy for insomnia in cancer patients: A cost-effective alternative. *Psychooncology, 30* (1), 44–51. https://doi.org/10.1002/pon.5532.

Sivertsen, B., Overland, S., Bjorvatn, B., Mæland, J. G., & Mykletun, A. (2009). Does insomnia predict sick leave? The Hordaland Health Study. *Journal of Psychosomatic Research, 66*, 67–74.

Spiegel, K., Sheridan, J. F., & Van Cauter, E. (2002). Effect of sleep deprivation on response to immunization. *JAMA*, *288* (12), 1471–1472. https://doi.org/10.1001/jama.288.12.1471-a.

Spiegelhalder, K., Scholtes, C., & Riemann, D. (2010). The association between insomnia and cardiovascular diseases. *Nature and Science of Sleep*, *2*, 71–78. https://doi.org/10.2147/nss.s7471.

van der Wardt, V., Logan, P., Conroy, S., Harwood, R., & Gladman, J. (2014). Antihypertensive treatment in people with dementia. *Journal of the American Medical Directors Association*, *15* (9), 620–629. https://doi.org/10.1016/j.jamda.2014.03.005.

Wu, J. Q., Appleman, E. R., Salazar, R. D., & Ong, J. C. (2015). Cognitive behavioral therapy for insomnia comorbid with psychiatric and medical conditions: A meta-analysis. *JAMA Internal Medicine*, *175* (9), 1461–1472. https://doi.org/10.1001/jamainternmed.2015.3006.

15

CBT-I Protocol for Insomnia Co-morbid with Chronic Pain

Nicole K. Y. Tang

Key points

- Insomnia is one of the most debilitating co-morbidities for which people with chronic pain want treatment.
- Insomnia is not a mere symptom of chronic pain, but a key driver of pain and poor health.
- Timely and appropriate sleep treatment could improve the quality of life and prevent adverse health outcomes.
- In published clinical trials, the most commonly used CBT-I components for treating insomnia co-morbid with chronic pain are sleep hygiene, stimulus control and sleep restriction therapy.
- Specific adaptions to these CBT-I components could enhance adherence and optimise outcomes of insomnia treatment in chronic pain.
- Given the bi-directional relationship between sleep and pain, a hybrid CBT combining select components of CBT-I and CBT for pain management may improve treatment efficiency and reap synergetic benefits.

Learning objectives

- To appreciate that insomnia is a common but distressing and disabling co-morbidity of chronic pain.
- To understand the scientific rationale behind the application of CBT-I and hybrid CBT in chronic pain.
- To learn that it is feasible to successfully address insomnia despite the presence of chronic pain.
- To consider essential adaptations to the usual CBT-I components for enhancing adherence and treatment outcomes.

Abstract

Insomnia co-morbid with chronic pain is common and debilitating. The majority of people with chronic pain present with insomnia of severity that warrants clinical intervention. Chronic pain often does not have a well-defined underlying pathology, and once established, it often does not remit with treatments including drugs, physical therapies, injections and surgeries. Sleep disturbances triggered whether by pain or not can persist, aggravating pain and dampening pain management efforts as a result.

Cognitive behaviour therapy for insomnia (CBT-I) has been applied to tackle pain-related insomnia with some success. This chapter will outline the scientific evidence underpinning such application and consider practical adaptations to CBT-I components that could be made to meet the specific needs of chronic pain patients. It is envisaged that these adaptations could lead to better adherence and hence optimise the treatment outcomes. It is also suggested that given the bi-directional relationship between sleep and pain, synergistic benefits can be gained by adopting a hybrid CBT approach combining select components of CBT-I and CBT for pain management to improve treatment efficiency. However, further research is required to establish clinical and cost effectiveness of the hybrid CBT approach.

Keywords *Insomnia, sleep disturbances, chronic pain, CBT for insomnia (CBT-I), hybrid CBT*

Cognitive-Behavioural Therapy for Insomnia (CBT-I) Across the Life Span: Guidelines and Clinical Protocols for Health Professionals, First Edition. Edited by Chiara Baglioni, Colin A. Espie and Dieter Riemann.

Introduction of chronic pain and co-morbid insomnia

In Europe, around one in five adults is living with severe chronic pain for which long-term management is required (Breivik, Collett, Ventafridda, Cohen & Gallacher, 2006). Unlike acute pain that can be traced to a recent injury, chronic pain often does not have a well-defined underlying pathology and is primarily defined by its persistence beyond the expected healing time (3–6 months) (International Association for the Study of Pain, 2020). For many patients, the pain persists and is not relieved by drugs, physical therapies, injections or surgeries.

Insomnia is one of the most debilitating co-morbidities that people with chronic pain want treatment for (Turk et al., 2008). Between 50 and 80% of mixed groups of chronic pain patients experience clinical insomnia (Alsaadi, McAuley, Hush & Maher, 2011; McCracken, Williams & Tang, 2011; Tang, Wright & Salkovskis, 2007), and as many as 90% of patients with fibromyalgia report significant sleep disturbances (Theadom & Cropley, 2008). Typical problems experienced are frequent awakenings, short sleep duration and poor sleep quality (Dubrovsky et al., 2014; Morin, Kowatch & Wade, 1989). These complaints are corroborated by polysomnographic abnormalities such as reduced sleep spindles during N2 sleep, reduced slow wave sleep, intrusion of alpha EEG activity during slow wave sleep, more frequent brief arousals and increased cyclical alternating pattern of EEG activity that signifies sleep instability; although none of these is a specific biomarker of sleep disturbance experienced by people with chronic pain.

Insomnia as a valid treatment starting point

Contrary to the assumption that insomnia is a mere symptom of chronic pain, several lines of research have converged to suggest that sleep disruption (triggered by pain or not) is a key driver of pain and poor health.

First, in cross-sectional studies, it has been found that individuals with both chronic pain and insomnia report lower pain tolerance, greater pain intensity, pain spread, psychological distress and physical disability than those reporting no insomnia (Alföldi, Dragioti, Wiklund & Gerdle, 2017; McCracken & Iverson, 2002; Sivertsen et al., 2015). Further, studies performing mediation analysis have revealed that negative mood, anxiety and depression symptoms, attention to pain, pain helplessness, stress and fatigue are possible pathways through which insomnia could intensify pain (Whibley et al., 2019).

Second, in well-controlled experimental studies of healthy normal sleepers, the introduction of acute and repeated sleep deprivation or fragmentation has been shown to result in greater pain reports and lower pain thresholds during quantitative sensory testing (Haack & Mullington, 2005; Haack, Sanchez & Mullington, 2007; Onen, Alloui, Gross, Eschallier & Dubray, 2001; Simpson, Scott-Sutherland, Gautam, Sethna & Haack, 2018; Smith, Edwards, McCann & Haythornthwaite, 2007).

Third, several micro-longitudinal studies have applied ecological momentary assessment and multilevel modelling techniques to decipher the temporal effect of sleep on pain among chronic pain patients in naturalistic settings. These studies examine sleep and pain as interacting daily processes and have found that, in the absence of any intervention/experimental manipulation, a night of poorer sleep quality is typically followed by a day of more pain (Lewandowski, Palermo, Motte & Fu, 2010; Tang, Goodchild, Sanborn, Howard & Salkovskis, 2012) and less physical activity (Tang & Sanborn, 2014).

Finally, a number of macro-longitudinal studies with long-term follow-ups have identified insomnia as a significant risk factor for future onset of pain in pain-free adults (Chen et al., 2018; Mork & Nilsen, 2012), and among individuals with chronic pain, insomnia onset has been found to triple the risk of subsequent incidence of major depression (Campbell et al., 2013).

These findings point to sleep as a profitable nightly treatment target, for improving quality of life and preventing adverse health outcomes. In fact, a 2015 systematic review and meta-analysis of 11 RCTs has found the use of non-pharmacological interventions for sleep in chronic cancer and non-cancer pain to be associated with improvements across self-reported outcome measures on sleep quality (SMD = 0.78), pain (SMD = 0.18) and fatigue (SMD = 0.38) at post-treatment (Tang et al., 2015). These gains in sleep quality and fatigue were largely maintained at follow-up and were accompanied by a reduction in depression symptoms (SMD = 0.31) (Tang et al., 2015). Consistently, a 2019 trial has shown that when CBT-I was applied to individuals with fibromyalgia, significant improvements in sleep diary WASO, SE, SQ and sleep-related beliefs and attitude were evident compared with baseline and with those who were on the waitlist or who received CBT for pain management only (McCrae et al., 2019).

General approach

The most commonly used CBT-I components for treating insomnia co-morbid with chronic pain are sleep hygiene (SH), stimulus control (SC) and sleep restriction therapy (SRT) (see Chapter 2). Depending on the length and intensity of the treatment, additional relaxation training and cognitive therapy are sometimes found in more comprehensive intervention programmes.

Extensive adaptations to these treatment contents – beyond adding psychoeducation on relevant pain conditions – have not been reported in published trials that tested the effect of CBT-I in chronic pain populations (Currie, Wilson, Pontefract & deLaplante, 2000; Edinger, Wohlgemuth, Krystal & Rice, 2005; Martínez et al., 2013; McCrae et al., 2019; Miró et al., 2011). However, based on emerging research, the following adaptions could potentially enhance adherence and optimise outcomes of insomnia treatment in chronic pain.

Setting the expectations right

Although the importance of sleep is well recognised by both patients and health care professionals in the pain community, it is not within patients' normal expectations to receive standalone sleep treatment prior to finding a reliable pain management strategy. The offering of sleep treatment may be puzzling to patients who believe pain is the sole cause of their insomnia and that there is nothing that can be done about it. These beliefs, if held strongly, can be a barrier to treatment engagement (Tang et al., 2020). Therapists may find it helpful to schedule in some early cognitive therapy to address these beliefs, helping patients see that CBT-I is a sensible alternative treatment starting point.

Afolalu, Moore, Ramley, Goodchild & Tang (2016) have developed the Pain-Related Beliefs and Attitudes about Sleep (PBAS) Scale for the assessment of these common beliefs in chronic pain. The PBAS is a 10-item scale with two factors: 'pain as the primary cause of insomnia' and 'inevitable consequences of insomnia on pain and coping'. The PBAS have good internal consistency ($\alpha = 0.84$), item-total correlation (range = 0.46–0.63), temporal stability ($r = 0.91$ between two measurements, 1 week apart) and are sensitive to the treatment effect. They correlated positively with the Insomnia Severity Index ($r = 0.37$–0.64, ISI; Bastien, Vallières & Morin, 2001), the Dysfunctional Beliefs and Attitudes about Sleep ($r = 0.57$–0.65, DBAS; Morin, Vallières & Ivers, 2007) and the Anxiety and Preoccupation about Sleep Questionnaire ($r = 0.45$–0.57, APSQ; Jansson-Frojmark, Harvey, Lundh, Norell-Clarke & Linton, 2011; Tang & Harvey, 2004) and was a significant predictor of not only insomnia severity but also pain interference in chronic pain samples recruited from hospital-based pain clinics.

Table 15.1 presents the PBAS items along with possible alternative viewpoints. They are meant to be presented as additional information, rather than a cognitive restructuring exercise. The therapist brings these up in session for discussion, not to 'correct' the patient's thinking but to inform and to help loosen up these beliefs, setting the stage for insomnia treatment.

Psychoeducation about pain–sleep interaction

When CBT-I is carried out to treat insomnia co-morbid with chronic pain, a large part of the psychoeducation should be about the pain–sleep interaction, illustrating the reciprocal relationship with pain worsening sleep and poor sleep aggravating pain and blunting day-time pain management. Aside from verbal discussion (like the discussion of PBAS items described above), a powerful way to allow patients to examine their own pain–sleep interaction on a day-to-day basis is through the use of a sleep diary. However, a typical sleep diary does not contain items on pain and hence it is advisable to add a pain rating (0 = 'no pain at all' to 10 = 'a lot of pain') in both the morning and evening sections of the consensus sleep diary (Carney et al., 2012). The pain rating could be phrased as 'What is the level of pain right now?', with reference to the present pain intensity item in the widely used Brief Pain Inventory (Cleeland & Ryan, 1994), which is a recommended outcome measure in chronic pain trials (Turk et al., 2003). It is also recommended to add a question asking about pain medication used, in particular any PRN medication taken to provide emergency pain relief.

With this hybrid diary tool, the therapist and the patient can work together as a team to co-investigate any pattern of correspondence between pain and sleep and to use the patient's own data to address concerns (Clark & Fairburn, 1997). For example, if the patient is particularly apprehensive about pain making it difficult to fall asleep (e.g., 'On nights when my pain is bad, it will take me hours to get comfortable enough to fall asleep'), the therapist could help the patient approach

Table 15.1 Pain-related beliefs and attitudes about sleep (PBAS). Scale items and possible response/ discussion points for therapists.

	PBAS item	Possible response/discussion points for therapists
1	My insomnia is largely a result of the pain and there is nothing I can do about it.	• Pain may not be the only cause of sleep trouble, especially if the sleep problems have been around for some time. • A number of factors are involved in the regulation of sleep. Consider the roles of age, circadian rhythm, homeostasis, biological factors, environmental factors, lifestyle, thoughts, behaviours and emotions. These factors may affect sleep individually or jointly with pain. • Research with people with chronic pain has found worries and pain-related thoughts better predictors of sleep disturbance than pain severity. • In the absence of a pain cure, it is possible to work on other factors linked to insomnia to improve sleep and quality of life.
2	With the pain, I can never get myself comfortable in bed.	• There are practical steps one can take to increase the level of comfort in bed. It may involve getting the right mattress and pillow, and adopting sleep positions that do not add strain to muscles, nerves and the spine. These strategies can be individualised to get yourself comfortable enough to fall asleep. • Remember the last time you dropped off to sleep in the sofa, on a bus or in a hotel bedroom whilst you were on holiday. You might not be pain-free, but you managed to get yourself calm and comfortable enough to fall asleep.
3	The pain is always there when you try to have a good night's sleep	• Physiologically, pain increases as the day progresses. This is because of the accumulation of pain/fatigue from physical activities and the natural dip in endorphins – a natural pain killer produced within our bodies – during the night. • Psychologically, the lack of distraction in the evening and the quietness of the surroundings make us particularly aware of what is going on within our bodies. The more we focus on our bodily sensations, the more pain we will feel. • Pain is particularly noticeable at night when one is trying to get a good night's sleep, but the good news is that pain perception is an active process, and with training one can learn to alter the focus of attention during the pre-sleep period, to notice less pain and be less bothered by pain as you fall asleep.
4	When I am in pain, I simply can't get to sleep no matter how hard I try.	• Pain may not be the culprit, trying is. The harder one tries to get to sleep the more worked up one will become. The resultant increase in anxiety, frustration and bodily tension are not conducive to sleep. • There are things one can do to facilitate sleep (e.g., increasing sleep pressure by staying awake during the day, reducing stimulation at or around bed-time), but the key is not to try too hard.
5	I know I can't sleep through the night because the pain will wake me up.	• Sleep occurs in stages. During the lighter stages of sleep, we can still process a range of sensory stimuli from the environment and briefs awakenings from sleep are not unusual consequences. The ability to wake up from sleep and respond to potential threats is considered to be of evolutionary importance to survival. • Most of us experience a number of awakenings during a normal night of sleep. We may or may not remember these awakenings, depending on their length and what happens during these awakenings. The longer the awakening time and the more physically and mentally active we become during these awakenings, the more likely we would register these awakenings in our memory. Our reactions to these awakenings are crucial to our perception of how well we sleep. • Some psychological experiments have demonstrated that worrying about pain and the fact that one is not sleeping could make it harder to go back to sleep.
6	I get very annoyed when the pain wakes me up.	• Whilst this is an understandable reaction, frustration will only make sleep worse. If sleep is the ultimate goal, changing one's expectation and emotional reactions to mid-night awakenings may help. • If you get annoyed because you think you *should* sleep through the night, you may find consolation in knowing that even the best sleepers in the world would experience a couple of brief awakenings during the night. You don't have to sleep through the night in one block in order to feel refreshed. • If you get annoyed because you worry that you won't be able to function well without a perfect night of sleep, be assured that you can survive without a perfect night of sleep.

Table 15.1 (Continued)

	PBAS item	Possible response/discussion points for therapists
7	Not sleeping well is going to make my pain worse the next day.	• Although there are times that worse pain will follow a poorer night of sleep, there are also times that the amount of pain will stay just about the same regardless of how well or poorly was the sleep the night before. • Research has suggested that the relationship between pain and sleep may be more complicated than it seems. How much pain we perceive during the day could be influenced by not just the sleep obtained the night before, but also our mood, the amount of attention we pay to the pain and the activity we do during the day. In other words, not having a good night's sleep doesn't necessarily lead to worse pain the following day. • There are individual differences. You're encouraged to monitor your sleep and pain throughout 1-2 weeks to identify your own pattern of sleep-pain relationship.
8	I won't be able to cope with the pain if I don't sleep well.	• Successful management of pain doesn't happen overnight, and it is unlikely that a night of poor sleep can cancel out all the effort you've put into coping with your pain. • Pain management skills you've acquired over the years will stay with you even if you don't sleep well occasionally. • Research has indicated that sleep is one of many factors that determine our levels of functioning during the day. Whilst some may feel noticeably more irritated and tired following a poor night of sleep, how we deal with these feelings and what we do during the day are important determinants of the levels of enjoyment and achievement. You are encouraged to test out whether or not this applies to you by designing your own real-life experiments.
9	Unless I get rid of the pain, I won't sleep well.	• Whilst insomnia is common in chronic pain, some people with chronic pain report no significant issue with sleep. • Research has shown that (1) people on pain medication for years continue to have a problem sleeping, (2) people who have completed pain management programmes do not necessarily show substantial improvement in their sleep, (3) people with chronic pain and insomnia responded to treatment for insomnia. • Conventional treatments for pain do not necessarily help you sleep better and you don't have to wait till you get rid of the pain before you do something to improve your sleep.
10	The insomnia is taking away one of my few respites from pain.	• Your frustration is understandable! What's important is that you are taking concrete actions to address your sleep problems. • Whilst you're working on improving your sleep, you may want to think about other ways to gain respites from pain. For example, learning new methods of relaxation rather than only getting rest from sleep, developing a hobby that is so absorbing that you forget about your pain (or you would feel lively and fulfilling despite the pain).

their bed-time with relative calmness simply by checking out their sleep-onset latency between nights of varying pain levels. Quite often, the patient would be pleasantly surprised by the differences between how they thought they sleep and what their own daily recordings suggest. During the SRT phase, they would also be surprised by how their body responds to sleep homeostasis and that pain is no longer as big a barrier to sleep onset than they once remembered.

This kind of self-monitoring and pattern-finding exercise can improve patient's awareness of their own sleep pattern. It can also be set up as a behavioural experiment in CBT terms (Bennett-Levy et al., 2004) to tackle sleep-related anxiety and their underpinning beliefs, if explicit hypotheses were co-developed with the patient upfront and reviewed after data collection. The use of behavioural experiments can be especially helpful during the initial stage of implementing the sleep restriction therapy ('My pain will be off the chart if I don't get a solid 7 hours of sleep' – to test out the actual impact of a slightly shorter sleep duration on pain) and in understanding that the effect of pain medication on sleep ('If I don't take my pain killer, I won't be able to go to sleep' – to test out if pain killers are a prerequisite to sleep).

Related to this, another important aspect of psychoeducation for CBT for pain-related insomnia is the positive and negative effects of various pain and mood medications on sleep (Table 15.2). Most patients with chronic pain who require treatment for sleep problems are taking some form of analgesics (e.g., non-steroid anti-inflammatory drugs, opioids), anticonvulsants (e.g., gabapentin, pregabalin) and/or antidepressants (e.g., amitriptyline, duloxetine), and have been doing so for years to manage their pain. However, the effects of these drugs on their sleep are not usually clearly explained or understood. For example, whilst more is learnt about the danger of using opioids with evidence of excess mortality

Table 15.2 Effects of medications commonly used for the management of chronic pain on sleep and other side effects.

	Positive effect on sleep	Negative effect on sleep	Other side effects
Non-opioid analgesics e.g., Ibuprofen High-dose aspirin Diclofenac Naproxen Paracetamol (Acetaminophen)	No clear benefit	Delay sleep onset Increase awakenings Increase Stage 2 Decrease SWS and delay SWS latency Decrease sleep efficiency	Indigestion Stomach ulcers Headache Dizziness
Opioids e.g., Morphine Buprenorphine Fentanyl Oxycodone Oxymorphone Hydromorphone Methadone	Reduce body/leg movement Improve self-reported sleep quality	Increase sleep-disordered breathing Shorten REM sleep onset and suppress REM Excessive day-time sleepiness/drowsiness Fatigue	Nausea/dizziness Vomiting Constipation Stomach pain Headache Opioid induced hyperalgesia Tolerance and dependence Lethality in overdose
Anticonvulsants e.g., Gabapentin Pregabalin Carbamazepine	Shorten sleep onset latency Reduce awakenings Increase total sleep time Improve pain-related sleep interference and insomnia symptoms Increase duration and percentage of SWS	Excessive day-time sleepiness/drowsiness Fatigue Reduced REM duration	Headaches Dizziness Nausea Diarrhoea Peripheral oedema Blurred vision Erectile dysfunction Weight gain Memory problems Lethality in overdose
Antidepressants e.g., Amitriptyline Nortriptyline Fluoxetine Venlafaxine Paroxetine Trazadone Mirtazapine	Increase TST Increase sleep efficiency Improve self-reported sleep quality	Reduce REM sleep and Increase REM latency Increase awakening after sleep onset Excessive day-time sleepiness/drowsiness Fatigue	Dry mouth and thirst Morning grogginess Nausea Blurred vision Difficulty thinking clearly Constipation Weight gain Orthostatic hypotension Anticholinergic effects Cardiovascular effects Tolerance and dependence Lethality in overdose

(Volkow & McLellan, 2016), data from trials revealed that many people still consider opioids as effective pain killers that hasten sleep and improve sleep quality (Tang, Stella, Banks, Sandhu, & Berna, 2019). The respiratory depression effect of opioids, as well as the ability of the drug to alter sleep architecture, cause excessive day-time drowsiness, and interact with benzodiazepines is not as clearly publicised as they should (Jann, Kennedy & Lopez, 2014). In the real world, it is not usually feasible to expect patients to be off their medications prior to commencing CBT-I (e.g., resistance, withdrawal and symptoms aggravation). The patients can simply be asked to keep their medication use steady throughout the CBT-I programme. Using the hybrid diary, they should be encouraged to note down any changes to medication use during CBT-I and pay attention to changes in their sleep patterns, whilst keeping their medication regime by and large unchanged.

Modifying sleep restriction therapy and stimulus control rules with flexibility

Chronic pain is not identified as a condition that contraindicates the use of SRT (Smith & Perlis, 2006), but experimental studies with healthy volunteers have shown that acute sleep deprivation and sleep fragmentation can lead to an increased level of spontaneous pain (Simpson et al., 2018; Smith et al., 2007). There is also qualitative evidence suggesting that SRT could lead to pain flare-ups and subsequent discontinuation of SRT in patients with chronic pain and co-morbid insomnia (Tang et al., 2020). The pace of the SRT should be implemented with care, depending on the patient's baseline sleep pattern and their readiness to cope with a potential increase in pain sensitivity during the initial SRT phase.

The associated increase in and/or extension of physical activity late into the evening is another aspect of SRT that chronic pain patients often find challenging. Advanced planning is needed to pace the activity and to identify ways to stay up without intensifying the pain (e.g., gentle stretching on the floor, sitting in a comfy chair to do some non-stimulating activities). Overexertion during SRT can considerably slow down the progress as it generally takes at least a few days for the pain to calm down. It is demoralising and may cause the patient to lose confidence in the overall treatment programme.

Several adaptations can make SRT and SCT more tolerable:

i) Start gently and give a little more room for the patient to ease into the new sleep schedule, e.g., when calculating the initial total time in bed, add 60 instead of 30 minutes to the average total sleep time in the past week. The TIB window could be shortened in the following week if required to further condense sleep.
ii) Getting in and out of bed can be challenging for patients with chronic back pain. Compliance to the 'get out of bed and go to a different room, if not sleeping within 15–20 minutes' rule should be encouraged with flexibility. Where getting out of bed and going to a different room is practically difficult, patients could be advised to sit in a chair next to the bed or simply just sit up in bed instead. This will interrupt the effort of trying to fall asleep and/or the frustration about not sleeping that will follow, but will maintain the core association between sleeping and the sleeping position (and the intention to fall asleep).
iii) Day-time naps are highly prevalent for certain subgroups of patients with chronic pain, e.g., fibromyalgia (Theadom, Cropley & Kantermann, 2015). For individuals who need a nap in the day, they should be advised to keep the nap short (<45 minutes) and in the early afternoon (e.g., no later than 3 p.m.). Also, they should be advised to keep this schedule regular and to use an alarm clock to help them wake up at the end of the nap period.

Side effects of SRT and SC as applied to chronic pain populations have not been extensively studied. A 2020 feasibility study has, however, identified increased day-time sleepiness and pain flare-ups as possible undesirable outcomes (Tang et al., 2020). Additional discussions around safety are warranted. Aside from not driving or operating machines when drowsy, the therapist should also discuss the safety limits (e.g., maximum dose) of PRN pain medication for the management of pain flare-ups and the typical length of a transition from drowsiness to full alertness where day-time naps are allowed.

Conclusion

The above adaptations should be carried out before and during CBT-I has the potential to enhance adherence and optimise outcomes. When the treatment is working and patients are getting better quality sleep, care must also be taken to prevent patients from reacting to the new-found energy with a boom-and-bust activity cycle. Previous research has found that following a night of better quality sleep, individuals with chronic pain tend to have a higher spontaneous level of physical activity during the day and report greater evening pain in the evening (Tang & Sanborn, 2014). This pattern of findings reflects the risk for people to overexert themselves (to catch up on life) on 'good days' when they have been restored by better sleep.

Hence, there are synergistic benefits in combining select pain management strategies, e.g., goal setting and physical activity management, with CBT-I. Such a hybrid approach has been developed and evaluated in several feasibility studies and randomised controlled trials, with treatment delivered in group or individually with mixed chronic pain patients, older adults with arthritis and patients with fibromyalgia (Jungquist et al., 2010; Pigeon et al., 2012; Prados et al., 2020; Tang, Goodchild & Salkovskis, 2012; Tang et al., 2020; Vitiello et al., 2013). The headline findings are that hybrid CBT for pain and insomnia are feasible, associated with better results in not only sleep but also mood, fatigue and other quality of life outcomes compared to waitlist control. The hybrid option appears to be superior to unimodal treatment in improving patient outcome measures of pain and insomnia, with early improvements in sleep predicting long-term gains in pain and quality of life outcomes (Vitiello et al., 2014) and those with more severe pain and insomnia outcomes more likely to gain sustained benefits (McCurry et al., 2014). The concept of hybrid CBT is gaining traction in the pain community for its promise in improving treatment efficiency and reducing polypharmacy (Herrero Babiloni et al., 2021), but more research is required to demonstrate treatment efficacy across clinical subgroups and cost-effectiveness in definitive trials. The wider dissemination of such treatment strategies would also require support from the health care infrastructure with trained personnel (Collard et al., 2021), which is a logistic challenge shared by conventional CBT-I (Baglioni et al., 2020).

References

Afolalu, E. F., Moore, C., Ramlee, F., Goodchild, C. E., & Tang, N. K. Y. (2016). Development of the pain-related beliefs and attitudes about sleep (PBAS) scale for the assessment and treatment of insomnia comorbid with chronic pain. *Journal of Clinical Sleep Medicine*, *12* (9), 1269–1277. doi: 10.5664/jcsm.6130.

Alföldi, P., Dragioti, E., Wiklund, T., & Gerdle, B. (2017). Spreading of pain and insomnia in patients with chronic pain: Results from a national quality registry (SQRP). *Journal of Rehabilitation Medicine*, *49* (1), 63–70. doi: 10.2340/16501977-2162.

Alsaadi, S. M., McAuley, J. H., Hush, J. M., & Maher, C. G. (2011). Prevalence of sleep disturbance in patients with low back pain. *European Spine Journal*, *20* (5), 737–743. doi:10.1007/s00586-010-1661-x

Baglioni, C., Altena, E., Bjorvatn, B., Blom, K., Bothelius, K., Devoto, A., & Riemann, D. (2020). The European Academy for Cognitive Behavioural Therapy for Insomnia: An initiative of the European Insomnia Network to promote implementation and dissemination of treatment. *Journal of Sleep Research*, *29* (2), e12967. https://doi.org/10.1111/jsr.12967.

Bastien, C. H., Vallières, A., & Morin, C. M. (2001). Validation of the Insomnia Severity Index as an outcome measure for insomnia research. *Sleep Medicine*, *2* (4), 297–307. doi: 10.1016/s1389-9457(00)00065-4.

Bennett-Levy, J., Butler, G., Fennell, M., Hackmann, A., Mueller, M., & Westbrook, D. (Eds.). (2004). *Oxford guide to behavioural experiments in cognitive therapy*. Oxford, UK: Oxford University Press.

Breivik, H., Collett, B., Ventafridda, V., Cohen, R., & Gallacher, D. (2006). Survey of chronic pain in Europe: Prevalence, impact on daily life, and treatment. *European Journal of Pain*, *10* (4), 287–333.

Campbell, P., Tang, N. K. Y., McBeth, J., Lewis, M., Main, C., Croft, P., & Dunn, K. (2013). The role of sleep problems in the development of depression among those with chronic pain: A prospective cohort study. *Sleep*, *36* (11), 1693–1698.

Carney, C. E., Buysse, D. J., Ancoli-Israel, S., Edinger, J. D., Krystal, A. D., Lichstein, K. L., & Morin, C. M. (2012). The consensus sleep diary: Standardizing prospective sleep self-monitoring. *Sleep*, *35* (2), 287.

Chen, T.-Y., Lee, S., Schade, M. M., Saito, Y., Chan, A., & Buxton, O. M. (2018). Longitudinal relationship between sleep deficiency and pain symptoms among community-dwelling older adults in Japan and Singapore. *Sleep*, *42* (2). doi: 10.1093/sleep/zsy219.

Clark, D. M., & Fairburn, C. G. (Eds.). (1997). *Science and practice of cognitive behaviour therapy*. Oxford, UK: Oxford University Press.

Cleeland, C. S., & Ryan, K. M. (1994). Pain assessment: Global use of the Brief Pain Inventory. *Annals of the Academy of Medicine Singapore*, *23* (2), 129–138.

Collard, V. E. J., Moore, C., Nichols, V. P., Ellard, D. R., Patel, S., Sandhu, H. K., & Tang, N. K. Y. (2021). Challenges and visions for managing pain-related insomnia in primary care: A small-scale qualitative interview study with GPs, nurses, and practice managers. *BMC Family Practice, 22*, 210. https://doi.org/10.1186/s12875-021-01552-3.

Currie, S. R., Wilson, K. G., Pontefract, A. J., & deLaplante, L. (2000). Cognitive-behavioral treatment of insomnia secondary to chronic pain. *Journal of Consulting Clinical Psychology, 68* (3), 407–416. Retrieved from PM:10883557.

Dubrovsky, B., Raphael, K. G., Lavigne, G. J., Janal, M. N., Sirois, D. A., Wigren, P. E., & Krieger, A. C. (2014). Polysomnographic investigation of sleep and respiratory parameters in women with temporomandibular pain disorders. *Journal of Clinical Sleep Medicine, 10* (02), 195–201. doi: 10.5664/jcsm.3452.

Edinger, J. D., Wohlgemuth, W. K., Krystal, A. D., & Rice, J. R. (2005). Behavioral insomnia therapy for fibromyalgia patients: A randomized clinical trial. *Archives of Internal Medicine, 165* (21), 2527–2535. Retrieved from http://dx.doi.org/10.1001/archinte.165.21.2527.

Haack, M., & Mullington, J. M. (2005). Sustained sleep restriction reduces emotional and physical well-being. *Pain, 119* (1), 56–64.

Haack, M., Sanchez, E., & Mullington, J. M. (2007). Elevated inflammatory markers in response to prolonged sleep restriction are associated with increased pain experience in healthy volunteers. *Sleep, 30* (9), 1145.

Herrero Babiloni, A., Beetz, G., Tang, N. K. Y., Heinzer, R., Nijs, J., Martel, M. O., & Lavigne, G. J. (2021). Towards the endotyping of the sleep–pain interaction: A topical review on multitarget strategies based on phenotypic vulnerabilities and putative pathways. *PAIN, 162* (5), 1281–1288. doi: 10.1097/j.pain.0000000000002124.

International Association for the Study of Pain (2020). *Classification of chronic ain* (2nd (revised) ed.). Retrieved from: https://www.iasp-pain.org/PublicationsNews/Content.aspx?ItemNumber=1673. <AU: Publisher and location?>no other info for this

Jann, M., Kennedy, W. K., & Lopez, G. (2014). Benzodiazepines: A major component in unintentional prescription drug overdoses with opioid analgesics. *Journal of Pharmacy Practice, 27* (1), 5–16. doi: 10.1177/0897190013515001.

Jansson-Frojmark, M., Harvey, A. G., Lundh, L. G., Norell-Clarke, A., & Linton, S. J. (2011). Psychometric properties of an insomnia-specific measure of worry: The Anxiety and Preoccupation about Sleep Questionnaire. *Cognitive Behaviour Therapy, 40* (1), 65–76. doi: 10.1080/16506073.2010.538432.

Jungquist, C. R., O'Brien, C., Matteson-Rusby, S., Smith, M. T., Pigeon, W. R., Xia, Y., Lu, N., & Perlis, M. L. (2010). The efficacy of cognitive-behavioral therapy for insomnia in patients with chronic pain. *Sleep Medicine, 11* (3), 302–309. https://doi.org/10.1016/j.sleep.2009.05.018.

Lewandowski, A. S., Palermo, T. M., Motte, S. D. L., & Fu, R. (2010). Temporal daily associations between pain and sleep in adolescents with chronic pain versus healthy adolescents. *Pain, 151* (1), 220–225.

Martínez, M. P., Miró, E., Sánchez, A. I., Díaz-Piedra, C., Cáliz, R., Vlaeyen, J. W., & Buela-Casal, G. (2013). Cognitive-behavioral therapy for insomnia and sleep hygiene in fibromyalgia: A randomized controlled trial. *Journal of Behavioral Medicine*, 1–15.

McCracken, L. M., & Iverson, G. L. (2002). Disrupted sleep patterns and daily functioning in patients with chronic pain. *Pain Research and Management, 7*, 75–79.

McCracken, L. M., Williams, J. L., & Tang, N. K. Y. (2011). Psychological flexibility may reduce insomnia in persons with chronic pain: A preliminary retrospective study. *Pain Medicine, 12* (6), 904–912.

McCrae, C. S., Williams, J., Roditi, D., Anderson, R., Mundt, J. M., Miller, M. B., Curtis, A. F., Waxenburg, L. B., Staud, R., Berry, R. B., & Robinson, M. E. (2019). Cognitive behavioral treatments for insomnia and pain in adults with comorbid chronic insomnia and fibromyalgia: Clinical outcomes from the SPIN randomized controlled trial. *Sleep, 42* (3), zsy234. https://doi.org/10.1093/sleep/zsy234.

McCurry, S. M., Shortreed, S. M., Von Korff, M., Balderson, B. H., Baker, L. D., Rybarczyk, B. D., & Vitiello, M. V. (2014). Who benefits from CBT for insomnia in primary care? Important patient selection and trial design lessons from longitudinal results of the Lifestyles trial. *Sleep, 37* (2), 299–308. doi: 10.5665/sleep.3402.

Miró, E., Lupiáñez, J., Martínez, M. P., Sánchez, A. I., Díaz-Piedra, C., Guzmán, M. A., & Buela-Casal, G. (2011). Cognitive-behavioral therapy for insomnia improves attentional function in fibromyalgia syndrome: A pilot, randomized controlled trial. *Journal of Health Psychology, 16* (5), 770–782. doi: 10.1177/1359105310390544.

Morin, C. M., Kowatch, R. A., & Wade, J. B. (1989). Behavioral management of sleep disturbances secondary to chronic pain. *Journal of Behaviour Therapy in Experimental Psychiatry, 20* (4), 295–302. Retrieved from: PM:2534597.

Morin, C. M., Vallières, A., & Ivers, H. (2007). Dysfunctional beliefs and attitudes about sleep (DBAS): Validation of a brief version (DBAS-16). *Sleep, 30* (11), 1547–1554. doi:10.1093/sleep/30.11.1547.

Mork, P. J., & Nilsen, T. I. L. (2012). Sleep problems and risk of fibromyalgia: Longitudinal data on an adult female population in Norway. *Arthritis & Rheumatism*, *64* (1), 281–284. doi: 10.1002/art.33346.

Onen, S. H., Alloui, A., Gross, A., Eschallier, A., & Dubray, C. (2001). The effects of total sleep deprivation, selective sleep interruption and sleep recovery on pain tolerance thresholds in healthy subjects. *Journal of Sleep Research*, *10* (1), 35–42.

Pigeon, W. R., Moynihan, J., Matteson-Rusby, S., Jungquist, C. R., Xia, Y., Tu, X., & Perlis, M. L. (2012). Comparative effectiveness of CBT interventions for co-morbid chronic pain & insomnia: A pilot study. *Behaviour Research Therapy*, *50* (11), 685–689. doi: 10.1016/j.brat.2012.07.005.

Prados, G., Miró, E., Martínez, M. P., Sánchez, A. I., Lami, M. J., & Cáliz, R. (2020). Combined cognitive-behavioral therapy for fibromyalgia: Effects on polysomnographic parameters and perceived sleep quality. *International Journal of Clinical Health Psychology*, *20* (3), 232–242. doi: 10.1016/j.ijchp.2020.04.002.

Simpson, N. S., Scott-Sutherland, J., Gautam, S., Sethna, N., & Haack, M. (2018). Chronic exposure to insufficient sleep alters processes of pain habituation and sensitization. *Pain*, *159* (1), 33–40.

Sivertsen, B., Lallukka, T., Petrie, K. J., Steingrímsdóttir Ó, A., Stubhaug, A., & Nielsen,C. S. (2015). Sleep and pain sensitivity in adults. *Pain*, *156* (8), 1433–1439. doi: 10.1097/j.pain.0000000000000131.

Smith, M. T., Edwards, R. R., McCann, U. D., & Haythornthwaite, J. A. (2007). The effects of sleep deprivation on pain inhibition and spontaneous pain in women. *Sleep*, *30* (4), 494–505. Retrieved from: PM:17520794.

Smith, M. T., & Perlis, M. L. (2006). Who is a candidate for cognitive-behavioral therapy for insomnia? *Health Psychology*, *25* (1), 15–19. doi: 10.1037/0278-6133.25.1.15.

Tang, N. K. Y., Goodchild, C. E., & Salkovskis, P. M. (2012). Hybrid cognitive-behaviour therapy for individuals with insomnia and chronic pain: A pilot randomised controlled trial. *Behaviour Research and Therapy*, *50* (12), 814–821. doi: 10.1016/j.brat.2012.08.006.

Tang, N. K. Y., Goodchild, C. E., Sanborn, A. N., Howard, J., & Salkovskis, P. M. (2012). Deciphering the temporal link between pain and sleep in a heterogeneous chronic pain patient sample: A multilevel daily process study. *Sleep*, *35* (5), 675–687.

Tang, N. K. Y., & Harvey, A. G. (2004). Correcting distorted perception of sleep in insomnia: A novel behavioural experiment? *Behaviour Research and Therapy*, *42* (1), 27–39. doi: 10.1016/s0005-7967(03)00068-8.

Tang, N. K. Y., & Sanborn, A. N. (2014). Better quality sleep promotes daytime physical activity in patients with chronic pain? A multilevel analysis of the within-person relationship. *PLoS One*, *9* (3), e92158.

Tang, N. K. Y., Stella, M. T., Banks, P. D., Sandhu, H. K., & Berna, C. (2019). The effect of opioid therapy on sleep quality in patients with chronic non-malignant pain: A systematic review and exploratory meta-analysis. *Sleep Medicine Reviews*, *45*, 105–126. https://doi.org/10.1016/j.smrv.2019.03.005.

Tang, N. K. Y., Wright, K. J., & Salkovskis, P. M. (2007). Prevalence and correlates of clinical insomnia co-occurring with chronic back pain. *Journal of Sleep Research*, *16* (1), 85–95.

Tang, N. K. Y., Lereya, S. T., Boulton, H., Miller, M. A., Wolke, D., & Cappuccio, F. P. (2015). Nonpharmacological treatments of insomnia for long-term painful conditions: A systematic review and meta-analysis of patient-reported outcomes in randomized controlled trials. *Sleep*, *38* (11), 1751–1764. doi: 10.5665/sleep.5158.

Tang, N. K. Y., Moore, C., Parsons, H., Sandhu, H. K., Patel, S., Ellard, D. R., Nicols, V. P., Madan, J., Collard, V. E. J., Sharma, U., & Underwood, M. (2020). Implementing a hybrid cognitive-behavioural therapy for pain-related insomnia in primary care: Lessons learnt from a mixed-methods feasibility study. *BMJ Open*, *10* (3), e034764. doi: 10.1136/bmjopen-2019-034764.

Theadom, A., & Cropley, M. (2008). Dysfunctional beliefs, stress and sleep disturbance in fibromyalgia. *Sleep Medicine*, *9*, 376–381.

Theadom, A., Cropley, M., & Kantermann, T. (2015). Daytime napping associated with increased symptom severity in fibromyalgia syndrome. *BMC Musculoskeleton Disorder*, *16*, 13. doi: 10.1186/s12891-015-0464-y.

Turk, D. C., Dworkin, R. H., Allen, R. R., Bellamy, N., Brandenburg, N., Carr, D. B., Cleeland, C., Dionne, R., Farrer, J. T., Galer, B. S., Hewitt, D. J., Jadad, A. R., Katz, N. P., Kramer, L. D., Manning, D. C., McCormick, C. G., McDermott, M. P., McGrath, P., Quessy, S., Rappaport, B. A., & Witter, J. (2003). Core outcome domains for chronic pain clinical trials: IMMPACT recommendations. *Pain*, *106*, 337–345. https://doi.org/10.1016/j.pain.2003.08.001.

Turk, D. C., Dworkin, R. H., Revicki, D., Harding, G., Burke, L. B., Cella, D., Cleeland, C. S., Cowen, P., Farrer, J. T., Hertz, S., Max, M. B., & Rappaport, B. A. (2008). Identifying important outcome domains for chronic pain clinical trials: An IMMPACT survey of people with pain. *Pain*, *137* (2), 276–285. doi: http://dx.doi.org/10.1016/j.pain.2007.09.002.

Vitiello, M. V., McCurry, S. M., Shortreed, S. M., Balderson, B. H., Baker, L. D., Keefe, F. J., Rybarczyk, B. D., & Korff, M. (2013). Cognitive-behavioral treatment for comorbid insomnia and osteoarthritis pain in primary care: The Lifestyles Randomized Controlled Trial. *Journal of the American Geriatrics Society, 61* (6), 947–956. https://doi.org/10.1111/jgs.12275.

Vitiello, M. V., McCurry, S. M., Shortreed, S. M., Baker, L. D., Rybarczyk, B. D., Keefe, F. J., & Von Korff, M. (2014). Short-term improvement in insomnia symptoms predicts long-term improvements in sleep, pain, and fatigue in older adults with comorbid osteoarthritis and insomnia. *Pain, 155* (8), 1547–1554. doi: 10.1016/j.pain.2014.04.032.

Volkow, N. D., & McLellan, A. T. (2016). Opioid abuse in chronic pain – Misconceptions and mitigation strategies. *New England Journal of Medicine, 374* (13), 1253–1263. doi: 10.1056/NEJMra1507771.

Whibley, D., AlKandari, N., Kristensen, K., Barnish, M., Rzewuska, M., Druce, K. L., & Tang, N. K. Y. (2019). Sleep and pain: A systematic review of studies of mediation. *The Clinical Journal of Pain, 35* (6), 544–558. doi: 10.1097/AJP.0000000000000697.

16

CBT for Insomnia Co-morbid with Other Sleep Disorders

Laura Palagini and Chiara Baglioni

Key points

- Insomnia and other sleep disorders are frequently co-morbid.
- Data indicate that insomnia is often underdiagnosed and undertreated in other sleep disorders.
- Emergent empirical evidences support the use of CBT-I when insomnia is co-morbid with other sleep disorders.
- Specific clinical protocols for insomnia co-morbid with others sleep disorders are provided.

Learning objectives

- To understand clinical aspects of insomnia considering other sleep disorders.
- To understand the scientific and clinical importance of offering treatment for insomnia when insomnia is co-morbid to other sleep disorders.
- To learn CBT-I protocol adaptations for specific sleep disorders.

Abstract

Poor sleep and insomnia are important factors influencing the quality of life of patients with other sleep disorders. Patients suffering from co-morbid insomnia experience the additive detrimental night-time and day-time symptoms of each disorder with greater impairments to day-time functioning and quality of life. Implementing CBT-I adaptations in the treatment of insomnia in patients with other sleep disorders is a priority. To this end, this chapter aims at providing clinical guidelines for professionals for offering high quality CBT for insomnia to patients suffering for other sleep disorders such as sleep apnoea, narcolepsy, parasomnia, sleep–wake schedule disorders and restless legs syndrome.

Keywords *CBT-I, insomnia, sleep apnoea, narcolepsy, parasomnia, sleep–wake schedule disorders, restless legs syndrome*

Insomnia and sleep apnoea: Specific theoretical issues

Obstructive sleep apnoea (OSA) is one of the most common sleep disorders, found in approximately 10% of the general population and characterized by repetitive brief obstruction (apnoea) or narrowing (hypopnea) of the upper airway during sleep (American Academy of Sleep Medicine (AASM), 2014). It is associated with feelings of non-restorative sleep, day-time sleepiness and fatigue, reduced quality of life and increased risk of cardiovascular disease and motor vehicle accidents (AASM, 2014). Several publications have addressed the co-occurrence of chronic insomnia disorder and OSA (co-morbid insomnia and sleep apnoea, COMISA) (Sweetman et al., 2019; Zhang et al., 2019; Ong, Crawford &

Cognitive-Behavioural Therapy for Insomnia (CBT-I) Across the Life Span: Guidelines and Clinical Protocols for Health Professionals,
First Edition. Edited by Chiara Baglioni, Colin A. Espie and Dieter Riemann.

Wallace, 2020). In a recent systematic review and meta-analysis, Zhang et al. (2019) evaluated the prevalence of insomnia and insomnia symptoms co-presenting with OSA. A total of 37 studies was included in their analysis. In OSA patients, high rates were found for overall prevalence of insomnia (38%), any insomnia complaints (36%), difficulty falling asleep (18%), difficulty maintaining sleep (42%) and early morning awakenings (21%). Findings suggest that OSA and insomnia mutually overlap in approximately one-third of cases. Patients suffering from COMISA experience the additive detrimental night-time and day-time symptoms of each disorder (Sweetman et al., 2019; Ong et al., 2020).

Importantly, COMISA patients experience greater impairments to day-time functioning and quality of life, compared to those with either insomnia, or OSA alone. COMISA patients express greater emotional and cognitive impairments, including irritability, reduced concentration, depressive symptoms and anxiety. A large number of studies indicated an additive and substantial impairment to sleep, day-time functioning, depressive and psychiatric symptoms and quality of life among COMISA patients (Sweetman et al., 2019; Ong et al., 2020).

Recommended treatment for moderate and severe OSA is continuous positive airway pressure (CPAP) therapy (AASM, 2014). Although CPAP effectively stabilizes the upper airway and improves clinical manifestations of OSA, patient acceptance and long-term adherence to CPAP remains a significant barrier to treatment. Importantly, recent research indicates that OSA patients with co-morbid insomnia are less likely to accept and use CPAP therapy compared to OSA patients without insomnia (Sweetman et al., 2019; Janssen, Venekamp, Peeters, Pijpers & Pevernagli, 2019; Ong et al., 2020).

A mutual reinforcement of negative effects, a 'positive feedback loop', may occur when OSA and insomnia are both present. Repeated obstructive respiratory events are associated with cortical arousals from sleep, hence precipitating insomnia. These short sleep interruptions may be perceived as awakenings and some patients may develop dysfunctional beliefs about sleep and expand the time in bed to compensate for day-time sleepiness, contributing to perpetuate insomnia (Janssen et al., 2019; Sweetman et al., 2019; Ong et al., 2020). It is also possible that among COMISA patients, post-apnoeic awakenings are also associated with sleep-state misperceptions, culminating in perceptions of prolonged time to fall asleep initially or prolonged awakenings during the night and thus an insomnia complaint (Sweetman et al., 2019). Patients may take periods of rest during day-time and increase caffeine intake. Such measures to alleviate day-time somnolence may contribute to perpetuate insomnia (Janssen et al., 2019; Ong et al., 2020). In addition, apnoea-induced arousals that are associated with sensations of breathlessness may promote anxiety, which in turn may prime cognitive processes towards increased alertness.

On the other hand, insomnia may contribute to OSA. In particular, frequent awakenings and subsequent transitions to sleep invariably invoke withdrawal of the wakefulness stimulus, which causes breathing instability and predisposes to upper airway obstruction (Janssen et al., 2019). Insomnia disorder may be associated with a reduced respiratory arousal threshold, which may predispose patients to prematurely awaken to respiratory events. In addition, it is possible that multiple consecutive or intermittent nights of partial sleep loss experienced by patients with chronic insomnia may contribute to the development or exacerbation of OSA by reducing upper-airway muscle tone (Janssen et al., 2019; Sweetman et al., 2019; Ong et al., 2020). Therefore, medical specialists are faced with difficult diagnostic and treatment decisions, and typically effective treatments for each disorder are impaired.

Evidence for CBT-I in insomnia co-morbid with sleep apnoea

Preliminary evidence suggests that CBT-I is an effective treatment for insomnia in the presence of co-morbid OSA. CBT-I resulted in durable improvements in insomnia symptoms, sleep parameters, day-time symptoms and promotes a 15% decrease in OSA severity. In addition, CBT-I allows COMISA patients to initiate and maintain sleep while wearing CPAP, and thus increased CPAP acceptance and long-term use. Therefore, several research groups have suggested that COMISA patients' insomnia should be treated initially, to increase subsequent acceptance and use of CPAP therapy (Janssen et al., 2019; Sweetman et al., 2019; Ong et al., 2020). Several studies have provided support for CBT-I delivered by trained therapists compared to self-administered (bibliotherapy) CBT-I materials for COMISA patients.

A first pilot study was conducted in 2004 (Krakow et al., 2004) in 19 COMISA patients, finding that improvements in self-reported insomnia indices were related to improvement of CPAP therapy compliance. Treatment studies that targeted both insomnia and OSA were associated with improvements in insomnia symptoms, day-time functioning, sleep quality and total sleep time. Another study was conducted in 30 patients with complaints of insomnia and mild OSA and tested sequences of CBT-I before or after ear/nose/throat surgery. Using a prospective crossover design, Guilleminault and colleagues (Guilleminault, Davis and Huynh, 2008) revealed that the optimal pathway for improving objective and subjective measures of sleep involved surgical intervention for OSA followed by CBT-I. Although these two studies provided preliminary evidence to support the use of CBT-I in combination with established OSA treatment, patient-centred issues related to education about treatment pathways and acceptability of a multidisciplinary approach were not reported. Another randomized controlled study was conducted in 140 patients with chronic insomnia and OSA (Crawford, Turner, Wyatt, Fogg & Ong, 2016). Participants were randomized to receive sequential treatment beginning with CBT-I followed by CPAP, or CBT-I and CPAP administered concurrently. These treatment arms were compared to a control condition, treatment where individuals received CPAP alone. CBT-I treatment consisted in four weekly CBT-I sessions. Standard CBT-I protocol in this study was reduced to four individual sessions including stimulus control, sleep restriction, sleep hygiene education and cognitive therapy to minimize the delay prior to CPAP and allowed to discuss instructions for OSA treatments. Since transient day-time sleepiness and lapses in attention/vigilance were considered potential adverse events related to CBT-I and to sleep restriction, weekly sleepiness ratings and other adverse events have been reviewed to ensure patient safety. Findings provided evidence of clinical benefits of treating insomnia disorder in the context of OSA and sequential treatment beginning with CBT-I followed by CPAP to be the most effective (Crawford et al., 2016). Ong et al. (2017) used a mixed-methods approach to examine clinical and patient-centred measures for 34 patients who received positive-airway pressure and/or cognitive-behaviour therapy for insomnia. Results revealed baseline-to-follow-up improvements on several self-reported sleep parameters and measures of day-time functioning. Qualitative analyses from patient interviews revealed three themes: importance of conceptual distinctions about each sleep disorder, importance of treating both sleep disorders and benefits of sequential treatment beginning with CBT-I followed by CPAP.

Bjorvatn and colleagues recently reported an RCT in which 134 COMISA patients were randomized to receive either a self-help CBT-I book or sleep hygiene information while commencing CPAP therapy (Bjorvatn, Berge, Lehmann, Pallesen & Saxvig, 2018). Although both CBT-I book and sleep hygiene control groups reported significant improvement of insomnia symptoms from pre- to post-treatment there was no difference in improvements between groups. Similarly, there were also no differences in objective CPAP adherence over the first three months of treatment between groups (2.54 hours, versus 2.55 hours in the sleep hygiene and CBT-I book groups respectively). This lack of differences in insomnia and CPAP outcomes may be due to this sample reflecting patients primarily recruited for management of OSA, who were potentially less motivated to read and adhere to the instructions of the CBT-I book. Indeed, 22% of the COMISA patients reported that they did not read the CBT-I material, compared to only 5% of insomnia patients investigated in the previous RCT. As the CBT-I book and CPAP were commenced concurrently, it is also possible that patients derived sufficient benefit from CPAP alone, and did not perceive a need to utilize the CBT-I intervention.

Alessi and colleagues (2018) recently reported preliminary results of an RCT comparing the effect of five sessions of a combined CBT-I and behavioural CPAP adherence program delivered by trained 'sleep coaches', versus a sleep education control program, on insomnia improvement and CPAP use with a six month follow-up. The CBT-I/adherence intervention was delivered concurrently with CPAP therapy. Authors recruited 125 adult veterans with insomnia and moderate and severe OSA. Compared to sleep education control, the CBT-I group showed greater improvement of diary- and actigraphy-measured sleep parameters, greater ISI reduction and 78 to 48 minutes of greater adherence to CPAP therapy at the three- and six-months follow-up respectively. Together, these recent larger RCTs provided tentative support for the effect of therapist-administered CBT-I in improving insomnia symptoms and increasing subsequent use of CPAP therapy in COMISA patients. It appears that CBT-I delivered by trained therapists may be more effective than self-administered (bibliotherapy) CBT-I materials for COMISA patients.

Another randomized controlled trial in participants with OSA and co-occurring insomnia was conducted with 145 patients who were randomized to either four sessions of CBT-I or treatment as usual before commencing CPAP therapy until six months post-randomization. A manualised CBT-I programme including sleep-hygiene education, bed-time restriction therapy, sleep misperception feedback, cognitive therapy and relapse prevention was delivered by seven experienced psychologists during 4/45-minute sessions administered over a six-week period. The CBT-I group showed greater improvement of global insomnia severity, and dysfunctional sleep-related cognitions by 6 months, and greater improvement in sleep impairment measures immediately following CBT-I. The authors concluded that in COMISA participants, CBT-I prior to initiating CPAP treatment improves CPAP use and insomnia symptoms compared to commencing CPAP without CBT-I (Sweetman et al., 2019). The same group conducted a study involving 145 patients with untreated physician-diagnosed OSA and insomnia. Patients were randomized to a four-week CBT-I program (n = 72) or no-treatment control (n = 73). There were no differences in changes in day-time sleepiness during treatment between CBT-I and control groups or OSA-severity groups. CBT-I appears to be a safe and effective treatment in the presence of co-morbid moderate and severe OSA. Nevertheless, patients living with co-morbid insomnia and sleep apnoea and treated with CBT-I should be monitored closely for increased day-time sleepiness during the initial weeks of bed-time restriction therapy (Sweetman et al., 2020). Another study conducted by the same group showed that CBT-I consolidates sleep periods and promotes a 15% decrease in OSA severity in patients with co-morbid insomnia and OSA (Sweetman et al., 2019). In another study, 121 COMISA patients were randomized to receive CBT-I followed by CPAP, CBT-I concurrent with CPAP or CPAP only. Findings from this study indicated that combining CBT-I with CPAP was superior to CPAP alone on insomnia outcomes (Ong et al., 2020).

In another study, the Apnea and Insomnia Research (AIR) Trial (Edinger et al., 2021), 276 patients were randomized to either a fully digital, online version of Cognitive Behavioral Insomnia Therapy (CBT-I) or no additional treatment beyond their CPAP therapy (CTRL). After eight weeks of treatment all patients were reassessed. Those receiving online CBT-I showed greater reductions in their insomnia symptoms from the baseline to the end of the initial eight-week treatment phase than did those in the CTRL group ($p = 0.0001$) and moved from moderately severe insomnia to mild insomnia symptoms. In contrast, no differences were noted between the online CBT-I and CTRL groups in regard to pre- to post-treatment changes on day-time sleepiness or amount of CPAP use. Authors concluded that whereas online CBT-I does not seem to reduce day-time sleepiness or improve CPAP adherence among patients with co-morbid sleep apnea and insomnia, it appears to be an effective intervention for reducing insomnia severity for this patient group.

CBT-I adaptations for insomnia co-morbid with sleep apnoea

Insomnia in COMISA patients can be treated using standard protocol (Chapter 2), and following general principles of the stepped care model (Section V; see Chapter 23, Figure 23.1). Several research groups have suggested that COMISA patients' insomnia should be treated initially, to increase subsequent acceptance and use of CPAP therapy and that CBT-I delivered by trained therapists may be more effective than self-administered CBT-I materials for COMISA patients. Nevertheless, standard CBT-I protocol in some studies was reduced to four individual sessions including stimulus control, sleep restriction, sleep hygiene education and cognitive therapy to minimize the delay prior to CPAP and enable discussion of OSA treatments. CBT-I interventions administered generally have included multifaceted approaches to target insomnia and some intervention included weekly sleepiness ratings to address patients' excessive day-time sleepiness and others included interventions to address sleep misperception. Other studies used a combination of CBT-I components and CPAP-adherence strategies to simultaneously improve insomnia and encourage greater CPAP outcomes. Since motivational interviewing and educational strategies have been shown to be effective in improving CPAP acceptance and use, this combined strategy may prove to be the most effective for COMISA patients treated in clinical settings (Sweetman et al., 2019). These modifications can be summarized as follows:

- Standard CBT-I protocol should be reduced to four individual sessions to minimize the delay prior to CPAP.
- Sleep psychoeducation should be adapted to COMISA (Table 16.1).

Table 16.1 Sleep psychoeducation for co-morbid insomnia and sleep apnea patients (COMISA).

What is OSA? What is insomnia?	**Discuss the insomnia model, discuss OSA and introduce its treatment**
OSA and insomnia	Discuss OSA and insomnia overlap and the additive night-time and day-time symptoms of each disorder. Discuss OSA as a precipitating factor for insomnia and perpetuating factors that may intervene (extension of time in bed, caffeine intake and other measures to alleviate day-time somnolence, sleep-state misperceptions or cognitive factors, anxiety related to the sensations of breathlessness)
Consequences of their association	Discuss the mutual reinforcement occurring when OSA and insomnia are both present and their consequences on mental and physical health
Sleep hygiene	Healthy eating, regular and well-balanced physical activity, and healthy sleep interact dynamically. In particular discuss caffeine intake, and of other behaviours that may be used to alleviate day-time somnolence related to OSA and insomnia

Table 16.2 Suggested four-week CBT-I programme for COMISA patients.

First session	Psychoeducation adapted to COMISA patients
Second session	Sleep restriction therapy (SRT) and Stimulus Control (SC) modified, weekly discussion about day-time sleepiness
Third session	Cognitive therapy and/or sleep misperception techniques (e.g., discuss time estimation ability and ability to perceive sleep, differences between objective/subjective measures of sleep obtained, differences in arousal levels across different sleep stages and stage sleep transition, discuss sleep inertia)
Fourth session	Sleep hygiene education – particularly measures to alleviate day-time somnolence
Fifth session	Conclusion and prevention of relapses, discussion of CPAP-adherence strategies

- Sleep restriction therapy (SRT) should be modified to reduce excessive related increase in day-time sleepiness in COMISA patients (e.g., by adding 30 minutes: SRT + 30 minutes or 6 hours at least. Some authors suggest the use of SRT with limited time in bed ≥ 6 hours). Otherwise, day-time sleepiness should be monitored, discussed and addressed weekly.
- Sleep misperception strategies might be included in the protocol (Table 16.2).
- CPAP-adherence strategies, in particular motivational interviewing and educational strategies, might be discussed at the end of CBT-I protocol.

Conclusion

CBT-I for co-morbid insomnia and sleep apnoea patients has important benefits including improvement of insomnia symptoms, sleep parameters, day-time symptoms and OSA severity. In addition, CBT-I may allow COMISA patients to initiate and maintain sleep while wearing CPAP, and thus increased CPAP acceptance and long-term use. In Table 16.2 a possible five sessions of CBT-I intervention for COMISA patients is proposed.

Sleep–wake schedule disorders: Specific theoretical issues

Sleep–wake schedule disorders share the common feature of a disruption in the timing of sleep (American Psychiatric Association (APA), 2013). The circadian system is a hierarchical organization of endogenous, oscillating clocks throughout the body that are regulated by the supra-chiasmatic nuclei (SCN), located in the hypothalamus. The endogenous circadian rhythm is synchronized or entrained to the 24-hour rhythm of the external environments daily by synchronizing agents, including light, physical activity, social behaviours and melatonin. Either disruption of the endogenous circadian control mechanism or misalignment between internal circadian rhythms with the 24-hour outside environment could result in circadian rhythm disorders with adverse consequences on sleep as well on several other aspects of human health (Foster, 2020; Geoffroy & Palagini, 2021). The sleep–wake cycle is regulated by a complex interaction between the homeostatic process, such as a drive for sleep that builds up during wakefulness and declines during sleep and the circadian process. Therefore, proper alignment between homeostatic and circadian processes is critical for optimal sleep quality and performance. Sleep–wake schedule disorders arise from a chronic or recurrent pattern of sleep and wake disturbance that is due to dysfunction of the circadian clock system, such as delayed sleep phase disorder, advanced sleep phase disorder, irregular sleep–wake rhythm and free-running disorder, or misalignment between timing of the endogenous circadian rhythm and externally imposed social and work cycles, such as, for example, jet lag and shift work disorder (APA, 2013; Wilson et al., 2019). Patients with sleep–wake schedule disorders commonly present with symptoms of insomnia and/or excessive sleepiness and severity of impairment in day-time functioning. Insomnia is particularly frequent in delayed, irregular and shift work sleep–wake schedule disorders: sleep–wake schedule disorders may act as predisposing, precipitating and perpetuating factors for insomnia. Insomnia and sleep–wake schedule disorder are frequently co-morbid conditions in special populations, such as adolescence and patients with mental disorders (see Sections II and III).

In addition, circadian sleep disorders and insomnia are very common in the working population with negative day-time consequences such as work-related stress, health complaints and impaired work performance (Wickwire, Geiger-Brown,

Scharf & Drake, 2017; Kerkhof, 2018). Shift workers' irregular sleep–wake patterns are a challenge in the screening and treatment of insomnia and it may be difficult to distinguish between insomnia disorder and shift work disorder (see Chapter 9).

The management of sleep–wake schedule disorders is a particular challenge and requires a combined approach comprising chronotherapies that include behavioural techniques, manipulation of light/dark exposure with timed bright light therapy and pharmacological agents such as exogenous melatonin (Wilson et al., 2019; see also Chapter 10). The behavioural approach, following sleep hygiene rules, encourages changes to improve sleep and to develop good sleep habits for maintaining regular sleep–wake times, avoiding naps and developing a regular routine. Good sleep hygiene practices are considered a critical step in any sleep treatment approach, indeed compared to CBT-I, there is also little evidence that sleep hygiene education alone is effective in the treatment of insomnia (Morin et al., 2015; Riemann et al., 2017). Hence in populations with circadian sleep disorders a structured approach for insomnia treatment is often needed and some CBT-I protocol adaptations have been developed. CBTI in the workplace has been already applied with positive effect, not only on insomnia but also on workers' health, productivity, presenteeism and job burnout (Vega-Escaño et al., 2020).

Evidence CBT-I for insomnia co-morbid with sleep–wake schedule disorders

Evidence suggests that CBT-I is an effective treatment for insomnia in the presence of delayed sleep phases and irregular sleep phases in special populations such as adolescents, patients with affective disorders, dementia and shift workers (see Sections II and III).

CBT-I protocol adaptations for insomnia co-morbid with sleep–wake schedule disorders

Insomnia co-morbid with sleep–wake schedule disorder and insomnia can be treated using the standard protocol (Chapter 2) and following general principles of the stepped care model (Section VI). Nevertheless, the standard CBT-I protocol has typically been modified in studies including insomnia patients with co-morbid sleep–wake schedule disorders. These modifications can be summarized as follows:

1) The standard CBT-I protocol should be reduced to 4–6 sessions to favour the implementation of chronotherapies and could be administered via group interventions, self-help approaches or through internet-based CBT-I. This is because the sleep co-morbidity may be harder to treat, and in order to implement more complex protocols for the different elements, CBT-I should be kept brief and reduced to a more limited number of sessions.
2) The CBT-I protocol for insomnia should be implemented along with bright light therapy and/or melatonin supplementation as chronotherapies to regularize dark/light exposition based on circadian principles (Table 16.3).
3) Sleep psychoeducation and sleep hygiene should include circadian principles relevant to a sleep–wake schedule disorder.

Conclusion

CBT-I for co-morbid insomnia and sleep–wake schedule disorder patients has important benefits including improvement of insomnia symptoms, sleep parameters, day-time symptoms, mood and stress symptoms. In Table 16.3 a possible 5–6 sessions of CBT-I intervention for patients with insomnia and sleep–wake schedule disorders is proposed.

Parasomnias: Specific theoretical issues

Parasomnias are a group of sleep disorders defined as undesirable physical events or experiences that occur during the initiation of sleep, during sleep or during arousal from sleep (AASM, 2014). Although they are more common in children, parasomnias can occur at any age. When they occur during adulthood, they are particularly related to impaired sleep quality, day-time dysfunction, and occasionally with violent and harmful nocturnal behaviours (Ntafouli, Galbiati, Gazea, Bassetti & Bargiotas, 2020). Parasomnias are disorders of arousal from NREM sleep or from REM sleep. These disorders are presumed to be triggered by sleep deprivation or sleep fragmentation related to pain, other sleep disorders including insomnia, febrile illness, sedating/antidepressant medications and alcohol (AASM, 2014). Vice versa, parasomnias may precipitate and contribute to insomnia perpetuation. NREM parasomnias are classified on the basis of the behaviours

Table 16.3 Suggested 5–6-week CBT-I programme for patients with insomnia co-morbid with sleep–wake schedule disorder.

	Sleep–wake schedule disorder
First session	Psychoeducation adapted, including circadian sleep regulation and light/dark exposure, introduction to bright light therapy
Second session	SRT and SC modified to reschedule sleep time based on circadian principles, combine with bright light therapy and/or melatonin supplementation, regulate/reschedule exposure to dark/light
Third session	Cognitive therapy
Fourth session	Sleep hygiene education including circadian rhythm regulation
Fifth session	Conclusion and relapse prevention plan
Bright light therapy, Melatonin supplementation, Behavioural approach based on circadian principles	**Delayed Sleep Phase Type**: Delayed bed time and wake times. Bed time: 2–6 a.m.; Wake time: 10 a.m.–1 p.m. Bright light: 1–3 hours of 2000–10,000 or 30 min 10.000 lux between 7 and 9 a.m. Melatonin: 0.3–3 mg 5 hours before bed timeChronotherapy: progressively advance bed times
	Advanced Sleep Phase Type: Advanced bed time and wake times. Bed time: 6–9 p.m.; Wake time: 2–5 a.m. Bright light: 1–3 hours of 2000–10,000 lux or 30 min 10.000 lux between 7 and 9 p.m. Chronotherapy: progressively advance bed times Melatonin: 0.3–0.5 mg between 7 and 9 a.m. Chronotherapy: progressively delay bed times
	Irregular sleep–wake Type: No regular bed times or wake times Frequent short naps throughout the day and nightBright light: 2 hours of 3000 to 5000 lux in the morning Decrease exposure to light and noise during the night Structured activity: increase physical and social activity during the day

displayed by the patient during the episode and include confusional arousals, sleep terrors, sleep-related eating disorders and sleepwalking. The general criteria for these disorders of arousal include: (a) recurrent episodes of incomplete awakening, (b) absent or inappropriate responsiveness, (c) limited or no cognition of dream report and (d) partial or complete amnesia for the episode. Two main REM parasomnias are recognized: nightmare disorder and REM sleep behaviour disorder (RBD), which are the most frequent parasomnia in adults. In particular, nightmares are defined as disturbing mental experiences that often awaken the sleeper from REM sleep. The experience generated internally by the dreamer seems real and vivid and can cause a wide range of negatively toned experiences including anxiety, fear or terror that may result in somatic manifestations like tachycardia, sweating and tachypnoea. Nightmares represent the most common parasomnia in adults and is frequently associated with insomnia and with mental disorders, especially Post-traumatic Stress Disorder (PTSD). Nightmares are also present in major depression, and they pose an independent risk to suicidality. REM sleep behaviour disorder (RBD) is a parasomnia characterized by the absence of sleep atonia during REM sleep and acting out of dreams, leading to injurious or potentially dangerous behaviours to the patients or bedmates. RBD can occur in a chronic as well as acute form. Acute forms are connected mainly with withdrawal states from sedative-hypnotic agents and alcohol and some serotonergic antidepressants are known to cause RBD. Few studies concern the treatment of these conditions, and most of these studies are uncontrolled and based mainly on case reports. Pharmacological treatments are available for these disorders, but evidence of their efficacy is variable. Consequently, behavioural and cognitive-behavioural treatments of sleep disorders have received growing attention in the last decades. However, evidence-based approaches are limited (Ntafouli et al., 2020).

For NREM parasomnia, behavioural methods include treatments for addressing predisposing factors, such as other sleep disorders including insomnia, and addressing triggering factors, which include regulating the sleep pattern to reduce the number of arousals and promote sleep continuity (Ntafouli et al., 2020). Psychoeducation about sleep, about how to avoid sleep deprivation and maintain good sleep hygiene, scheduled awakening and relaxation therapy have been used for this purpose in parasomnia treatment. Education about ensuring environmental safety is another fundamental intervention for parasomnia. There are several behavioural and cognitive-behavioural techniques for the treatment of nightmares in the literature, including imagery rehearsal therapy (IRT). In IRT the patient is asked to modify the plot of the recurring nightmare during wakefulness by verbal or written means, with a new self-made script in which the unpleasant part and/or the ending of the nightmare is replaced with a more pleasant one. Exposure techniques consist of gradually exposing the patient to the source of the negative component of the nightmare during wakefulness, and in safe surroundings. Exposure, relaxation and rescripting therapy (ERRT) includes different types of intervention, such as psychoeducation, sleep hygiene, progressive muscle relaxation and rescripting the nightmare as exposures are combined together. Lucid dreaming therapy (LDT) is a restructuring cognitive technique. The patient is taught to become lucid in his or her nightmare through daily exercises. Consequently, he or she will be able to perform actions during the nightmare that will modify its storyline. At the moment IRT is the approach that is recommended for the treatment of nightmares in adults.

CBT-I protocol adaptations for insomnia co-morbid with parasomnia

Insomnia co-morbid with parasomnias can be treated using the standard protocol (Chapter 2) and following general principles of the stepped care model (Section V). Behavioural methods used in the treatment of parasomnias, which include regulating the sleep pattern to reduce the number of arousals and to promote sleep continuity, psychoeducation about sleep and to avoid sleep deprivation and to keep a correct sleep hygiene, and relaxation therapy, are key components of CBT-I protocols. Nevertheless, psychoeducation about sleep and sleep hygiene should be adapted to patients with parasomnia and sleep restriction and stimulus control should be modified in order to avoid sleep deprivation. When nightmares are present standard CBT-I protocols should be implemented with imagery rehearsal therapy (IRT). These proposed modifications to the standard CBT-I protocols in patients with parasomnia can be summarized as follows:

1) Sleep psychoeducation and sleep hygiene should be adapted to parasomnias (Table 16.4).
2) SRT and stimulus control (SC) should be modified allowing extra time in bed (e.g., adding 30 minutes: SRT + 30 minutes or 6 hours at least; some authors suggest SRT with a minimal time in bed ≥ 6 hours or using sleep compression) in order to regulate the sleep pattern, to reduce the number of arousals, to promote sleep continuity and to avoid sleep deprivation.
3) Relaxation strategies should be included in the CBT-I protocol.
4) When nightmares are present CBT-I protocols should be implemented with imagery rehearsal therapy (IRT) (Table 16.5).

Table 16.4 Sleep psychoeducation for insomnia co-morbid with parasomnia.

Parasomnia and Insomnia	Discuss parasomnia models and their role as predisposing/precipitating factors. Discuss insomnia models.
Consequences of their association	Discuss the mutual reinforcement occurring when these sleep disorders are present at the same time.
Sleep hygiene	Healthy eating, regular and well-balanced physical activity and healthy sleep are dynamically interrelated. Reschedule sleep time in order to avoid sleep deprivation, discuss how to avoid precipitating factors for parsomnia. Discuss how to manage environmental safety

Table 16.5 Suggested 6 week of CBT-I programme for patients with insomnia co-morbid with parasomnia.

First session	Psychoeducation adapted to parasomnia including how to ensure environmental safety, for nightmares discuss models and use nightmare diary (psychoeducation about nightmares)
Second session	SRT and SC modified to reschedule sleep time in order to reduce the number of arousals, promote sleep continuity and avoid sleep deprivation
Third session	Sleep hygiene education adapted to parasomnia and to precipitating factors
Fourth session	Relaxation techniques
Fifth session	Cognitive therapy and/or imagery rehearsal therapy (IRT) if nightmares are present IRT comprises review of nightmare diaries, pleasant imagery practice, rewriting of the dream with a new scenario, imagery rehearsal of the dream with new scenario
Sixth session	Conclusion and prevention of relapses

Conclusion

Behavioural methods used in the treatment of parasomnia are key components of CBT-I protocols. Nevertheless, some CBT-I protocol adaptations may be necessary for treating insomnia co-morbid with parasomnia. In Table 16.5 a possible six sessions CBT-I adapted protocol is proposed.

Restless legs syndrome: Specific theoretical issues

Restless legs syndrome (RLS) is a common neurological sensorimotor disorder characterized by an urge to move the legs during periods of rest or inactivity (AASM, 2014). The International Restless Legs Syndrome Study Group (IRLSSG) (Allen et al., 2014) has described four mandatory clinical features to establish the diagnosis of RLS, namely: (i) an urge to move the legs, usually accompanied or caused by uncomfortable and unpleasant sensations in the legs; (ii) these symptoms begin or worsen during periods of rest or inactivity, such as lying or sitting; (iii) they are partially or totally relieved by movement; and (iv) they are worse in the evening or night-time. Between 5 and 15% of the adult population may have RLS and from 11 to 29% of pregnant women are affected. RLS can be secondary as well as primary. Secondary RLS can arise from aetiologies such as peripheral neuropathy, end-stage renal disease and iron deficiency (e.g., during pregnancy). RLS may precipitate and perpetuate insomnia; hence the two disorders are frequently co-morbid. Pharmacological treatments are considered as the first line approach but *behavioural interventions* may provide relief in persons with mild to moderate symptoms of RLS. These interventions include avoiding or decreasing the use of alcohol and tobacco, or drugs that may exacerbate symptoms, such as antidepressants, antipsychotics, dopamine-blocking antiemetics and centrally acting antihistamines, changing or maintaining a regular sleep pattern, programmes of moderate exercise or gentle activities like yoga, cycling and swimming. Indications for temporary relief include massaging the legs, taking a warm bath or using a heating pad or ice pack. Relaxation, aerobic and leg-stretching exercises to relax muscles are suggested and may provide some relief from mild symptoms.

CBT-I protocol adaptation for insomnia co-morbid with restless legs syndrome

No specific CBT-I protocol adaptations have been developed for insomnia co-morbid with RLS; hence insomnia can be treated using the standard protocol (Chapter 2) and following general principles of the stepped care model (Section V). Indeed, behavioural methods used in alleviating RLS symptoms, which include regulating the sleep pattern, maintaining good sleep hygiene and the use of relaxation techniques are key components of CBT-I protocols. Nevertheless, psychoeducation about sleep and sleep hygiene should be adapted to patients with RLS. These proposed modifications to the standard CBT-Insomnia protocols in patients with RLS can be summarized as follows:

1) Sleep psychoeducation and sleep hygiene should be adapted to RLS (Table 16.6).
2) SRT and SC should be modified and applied in order to keep the sleep pattern regular; they should also be modified to avoid sleep deprivation (e.g., by adding 30 minutes: SRT + 30 minutes or 6 hours at least. Some authors suggest using SRT with a minimal time in bed of ≥ 6 hours or by using sleep compression).
3) Relaxation strategies with yoga, aerobic and leg-stretching exercises should be included in the CBT-I protocol.

Table 16.6 Sleep psychoeducation for insomnia co-morbid with RLS.

RLS and insomnia	Discuss RLS causes and how RLS contributes to precipitate and perpetuate insomnia.
Consequences of their association	Discuss the mutual reinforcement occurring when these sleep disorders present at the same time. Discuss how to reduce symptoms including massaging the legs, taking a warm bath, or using a heating pad or ice pack.
Sleep hygiene	Healthy eating, regular and well-balanced physical activity, and healthy sleep dynamically interact. Eating a balanced diet is important, and get enough vitamins and minerals, especially iron, important for treating RLS.
	Discuss avoiding or decreasing the use of alcohol and tobacco, or drugs that may exacerbate symptoms. Discuss programs of moderate exercise, gentle activities like yoga, cycling and swimming to be introduced into the daily life, relaxation, aerobic and leg-stretching exercises to favour muscle relaxation.

Conclusion

Behavioural methods used in alleviating RLS symptoms are key components of CBT-I protocols. Nevertheless, some CBT-I protocol adaptations may be necessary for treating insomnia co-morbid with RLS. In Table 16.7 a possible six sessions of the CBT-I adapted protocol is proposed.

Narcolepsy: Specific theoretical issues

Narcolepsy is a disabling *sleep disorder* that consists of a set of core symptoms known as the 'narcoleptic tetrad' (AASM, 2014). These symptoms include excessive day-time sleepiness with sudden sleep attacks during the day, *cataplexy*, *loss of muscle tone* during intense emotions and *sleep paralysis*, feeling unable to move when waking up, *hypnagogic hallucinations*, active hallucinations prior to the onset of sleep and dream pattern alterations, as well as secondary symptoms that accompany the disorder, such as automatic behaviours and *cognitive deficits*. Despite being a disorder of excessive sleepiness, nocturnal insomnia symptoms occur frequently in narcoleptic patients. Narcolepsy may act as a predisposing, precipitating and perpetuating factor for insomnia in these patients.

Narcolepsy typically has a significant negative impact in quality of life. The treatment of choice for narcolepsy consists of prescribing stimulants to mitigate excessive day-time sleepiness and antidepressants to treat parasomnias and associated cataplexy. Drug therapy has been highly recommended and supported by well-designed research that shows its effectiveness. Conversely, the implementation of behavioural interventions has not been well studied with regard to narcolepsy, even if its effectiveness has been recognized for improving sleep quality and hypersomnia/insomnia symptoms in these patients (Marín Agudelo et al., 2014). These interventions include structuring nocturnal sleep habits, avoiding sleep deprivation and changes in sleep time, maintaining a regular schedule of nocturnal sleep, practising relaxation techniques before nocturnal sleep, regularly scheduled naps and diet recommendations.

Sleep satiation is another technique that has been used to regulate sleep and alertness in narcolepsy and consists of a scheduled extension of nocturnal sleep during the day. This technique, which is based on the theory of sleep homeostasis, is effective for certain patients when combined with other measures. Overall, a clearer consensus exists with regard to scheduling 15-minute naps in the afternoon, depending on the difficulty and level of disruption that patients experience. The lucid dreaming technique has also been applied in the treatment of hypnagogic hallucinations in patients with narcolepsy (Franceschini, Pizza, Antelmi, Folli & Plazzi, 2020).

CBT-I protocol adaptation for insomnia co-morbid with narcolepsy

While no psychological intervention has been proposed for insomnia co-morbid with narcolepsy, a cognitive behavioural multimodal approach for narcolepsy has been proposed (CBT-N). This protocol includes some components of CBT-I protocols. These proposed modifications can be summarized as follows:

1) Sleep psychoeducation and sleep hygiene should be adapted to Narcolepsy (Table 16.8).
2) SRT and SC should be modified allowing extra *time in bed* (e.g., by adding 30 minutes: SRT + 30 minutes or 6 hours at least; some authors suggest using SRT with a minimum limited time in bed of ≥ 6 hours or by using sleep compression) including naps, in order to regulate sleep pattern, to avoid sleep deprivation and maintain a regular schedule of nocturnal sleep. Scheduled naps should be programmed to mitigate excessive day-time sleepiness. Naps can range from 15 to 20 minutes to over 1 hour.
3) Relaxation strategies should be included in the CBT-I protocol.
4) If hypnagogic hallucinations present, a lucid dream technique could be implemented.

Table 16.7 Suggested 6 weeks of CBT-I programme for patients with insomnia co-morbid with RLS.

First session	Psychoeducation adapted to RLS
Second session	SRT and SC modified to reschedule sleep time and keep it regular
Third session	Sleep hygiene education adapted to RLS
Fourth session	Relaxation techniques and leg-stretching exercises to favour muscle relaxation
Fifth session	Cognitive therapy
Sixth session	Conclusion and prevention of relapses

Table 16.8 Sleep psychoeducation for insomnia co-morbid with narcolepsy.

Narcolepsy	Discuss factors that may dysregulate sleep pattern and increase poor sleep quality, insomnia and hypersomnia in narcolepsy. Discuss the importance of maintaining a structured sleep schedule and avoiding sleep deprivation. Discuss the importance of programmed naps to address day-time sleepiness.
Sleep hygiene	Healthy eating habits, limitating the intake of sweets and carboydrates, regular and well-balanced physical activity and healthy sleep are dynamically interrelated. Over-the-counter stimulants (e.g., tea, coffee) should only be used on a planned schedule and according to doctor's recommendations. Discuss avoiding or decreasing the use of alcohol or drugs that may exacerbate symptoms (especially REM suppressant drugs or hypnotics).

Table 16.9 Suggested 6 weeks of CBT-I programme for patients with insomnia co-morbid with narcolepsy.

First session	Psychoeducation about sleep adapted to narcolepsy and to show how narcolepsy is associated with disrupted sleep.
Second session	SRT and SC should be applied to ameliorate insomnia symptoms and to target disrupted night-time sleep. These techniques should be modified to reschedule sleep time and keep it regular, allowing extra time in bed and scheduling programmed day-time naps.
Third session	Sleep hygiene education adapted to narcolepsy.
Fourth session	Relaxation techniques.
Fifth session	Cognitive therapy/lucid dream technique if hypnagogic hallucinations are present.
Sixth session	Conclusion and prevention of relapses.

Conclusion

Behavioural methods used in treating narcolepsy are key components of CBT-I protocols. Nevertheless, some CBT-I protocol adaptations may be necessary for treating insomnia in narcoleptic patients. By treating insomnia in narcolepsy we may contribute to regularizing sleep patterns and hence addressing day-time and night-time symptoms of narcolepsy. In Table 16.9 a possible six session CBT-I adapted protocol is proposed.

References

Alessi, C., Martin, J., Fung, C., Dzierzewski, J., Fiorentino, L., Stepnowsky, C., Song, Y., Rodriguez, R. C., Zeidler, M., & Mitchell, M. (2018). Randomized controlled trial of an integrated behavioral treatment in veterans with obstructive sleep apnea and coexisting insomnia. *Sleep*, *41* (Suppl. 1), A155. doi: 10.1093/sleep/zsy061.40.

Allen, R. P., Picchietti, D. L., Garcia-Borreguero, D., Ondo, W. G., Walters, A.S., Winkelman, J. W., Zucconi, M., Ferri, R., Trenkwalder, C., & Lee, H.B. (2014). International Restless Legs Syndrome Study Group. Restless legs syndrome/Willis-Ekbom disease diagnostic criteria: updated International Restless Legs Syndrome Study Group (IRLSSG) consensus criteria History, rationale, description, and significance. *Sleep Medicine, Aug.,15* (8), 860–873.

American Academy of Sleep Medicine (2014). *International classification of sleep disorders* (3rd ed.), *Diagnostic and coding manual*. Westchester, IL: American Academy of Sleep Medicine.

American Psychiatric Association (APA) (2013). *Diagnostic and statistical manual of mental disorders* (5th ed.). Arlington, VA: American Psychiatric Association.

Bjorvatn, B., Berge, T., Lehmann, S., Pallesen, S., & Saxvig, I. W. (2018). No effect of a self-help book for insomnia in patients with obstructive sleep apnea and comorbid chronic insomnia – A randomized controlled trial. *Front Psychology*, *9*, 2413.

Crawford, M. R., Turner, A.D., Wyatt, J. K., Fogg, L. F., & Ong, J.C. Evaluating the treatment of obstructive sleep apnea comorbid with insomnia disorder using an incomplete factorial design. *Contempory Clinical Trials*, Mar., *47*, 146–152.

Edinger, J. D., & Manber, R. (2021). The Apnea and Insomnia Research (AIR) Trial: A preliminary report. *Sleep*, *43*, 195.

Foster, R. G. (2020). Sleep, circadian rhythms and health. Interface. *Focus*, June, *10* (3), 20190098.

Franceschini, C., Pizza, F., Antelmi, E., Folli, M. C., & Plazzi, G. (2020). Narcolepsy treatment: Pharmacological and behavioral strategies in adults and children. *Sleep Breathing*, 2020 June, *24* (2), 615–627.

Geoffroy, P. A., & Palagini, L. (2021). Biological rhythms and chronotherapeutics in depression. *Progress in Neuropsychopharmacology and Biological Psychiatry*, *106*, 110158.

Guilleminault, C., Davis, K., & Huynh, N. T. (2008). Prospective randomized study of patients with insomnia and mild sleep disordered breathing. *Sleep*, Nov., *31* (11), 1527–1533.

Janssen, H. C. J. P., Venekamp, L. N., Peeters, G. A. M., Pijpers, A., & Pevernagie, D. A. A. (2019). Management of insomnia in sleep disordered breathing. *European Respiratory Review*, *28* (153), 190080.

Kerkhof, G.A. (2018). Shift work and sleep disorder comorbidity tend to go hand in hand. *Chronobiology International*, Feb., *35* (2), 219–228.

Krakow, B., Melendrez, D., Lee, S. A., Warner, T. D., Clark, J.O., & Sklar, D. (2004). Refractory insomnia and sleep-disordered breathing: A pilot study. *Sleep Breathing, Mar.*, *8* (1), 15–29.

Marín Agudelo, H.A., Jiménez Correa, U., Carlos Sierra, J., Pandi-Perumal, S. R., & Schenck, C.H. (2014). Cognitive behavioral treatment for narcolepsy: Can it complement pharmacotherapy? *Sleep Science*, Mar. *7* (1), 30–42.

Morin, C. M., Drake, C. L., Harvey, A. G., Krystal, A. D., Manber, R., Riemann, D., & Spiegelhalder, K. (2015). Insomnia disorder. *National Review of Disease Primers*, Sep. *3* (1),15026.

Ntafouli, M., Galbiati, A., Gazea, M., Bassetti, C. L. A., & Bargiotas, P. (2020). Update on nonpharmacological interventions in parasomnias. *Postgraduate Medicine*, Jan., *132* (1), 72–79. doi: 10.1080/00325481.2019.1697119. Epub:11.PMID: 31760836.

Ong, J. C., Crawford, M. R., & Wallace, D. M. (2020). Sleep apnea and insomnia: Emerging evidence for effective clinical management. *Chest*, Dec., *10*, S0012–3692(20)35348-4.

Ong, J. C., Crawford, M. R., Kong, A., Park, M., Cvengros, J. A., Crisostomo, M. I., Alexander, E.I., & Wyatt, J. K. (2017). Management of obstructive sleep apnea and comorbid insomnia: A mixed-methods evaluation. *Behavioral Sleep Medicine*, May–June, *15* (3), 180–197.

Ong, J. C., Crawford, M. R., Dawson, S. C., Fogg, L. F., Turner, A. D., Wyatt, J.K., Crisostomo, M. I., Chhangani, B. S., Kushida, C. A., Edinger, J. D., Abbott, S. M., Malkani, R. G., Attarian, H. P., & Zee, P. C. (2020). A randomized controlled trial of CBT-I and PAP for obstructive sleep apnea and comorbid insomnia: Main outcomes from the MATRICS study. *Sleep*, Sep., *43* (9), zsaa041.

Riemann, D., Baglioni, C., Bassetti, C., Bjorvatn, B., Dolenc Groselj, L., Ellis, J. G., Espie, C. A., & Spiegelhalder, K. (2017). European guideline for the diagnosis and treatment of insomnia. *Journal of Sleep Research*, *26* (6), 675–700.

Sweetman, A., Lack, L., Catcheside, P. G., Antic, N. A., Smith, S., Chai-Coetzer, C. L., Douglas, J., O'grady, A., Dunn, N., Robinson, J., Paul, D., Williamson, P., & McEvoy, R. D. (2019). Cognitive and behavioral therapy for insomnia increases the use of continuous positive airway pressure therapy in obstructive sleep apnea participants with comorbid insomnia: A randomized clinical trial. *Sleep*, Dec., *42* (12), zsz178.

Sweetman, A., McEvoy, R. D., Smith, S., Catcheside, P.G., Antic, N. A., Chai-Coetzer, C. L., Douglas, J., O'Grady, A., Dunn, N., Robinson, J., Paul, D., Williamson, P., & Lack, L. (2020). The effect of cognitive and behavioral therapy for insomnia on week-to-week changes in sleepiness and sleep parameters in patients with comorbid insomnia and sleep apnea: A randomized controlled trial. *Sleep*, July, *13*, 43 (7), zsaa002.

Vega-Escaño, J., Porcel-Gálvez, A. M., Diego-Cordero, R., Romero-Sánchez, J. M., Romero-Saldaña, M., Barrientos-Trigo, S. (2020). Insomnia interventions in the workplace: A systematic review and meta-analysis. *International Journal of Environmental Research for Public Health*, Sep., *17* (17), 6401.

Wickwire, E. M., Geiger-Brown, J., Scharf, S. M., & Drake, C. L. (2017). Shift work and shift work sleep disorder: Clinical and organizational perspectives. *Chest*, May, *151* (5), 1156–1172.

Wilson, S., Anderson, K., Baldwin, D., Dijk, D. J., Espie, A., Espie, C.A., Gringas, P., Krystal, A., Nutt, D., Selsick, H., & Sharpley, A. (2019). British Association for Psychopharmacology consensus statement on evidence-based treatment of insomnia, parasomnias, and circadian rhythm disorders: An update. *Journal of Psychopharmacology*, *33* (8), 923–947.

Zhang, Y., Ren, R., Lei, F., Zhou, J., Zhang, J., Wing, Y. K., Sanford, L. D., & Tang, X. (2019). Worldwide and regional prevalence rates of co-occurrence of insomnia and insomnia symptoms with obstructive sleep apnea: A systematic review and meta-analysis. *Sleep Medical Review*, *45*, 1–17.

Section IV

A Focus on Emotional Processes and New Avenues

Section Editor: Colin A. Espie

17

Mindfulness and Insomnia Disorder

Chiara Baglioni

Key points

- Patients with insomnia present high levels of emotional arousal.
- Indicates that it standard CBT-I protocol includes relaxation techniques, though empirical evidence may not be sufficient to effectively treat emotional aspects of insomnia disorder.
- New emergent approaches to the treatment of the disorder suggest that the standard CBT-I protocol may benefit from addition of strategies targeting emotions and emotion regulation skills that have a direct impact on hyperarousal.
- The chapter briefly introduces the programme proposed by Ong, Shapiro and Manber (2009) on Mindfulness Based Training for Insomnia (MBTI), which targets emotional aspects associated with insomnia disorder.
- The programme MBTI is based on a theoretical framework that stresses the role of metacognitive processes in the disorder of insomnia.
- Populations with long-lasting effects of insomnia such as the elderly and patients with co-morbid disorders may have the greatest benefit from MBTI compared to other patients with insomnia.

Learning objectives

- To understand MBTI and its components.
- To focus on the relevance of emotional aspects associated with insomnia disorder.
- To consider metacognitive processes in insomnia disorder.
- To learn which patients may benefit the most from MBTI.

Abstract

Theoretical models of insomnia underline the role of heightened emotional reactivity to sleep-related stimuli in the maintenance of symptoms. Nevertheless, standard CBT-I protocol does not include specific strategies that target emotional aspects of the disorder. In 2009, Ong, Shapiro and Manber proposed a clinical protocol that suggested the application of mindfulness principles to the treatment of insomnia. This is now referred to as Mindfulness Based Training for Insomnia (MBTI). The intervention is composed of eight sessions, each one combining standard CBT-I strategies with mindfulness practices specifically targeting insomnia-related issues. Specifically, MBTI focuses on metacognitive processes, that is, cognitive and emotional aspects of how patients with insomnia relate to thoughts about sleep deficit. These processes, also called 'secondary-level arousal' include the emotional valence, charge, bias and attachment that the individual associates with sleep-related dysfunctional beliefs and behaviours.

Keywords *insomnia, mindfulness, emotion regulation, secondary-level arousal*

Cognitive-Behavioural Therapy for Insomnia (CBT-I) Across the Life Span: Guidelines and Clinical Protocols for Health Professionals,
First Edition. Edited by Chiara Baglioni, Colin A. Espie and Dieter Riemann.

Introduction

Theoretical models of insomnia underline the role of heightened emotional reactivity to sleep-related stimuli for the maintenance of symptoms (Espie, 2002; Baglioni, Spiegelhalder, Lombardo & Riemann, 2010). Nevertheless, standard CBT-I clinical protocols mainly focus on factors influencing sleep regulation (see Chapter 2) while emotional aspects may not receive full consideration. Specifically important with respect to psychopathology is the ability to regulate emotions, which reflects variations in how well people adjust emotional responses to meet current situational demands (Gross & Thompson, 2007). The common experience of a few nights of poor sleep would be associated in some predisposed individuals with cognitive hyperarousal, often including worries and preoccupations about consequences of sleeping badly. This cognitive activity is negatively toned (Harvey, 2002) and the individual associates feelings of discomfort and stress with the nights of poor sleep. With sleep being an experience of everyday life, increased negative emotions associated with sleep difficulties are likely to spread to other aspects of daily life the more the disorder becomes chronic. In order to cope with the intense negative emotions experienced, patients with insomnia disorder may attempt to monitor and reduce them. Nevertheless, these attempts are often not effective and instead further increase the intensity of the negative emotions. That is, people with insomnia disorder may show difficulties in regulating emotions, especially if intense, negative and associated with the experience of poor sleep. Despite this theoretical background, the standard CBT-I protocol does not include strategies directly targeting emotions and emotion regulation skills.

This chapter aims at providing brief useful practical information for clinicians on Mindfulness-Based Therapy for Insomnia (MBTI), which was proposed by Ong, Shapiro and Manber (2009). This intervention will be summarized briefly here, as a full clinical manual has been previously published (refer to Ong, 2017).

Mindfulness-based therapy for insomnia (MBTI)

It is beyond the scope of the present chapter to explore in depth the concept of mindfulness and of mindfulness psychotherapy. In simple terms, mindfulness is defined as an intentional state in which the individual brings awareness to the present moment in a non-judgemental manner (Kabat-Zinn, 1990). Mindfulness training in psychotherapy aims at working on the individuals' relationship with their negative and dysfunctional thoughts and behaviours, instead of changing their thoughts and behaviours. In the case of treatment for insomnia, while CBT-I strategies focus on modifying dysfunctional sleep-related attitudes, behaviours and beliefs (see Chapter 2), mindfulness treatment applied to insomnia focuses on changing the emotional charge and attachment to these behaviours and cognitions.

Metacognitive model of insomnia

Based on Morin's model of perpetuating factors associated to insomnia disorder (Morin, 1993), maladaptive behaviours (such as prolonging time in bed or napping during the day) and dysfunctional beliefs (such as excessive worries about consequences of poor sleep) trigger increased levels of physical and cognitive arousal. Hyperarousal is a key central aspect of patients with insomnia, which is reported both during the night and the day (see Chapter 1). Ong, Ulmer and Manber (2012) hypothesised that this 'primary-level arousal' triggers a 'secondary-level arousal', which is defined by the emotional valence, charge, bias and attachment the individual associates with the dysfunctional beliefs and behaviours. For example, the belief that a poor night of sleep has a strong impact on next day performances is generally associated in patients with insomnia, with negative emotions and urgency to direct efforts on controlling sleep processes, similar to the Espie, Broomfield, MacMahon, Macphee and Taylor (2006) attention–intention–effort model. While primary arousal refers to worry relating to poor daily performance because of loss of sleep, secondary arousal refers to negative emotions and rigidity and attachment to this thought. The metacognitive model of insomnia (Ong et al., 2012) focuses on secondary arousal and provides the rationale for mindfulness treatment for insomnia disorder.

Mindfulness-based treatment for insomnia (MBTI)

MBTI includes eight sessions lasting about 2.5 hours each, often delivered in group therapy. Group sizes are generally around 6–8 individuals. The aim of the intervention is to help the patient to shift from an *outcome-oriented approach*, that is, taking action to reduce stress and negative emotions, to a *process-oriented approach*, that is, changing the relationship with stress and negative emotions by observing that one is stressed without trying to change the source of stress. Patients are guided to learn to regulate their attention to internal experiences in a non-judgemental manner. MBTI works on an emotional secondary arousal of insomnia disorder to promote a change in the relationship with stress and increased arousal. Patients are guided through meditative exercises to awareness of the influence of secondary arousals on their stress and arousal state. This in turn promotes de-attachment to sleep-related outcomes and beliefs and a consequent decrease of arousal levels. Indirectly, the treatment promotes individuals' abilities to restore baseline levels of arousal that are compatible with sleep-onset processes. Compared to relaxation therapy, including progressive muscle relaxation or imagery techniques, MBTI considers diverse aspects of hyperarousal, including emotional attachment to dysfunctional beliefs about sleep, cognitive rigidity, and acceptance of intrusive thoughts. The goal of MBTI is not necessarily to induce relaxation, but, instead, to improve patients' skills in awareness, acceptance and modulation of negative experiences associated with sleep.

Table 17.1 summarizes the content of the eight sections of MBTI. Each session is structured as follows: (a) formal meditations; (b) period of discussion; (c) insomnia-related activities and instructions. Standard CBT-I behavioural

Table 17.1 MBTI: Summary of the eight sessions of the treatment (based on Ong, 2017).

Session	Topic	Session content	Homeworks
1	Introduction to: 1) Clinical program 2) Theoretical models 3) Mindfulness meditation training 4) Work with sleep diaries	Overview of the intervention; Discussion on patients' expectations; Psychoeducation on mindfulness training and on theoretical models of insomnia disorder; Mindfulness meditations exercises	a) Practise mindfulness meditation b) Fill in meditation diaries c) Fill in sleep diaries
2	1) Introduce the concept of awareness to the mind and body 2) Sleep hygiene psychoeducation	Develop an individual's meditation program; Mindfulness meditations exercises; Principles of sleep hygiene	1) Practise mindfulness meditation 2) Fill in meditation diaries 3) Fill in sleep diaries 4) Introduce sleep hygiene behaviours in daily routines
3	1) Strengthen meditation skills 2) Work on day-time symptoms of insomnia 3) Sleep consolidation	Mindfulness meditation exercises; Discuss day-time symptoms and exercise awareness to body and mind signals for sleepiness; Set a sleep consolidation programme for each patient.	1) Practice mindfulness meditation 2) Fill in meditation diaries 3) Fill in sleep diaries 4) Practice sleep consolidation
4	1) Strengthen meditation skills 2) Evaluate sleep consolidation outcomes 3) Sleep reconditioning 4) Work on sleepiness in the evening through sleep reconditioning	Mindfulness meditation exercises; Discuss day-time symptoms; Set a sleep reconditioning programme for each patient.	a) Practice mindfulness meditation b) Fill in meditation diaries c) Fill in sleep diaries d) Practice sleep consolidation and sleep reconditioning
5	1) Strengthen the acquired skills 2) Discuss the 'territory' of insomnia, i.e., the individual's experience of insomnia before and during treatment	Mindfulness meditation exercises; Discuss the territory of insomnia; Discuss and adapt the sleep consolidation and reconditioning programme for each patient.	1) Practice mindfulness meditation 2) Fill in meditation diaries 3) Fill in sleep diaries 4) Practice sleep consolidation and sleep reconditioning
6	1) Introduce the principles of acceptance and letting go 2) Apply the discussion on the territory of insomnia to sleep-related thoughts and feelings	Discuss the principles of acceptance and letting go; Connect this discussion to the territory of insomnia; Discuss and adapt the sleep consolidation and reconditioning programme for each patient.	1) Practice mindfulness meditation 2) Fill in meditation diaries 3) Fill in sleep diaries 4) Practice sleep consolidation and sleep reconditioning

(*Continued*)

Table 17.1 (Continued)

Session	Topic	Session content	Homeworks
7	1) Revisiting the relationship with sleep 2) Introduce the principles of self-care and self-compassion in the context of insomnia 3) Introduce informal mindfulness practices and attitudes into daily life	Discuss the individual's relationship with sleep for each patient; Discuss the principles of self-care and self-compassion; Connect this discussion to the territory of insomnia; Discuss and adapt the sleep consolidation and reconditioning programme for each patient.	1) Practice mindfulness meditation 2) Fill in meditation diaries 3) Fill in sleep diaries 4) Practice sleep consolidation and sleep reconditioning
8	1) Action plan for future episodes of insomnia 2) Concluding remarks	Discuss how to implement and keep mindfulness formal and informal practice after MBTI; Set an action plan to cope with future episodes of insomnia; Provide a sense of closure to the programme.	

techniques are revised here and adapted for mindfulness theoretical concepts. Sleep restriction strategy is reconceptualized in the so-called 'consolidation' strategy. Patients are instructed to set regular sleep times. Especially, waking time should be fixed and awareness of body signals should be developed for deciding when going to bed in the evening. A sleep window is planned together with the therapist, with the aim of minimizing the time spent awake in bed. Bed time should not be before the planned sleep window, but it could be after if the patient feels not yet tired at the set time to go to bed. Waking time, instead, should be kept fixed. Stimulus control therapy is adapted in the so-called 'sleep reconditioning' strategy. Patients are instructed to stop putting too much effort in trying to sleep when in bed at night. In addition, they should pay attention to their mind and body signals: if they notice that they are beginning to move or to ruminate, they are instructed to become aware of this state of wakefulness. As a consequence, patients should go out of bed and go into another room. If leaving bed is perceived as too difficult, sitting in bed may be allowed. In this case, a dim light may be recommended for reading. Alternatively, patients may practice meditation exercises, which, however, should not replace those assigned for daily practice.

Conclusions

Despite insomnia being characterised by increased emotional arousal, the standard CBT-I protocol does not directly target emotional processes involved in the maintenance of the disorder. Based on emergent therapies that focus on training patients to effectively regulate emotions and attachment to rigid and dysfunctional thoughts, Ong et al. (2009) have proposed a clinical protocol that combines standard CBT-I techniques with mindfulness practices. Adding clinical modules on emotion regulation skills may be important to address directly and effectively the daytime component of the disorder (e.g. Benz et al., 2020). A recent meta-analysis on the efficacy of several interventions for insomnia that are not currently recommended suggested that meditative movement therapies, including mindfulness, meditation, yoga and tai chi, ameliorated perceived sleep efficiency and severity of insomnia, but not for other outcome variables (Baglioni et al., 2020). Similarly, a meta-analysis focusing specifically on mindfulness training for sleep quality suggested also that this intervention may benefit specific aspects of sleep disturbances (Rusch et al., 2019). These results indicated that these interventions could be efficacious as supportive to the standard CBT-I protocol, but not as therapies standing alone. Evidence is, however, still relatively recent and further investigation is needed.

References

Baglioni, C., Spiegelhalder, K., Lombardo, C., & Riemann, D. (2010). Sleep and emotions: A focus on insomnia. *Sleep Medicine Reviews, 14* (4): 227–238. doi: 10.1016/j.smrv.2009.10.007.

Benz, F., Knoop, T., Ballesio, A., Bacaro, V., Johann, A.F., Rücker, G., Feige, B., Riemann, D., & Baglioni, C. (2020). The efficacy of cognitive and behavior therapies for insomnia on daytime symptoms: A systematic review and network meta-analysis. *Clinical Psychology Review, 80*, 101873. doi: 10.1016/j.cpr.2020.101873.

Espie, C. A. (2002). Insomnia: Conceptual issues in the development, persistence and treatment of sleep disorders in adults. *Annual Reviews of Psychology, 53*, 215–243. doi: 10.1146/annurev.psych.53.100901.135243.

Espie, C. A., Broomfield, N. M., MacMahon, K. M., Macphee, L. M., & Taylor, L. M. (2006). The attention–intention–effort pathway in the development of psychophysiologic insomnia: A theoretical review. *Sleep Medicine Reviews, 10* (4), 215–245. https://doi.org/10.1016/j.smrv.2006.03.002.

Gross, J. J., & Thompson, R. A. (2007). Emotion Regulation: Conceptual Foundations. In J. J. Gross (Ed.), *Handbook of emotion regulation* (pp. 3–24). New York: Guilford Press.

Harvey, A. G. (2002). A cognitive model for insomnia. *Behaviour Research and Therapy, 40* (8), 869–893. doi: 10.1016/s0005-7967(01)00061-4.

Kabat-Zinn, J. (1990). *Full catastrophe living: Using the wisdom of your body and mind to face stress, pain, and illness*. New York: Delacorte Press.

Morin C. M. (1993). *Insomnia, psychological assessment and management*. New York: Guilford Press.

Ong, J. C. (2017). *Mindfulness-based therapy for insomnia*. Washington, DC: American Psychological Association.

Ong, J. C., Shapiro, S. L., & Manber, R. (2009). Mindfulness mediation and cognitive behavioural therapy for insomnia: A naturalistic 12-months follow up. *EXPLORE: The Journal of Science and Healing, 5*, 30–36. doi: 10.1016/j.explore.2008.10.004.

Ong, J. C., Ulmer, C. S., & Manber, R. (2012). Improving sleep with mindfulness and acceptance: A metacognitive model of insomnia. *Behaviour Research and Therapy, 50*, 651–660. doi: 10.1016/j.brat.2012.08.001.

Rusch, H. L., Rosario, M., Levison, L. M., Olivera, A., Livingston, W. S., Wu, T., & Gill, J. M. (2019). The effect of mindfulness meditation on sleep quality: a systematic review and meta-analysis of randomized controlled trials. *Annals of the New York Academy of Sciences, 1445* (1), 5–16. doi: 10.1111/nyas.13996.

18

Acceptance and Commitment Therapy (ACT) for Insomnia

Theoretical Issues and Principles and Interventional Strategies and Instruments

Anna F. Johann and Elisabeth Hertenstein

Key points

- A substantial number of patients do not fully respond to CBT-I.
- Untreated insomnia is a risk factor for physical and mental illness.
- Untreated insomnia is associated with reduced quality of life.
- Early evidence proves that ACT may be a beneficial adjunct to CBT-I in chronic insomnia.

Learning objectives

- To understand limitations of CBT-I.
- To learn how to add ACT to CBT-I.

Abstract

CBT-I is the first-line treatment for insomnia and widely proven to be very effective. However, a number of patients do not, or do not fully, respond to CBT-I. This chapter outlines how Acceptance and Commitment Therapy (ACT) can be introduced as an add-on therapy to CBT-I. ACT centres on two therapeutic modules: first, acceptance of thoughts, emotions and sensations and, second, commitment to individual life goals. In the first module, patients practise mindful, non-judgemental awareness to promote acceptance. In the second module, patients clarify their personal values and develop goal-oriented behaviour. ACT has the potential to target characteristic clinical features of insomnia such as intentional sleep-related effort ('non-acceptance') and avoidance or safety behaviours.

Keywords *insomnia, add-on, adjunct, non-responder, ACT, CBT-I*

Introduction

Insomnia disorder is a major health problem worldwide, substantially reducing the quality of life of affected individuals (Ohayon, 2002). In addition, it is a risk factor for the *de novo* onset and maintenance of other disorders, including physical illness such as cardiovascular disease (Johann et al., 2020) and mental illness, such as affective disorders (Baglioni et al., 2011). Cognitive Behavioural Therapy for insomnia (CBT-I) is the most effective treatment according to current guidelines (Riemann et al., 2017). However, 40% of patients do not respond to CBT-I and 60% of patients show no remission of insomnia (Morin et al., 2009). That is, CBT-I leads to a marked improvement of insomnia in the majority of patients, yet a substantial number of patients are considered to be non-responders or non-remitters (Morin et al., 2009).

Cognitive-Behavioural Therapy for Insomnia (CBT-I) Across the Life Span: Guidelines and Clinical Protocols for Health Professionals,
First Edition. Edited by Chiara Baglioni, Colin A. Espie and Dieter Riemann.

The aim of this chapter is to outline how Acceptance and Commitment Therapy (ACT) can be used as an add-on or adjunct therapy to CBT-I. ACT is based on the therapy manual by Hayes (2005), but has been adapted for patients with insomnia by Hertenstein et al. (2014), who conducted an uncontrolled pilot study and found that ACT is feasible in patients with insomnia and reported the first evidence of its potential efficacy.

Current pathophysiological models (see Chapter 1 for more details) highlight that insomnia is a multidimensional disorder. More specifically, excessive sleep-related attention, intention and effort (A-I-E model; Espie, Broomfield, MacMahon, Macphee & Taylor, 2006), sleep-interfering cognitive hyperarousal and dysfunctional sleep-related beliefs (Lundh und Broman, 2000; Riemann et al., 2010) have been identified as mediators of impaired sleep and reduced quality of life in patients with chronic insomnia. Importantly, current pathophysiological models characterize insomnia as a 24-hour disorder, indicating that the identified pathomechanisms refer to both night-time and day-time symptoms. In this chapter we outline how specific ACT interventions can be used to address crucial pathophysiological aspects of insomnia disorder.

ACT centres on the acceptance of inner experience, 'being present' (mindfulness), defusion from dysfunctional beliefs and the strengthening of value-based behaviour (Hayes, 2005), and so might be particularly well-suited to target some critical components of the pathophysiology of insomnia. First, in more detail, the 'acceptance' component of ACT may be suitable to reduce sleep effort (Espie, 2002). The A-I-E pathway in the development of insomnia describes good sleepers as essentially passive concerning their sleep. A central aim of ACT is to promote a discrimination between controllable and uncontrollable experiences. ACT emphasizes that control and effort are counterproductive for sleep-onset and maintenance, and aims to increase the acceptance of unpleasant experiences, such as remaining awake.

Second, 'being present' is an element of ACT that includes cognitive deactivation techniques (Lundh, 2005) and is expected to reduce cognitive hyperarousal. The hyperarousal model, one of the leading psychophysiological models of insomnia, is in line with the cognitive model by Lundh and Broman and describes cognitive hyperarousal as an important pathophysiological factor in insomnia disorder (Lundh und Broman, 2000; Riemann et al. 2010, 2015). In ACT, patients practise reducing their cognitive activation by focusing on the present moment in a non-judgemental way. Since cognitive deactivation is likely to promote sleep, 'being present' is assumed to facilitate sleep onset (Lundh, 2005).

Third, 'defusion' is a component of ACT that can be used to address dysfunctional beliefs (Moffitt, Brinkworth, Noakes & Mohr, 2012), which are commonly observed in patients with insomnia. Defusion aims at taking a meta-perspective on the thinking process and reducing the impact of dysfunctional thoughts. It may be easier to use and apply compared to cognitive restructuring, which is commonly used in classical cognitive therapy (Moffitt et al., 2012). This seems especially important for patients with insomnia, since therapeutic techniques should be as effortless as possible in order to prevent a further increase in arousal and interference with sleep. By shifting the focus away from the content of dysfunctional thoughts, defusion seeks to reduce attentional bias to sleep-related thoughts.

Fourth, patients with insomnia might benefit from the 'values and commitment' component of ACT, which refers to the clarification of personal values and value-based action planning. This idea arises from the clinical observation that insomnia patients often place an exaggerated value on sleep, show avoidance behaviour and neglect valued aspects of their lives beyond sleep (Harvey, 2002; Hood, Carney & Harris, 2011).

Therapeutic techniques

ACT belongs to the so-called 'third wave' of behaviour therapy. Its main focus is not the reduction of symptoms, but the improvement of quality of life. In the context of insomnia, this means that the treatment is not only centred on night-time sleep, but mainly focuses on behaviour and well-being during the day. The main therapeutic goals are accepting difficult thoughts, emotions and sensations and living one's life according to personal values. ACT uses a multitude of metaphors and experiential exercises to illustrate and initiate discussions about these topics. The therapeutic program can be adapted to different disorders or problems by choosing suitable metaphors and exercises. ACT is conceptually related to mindfulness-based treatment. In fact, mindfulness exercises are a part of ACT. However, ACT includes additional treatment elements not included in classical mindfulness-based treatment, such as the identification of personal values and setting individual life goals.

As outlined above, scientific models of the pathophysiology of insomnia emphasize sleep effort, dysfunctional sleep-related beliefs and attitudes, somatic and cognitive hyperarousal and safety behaviours. These characteristic features of insomnia can be addressed with ACT interventions.

Sleep effort and acceptance

Though sleep can indirectly be modulated through behaviour, falling asleep per se is an involuntary process. Good sleepers are characterized by paying little attention towards sleep and by falling asleep effortlessly (Espie et al., 2006). Typical good sleepers cannot describe how they manage to sleep well. In contrast, attention towards sleep is high in patients with insomnia. The sleep onset phase is characterized by direct efforts to fall asleep quickly. This may be an understandable consequence of prolonged periods of poor sleep – however, focused attention towards sleep and intense sleep effort, together with anxious arousal, maintain sleep difficulties in an ensuing vicious cycle.

While this seems relatively straightforward, the opposite is true for many other everyday problems. We learn from an early age that the more effort we put into solving a problem, the likelier it becomes that this problem can be solved. Naturally, the same principle is often applied to sleeping problems (consciously or unconsciously). In ACT, patients learn to distinguish between things that can easily be controlled (many behaviours; e.g., when do I go to bed) and things that cannot be controlled (emotions and involuntary processes; e.g., when do I fall asleep). Patients learn to change things that can be changed (e.g., keep a healthy sleep–wake behaviour and level of activity), and adopt an open, non-judgemental attitude towards those things that cannot be controlled. This attitude is practised with mindfulness exercises. Interestingly, a comparison study between patients with psychophysiological insomnia and idiopathic (lifelong, since childhood) insomnia suggests that especially patients with idiopathic insomnia may benefit from an acceptance-based approach (Espie, Barrie & Forgan, 2012). The concept of acceptance is introduced and discussed with the help of metaphors. One metaphor is the tug-of-war with a monster. Here, patients engage in an actual tug-of-war with the therapist or a peer. They experience that the harder they pull, the harder pulls their opponent, resulting in a more and more exhausting 'war', symbolizing a futile fight against something that cannot be controlled (sleep). They learn that the only way of ending this fight is to let go of the rope. This metaphor is then used to identify futile strategies to control sleep and discuss ways of 'letting go' in real life.

Arousal and mindfulness

Compared with healthy controls, patients with insomnia have higher physiological, cognitive and emotional arousal during the day and during the night. The hyperarousal model is one of the leading psychophysiological models of insomnia (Riemann et al., 2010). High physiological arousal manifests, for example, in increased heart rate, increased cortisol response, and increased fast frequencies (beta/gamma) in the EEG during sleep. Interestingly, patients with insomnia have difficulties sleeping also during the day – contrary to what one would expect in someone with a major sleep deficit (Bonnet & Arand, 2000). Cognitive arousal refers to a tendency to worry and ruminate as well as anxious preoccupation with sleep. Emotional arousal refers to negative emotions such as anxiety, anger or helplessness associated with sleep. It is not entirely clear whether high arousal is a reason for or a consequence of poor sleep (or both). In any case, a reduction of arousal is likely to benefit sleep and the day-time condition.

Mindfulness meditation training as an important part of ACT has the potential to reduce arousal. Mindfulness is defined as a state of focused, non-judgemental awareness of the present moment. In other words, attention is focused on current sensual experience, for example one's own breath, a sound, a taste, or an object. When attention drifts away (which it naturally does), it should simply be brought back to the present moment. While focusing attention on the present moment, the practising person learns to observe, acknowledge and accept all upcoming experiences, thoughts and feelings. This latter part is the most difficult and requires a lot of practice. Ideally, mindfulness exercises are introduced in the session with the therapist and then practised daily by the patient, who can choose from different mindfulness exercises such as breathing meditation, a 'bodyscan' where attention is focused on sensations in different parts of the own body, mindful walking or mindfully executing everyday activities.

Regular mindfulness practice reduces indices of stress and anxiety (Hoge et al., 2018). After an 8-week mindfulness training, compared to a control group, cognitive and somatic arousal when trying to fall asleep was reduced in patients with insomnia (Hoge et al., 2018). Since hyperarousal persists for 24 hours in some patients with insomnia, reducing arousal with the help of mindfulness may be helpful to improve sleep as well as day-time well-being. With the help of mindfulness, patients can learn to notice and interrupt rumination and negative thinking in general. Research also suggests that trait-mindfulness moderates the relationship between subjective stress and physiological stress-markers such as cortisol (Jacobs et al., 2013). An interpretation of this result is that individuals with high mindfulness still experience stressful situations, but react less on a physiological level. To sum up, mindfulness is an integral part of ACT; however, ACT is more than a mindfulness training because it includes work on personal values and goals. The difference can be explained with the help of a metaphor: When there is a puddle of mud in the middle of the road, a mindful and accepting attitude will help you walk through it. Knowing personal values and goals will help you evaluate whether there is something worthwhile at the other side of the puddle and whether it makes any sense for you to walk through it.

Dysfunctional thoughts and attitudes about sleep and defusion

Dysfunctional thoughts and attitudes about sleep are common in patients with insomnia. These, broadly speaking, can be divided in two categories: factually inaccurate assumptions and dysfunctional thoughts with a certain element of truth. Inaccurate assumptions are, for example, that every human has a sleep need of around 8 hours, or that sleep before midnight is particularly important and restful. For this first category, it is important to provide information and clarify misunderstandings. 'If I cannot sleep tonight, I will have difficulties concentrating tomorrow', in contrast, is a thought with an element of truth in it. This belief may be exaggerated in patients, is not totally wrong, but is certainly not helpful in falling asleep. Defusion is a way of dealing with the latter category of thoughts in ACT. It can also be a way of dealing with the first category of thoughts, if patients have understood the incorrectness of their thought on a cognitive level, but still feel emotionally attached to it.

Defusion is practised in three steps: identification, observation and letting go. To work with specific thoughts, they first need to be identified and named as thoughts. Mindfulness and thought diaries can help in this process. Second, patients observe the thought. In this process, they can categorize the thought (e.g., memory, prediction of the future, judgement) and decide whether or not this thought is helpful and whether or not they want to react to it behaviourally. If the thought is labelled as not helpful, patients practise letting go of this thought and not reacting to it.

There is a multitude of ACT exercises to learn and practise defusion, provided, for example, in Luoma, 2008. One of them is the 'leaves on a stream' exercise. In this exercise, patients are instructed to imagine a stream/river with lots of fallen leaves on top. In their imagination, they put each thought they can identify on one of the leaves and watch this leaf float down the river. The exercise illustrates that thoughts always come and go and that one does not need to react to every thought. The aim of the exercise is not to get rid of thoughts, but to observe their natural flow without reacting. In addition, experiential exercises and metaphors can help patients to perceive their thoughts in a different context, for example imagining one's own mind as an ambitious trainee who hands his supervisor lots of different tools (thoughts), but not all of them are useful. Or the mind as a 'helicopter-parent' who has the best intentions, gives lots of advice, but not all of it needs to be followed.

Defusion differs from classical cognitive therapy, where thoughts are identified and disputed. The main difference is that cognitive therapy focuses on the content of the thought and finds arguments against it, whereas defusion takes a meta-perspective on the process of thinking itself and tries to move attention away from unhelpful thoughts. Both approaches can be helpful. Depending on the amount of 'truth' in the thought, one or the other may be more promising.

Safety behaviours and values/commitment

Many patients with insomnia engage in safety behaviours with the aim of protecting their sleep. Examples are skipping evening activities, sleeping apart from the partner or choosing an especially quiet and undisturbed living environment. Avoiding activities due to the fear of not being rested enough is also common. These safety behaviours are rather unlikely to solve the sleep problem. Typically, patients have engaged in these behaviours for a long time and still suffer from insomnia when they begin therapy. Safety behaviours maintain an anxious focus on sleep and reinforce the belief that measures must be taken in order to sleep well (in contrast to an effortless, accepting attitude that could actually benefit sleep). In addition, they can directly reduce the quality of life.

The goal of the 'commitment' part of ACT is to reduce avoidance, safety behaviours and increase the quality of life. With the help of metaphors and experiential exercises, personal values are identified. The term 'values' refers to valued directions of life that are important to the patient (not ethical values, etc.). Examples for values are: being a loving and supportive partner, being well educated and being an engaged and creative employee. Importantly, values give a direction but can never be 'reached' (one can always be a bit more engaged and creative). Once the values are identified, short-term, medium-term and long-term goals associated with these values are developed. Goals, in contrast to values, are meant to be specific, scheduled and realistic. A goal could be to ask the partner out for a romantic evening dinner the next week or to participate in a training course at work. Patients are encouraged to work towards these goals in small steps, even if sleep-related problems make it difficult.

In insomnia, working with personal values and goals may be helpful for another reason. Every therapy targeting sleep directly bears the risk of increasing sleep-related attention and effort and thereby, as a side effect, worsening sleep. Working with values may shift attention away from sleep and towards relevant aspects of life. Patients will learn that aspects of their life can be improved without directly improving sleep. This can be helpful to break the vicious cycle of sleep difficulties, sleep-related attention, sleep effort and poorer sleep.

Assessment

We recommend using the following instruments:

- Insomnia Severity Index (Bastien, Vallières & Morin, 2001)
- The consensus sleep diary: standardizing prospective sleep self-monitoring (Carney et al., 2012)
- Glasgow Sleep Impact Index (Kyle et al., 2013)
- Acceptance and Action Questionnaire-II (Bond et al., 2011)

The Glasgow Sleep Impact Index measures the sleep-related quality of life. The three most important areas of life impaired due to insomnia are defined by the patient. The degree of impairment is rated on a visual analogue scale. This instrument helps identify the most important treatment target for ACT: that is, the degree of impairment in valued areas of life (in contrast to symptom severity). The Acceptance and Action Questionnaire (AAQ) measures experiential avoidance, that is the tendency to avoid certain situations or actions because they may evoke unpleasant feelings. The AAQ is a more global, non-sleep-related, measure of day-time impairment.

Case Discussion

Mrs B. is a 58-year-old secretary who lives with her husband and has two adult sons: Nathan, 32 years old, who works as a teacher and is married, and Andrew, 29 years old, who lives alone, is currently unemployed and has been diagnosed with schizophrenia. Mrs B.'s insomnia started around 33 years ago with her first pregnancy. During that time, she started feeling a lot of responsibility for her family and found it increasingly difficult to cope with the pressure to be successful at work and at home. During all these years, she experienced phases of milder insomnia and phases of severe insomnia, depending on her level of stress at work and in her private life. She says that she never slept well again after the start of her insomnia. She estimates her sleep need to be 8 hours. Her actual sleep time is between 4 and 6 hours. During the day, she feels tired and worn out, but, according to her boss and her co-workers, performs very well at work. She never sought professional help and never took medication because she thought that her problem was 'not really bad' and that other people need the help of a psychologist/psychiatrist more than her. A year ago, she got more responsibility at her workplace because she was promoted to be a head secretary. In addition, her son Andrew moved from the family home to his own flat and started using cannabis on a regular basis, which worsened his psychotic symptoms and caused her a lot of sorrow and worry. In this context, her insomnia worsened and she only slept 3 hours or less per night. For this reason, a year ago, she presented in our sleep clinic.

Mrs B. was diagnosed with psychophysiological insomnia. Clinically and in a diagnostic polysomnography, there was no indication of an intrinsic sleep disorder. Her 'objective' sleep time was 6 and a half hours. As a first therapeutic step, she received eight individual sessions of CBT-I with a psychologist (EH). During sleep restriction, her bed time was reduced from 9 and a half hours to 5 hours. When her sleep efficiency gradually increased, her time in bed was increased to 7 hours and her sleep time increased to 6 and a half hours. Progressive muscle relaxation helped her fall asleep within approximately 30 minutes. She learned that her intrinsic sleep need is most likely between 6 and 7 hours (not 8 hours as she previously assumed) because she never slept more than 7 hours on a nightly basis and she was never sleepy during the day. After the eight sessions, Mrs B. stated that she was happy about the substantial improvement of her sleep. On the other hand, she was very disappointed because during the day, she still often felt tired and found it difficult to motivate herself to get up and go to work. She still felt stressed out – because of her workload during the week, and because she spent most weekends with her son Andy discussing his health and his substance abuse. Mrs B. found this very disappointing because she had been sure that if only she could sleep better, everything else in her life would also be better. She now noticed that this was not the case. Mrs B. and her psychologist agreed to try another 10 sessions of ACT. ACT was introduced as a new treatment that was not insomnia-specific, but targeted difficult feelings in general in order to help improve quality of life. Mrs B. agreed that this may be something that could help her because she found that her sleeping problem was closely related to other aspects of her life, such as work stress and her private life.

During these sessions, all elements of ACT were discussed with the help of metaphors and experiential exercises. The tug-of war with a monster metaphor (see the section 'sleep effort and acceptance') was used to illustrate that Mrs B. was in the middle of a fight against her son's illness that she cannot win. Mrs B. found the values-and-commitment part of ACT especially helpful. She found out that she would love to be calm, loving and supportive, but realized that she often perceived herself as stressed, hectic and irritable. She set goals such as implementing 'me-time' at least 45 minutes every day, where she would sit down and read magazines, paint her nails or have a coffee while chatting with friends on the phone. She discovered hiking as a hobby together with her husband and started spending weekends out in the mountains. The 'acceptance' part helped her to struggle a bit less with her son's illness and hand over part of the responsibility to his psychiatrist, her husband and her other son Nathan. She found that her relationship with Andrew unexpectedly improved when she stopped calling him daily and started interfering a bit less with his decisions. The two still met several times per week and went for walks together, where she practised 'being like a good friend to him rather than trying to fight his illness'. She practised defusion with difficult thoughts like 'I'm a bad mother if I think of my own well-being' and 'Others will start talking behind my back if I make any mistakes at work'. In addition to improving her sleep, ACT helped her also to improve her quality of life. Throughout the ACT part, Mrs B. kept sleep diaries that were discussed at the beginning of each session. She kept implementing sleep restrictions. When she experienced difficulties getting back to sleep at night, she was instructed to implement acceptance strategies to focus away from sleep and not get into an effortful 'struggle'.

Mrs B.'s total score on the insomnia severity index was 25 (severe insomnia) before therapy, 11 (subthreshold insomnia) after CBT-I and 7 (no clinically significant insomnia) after ACT. Her score on the Glasgow Sleep Impact Index (sleep-related quality of life) was 25 before therapy, 45 after CBT-I and 70 after ACT. CBT-I seemed effective enough to improve insomnia considerably and the further reduction of insomnia severity throughout the ACT part of therapy may be explained fully by the continued implementation of sleep restriction. ACT, however, helped to complete the treatment response in terms of an improvement of sleep-related quality of life.

References

Baglioni, C., Battagliese, G., Feige, B., Spiegelhalder, K., Nissen, C., Voderholzer, U., Lombardo, C., & Riemann, D. (2011). Insomnia as a predictor of depression: A meta-analytic evaluation of longitudinal epidemiological studies. *Journal of Affective Disorders*, *135* (1–3), 10–19.

Bastien, C. H., Vallières, A., & Morin, C. M. (2001). Validation of the Insomnia Severity Index as an outcome measure for insomnia research. *Sleep Medicine*, *2* (4), 297–307.

Bond, F. W., Hayes, S. C., Baer, R. A., Carpenter, K. M., Guenole, N., Orcutt, H. K., Waltz, T., & Zettle, R. D. (2011). Preliminary psychometric properties of the Acceptance and Action Questionnaire–II: A revised measure of psychological inflexibility and experiential avoidance. *Behavior Therapy*, *42* (4), 676–688.

Bonnet, M. H., & Arand, D. L. (2000). Activity, arousal, and the MSLT in patients with insomnia. *Sleep*, *23* (2), 205–212.

Carney, C. E., Buysse, D. J., Ancoli-Israel, S., Edinger, J. D., Krystal, A. D., Lichstein, K. L., & Morin, C. M. (2012). The consensus sleep diary: Standardizing prospective sleep self-monitoring. *Sleep*, *35* (2), 287–302.

Espie, C. A. (2002). Insomnia: Conceptual issues in the development, persistence, and treatment of sleep disorder in adults. *Annual Review of Psychology*, *53*, 215–243.

Espie, C. A., Barrie, L. M., & Forgan, G. S. (2012). Comparative investigation of thepsychophysiologic and idiopathic insomnia disorder phenotypes: Psychologic characteristics, patients' perspectives, and implications for clinical management. *Sleep*, *35* (3), 385–393.

Espie, C. A., Broomfield, N. M., MacMahon, K. M., Macphee, L. M., & Taylor, L. M. (2006). The attention–intention–effort pathway in the development of psychophysiologic insomnia: A theoretical review. *Sleep Medicine Reviews*, *10* (4), 215–245.

Harvey, A. G. (2002). Identifying safety behaviors in insomnia. *The Journal of Nervous and Mental Disease*, *190* (1), 16–21.

Hayes, S. C. (2005). *Get out of your mind and into your life: The new acceptance and commitment therapy*. Oakland, CA: New Harbinger Publications.

Hertenstein, E., Thiel, N., Lüking, M., Külz, A. K., Schramm, E., Baglioni, C., Spiegelhalder, K., Riemann, D., & Nissen, C. (2014). Quality of life improvements after acceptance and commitment therapy in nonresponders to cognitive behavioral therapy for primary insomnia. *Psychotherapy and Psychosomatics*, *83* (6), 371–373.

Hoge, E. A., Bui, E., Palitz, S. A., Schwarz, N. R., Owens, M. E., Johnston, J. M., Pollack, M. H., & Simon, N. M. (2018). The effect of mindfulness meditation training on biological acute stress responses in generalized anxiety disorder. *Psychiatry Research*, *262*, 328–332.

Hood, H. K., Carney, C. E., & Harris, A. L. (2011). Rethinking safety behaviors in insomnia: Examining the perceived utility of sleep-related safety behaviors. *Behavior Therapy*, *42* (4), 644–654.

Jacobs, T. L., Shaver, P. S., Epel, E. S., Zanesco, A. P., Aichele, S. R., Bridwell, D. A., Rosenberg, E. L., King, B. G., Maclean, K. A., Sahdra, B. K., Kemeny, M. E., Ferrer, E. B., Wallace, A., & Saron, C. D. (2013). Self-reported mindfulness and cortisol during a Shamatha meditation retreat. *Health Psychology*, *32* (10), 1104–119. doi: 10.1037/a0031362.

Johann, A. F., Hertenstein, E., Feige, B., Akram, U., Holub, F., Baglioni, C., Domschke, K., Schramm, E., Nissen, C., Kyle, S. D., Riemann, D., Biermann, J., & Spiegelhalder, K. (2020). Cognitive behavioural therapy for insomnia does not appear to have a substantial impact on early markers of cardiovascular disease: A preliminary randomized controlled trial. *Journal of Sleep Research*, *29* (5), e13102.

Kyle, S. D., Crawford, M. R., Morgan, K., Spiegelhalder, K., Clark, A. A., & Espie, C. A. (2013). The Glasgow Sleep Impact Index (GSII): A novel patient-centred measure for assessing sleep-related quality of life impairment in insomnia disorder. *Sleep Medicine*, *14* (6), 493–501.

Lundh, L. G. (2005). The role of acceptance and mindfulness in the treatment of insomnia. *Journal of Cognitive Psychotherapy*, *19* (1), S. 29–39.

Lundh, L. G., & Broman, J. E. (2000). Insomnia as an interaction between sleep-interfering and sleep-interpreting processes. *Journal of Psychosomatic Research*, *49* (5), 299–310.

Luoma, J. B. (2008). *Learning ACT: An acceptance & commitment therapy skills-training manual for therapists (Pap/DVD Edition)*. Oakland, CA: New Harbinger.

Moffitt, R., Brinkworth, G., Noakes, M., & Mohr, P. (2012). A comparison of cognitive restructuring and cognitive defusion as strategies for resisting a craved food. *Psychology & Health*, *27* (Suppl. 2), 74–90.

Morin, C. M., Vallières, A., Guay, B., Ivers, H., Savard, J., Mérette, C., Bastien, C., & Baillargeon, L. (2009). Cognitive behavioral therapy, singly and combined with medication, for persistent insomnia: A randomized controlled trial. *JAMA*, *301* (19), 2005–2015.

Ohayon, M. M. (2002). Epidemiology of insomnia: What we know and what we still need to learn. *Sleep Medicine Reviews*, *6* (2), 97–111.

Riemann, D., Spiegelhalder, K., Feige, B., Voderholzer, U., Berger, M., Perlis, M., & Nissen, C. (2010). The hyperarousal model of insomnia: A review of the concept and its evidence. *Sleep Medicine Reviews*, *14* (1), 19–31.

Riemann, D., Nissen, C., Palagini, L., Otte, A., Perlis, M. L., & Spiegelhalder, K. (2015). The neurobiology, investigation, and treatment of chronic insomnia. *The Lancet Neurology*, *14* (5), 547–558.

Riemann, D., Baglioni, C., Bassetti, C., Bjorvatn, B., Dolenc Groselj, L., Ellis, J. G., Espie, C. A., Garcia-Borreguero, D., Gjerstad, M., Goncalves, M., Hertenstein, E., Jansson-Fröjmark, M., Jennum, P. J., Leger, D., Nissen, C., Parrino, L., Paunio, T., Pevernagie, D., Verbraecken, J., Weess, H. G., Wichniak, A., Zavalko, I., Arnardottir, E. S., Deleanu, O. C., Strazisar, B., Zoetmulder, M., & Spiegelhalder, K. (2017). European guideline for the diagnosis and treatment of insomnia. *Journal of Sleep Research*, *26* (6), 675–700. https://doi.org/10.1111/jsr.12594.

19

Training for Emotion Regulation in Patients with Insomnia Disorder

A novel therapeutic in the early stage of development

Silvia Cerolini and Caterina Lombardo

Key points

- Although the interplay between insomnia and emotion regulation (ER) is well recognized, ER strategies have not yet been included or combined with the standard CBT-I programs, with only a few exceptions.
- A new protocol is presented consisting of eight sessions combining techniques addressing sleep difficulties (four sessions) and techniques promoting emotion regulation (four sessions).
- Preliminary evidence from university students and a clinical case in support of this protocol are presented.

Learning objectives

- To learn the theoretical bases of a new eight-session protocol promoting both good sleep and emotion regulation.
- To learn how to use the techniques promoting the regulation of emotions in patients with insomnia disorder.
- To practice with actual clinical challenges in using this protocol.

Abstract

As a growing body of literature suggests, insomnia and emotion regulation (ER) are closely linked, and there is a complex interplay between them, possibly bidirectional. Nevertheless, ER strategies have not yet been included or combined with the standard CBT-I programmes, with only a few exceptions.

The aim of the chapter is to outline a new therapeutic eight-session protocol that may help the clinician to target sleep difficulties in conjunction with emotional problems. Specifically, the first four sessions target sleep difficulties through a standard CBT-I training, including the manualized CBT-I techniques, while the last four sessions provide an add-on or adjunct to CBT-I, focusing upon emotion regulation ability and strategies. The structure of the ER training is presented in detail. Both the CBT-I training and the ER training were preliminary tested for efficacy, showing promising results. A clinical case study is presented of a 54-year-old woman with chronic insomnia of about 20 years duration who underwent the combined training.

Future studies should evaluate the efficacy of this eight-session combined training (CBT-I + ER) in reducing insomnia symptoms and emotion regulation difficulties using randomized controlled trials. However, its brevity, structure and the topics presented allow clinicians and researchers to apply and adapt the proposed protocol to different conditions and populations with a degree of flexibility.

Keywords *emotion regulation training, insomnia, potentiated CBT-I protocol*

Cognitive-Behavioural Therapy for Insomnia (CBT-I) Across the Life Span: Guidelines and Clinical Protocols for Health Professionals,
First Edition. Edited by Chiara Baglioni, Colin A. Espie and Dieter Riemann.

An original clinical protocol targeting emotion regulation in insomnia disorder

The efficacy of mindfulness-based interventions for many mental disorders is well demonstrated (e.g., Eisendrath, 2016; see Chapter 17). However, several limitations to their applicability, efficacy and acceptability should also be acknowledged. First of all, evidence related to its usefulness for treating insomnia is still preliminary (Ong, 2017). Second, some data suggest that trait mindfulness, defined as the innate capacity of paying and maintaining attention to present-moment experiences with an open and non-judgemental attitude (Tang & Tang, 2020; Brown & Ryan, 2003), may mediate the efficacy and acceptability of mindfulness-based interventions (e.g., Carswell and Frewen, 2017). Still, we do not know whether this is also true for mindfulness-based interventions for insomnia (MBTI) (Ong, 2017). Finally, evidence suggests that subjective measures may change after training, while objective parameters do not. For instance, Lee et al. (2020) conducted a meta-analysis combining studies evaluating the effectiveness of mindfulness-based stress reduction (MBSR) programmes in people with elevated blood pressure (BP). Results found a reduction in office-based BP and self-reported depressive, anxiety and stress symptoms after MBSR but failed to find a significant reduction in 24-hour, day-time and nocturnal BP.

Moreover, in MBTI, Ong (2017) included strategies to address the emotional charge and attachment to sleep-related behaviours and cognitions, particularly focusing on mindfulness meditation strategies to reduce sleep-related psychophysiological arousal. However, this type of treatment is focused on emotions associated with sleep difficulties, thus leaving out other broader aspects of emotion regulation such as emotion regulation strategies (i.e., expressive suppression or cognitive reappraisal), which have been documented to be connected with negative health outcomes (e.g., Aldao, Nolen-Hoeksema & Schweizer, 2010; Ellis, Prather, Grenen & Ferrer, 2019; Fairholme et al., 2013; Gross & John, 2003; Hu et al., 2014; Latif, Hughes & Bendall, 2019; Palmer, Oosterhoff, Bower, Kaplow & Alfano, 2018). Emotion regulation is a construct that includes a set of strategies, either adaptive or maladaptive, by which individuals monitor and manage emotional experiences and responses (e.g., Gross, 2014).

As a growing body of literature suggests, insomnia and emotion regulation (ER) are closely linked (Baglioni, Spiegelhalder, Lombardo & Riemann, 2010) and people suffering from sleep problems, such as insomnia, are often characterized by emotion dysregulation (Jansson-Fröjmark, Norell-Clarke & Linton, 2016) and there is a complex interplay between them, possibly bidirectional (Cerolini, Ballesio & Lombardo, 2015). For instance, Mauss and co-workers (2013) demonstrated that poor sleep quality in the past week reduces the effective use of cognitive reappraisal during a laboratory paradigm. Other evidence suggests that sleep deprivation affects emotional processing, emotional reactivity and impairs emotion regulation, thus increasing the risk of poor sleep the subsequent night (Vandekerckhove and Wang, 2018). Therefore, providing patients with strategies useful to increase their ability in regulating emotions during the day may help them to reduce the negative impact of a bad night of sleep. This may lead them to adopt a more efficient emotion regulation style, thus preventing its detrimental influences on their sleep activity and avoiding a 'vicious cycle', in which poor sleep impairs emotion regulation, which in turn disrupts sleep, leading to further impairments in emotional well-being (Vandekerckhove and Wang, 2018). Nevertheless, ER strategies have not yet been addressed within the standard CBT-I programmes.

For these reasons, we propose an eight-session protocol that may help the clinician to target sleep difficulties and at the same time the daily emotional dysregulation, which is possibly exacerbated by sleep difficulties. The proposed protocol addresses sleep difficulties at the beginning of the training and then focuses on ER (i.e., the capacity to implement strategies to change the intensity or valence of an emotion; Gross, 2015). The protocol may be delivered individually or in groups, but the format that is described below was tested in a group setting. The first four sessions target sleep difficulties through standard CBT-I training, including the manualized CBT-I techniques like stimulus control, sleep restriction, sleep hygiene, relaxation, cognitive restructuring, and cognitive control (see Chapter 2 and Riemann et al., 2017).

Similarly, the ER training consists of four sessions. They include psychoeducation, experiential activities in groups and homework. Psychoeducation addresses emotional knowledge and ER strategies. Experiential moments encourage participants to share and discuss personal experiences and thoughts triggered by videos, images, and exercises. Homework aims at facilitating insight, coping and generalization. The theoretical framework used is based on Gross's model of ER (e.g., Gross, 2015), and the proposed techniques are derived by the standard and third-generation CBT. According to Gross, ER refers to the process by which subjects influence the quality and intensity of their emotions according to their goals (Gross, 1999). Emotion regulation strategies are intrinsic processes that people use to regulate both positive and negative emotions. Some emotion-regulation strategies have been considered to be risk factors for psychopathology, while others have been indicated as protective factors (for a review, see Aldao et al., 2010). However, as suggested also by Gross (2014), no strategy is dysfunctional per se but it becomes dysfunctional if it is used without taking into account situational demands. For this reason, Bonanno and Burton (2013) suggested the emergence of a broader construct defined as 'regulatory flexibility'.

The new training we are proposing aims at stimulating and developing the ability to adaptively and flexibly regulate emotion, which is crucial for social functioning and mental health (Gresham & Gullone, 2012; Gross, 2014; Gross & John, 2003), integrating psychoeducation, group discussions and techniques and exercises described in the practitioner handbook of Leahy, Tirch and Napolitano (2011). Each of the eight group sessions lasts about 2.5 hours, but we recommend shorter (e.g., 1 hour) sessions for individual settings.

The 4 ER sessions

The first session has the objective of helping participants to recognize and distinguish their emotions by identifying their triggers and the emotional experience both on a bodily, cognitive and behavioural level (the ABC technique on the emotions of anger, sadness and joy). Participants are encouraged to identify the functions of the emotions and explore functional ways to share emotional states with others, thus contrasting expressive suppression, which has been associated with sleep difficulties (Ellis et al., 2019; Latif et al., 2019; Palmer et al., 2018). Moreover, they are also encouraged to identify dysfunctional responses to invalidation (i.e., the feeling of not being understood and supported by the others) and to find new adaptive alternatives, in order to prevent anger, rumination or perseverative negative thinking, which are known to strongly interfere with sleep (Ballesio, Cerolini, Vacca, Lucidi & Lombardo, 2020).

The second session has the aim of recognizing the ER strategies frequently used, especially referring to participants' experiences, e.g., the frequent use of rumination, suppression or catastrophizing that can elicit anxiety and worries, thus increasing pre-sleep arousal or altering sleep maintenance (Ballesio et al., 2018); identifying their strengths and weaknesses in the short and long term; and expanding the range of regulatory strategies and comparing them with alternatives, thus practising regulatory flexibility (Bonanno & Burton, 2013). In particular, the use of alternative strategies such as problem solving, cognitive reappraisal, de-catastrophizing and acceptance are stimulated in different ways such as practical exercises (derived from Hayes, Strosahl & Wilson, 1999).

The third session is aimed at helping the participants to recognize the use of automatic irrational thoughts and the influence that they have in triggering or worsening their emotional experience. The ABC technique is proposed with the aim of monitoring participants' automatic thoughts and mental states. This technique may be useful to create and develop awareness on emotional experience in contrast with experiential avoidance and emotional suppression, which in turn may alter sleep (Zakiei et al., 2021). Finally, compassion for oneself and one's emotional experience is stimulated through practical exercises (based on Leahy et al., 2011).

Lastly, the fourth session has two aims: to encourage participants to identify the most useful ER skills and to flexibly apply them to their daily life; to prevent future relapses, in terms of returning to the inflexible use of dysfunctional cognitive and behavioural ER strategies.

Most techniques used come from third-wave CBT approaches (i.e., acceptance and commitment therapy, compassion focused therapy, cognitive therapy), which have been demonstrated to improve and increase emotional well-being (Leahy et al., 2011), and also in non-responders to CBT-I (Hertenstein et al., 2014). Moreover, emerging evidence is supporting their use to improve sleep quality and quantity (Zakiei et al., 2021; Chapoutot et al., 2021). The contents of the sessions are summarized in Table 19.1.

Applicability and potential beneficiaries

Up to now, both the CBT-I training and the ER training have been offered separately within the Clinical Psychology and Consultancy Service of the Department of Psychology at the Sapienza University of Rome with students or patients who accessed the service or in practical laboratories within the lessons of the Master's degree courses. Both parts of the training were independently tested for efficacy (Ballesio, Devoto & Lombardo, 2018; Cerolini et al., 2019). Specifically, the ER training has been demonstrated to reduce the use of expressive suppression (namely the tendency to conceal one's emotions to others or the denial of the emotional experience), an ER strategy largely associated with dysfunctional health and poorer psychological outcomes (e.g., Aldao et al., 2010; Fairholme et al. 2013; Gross & John, 2003; Hu et al., 2014) including poorer sleep quality (Ellis et al., 2019; Latif et al., 2019; Palmer et al., 2018). Moreover, Cerolini et al. (2019) demonstrated that the ER training, used alone, yielded marginally significant reductions of insomnia symptoms when compared to an active control group where people with insomnia received standard group CBT-I.

Table 19.1 ER training: summary of the four sessions of the protocol.

Session	Topic	Session content	Homework
1	1) Psychoeducation on emotions 2) Emotion validation	a) Help participants to recognize and distinguish their emotions by identifying their triggers and the emotional experience at the body, cognitive and behavioural levels (ABC technique on the emotions of anger and joy); b) Identify the functions of the emotions; c) Explore ways to share emotional states with others; d) Discuss the topic of emotion validation (interpreted as the feeling of being understood and supported by the others); e) Stimulate reflection on the moments and ways in which participants feel validated or not validated by others with respect to their emotional state, identifying their dysfunctional behavioural responses, to invalidation through some exercises.	a) ABC of an episode feeling sadness b) Monitor: - episodes in which I feel validated and not validated - dysfunctional emotional communication modalities - what can I say or what can I do when I feel invalidated (Leahy et al., 2011) c) Fill in emotional diaries
2	1) Emotion regulation strategies 2) Adaptive and maladaptive strategies 3) Introduce the concept of regulatory flexibility (Bonanno & Burton, 2013)	a) Recognize the ER strategies frequently used, especially referring to participants' experience; b) Identify their strengths and weaknesses in the short and long term; c) Expand the range of regulatory strategies and compare them with alternatives; d) Stimulate the use of alternative strategies such as problem solving, cognitive reappraisal, de-catastrophizing and acceptance in different ways such as practical exercises, sharing life experiences and reading the text,'The monsters of bus', taken from Hayes, Strosahl and Wilson (1999).	a) Monitor emotion regulation strategies used b) Identify alternative strategies to use or used during the week
3	1) Automatic irrational thoughts 2) Mental states and content 3) Introduce the concept of compassion and compassionate mind	a) Help participants to recognize the use of automatic irrational thoughts and the influence that they have in triggering or worsening emotional experience; b) Monitor participants' automatic thoughts and mental states through the ABC technique; c) Stimulate compassion for oneself and one's emotional experience through the explanation of the compassionate letter task, in which participants are asked to address a letter to themselves by adopting the point of view of a person who is deeply compassionate and wise (Leahy et al., 2011).	a) Write the compassionate letter
4	4) Summary of the content and techniques 5) Active plan for the future 6) Prevent relapses 7) Concluding remarks	a) Discuss the contents and techniques of the previous meetings, evidencing benefits and difficulties; b) Encourage participants to identify the most useful ER skills and to flexibly apply them to their daily life (planning future applicability); c) Promote a maintenance plan for their use over time, in order to prevent future relapses (considered as returning to the use of less functional cognitive and behavioural modalities and ER strategies for one's psychological well-being).	

The proposed clinical protocol has been offered within the university student community, recognized as a high-risk population for insomnia disorder (Sivertsen et al., 2019) and emotional difficulties (Auerbach et al., 2018). However, it may also be accepted by a wider clinical population of patients with insomnia disorders and co-morbid emotional problems (e.g., anxiety and mood problems, eating behaviour difficulties, etc.), as preliminarily evidenced by responses of a couple of adult patients who participated in a pilot trial (one of these is described below).

Future studies should evaluate the efficacy of the eight sessions of combined training (CBT-I + ER) in reducing insomnia symptoms and emotion regulation difficulties using randomized controlled trials. However, its brevity, structure and topics allow clinicians and researchers to apply and adapt the proposed protocol to different conditions and populations with a degree of flexibility. It might be useful in the context of a public or university service in which there is a large flow of people and few specialized resources allocated.

A clinical case study

Sara (name changed for anonymity) was a 54-year-old woman with chronic insomnia for about 20 years. She worked as a speech and language therapist/logopedic. When she accessed the clinical service, she reported moderate-to-severe difficulties in falling asleep (SOL from 20 min to > 1.3 h), maintaining sleep (5–6 awakenings per night > 5–10 min), and early awakenings (30 min–1 h before the desired time). She also had a long history of using medications: she had been taking a benzodiazepine (Lormetazepam, 0.4–1.4 mg) and melatonin (1 mg) for around 10 years. She had a diagnosis of Fibromyalgia, scoliosis, irritable bowel syndrome and was menopausal for 4 years. She was used to practising yoga, physical activity and meditation. She reported a good sleep hygiene. She had difficulties with chronic pain related to Fibromyalgia and consequent mild mood problems. She had received psychoanalysis for 20 years before intake and she interrupted this treatment intending to look for something more effective for her sleep and emotion regulation problems.

She started a patient-tailored individual CBT-I program (about six sessions of 1 h). After an initial improvement in sleep quality and quantity, she still referred to persistent mood and emotion regulation problems. She then started the emotion regulation training in four group sessions. After the group, she was enthusiastic about her improvements and her stability with sleep after all those years of persistent chronic insomnia and mood difficulties. At three years of follow-up, she reported good sleep quality and quantity and minimum problems in emotion regulation and mood, as evidenced in Figure 19.1 (Panel A for sleep and Panel B for mood).

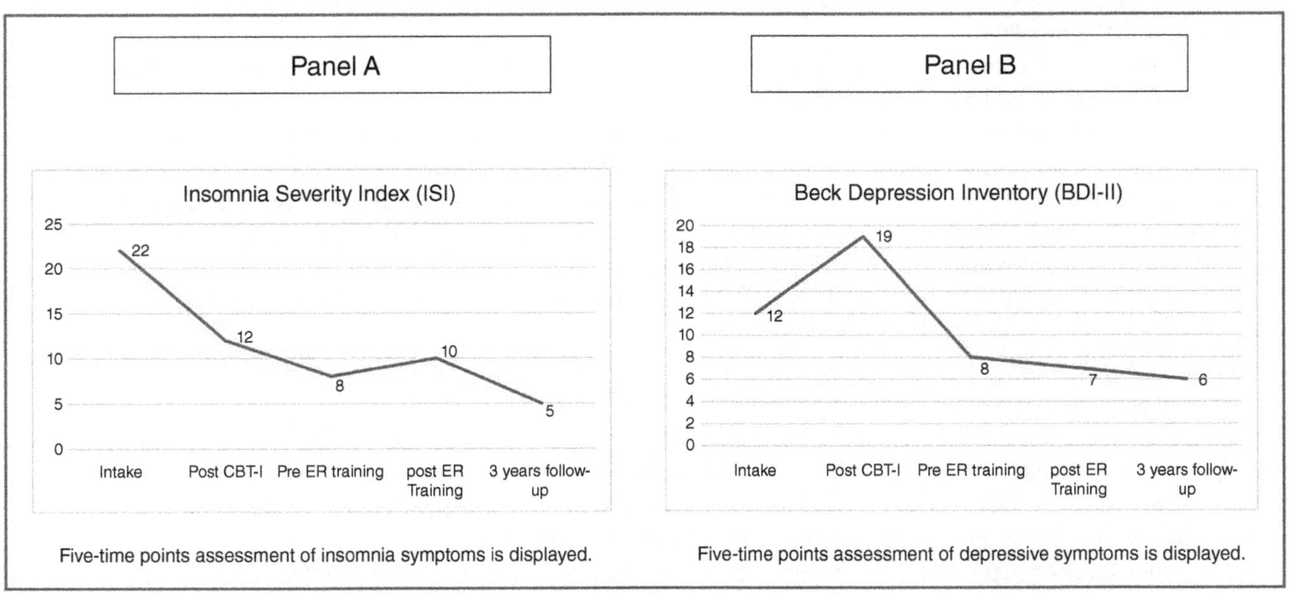

Figure 19.1 Patient's score of insomnia symptoms (Panel A) and depressive symptoms (Panel B) over the time.

Conclusion

The ability to adaptively and flexibly regulate emotion is crucial for social functioning and mental health and may be altered in patients with insomnia, especially regarding thoughts about sleep need and consequences of poor sleep. The current standard CBT-I protocol (see Chapter 2) does not include well-defined strategies targeting specifically emotion regulatory skills. The first evidence, described in this chapter, shows that training for emotion regulation has potential effects on insomnia disorder. Future clinical protocols could evaluate the efficacy of combined CBT-I and emotion regulation therapies for insomnia disorder, especially for day-time symptoms.

References

Aldao A, Nolen-Hoeksema S, Schweizer S (2010). Emotion-regulation strategies across psychopathology: A meta-analytic review. *Clinical Psychology Review*, *30*, 217–237.

Auerbach, R. P., Mortier, P., Bruffaerts, R., Alonso, J., Benjet, C., Cuijpers, P., & Kessler, R. C. (2018). WHO World Mental Health Surveys International College Student Project: Prevalence and distribution of mental disorders. *Journal of Abnormal Psychology*, *127* (7), 623.

Baglioni, C., Spiegelhalder, K., Lombardo, C., & Riemann, D. (2010). Sleep and emotions: A focus on insomnia. *Sleep Medicine Reviews*, *14* (4), 227–238.

Ballesio, A., Cerolini, S., Vacca, M., Lucidi, F., & Lombardo, C. (2020). Insomnia symptoms moderate the relationship between perseverative cognition and backward inhibition in the task-switching paradigm. *Frontiers in Psychology*, *11*.

Ballesio, A., Devoto, A., & Lombardo, C. (2018). Cognitive behavioural therapy for insomnia reduces ruminative thinking. *Sleep and Biological Rhythms*, *16* (3), 371–372.

Ballesio, A., Mallia, L., Cellini, N., Cerolini, S., Jansson-Fröjmark, M., & Lombardo, C. (2018). Italian adaptation of the Insomnia Catastrophising Scale (ICS): A tool to evaluate insomnia-specific catastrophic thinking. *Sleep and Biological Rhythms*, *16* (4), 423–429.

Bonanno, G. A., & Burton, C. L. (2013). Regulatory flexibility: An individual differences perspective on coping and emotion regulation. *Perspectives on Psychological Science*, *8* (6), 591–612.

Brown, K. W., & Ryan, R. M. (2003). The benefits of being present: Mindfulness and its role in psychological well-being. *Journal of Personality and Social Psychology*, *84* (4), 822.

Carswell, J., & Frewen, P. (2017). Experiences of psychopathology distract from focused attention during mindfulness meditation: Assessment in relation to meditation breath attention scores in mental health help-seeking participants. *Mindfulness*, *8* (4), 943–948.

Cerolini, S., Ballesio, A., & Lombardo, C. (2015). Insomnia and emotion regulation: Recent findings and suggestions for treatment. *Journal of Sleep Disorders and Management*, *1* (1).

Cerolini, S., Terrasi, M., Ballesio, A., Devoto, A., Bacaro, V., Vacca, M., & Lombardo, C. (2019). Efficacia di un training di regolazione delle emozioni in un gruppo di studenti universitari. *Cognitivismo Clinico*, *16* (1).

Chapoutot, M., Peter-Derex, L., Schoendorff, B., Faivre, T., Bastuji, H., & Putois, B. (2021). Telehealth-delivered CBT-I programme enhanced by acceptance and commitment therapy for insomnia and hypnotic dependence: A pilot randomized controlled trial. *Journal of Sleep Research*, *30* (1), e13199. doi: 10.1111/jsr.13199.

Eisendrath, S. J. (2016). Mindfulness-based cognitive therapy. Mindfulness and Acceptance: Expanding the Cognitive-Behavioral Tradition.

Ellis, E. M., Prather, A. A., Grenen, E. G., & Ferrer, R. A. (2019). Direct and indirect associations of cognitive reappraisal and suppression with disease biomarkers (2019). *Psychological Health*, *34* (3), 336–354.

Fairholme, C. P., Nosen, E. L., Nillni, Y. I., Schumacher, J. A., Tull, M. T., & Coffey, S. F. (2013). Sleep disturbance and emotion dysregulation as transdiagnostic processes in a comorbid sample. *Behaviour Research and Therapy*, *51*, 540–546.

Gresham, D., & Gullone, E. (2012). Emotion regulation strategy use in children and adolescents: The explanatory roles of personality and attachment. *Personality and Individual Differences*, *52*, 616–621.

Gross, J. J. (1999). Emotion regulation: Past, present, future. *Cognition and Emotion* 13, 551–573. https://doi.org/10.1080/026999399379186.

Gross, J. J. (2014). *Handbook of Emotion Regulation* (2nd ed.). New York: Guilford Press.

Gross, J. J. (2015). Emotion regulation: Current status and future prospects. *Psychological Inquiry*, *26*, 1–26.

Gross, J. J., & John, O. P. (2003). Individual differences in two emotion regulation processes: Implications for affect, relationships, and well-being. *Journal of Personality and Social Psychology*, *85* (2), 348–362.

Hayes, S. C., Strosahl, K. D., & Wilson, K. G. (1999). *Acceptance and Commitment Therapy: An experimental approach to behavior change*. New York: Guilford Press.

Hertenstein, E., Thiel, N., Lüking, M., Külz, A. K., Schramm, E., Baglioni, C., Spiegelhalder, K., Riemann, D., & Nissen, C. (2014). Quality of life improvements after acceptance and commitment therapy in nonresponders to cognitive behavioral therapy for primary insomnia. *Psychotherapy and Psychosomatics*, *83* (6),371–373.

Hu, T., Zhang, D., Wang, J., Mistry, R., Ran, G., & Wang, X. (2014). Relation between emotion regulation and mental health: A meta-analysis review. *Psychological Reports*, *114*, 341–362.

Jansson-Fröjmark, M., Norell-Clarke, A., and Linton, S. J. (2016). The role of emotion dysregulation in insomnia: Longitudinal findings from a large community sample. *British Journal of Health Psychology*, *21*, 93–113. doi: 10.1111/bjhp.12147.

Latif, I., Hughes, A. T., & Bendall, R. C. (2019). Positive and negative affect mediate the influences of a maladaptive emotion regulation strategy on sleep quality. *Frontiers in Psychiatry*, *10*, 628. https://doi.org/10.3389/fpsyt.2019.00628.

Leahy, R. L., Tirch, D., & Napolitano, L. A. (2011). *Emotion regulation in psychotherapy: A practitioner's guide*. New York: Guilford Press.

Lee, E. K., Yeung, N. C., Xu, Z., Zhang, D., Yu, C. P., & Wong, S. Y. (2020). Effect and acceptability of mindfulness-based stress reduction program on patients with elevated blood pressure or hypertension: A meta-analysis of randomized controlled trials. *Hypertension*, *76* (6), 1992–2001.

Mauss, I. B., Troy, A. S., & LeBourgeois, M. K. (2013). Poorer sleep quality is associated with lower emotion-regulation ability in a laboratory paradigm. *Cognition & Emotion*, *27* (3), 567–576.

Ong, J.C. (2017). *Mindfulness-based therapy for insomnia*. Washington, DC: American Psychological Association.

Palmer, C. A., Oosterhoff, B., Bower, J. L., Kaplow, J. B., & Alfano, C. A. (2018). Associations among adolescent sleep problems, emotion regulation, and affective disorders: Findings from a nationally representative sample. *Journal of Psychiatry Research*, *96*, 1–8.

Riemann, D., Baglioni, C., Bassetti, C., Bjorvatn, B., Dolenc Groselj, L., Ellis, J. G., & Spiegelhalder, K. (2017). European guideline for the diagnosis and treatment of insomnia. *Journal of Sleep Research*, 26 *(6)*, 675–700.

Sivertsen, B., Vedaa, Ø., Harvey, A. G., Glozier, N., Pallesen, S., Aarø, L. E., & Hysing, M. (2019). Sleep patterns and insomnia in young adults: A national survey of Norwegian university students. *Journal of Sleep Research*, *28* (2), e12790.

Tang, Y. Y., & Tang, R. (2020). *The neuroscience of meditation: Understanding individual differences*. Academic Press.

Vandekerckhove, M., & Wang, Y. L. (2018). Emotion, emotion regulation and sleep: An intimate relationship. *Aims Neuroscience*, *5* (1), 1.

Zakiei, A., Khazaie, H., Rostampour, M., Lemola, S., Esmaeili, M., Dürsteler, K., & Brand, S. (2021). Acceptance and commitment therapy (ACT) improves sleep quality, experiential avoidance, and emotion regulation in individuals with insomnia – Results from a randomized interventional study. *Life*, *11* (2), 133.

Section V

Developing and Delivering Services for People with Insomnia

Section Editor: Chiara Baglioni

20

CBT-I Strategies for General Practitioners (GPs)

Bjørn Bjorvatn

Key points

- General Practitioners (GPs) are ideally placed in the health care system to assess and manage patients with insomnia.
- Insomnia is very common among patients visiting the GPs.
- GPs need to consider co-morbid psychological and somatic conditions when managing patients with insomnia.
- GPs need to receive formal training in CBT-I.

Learning objectives

- To understand how common and important insomnia is among patients in general practice.
- To appreciate the role GPs may have in management and care of insomnia patients.
- GPs need to understand the basics of CBT-I.
- Due to time limitations etc. within general practice, to focus on sleep restriction as a single treatment modality is recommended.

Abstract

This chapter focuses on insomnia within the setting of general practice. As insomnia is often co-morbid with other psychological and somatic disorders, the prevalence of insomnia among patients visiting their GPs is very high. As most patients attend the GP office on a regular basis, GPs are ideally placed within the health care system to manage patients with insomnia. However, GPs may not be aware of how common insomnia is among their patients, and most GPs are certainly not trained in non-pharmacological treatment of insomnia. Furthermore, it may be difficult for GPs to provide full CBT-I due to constraints within the general practice environment (e.g., short consultation time). I will therefore recommend GPs to start with sleep restriction as a single treatment modality. Sleep restriction will likely improve insomnia symptoms in most patients. If not successful, patients may be referred to self-help therapies such as digital CBT-I or self-help books or to secondary care specialists – consistent with the suggested stepped care model.

Keywords *general practice, GP, insomnia, CBT-I, sleep restriction*

Cognitive-Behavioural Therapy for Insomnia (CBT-I) Across the Life Span: Guidelines and Clinical Protocols for Health Professionals, First Edition. Edited by Chiara Baglioni, Colin A. Espie and Dieter Riemann.

General practitioners' unique position in the health care system

General practitioners (GPs) are at the forefront of health care delivery in most European countries as well as in many other countries worldwide. In several countries, including Norway, each citizen is through legislation entitled to be part of a GP's patient list, and the GP has obligations to provide adequate health care. Policymakers envision that such a strong primary care service is essential for cost-effective health care. GPs serve as gatekeepers for referrals to secondary care specialists and hospitals. The GP often has a long-term relationship with each patient and is familiar with possible problematic issues at home or at work, and the patient's previous and current psychiatric and somatic history. In such a health care system GPs are ideally placed to assess, diagnose and manage patients with all types of disorders and diseases, including insomnia.

GPs' role in the management of insomnia

One may question whether GPs are able to fulfil this role in the management of insomnia. Will GPs be able to provide CBT-I? Are GPs aware of how common insomnia is among their patients? As sleep problems frequently co-occur with other psychological and somatic conditions (Hohagen et al., 1993; Katic et al., 2015; Terzano et al., 2004), the prevalence of insomnia is likely to be higher in patients visiting GPs compared to the prevalence in epidemiological studies. This is corroborated by studies from several countries including Italy (Terzano et al., 2004), Canada (Blais, Morin, Boisclair, Grenier & Guay, 2001), New Zealand (Arroll et al., 2012), USA (Shochat, Umphress, Israel & Ancoli-Israel, 1999), Switzerland (Maire et al., 2020) and Germany (Hohagen et al., 1993) with prevalences ranging from 19% to 44%. Moreover, in a Norwegian study among consecutive and unselected patients visiting their GPs, the prevalence of chronic insomnia disorder using DSM-IV criteria was as high as 53.6% and 16.2% of the patients used hypnotics (Bjorvatn, Meland, Flo & Mildestvedt, 2017). Non-restorative sleep has been removed from the diagnostic criteria in DSM-5 and ICSD-3 (see Chapter 1), but the prevalence of insomnia among patients visiting their GPs remained very high (47.4%), even when this criterion was removed (Bjorvatn et al., 2017).

GPs do not seem to be aware of how common insomnia is among the patients visiting their practice. In one study the GPs estimated the prevalence of sleep problems among their patients to be 11% (Sivertsen, Nordhus, Bjorvatn & Pallesen, 2010). Another study showed that GPs did not know that their patients suffered from chronic insomnia in more than half of the cases (Hohagen et al., 1993). Furthermore, in most cases the GPs do not ask about insomnia symptoms (Hohagen et al., 1993). One study showed that less than 8% of the GPs assessed sleep problems with sleep diaries or sleep questionnaires (Sivertsen et al., 2010), even though these are the recommended assessment tools (Everitt et al., 2014; Morin & Benca, 2012; Riemann et al., 2017). Moreover, one study indicated that 79% of GPs see patients with a sleep complaint at least once a week (Everitt et al., 2014). Prevalence studies in the general population may possibly lead GPs to underestimate the likelihood of insomnia among their patients. This is unfortunate, as patients with insomnia are shown to have twice as many admissions to hospital and more visits (+14%) and phone calls (+8%) to the GP compared to patients without insomnia (Terzano et al., 2004).

Cognitive behavioural therapy

The treatment-of-choice for chronic insomnia disorder is cognitive behavioural therapy (CBT-I), in which the behavioural treatment components *sleep restriction* and *stimulus control* constitute the most effective components (Brasure et al., 2016; Morin, Culbert & Schwartz, 1994; Riemann et al., 2017; see Chapter 2). Sleep restriction is a behavioural treatment method in which time in bed is restricted to the actual time the patient sleeps, usually based on estimations from sleep diaries. Patients with chronic insomnia disorder typically spend 8–10 hours in bed each night, but only report an average of 5 or less hours of sleep. Initially, the patient is instructed to stay in bed only for this estimated sleep duration (called the sleep window). Although there is no consensus, most sleep clinicians do not recommend starting treatment with a sleep window below 5 hours – even if the patient reports less than 5 hours of sleep. Adjustments in this sleep window are made, usually on a weekly basis, depending on the progress. Again, there is no consensus, but for GPs I recommend increasing the sleep window by 15 minutes when sleep efficiency (total sleep time divided by time in bed x 100%) is 80% or above. However, individual tailoring is recommended. Stimulus control refers to a set of instructions in which the patient is recommended not to stay in bed if sleep does not ensue. This means that the patient is instructed to get out of bed when unable to sleep and to stay up until sleepiness resumes. The bedroom should only be used for sleep (and sex), and not for work, TV watching or use of electronic media. These stimulus control instructions aim to re-associate the bed and bedroom with sleep, and to re-establish a proper sleep–wake pattern. In addition to behavioural treatment components, CBT-I also includes cognitive strategies to identify, challenge and to change faulty beliefs and misconceptions about sleep and insomnia (Riemann et al., 2017; see Chapter 2). Such cognitive therapy may be more difficult for GPs to manage, as compared to the pure behavioural instructions. Other treatment components sometimes included in CBT-I comprise sleep hygiene, which is basic advice (e.g., not drink coffee too late) on how to promote sleep, and various relaxation techniques to counteract physiological, emotional and cognitive activation.

Unfortunately, CBT-I is often not available for patients with chronic insomnia, and most patients still receive insomnia treatment in terms of medications and/or general sleep hygiene advice (Cheung, Jarrin, Ballot, Bharwani & Morrin, 2019; Everitt et al., 2014). This is certainly true also in primary care settings (Everitt et al., 2014; Sivertsen et al., 2010). In fact, a recent study among Swiss GPs showed that only 1% of the patients with chronic insomnia disorder had received CBT-I (Maire et al., 2020). However, even though hypnotics may be effective in the short term, there is lack of evidence for their effectiveness and safety beyond a few weeks of use (Rios et al., 2019). Moreover, hypnotics are known to be associated with unwanted effects like sedation, falls, accidents, amnesia, tolerance, dependence and abuse, and research also shows that such use may increase infection rates and mortality (Kripke, 2000; Parsaik et al., 2016; see Chapter 6). Of great interest, when asking patients who use hypnotics what they would prefer, 80% say they prefer non-pharmacological therapy compared with medications (Omvik et al., 2010). However, less than 10% of this group of hypnotic users had ever been offered anything other than pharmacological treatment (Omvik et al., 2010). Thus, easily implementable therapies in primary care are clearly needed. Several randomized controlled trials show that CBT-I delivered through the internet (Espie et al., 2012; Ritterband et al., 2009) or through self-help books (Bjorvatn, Fiske & Pallesen, 2011; Jernelov et al., 2012) are effective. However, in my view there are major advantages in involving GPs in the management of insomnia. For instance, many patients with insomnia also suffer from co-morbid conditions that need assessment and management. My concern is that to just rely on self-help therapies, many patients may receive suboptimal assessment and treatment of their sleep problems and co-morbid conditions.

CBT-I in the GP office

Although few studies are published, CBT-I, or components of CBT-I, is also effective when given in general practice (Baillargeon, Demers & Ladouceur, 1998; Cheung et al., 2019; Falloon, Elley, Fernando, Lee & Arroll, 2015; Katofsky et al., 2012). In a study from general practice in New Zealand, sleep restriction impressively improved sleep among patients with chronic insomnia as compared with sleep hygiene advice (Falloon et al., 2015). Among the issues often mentioned as precluding access to CBT-I by GPs is the limited consultation time in general practice. However, GPs already have extensive knowledge about their patients and a long consultation time may not be necessary. Furthermore, hypnotics seldom cure the patients and GPs therefore also spend a lot of time prescribing such drugs in patients who are not improving. To treat patients with CBT-I may therefore not necessarily take more time in the long run. I would recommend GPs to focus on sleep restriction as a single treatment modality. It may be difficult to provide full CBT-I due to constraints within the general practice environment, but sleep restriction will likely improve the insomnia symptoms in most patients (see Table 20.1 for specific guidelines). The rationale behind sleep restriction is easy to convey to GPs and I believe that education about how different treatment modalities affect insomnia is important for convincing clinicians to use this kind of therapy. I strongly believe that GPs will implement sleep restriction among their patients with insomnia disorder when given the rationale and explanations for why such treatment is preferable. Therefore, GPs need to get formal training in CBT-I (Baglioni et al., 2020).

Sleep restriction (and other components of CBT-I) may cause excessive daytime sleepiness during the initial treatment phase. All clinicians managing insomnia need to be cautious when treating patients in which increased sleepiness may pose a risk, e.g., among professional drivers. In such cases, patients may be recommended to be on sick leave during the first days/weeks of CBT-I. Some patients find the sleep restriction rules difficult to follow. In such cases, GPs need to motivate the patients. Even though sleep restriction is stressful and may cause increased sleepiness and fatigue, improvement usually comes within the first or second week of treatment.

Table 20.1 Assessment and treatment guidelines for GPs.

1) Does the patient fulfil the criteria for chronic insomnia disorder?
   a) Problems sleeping at night with day-time consequences at least three days per week for a duration of at least three months.
   b) The insomnia symptoms are not better explained by another sleep disorder.
      i) Consider obstructive sleep apnea.
      ii) Consider circadian rhythm sleep–wake disorders.
      iii) Consider restless legs syndrome.
2) Consider whether the patient has co-morbid conditions that also need to be managed.
3) Use a sleep diary for 1–2 weeks to assess the insomnia symptoms.
4) Start treatment with sleep restriction – that is, restrict time in bed to the estimated sleep duration calculated from the sleep diary (but do not restrict to below 5 hours in bed).
5) Follow-up after one week: Increase time in bed by 15 minutes if sleep efficiency is increased to 80% or above. If sleep efficiency is below 80%, continue unchanged.
6) Follow-ups with intervals of 1–2 weeks: Increase time in bed on a weekly basis according to bullet point 5. Use sleep diaries for assessment.
7) If no improvement within a few weeks, consider adding stimulus control and/or cognitive strategies, or referral to secondary care or sleep specialists.

If the patient is taking hypnotics, I recommend to start with sleep restriction without changing the dose. When the patient's sleep improves, the hypnotic may be gradually tapered over several weeks (see Chapter 6).

Insomnia and co-morbidity

My recommendation is that all patients with sleep problems should undergo a thorough assessment by their GP (see also Chapter 1 for details). Co-morbid conditions such as psychological or somatic conditions need to be diagnosed and managed – in addition to the sleep problem. Blood tests need to be considered, as hypothyroidism and many other disorders and diseases may cause sleep problems. Studies clearly show that sleep problems are associated with a multitude of health problems, such as anxiety, depression, suicidal ideation, obesity, cardiovascular diseases, cancer and dementia (Kecklund & Axelsson, 2016; Riemann et al., 2017), all of which need to be assessed and managed, and where the GP has a major role. Furthermore, patients with severe insomnia may need sick leave, a service provided by GPs.

It is furthermore important to note that patients with insomnia symptoms may in fact suffer from other sleep disorders than insomnia disorder (see Chapter 16). Patients with obstructive sleep apnea (OSA) and circadian rhythm sleep–wake disorders may present with symptoms or complaints that resemble insomnia disorder, but where the treatment-of-choice differs substantially. Importantly, the diagnostic criteria for insomnia disorder specify that the diagnosis should only be used when the symptoms are not better explained by another sleep disorder (see the introductory chapter). Sometimes it is difficult to determine whether the patient has insomnia disorder or whether the symptoms are due to another sleep disorder. GPs need training to be able to differentiate between different sleep disorders. Some patients may suffer from both insomnia disorder and another sleep disorder with insomnia symptoms. For instance, it is not uncommon for patients with OSA to also have insomnia disorder, that is, co-morbid insomnia and OSA (so-called COMISA) (Sweetman, Lack & Bastien, 2019). Hence, thorough clinical assessment and proper diagnostic evaluation are of great importance, as the final diagnosis reached has treatment implications. CBT-I is very effective in patients with insomnia disorder but may not be effective if the insomnia symptoms are purely due to another sleep disorder. In line with this, and due to limited research on the use of CBT-I with other patient groups, CBT-I, and especially sleep restriction, are not advised in patients with OSA or delayed sleep–wake phase disorder, as such treatment may cause adverse effects, e.g., increased day-time sleepiness. If the patient suffers from OSA, and it seems likely that the apnoeas and hypopneas are causing the insomnia symptoms, treatment with CPAP will likely reduce the symptoms (Bjornsdottir et al., 2013; Mysliwiec et al., 2020). Similarly, if the insomnia symptoms are due to delayed sleep–wake phase disorder, bright light and/or exogenous melatonin administration may effectively reduce the insomnia symptoms (Saxvig et al., 2014).

However, as mentioned, it is sometimes difficult to determine whether the patients suffer from insomnia disorder or insomnia symptoms due to another sleep disorder, or whether the patient in fact suffers from co-morbidity, that is, both insomnia disorder and another sleep disorder. In line with this, several recent studies show that treatment with CBT-I reduces the insomnia complaints in patients with COMISA (co-morbid insomnia and OSA) (Ong et al., 2020; Sweetman, Lack, Lambert, Gradisar & Harris, 2017; Sweetman et al., 2020). Thus, in co-morbid conditions, the recommended treatment is to focus on both disorders (Ong et al., 2020).

Although CBT-I may not be indicated in cases where insomnia symptoms clearly are secondary to another condition, GPs need to be aware that insomnia symptoms may prevail (e.g., due to irrational compensatory behaviour and negative conditioning) after successful treatment of the main disorder/disease. In such cases the GP should consider focusing on the insomnia symptoms and start treatment with sleep restriction.

Insomnia – a heterogenic disorder

Insomnia is a heterogenic disorder with many subtypes. For instance, some patients complain mainly of sleep onset problems, whereas other patients complain mainly of sleep maintenance problems. Most patients with insomnia disorder, however, complain of both sleep onset and maintenance problems (Bjoroy, Jorgensen, Pallesen & Bjorvatn, 2020). In clinical practice, such different subtypes may respond differently to treatment (Riemann et al., 2017). For instance, CBT-I may be more effective in patients with sleep onset problems than among patients with pure early morning awakening.

Importantly, if treatment with sleep restriction provided by the GP is not effective, adding other CBT-I components such as stimulus control and cognitive therapy should be considered. For unsuccessful cases, the GP may also refer the patient to self-help therapies such digital CBT-I or self-help books or consider referring the patient to secondary care specialists – consistent with the suggested stepped care model (Baglioni et al., 2020; Espie, 2009).

References

Arroll, B., Fernando, A., 3rd, Falloon, K., Goodyear-Smith, F., Samaranayake, C., & Warman, G. (2012). Prevalence of causes of insomnia in primary care: A cross-sectional study. *British Journal of General Practice*, *62* (595), e99–103. https://doi.org/10.3399/bjgp12X625157.

Baglioni, C., Altena, E., Bjorvatn, B., Blom, K., Bothelius, K., Devoto, A., Espie, C. A., Frase, L., Gavriloff, D., Tuuliki, H., Hoflehner, A., Hogl, B., Holzinger, B., Jarnefelt, H., Jernelov, S., Johann, A. F., Lombardo, C., Nissen, C., Palagini, L., Peeters, G., Perlis, M. L., Posner, D., Schlarb, A., Spiegelhalder, K., Wichniak, A., & Riemann, D. (2020). The European Academy for Cognitive Behavioural Therapy for Insomnia: An initiative of the European Insomnia Network to promote implementation and dissemination of treatment. *Journal of Sleep Research*, *29* (2), e12967. https://doi.org/10.1111/jsr.12967.

Baillargeon, L., Demers, M., & Ladouceur, R. (1998). Stimulus-control: nonpharmacologic treatment for insomnia. *Canadian Family Physician*, *44*, 73–79. http://www.ncbi.nlm.nih.gov/entrez/query.fcgi?cmd=Retrieve&db=PubMed&dopt=Citation&list_uids=9481465.

Bjornsdottir, E., Janson, C., Sigurdsson, J. F., Gehrman, P., Perlis, M., Juliusson, S., Arnardottir, E. S., Kuna, S. T., Pack, A. I., Gislason, T., & Benediktsdottir, B. (2013). Symptoms of insomnia among patients with obstructive sleep apnea before and after two years of positive airway pressure treatment. *Sleep*, *36* (12), 1901–1909. https://doi.org/10.5665/sleep.3226.

Bjoroy, I., Jorgensen, V. A., Pallesen, S., & Bjorvatn, B. (2020). The prevalence of insomnia subtypes in relation to demographic characteristics, anxiety, depression, alcohol consumption and use of hypnotics. *Frontiers in Psychology*, *11*, 527. https://doi.org/10.3389/fpsyg.2020.00527.

Bjorvatn, B., Fiske, E., & Pallesen, S. (2011). A self-help book is better than sleep hygiene advice for insomnia: a randomized controlled comparative study. *Scandinavian Journal of Psychololgy*, *52* (6), 580–585. https://doi.org/10.1111/j.1467-9450.2011.00902.x.

Bjorvatn, B., Meland, E., Flo, E., & Mildestvedt, T. (2017). High prevalence of insomnia and hypnotic use in patients visiting their general practitioner. *Family Practice*, *34* (1), 20–24. https://doi.org/10.1093/fampra/cmw107.

Blais, F. C., Morin, C. M., Boisclair, A., Grenier, V., & Guay, B. (2001). Insomnia. Prevalence and treatment of patients in general practice. *Canadian Family Physician*, *47*, 759–767. http://www.ncbi.nlm.nih.gov/pubmed/11340757 (L'insomnie. Prevalence et traitement chez les patients consultant en medecine generale).

Brasure, M., Fuchs, E., MacDonald, R., Nelson, V. A., Koffel, E., Olson, C. M., Khawaja, I. S., Diem, S., Carlyle, M., Wilt, T. J., Ouellette, J., Butler, M., & Kane, R. L. (2016). Psychological and behavioral interventions for managing insomnia disorder:

An evidence report for a clinical practice guideline by the American College of Physicians. *Annals of Internal Medicine, 165* (2), 113–124. https://doi.org/10.7326/M15-1782.

Cheung, J. M. Y., Jarrin, D. C., Ballot, O., Bharwani, A. A., & Morin, C. M. (2019). A systematic review of cognitive behavioral therapy for insomnia implemented in primary care and community settings. *Sleep Medicine Reviews, 44*, 23–36. https://doi.org/10.1016/j.smrv.2018.11.001

Espie, C. A. (2009). 'Stepped care': A health technology solution for delivering cognitive behavioral therapy as a first line insomnia treatment. *Sleep, 32* (12), 1549–1558. http://www.ncbi.nlm.nih.gov/entrez/query.fcgi?cmd=Retrieve&db=PubMed&dopt=Citation&list_uids=20041590.

Espie, C. A., Kyle, S. D., Williams, C., Ong, J. C., Douglas, N. J., Hames, P., & Brown, J. S. (2012). A randomized, placebo-controlled trial of online cognitive behavioral therapy for chronic insomnia disorder delivered via an automated media-rich web application. *Sleep, 35* (6), 769–781. https://doi.org/10.5665/sleep.1872.

Everitt, H., McDermott, L., Leydon, G., Yules, H., Baldwin, D., & Little, P. (2014). GPs' management strategies for patients with insomnia: A survey and qualitative interview study. *British Journal of General Practice, 64* (619), e112–119. https://doi.org/10.3399/bjgp14X677176.

Falloon, K., Elley, C. R., Fernando, A., 3rd, Lee, A. C., & Arroll, B. (2015). Simplified sleep restriction for insomnia in general practice: A randomised controlled trial. *British Journal of General Practice, 65* (637), e508–515. https://doi.org/10.3399/bjgp15X686137.

Hohagen, F., Rink, K., Kappler, C., Schramm, E., Riemann, D., Weyerer, S., & Berger, M. (1993). Prevalence and treatment of insomnia in general practice. A longitudinal study. *European Archives of Psychiatry and Clinical Neuroscience, 242* (6), 329–336. http://www.ncbi.nlm.nih.gov/entrez/query.fcgi?cmd=Retrieve&db=PubMed&dopt=Citation&list_uids=8323982.

Jernelov, S., Lekander, M., Blom, K., Rydh, S., Ljotsson, B., Axelsson, J., & Kaldo, V. (2012). Efficacy of a behavioral self-help treatment with or without therapist guidance for co-morbid and primary insomnia – A randomized controlled trial. *BMC Psychiatry, 12*, 5. https://doi.org/10.1186/1471-244X-12-5.

Katic, B., Heywood, J., Turek, F., Chiauzzi, E., Vaughan, T. E., Simacek, K., Wicks, P., Jain, S., Winrow, C., & Renger, J. J. (2015). New approach for analyzing self-reporting of insomnia symptoms reveals a high rate of comorbid insomnia across a wide spectrum of chronic diseases. *Sleep Medicine, 16* (11), 1332–1341. https://doi.org/10.1016/j.sleep.2015.07.024.

Katofsky, I., Backhaus, J., Junghanns, K., Rumpf, H. J., Huppe, M., von Eitzen, U., & Hohagen, F. (2012). Effectiveness of a cognitive behavioral self-help program for patients with primary insomnia in general practice – a pilot study. *Sleep Medicine, 13* (5), 463–468. https://doi.org/10.1016/j.sleep.2011.12.008.

Kecklund, G., & Axelsson, J. (2016). Health consequences of shift work and insufficient sleep. *British Medical Journal, 355*, i5210. https://doi.org/10.1136/bmj.i5210.

Kripke, D. F. (2000). Chronic hypnotic use: Deadly risks, doubtful benefit. *Sleep Medicine Reviews, 4* (1), 5–20. https://doi.org/10.1053/smrv.1999.0076.

Maire, M., Linder, S., Dvorak, C., Merlo, C., Essig, S., Tal, K., Del Giovane, C., Syrogiannouli, L., Duss, S. B., Heinzer, R., Nissen, C., Bassetti, C. L. A., & Auer, R. (2020). Prevalence and management of chronic insomnia in Swiss primary care: Cross-sectional data from the 'Sentinella' practice-based research network. *Journal of Sleep Research, 29* (5), e13121. https://doi.org/10.1111/jsr.13121.

Morin, C. M., & Benca, R. (2012). Chronic insomnia. *Lancet, 379* (9821), 1129–1141. https://doi.org/10.1016/S0140-6736(11)60750-2.

Morin, C. M., Culbert, J. P., & Schwartz, S. M. (1994). Nonpharmacological interventions for insomnia: A meta-analysis of treatment efficacy. *American Journal of Psychiatry, 151* (8), 1172–1180. http://www.ncbi.nlm.nih.gov/entrez/query.fcgi?cmd=Retrieve&db=PubMed&dopt=Citation&list_uids=8037252.

Mysliwiec, V., Martin, J. L., Ulmer, C. S., Chowdhuri, S., Brock, M. S., Spevak, C., & Sall, J. (2020). The management of chronic insomnia disorder and obstructive sleep apnea: Synopsis of the 2019 U.S. Department of Veterans Affairs and U.S. Department of Defense Clinical Practice Guidelines. *Annals of Internal Medicine, 172* (5), 325–336. https://doi.org/10.7326/M19-3575.

Omvik, S., Pallesen, S., Bjorvatn, B., Sivertsen, B., Havik, O. E., & Nordhus, I. H. (2010). Patient characteristics and predictors of sleep medication use. *International Clinical Psychopharmacology, 25* (2), 91–100. https://doi.org/10.1097/YIC.0b013e328334e5e6.

Ong, J. C., Crawford, M. R., Dawson, S. C., Fogg, L. F., Turner, A. D., Wyatt, J. K., Crisostomo, M. I., Chhangani, B. S., Kushida, C. A., Edinger, J. D., Abbott, S. M., Malkani, R. G., Attarian, H. P., & Zee, P. C. (2020). A randomized controlled trial of CBT-I and PAP for obstructive sleep apnea and comorbid insomnia: Main outcomes from the MATRICS study. *Sleep, 43* (9). https://doi.org/10.1093/sleep/zsaa041.

Parsaik, A. K., Mascarenhas, S. S., Khosh-Chashm, D., Hashmi, A., John, V., Okusaga, O., & Singh, B. (2016). Mortality associated with anxiolytic and hypnotic drugs – A systematic review and meta-analysis. *The Australian and New Zealand Journal of Psychiatry, 50* (6), 520–533. https://doi.org/10.1177/0004867415616695.

Riemann, D., Baglioni, C., Bassetti, C., Bjorvatn, B., Dolenc Groselj, L., Ellis, J. G., Espie, C. A., Garcia-Borreguero, D., Gjerstad, M., Goncalves, M., Hertenstein, E., Jansson-Frojmark, M., Jennum, P. J., Leger, D., Nissen, C., Parrino, L., Paunio, T., Pevernagie, D., Verbraecken, J., Weess, H. G., Wichniak, A., Zavalko, I., Arnardottir, E. S., Deleanu, O. C., Strazisar, B., Zoetmulder, M., & Spiegelhalder, K. (2017). European guideline for the diagnosis and treatment of insomnia. *Journal of Sleep Research, 26* (6), 675–700. https://doi.org/10.1111/jsr.12594.

Rios, P., Cardoso, R., Morra, D., Nincic, V., Goodarzi, Z., Farah, B., Harricharan, S., Morin, C. M., Leech, J., Straus, S. E., & Tricco, A. C. (2019). Comparative effectiveness and safety of pharmacological and non-pharmacological interventions for insomnia: An overview of reviews. *Systematic Reviews, 8* (1), 281. https://doi.org/10.1186/s13643-019-1163-9.

Ritterband, L. M., Thorndike, F. P., Gonder-Frederick, L. A., Magee, J. C., Bailey, E. T., Saylor, D. K., & Morin, C. M. (2009). Efficacy of an internet-based behavioral intervention for adults with insomnia. *Archives of General Psychiatry, 66* (7), 692–698. https://doi.org/66/7/692 [pii]10.1001/archgenpsychiatry.2009.66.

Saxvig, I. W., Wilhelmsen-Langeland, A., Pallesen, S., Vedaa, O., Nordhus, I. H., & Bjorvatn, B. (2014). A randomized controlled trial with bright light and melatonin for delayed sleep phase disorder: Effects on subjective and objective sleep. *Chronobiology International, 31* (1), 72–86. https://doi.org/10.3109/07420528.2013.823200.

Shochat, T., Umphress, J., Israel, A. G., & Ancoli-Israel, S. (1999). Insomnia in primary care patients. *Sleep, 22* (Suppl. 2), S359–365. http://www.ncbi.nlm.nih.gov/pubmed/10394608.

Sivertsen, B., Nordhus, I. H., Bjorvatn, B., & Pallesen, S. (2010). Sleep problems in general practice: A national survey of assessment and treatment routines of general practitioners in Norway. *Journal of Sleep Research, 19* (1, Pt 1), 36–41. https://doi.org/10.1111/j.1365-2869.2009.00769.x.

Sweetman, A., Lack, L., & Bastien, C. (2019). Co-morbid insomnia and sleep apnea (COMISA): Prevalence, consequences, methodological considerations, and recent randomized controlled trials. *Brain Sciences, 9* (12). https://doi.org/10.3390/brainsci9120371.

Sweetman, A., Lack, L., Lambert, S., Gradisar, M., & Harris, J. (2017). Does comorbid obstructive sleep apnea impair the effectiveness of cognitive and behavioral therapy for insomnia? *Sleep Medicine, 39*, 38–46. https://doi.org/10.1016/j.sleep.2017.09.003.

Sweetman, A., Lack, L., McEvoy, R. D., Antic, N. A., Smith, S., Chai-Coetzer, C. L., Douglas, J., O'Grady, A., Dunn, N., Robinson, J., Paul, D., Eckert, D., & Catcheside, P. G. (2020). Cognitive behavioural therapy for insomnia reduces sleep apnoea severity: A randomised controlled trial. *ERJ Open Research, 6* (2): 00161–2020. https://doi.org/10.1183/23120541.00161-2020.

Terzano, M. G., Parrino, L., Cirignotta, F., Ferini-Strambi, L., Gigli, G., Rudelli, G., Sommacal, S., & Studio Morfeo, C. (2004). Studio Morfeo: Insomnia in primary care, a survey conducted on the Italian population. *Sleep Medicine, 5* (1), 67–75. http://www.ncbi.nlm.nih.gov/pubmed/14725829.

21

CBT-I Applied to Acute Insomnia

Jason G. Ellis, Pamela Alfonso-Miller and Greg Elder

Key points
• Acute insomnia should be characterised by vulnerability to on-going stressors in addition to life events. • A CBT-I framework is more appropriate for acute insomnia than a stress-reduction paradigm. • The 'One-Shot' is an effective strategy to manage acute insomnia. • The 'One-Shot' can be used in groups and with vulnerable populations.

Learning objectives
• To be able to differentiate acute insomnia from chronic insomnia. • To understand when the 'one-shot' should be used. • To be able to deploy the 'one-shot' in practice. • To determine when modifications to the 'one-shot' are necessary.

Abstract

Whilst CBT-I is considered the optimal treatment for insomnia disorder, there is limited research in terms of its prophylactic properties. This chapter examines the use of a brief variant of CBT-I in the context of acute insomnia. Starting with the definition of acute insomnia, the chapter moves on to outline the only non-pharmacological strategy aimed to circumvent the transition from acute to chronic insomnia (i.e., the 'one-shot) and show how it can be used in practice. The results from the trials of the 'one-shot' demonstrate its use in acute insomnia and the potential for its utility in more complex situations and environments.

Keywords *acute insomnia, sleep diary, prevention, single session, self-help*

Defining acute insomnia

Before discussing the treatment of acute insomnia, it is wise to provide a definition for the context of treatment. Until relatively recently it appeared that acute insomnia was diagnosed on the basis of exclusion as no formal diagnosis existed beyond 'adjustment insomnia' outlined in the ICSD-2 (American Association Sleep Medicine (AASM), 2005). Under that framework it was noted that acute insomnia was triggered by a life event, occurs over a short term (up to one week was defined as acute insomnia and between one week and three months was defined as sub-acute insomnia) and would resolve naturally.

Cognitive-Behavioural Therapy for Insomnia (CBT-I) Across the Life Span: Guidelines and Clinical Protocols for Health Professionals,
First Edition. Edited by Chiara Baglioni, Colin A. Espie and Dieter Riemann.

Currently, the rather arbitrary duration criteria, outlined in the DSM-5 and ICSD-3, would suggest, again by exclusion, that acute insomnia occurs when all other criteria for insomnia disorder are met, except that it has been present for less than three months (American Psychiatric Association (APA), 2013; American Association of Sleep Medicine (AASM), 2014). That said, Ellis Gehrman, Espie, Riemann & Perlis (2012), for the first time, outlined specific criteria for a diagnosis of acute insomnia, which included a pre-transient – presumed adaptive – period (0–14 days), a transient period (14 days–1 month) and a pre-chronic period (1–3 months). Additionally, unlike the ICSD-2, this definition suggested that the triggering event need not be a significant life event, per se, but those who were undergoing chronically stressful circumstances (e.g., as a caregiver) and/or an accumulation of daily hassles and stressors could also lead to acute insomnia. This latter point is important when we start to consider identifying individuals vulnerable to acute insomnia in terms of targeted prevention or early intervention.

Why a CBT-I approach?

Whilst it might stand to reason, taking into account Spielman's 3P model of insomnia (Spielman, 1986; Spielman, Caruso & Glovinsky, 1987) that a stress reduction paradigm may be a more pertinent management strategy in the context of acute insomnia, several considerations suggest CBT-I, or a variant thereof, may be more appropriate. On theoretical grounds, even though Spielman suggested precipitating factors would be the main issue driving insomnia during the acute phase, (i) we still do not empirically know when acute insomnia becomes insomnia disorder and (ii) Spielman's model suggests the introduction of perpetuating factors prior to insomnia becoming chronic. As such, whilst employing the current three-month criterion for insomnia disorder, stress-reduction techniques may be too late and are certainly not appropriate in the early management of sleep-incompatible attitudes, beliefs and behaviours. Underscoring this latter point, one study found that although precipitating factors (perceived stress, anxiety and depression) differentiate those who sleep 'normally' from those with acute insomnia, these factors do not predict the transition to chronic insomnia and that perpetuating factors, such as dysfunctional beliefs, sleep preoccupation and pre-sleep arousal, are evident during the acute insomnia period (Ellis et al., 2021). There is also evidence, albeit scarce, that there are no differences in the severity of complaint and levels of stress between those in the acute period of insomnia and those with chronic insomnia (Man, Freeston, Ellis & Lee, 2015), further underscoring why stress-reduction techniques may not be appropriate.

When to use a CBT-I approach in the context of acute insomnia

Whilst it could then be suggested that CBT-I, or a variant thereof, be used as soon as an individual has a few nights of poor sleep, we would caution against it being deployed too soon. If, as suggested by Perlis and colleagues (Perlis, Ellis, Kloss & Riemann, 2016), the initiation of insomnia is adaptive (i.e., part of the fight or flight response) then treating it too soon may be detrimental to any natural adaptive response. The recommendation, and evidence (see Does the One-Shot Work?), suggests a treatment period between two-weeks and three months.

Components and structure

To date, there has only been one non-pharmacological approach designed to manage acute insomnia preventing the transition to chronic insomnia (the 'one-shot'; Ellis, 2019). This variant of CBT-I is very brief but still designed to address sleep-incompatible thoughts, feelings and behaviours. It also aligns with the stepped-care model of insomnia (Espie, 2009), whereby it could be considered that as dysfunctional cognitions and behavioural coping strategies would be in their infancy during acute insomnia, a less intensive version of CBT-I would be appropriate.

There are two main components to the 'one-shot'; a self-help pamphlet and a single face-to-face treatment session (lasting approximately 50–60 minutes; see Table 21.1). The first thing to note is that the pamphlet is entitled 'Coping with stress-related sleep loss' and this is largely due to our early research and clinical experience whereby individuals do not readily self-identify as having acute insomnia but rather say they are not sleeping well due to stress. The pamphlet starts with a

Table 21.1 Overview of one-shot components and structure.

Pamphlet	Component
Informational	
	Definition of Acute Insomnia
	Instructions for Creating a Sleep Diary
	When to see a Healthcare Professional
Active Elements	
	Managing the Bedroom Environment
	Stimulus Control Instructions
	Cognitive Control Instructions
	Distraction Techniques
Single Session	
Informational	
	Sleep Education
	Measuring Sleepiness
	Checking patient understands leaflet components
Active Elements	
	Managing Barriers
	Sleep Rescheduling (including titration rules)

general definition of acute (short-term) insomnia, noting that it is a 'normal' adaptive response to stress and in many cases will resolve naturally. Further, it notes that although it is unlikely that the bedroom environment is causing the insomnia it can make the problem worse and to keep the bedroom cool, dark and quiet. The more active components of the pamphlet are framed in a simple 3D's format (Detect, Detach, Distract). 'Detect' outlines how to record a sleep diary, being mindful of patterns, and when to see a healthcare professional about your sleep. 'Detach' is mainly focused on stimulus control instructions (e.g., if you are in bed and cannot sleep, get out of the bed and return when tired, only sleep in bed), but also emphasises the importance of keeping a consistent wake time. More recently, this section was updated to include counter control as there may be situations where leaving the bedroom is impractical or ill advised (e.g., frailty, physical immobility or prison). The other aspects of 'Detach' are focused on putting the day to bed before you go to bed. These are framed as setting aside time in the early evening to compile a to-do-list and write down and prioritise any worries and concerns you have (constructive worry time). Finally, 'Distract' discusses creating a mental technique that is challenging but contains no emotion in order to manage intrusive thoughts and a couple of examples are included (e.g., counting backwards from 1000 in 7s).

The face-to-face session serves two purposes; to tailor and deliver a programme of sleep restriction therapy, if necessary, and to ensure the patient understands the rationale for the techniques provided in the pamphlet whilst addressing any potential barriers. This session also allows for day-time sleepiness to be assessed (see Chapter 5). The sleep restriction protocol (although termed 'sleep rescheduling' in session due to the counterproductive nature of the term sleep restriction) follows established norms whereby Total Sleep Time from the sleep diary is used as the starting point for the patients' prescribed Time In Bed (TIB) and from which an anchored wake time can be established. In terms of titration, whilst instructions are provided on how and when to titrate (i.e., weekly and on the basis of sleep efficiency of 85–90%, keep the same sleep/wake time, and if ≥90% increase time in bed by 15 minutes), no instruction is provided on decreasing time in bed if sleep efficiency falls below 85%. The main rationale for this is for safety reasons when considering that titration will be done remotely and so it would be difficult to determine whether sleep efficiency had fallen below 85% or if it was a miscalculation. As with any CBT-I protocol, the most reinforced instruction(s) during the session is that the patient is never to go below 5 hours TIB and if they feel excessively sleepy during the day (i.e., I need a nap as opposed to wanting a nap), then they should stop sleep restriction/sleep rescheduling and seek specialist help.

It is assumed that the pamphlet is provided at least one week in advance of the session in order for the patient to complete an initial sleep diary before the session. In practice, however, there have been occurrences whereby the pamphlet has been provided during an initial meeting/session. Whilst the obvious advantage to this approach is that every aspect of the 'one-shot' can be addressed comprehensively in a single session, we must be mindful that the session may then be longer due to explanations about the sleep diary.

Does it work?

To date there have been three trials of the 'one-shot'. The first, a randomized control trial in a community sample, the second a comparison of group versus individual treatment, again in a community sample, and the final study an open-label trial with male prisoners (Ellis, Cushing & Germain, 2015; Boullin, Ellwood & Ellis, 2016; Randall, Nowakowski & Ellis, 2019). In each case, moderate to large effect sizes were observed in terms of the Insomnia Severity Index (Bastien, Vallières & Morin, 2001) and sleep latency and wake after sleep onset from the sleep diaries. There were also significant reductions, observed in the second and third trials, in terms of anxiety (using the GAD-7; Spitzer, Krohnke, Williams & Löwe, 2006) and depression (using the PHQ-9; Kroenke, Spitzer & Williams, 2001). This latter finding has prompted its integration into several services, alongside standard CBT approaches for anxiety and depression, with promising results (Orchard et al., 2019).

Conclusion

Whilst there is still much work to do in both understanding acute insomnia and its management, the one-shot demonstrates promise in preventing the transition to chronic insomnia. Further research is necessary, however, to determine its definitive place within the stepped care model of insomnia (see Chapter 23, Figure 23.1).

References

American Academy of Sleep Medicine (AASM) (2005). *International classification of sleep disorders* (2nd ed.). Rochester, MN: American Academy of Sleep Medicine.

American Academy of Sleep Medicine (AASM) (2014). International classification of sleep disorders (3rd ed., ICSD-3). Darien, IL: American Academy of Sleep Medicine.

American Psychiatric Association (APA) (2013). *Diagnostic and statistical manual of mental disorders* (DSM-5®). Washington, DC: American Psychiatric Publishers.

Bastien, C. H., Vallières, A., & Morin, C. M. (2001). Validation of the Insomnia Severity Index as an outcome measure for insomnia research. *Sleep Medicine*, *2* (4), 297–307.

Boullin, P., Ellwood, C., & Ellis, J. G. (2016). Group versus individual therapy for acute insomnia: A pilot investigation of a 'one-shot' treatment strategy. *Brain Sciences*, 7, 1–9.

Ellis, J. G. (2019). Cognitive behavioral therapy for insomnia and acute insomnia: considerations and controversies. *Sleep Medicine Clinics*, *14* (2), 267–274.

Ellis, J. G., Cushing, T., & Germain, A. (2015). Treating acute insomnia: A randomised control trial of a 'single-shot' of cognitive behavior therapy for insomnia. *Sleep*, *38* (6), 971–978.

Ellis, J., Gehrman, P., Espie, C. A., Riemann, D., & Perlis, M. (2012). Acute insomnia: Current conceptualizations and future directions. *Sleep Medicine Reviews*, *16*, 5–14.

Ellis, J. G., Perlis, M. L., Espie, C. A., Grandner, M. A., Bastien, C. H., Barclay, N. L., Altena, E., & Gardani, M. (2021). The natural history of insomnia: Predisposing, precipitating, coping, and perpetuating factors over the early developmental course of insomnia. *Sleep*, *44* (9), zsab095.

Espie, C. A. (2009). 'Stepped care': a health technology solution for delivering cognitive behavioral therapy as a first line insomnia treatment. *Sleep*, *32*(12), 1549–1558.

Kroenke, K., Spitzer, R. L., & Williams, J. B. (2001). The PHQ-9: Validity of a brief depression severity measure. *Journal of General Internal Medicine*, *16* (9), 606–613.

Man, S., Freeston, M., Ellis, J. G., & Lee, D. R. (2015) Examining the Attention, Intention, Effort pathway in acute insomnia: A preliminary investigation on differences in sleep and life preoccupations. *Sleep Medicine Research*, *4* (2), 43–50.

Orchard, F., Pass, L., Chessell, C., Moody, A., Ellis, J., & Reynolds, S. (2019). Adapting brief CBT-I for depressed adolescents: A case illustration of the Sleeping Better Program. *Cognitive and Behavioral Practice.*

Perlis, M., Ellis, J., Kloss, J., & Riemann, D. (2016). Insomnia: Etiology and pathophysiology of insomnia. *Principles and practice of sleep medicine* (6th ed.), pp. 769–784. Maryland Heights, MO: Elsevier Saunders.

Randall, C., Nowakowski, S., & Ellis, J. (2019). Managing acute insomnia in prison: Evaluation of a 'one-shot' cognitive behavioural therapy for insomnia (CBT-I) intervention. *Behavioral Sleep Medicine*, *17* (6), 827–836.

Spielman, A. J. (1986). Assessment of insomnia. *Clinical Psychology Review*, *6* (1), 11–25.

Spielman, A. J., Caruso, L. S., & Glovinsky, P. B. (1987). A behavioral perspective on insomnia treatment. *Psychiatric Clinics*, *10* (4), 541–553.

Spitzer, R. L., Kroenke, K., Williams, J. B., & Löwe, B. (2006). A brief measure for assessing generalized anxiety disorder: The GAD-7. *Archives of Internal Medicine*, *166* (10), 1092–1097.

22

Addressing Insomnia Using Group CBT-I

Kai Spiegelhalder

Key points

- Group CBT-I aims at disseminating the first-line treatment for insomnia by increasing cost-effectiveness in comparison with individual CBT-I.
- The available meta-analytical evidence shows that group CBT-I is an effective treatment. No inferiority of group CBT-I versus individual CBT-I was found; however, only a few studies have directly compared the two formats.
- Examples of advantages (meeting other patients with insomnia, increasing motivation for behaviour change) and disadvantages (less individual therapeutic interaction, logistic challenges) of group CBT-I are discussed.

Learning objectives

- To become familiar with the empirical literature on group CBT-I.
- To be able to identify and discuss specific advantages and disadvantages of group CBT-I.

Abstract

Group CBT-I aims at disseminating the first-line treatment for insomnia by increasing cost-effectiveness in comparison to individual CBT-I. Since less therapist time is usually needed per patient in group therapy, each therapist can treat a larger number of patients per time. Meta-analytical data clearly shows that group CBT-I is an effective treatment. In addition, so far, no inferiority of group CBT-I versus individual CBT-I was found; however, only a few studies have directly compared the two formats with each other. Meeting other patients with insomnia in the context of group CBT-I helps many patients to overcome feelings of loneliness and isolation and gives them the chance to learn from others who are in a similar situation. Moreover, the presence of a group may motivate some patients to adhere to the challenging behavioural changes of sleep restriction therapy and stimulus control therapy. A disadvantage of group CBT-I is that therapists have less time for the interaction with each individual patient, which may complicate tailoring the intervention to the specific needs of each patient. In addition, group therapy is a logistic challenge outside of the inpatient setting.

Keywords *group CBT-I, group therapy*

Introduction

Cognitive-behavioural treatment for insomnia (CBT-I) is the first-line treatment for insomnia, but it is not widely available. For example, comparing epidemiological data on the prevalence of insomnia in Germany (Schlack, Hapke, Maske, Busch & Cohrs, 2013) with health insurance data from the BARMER, a large German health insurance (Grobe, Steinmann & Gerr, 2019),

Cognitive-Behavioural Therapy for Insomnia (CBT-I) Across the Life Span: Guidelines and Clinical Protocols for Health Professionals,
First Edition. Edited by Chiara Baglioni, Colin A. Espie and Dieter Riemann.

indicates that, at best, 3% of all insomnia patients in Germany receive a psychotherapeutic treatment. Many more insomnia patients are treated with benzodiazepine receptor agonists or sedating antidepressants on a long-term basis, treatments that are potentially harmful and not recommended as a first-line method by clinical guidelines (Riemann et al., 2017).

Different pathways have been suggested to overcome the limited number of CBT-I providers, e.g., training health professionals other than physicians and clinical psychologists/ psychotherapists to provide CBT-I or establishing fully automated online treatments. Group CBT-I also aims at disseminating the first-line treatment for insomnia by increasing the cost-effectiveness of the treatment in comparison to individual CBT-I. Since less therapist time is usually needed per patient in group therapy, each therapist can treat a larger number of patients per unit time. Because of this, group CBT-I is probably the most common way of providing this treatment in at least some countries, and it has been suggested to be an appropriate first clinician-led treatment in a stepped care model for insomnia treatment (Espie, 2009; see Chapter 23, Figure 23.1).

Evidence

A meta-analysis published 6 years ago found eight randomised controlled trials that investigated group CBT-I versus waitlist, treatment as usual or placebo control groups (Koffel, Koffel & Gehrman, 2015). Small to large effect sizes were found for subjective sleep-related outcomes, namely sleep efficiency (0.84), sleep onset latency (0.47) and wake after sleep onset (0.65), at post-treatment. In addition, small to medium effect sizes were found for the same variables at 3–12 months follow-up (sleep efficiency: 0.48; sleep onset latency: 0.45; wake after sleep onset: 0.39). Using somewhat different inclusion criteria a couple of years later, the more recent meta-analysis on CBT-I efficacy by van Straten et al. (2018) included 35 randomised controlled trials on group CBT-I. In this meta-analysis, pre- to post-treatment effect sizes for group CBT-I were 0.90 for sleep efficiency, 0.59 for sleep onset latency and 0.98 for the Insomnia Severity Index. The individual trials also showed that group CBT-I has stable long-term effects (Castronovo et al., 2018), can be successfully implemented in different settings, e.g., in primary care (Espie et al., 2007; Cape, Leibowitz, Whittington, Espie & Pilling, 2016; Davidson, Dawson & Krsmanovic, 2019) or at the workplace (Schiller, Söderström, Lekander, Rajaleid & Kecklund, 2018), and can be offered to different patient populations, e.g., middle-aged adults with insomnia and depression (Norell-Clarke, Jansson-Fröjmark, Tillfors, Holländare & Engström, 2015), patients with concurrent health conditions such as cancer (Espie et al, 2008) and older adults with different co-morbidities (Ludwin, Bamonti & Mullingan, 2018).

Of particular importance, no inferiority of the group format compared to individual therapy was found in the meta-analysis of van Straten et al. (2018). However, it should be noted that, up to now, only a few studies have directly compared group CBT-I with individual CBT-I. Most notably, Bastien, Morin, Ouellet, Blais & Bouchard (2004) compared group CBT-I ($n = 16$) with individual CBT-I ($n = 15$) in a randomised clinical trial and found no significant effect of the treatment format on sleep-related outcomes. Non-randomised comparative studies, however, yielded mixed results with two studies suggesting no major effect of the treatment format (Verbeek, Konings, Aldenkamp, Declerck & Klip, 2006; Boullin, Ellwood & Ellis, 2016), with one study suggesting a potential superiority of the individual format (Yamadera et al., 2013). Thus, in the future, an adequately powered and well-designed non-inferiority trial with the same therapeutic content and the same level of therapist qualification in both conditions would provide important evidence for therapists and healthcare policy makers, especially when a health-economic evaluation would be included. For comparison, meta-analytical data suggests that cognitive behavioural treatment for depression is moderately superior in the individual format compared to the group format (Huntley, Araya & Salisbury, 2012), while a transdiagnostic meta-analysis on the comparison between group and individual psychotherapy reported no significant differences between the two formats (Burlingame et al., 2016).

Issues related to group CBT-I

Several advantages and disadvantages of group CBT-I have been identified. Some examples of these are described in this chapter.

Meeting other patients with insomnia

Qualitative studies have highlighted the fact that patients with insomnia perceive it as informative and emotionally supportive to meet other people with insomnia who share their suffering (Sandlund, Kane, Ekstedt & Westman, 2018; Barnes,

Lawrence, Khondoker, Stewart & Brown, 2019). This is particularly important since – without a group treatment – many patients with insomnia feel isolated because of their disorder and a lack of understanding from others (Kyle, Espie & Morgan, 2010). Thus, the group format helps many patients with insomnia to overcome feelings of loneliness and isolation and gives them the chance to learn from others who are in a similar situation. The general psychotherapy literature suggests that this has probably a positive effect on treatment outcomes since the quality of the relationships between group members as well as between group members and therapists has been clearly linked to the efficacy of group psychotherapy (Burlingame, McClendon & Yang, 2018).

Increasing motivation for behaviour change

In the author's view, the relationships within a psychotherapy group may be an important factor for behaviour change, especially when it comes to very challenging behavioural changes like the ones suggested during sleep restriction therapy or stimulus control therapy. In line with this, a qualitative study of group CBT-I has identified 'being together with others pushes you forward' as a central theme that describes the experience of patients with group treatment (Sandlund et al., 2018). This is nicely captured in the quote of one patient: 'And once you've started in this kind of a group, you can't let it down. Instead, you have to do your bit. If you had done it by yourself, you might have thought that no, this was too tough. But if you start it, you have to complete it, so to speak.' Further support for this assumption comes from the notion that some patients seek out other people's experiences of sleep restriction therapy for motivation (Kyle, Morgan, Spiegelhalder & Espie, 2011).

Less individual therapeutic interaction

A disadvantage of the cost-effectiveness of group CBT-I is, of course, that therapists have less time for the interaction with each individual patient. In the author's view, this is not particularly problematic in the context of highly standardised psychoeducational sessions or in the context of providing a rationale for relaxation therapy, sleep restriction therapy or stimulus control therapy. However, tailoring the intervention to the specific needs of each patient, e.g., when it comes to cognitive restructuring, is more challenging in the group format because of time constraints. Moreover, it is generally more difficult for the therapist to keep track of each individual's therapeutic course in the group format due to limited information processing capacity. In larger groups, this even holds true for simple information such as the timing and length of prescribed sleep windows. Another very basic example of the potential negative effects of reduced therapeutic interaction is the calculation of the last week's average sleep duration for sleep restriction therapy (see Chapter 2). In the author's clinical experience, this calculation is far from trivial when the data are given in hours and minutes in a pen-and-paper sleep diary. In this case, it can be helpful to calculate the average sleep duration together with each patient which is, however, time-consuming and less practical in larger groups.

Logistic challenges

Outside of the inpatient setting (see also Crönlein, Langguth, Geisler, Wetter & Eichhammer, 2014), group therapy is logistically more challenging than individual therapy. Therapists need to find a sufficient number of patients with insomnia to start a group, and need to resolve difficulties scheduling the appointments with multiple group members. Moreover, depending on the specific healthcare system, there are issues with or requirements for the reimbursement of group therapies. Given these logistical challenges, evidence-based strategies to improve the outcome of group therapy, such as, for example, structuring the group composition according to the similarity of its members (see Firth, Delgadillo, Kellett & Lucock, 2020) is usually not a realistic option.

Conclusion

CBT-I, being a relative short and standardized intervention, can be offered easily in group contexts. This has several advantages, both practical (e.g., treating more patients in a short time) and theoretical (e.g., many patients benefit from social interaction and sharing experiences). Nevertheless, individual tailored therapy may be more difficult to implement in group contexts; thus, it should be considered carefully in the assessment phase when it is decided which patients may benefit by group CBT-I and which not. Evidence data support the efficacy of group CBT-I, though future research should focus more on specific populations to guide clinical practice. For example, group CBT-I may be especially important in primary care to treat insomnia in groups that may be exposed to development life periods, which are known to be associated with higher vulnerability for health issues (e.g., pregnant women, older adults, adolescents).

References

Barnes, G. L., Lawrence, V., Khondoker, M., Stewart R., & Brown, J. S. (2019). Participant experiences of attending a community CBT workshop for insomnia: A qualitative six-year follow-up. *Behavioral Sleep Medicine*, *17*, 156–173.

Bastien, C. H., Morin, C. M., Ouellet, M. C., Blais, F. C., & Bouchard, S. (2004). Cognitive-behavioral therapy for insomnia: Comparison of individual therapy, group therapy, and telephone consultations. *Journal of Consulting and Clinical Psychology*, *72*, 653–659.

Boullin, P., Ellwood, C., & Ellis, J. G. (2016). Group vs. individual treatment for acute insomnia: A pilot study evaluating a 'one-shot' treatment strategy. *Brain Sciences*, *7*, 1.

Burlingame, G. M., McClendon, D. T., & Yang, C. (2018). Cohesion in group therapy: A meta-analysis. *Psychotherapy*, *55*, 384–398.

Burlingame, G. M., Seebeck, J. D., Janis, R. A., Whitcomb, K. E., Barkowski, S., Rosendahl, J., & Strauss, B. (2016). Outcome differences between individual and group formats when identical and nonidentical treatments, patients, and doses are compared: A 25-year meta-analytic perspective. *Psychotherapy*, *53*, 446–461.

Cape, J., Leibowitz, J., Whittington, C., Espie, C. A., & Pilling, S. (2016). Group cognitive behavioural treatment for insomnia in primary care: A randomized controlled trial. *Psychological Medicine*, *46*, 1015–1025.

Castronovo, V., Galbiati, A., Sforza, M., Poletti, M., Giarolli, L, Kuo, T., Zucconi, M., Manconi, M., Hensley, M., Morin, C., & Ferini-Strambi, L. (2018). Long-term clinical effect of group cognitive behavioral therapy for insomnia: A case series study. *Sleep Medicine*, *47*, 54–59.

Crönlein, T., Langguth, B., Geisler, P., Wetter, T. C., & Eichhammer, P. (2014). Fourteen-day inpatient cognitive-behavioural therapy for insomnia: A logical and useful extension of the stepped-care approach for the treatment of insomnia. *Psychotherapy and Psychosomatics*, *83*, 255–256.

Davidson, J. R., Dawson, S., & Krsmanovic, A. (2019). Effectiveness of group cognitive behavioral therapy for insomnia (CBT-I) in a primary care setting. *Behavioral Sleep Medicine*, *17*, 191–201.

Espie, C. A. (2009). 'Stepped care': A health technology. *Sleep*, *32*, 1549–1558.

Espie, C. A., MacMahon, K. M., Kelly, H. L., Broomfield, N. M., Douglas, N. J., Engleman, H. M., McKinstry, B., Morin, C. M., Walker, A., & Wilson, P. (2007). Randomized clinical effectiveness trial of nurse-administered small-group cognitive behavior therapy for persistent insomnia in general practice. *Sleep*, *30*, 574–584.

Espie, C. A., Fleming, L., Cassidy, J., Samuel, L., Taylor, L. M., White, C. A., Douglas, N. J., Engleman, H. M., Kelly, H. L., & Paul, J. (2008). Randomized controlled clinical effectiveness trial of cognitive behavior therapy compared with treatment as usual for persistent insomnia in patients with cancer. *Journal of clinical oncology: official journal of the American Society of Clinical Oncology*, *26* (28), 4651–4658. https://doi.org/10.1200/JCO.2007.13.9006.

Firth, N., Delgadillo, J., Kellett, S., & Lucock, M. (2020). The influence of socio-demographic similarity and difference on adequate attendance of group psychoeducational cognitive behavioural therapy. *Psychotherapy Research*, *30*, 362–374.

Grobe, T. G., Steinmann, S., & Gerr, J. (2019). *Gesundheitsreport 2019 – Schlafstörungen. Schriftenreihe zur Gesundheitsanalyse – Band 17*. Schwäbisch-Gmünd: BARMER.

Huntley, A. L., Araya, R., & Salisbury, C. (2012). Group psychological therapies for depression in the community: Systematic review and meta-analysis. *British Journal of Psychiatry*, *3*, 184–190.

Koffel, E. A., Koffel, J. B., & Gehrman, P. R. (2015). A meta-analysis of group cognitive behavioral therapy for insomnia. *Sleep Medicine Reviews*, *19*, 6–16.

Kyle, S. D., Espie, C. A., & Morgan, K. (2010). '. . .Not just a minor thing, it is something major, which stops you from functioning daily': Quality of life and daytime functioning in insomnia. *Behavioral Sleep Medicine*, *8*, 123–140.

Kyle, S. D., Morgan, K., Spiegelhalder, K., & Espie, C. A. (2011). No pain, no gain: An exploratory within-subjects mixed-methods evaluation of the patient experience of sleep restriction therapy (SRT) for insomnia. *Sleep Medicine*, *12*, 735–747.

Ludwin, B. M., Bamonti, P., & Mulligan, E. A. (2018). Program evaluation of group-based cognitive behavioral therapy for insomnia: A focus on treatment adherence and outcomes in older adults with co-morbidities. *Clinical Gerontologist*, *41*, 487–497.

Norell-Clarke, A., Jansson-Fröjmark, M., Tillfors, M., Holländare, F., & Engström, I. (2015). Group cognitive behavioural therapy for insomnia: Effects on sleep and depressive symptomatology in a sample with comorbidity. *Behaviour Research and Therapy*, *74*, 80–93.

Riemann, D., Baglioni, C., Bassetti, C., Bjorvatn, B., Dolenc Groselj, L., Ellis, J. G., Espie, C. A., Garcia-Borreguero, D., Gjerstad, M., Gonçalves, M., Hertenstein, E., Jansson-Fröjmark, M., Jennum, P. J., Leger, D., Nissen, C., Parrino, L., Paunio, T., Pevernagie, D., Verbraecken, J., Weeß, H. G., Wichniak, A., Zavalko, I., Arnardottir, E. S., Deleanu, O. C., Strazisar, B., Zoetmulder, M., & Spiegelhalder, K. (2017). European guideline for the diagnosis and treatment of insomnia. *Journal of Sleep Research*, *26*, 675–700.

Sandlund, C., Kane, K., Ekstedt, M., & Westman, J. (2018). Patients' experiences of motivation, change, and challenges in group treatment for insomnia in primary care: A focus group study. *BMC Family Practice*, *19*, 111.

Schiller, H., Söderström, M., Lekander, M., Rajaleid, K., & Kecklund, G. (2018). A randomized controlled intervention of workplace-based group cognitive behavioral therapy for insomnia. *International Archives of Occupational and Environmental Health*, *91*, 413–424.

Schlack, R., Hapke, U., Maske, U., Busch, M., & Cohrs, S. (2013). Frequency and distribution of sleep problems and insomnia in the adult population in Germany: Results of the German Health Interview and Examination Survey for Adults (DEGS1) [Article in German]. *Bundesgesundheitsblatt – Gesundheitsforschung – Gesundheitsschutz*, *56*, 740–748.

van Straten, A., van der Zweerde, T., Kleiboer, A., Cuijpers, P., Morin, C. M., & Lancee, J. (2018). Cognitive and behavioral therapies in the treatment of insomnia: A meta-analysis. *Sleep Medicine Reviews*, *38*, 3–16.

Verbeek, I. H., Konings, G. M., Aldenkamp, A. P., Declerck, A. C. & Klip, E. C. (2006). Cognitive behavioral treatment in clinically referred chronic insomniacs: Group versus individual treatment. *Behavioral Sleep Medicine*, *4*, 135–151.

Yamadera, W., Sato, M., Harada, D., Iwashita, M., Aoki, R., Obuchi, K., Ozone, M., Itoh, H., & Nakayama, M. (2013). Comparisons of short-term efficacy between individual and group cognitive behavioral therapy for primary insomnia. *Sleep and Biological Rhythms*, *11*, 176–184.

23

Digital CBT for Insomnia

Annemarie I. Luik and Colin A. Espie

Key points
• Digital Cognitive Behavioural Therapy (dCBT) is an evidence-based psychological therapy delivered with extensive involvement of digital means. • dCBT for insomnia typically takes the form of dCBT as support guided dCBT or fully automated dCBT. • Digital Medicine and dCBT for insomnia allow for scalability, increased treatment quality, a personalized medicine approach, advancement, accessibility and affordability. • dCBT for insomnia is an effective treatment for insomnia across populations, going beyond treating insomnia alone.

Learning objectives
• To understand what a digital medicine approach means for CBT for insomnia. • To explain how dCBT can address current limiting factors in the provision of CBT. • To have learned the current state of evidence for the use of dCBT.

Abstract

Complaints of insomnia are common, yet provision of the recommended treatment, Cognitive Behavioural Therapy (CBT), is limited. In this chapter we discuss how a digital medicine approach, in the form of CBT delivered by web or mobile (dCBT), could have a transformative impact on insomnia care provision by enabling universal implementation of clinical guidelines for the treatment of insomnia, with consequent improvement in patient outcomes, and patient and clinician satisfaction. We summarize the evidence that supports the potential of dCBT as an evidence-based intervention for insomnia and illustrate ways to advance the implementation of digital medicine for the treatment of insomnia.

Keywords *digital, online, internet, sleep, insomnia, cognitive behavioural therapy*

Introduction

A substantial proportion of the population experiences insomnia: estimates range up to 10% for insomnia disorder and 25% for insomnia symptoms (Morin et al., 2011). Insomnia disorder is most often treated with medication (Morin et al., 2015; Roy & Smith, 2010), but the recommended first line treatment for insomnia is CBT (Qaseem et al., 2016; Riemann et al., 2017; Edinger et al., 2021). In addition, CBT has been reported as the preferred treatment for insomnia by the majority of patients (Sato, Sutoh, Seki, Nagai & Shimizu, 2019; Vincent & Lionberg, 2001).

Cognitive-Behavioural Therapy for Insomnia (CBT-I) Across the Life Span: Guidelines and Clinical Protocols for Health Professionals,
First Edition. Edited by Chiara Baglioni, Colin A. Espie and Dieter Riemann.

Although CBT is the recommended and preferred treatment (Qaseem et al., 2016; Riemann et al., 2017), the dissemination of CBT to those with insomnia remains extremely low, primarily due to the limited number of professionals who are trained in CBT for insomnia. Published guidelines therefore have little option but to incorporate the suggestion of treating insomnia with medication when CBT is not available (Riemann et al., 2017). We argue, however, that the advent of 'digital medicine' (Espie, Hames & McKinstry, 2013; Espie, Kyle, Gehrman, Ong & Hames, 2014; Luik, Kyle & Espie, 2017) offers new possibilities, not just to increase access to CBT for insomnia, but to make the availability of CBT completely ubiquitous.

In this chapter, we will explain what we mean by digital medicine and why we believe it is central to the real-world delivery of clinical guidelines. We will also summarise the evidence for digital CBT (dCBT) for insomnia and outline how we can, and should, apply digital medicine for insomnia to everyday practice.

What is digital medicine?

The digital revolution is gathering pace. We cannot do our jobs without internet access, we are dependent on our smartphones to find the way and it is estimated that up to 45% of people have used, or currently use, a fitness tracker (Price Waterhouse Coopers, 2016). Such digital advances have also translated into health care. For example, diagnoses are faster and potentially more accurate thanks to new technologies (Peeling, 2015), while storing medical records electronically yields 'big data', which can be used as a powerful evidence base (Murdoch & Detsky, 2013), also offering new potential for the field of insomnia.

Over the past few years, we have refined what we mean by 'digital medicine' (Espie et al., 2013; Luik, Kyle & Espie, 2017). Our focus is on digital medicine as evidence-based psychological therapy when delivered with extensive involvement of digital means. Other terms such as 'computerised', 'electronic', 'online' or 'internet' have been used for such phenomena, but we prefer the contemporary term 'digital'. We want to encourage insights into what should become possible with world-leading technology, and to recognize that the future is certain to surpass our most radical imagination, as is the norm in relation to technological advance.

Digital provision of CBT comes in many shapes and forms but is typically offered in three main ways (Luik et al., 2017; see Table 23.1). First, *dCBT as support*. This is where dCBT is used mainly as a support function to individual face-to-face or to group therapy, but the in-person therapy remains primary; for example, offering additional background information, automated sleep diaries or help with treatment implementation. This form of CBT has also been described as 'digitally-assisted' therapy. Second, *guided dCBT*. This is perhaps the most common form of digital CBT at present. In guided dCBT, actual therapy content is communicated to the patient by a professional with the help of web pages or a mobile app containing text, images, videos, audio or animations. Sleep diary data may be shared with a clinical professional who feeds back and gives tailored advice to the patient, most commonly after each session, perhaps using email or integrated text functions. Third is *fully automated dCBT*. This form of dCBT offers the full advantages of the digital medicine approach and has the greatest potential for scalability. Personalization is built into the automated program using algorithms to tailor the therapy based on sleep diaries, questionnaires and patient progress scores. Feedback and

Table 23.1 dCBT as support, guided dCBT and fully automated dCBT compared. (Luik et al., 2017.)

	dCBT as support	Guided dCBT	Fully automated dCBT
Definition	dCBT elements are used to support conventional therapy	Automated dCBT with guidance of trained clinicians	Fully automated and tailored dCBT without in-person clinical support
Automatization	Limited	Partly	Fully
Costs	Clinician time Development and maintenance dCBT	Clinician time Development and maintenance dCBT	No clinician time Development and maintenance dCBT
Scalability	Capped by availability of trained clinicians	Capped by availability of trained clinicians	Fully extensible
Clinician involvement in delivery	Comparable to conventional CBT	Up to 2 hours	None

reminders are also automated. Additional components such as expert videos, a user community, or live online sessions with a clinical expert have been used in fully automated dCBT to mimic contact with health professionals and/or other people with insomnia.

We cannot emphasize strongly enough that, in our opinion, digital medicine should be a highly refined 'product'. Clinicians and citizens would expect medication to be pharmaceutical grade; produced to impeccable standards, reproducible, and safe and effective wherever given or taken worldwide. As digital medicine is intended as a treatment for a condition, and therefore Software as a Medical Device (SaMD), we should expect the same standards for digital medicine for insomnia as we do for medication or medical devices. We therefore want to emphasize the importance of clinical governance, in particular for fully automated solutions, because there is likely to be no direct contact with users. The UK National Health Services (NHS) identifies six components of clinical governance: (1) risk management, (2) clinical audits, (3) continuing professional development, (4) evidence bases, (5) patient and care experience, and (6) staffing and staff management. Like any other treatment, any digital product or therapy aiming to target mental of physical health ought to address these in a satisfactory way, in addition to any data security regulations such as, for example, the European General Data Protection Regulation (GDPR), the UK GDPR and the US Health Insurance Portability and Accountability Act of 1996 (HIPAA). As digital medicine becomes increasingly common, regulatory bodies (e.g., US Food and Drug Administration (FDA), UK's Medicines and Healthcare products Regulatory Agency (MHRA) and the European Medicines Agency (EMA)) have implemented new pathways to provide oversight of digital medicine. This will ensure that digital interventions adhere to rigorous standards relating to efficacy, data security and privacy, and safety, with any claims supported by robust clinical research evidence. Indeed, Somryst (Shut-i), a fully automated dCBT program for insomnia was recently cleared by the FDA as a prescription digital intervention (Morin, 2020) requiring a physician to prescribe. Certainly, if digital medicine wishes to be seen as credible by both providers and patients, rigorous evidence standards must be adhered to (Espie & Henry, 2022), but a physician prescription may not be the only pathway. The dCBT Sleepio, for example, is provided to members and patients as an integrated component to the health or benefits system.

Why is digital medicine needed?

We believe that there are six main reasons to suggest that a digital approach to CBT is the radical change that would be needed to meet our duty of clinical guideline care of providing CBT as a first line insomnia treatment.

1) *Need for scalability*: Consider this example. There are an estimated 50 million users of sleep medication in the UK and US. If we would want to treat only 50% of those users with face-to-face CBT, about 75 million therapist hours would be required as a conservative estimate based on 3 hours of therapist time per patient. This would equate to hiring 1.9 million full-time employed therapists to provide CBT to insomnia patients, making delivering against the clinical guideline not even remotely possible. Because fully automated digital medicine can function without any therapist intervention and software can be scaled up without any limits, SaMD as digital medicine has the potential to make waiting time for CBT for insomnia a thing of the past.
2) *Need for reliability of treatment quality*: One distinct advantage of digital medicine is that it can be standardized and employ pre-defined algorithms, which ensures that its performance, and hence its treatment effectiveness, is independent of factors such as therapist experience, group size, medium of delivery or allocated time. Moreover, using algorithms and machine learning could enable digital medicine to adapt and personalize the course of treatment at any given time. Readily accessible technology also offers more immersive support to motivate and engage patients between sessions.
3) *Need for personalized medicine:* A personalized medicine approach to CBT seems plausible, and we have previously suggested how a CBT for insomnia stepped care 'triage' system might work (Espie, 2009; Espie et al., 2013; Espie, Kyle et al., 2014; see Figure 23.1). Stepped care is often conceptualized as a pyramid consisting of different levels with at the bottom the least specialized help applicable for those with less severe and more generic complaints and highly specialized help for those with more severe and rare problems as the top. Digital medicine might be particularly suitable to be one of the entry level methods for the treatment of insomnia, as it has a large scalability. However, integration of digital medicine should not only affect the bottom step of the stepped care pyramid; digital medicine can also be a helpful tool for those needing more specialized care.

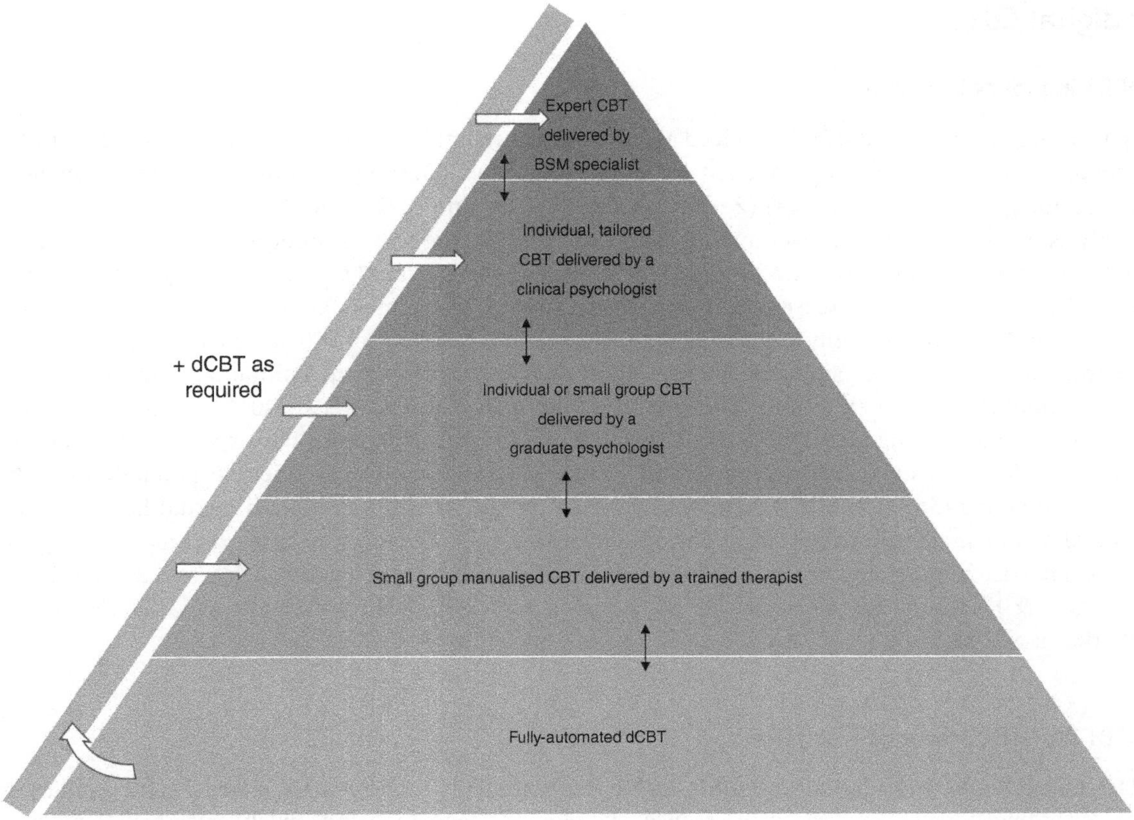

Figure 23.1 Stepped care model for the treatment of insomnia adapted to incorporate dCBT. Black arrows represent potential movement/referral pathways. White arrows indicate where dCBT could supplement other treatment modalities at each level. (Adapted from Espie, C. A. (2009). 'Stepped care' a health technology solution for delivering cognitive behavioural therapy as a first-line insomnia treatment. *Sleep, 32,* 1549–1558 and Espie, C. A., Hames, P., & McKinstry, B. (2013). Use of the internet and mobile media for delivery of cognitive behavioral insomnia therapy. *Sleep Medicine Clinic, 8,* 407–419.)

4) *Need for professional advancement*: Digital medicine is not merely the modern equivalent of a worthy self-help book or an approach that will help take care of mild to moderate problems at scale. For comparison, it would be inconceivable nowadays that medical doctors would have no access to world-leading technology to develop and instrument their diagnostics, and equally inconceivable that they would have no reliable, evidence-based medications or advanced precision surgical methods to treat disorders. Likewise, we suggest that digital medicine offers a transformative agenda to clinical psychology and behavioural medicine. Recent work showed that 47% indicated to prefer a digital treatment over a face-to-face treatment (Sato et al., 2019).
5) *Need for affordability to cope with pressured health budgets*: Health care costs are under pressure across the world. Budgets are not sufficient to fund face-to-face CBT to everyone in need. Digital medicine, however, could be a very affordable alternative with better outcomes for patients and fewer side-effects than drugs, provided in less clinician time and at reduced costs. The available literature indeed suggests that dCBT is a cost-effective approach, where cost-savings are mostly due to the lower costs of dCBT than conventional forms of CBT (Baka, van der Zweerde, Lancee, Bosmans & van Straten, 2021; Darden et al., 2021; De Bruin, van Steensel & Meijer, 2016; Thiart et al., 2013).
6) *Need for accessibility in the 24/7 society*: Another argument in support of digital medicine is its 24/7 availability, meaning that patients can take sessions at their convenience and can get support for their sleep problem at times they most need it. For patients who have difficulty travelling to a clinic or who are in remote locations, access from any location might be a particularly promising attribute (Moloney, Dunfee, Rutledge & Schoenberg, 2020). Being able to get help for your insomnia from your own home could also help treating those who experience stigmatization when visiting a psychological clinic. In addition, when there is a lack of willingness to talk to a stranger about personal problems, online communication may have a facilitating effect.

Evidence for digital CBT

Evidence that dCBT improves insomnia

A series of RCTs have demonstrated that dCBT is indeed an effective treatment for insomnia. Suggested pooled effects are large for insomnia severity (Hedges's g adjusted for publication bias: 0.89) and medium for sleep efficiency (Hedges's g adjusted for publication bias: 0.49) (Zachariae, Lyby, Ritterband & O'Toole, 2015), *n* of studies = 11. Another meta-analysis, which includes an overlapping sample of studies, suggests an improvement of 7% in sleep efficiency (95% CI: 5% to 9%), increased total sleep time of 20 minutes (95% CI: 9 to 31), decreased sleep onset latency of 11 minutes (95% CI: −16 to −5) and decreased wake after sleep onset of 20 minutes (95% CI: −35 to −6) after dCBT (Seyffert et al., 2016). Guided dCBT and fully automated dCBT appear to have effect sizes in a similar range, although no formal comparison has been made. In addition, the benefits of dCBT on insomnia are maintained, even after multiple year follow-up periods (Blom, Jernelov, Ruck, Lindefors & Kaldo, 2016; Ritterband et al., 2017; Vedaa et al., 2019), and increased health resilience during the COVID-19 pandemic in individuals who previously experienced insomnia (Cheng, Casement, Kalmbach, Castelan & Drake, 2021). dCBT has also been used in a variety of populations with co-morbid disorders, demonstrating that dCBT improves insomnia in patients with co-morbid mental health disorders, such as depression and anxiety, and co-morbid physical disorders, such as cancer, tinnitus, asthma and heightened blood pressure, and also in pregnant women (e.g., Beukes, Baguley, Allen, Manchaiah & Anderson, 2018; Felder, Epel, Neuhaus, Kyrstal & Prather, 2020; Henry et al., 2021; Kalmbach et al., 2020; Luyster et al., 2020; McGrath et al., 2017; Zachariae et al., 2018).

Evidence that dCBT has effects beyond insomnia

The effects of dCBT are not limited to improving insomnia, and the evidence for improvements in mental health symptoms has been growing. According to a meta-analysis, dCBT reduces symptoms of depression and anxiety with small to moderate effect sizes (ES: −0.36, 95% CI: −0.47 to −0.26 and ES: −0.35, 95% CI: −0.46 to −0.25 respectively) (Ye et al., 2015), and effects have been suggested to be long-term (Cheng et al., 2019a). Research also suggests that this is a causal relationship, with mental health symptom improvement being mediated by insomnia change (Espie et al., 2019; Freeman et al., 2017; Henry et al., 2021). Moreover, improvements in cognitive complaints, work performance and work behaviour have been reported after dCBT to some extent (Barnes, Miller & Bostock, 2017; Bostock, Luik & Espie, 2016; de Bruin, Dewald-Kaufmann, Oort, Bogels & Meijer, 2015; Kyle et al., 2020; Shaffer et al., 2020).

Evidence on comparability of dCBT to other forms of CBT for insomnia

One of the most frequently asked questions with regard to dCBT is whether the effects are comparable to those of face-to-face CBT. The evaluation of digital therapy versus face-to-face therapy has been rather limited. Meta-analyses suggest that the effects of dCBT are in the range of face-to-face-CBT (Seyffert et al., 2016; Zachariae et al., 2015), although one study comparing face-to-face CBT to guided dCBT suggest that face-to-face CBT outperforms guided dCBT (Lancee, van Straten, Morina, Kaldo & Kamphuis, 2016). On the other hand, two studies did not find any differences in effect size when comparing guided dCBT with group CBT (Blom et al., 2015; De Bruin et al., 2016).

Evidence on who benefits from dCBT

Only a few studies have investigated predictors of improvement following dCBT. A younger age and higher educational level have been reported as a positive predictor for improvement with dCBT, although the effects are small (Espie, Bostock, Kyle, Paluzzi & Hames, 2014; Vincent, Walsh & Lewycky, 2013). More recent work, however, suggests that demographics including age, race or gender and socio-economic status do not affect the effectiveness of dCBT (Cheng et al., 2019b). If we focus on the predictive value of baseline sleep characteristics, co-morbid sleep disorders, a higher sleep efficiency, a lower insomnia severity and a longer total sleep time predict less successful treatment or non-completion (Espie, Bostock et al., 2014; Vincent et al., 2013; Yeung, Chung, Ho & Ho, 2015), which is also true for face-to-face CBT. One opportunity afforded by dCBT is that recruitment can occur at an order of magnitude larger than for trials of face-to-face CBT, and it also permits evaluation of effects using a standardized intervention, removing the variability associated with individual therapists. For example, individual participant data from 8509 participants across 12 published RCTs of Sleepio was combined into an individual participant data (IPD) meta-analysis to evaluate moderators of treatment effects. Results show that Sleepio is highly effective across many different clinical and demographic groups of participants (e.g., age, insomnia severity, presence of co-morbidities, relationship status, income, race and ethnicity, insomnia duration and sleep medication use) and should be used in adults (18 years+) with symptoms of insomnia (see Miller, Henry and Espie, 2019, and also manuscript in preparation, PROSPERO: https://www.crd.york.ac.uk/prospero/display_record.php?RecordID=105424).

Evidence on dCBT and sleep medication

dCBT has mostly been studied independent of sleep medication use, making this is an important gap in the literature. Even more so because, as we have suggested, dCBT has the potential to become a direct alternative to, or replacement for, sleep medication. Often participants within studies have been advised to keep medication constant for study purposes. Although this suggests that dCBT and sleep medication can be used in conjunction, the question as to whether dCBT helps people reduce and withdraw from sleep remains. What evidence there is suggests that, when tapering of medication is specifically addressed during the program, dCBT can lower medication use (Blom et al., 2016; Kaldo et al., 2015). However, reductions in medication use have been observed when no tapering protocols were used, with effects maintained at 48 weeks for non-prescription medication but not for prescription medication (Luik et al., 2020).

Making digital medicine available

Although the intrinsic advantages of fully automated digital medicine are clear and clinical evidence has been mounting, the dissemination of dCBT so far has been very limited. It is not that clinicians are disinterested. Of the health professionals approached in one study, as many as 60% were very interested in referring to an insomnia program and less than 7% was indifferent or disinterested (Beaulac, Vincent & Walsh, 2015). Innovation tends to gather pace over time, and we are probably at an early stage, but we should be encouraged by the potential of digital medicine to offer transformative and not just incremental change.

We suggest there are two main routes through which digital medicine could reach those in need. First, digital medicine can be integrated within traditional care by being offered by general practitioners and specialists. The few reports published on the integration of dCBT in existing healthcare are positive. In a UK-based psychological service, patients worked through a dCBT program on their own, with weekly support calls to enquire about progress/engagement with the program. The program led to improvements in insomnia, depression and anxiety. It is encouraging that 59% of patients achieved a reliable recovery, with 88% completing four or more sessions (Luik, Bostock, et al., 2017). Similar benefits to sleep and mental health were observed in adolescents aged 14–17 attending a child and adolescent mental health service who received dCBT alongside weekly support calls (Cliffe, Croker, Denne, Smith & Stallard, 2020). Second, digital medicine might be made available directly to anyone interested by means of self-referral. There are of course limitations to self-referral, but in the case of dCBT for insomnia self-referral could be a solution. On the one hand, because the treatment side effects are limited and carry little clinical risk, this makes strict regulation by a clinician for each patient less essential. On the other hand, treatment has been largely unavailable via traditional care so far, and this may be compensated by the ease of accessing digital medicine without intervention of a health professional per se.

Conclusion

Digital medicine has the potential to transform insomnia care and to make CBT as ubiquitous a treatment for insomnia as sleep medication. Pharmaceutical treatment currently has the monopoly on insomnia care provision, but by no means the best evidence. As research on digital medicine for insomnia grows, bearing in mind also the potential to enrol thousands of participants per study, and as this new industry gains traction, we predict that digital medicine will steadily start dominating the insomnia treatment landscape in the years to come.

References

Baka, A., van der Zweerde, T., Lancee, J., Bosmans, J. E., & van Straten, A. (2021). Cost-effectiveness of guided internet-delivered cognitive behavioral therapy in comparison with care-as-usual for patients with insomnia in general practice. *Behavioral Sleep Medicine*, 1–16. doi: 10.1080/15402002.2021.1901708.

Barnes, C. M., Miller, J., & Bostock, S. (2017). Helping employees sleep well: Effects of cognitive behavioral therapy for insomnia on work outcomes. *Journal of Applied Psychology*, *102*, 104–113.

Beaulac, J., Vincent, N., & Walsh, K. (2015). Dissemination of an internet-based treatment for chronic insomnia into primary care. *Behavioral Sleep Medicine*, *13* (2), 124–139. doi: 10.1080/15402002.2013.845780.

Beukes, E. W., Baguley, D. M., Allen, P. M., Manchaiah, V., & Andersson, G. (2018). Audiologist-guided internet-based cognitive behavior therapy for adults with tinnitus in the United Kingdom: A randomized controlled trial. *Ear and Hearing*, *39* (3), 423–433. doi: 10.1097/AUD.0000000000000505.

Blom, K., Jernelov, S., Ruck, C., Lindefors, N., & Kaldo, V. (2016). Three-year follow-up of insomnia and hypnotics after controlled internet treatment for insomnia. *Sleep*, *39* (6), 1267–1274. doi: 10.5665/sleep.5850.

Blom, K., Tarkian Tillgren, H., Wiklund, T., Danlycke, E., Forssén, M., Söderström, A., Johansson, R., Hesser, H., Jernelöv, S., Lindefors, N., Andersson, G., & Kaldo, V. (2015). Internet-vs. group-delivered cognitive behavior therapy for insomnia: A randomized controlled non-inferiority trial. *Behaviour Research and Therapy*, *70*, 47–55. doi: 10.1016/j.brat.2015.05.002

Bostock, S., Luik, A. I., & Espie, C. A. (2016). Sleep and productivity benefits of digital cognitive behavioral therapy for insomnia: A randomized controlled trial conducted in the workplace environment. *Journal of Occupational and Environmental Medicine*, *58* (7), 683–689. doi: 10.1097/JOM.0000000000000778.

Cheng, P., Casement, M. D., Kalmbach, D. A., Castelan, A. C., & Drake, C. L. (2021). Digital cognitive behavioral therapy for insomnia promotes later health resilience during the coronavirus disease 19 (COVID-19) pandemic. *Sleep*, *44* (4). doi: 6010120 [pii].10.1093/sleep/zsaa258.

Cheng, P., Kalmbach, D. A., Tallent, G., Joseph, C. L., Espie, C. A., & Drake, C. L. (2019a). Depression prevention via digital cognitive behavioral therapy for insomnia: a randomized controlled trial. *Sleep*, *42* (10). doi: 5571183 [pii].10.1093/sleep/zsz150.

Cheng, P., Luik, A. I., Fellman-Couture, C., Peterson, E., Joseph, C. L. M., Tallent, G., Tran, K. M., Ahmedani, B. K., Roehrs, T., Roth, T., & Drake, C. L. (2019b). Efficacy of digital CBT for insomnia to reduce depression across demographic groups: A randomized trial. *Psychological Medicine*, *49* (3), 491–500.

Cliffe, B, Croker, A., Denne, M., Smith, J., & Stallard, P. (2020). Digital cognitive behaviour therapy for insomnia (CBTi) for adolescents with mental health problems. Results from a feasibility open trial. *JMIR Mental Health*, *7*(3). doi:10.2196/14842

Darden, M., Espie, C. A., Carl, J. R., Henry, A. L., Kanady, J. C., Krystal, A. D., & Miller, C. B. (2021). Cost-effectiveness of digital CBT (Sleepio) for insomnia: A Markov simulation model in the United States. *Sleep, Apr.*, *44* (4), zsaa223. doi: 10.1093/sleep/zsaa22.

De Bruin, E. J., Dewald-Kaufmann, J. F., Oort, F. J., Bogels, S. M., & Meijer, A. M. (2015). Differential effects of online insomnia treatment on executive functions in adolescents. *Sleep Medicine*, *16* (4), 510–520. doi: 10.1016/j.sleep.2014.12.009.

De Bruin, E. J., van Steensel, F. J., & Meijer, A. M. (2016). Cost-effectiveness of group and internet cognitive behavioral therapy for insomnia in adolescents: Results from a randomized controlled trial. *Sleep*, *39* (8), 1571–1581. doi: 10.5665/sleep.6024.

Edinger, J. D., Arnedt, J. T., Bertisch, S. M., Carney, C. E., Harrington, J. J., Lichstein, K. L., Sateia, M. J., Troxel, W. M., Zhou, E. S., Kazmi, U., Heald, J. L., & Martin, J. L. (2021). Behavioral and psychological treatments for chronic insomnia disorder in adults: An American Academy of Sleep Medicine clinical practice guideline. *Journal of Clinical Sleep Medicine*, *17* (2), 255–262. https://doi.org/10.5664/jcsm.8986.

Espie, C. A. (2009). 'Stepped care': A health technology solution for delivering cognitive behavioral therapy as a first line insomnia treatment. *Sleep, Dec.*, *32* (12), 1549–1558. doi: 10.1093/sleep/32.12.1549. PMID: 20041590; PMCID: PMC2786038.

Espie, C. A., Bostock, S., Kyle, S. D., Paluzzi, B., & Hames, P. (2014). Who benefits from online CBT for insomnia? Factors associated with change in sleep efficiency in a large online treatment cohort. *Sleep*, *37*, A205.

Espie, C. A., Hames, P., & McKinstry, B. (2013). Use of the internet and mobile media for delivery of cognitive behavioral insomnia therapy. *Sleep Medicine Clinics*, *8* (3), 407–419. doi: 10.1016/j.jsmc.2013.06.001.

Espie, C. A., & Henry, A. L. (2022). Designing and delivering a DTx Clinical Research Program: No Need to Re-invent the Wheel. In A. Sverdlov & J. VanDam (Eds.), *Digital therapeutics: Scientific, statistical, clinical, and regulatory development aspects*. London: CRC Press.

Espie, C. A., Kyle, S. D., Gehrman, P., Ong, J. C., & Hames, P. (2014). Tailoring cognitive-behavioural therapy for insomnia to specific needs: A personalized behavioural medicine approach. In C. Bassetti, Z. Dogas & P. Peigneux (Eds.), *ESRS European Sleep Medicine Textbook*. Regensburg: European Sleep Research Society (ESRS).

Espie, C. A., Emsley, R., Kyle, S. D., Gordon, C., Drake, C. L., Siriwardena, A. N., Cape, J., Ong, J. C., Sheaves, B., Foster, R., Freeman, D., Costa-Font, J., Marsden, A., & Luik, A. I. (2019). Effect of digital cognitive behavioral therapy for insomnia on health, psychological well-being, and sleep-related quality of life: A randomized clinical trial. *JAMA Psychiatry*, *76* (1), 21–30. doi: 2704019 [pii]. 10.1001/jamapsychiatry.2018.2745.

Felder, J. N, Epel, E. S., Neuhaus, J., Krystal, A.D., & Prather, A.A. (2020). Efficacy of digital cognitive behavioral therapy for the treatment of insomnia symptoms among pregnant women. *JAMA Psychiatry, May*, *77* (5), 484–492. doi: 10.1001/jamapsychiatry.2019.4491.

Freeman, D., Sheaves, B., Goodwin, G. M., Yu, L. M., Nickless, A., Harrison, P. J., Emsley, R., Luik, A. I., Foster, R. G., Wadekar, V., Hinds, C., Gumley, A., Jones, R., Lightman, S., Jones, S., Bentall, R., Kinderman, P., Rowse, G., Brugha, T., Blagrove, M., Gregory, A. M., Fleming, L., Walklet, E., Glazebrook, C., Davies, E. B., Hollis, C., Haddock, G., John, B., Coulson, M., Fowler, D., Pugh, K., Cape, J., Moseley, P., Brown, G., Hughes, C., Obonsawin, M., Coker, S., Watkins, E., Schwannauer, M., MacMahon, K., Siriwardena, A. N., & Espie, C. A. (2017). The effects of improving sleep on mental health (OASIS): A randomised controlled trial with mediation analysis. *Lancet Psychiatry*, *4* (10), 749–758. doi: 10.1016/S2215-0366(17)30328-0.

Henry, A. L., Miller, C. B., Emsley, R., Sheaves, B., Freeman, D., Luik, A. L., Littlewood, D. L., Saunders, K., Kanady, J. C., Carl, J. R., Davis, M. L., Kyle, S.D., & Espie, C. A. (2021). Insomnia as a mediating therapeutic target for depressive symptoms: A sub-analysis of participant data from two large randomized controlled trials of a digital sleep intervention. *Journal of Sleep Research*, *30* (1), e13140. doi: 10.1111/jsr.13140.

Kaldo, V., Jernelöv, S., Blom, K., Ljótsson, B., Brodin, M., Jörgensen, M., Kraepelien, M., Rück, C., & Lindefors, N. (2015). Guided internet cognitive behavioral therapy for insomnia compared to a control treatment – A randomized trial. *Behaviour Research and Therapy*, *71*, 90–100. doi: 10.1016/j.brat.2015.06.001.

Kalmbach, D., O'Brien, L. M., Swanson, L. M., Sangha, R., Sen, S., Guille, C., Cuamatzi-Castelan, A., Henry, A. L., Roth, T., & Drake, C. L. (2020). A randomized controlled trial of digital CBT for insomnia in pregnant women. *Sleep Medicine*, *72*, 82–92. doi: 10.1016/j.sleep.2020.03.016.

Kyle, S. D., Hurry, M. E. D., Emsley, R., Marsden, A., Omlin, X., Juss, A., Spiegelhalder, K., Bisdounis, L, Luik, A. I., Espie, C. A., & Sexton, C. E. (2020). The effects of digital cognitive behavioural therapy for insomnia on cognitive function: A randomised, controlled trial. *Sleep, Sep.*, *43* (9), zsaa034. doi: 10.1093/sleep/zsaa034.

Lancee, J., van Straten, A., Morina, N., Kaldo, V., & Kamphuis, J. H. (2016). Guided online or face-to-face cognitive behavioral treatment for insomnia: A randomized wait-list controlled trial. *Sleep*, *39* (1), 183–191. doi: 10.5665/sleep.5344.

Luik, A. I., Kyle, S. D., & Espie, C. A. (2017). Digital cognitive behavioral therapy (dCBT) for insomnia: A state-of-the-science review. *Current Sleep Medical Reports*, *3* (2), 48–56. doi: 10.1007/s40675-017-0065-4.

Luik, A. I., Bostock, S., Chisnall, L., Kyle, S. D., Lidbetter, N., Baldwin, N., & Espie, C. A. (2017). Treating depression and anxiety with digital cognitive behavioural therapy for insomnia: A real world NHS evaluation using standardized outcome measures. *Behavioural and Cognitive Psychotherapy*, *45*, 91–96. doi: 10.1017/S1352465816000369.

Luik, A. I., Marsden, A., Emsley, R., Henry, A. L., Stott, R., Miller, C. B., & Espie, C. A. (2020). Long-term benefits of digital cognitive behavioural therapy for insomnia: Follow-up report from a randomized clinical trial. *Journal of Sleep Research*, *29*, e13018. doi: 10.1111/jsr.13018.

Luyster, F. S., Ritterband, L. M., Sereika, S. M., Buysse, D. J., Wenzel, S. E., & Strollo, P. J. (2020). Internet-based cognitive-behavioral therapy for insomnia in adults with asthma: A pilot study. *Behavioral Sleep Medicine*, *18* (1), 10–22. doi: 10.1080/15402002.2018.1518229.

McGrath, E. R., Espie, C. A., Power, A., Murphy, A. W., Newell, J., Kelly, C., Duffy, N., Gunning, P., Gibson, I., Bostock, S., & O'Donnell, M.J. (2017). Sleep to lower elevated blood pressure: A randomized controlled trial (SLEPT). *American Journal of Hypertension*, *30*, 319–327. doi: 10.1093/ajh/hpw132.

Miller, C. B., Henry, A. L., & Espie, C. A. (2019). Effects of a digital therapy (Sleepio) for the treatment of insomnia: A collaborative individual participant data meta-analysis of randomised controlled trials. PROSPERO: International Prospective Register of Systematic Reviews. Available from: https://www.crd.york.ac.uk/prospero/display_record.php?RecordID=105424.

Moloney, M. E., Dunfee, M., Rutledge, M., & Schoenberg, N. (2020). Evaluating the feasibility and acceptability of internet-based cognitive behavioral therapy for insomnia in rural women. *Womens Health Report (New Rochelle)*, *1* (1), 114–122. doi: 10.1089/whr.2020.0053 [pii].

Morin, C. M. (2020). Profile of Somryst Prescription Digital Therapeutic for Chronic Insomnia: Overview of safety and efficacy. *Expert Review of Medical Devices*, *17* (12), 1239–1248. doi: 10.1080/17434440.2020.1852929.

Morin, C. M., LeBlanc, M., Belanger, L., Ivers, H., Merette, C., & Savard, J. (2011). Prevalence of insomnia and its treatment in Canada. *Canadian Journal of Psychiatry*, *56* (9), 540–548. doi: 10.1177/070674371105600905.

Morin, C. M., Drake, C. L., Harvey, A. G., Krystal, A. D., Manber, R., Riemann, D., & Spiegelhalder, K. (2015). Insomnia disorder. *Nature Reviews Disease Primers*, *1*, 15026. doi: 10.1038/nrdp.2015.26.

Murdoch, T. B., & Detsky, A. S. (2013). The inevitable application of big data to health care. *JAMA*, *309* (13), 1351–1352. doi: 10.1001/jama.2013.393.

Peeling, R. W. (2015). Diagnostics in a digital age: An opportunity to strengthen health systems and improve health outcomes. *International Health*, *7* (6), 384–389. doi: 10.1093/inthealth/ihv062.

Price Waterhouse Coopers (2016). *The Wearable Life 2.0. Connected living in a wearable world*. Retrieved from http://www.pwc.se/sv/pdf-reports/the-wearable-life-2-0.pdf.

Qaseem, A., Kansagara, D., Forciea, M. A., Cooke, M., Denberg, T. D., & Clinical Guidelines Committee of the American College of Psychiatry (2016). Management of chronic insomnia disorder in adults: A Clinical Practice Guideline from the American College of Physicians. *Annals of Internal Medicine*, *165* (2), 125–133. doi: 10.7326/M15-2175.

Riemann, D., Baglioni, C., Bassetti, C., Bjorvatn, B., Dolenc Groselj, L., Ellis, J. G., Espie, C. A., Garcia-Borreguero, D., Gjerstad, M., Gonçalves, M., Hertenstein, E., Jansson-Fröjmark, M., Jennum, P. J., Leger, D., Nissen, C., Parrino, L., Paunio, T., Pevernagie, D., Verbraecken, J., Weeß, H. G., Wichniak, A., Zavalk, I., Arnardottir, E. S., Deleanu, O. C., Strazisar, B., Zoetmulder, M., & Spiegelhalder, K. (2017). European guideline for the diagnosis and treatment of insomnia. *Journal of Sleep Research*, *26* (6), 675–700. doi: 10.1111/jsr.12594.

Ritterband, L. M., Thorndike, F. P., Ingersoll, K. S., Lord, H. R., Gonder-Frederick, L., Frederick, C., Quigg, M. S., Cohn, W. F., & Morin, C. M. (2017). Effect of a web-based cognitive behavior therapy for insomnia intervention with 1-year follow-up: A randomized clinical trial. *JAMA Psychiatry*, *74* (1), 68–75. doi: 10.1001/jamapsychiatry.2016.3249.

Roy, A. N., & Smith, M. (2010). Prevalence and cost of insomnia in a state Medicaid fee-for-service population based on diagnostic codes and prescription utilization. *Sleep Medicine*, *11* (5), 462–469. doi: 10.1016/j.sleep.2009.09.012.

Sato, D., Sutoh, C., Seki, Y., Nagai, E., & Shimizu, E. (2019). Treatment preferences for internet-based cognitive behavioral therapy for insomnia in Japan: Online survey. *JMIR Formative Research*, *3* (2), e12635. doi: v3i2e12635 [pii] 10.2196/12635.

Seyffert, M., Lagisetty, P., Landgraf, J., Chopra, V., Pfeiffer, P. N., Conte, M. L., & Rogers, M. A. (2016). Internet-delivered cognitive behavioral therapy to treat insomnia: A systematic review and meta-analysis. *PLoS One*, *11* (2), e0149139. doi: 10.1371/journal.pone.0149139.

Shaffer, K. M., Finkelstein, E. A., Camacho, F., Ingersoll, K. S., Thorndike, F., & Ritterband, L. M. (2021). Effects of an internet-based cognitive behavioral therapy for insomnia program on work productivity: A secondary analysis. *Annals of Behavioral Medicine, June*, 55 (6), 592–599. doi: 5923960 [pii] 10.1093/abm/kaaa085.

Thiart, H., Lehr, D., Ebert, D. D., Sieland, B., Berking, M., & Riper, H. (2013). Log in and breathe out: Efficacy and cost-effectiveness of an online sleep training for teachers affected by work-related strain – Study protocol for a randomized controlled trial. *Trials*, *14*, 169. doi: 10.1186/1745-6215-14-169.

Vedaa, Ø., Hagatun, S., Kallestad, H., Pallesen, S., Smith, O. R. F., Thorndike, F. P., Ritterband, L. M., & Sivertsen, B. (2019). Long-term effects of an unguided online cognitive behavioral therapy for chronic insomnia. *Journal of Clinical Sleep Medicine*, *15* (1), 101–110.

Vincent, N., & Lionberg, C. (2001). Treatment preference and patient satisfaction in chronic insomnia. *Sleep*, *24* (4), 411–417.

Vincent, N., Walsh, K., & Lewycky, S. (2013). Determinants of success for computerized cognitive behavior therapy: Examination of an insomnia program. *Behavioural Sleep Medicine*, *11* (5), 328–342. doi: 10.1080/15402002.2012.700662.

Ye, Y. Y., Zhang, Y. F., Chen, J., Liu, J., Li, X. J., Liu, Y. Z., Lang, Y., Lin, L., Yang, X. J., & Jiang, X. J. (2015). Internet-based cognitive behavioral therapy for insomnia (ICBT-i) improves comorbid anxiety and depression – A meta-analysis of randomized controlled trials. *PLoS One*, *10* (11), e0142258. doi: 10.1371/journal.pone.0142258.

Yeung, W. F., Chung, K. F., Ho, F. Y., & Ho, L. M. (2015). Predictors of dropout from internet-based self-help cognitive behavioral therapy for insomnia. *Behaviour Research and Therapy*, *73*, 19–24. doi: 10.1016/j.brat.2015.07.008.

Zachariae, R., Lyby, M. S., Ritterband, L. M., & O'Toole, M. S. (2015). Efficacy of internet-delivered cognitive-behavioral therapy for insomnia – A systematic review and meta-analysis of randomized controlled trials. *Sleep Medicine Review*, *30*, 1–10. doi: 10.1016/j.smrv.2015.10.004.

Zachariae, R., Amidi, A., Damholdt, M. F., Clausen, C. D., Dahlgaard, J., Lord, H., . . . & Ritterband, L. M. (2018). Internet-delivered cognitive-behavioral therapy for insomnia in breast cancer survivors: A randomized controlled trial. *JNCI: Journal of the National Cancer Institute*, *110* (8), 880–887. doi: 10.1093/jnci/djx293.

Section VI

Training in CBT-I

Section Editor: Chiara Baglioni

24

Recommendation of the European Academy for Cognitive-Behavioural Therapy for Insomnia (CBT-I) for high quality training for health professionals

Chiara Baglioni, Colin A. Espie, Kai Spiegelhalder, Dimitri Gavriloff and Dieter Riemann

Key points

- The European Academy for Cognitive-Behavioural Therapy for Insomnia (CBT-I) is a task force of the European Insomnia Network (EIN) and of the European Sleep Research Society (ESRS) composed of experts in evidence-based psychological treatment of insomnia.
- The Academy aims at increasing the number of health professionals, who are experts in CBT-I, to improve the focus on effective clinical practice in insomnia care and to reduce treatment variability across clinicians.
- It is the Academy's suggestion that, in Europe, expert providers of CBT-I would be by definition health professionals with a recognized licence to provide clinical psychology/psychotherapy/mental healthcare. Moreover, expert providers of CBT-I should have further received qualification and associated supervised education and practice in sleep medicine and sleep clinical psychology.
- The Academy has identified three levels of expertise for providers of CBT-I: expert level, advanced level and foundation level. CBT-I providers with expert level may operate also as CBT-I trainers and supervisors.
- The Academy has identified minimal criteria for high quality courses on CBT-I.

Learning objectives

- To understand the reason why it is a primary health aim to strengthen the CBT-I offer in European health care.
- To understand the stepped-care model for CBT-I offer in health care.
- To understand minimal criteria for CBT-I courses directed to different expertise levels.
- To understand the European CBT-I Academy's aims and resources.

Abstract

European clinical guidelines clearly identified Cognitive Behavioural Therapy for Insomnia (CBT-I) as first line of treatment for insomnia disorder. Yet, despite these indications, so far CBT-I is rarely offered in clinical practice and pharmacotherapy is still the dominant clinical practice. In order to promote a change in clinical practice, a Task Force of the European Sleep Research Society and the European Insomnia Network was established with the aim of enabling a Europe-wide system of CBT-I training and training centre accreditation. This, in turn, would correspond to a wider offer of CBT-I in Europe, to similar standards and with comparable levels of dissemination within countries. Specifically, this would be achieved by extending knowledge and skills relating to insomnia and its psychological treatment from the area of sleep medicine to the areas of clinical psychology, evidence-based psychotherapy and psychiatry, as well as primary care and health care practice (e.g., general practicioners, paediatricians). It is the Academy's suggestion that, in Europe, expert providers of CBT-I would be by definition health professionals with a recognized

Cognitive-Behavioural Therapy for Insomnia (CBT-I) Across the Life Span: Guidelines and Clinical Protocols for Health Professionals,
First Edition. Edited by Chiara Baglioni, Colin A. Espie and Dieter Riemann.

licence to provide clinical psychology/psychotherapy/mental healthcare. Moreover, expert providers of CBT-I should have further received qualification and associated supervised education and practice in sleep medicine and sleep-related aspects of clinical psychology. The Academy has identified different levels of CBT-I providers expertise, depending on clinical qualification and target patient population. Furthermore, the Academy provided minimal criteria for high quality CBT-I courses directed towards health professionals. This chapter aims at summarizing the deliberations and the initiatives of the CBT-I Academy to promote training and knowledge of CBT-I to health professionals.

Keywords *cognitive-behavioural treatment for insomnia, CBT-I Academy, CBT-I expertise levels, CBT-I training*

Introduction

Recent guidelines in the US and Europe unequivocally conclude that cognitive-behavioural therapy for insomnia (CBT-I) should be the first-line treatment for the disorder (see Chapter 1). Based on a very large evidence-based literature (see Chapter 3), experts in insomnia and its treatment around the world endorse a radical shift in clinical recommendations in favour of CBT-I and away from the use of sleeping pills. Nevertheless, as often happens, advances in evidence-based research are not yet reflected in clinical practice. Indeed, data from different sources indicate that at present CBT-I is offered only to a very small proportion of patients suffering from chronic insomnia (e.g., Koffel, Bramoweth & Ulmer, 2018). Furthermore, pharmacotherapy is still by far the most prevalent intervention for insomnia in routine healthcare worldwide. Consistently, clinical psychologists, psychotherapists, psychiatrists, medical doctors from other specialisations and other health professionals know little about the diagnosis and treatment of sleep disorders, especially insomnia (e.g., Baglioni et al., 2020; Meltzer, Phillips & Mindell, 2009). This is likely to be dependent on historical factors. Expertise on clinical aspects regarding insomnia disorder is currently a branch of sleep medicine; however, it is often not included in clinical psychology/psychiatry/psychotherapy training. Indeed, insomnia has been classically interpreted as a symptom, rather than as a disorder. As a consequence, the clinical approach was to treat the primary disorder (which was mainly considered to be depression). Several research studies in the last 20 years have demonstrated that insomnia does not respond primarily to the treatment of depression or other disorders, but it responds best to its specific therapy (i.e., CBT-I). Moreover, in recent times sleep and insomnia have been proposed as transdiagnostic processes in psychopathology (e.g., Harvey, Murray, Chandler & Sochner, 2011; Dolsen, Asarnow & Harvey, 2014) involved in the causation and maintenance of the most common mental disorders, and the classical distinction between primary and co-morbid insomnia has been abandoned with the publication of the fifth edition of the *Diagnostic and Statistical Manual for Mental Disorders* (DSM-5, American Psychiatric Association (APA), 2013). This has led to the new interpretation of insomnia as an independent psychophysiological disorder, which should be treated with its specific therapy. These changes in interpretation need, however, to be followed by important modifications in clinical practice.

In order to promote this change in interpretation, a Task Force of the European Sleep Research Society and the European Insomnia Network was established with the aim of enabling a Europe-wide system of CBT-I training and of training centre accreditation. This, in turn, would correspond to a wider offer of CBT-I in Europe, to similar standards and with comparable levels of dissemination within countries. Specifically, this would be reached by extending the knowledge and skills on insomnia and its psychological treatment from the area of sleep medicine to the areas of clinical psychology, evidence-based psychotherapy and psychiatry. Furthermore, basic understanding of clinical sleep psychology would be ideally offered to primary care health professionals, such as general practitioners and other health professionals such as paediatricians. It is the Academy's suggestion that, in Europe, expert providers of CBT-I would be by definition health professionals with a recognized licence to provide clinical psychology/psychotherapy/mental healthcare. Moreover, expert providers of CBT-I should have further received qualification and associated supervised education and practice in sleep medicine and sleep clinical psychology. This aim of the European CBT-I Academy is schematically illustrated in Figure 24.1.

This section is based on the guidelines developed by the Academy in terms of training standards, which have been extensively described in a paper published in *Journal of Sleep Research* (Baglioni et al., 2020).

Preconditions for CBT-I practice

Professionals who wish to become practicing CBT-I clinicians should be fully licenced and insured for all of their working healthcare practice and should practice within the boundaries of their professional training in their home country. The CBT-I Academy is not a legal organization. That is, it is not the role of the Academy to recognize titles, which are

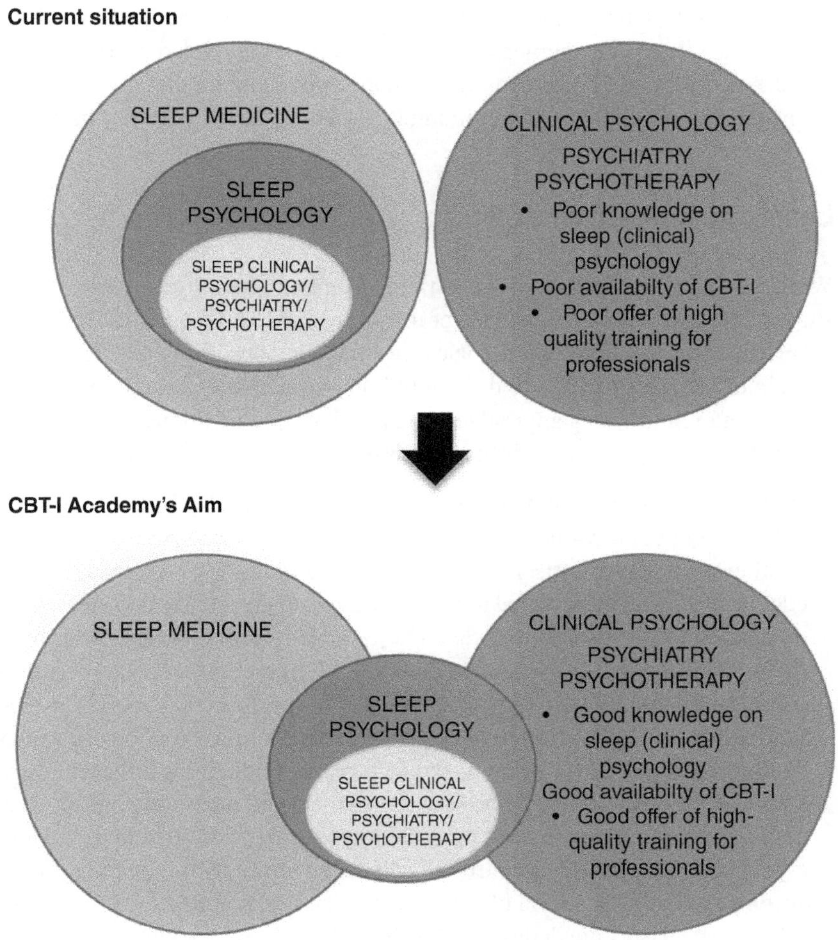

Figure 24.1 Expert providers of CBT-I would be by definition health professionals with a recognized licence to provide clinical psychology/psychotherapy/mental healthcare. Moreover, expert providers of CBT-I should have further received qualification and associated supervised education and practice in sleep medicine and sleep clinical psychology.

defined by each country's legal health organizations. Rather, the Academy acts as a standard setting agency to identify hallmarks of good quality training.

Accordingly, CBT-I practitioners must already possess a licence to practice clinically. As a consequence, simply undertaking a CBT-I course does not in itself confer a licence to see patients. There is a parallel here with medical management in that a licensed physician is intrinsically qualified to prescribe medication, but is likely to require further orientation to and training in a particular therapy or therapeutic approach. In the same way, a licensed clinical or practitioner psychologist, psychotherapist or psychiatrist is already qualified to see patients and to take clinical responsibility based on their national laws and professional regulations, and is best placed to extend his or her skills into the CBT/insomnia area. It is assumed that until this point no European country has a governing body controlling whether or not somebody is competent to practice CBT-I. On the other hand, most European countries have governing bodies controlling who is permitted to practise clinical psychology or psychotherapy, or to call themselves a psychotherapist.

Preconditions for health professionals to conduct and teach CBT-I

The aim of the Academy is to facilitate an increase in the number of professionals working in CBT-I, to improve the focus on effective clinical practice in insomnia care and to reduce treatment variability across clinicians. This needs to be achieved through adequate training and supervision and needs to be provided by clinicians with expert credentials in insomnia research and CBT-I (see the definition of an expert below). As stated above, in establishing the CBT-I Academy our starting assumption is that eligible individuals have a legitimate license to practice in a clinical context. That is, the CBT-I skills obtained on a course can only be an extension of a person's practising certificate. It is that certification (e.g., as a physician, clinical psychologist, health or practitioner psychologist, or psychotherapist) that provides the governance structure enabling a person to see patients, and thus to be regulated as a professional in their country of practice.

Consequently, CBT-I expert clinicians who run training courses as a minimum will be health professionals who have: (a) a licence to practice clinically and (b) who have completed accredited CBT-I training themselves and/or have recognized expertise in sleep behavioural medicine and insomnia therapy.

The next section will focus on different levels of expertise that may be gained from different CBT-I courses.

Levels of expertise in CBT-I

While clinical qualification to see patients in mental health care is a necessary precondition for all, CBT-I practitioners should also have a good knowledge of insomnia and sleep medicine. This is necessary, as practitioners should have a good knowledge of sleep basic physiological mechanisms, insomnia aetiology and pathophysiology and basic CBT-I strategies and should be able to provide differential diagnosis. Nevertheless, this may apply to different levels of expertise, which require different training approaches and previous qualifications.

The Academy has identified three levels of expertise that should be considered:

Expert level: This level of expertise would allow licensed health professionals to be expert CBT-I practitioners, who are able to conduct individually tailored CBT-I. This level of expertise is suited to clinical and healthcare psychologists, psychotherapists, psychiatrists and sleep experts whose CBT-I expertise is core to their professional clinician level knowledge. They would be expected to have attended a high-quality, certified course, endorsed by the Academy and specifically directed to this level of knowledge. They should have followed at least three cases over the course of 3–6 months under the guidance of a CBT-I qualified expert. CBT-I practitioners with certificated knowledge in sleep medicine and sleep clinical psychology could operate also as CBT-I trainers and supervisors (see above).

Advanced level: This advanced level of expertise would allow health professionals to be trained therapists who could conduct manualized CBT-I delivered face to face or digitally, under the supervision of an expert-level CBT-I supervisor. This level of expertise would be suited to clinical and health psychology master's graduates and psychiatrists in training and, in some countries, nurses or social workers. To be entitled to an advanced level of expertise, practitioners would be expected to have attended a certified course, endorsed by the Academy, including interactive and supervising activities.

Foundation level: This level of expertise is specifically suited to GPs (or paediatricians, gynaecologists, etc.) and should reflect more basic knowledge of CBT-I behavioural strategies and sleep medicine obtained through attendance at a CBT-I Academy certified course.

Table 24.1 summarizes schematically the three levels of expertise in CBT-I in terms of skills.

Table 24.1 Definition of CBT-I skills for each level of expertise.

Skill/level of expertise	Foundation level	Advanced level	Expert level
Diagnostics of Insomnia Disorder (Questionnaires, sleep logs, actigraphy, polysomnography)	YES	YES	YES
Differential diagnosis	YES	YES	YES
Core behavioural components (bedtime restriction and stimulus control must be included)	YES	YES	YES
Knowledge on basic elements of sleep mechanisms (e.g., sleep psychophysiology)	YES	YES	YES
Knowledge of insomnia pathophysiology	YES	YES	YES
Basic knowledge of CBT-I stepped care model	YES	YES	YES
Cognitive components	NO	YES	YES
CBT-I for specific populations: e.g., infants, toddlers, children, preadolescents, adolescents, women (e.g., pregnancy, menopause), elderly, persons with disabilities, shift workers, psychiatric populations, etc.)	NO	YES	YES
Delivering a manual-based cognitive-behavioural treatment for insomnia	NO	YES	YES
Additional CBT-I components (e.g., motivational and emotional interventions)	NO	NO	YES
Medication tapering	NO	NO	YES
Individual tapered interventions	NO	NO	YES
Promote a CBT-I course	NO	NO	YES

Training principles and characteristics

Courses for aspiring CBT-I practitioners at foundation and/or advanced levels should be of a minimum of 2 days in duration and may be offered to people with pre-existing qualifications in different healthcare areas with a recognized licence to see patients in mental healthcare contexts. Courses should include teaching on sleep itself, on insomnia disorder and its assessment, as well as on core CBT-I components (such as behavioural and cognitive intervention). Courses directed at a foundation level of expertise may focus specifically on diagnostic aspects and CBT-I behavioural components. Courses should include conceptual elements covering sleep mechanisms and pathophysiology, theoretical underpinnings of insomnia development and maintenance and formulation of CBT as an intervention. The stepped-care model of insomnia service delivery may also be taught. Courses should cover basic principles of CBT therapy. Courses should be organized to be interactive (e.g., role playing, working in small groups and difficult situations) and case supervision should be offered. It is possible that some elements of the CBT-I programme could involve interactive training and be offered online. Courses directed at an advanced level should further include specific focus on cognitive techniques and delivery of manualized CBT-I. A module on sleep, insomnia and associated treatment in specific populations seem relevant to this level.

Finally, courses directed at the expert level may necessitate longer-term duration and/or follow-up refresher courses, or should be directed to those practitioners who have already gained through their professional training good knowledge of sleep medicine, insomnia and clinical practice. At this level, modules on additional CBT-I components (such as emotional and motivational strategies) should be added. A module on sleep medication and tapering off/withdrawing medication should be included. Depending on national laws, some health professionals may be prohibited from discussing any change in medication status with patients as they do not have the necessary professional competences. Nevertheless, any health professional dealing with patients with insomnia at a clinical level should be aware of sleep medication mechanisms and effects during use and withdrawal. For the expert level, courses should comprise extensive teaching of the individual tailoring of treatment, advanced knowledge on sleep medicine, insomnia and CBT principles, clinical experience (e.g., at least three case studies), and either have a longer-term duration or include a follow-up/refresher course to discuss cases. Trainers should all be expert-level CBT-I professionals. Table 24.2, which is an adaptation of the table published in the statement paper of the Academy (Baglioni et al., 2020), summarizes the CBT-I course criteria identified by the Academy.

Further specifications for course levels were recently offered by the Academy's board and can be summarized as follows:

a) *Basic foundation level*: The course offers theoretical and practical knowledge on main CBT-I ingredients as defined in the course form proposal. This level is directed to those professionals who have little or no experience with CBT-I.
b) *Advanced level*: The course offers theoretical and practical knowledge on CBT-I specific aspects, as possible problems in applying the strategies, specific populations, additional motivational and emotional strategies. Participants are expected

Table 24.2 CBT-I courses criteria identified by the European Academy for Cognitive-Behavioural Treatment for Insomnia.

	Duration	Teachers	Participants	Teaching content and methods
Criteria	At least 2 days	Expert level CBT-I practitioners	Health professionals with a recognized licence to provide clinical psychology, psychotherapy, mental health care. CBT-I clinicians should be fully insured for all of their work in health-care practice and should practice within the boundaries of their professional training.	All courses should offer comprehensive knowledge on sleep physiology and insomnia pathophysiology. CBT-I core strategies should be taught with a practical interactive approach (e.g., using practical experiences and clinical cases exposition). The stepped care model should be explained. Courses may be offered face-to-face or online.
Notes	For expert level, courses may necessitate long-term duration and/or follow-up refresher courses or should be directed to those practitioners who have already gained in their professional training good knowledge in sleep medicine, insomnia and clinical practice.		For expert level: Qualified and essential further supervised education in sleep medicine should be given during the course or previously obtained. For advanced and foundation levels: Basic relevant education in sleep medicine and insomnia should be given during the course.	For expert level, supervision of clinical cases should be provided.

to discuss their own cases. This level is directed to those professionals who already have participated to a foundation level course and/or already have some CBT-I knowledge and experience.

c) *Expert level*: The course offers longer-term theoretical and practical knowledge on CBT-I, covering both the main CBT-I ingredients and specific CBT-I aspects. Case supervision is provided. This level is directed to all those professionals who want to gain a deep expertise in CBT-I and of ways to offer the treatment and to train other professionals.

These criteria are not intended to be overly prescriptive, but neither are they completely comprehensive. However, we have attempted to set expectations and minimum standards for what may be regarded as necessary and feasible. Furthermore, it has to be underlined that these criteria apply to the ideal situation in which each country offers the full range of CBT-I courses for different levels of expertise and across different areas of healthcare. A more realistic current situation may be that a course offers learning content consistent with both foundation and advanced levels of expertise and be attended by different health professionals, such as, for example, clinical psychologists and general practitioners. In this case, it is the clinical qualification and aims of the professionals attending that might define the level of expertise at which CBT-I training is offered.

Sources of the Academy

The proposal form for CBT-I courses for those CBT-I practitioners with expert level who may wish to promote a CBT-I course in his/her own country may be downloaded from the Academy's website: https://esrs.eu/the-european-cbt-i-academy/. On this website, further information on founding members of the Academy, members of the Steering Committee, currently endorsed courses around Europe and further initiatives of the Academy can be found.

References

American Psychiatric Association (2013). *Diagnostic and statistical manual of mental disorders* (5th ed.): *DSM-5*. Washington, DC: American Psychiatric Association Publishing.

Baglioni, C., Altena, E., Bjorvatn, B., Blom, K., Bothelius, K., Devoto, A., Espie, C. A., Frase, L., Gavriloff, D., Tuuliki, H., Hoflehner, A., Högl, B., Holzinger, B., Järnefelt, H., Jernelöv, S., Johann, A. F., Lombardo, C., Nissen, C., Palagini, L., Peeters, G., Perlis, M. L., Posner, D., Schlarb, A., Spielgelhalder, K., Wichniak, A., & Riemann, D. (2020). The European Academy for Cognitive Behavioural Therapy for Insomnia: An initiative of the European Insomnia Network to promote implementation and dissemination of treatment. *Journal of Sleep Research, Apr. 29* (2), e12967. https://doi.org/10.1111/jsr.12967.

Dolsen, M. R., Asarnow, L. D., & Harvey, A. G. (2014). Insomnia as a transdiagnostic process in psychiatric disorders. *Current Psychiatry Reports, 16* (9), 471. doi: 10.1007/s11920-014-0471-y.

Harvey, A. G., Murray, G., Chandler, R. A., & Soehner, A. (2011). Sleep disturbance as transdiagnostic: consideration of neurobiological mechanisms. *Clinical Psychology Review, 31* (2), 225–235. https://doi.org/10.1016/j.cpr.2010.04.003.

Koffel, E., Bramoweth, A. D., & Ulmer, C. S. (2018). Increasing access to and utilization of cognitive behavioral therapy for insomnia (CBT-I): A narrative review. *Journal of General Internal Medicine, 33* (6), 955–962. https://doi.org/10.1007/s11606-018-4390-1.

Meltzer, L. J., Phillips, C., & Mindell, J. A. (2009). Clinical psychology training in sleep and sleep disorders. *Journal of Clinical Psychology, 65* (3), 305–318. doi: 10.1002/jclp.20545.

Name Index

Cognitive-Behavioural Therapy for Insomnia (CBT-I) Across the Life Span: Guidelines and Clinical Protocols for Health Professionals,
First Edition. Edited by Chiara Baglioni, Colin A. Espie and Dieter Riemann.

Subject Index

Please note that page references to Figures will be followed by the letter 'f', to Tables by the letter 't'

Cognitive-Behavioural Therapy for Insomnia (CBT-I) Across the Life Span: Guidelines and Clinical Protocols for Health Professionals, First Edition. Edited by Chiara Baglioni, Colin A. Espie and Dieter Riemann.